SKIING USA

THE GUIDE FOR SKIERS AND SNOWBOARDERS

By Clive Hobson

Fodor's Travel Publications, Inc.
New York • Toronto • London • Sydney • Auckland
www.fodors.com/

Second Edition

ISBN 0–679–03534–6

Fodor's Skiing USA: The Guide for Skiers and Snowboarders

EDITOR: Donna Cornachio
Contributors: Karen Cure, Jane McConnell, Daniel Mangin, Effin Older, Jules Older, Dennis Steele, Robbe Stimson, Nancy van Itallie
Editorial Production: Tracy Patruno
Maps: Mapping Specialists, Inc., *cartographer*; Robert Blake, *map editor*
Design: Fabrizio La Rocca, *creative director*; Guido Caroti, *associate art director*; Jolie Novak, *photo editor*
Text Design: Teri McMahon
Cover Design: Allison Saltzman
Production/Manufacturing: Robert B. Shields
Cover Photograph: J. F. Causse/TSW

Special Sales

Fodor's Travel Publications are available at special discounts for bulk purchases for sales promotions or premiums. Special editions, including personalized covers, excerpts of existing guides, and corporate imprints, can be created in large quantities for special needs. For more information, contact your local bookseller or write to Special Markets, Fodor's Travel Publications, 201 East 50th Street, New York, NY 10022. Inquiries from Canada should be directed to your local Canadian bookseller or sent to Random House of Canada, Ltd., Marketing Department, 1265 Aerowood Drive, Mississauga, Ontario L4W 1B9. Inquiries from the United Kingdom should be sent to Fodor's Travel Publications, 20 Vauxhall Bridge Road, London SW1V 2SA, England.

CONTENTS

The American ski scene has grown and matured mightily in the past decade, and its kingpin resorts now have a place in the pantheon of international destinations. Giants such as Vail, Snowbird, Jackson Hole, Sun Valley, and Aspen are mentioned in the same breath as legendary destinations such as St. Anton, Chamonix, Val d'Isère, Whistler/Blackcomb, or Verbier, their merits endlessly debated by the cognoscenti of the sport. It's a haughty, arbitrary rating system, but in terms of customer satisfaction the American ski resorts in this book—and indeed many others not mentioned—are hard to beat for the overall quality of the product. Convenient (there are four first-class resorts within 40 minutes of Salt Lake City, and most others are reached on safe, paved highways), modern (American resorts lead the world in high-speed quad chairs, and European resort operators regularly take tutorials from their American counterparts on computerized snowmaking and slope grooming, a skill U.S. resorts have honed to a fine art), and the most reasonably priced of those in traditional ski countries, American resorts attract skiers from around the world.

There are more than 300 ski resorts in the United States, ranging from the tiniest of day areas to the mightiest of megamountains. A trip to your local day hill doesn't take much planning, but a commitment for a week of skiing at a distant, unknown resort does.

CHOOSING THE RIGHT RESORT

In many ways there are no bad ski resorts. Certainly all resorts strive to make customers happy—they wouldn't stay in business otherwise—and some do it better than others. If you hear that someone has had a bad experience at a ski resort, you can usually attribute it to a couple of key factors, one of which you can do something about and the other you have only a modicum of control over. The latter is weather: unfortunately, the capriciousness of mountain systems and microclimates makes it a roll of the dice. The most you can do is avoid early season if you want the entire resort open and mid-January if you absolutely hate cold weather. Overall, you take what you get and try to keep smiling.

The main reason most people don't enjoy their resort experience is that they don't choose the right resort. It's hard to go wrong if you first ask yourself what you're looking for in a week's ski vacation. Do you put a premium on skiing or resort amenities? Do you want a busy lifestyle resort, or are you happy with a quieter, more homespun experience? Are you comfortable in natural powder snow, or do you prefer executive grooming? Do you want a week of cruising or a week of challenge? Are you traveling alone, as part of a group, or in a family? What's your budget? You should consider all of these questions when shopping for your next ski vacation—especially if you're heading to a major western resort for the first time. To keep it simple, consider these guidelines:

How important is snow to you? This seems like an obvious question, but you can actually have too much of a good thing. If you can't handle deep, ungroomed powder, for instance, it's not a good idea to consider places like Snowbird or Alta, where deep powder is the main attraction. A better choice would be Snowmass or Park City, where groomed runs are the norm, or, better still, places like Deer Valley or Beaver Creek, where grooming is everything. Powder is great stuff when you can ski it, and you'll usually get a taste of it at any western resort, but it's a tough introduction to western skiing. Don't be misled by impressive snowfall statistics; if you like to see the tops of your skis all the time, you'll have more fun skiing something you can handle.

What kind of resort atmosphere do you want? All the resorts featured in this book have a self-contained ski-village center, but some are more contained than others, and some are definitely livelier than others when skiing is done for the day. If you want wide and varied nightlife, shopping binges, or haute cuisine in your ski vacation, you should consider larger areas with well-established communities—places like Aspen, Vail, or Heavenly. If you are content to provide your own entertainment and dining à la condo and to just ski yourself into daily exhaustion, then places like Big Sky, Squaw Valley, or Winter Park might be a better choice. Resorts with strong community roots—Crested Butte, Telluride, Steamboat, Jackson Hole—are a better option if you want to combine slopeside condo convenience with nightlife in town, close at hand.

WHEN TO GO

Wherever possible, avoid peak periods. That's easy to say, but for most of us almost impossible to do. That's why traditional holiday weeks such as Christmas, March break, and Easter are the busiest at most resorts and also the most expensive. If this is your only choice for a ski vacation, make the most of it by booking early (some establishments take reservations from one holiday period to the next for regular guests) and packing your patience. Early booking should include arrangements for your transportation (air, shuttle reservations, rental car) and such extras as lessons and equipment rental. You can avoid restaurant lines by choosing condo-style accommodations with kitchen and dining facilities, avoid parking-lot and shuttle-bus snarls by staying within walking distance of the lifts, and avoid some of the general crush by going to lesser known resorts.

WHERE TO STAY

Ski-resort accommodations are remarkably varied, with everything from log cabins to Ralph Lauren designer suites. The right choice for you may lie somewhere in between. You can break the broad options into three groups:

Full-Service Hotels

This is usually the most expensive option on a per-person, per-day basis, but it comes with all the trimmings. If you are prepared to pay a premium, you should get things like concierge and bell service, room service, fitness and spa facilities, valet parking, and shuttle services in the price of your stylish, spacious room or suite. Full-service hotels range in size from 500 rooms to less than a dozen—but all place the emphasis on guest services and distinctive touches.

Condominium Suites

Be careful when you hear the word *suite* used to describe a condo in ski country. This is the most popular form of accommodation, and certain liberties have been taken with the use of the term; more than one guest has been taken aback at an airless, 10-foot-by-10-foot cubicle with a wall bed and collapsible dining-room table that had been described in brochure-speak as an "intimate and self-contained mountainside condominium suite." Fortunately, examples like these become less frequent as condo quality improves and new developments appear. The term condo (referred to as "unit" in this book) is a

catchall that can mean anything from a one-bedroom in a high-rise tower to a five-bedroom town house–style unit with a private lap pool. It can also mean prices that range from $100 to $1,000 per day, but on a per-person basis condos are generally cheaper than hotel rooms of comparable quality. There's also a wide range in quality; low-end units often have utilitarian decor and inferior furnishings and household appliances, but upscale units may have handwoven rugs, en suite hot tubs and saunas, and high-tech kitchens. In general, you get what you pay for, but when shopping for the right unit consider the following:

Location

Generally speaking, the closer the unit is to the lifts, the more expensive it will be. Weigh that against the cost of renting a car, and the condo may be a better deal. On the other hand, if a car is desirable for getting around, consider units farther away from the slopes, where you can probably get more space for the price of a smaller slopeside unit.

Size

How much time do you plan to spend in your accommodations? If you plan to have most meals and entertainment at home, look for a fireplace, a full-size kitchen, and a separate dining area; otherwise opt for smaller units and spend the savings on restaurant meals. Check the bed count carefully: "suitable for 8" may mean four to a room or sofa beds in the living room; if you value privacy, count bedrooms, not beds. Bathrooms are key, too: Six skiers lining up for one bathroom can turn things ugly in the early morning rush to the slopes.

Amenities

Are there spa facilities, a pool, exercise rooms, and daily maid service? Do you want all the extras? If you don't, why pay for them? Daily housekeeping is a worthwhile extra (it's not standard with all condos) if you don't want to deal with beds and dishes, and the recreational amenities can be important for families.

Small Inns, Bed-and-Breakfasts, and Motels

This is the most varied category of accommodations, and it includes some real gems as well as your basic no-frills motel room. Prices vary accordingly, and keep in mind that many smaller establishments have a per-person rate rather than a per-room rate. Some include breakfast and/or dinner in the basic rate, and some of the more expensive places provide afternoon snacks and libations.

HOW TO GO

By Car

This is the easiest, most practical option, and if your destination is within 500 miles, it's your best bet. An alternative to loading up the family wagon is a rental car. Book in advance for a weekly rate, and the couple hundred dollars it costs to rent a car will help save wear and tear on your own vehicle. Whatever the car, make sure it's equipped for winter driving, which can range from the sublime to the horrific. That means winter tires—chains, if they're required—good wipers, topped-up fluids, and emergency supplies such as flares, candles, and a flashlight. Keep windows free from baggage, carry all skis and poles in bags on a well-secured roof rack, and pack lots of snacks.

If you're traveling to the resort by some other means but need a car once you get there, make sure you book well in advance for the best rate. Request a vehicle with a ski rack and winter tires; inquire about local chain regulations. Most airport rental agencies provide a map to your destination, and many run winter promotions in conjunction with the resorts. Make sure you sign at least two drivers on the vehicle registration, and make sure you understand the implications of the insurance waiver or surcharge. Finally, take it easy. The temptation to get to the slopes should be tempered with an eye to the driving conditions.

By Plane

Booking early is the key to getting the best possible airfare, and attention to this detail can save you hundreds of dollars. Wherever possible, schedule your arrival at the destination airport as early in the day as possible. In some places, like Salt Lake City, you may be able to get in an afternoon of skiing, but in most cases an early arrival just makes it easier if you are driving to the resort, especially if the weather is bad or you have high mountain passes to cross. Most airlines accept skis as a regular part of the luggage allotment, but at many airports they have to be checked at a special service desk and retrieved at your destination in an area separate from the main luggage carousel. Make sure you have identification tags on all bags, and carry your boots on board if possible. Lost skis can be rented easily enough, but rented boots are another story.

By Train

This is becoming an increasingly popular option, but it's not always the most convenient. If you yearn to ride the rails, Amtrak (tel. 800/872–7245) has somewhat regular service to most major cities near the resorts in this book. Several resorts, such as Winter Park and Squaw, come close. Check with Amtrak for options.

PACKING FOR A SKI VACATION

When it comes to taking a trip, I'm viewed as a totalitarian by my family as a result of the one-bag edict. For a ski trip, though, I soften and allow an abundance of accessories because the trip just seems to demand it. Besides, in addition to a regular piece of luggage, you can stuff all those needed extras into ski bags and boot bags with almost reckless abandon. These four pieces of luggage are what you need to tote your stuff to the slopes:

Duffle or Equipment Bag

This is your main piece of luggage, and larger is definitely better. A well-made, waterproof model will cost between $80 and $150 but will outlast most of your ski equipment. Don't scrimp—look for quality materials, reinforced stitching and seam welding, a heavy-duty two-way zipper, sturdy handles stitched around the bottom of the bag (not just to the top), and a shoulder strap that can be detached. Some models have external pockets; this is useful for keeping gear organized or isolating wet footwear.

Boot Bag

Doesn't it amaze you that some skiers spend hundreds of dollars on a pair of ski boots, then subject them to the torture test of an airline luggage system without protecting them in a boot bag? Besides protecting your most valuable piece of equipment, the boot bag is a bonus for packing extra gear. Again, think large in a boot bag, and avoid those nifty-looking versions in the shape of a boot that have little room for extras. Buy a good-quality bag with a sturdy zipper and shoulder strap, and once your boots are stowed you can fill up the rest of the space with those absolutely necessary extras.

Ski Bag

A ski bag is essential for protecting your skis, and like the boot bag it gives you a great deal of extra space. A good ski bag should be made from heavy-duty, waterproof material and have a full-length zipper and well-secured carrying and shoulder straps. Use extra space to pack sweaters, jackets, and other clothing, which also help protect your skis.

Day Pack

This is an important piece of luggage because it does double duty. Use it as carry-on luggage for your personal items—tickets, valuables, medications, sunglasses, and so on. At the resort you'll need it to carry your lunch, goggles, camera, and other items. The day pack shouldn't be too large, but it should have padded shoulder straps and many outside pockets with large zippers that are easy to open and close with gloves on.

With all this space at your disposal, here's a suggested list of clothing and other items you'll need for a week at a ski resort:

Ski Suit

Take two if you have them, and try for mix-and-match versatility. Layering is the key. You can add versatility by packing a wind shell or jacket, waterproof pants, a vest, or stretch pants.

Sweaters

Wool is good, fleece is just as good and perhaps a little more adaptable. Fleece pullovers can double as sweat tops or sweaters and dry quickly when wet.

Turtlenecks

One a day is a luxury, one for every other day is refreshing, anything less is likely to end up offending your companions.

Socks

A pair for every two days is the minimum unless you're going to wash them every night. Wear only good-quality ski socks: no sweat socks, work socks, or dress socks. For cold feet, pack a pair of silk sock liners.

Sweat Suit

This is a bulky but useful extra great for lounging, dashing to the outdoor hot tub, sleeping (when the heat fails), and insulating on extra cold days.

Gloves, Goggles, Hats, Headbands, Neck Warmers

Pack two of each, if for no other reason than that it will make you a popular person when a less organized companion comes looking for a spare.

Footwear

Take a good pair of hiking or other winter boots, plus other casual footwear and something that will double as a dress shoe if required.

Casual Clothing

Keep in mind that you'll spend at least two-thirds of your waking hours in ski wear, so your casual-clothing requirements will be fairly light. Most ski resorts are casual places, so chic evening clothes are likely to go unused.

Bathing Suit

This may be the most commonly forgotten item on a ski trip. Pack yours—even if there's no pool, just a sauna or hot tub.

And if room permits:

Repair Items

A Swiss army knife is indispensable (for everything from opening wine to unjamming a balky boot buckle), but also consider a small multihead screwdriver, vise grip, bastard file (for your edges), duct tape (for emergency repairs), elastic shock straps (for securing skis to roof racks), and a small flashlight.

Games and Other Diversions

Board games, cards, and reading material are all good additions for those not of the party-till-you-pass-out persuasion. Don't forget your camera, film, and spare batteries.

Sundries

Along with your basic toiletries, it's useful to include aspirin, antihistamine, plastic bandages, an elastic bandage, and an ice pack. Don't forget sunglasses, sun block, and an alarm clock.

How to Take It All

Don't waste space inside your boots or other footwear. Stuff them with breakable items, toiletries, cassette tapes, and goggles and top them off with socks. Use bags inside bags. Small nylon or fleece stuff sacks are good for organizing small items and making things easy to find. Keep all breakable items in the center of your biggest bag to afford extra protection.

Wear, don't pack, your bulkiest jacket.

Wrap your skis and poles with ski pants, turtlenecks, or long underwear. Don't overlook the cavity around the ski tips; there's always room for footwear or gloves.

Pack miscellaneous footwear in your boot bag, each pair wrapped in a plastic bag. This keeps them organized and is useful on the return journey when some may be wet or dirty.

Once you've packed, secure all zippers with a small lock or wire ties to prevent accidental spillage. Make sure each piece has a tag with your name and telephone number. Finally, make sure you can carry everything at once, if only for a short distance.

ABOUT PRICES

Prices vary wildly at ski resorts, peaking during key family-vacation periods and bottoming out during the early and late parts of the season. January is another period of relatively low rates. Be sure to check out packages, which should include lift tickets and may include ski rental or car rental. Call an individual resort's central reservations line to ask about lift ticket discounts as well as discounts for off-site purchases (at certain gro-cery stores, for example) and other promotions.

In this book, all prices quoted are based on the following:

Accommodations

All prices are based on a high-season, single-night 1997 rate with no advance booking. Unless noted otherwise, all rooms have a private bath, and all condo units have kitchens. Rates are per unit (standard double room, suite, or condo) unless otherwise indicated; if extras such as meals are included, that is also noted.

Dining

Restaurants are reviewed in three categories—expensive, moderate, and inexpensive. Specific prices are not quoted. As a guideline to price ranges use the following:

Expensive: $100 plus for dinner for two people, including one medium-price bottle of wine.

Moderate: $50–$100 for dinner for two people, including one medium-price bottle of wine.

Inexpensive: $25–$50 for dinner for two people, including one cocktail or glass of wine.

Places to eat on the mountain and best bets for breakfast fall into the moderate price range unless otherwise noted.

In the restaurants reviewed here dress is casual and reservations are not required unless noted otherwise.

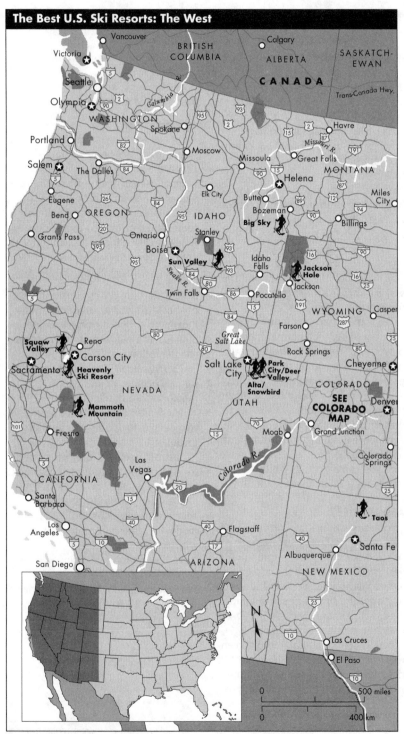

The Best U.S. Ski Resorts: The West

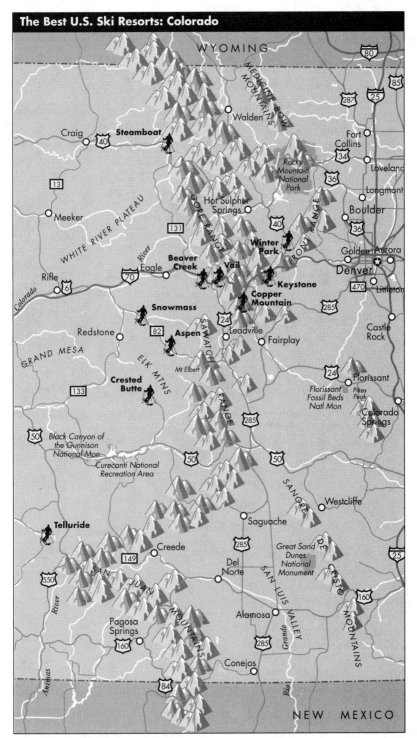

The Best U.S. Ski Resorts: Colorado

The Best U.S. Ski Resorts: The East

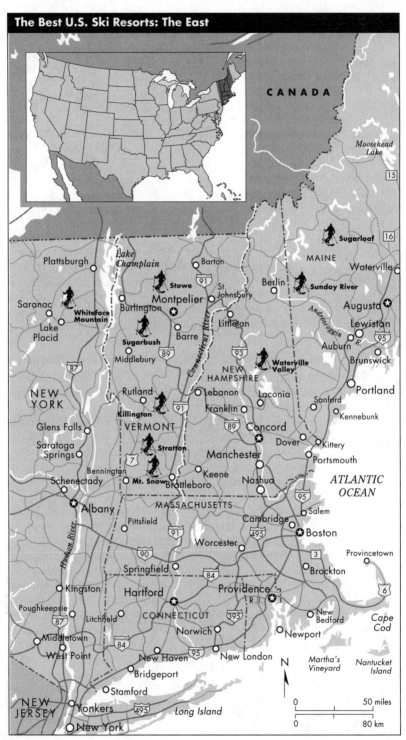

CANADA

Moosehead
Lake

15

Sugarloaf 16

MAINE

Plattsburgh
Lake
Champlain
Barton
St. Johnsbury
Berlin
Sunday River
Waterville

Stowe
91
Montpelier
Augusta

Saranac
Burlington
Littleton
Lewiston

Whiteface
Mountain
Barre
93
Auburn
95

Lake
Placid
Sugarbush
89
Middlebury
Sanford
Brunswick

NEW
YORK
Rutland
NEW
HAMPSHIRE
Waterville
Valley
Portland

Glens Falls
Killington
VERMONT
Lebanon
Laconia
Kennebunk

Saratoga
Springs
91
Franklin
Concord
Dover
Kittery

Schenectady
Bennington
Stratton
7
89
Manchester
Portsmouth

Mt. Snow
Brattleboro
Keene
Nashua
ATLANTIC
OCEAN

Albany
MASSACHUSETTS
Salem
95

Pittsfield
Cambridge
Boston

87
90
Worcester
495
3
Provincetown

Hudson River
91
Springfield
84
Brockton
6

Kingston
Hartford
Providence
R.I.
Cape
Cod

Poughkeepsie
87
Litchfield
CONNECTICUT
395
New
Bedford

Middletown
84
Norwich
Newport

West Point
New Haven
95
New London
N
Martha's
Vineyard
Nantucket
Island

Bridgeport

Stamford

NEW
JERSEY
Yonkers
495
Long Island
0   50 miles

New York
0   80 km

F or a state that is most often associated with sun, surfing, and vineyards, California has an astonishing variety of skiing. The mighty Sierra Nevada range stretches north from Los Angeles to the Oregon state line, yielding more than 30 ski areas, which range from the glittering two-state sprawl of Heavenly Ski Resort, in both California and Nevada, to the more isolated locals-oriented slopes such as June Mountain and Bear Valley. The region that includes Heavenly and Squaw Valley is called the Lake Tahoe basin.

This 300-by-150-mile wilderness area dominated by the wall of rugged sky-punching peaks is almost unknown outside California, but for the 55% of visitors to Lake Tahoe who are Californians, it is their winter playground. And as with most things Californian, nothing succeeds like excess. The resorts in this snow-blessed gift from the gods can variously lay claim as the biggest, the highest, the snowiest, the hippest, and the most star-studded resorts in America.

The Sierra Nevada—an unbroken monolith that is nearly as big as the Alps and boasts the highest peaks (many topping the 12,000-foot mark) outside Alaska, as well as the largest trees, the deepest valleys, and the highest waterfalls—is the most massive mountain block in North America. (Physically, the Rockies encompass a larger area, but they are a collection of ranges, separated by wide steppes and mesas.)

The ski resorts in this region are just as impressive: Heavenly—in the storied and striking Lake Tahoe basin—is the largest ski resort in the state, and maybe in the nation, depending on how you measure. Lofty Mammoth Mountain is annually smothered under more than 70 feet of snow; and Squaw Valley is one of only two U.S. resorts that have hosted the Winter Olympics. The skiing, weather, and snow conditions in the region certainly rival those found in Colorado and Utah.

GETTING TO CALIFORNIA RESORTS

By Plane

Reno/Tahoe International Airport, in Reno, Nevada, is the international facility closest to Lake Tahoe and Mammoth Mountain. **Alaska Airlines** (tel. 800/426–0333), **American** (tel. 800/433–7300), **America West** (tel. 800/247–5692), **Continental** (tel. 800/525–0280), **Delta** (tel. 800/221–1212), **Northwest** (tel. 800/225–2525), **Reno Air** (tel. 800/736–6247), **Sky West** (tel. 800/453–9417 in Nevada, Utah, Arizona, Idaho, and Wyoming only), **Southwest** (tel. 800/435–9792), **TWA** (tel. 800/221–2000), **United** (tel. 800/241–6522), and **US Airways** (tel. 800/428–4322) have direct or connecting service into Reno International from most major cities.

Car Rental

Avis (tel. 800/831–8000), **Budget** (tel. 800/527–0700), **Dollar** (tel. 702/739–8408), **Hertz** (tel. 800/654–3131), **National** (tel. 702/739–5391), and **Thrifty** (tel. 702/736–4706) have counters at Reno/Tahoe International Airport. Most rent winterized vehicles—four-wheel-drive cars or front-wheel-drive cars equipped with chains. Be sure to reserve one of these vehicle types: In the event of a storm, if you don't have a four-wheel-drive car and chains are required, you may have to purchase them for an exorbitant amount of money from one of the few gas stations on the highway; or worse, you may end up stranded for several days.

Shuttle Service

From Reno/Tahoe International Airport look for the **Tahoe Casino Express** (tel. 702/785–2424 or 800/446–6128), which has an average of 15 round-trips daily; the cost is $17 each way.

By Bus

Greyhound Lines (tel. 916/541–2222 or 800/231–2222) serves South Lake Tahoe with daily nonstop service to and from the Sacramento and San Francisco areas (2½ and 4 hours, respectively). Sierra Nevada Gray Line (tel. 702/331–1147 or 800/822–6009) has regularly scheduled service from Reno to South Lake Tahoe.

By Train

The **Amtrak** (tel. 800/872–7245) *California Zephyr* bound for Chicago has daily service from the San Francisco/Oakland train station to both Reno and Truckee (20 miles from the north shore of Lake Tahoe and 60 miles from the south shore). It's a spectacular ride up the coast and over the Donner Pass, with stops in Richmond, Martinez, Fairfield, Davis, Sacramento, Roseville, and Colfax.

HEAVENLY SKI RESORT

Box 2180
Stateline, NV 89449
Tel. 702/586–7000

STATISTICALLY SPEAKING

Base elevation: 6,540 feet in California; 7,200 feet in Nevada

Summit elevation: 10,040 feet

Vertical drop: 3,500 feet

Skiable terrain: 4,800 acres

Number of trails: 79

Longest run: 5.5 miles

Lifts and capacity: 1 aerial tram, 3 high-speed quads, 8 triples, 7 doubles, 5 surface; 29,000 skiers per hour

Daily lift ticket: $46

Average annual snowfall: 250 inches

Number of skiing days 1995–96: 150

Snowmaking: 3,100 acres; 65%

Terrain mix: N 20%, I 45%, E 35%

Snowboarding: yes

Heavenly Ski Resort is the largest of seven such areas dotting the shore of the achingly aquamarine Lake Tahoe. The vision of the lake prompted Mark Twain to write, "I thought it must surely be the fairest picture the whole earth affords." The 22-by-12-mile blue glacial jewel, rimmed by a necklace of white peaks and fed by 63 streams, offers a 72-mile drive that is among the most stunning in America.

Although its physical attributes are singularly spectacular, this is a resort of many contradictions. It is at once a gaudy, ostentatious casino and entertainment hot spot and a strikingly picturesque and diverse outdoor recreation nirvana. In fact, it is two towns divided by the state line between California and Nevada: Butting up against this man-made boundary are the towns of South Lake Tahoe, California, and Stateline, Nevada.

Although they share a common boundary, they are strikingly different in character. The Nevada side is flush with major casino action led by some of the most familiar names in the business—Caesars, Harvey's, Harrah's—all presenting towering edifices reflecting their success at separating you from your money yet making you as comfortable as possible while doing so. On the California side you'll find a town in transition—a faded lady, if you will, attempting to redefine its character after the decline of its belle epoque in the '30s and '40s, when the blue bloods of southern California made Tahoe their retreat, much the way East Coast millionaires carved their place in the Adirondack wilderness around Lake Placid. The grand homes on the shoreline still stand, alongside new multimillion-dollar houses, but unfortunately so does a shantytown with run-down motels that embarrassingly sits slap in the middle of town. However, a 10-year plan to revitalize the area has broken ground, with a new regulation-size ice-skating rink, parks, shops and hotels, and will eventually include an aerial tramway from the center of town to Heavenly.

In the meantime, this curious coexistence continually draws record crowds because it provides visitors with virtually every conceivable experience—from high-stakes poker to high-alpine touring. The region is an entertainment mecca, perhaps second to none

Area code: 916 (CA);
702 (NV)

Children's services: ski school,
tel. 702/586–7000

Snow phone:
tel. 916/541–7544

Police: CA, tel. 916/542–6100

Sheriff: NV, tel. 702/586–7250

California highway patrol:
tel. 916/587–3510

Medical center: California
Stateline Medical, tel. 702/
588–3561; Tahoe Urgent
Care, tel. 916/541–3277

Hospital: Barton Memorial
Hospital, tel. 916/541–3420

South Lake Tahoe Chamber of
Commerce: tel. 916/541–5255

Road conditions:
tel. 916/445–1534 (CA);
702/793–1313 (NV)

Towing: Welcome's,
tel. 916/541–8811

FIVE-STAR FAVORITES

Best run for vertical:
Gunbarrel

Best run overall: Big Dipper
Bowl to Stagecoach

Best bar/nightclub:
Thirsty Duck

Best hotel: Embassy Suites

Best restaurant: Evan's

in ski country, with its natural wonders at times playing second fiddle to the man-made variety. Still, overall, it is a resort area that has something for everyone—from high rollers in limousines to families in station wagons.

HOW TO GET THERE

By Plane

The closest major airport is Reno's **Reno-Tahoe International Airport** (*see* Getting to California Resorts, *above*), 90 minutes by car.

Shuttle Service

From South Lake Tahoe catch the airport shuttle (tel. 916/542–6180) for $6 to any major hotel on Route 50. From there you can hop aboard the free Heavenly shuttle.

By Car

From the Reno-Tahoe International Airport, take Route 395 south to Carson City, where you take Route 50 west over Spooner Summit and down into South Lake Tahoe and then to Heavenly. During the day and in good weather, the 55-mile drive along winding mountain roads is easy and scenically spectacular, but if you arrive late in the day, it's best to stay in Reno overnight rather than tackle the highways in darkness. From the San Francisco area it's about a 200-mile (3½-hour) journey—east on I–80 for about 90 minutes to Sacramento and then east on Route 50 for about 100 miles (two hours) directly to Lake Tahoe. Regardless of where your travels begin, the weather changes fast—especially in the high passes—and police and highway department crews will move equally quickly to close roads when the snows come or stop those without chains or four-wheel-drive vehicles.

Avis and **Hertz** operate out of South Lake Tahoe Airport.

GETTING AROUND

A car is not really necessary in Tahoe unless you want to do some touring. Parking at the resort is limited, the roads to it are congested, and often you'll have to park as much as a half mile from the lifts on holidays and weekends. Heavenly operates a free ski shuttle from most South Lake Tahoe lodging properties; also most casinos provide on-request shuttle service (tel. 702/586–7000) to and from the ski area every half hour between 8 and 5:20. Finally, a number of taxi services, including **Yellow Cab** (tel. 916/544–5555) and **Paradise Cab** (tel. 916/577–4708), cover the entire Heavenly and Lake Tahoe area.

THE SKIING

Heavenly is a vast, sprawling resort of nine peaks, two valleys, and three base-lodge areas straddling two states. It is by most measurements the largest ski area in the nation and has become one of my favorites. Like the resort area, the mountain has a little something for everyone, including some remarkable expert terrain that officially opened in 1991 and has so far appeased the critics who had complained that the resort lacked true challenge.

Curiously, when first seen from the base, the slopes on the California side look impossibly difficult, with the heart-stopping, unnerving view of mogul-choked Gunbarrel Run. What you see is not what you get, however, for Heavenly is an inverted mountain; the majority of the slopes are rated as intermediate and are located out of sight, on the top half.

This extensive intermediate terrain, combined with the prolific and reliable snow coverage and sunny weather, has always attracted large crowds of skiers, especially families. The world's largest snow-making system also guarantees good early and late-season coverage. The opening of the Mott and Killebrew canyons areas—with their steep chutes and thick-timbered slopes—has added a dimension that the resort admittedly had been missing. For the very few who relish the formidable, it's a reason to return to Heavenly, but for most of us, the 20 square miles of wide, well-groomed pistes present enough challenge.

Another knock against the sprawling Heavenly terrain is the number of flat traverses that must be negotiated between mountain sectors. It's true enough, and there's not too much you can do about it except to pay careful attention to the trail map and be prepared to carry some speed across the critical sections. The resort has made some effort to minimize this inconvenience with some well-placed signs and good grooming on the flat sections; overall, it's a small price to pay for the vastness and variety of the mountain.

Like the towns below the peaks, Heavenly can be busy and confusing, with three base lodges that help disperse the traffic on both sides of the resort. The California side is typically the most crowded in the morning; the tram is the fastest and most popular way to the midstation and the upper-mountain lifts. A double and a triple chair also go to the same place, providing an alternative to the long tram line. To avoid the crowds, you can set out from the slightly less busy Stagecoach or Boulder base lodges, on the Nevada side. Heading to the top from this side requires a three-lift ride from the Boulder base and two lifts from the Stagecoach, but during busy periods it ends up being a faster way to the top.

For snowboarders the entire mountain is your playground, particularly the airport snowboard park on the Nevada side. Snowboard classes from novice to expert are offered. In 1996 two Burton Snowboard Demo centers opened at the mountain, featuring all of Burton's premier snowboard models.

Novices

If you start your day from the California side, be prepared for a jaw-to-the-chest gape when you feast your eyes on the bump-studded front face under the tram. Don't worry, though; you'll never have to ski the famed Gunbarrel because just as the lift will whisk you up to tamer territory, so it can bring you down at the end of the day.

In fact, as one veteran Heavenly skier suggested, "Hardly anyone skis Gunbarrel because in the morning most are not ready for it, and at the end of the day most are too tired." First-timers starting from the California base can tackle the Poma Trail and the Enchanted Forest first—two short, smooth, gentle runs served by their own West Bowl Poma. Once you get a few runs under your boots, take the tram to midstation, where two chairs—Powderbowl and Waterfall—take you to several wide, well-groomed boulevards that will surely increase your confidence level. The easiest way down is via Maggies, but you can reach it only from the Waterfall lift. If you take the Powderbowl lift, there's a short blue section, fairly steep, to tackle before you get to Maggies. Also from the top of the Waterfall lift you can cut off Maggies to Mombo Meadows, which winds back under both lifts. Powderbowl Run, the other trail accessible from the top of either chair, is marked blue, but it's wide and groomed, with a fairly gentle pitch and no surprises. Try it once you've had your warm-ups on the green trails.

To move up a notch but still stay on wide, groomed trails, take the Canyon, Sky Express, or Ridge lifts (go to the top of the Waterfall lift and then ski down Maggies to the bottom of the Ridge chair or tackle the short, not-too-steep right-hand side of Maggies and carry on down to the bottom of the Canyon or Sky Express lifts) and go right off the lift, along the winding Ridge Run. The lower half, where it turns into Powderbowl, gets a little steeper, but you can always bail out at Mombo Meadows.

If you're a first-timer or early novice, your options are a bit limited if you're skiing on the Nevada side. But novice-intermediates should be able to make the transition successfully from green to blue here. To warm up, head for the Edgewood Bowl run, at the Boulder base, reached from the Boulder lift. From here take the Northbowl lift to mid-mountain and a plethora of blue runs that any solid snowplower should be able to handle. Right off the lift you come to Upper North Bowl, which starts out on a good pitch but is wide and well groomed and tends not to be busy because most folks have gone farther up the mountain. When it widens out more below the initial pitch, make sure you turn hard right (looking down), or you could end up on the North Bowl, a black run with lots of moguls. After you pass under the North Bowl chair, you come to a three-way split: 075 is groomed but tends to get bumped early in the day; Way Home is a wide speed-controlled zone that takes you to the bottom of the North Bowl lift; and the lower part of the Olympic Downhill, wide and groomed, takes you to the bottom of the Stagecoach chair.

Intermediates

This is your mountain, with an endless selection of medium-to-high-end intermediate runs, no matter from which side you set off in the morning. From the California base take the tram and follow the long, flat traverse over to the Sky Express lift and turn right off the lift along the Ridge Run for a choice of a half-dozen primo intermediate cruisers. As you ski along the Ridge Run trail, you'll have easy access to all the blues. For your first run, however, you might want to skip Liz's and start on Rusutsu, Canyon, or Betty's—a trio of fairly steep but wide and groomed leg warmers. Next time up the Sky Express lift try Liz's, which tends to be steeper than the others and is moguled.

Your next move from the top is to take the Skyline Trail, skirting the canyon to the Nevada side, and come down the mountain on Big Dipper, a long, high-speed cruiser. If you really want to burn your thighs and can carry some cautious speed, cut through the midstation day-lodge area and pick up Stagecoach, which will carry you all the way down to the Stagecoach base area. Another option is to cut left (looking down the mountain) instead of right just below midstation, get onto Pepi's to Upper North Bowl, and then 075 down to the Boulder base area. If you see that traffic is heavy on the Stagecoach, North Bowl, or Dipper lifts, cut right at midstation and head for the less busy Galaxy lift, where you'll find Galaxy and Perimeter, a pair of medium-paced blue runs. Perimeter is a well-groomed cruiser with steady pitch and some speed-checking rolls and dips, while Galaxy has sections of ungroomed bumps.

Maybe it's time to try some bowl and chute skiing (without losing your dignity in the canyons) in the Milky Way Bowl, which is mostly above tree line except for the lower third of the area. Take the Dipper Express and cut a hard left off the lift to the cat track that runs along the edge of the bowl. Although it's steep here, it's easy to pick your way down, taking advantage of the open space as you pause and ponder your next move. When you reach the control gates to the expert terrain in the canyon, you'll be steered to a steep, narrow exit trail that spits you out on a blue run, just a short scoot from the Dipper chair. The signs are clear. Skiing with your eyes closed would be the only way to end up in expert terrain without knowing it, so relax. Keep in mind that if you are based on the California side, you must start heading back that way no later than 3 PM, or you risk being stuck in Nevada. If this happens, you'll have to take a shuttle bus, which only stops at the accommodations, back into town. Your only other choice is a $10 cab ride.

Experts

You'll most certainly want to head for the Mott and Killebrew canyons with their chutes and couloirs, but in your rush for vertical, don't ignore some of the challenging tree runs that lie partly concealed on the front face. On this side you'll find stepladder steepness, big-tree closeness, and some of the best untouched snow on the mountain. The chance to brush teeth with mountain pine does not appeal to everyone; hence the snow often lies still and preserved for even several days after a storm. The fastest route from the California side is on the tram and the Sky Express lift to the top. To warm up, turn left off the tram to Ellie's, a satisfying blend of high-speed steeps, drop-offs, and a limitless number of excursions through the trees. Next time up follow the Skyline Trail to the Nevada side and take a few runs in the Big Dipper Bowl before heading for the wide-open spaces of the Milky Way Bowl, which is steep and wide and mostly above tree line, apart from some tasty and challenging little groves near the bottom.

You could easily explore the Milky Way for a half day, but when you crave just a little more steepness and fewer skiers, it's time to head for either Mott or Killebrew Canyon. There are a dozen or so designated runs, but this is really free-form skiing out of free-fall chutes and couloirs. Entry to the canyons is through clearly marked control gates, and once you pick your spot over the lip, recover your equilibrium, and restore your breathing to normal, you can fancy-dance your way down some of the sweetest tree-stuffed steeps you'll find anywhere. This is 800 acres of double-black-diamond terrain that's never groomed and features many hidden obstacles, tight knots of trees, and lots of untouched snow. Remember, if you're staying on the California side, head back by 3 PM and—if you dare—strut your stuff on Gunbarrel's school-bus-size moguls.

WHERE TO STAY

Reno is an option if you want to gamble more than ski or if you arrive on a late-evening flight and don't want to deal with the sometimes tricky route over Spooner Summit and down to South Lake Tahoe. The hotels and motels are numerous and somewhat indistinguishable, with the casinos claiming the high ground and a string of nondescript chain properties dominating the midrange choices. Rates are more than reasonable—most places aim to get your money some other way—and as winter tends to be low season in Reno, discount deals are available at most major hotels. This dusty Nevada gambling town is no Las Vegas, but it can amuse you for an evening.

If you're here to ski, your best bet is to stay closer to the slopes, in either Stateline or South Lake Tahoe, where many casino hotels have set up shop alongside the more traditional ski resort hotels and inns and altogether too many decidedly tacky motels. Yes, there are some truly awful motels and small hotels in this area, and although there is a possibility that many will be leveled in the near future, in the meantime they remain a blight on the town. Prices are very reasonable, especially package deals, and with some careful shopping you can get a three-, five-, or seven-day deal that works out to less than $50 a night.

In terms of access to Heavenly, it makes little difference whether you stay in Stateline, Nevada, or South Lake Tahoe, California, as shuttle buses run regularly from hotels to either the California or Nevada base lodges. Avoid using your car if possible, especially if you're going to the California side, where the traffic jams are fierce and some of the parking so far from the lifts that you need to take a shuttle bus back to the base area. Accommodations can be booked through central reservations at 800/243–2836 or by writing to Box 2180, Stateline, NV 89449.

Expensive

Christiana Inn
Perhaps, when the much-talked-about renovation of the area takes place, some thought will be given to building more small, European-style lodges such as the Christiana. Within walking distance of the lifts on the California side, this delightful spot has just two rooms and four suites, each tastefully decorated with custom furnishings and special touches like king-size beds and a complimentary decanter of brandy. The suites all have fireplaces—two even have a fireplace in the bedroom, and two others have an individual sauna and whirlpool bath. Although the suites will definitely handle a family of four, the inn is more suited to couples because of the generally low-key ambience. *3819 Saddle Rd., Box 18298, South Lake Tahoe, CA 96151, tel. 916/544–7337,* *fax 916/544–5342. 2 rooms, 4 suites. Facilities: restaurant, lounge, maid service, ski storage, laundry. MC, V. $75–$175, including Continental breakfast.*

Embassy Suites
A favorite full-service hotel in South Lake Tahoe for many reasons (including that it's *not* a gambling emporium), it sits just far enough away from the casino canyon and the tacky motel strip. Inside, the six-story atrium lobby gives you a sense of mountain-size space. The capacious feel is continued in all the extraspacious rooms, which are really two-room suites with minikitchens that include a fridge, a microwave, and a coffeemaker. A pullout couch expands sleeping capacity to four—ideal for small families. The daily rate includes an excellent buffet breakfast served in the atrium lobby along with a complimentary two-hour cocktail session each day. *4130 Lake Tahoe Blvd., South Lake Tahoe, CA 96150, tel. 916/544–5400 or 800/362–2779, fax 916/544–4900. 400 rooms. Facilities: restaurant, bar, lounge, exercise room, indoor pool, 24-hr desk service, maid service, ski storage, game room. AE, D, DC, MC, V. $198–$278.*

Harvey's Resort Hotel & Casino
Sometimes it can be difficult to distinguish between the various upscale casino hotels, but Harvey's—being a little more like a resort hotel than a gambling den—manages to rise above the competition. When you check in, you don't have to maneuver your baggage around the slot machines, and the ambience rises above the well-worn weariness of some others. The multitude of rooms and suites is defi-

nitely upscale, with elegant French provincial furnishings and lots of luxury extras, such as multiple telephones and TVs, a bar, and a refrigerator. Rooms and suites on the lakeside have the added attraction of a spectacular view. A family or two couples would be more than comfortable in a two-room suite with a balcony, a Jacuzzi, and a marble bathroom. Excellent deals exist on two- and three-night packages that include three nights' accommodation, dinner for two, a pitcher of margaritas, a daily buffet breakfast, daily box lunches for skiers, and two lift tickets. *Rte. 50, Box 128, Stateline, NV 89449, tel. 702/588–2411 or 800/427–8397, fax 702/782–4889. 742 rooms. Facilities: 8 restaurants, 5 bars, hot tub, outdoor heated pool, health club, 24-hr desk service, 24-hr room service, maid service, ski storage, laundry, game room. AE, D, DC, MC, V. $99–$195.*

Ridge Tahoe Resort

Its private 10-passenger gondola connects this fairly exclusive enclave of deluxe one- and two-bedroom condos directly to the slopes on the Nevada side of Heavenly. The condo units are ultraluxurious, with designer furnishings and decorations, large bedrooms with king- and queen-size beds, a full kitchen, a fireplace, a wet bar, and a stereo. It's an ideal spot for families because of its self-contained isolation, away from the bright lights and gaming of downtown Tahoe. *400 Ridge Club Dr., Box 5790, Stateline, NV 89449, tel. 702/588–3553, fax 702/588–7099. 480 rooms. Facilities: 2 restaurants, bar, 14 hot tubs, indoor pool, health club, 24-hr desk service, maid service, ski storage, laundry, game room. AE, D, MC, V. $160–$455.*

Moderate

Best Western Station House Inn

This good midrange property is about 2 miles from the resort. Although its rooms are not luxurious, they are comfortable, roomy, and equipped with enough amenities to satisfy all but the most fussy visitor. There are also several two- and three-bedroom cabins that will suit families or groups. Ski packages include breakfast, dinner, and daily lift ticket. *901 Park Ave., South Lake Tahoe, CA 96157, tel. 916/542–1101 or 800/822–5953, fax 916/542–1714. 102 rooms. Facilities: restaurant, bar, hot tub, ski storage. AE, D, DC, MC, V. $108–$175, including full breakfast.*

Inn by the Lake

These two three-story brown wooden buildings linked by heated brick walkways are in a pretty lakeside location. The spacious, no-nonsense rooms that can sleep four, and larger suites that sleep more, make this an ideal family spot. The rooms, furnished in light oak and earth-tone patterned fabrics, come with various bed configurations ranging from one king-size to two doubles or queen-size beds. The suites—some with a lake view—can sleep 12 comfortably; some have a full kitchen. *3300 Lake Tahoe Blvd., South Lake Tahoe, CA 96150, tel. 916/542–0330 or 800/877–1466, fax 916/541–6596. 87 rooms, 13 suites. Facilities: pool, whirlpool, sauna, ski storage. AE, D, DC, MC, V. $84–$395, including Continental breakfast.*

Lakeland Village Beach & Ski Resort

This big, sprawling lakefront resort complex, about a mile from town and the lifts, has units in the main lodge that range from small, comfortable studios to larger one-bedrooms with a loft. There are also one- to four-bedroom town houses, some with a great lake view, that come complete with fireplace, deck, and kitchen and can sleep 10. *3535 Lake Tahoe Blvd., Box 1356, South Lake Tahoe, CA 96150, tel. 916/541–7711 or 800/822–5969, fax 916/544–0193. 211 units. Facilities: pool, hot tub, sauna, ski storage. AE, MC, V. $89–$460.*

Pinewild Condominiums
You'll find these delightfully deluxe town houses and condominiums on the edge of the lake just 3 miles from the center of the action, but light years away in terms of solitude and serenity. All the three-bedroom, three-bath units are modern, well designed, and well furnished, with full kitchens, log-burning fireplaces, private decks, and washer/dryer combos; some even come with a hot tub or Jacuzzi. Many of the large units also have spectacular lakefront views. Parents might appreciate the quiet location, but the kids may find it a bit too quiet; there are few on-site amenities. *Box 11347, Zephyr Cove, NV 89448, tel. 702/588–2790 or 800/822–2790. 135 units. Facilities: ski storage, hot tub. MC, V. $125–$400; 2-night minimum.*

Tahoe Chalet Inn
This well-maintained hotel suits families, groups, or even couples, as units range from fairly spacious standard rooms to small suites with a kitchen to self-contained chalets and even elaborate theme suites. You can choose to stay in the opulent Marie Antoinette Suite, the King Arthur or the Cleopatra suites, among others.

For the less adventurous, the standard suites are more contemporary in furnishings but just as comfortable. *3860 Lake Tahoe Blvd., Rte. 50, South Lake Tahoe, CA 96150, tel. 916/544–3311 or 800/821–2656, fax 916/544–4069. 67 units. Facilities: hot tub, sauna, ski storage, laundry, game room. AE, D, DC, MC, V. $58–$205.*

Inexpensive
Camp Richardson Resort
This 1906 logging camp became a resort in the '20s, during Lake Tahoe's heyday. The two lodges and 47 log cabins are nestled among 80 acres of pines bordering the lake. The cabins sleep eight, with fireplaces or wood stoves. The log-cabin-style lodge has a great room with a rock fireplace and a big-screen TV. Rooms in the newer Beach Inn are the only ones with phones and TVs. *1900 Jameson Beach, South Lake Tahoe, CA 96157, tel. 916/ 542–6550. 36 lodge rooms, 47 cabins. Facilities: restaurant, grocery, cross-country skiing, ski storage, sleigh rides, ski shuttle. AE, MC, V. $59–$180.*

Cedar Lodge Lake Tahoe
This is a standard two-story wood-and-painted-brick motor lodge, but it's clean and comfortable and stands in a pleasant forest grove at the east end of Stateline/South Lake Tahoe. The quiet location is within walking distance of the bright lights and an easy shuttle bus ride from the slopes. The rooms have a rustic feel, with dark pine furniture and brown tones; they contain either one or two queen-size beds. Ski packages include lift tickets and all meals. *4069 Cedar Ave., Box 4547, South Lake Tahoe, CA 96157, tel. 916/544–6453 or 800/*

222–1177. 34 rooms. Facilities: outdoor hot tub. D, MC, V. $36–$72.

Lakeside Inn & Casino

If you don't want to spend the money
for a room at one of the mainstream
casinos, the Lakeside will give you a
taste of the action for about half the
price. The rooms may not be as lavish
as those offered by the big guns up
the street, but they are spacious and
clean and come with either one king-
or two queen-size beds. There are also
a number of larger suites with a separate bedroom. All come with a TV, a
coffeemaker, and little delights such
as Belgian chocolates and French
soap. Casino-style perks are plentiful,
including discounted drinks, the
supercheap buffet spreads, gaming
rebates, and free champagne. *Rte. 50,
Kingsbury Grd., Box 5640, Stateline,
NV 89449, tel. 702/588–7777 or 800/
624–7980, fax 702/588–4092. 124
rooms. Facilities: casino, games arcade,
dining room, gift shop, and bar. AE, D,
DC, MC, V. $59–$79.*

Montgomery Inn

This wood-exterior motor inn in a
pine grove not far from the action has
green-and-white rooms with rustic
wooden furniture. The two-bedroom
cabin has a kitchen, a fireplace, a
sleep sofa, and a hot tub. *966 Modesto
Ave., South Lake Tahoe, CA 96105, tel.
916/544–3871 or 800/624–8224, fax
916/542–4385. 25 rooms, 1 cabin.
Facilities: hot tub, ski storage. AE, D,
MC, V. $30–$90.*

WHERE TO EAT

There are more than 100 restaurants
in the Lake Tahoe area, and that's not
including the multitude of dining
rooms in the ubiquitous casino hotels.

You can go for high cuisine or basic
pub grub, and you can blast a hole in
your credit card or feed a family of
four for less than $20. Remember,
some of the best deals in town are the
casino buffets.

Expensive

Christiana Inn

You'll find that the dining room in
this inn is a quiet, elegant spot, with
impeccable service and an Ameri-
can/Continental menu. Particular
favorites are the combination dishes
such as quail and scallops on a
tomato coulis or prawns and lamb
served with a red onion confit. The
more traditional solo offerings also
get high marks, especially the beef
dishes—Wellington, tournedos, and
filet mignon—which are all cooked
precisely to your liking. If you don't
mind dining before 7, check out the
early skier's special. *3819 Saddle Rd.,
South Lake Tahoe, CA, tel. 916/544–
7337. MC, V.*

Evan's

Ask locals about the best upscale dining in town, and most will suggest
this delightful family-owned-and-
operated eatery. The vintage Tahoe
cottage, nestled in the pine trees, is
about 5 miles from the town center.
Inside, it's brimming with a warm,
woodsy atmosphere and faultless service. The menu is American, with a
changing lineup daily that includes
homemade soups and fish dishes. Try
the carpaccio of peppered ahi tuna,
the roast pepper venison steak with
dried blueberries and black-currant
glaze, or the baked salmon with
smoked salmon crust served with
asparagus and black caviar. *536 Emer-*

ald Bay Rd., South Lake Tahoe, CA, tel. 916/542–1990. MC, V.

Fresh Ketch

In an upbeat bistro atmosphere, this is an excellent spot for seafood, including a potpourri of fresh dishes such as tuna, swordfish, sole, salmon, crab legs, and any other piscatorial pleasures the daily markets produce. All are prepared to your choosing—charred, panfried, sautéed, baked, or blackened—and can be enjoyed with a number of interesting sauces. There's also a good selection of charbroiled steaks and a rack of lamb basted in a tangy Dijon batter. *2433 Venice Dr., South Lake Tahoe, CA, tel. 916/541–5683. AE, D, DC, MC, V.*

Zackary's

This bright, stylish dining room in the Embassy Suites Hotel manages to pull off—with no little panache—an unorthodox mix of wood-fired brick-oven pizzas and a smattering of upscale Continental cuisine. The pizzas are inventive, with an adventurous array of California-style toppings ranging from sprouts to goat cheese. The emphasis is mostly on light, nouvelle cooking, with a California twist, such as chicken tequila fettuccine. *Embassy Suites Hotel, 4130 Lake Tahoe Blvd., South Lake Tahoe, CA, tel. 916/543–2140. AE, D, DC, MC, V.*

Moderate

Beacon

This restaurant, in historic Camp Richardson Resort (see Lodging, above) offers the only lakeside dining on the South Shore. The decor is nautical, and the menu leans toward fish, although steaks and pastas are also well represented. It's a popular spot with locals. *1900 Jameson Beach, South Lake Tahoe, CA, tel. 916/541–0232. AE, MC, V.*

Cafe Fiore

If you're looking for a quiet, romantic atmosphere, and especially if you like northern Italian food, then try this relaxed, friendly place. The low lighting, tiny candlelighted tables, and attentive (but unobtrusive) service make it perfect for intimate evenings. The menu includes pastas, a selection of veal dishes including a divine parmigiana, rack of lamb, and some traditional European specialties, including a scrumptious beef bourguignonne and a daily fish special. *1169 Ski Run Blvd., South Lake Tahoe, CA, tel. 916/541–2908. AE, MC, V.*

The Met

This is a bit of a locals' hangout, as you'll see from the prices—particularly those in the bar during après-ski—and the reliable quality of the food. It's really an all-purpose menu that features excellent burgers, a 20-item salad bar, and a variety of specialty pizzas, such as spinach and garlic or the Roundhill combo, stacked mountain-high with just about everything you can imagine. *Round Hill Mall, Zephyr Cove, NV, tel. 702/588–8220. AE, D, MC, V.*

Siam

If you are a fan of Thai food, you will compare Siam favorably with almost any you've tried elsewhere. Good preparation and delicate seasoning—with occasional power spicing—complement all the traditional dishes. Satay comes in numerous styles, and there are other choices such as *pad thai*, noodles with bean sprouts, egg, sugar, salt, and red onion in a sweet-and-sour spice mix. There are numerous delicious soups perked up with lemongrass, zesty coconut with chicken, and delicately cooked fish dishes. *2180 Rte. 50, South Lake Tahoe, CA, tel. 916/544–0370. AE, MC, V.*

Inexpensive

The Cantina

Good, spirited Mexican fare accompanies a great après-ski atmosphere that tends to linger well into the evening after it spills over from the dining room into the bar. The fajitas get high marks, but so do most of the traditional dishes. There are also crab enchiladas and *carnitas,* roast pork leg served with a soft taco. Portions are generous, and even larger appetites can opt for mesquite-barbecued steaks or chicken. *765 Emerald Bay Rd., South Lake Tahoe, CA, tel. 916/544–1233. MC, V.*

Dixon's Brew Pub

This place is fast, friendly, and thrifty, with the added attraction of more than a dozen brews on tap. The extensive menu relies on good, contemporary American dining, with a variety of salads, healthy pastas, and specialties from south of the border, including good chicken fajitas. *675 Emerald Bay Rd., South Lake Tahoe, CA, tel. 916/542–3389. AE, MC, V.*

Best Bets for Breakfast

Casino Buffets

No self-respecting casino is without a high-speed breakfast buffet (the faster you get through the first meal of the day, the faster you can get back to losing your money), and if volume and price are your chief criteria, check out the all-you-can-eat affairs at the major gambling emporiums.

Ernie's

The waitstaff has been there so long their portraits are framed and hanging above the kitchen. And if you come often enough, you can get a coffee mug with your name on it. The service is fast and friendly in this diner. A selection of egg dishes will satisfy your cholesterol cravings, or you can opt for heart-healthy selections. The locally roasted Alpen Sierra Coffee will wake you up for a day on the slopes. *1146 Emerald Bay Rd., South Lake Tahoe, CA, tel. 916/541–2161. No credit cards.*

Jumpstart Jack's

The early (very early) morning crowd tends to be the mountain workers, so this is a great place to pick up some tips about weather and conditions. What attracts them, and everyone else, to this somewhat grungy little coffee hut is the best java in town, and that includes their cappuccino and espresso. A varied selection of pastries and bagels makes up most of the food menu. *4040 Lake Tahoe Blvd., South Lake Tahoe, CA, tel. 916/544–5522. No credit cards.*

NIGHTLIFE AND ENTERTAINMENT

Truly, there are few ski towns anywhere that can match the diversity and intensity of the nightlife and entertainment in South Lake Tahoe. Even if you eliminate the gambling from your après-ski activities, the lineup of headline acts, special events, and dozens of bars and nightclubs gives it the edge even over Aspen. The casinos want nothing more than to keep you happy by feeding you and entertaining you as they parade the temptation of the tables and the slots in front of your face. Thus bargains abound, with reduced drink prices, discount coupons by the bucket, and endless meal specials. For current live entertainment, check the local listings.

Après-Ski

California Bar

Make this bar your first stop after your last run. It's in the base lodge area on the California side, and it really cooks after skiing. You'll always find it packed with sun-flushed revelers, and the daily drink specials ensure that the glow doesn't fade. They also have regular live entertainment. *Base lodge area, Wildwood Rd. and Saddle Rd., South Lake Tahoe, CA, tel. 702/586–7000. AE, D, DC, MC, V.*

Loud and Lively/Dancing

The Brewery

This good brew pub has an excellent lineup of drafts, a lively atmosphere, and a good mix of locals and visitors. The crowd changes as it gets later, but for the better part of the evening it's mostly folks on the flusher side of 30. By midnight the younger partiers tend to gather in numbers. *3542 Lake Tahoe Blvd., South Lake Tahoe, CA, tel. 916/544–2739. AE, MC, V.*

Thirsty Duck

This place is not easy to find: Take Elk Point Road across from the Round Hill Mall, turn left at Dorla Court, and look for the building with the satellite dish on top. It's worth the search to discover this popular locals' hangout, with a friendly staff, an excellent lineup of draft beers, and an upbeat atmosphere. The decor runs to sports paraphernalia and posters, with multiple TVs providing nonstop sports viewing and a pool table and video poker machines at the bar. *400 Dorla Ct., Zephyr Cove, NV, tel. 702/588–3899. D, MC, V.*

More Mellow

Peak Lounge

Getting away from the contrived cacophony of the casinos is not easy, but the Peak Lounge in Harvey's stands out like a welcome oasis. Deep chairs, low-key piano music, and a quiet, civilized atmosphere are all yours for the price of a drink. *Harvey's Hotel, Rte. 50, Stateline, NV, tel. 702/588–2411. AE, D, DC, MC, V.*

St. Moritz Bar

This is the perfect place to sip and relax right after skiing or later in the evening, and it may be one of the best-kept secrets in Tahoe. There's a delightful fireside bar, a large fireplace, and lots of cozy couches and well-stuffed chairs. They have live jazz on the weekends. *Christiana Inn, 9819 Saddle Rd., South Lake Tahoe, CA, tel. 916/544–7337. MC, V.*

MAMMOTH SKI RESORT

Box 24
Mammoth Lakes, CA 93546
Tel. 619/934-2571

STATISTICALLY SPEAKING
Base elevation: 7,953 feet

Summit elevation: 11,053 feet

Vertical drop: 3,100 feet

Skiable terrain: 3,500 acres

Number of trails: 150

Longest run: 3 miles

Lifts and capacity: 6 quads
(2 high-speed detachable),
7 triples, 14 doubles, 2 gondolas, 2 surface; 53,000 skiers
per hour

Daily lift ticket: $45

Average annual snowfall:
335 inches

Number of skiing days
1995-96: 239

Snowmaking: 300 acres; 9%

Terrain mix: N 30%, I 40%,
E 30%

Snowboarding: yes

Mammoth says it all. Call it tautological, call it California size. Call it large, with a capital L. Mammoth is a monster, and if Heavenly can be compared to a Christmas cake, spiced with exotic and interesting ingredients, then Mammoth is best likened to a giant sundae, its conelike flanks smothered from November through June by some of the deepest snow in the Sierra Nevada. Such is the lure of this broad-shouldered conical peak that 10,000 to 12,000 skiers pack its slopes on some weekend days, most enduring a five- to six-hour drive from southern California and contributing to Mammoth's reputation as one of the busiest ski areas in America.

Mammoth, mind you, is more than up to the task of accommodating the crowds; its "dormant" volcanic mass, set against the craggy backdrop of the Minaret Peaks, consists of more than 3,500 acres of skiable terrain. At 11,000 feet, Mammoth is the highest resort in California and one of the highest in the country. It straddles the Sierra Crest in conical isolation, its north and south shoulders drooping down to 9,000 feet and its western and eastern slopes plunging more than 3,000 feet down to the San Joaquin Canyon on one side and the mountain village of Mammoth Lakes on the other.

Accommodations at the resort are limited, so the town of Mammoth Lakes is where the majority of people bunk. It's about a 4-mile drive between the main lodge and town—a route served by the Mammoth Area Shuttle—and like its namesake mountain, the town is a sprawling development that has often been referred to as the "condo city of the Sierra." It's an accurate appellation, given the preponderance of this type of accommodation. There's no real town center and few traditional hotels or gracious inns—just a gridwork of streets, many four lanes wide. Hotels, restaurants, shops, bars, and boutiques are strung out along a mile of Main Street, and at times the vehicular traffic can resemble Hollywood Boulevard at rush hour. In spite of this, Mammoth Lakes does have its charm, most of which comes from the stunning scenery that surrounds it and from the youthful vibrancy of its 5,000 permanent residents.

USEFUL NUMBERS
Area code: 619

Children's services: day care, tel. 619/934-0646; instruction, tel. 619/934-0658

Snow phone: tel. 619/934-6166

Police: tel. 911 or 619/934-2011

Medical center: tel. 619/934-2551

Hospital: Mammoth Hospital, tel. 619/934-3311

Mammoth Lakes Visitors Bureau: tel. 619/934-2712 or 800/367-6572

National Forest Visitor Center: tel. 619/934-2505

Taxi: tel. 619/934-3030

Road conditions: tel. 800/427-7623

Towing: Bill's Towing & Recovery, tel. 619/934-4264; Mammoth Towing, tel. 619/934-7137

Weather conditions: tel. 619/873-3213

FIVE-STAR FAVORITES
Best run for vertical: Cornice Bowl

Best run overall: Roadrunner

Best bar/nightclub: Whiskey Creek

Best hotel: Mammoth Mountain Inn

Best restaurant: Restaurant at Convict Lake

HOW TO GET THERE

By Plane
Reno-Tahoe International Airport (*see* Getting to California Resorts, *above*), about 165 miles away, is the closest major airport. The **Mammoth Lakes Airport** (tel. 619/934-3825) is about 10 minutes from the resort and is served by **Mountain Air Express** (tel. 310/595-1011 or 800/788-4247) from Long Beach.

Shuttle Service
There is no shuttle between Reno and Mammoth. The free **Mammoth Area Shuttle** (MAS; tel. 619/934-2571) meets flights at Mammoth Lakes Airport and takes passengers to resort-owned accommodations in Mammoth. **Mammoth Shuttle Systems** (tel. 619/934-3030) runs from the airport to town.

By Car
The resort is 325 miles from Los Angeles and Orange County on U.S. 395 north to U.S. 203 at Mammoth Lakes Junction. From Reno it's 165 miles southwest on U.S. 395. It's a 360-mile drive east from the San Francisco area on U.S. 80 or U.S. 50 to U.S. 395 south. No matter which direction you're driving from, carrying chains is recommended.

Major car-rental firms have desks at the Reno-Tahoe airport (*see* Getting to California Resorts, *above*). There are no car rentals at Mammoth Lakes Airport.

By Bus
Greyhound Lines (tel. 800/231-2222) provides daily service between Mammoth and both Los Angeles and Reno. A number of charter bus companies also travel daily from Los Angeles to Mammoth for $40–$50 round-trip.

By Train
See Getting to California Resorts, *above*.

GETTING AROUND
A car can be useful for exploring the region, but if you are just commuting between town and the resort, the free **Mammoth Area Shuttle** (MAS; tel. 619/934-2571), which runs throughout the town of

Mammoth and to the Main Lodge, Warming Hut II, and Outpost 15 areas at the resort, is your best bet. Parking is limited at the resort, and the roads are often so snow-covered that chains are essential. **KC Cabs** (tel. 619/934–4770) and **Mammoth Shuttle Systems** (tel. 619/934–3030) both run cars and small vans throughout the town and between the town and the lodge.

THE SKIING

Mammoth is so vast that even regulars who have been skiing the resort for years have not skied its entire Brobdingnagian mass, and for visitors it represents a confusing network of lifts numbered in the order that they were built, which results, for example, in Lift 22 going to an entirely different point on the mountain from Lift 23. That idiosyncrasy aside, Mammoth is actually well laid out; most of the expert runs lace the top half of its sloping shoulders, and the intermediate and novice runs network the lower half of the mountain.

Mammoth began life in prehistoric times as a volcano, and now with half its girth so much geological dust, the remaining ridge gives access to a dozen wide bowls, the largest one—once the interior of the cone—a staggering 13,000 feet across. Below this vast expanse are the lower peaks of Lincoln Mountain, Gold Hill, and Hemlock Ridge, where you'll find a 6½-mile-wide swath of groomed boulevards and moguled canyons.

It is those bowls that make it one of the most expansive ski resorts in America and that are the preoccupation of its owner, Dave McCoy, who first strapped on skis and explored the area more than 50 years ago. McCoy overcame considerable obstacles—isolation and money, just two of them—to create his vision of a ski resort. There are only two other resorts in the country that can be said to bear the personal stamp of their creators—Dick Bass's Snowbird in Utah and the late Ernie Blake's Taos Ski Valley. Even today, as Mammoth enjoys its place among the great resorts of America, McCoy is still actively involved in running it.

Loosely speaking, there are three main staging areas for tackling the mountain. At the far east side, closest to the town, is Outpost 15, with a mix of runs ranging from bunny slopes to black diamond plunges. Halfway up the access road to the resort is Warming Hut II, with lifts that serve the Lincoln Mountain area. At the end of the access road is the main base lodge area, which serves the west side of the mountain. All three areas are linked by either trails or lifts that intermediates and up can handle. Each base area is progressively more crowded as you approach the main base area. The best way to avoid crowds and enjoy the morning sun is to start at Outpost 15, move to the Warming Hut II area by midmorning, and then hit the main lodge area and the summit gondola by lunchtime, when the lifts in this area are slightly less busy. Just make sure you begin your return journey from the west to the east in time to catch all the required lifts.

For snowboarders Mammoth offers a huge terrain park on Bowling Alley, with quarter pipes, table tops, and lots of features designed for lift-off. The American Snowboard Tour and the National Snowboarding Championships are both held here.

Novices

You have three choices for starting your day: Outpost 15, the lift area closest to Mammoth Lakes; Warming Hut II, which is halfway up the Mammoth entrance road; and the main base lodge area. Outpost 15 gets the early morning sun and tends to be the least crowded, mainly because it has only two novice trails—Lupin and Sleepy Hollow—and once you grow bored with them, you can easily reach the Warming Hut II area by traversing the Chickadee or Swell trails and ending up on Clover Leaf. Conversely, the main base lodge area gets no early morning sun and is typically the most crowded place on the mountain.

Three lifts serve the novice terrain in this area. Runs such as Jill's Run, St. Moritz, and Gus's Pasture are wide open, meticulously groomed, and gently undulating. From Lifts 11 and 27 beginners can reach the most popular gentle slopes, Sesame Street and Road Runner.

A good compromise between the limited terrain and isolation of Outpost 15 and the congestion of the Main Base lodge area is Warming Hut II, where the sun makes an appearance by midmorning and two lifts (7 and 17) serve a mixture of green and gentle blue runs. Lift 7 lets you explore the novice trails of Hansel and Gretel—both wide and smooth—and Lift 17 will take you a little higher up the slope once you feel comfortable about tackling gentle blue runs such as Clover Leaf and Round Robin, both of which are well groomed and wide open—perfect for

trying those first intermediate turns. Unfortunately, there are no novice runs on the upper half of the mountain, so until you can comfortably link turns and handle a little more steepness, you'll have to stay below.

Intermediates

If you want to catch the early morning sun and avoid the crowds, it's a good idea to start at Outpost 15. Take either Lift 15 or Lift 24, turn left, and scoot down Holiday to Lift 25, which carries you to a point just below the double-black-diamond bowls of the upper mountain. You can take Repeat 22, a moderately steep and wide cruiser, to get the legs warmed up.

When you are ready to move on, cut left onto Holiday about halfway down Repeat 22 and follow a combination of Swell and Clover Leaf that will take you down to the base area at Warming Hut II. This is a good high-speed run with consistent pitch and a few interesting rolls and drop-offs; it's usually groomed. You can ride Lift 8 back up for a repeat shot or pick up Hully Gully (turn right off the lift) for a taste of some bumps. Your other choice is to take Lift 16, a high-speed quad, and follow Roller Coaster or Lost in the Woods, a pair of giant-slalom runs that let the skis track fast and smooth.

A slightly steeper and narrower alternative is Wall Street. Roller Coaster takes you back to the bottom of Lift 16, but Wall Street and Lost in the Woods take you to the bottom of Lift 18, which will take you high up into the sloping and wide-open bowl area just below the summit. Because this lift goes farther up, into more advanced territory, it tends to be less crowded than Lift 2, which runs in the same direction but stops near the summit gondola midstation.

From here you can continue down Stump Alley or Broadway. Both are wide and well groomed but tend to be extremely busy, especially Broadway, which ends up in the main base lodge area. From either point you can ride back up to the Mid-Chalet or the top of the upper gondola. From there you can take Chair 1 up to the top of the Wall, a steep black run; skip that and head over the back side and pick up Silver Tip. Follow it down to the lower bowls of the western ridge. This is wide-open intermediate bowl cruising and a good place to catch the afternoon sun. From the main base lodge area you can also take Gondola 1 and Gondola 2 up to the summit and turn right to follow Road Runner, a long, wide, and varied green cruiser that skirts the western summit ridge and gives you a spectacular view of the surrounding Minarets.

Experts

You can start the day in the sun at Outpost 15 by riding either Lift 24 or Lift 15 and then Lift 25 to the blue-black runs of Quicksilver, Back for More, or Haven't the Foggiest. When you're ready for more challenges, head over to the steep double-black terrain of Grizzly, Shaft, Viva, and Avalanche Chutes. These are all supersteep freefalls that slash through the trees like a frozen waterfall, and you can ski them intensely from Lift 22, which, to the amazement of locals, tends to be one of the least busy lifts on the mountain. From the top of Lift 22, you can turn left on

Repeat 22, a blue run that takes you to the bottom of Lift 9, another relatively unbusy lift, which gets you to the upper bowls on the eastern fringe of the summit ridge. Another option is to turn right off the top of Lift 22 and ski down to Lift 5. This lift—again, it tends to be relatively uncrowded—parallels the path of the gondola but stops short of the summit (on a different peak). From this point you get a taste of some ultrasteep chutes—Face of Five, Sanctuary, Silver, and Dry Creek.

When you're ready to move on, ski down to the base of Chair 18 and ride it up to Mid-Chalet. The gondola gets very busy by midmorning, so if you find yourself there at that time, a good alternative is to head for Lift 23—fed by Lift 19 from the main base area—which is usually less crowded. From either point (the gondola or Lift 23) you have the full expanse of Mammoth's bowls at your feet. The Cornice Bowl is a favorite for early morning powder, but as it gets tracked, skiers later head either east to the Dragon's Back off Lift 9 or west to Hemlock Ridge off Lift 14.

WHERE TO STAY

For a small, somewhat isolated community in the mountains, Mammoth Lakes has an astonishingly large bed base of almost 11,000. Unfortunately, the town's nickname of "condo city of the Sierra Nevada," is accurate, and there is a real shortage of small lodges, full-service hotels, and even true slope-side accommodation. Staying slope side is convenient but means a drive into town for nightlife.

Expensive

Mammoth Mountain Inn

Just a few hundred yards from the Mammoth day lodge and surrounded by forest and next to a tiny stream, this full-service hotel complex has a choice of spacious hotel rooms and suites as well as one- and two-bedroom condo-style units. The decor is mountain modern, with lots of wood trim and well-crafted pine furniture, offset by bright wall coverings and upholstery in warm colors. Both the rooms and the suites have lots of light, and the suites have well-equipped kitchens. *1 Minaret Rd., Box 353, Mammoth Lakes 93546, tel. 619/934–2581 or 800/228–4947, fax 619/934–0700. 213 units. Facilities: 2 restaurants, 2 bars, lounge, 3 whirlpools, 24-hr desk service, maid service, ski valet, ski storage, laundry, game room. AE, MC, V. $110–$395.*

Silver Bear

Just a few hundred yards from the lifts at Hut II, this condo complex combines traditional Euro-inn style with modern architecture and furnishings. The units are either two-bedroom or two plus a loft, making them perfect for families. Each unit has a dining area, a stone fireplace, and a combination of wood, wicker, and plush furnishings. *527 Lakeview Blvd., Box 7670, Mammoth Lakes 93546, tel. 619/934–5680 or 800/336–6543, fax 619/934–5306. 24 units. Facilities: sauna, whirlpool, indoor pool, ski storage, laundry, game room. No credit cards. $235–$350.*

Snowcreek Resort

A resort unto itself, on 335 acres about a five-minute drive from the mountain, this complex offers some of the more luxurious units available in Mammoth, especially the three- and four-bedroom town houses. The decor in both the condos and town houses is stylish and modern, with high vaulted ceilings, lots of windows, and a pleasant blend of wood and rock. All units come with a fireplace. *1254 Old Mammoth Rd., Box 1647, Mammoth Lakes 93546, tel. 619/934–3333 or 800/544–6007, fax 619/934–1619. 160 units. Facilities: health club, whirlpool, indoor pool, steam room, sauna, ski storage. D, MC, V. $130–$350.*

Moderate

Krystal Villa East

Close to Lift 15, this villa houses condo units in two sizes—one bedroom or one bedroom with loft, both roomy enough to handle groups of six. All have good, practical furnishings. The big, comfortable common area is decorated with a certain country charm, including hand-painted pine branches and acorns over each of the doorways. *137 Laurel Mountain Rd., Box 1132, Mammoth Lakes 93546, tel. 619/934–2669 or 800/237–6181, fax 619/934–1770. 24 units. Facilities: sauna, hot tub, maid service, ski storage, laundry. D, MC, V. $64–$155.*

Snowflower

These spacious three-story units right next to the Snow Creek golf course can sleep eight people and have a great view and comfortable, modern furnishings. They all have two bedrooms with baths downstairs, with a living room with fireplace, a dining room, a bathroom, and a full kitchen on the second floor, and a loft with queen-size bed. *Gateway Center, Box 1608, Mammoth Lakes 93546, tel. 619/934–2528 or 800/527–6273, fax 619/934–2317. 88 units. Facilities: 2 saunas, 2 hot tubs, ski storage, ski shuttle. D, MC, V. $235.*

Snowgoose Inn

Just off Main Street, this tidy little two-story lodge with a wood-plank exterior and a shingled roof is billed as a B&B, but it has a number of rooms and suites that come with kitchens. The well-furnished rooms are an ideal size for couples, while the suites—with one or two bedrooms—are a good bet for families or several couples. *57 Forest Trail, Box 387, Mammoth Lakes 93546, tel. 619/934–2660 or 800/874–7368, fax 619/934–5655. 19 units. Facilities: hot tub, maid service, ski storage, ski shuttle, games room. AE, D, DC, MC, V. $78–$168, including Continental breakfast.*

Tamarack Lodge

Tucked away on the edge of the John Muir Wilderness Area, this original 1924 log lodge was built by Mary Foy—mother of the famous vaudevillian family immortalized in the 1955 Bob Hope movie *The Seven Little Foys.* Whether you stay in the main lodge or in one of the surrounding cabins, you are guaranteed rustic solitude in a historic natural setting. Some of the rooms share bathroom facilities and can be fairly spartan in their furnishings. The cabins scattered around the resort's six acres range from rustic to luxurious and come in various sizes from smallish studio units all the way to large houses that sleep 10. The cabins all lack televisions, but they

are comfortable and functional, and some come with a wood-burning stove. *Twin Lakes Rd., Box 69, Mammoth Lakes 93546, tel. 619/934–2442 or 800/237–6879, fax 619/934–2281. 36 units. Facilities: restaurant, lounge, maid service, cross-country skiing, ski storage. D, MC, V. $55–$360.*

White Horse Inn Bed & Breakfast

This delightful bed-and-breakfast is small and homey but maintains a high level of style and good taste. Each of its rooms is distinctive for its furnishings and ambience. They may have Chinese, Austrian, or Italian antiques. The Tribal Room, with artifacts of the region's earliest Indian inhabitants, has three single beds and is ideal for small families. There's also a separate building housing a billiard room, which has a stone fireplace. *2180 Old Mammoth Rd., Box 2326, Mammoth Lakes 93456, tel. 619/924–3656 or 800/982–5657. 5 rooms. Facilities: ski storage. D, DC, MC, V. $115–$135, including full breakfast.*

Inexpensive

Austria Hof

A tidy, tiny wood-and-stucco Austrian-style chalet a short distance from the lifts at Warming Hut II, this place is clean, comfortable, modern, and convenient. Smaller rooms come with just a queen-size bed, while the larger ones have either two queens or a queen and two twins. *924 Canyon Blvd., Mammoth Lakes 93546, tel. 619/934–2764 or 800/922–2966, fax 619/934–1880. 22 units. Facilities: restaurant, bar, lounge, hot tub, maid service, ski storage. D, DC, MC, V. $78–$130.*

Mammoth Travelodge

These small side-by-side motel-type accommodations have combined into a single lodging. Ideally situated just off Main Street, the lodge has studios, one- and two-bedroom suites, and two-bedroom cottages complete with kitchen. The decor is simple rec-room style, and the furnishings and amenities are minimal, but the place also has an indoor swimming pool—something of a rarity in Mammoth. *6209 Minaret Rd., Mammoth Lakes 93546, tel. 619/934–8526 or 800/228–4947, fax 619/934–8007. 123 units. Facilities: indoor pool, 2 hot tubs, 2 saunas, maid service, ski storage, ski shuttle. AE, MC, V. $90–$150.*

White Stag Inn

The simple stained wood-plank exterior looks cute, and all rooms in this clean, comfortable two-story motor lodge right in the middle of town are large enough for four people. Some rooms come with a small kitchenette. *Main St. and Minaret St., Box 45, Mammoth Lakes 93546, tel. 619/934–7507. 21 rooms. Facilities: sauna, maid service, ski storage, ski shuttle. AE, D, MC, V. $44–$84.*

WHERE TO EAT

The dining and nightlife scene is spread all around the Mammoth resort area, from the slope-side hotels, to small inns and restaurants between the mountain and the town, and into the town itself. The most varied selection is found in town, although there are some noteworthy spots in the surrounding area that are worth making the effort to get to.

Expensive

The Lakefront

The 10-table dining room in the Tamarack Lodge is constructed completely of knotty pine—walls, floors, ceilings, and tables—with the exception of the oversize stone fireplace. The atmosphere is relaxed but definitely upscale, and celebrity-packed photographs of Mammoth's early glory days, in the 1930s and 1940s, bedeck the walls. The menu is Continental, with specialties such as rack of lamb; roast duckling with raspberry–green peppercorn sauce; eggplant Wellington, with eggplant substituting for the meat; veal scallopini; and a selection of steak, fish, and chicken dishes. *Twin Lakes Rd., Mammoth Lakes, tel. 619/934–3534. AE, MC, V.*

Mountainside Grill

The Grill is a beautifully serene dining room, with a vaulted ceiling, large picture windows, and a warm, woodsy motif that both absorbs large groups and sequesters quiet couples. The menu is a mix of traditional American and classic Continental, with such entrées as sautéed Long Island duck breast served with mango sauce; Iowa-style pork chop, broiled or blackened, with jalapeño-pineapple compote; generous cuts of prime rib; grilled mahimahi; chicken Kiev; and pepper steak. *Mammoth Mountain Inn, 1 Minaret Rd., Mammoth Lakes, tel. 619/934–0601. AE, MC, V.*

Restaurant at Convict Lake

Just 4 miles south of town you'll find one of the more luxurious dining experiences in Mammoth. This dining room with spectacular views of the surrounding countryside combines an atmosphere of rustic elegance with eclectic Californian cuisine. The decor is a mix of refined dark wood furniture and pale peach linen and crystal place settings. The menu offers a strong lineup of Continental offerings, such as steak Diane and oven-roasted duck with berry confit. There are also a number of fish dishes, including seared tuna and mahimahi in a chervil and butter sauce. *4 mi south of Mammoth Lakes off U.S. 395 at Convict Lake exit, tel. 619/934–3803. AE, D, MC, V.*

Skadi

A great high, oak-beamed ceiling dominates the dining room of this upscale restaurant, named for the Viking goddess of skiing. The decor is refined country, with dark wood tables and chairs, elegant wainscoting and other wood trim, and floral accents. The menu draws on mountain cuisines from around the world, with offerings like pasta with smoked chicken and wild mushrooms or roast duck with kiln-dried cherries. Venison is a mainstay here; the restaurant has its own venison ranch in southern California. A changing selection of decadent desserts will round out your meal. *587 Old Mammoth Rd., Mammoth Lakes, tel. 619/934–3902. AE, MC, V.*

Moderate

Austria Hof

This restaurant envelops you in a warm Old World Austrian atmosphere, the perfect setting for the best selection of schnitzels in town, including Wiener, chicken and Jaeger, as well as sauerbraten, thick goulash soups, and plump German sausages with sauerkraut. *924 Canyon Blvd., by*

Warming Hut II, Mammoth Lakes, tel. 619/934–2764. AE, D, DC, MC, V.

Cervinos

This Italian bistro with modern decor gets away from the red-and-white-checked-tablecloth syndrome. It is both elegant—with linen and crystal place settings, stylish art, and low lighting—and casual. The menu is diverse: The veal piccata served with sun-dried tomato and chive sauce is feathery light and succulent; there's an excellent lineup of fish entrées including swordfish and calamari, both buttered and pan seared, and a fine cioppino (fish stew), as well as pasta. *View Point Rd., Mammoth Lakes, tel. 619/934–4734. AE, D, DC, MC, V.*

Mogul Restaurant

In these four small dining rooms almost every table seems to have a secluded corner to itself. Landscapes by local artists hang on the mauve-painted walls, and the largest dining room has a great window looking out onto the mountain. It's a traditional steak house, with a grill in the center of the room. There's also an excellent prime rib, lobster and other seafood, chicken, and rack of lamb. *1528 Tavern Rd., Mammoth Lakes, tel. 619/ 934–3039. AE, MC, V.*

Ocean Harvest

This is the place to go for seafood. A fresh, woody smell wafts from the rough-sawed cedar siding of the interior, and old photos of local fishing heroes adorn the walls. The daily specials vary depending on the catch, and you can take your choice of sauce—such as the béarnaise over peppered ahi or the cajun spices over catfish—as well as such dishes as

Idaho rainbow trout (panfried), Canadian scallops on a skewer, and a delicious cioppino. *248 Old Mammoth Rd., Mammoth Lakes, tel. 619/934–8539. AE, D, DC, MC, V.*

Whiskey Creek

If you're looking for a light bite in a busy roadhouse atmosphere with a loud country/rock jukebox, try the oyster bar upstairs or just sample a few appetizers before heading down to the main dining room. It is larger and quieter, with a crackling fireplace and mellow background music. The menu relies heavily on grilled steaks and seafood with a variety of interesting homemade marinades and sauces. Among house specialties are shrimp and scallops Marguerite (sautéed in tequila-lime sauce) and New Zealand rack of lamb with jalapeño mint jelly. *Main St. and Minaret Rd., Mammoth Lakes, tel. 619/934–2555. AE, MC, V.*

Inexpensive

Angels

The antique decor and old wooden tables might give the place an upscale look, but this cheerful spot in the middle of town attracts a good number of locals because of its monster portions, friendly service, and reasonable prices. It has family-friendly food such as sandwiches and burgers— notably the avocado melt (a combo of tuna, avocado, and cheese)—and an excellent selection of giant salads, including an outstanding grilled Southwestern chicken. *20 Sierra Blvd., Mammoth Lakes, tel. 619/934–7427. AE, D, MC, V.*

Bergers

The simple decor—rough wooden tables and chairs, local artists' photos on walls, red carpeting—is modestly understated, allowing you to enjoy the beaming sunshine and glorious view of the Sherwin Mountains through the high windows up front. This place serves the best burgers in town, which come in a variety of flavors and sizes—try the jumbo buffalo burger. There's also a good selection of meal-size sandwiches, including turkey, pastrami, chicken breast, and beef brisket, along with pork ribs, fresh fish, and venison steak dinners. *6118 Minaret Rd., Mammoth Lakes, tel. 619/934–6622. MC, V.*

Carl's Jr.

Fast and funky, this is an excellent fast-food spot—complete with plastic booths, Formica tables, ubiquitous mirrors, and wood paneling—offering standard favorites from hamburger platters to chicken and sandwiches. There's also a good lineup of salads and other low-fat and low-cholesterol options. *437 Old Mammoth Rd., Mammoth Lakes, tel. 619/934–8812. No credit cards.*

Mammoth Stonehouse Brewery and Restaurant

Everyone—from sports fanatics to families—will feel welcome here. If you're not too full after potato nachos and a microbrew from the bar, try the baby-back ribs, barbecued chicken, or steak selections. There's a Monday-night football buffet and live entertainment on weekends. *361 Old Mammoth Rd., Mammoth Lakes, tel. 619/934–6196. AE, D, DC, MC, V.*

Best Bets for Breakfast

Schat's Bakery

Part restaurant, part bakery, and part community center, this family-run business serves everything from huge, superbly cooked omelets and other egg dishes to monster pancakes, awesome French toast, and a joyous selection of freshly baked breads and pastries. *Main St., Mammoth Lakes, tel. 619/934–6055. MC, V.*

The Stove

Leading the breakfast hit parade here—apart from the friendly service—are four-egg omelets, oversize pancakes, and cinnamon French toast. *644 Old Mammoth Rd., Mammoth Lakes, tel. 619/934–2821. AE, MC, V.*

NIGHTLIFE AND ENTERTAINMENT

Après-Ski

Dry Creek Bar

This bar is in a quiet spot in the Mammoth Mountain Inn. A guitarist and/or pianist usually keeps the mood mellow, and bar snacks are served daily. *Mammoth Mountain Inn, 1 Minaret Rd., Mammoth Lakes, tel. 619/934–2581. AE, MC, V.*

Yodler Restaurant and Bar

This is a funky wooden chalet bar with several different rooms. It gets cheek to jowl around the bar area, but you can also spread out in front of the fireplace. There's music, occasionally a live entertainer, and a TV pumping out ski movies. *Mammoth Mountain Inn, 1 Minaret Rd., Mammoth Lakes, tel. 619/934–2581. AE, MC, V.*

Loud and Lively/Dancing

Goat's Bar

A good all-purpose hangout, this is the closest thing to a traditional neighborhood pub in Mammoth Lakes. It has a pool table, darts, and multiple TVs for tube junkies. *Red Rooster Mall, upstairs, Mono and Main Sts., Mammoth Lakes, tel. 619/934–4629.*

La Sierra's Cantina

A combination of live rock and blues acts, Mammoth's largest dance floor, and (at last count) at least 10 televisions explain the popularity of this spot. The numerous drink and food specials make it fun to part with your money. *3789 Main St., Mammoth Lakes, tel. 619/934–8083.*

Whiskey Creek

Definitely your best choice for live entertainment, this place has an ever-changing lineup of club bands from across the state. You can count on large, youthful crowds on Friday and Saturday. *Main St. and Minaret Rd., Mammoth Lakes, tel. 619/934–2555. AE, MC, V.*

More Mellow

Aspen Grill

The cigar bar adjacent to the restaurant of the same name offers a quiet place to relax in front of the fire. Jazz or blues is featured nightly and is live on weekends. *202 Old Mammoth Rd., tel. 619/934–2537. AE, D, DC, MC, V.*

Looney Bean

This throwback to the days of coffeehouse hippiedom has live acoustic and folk entertainers every weekend night. They don't serve beer or alcohol, but you will find the best selection of coffee in town. *Main St., Mammoth Lakes, tel. 619/934–1345. No credit cards.*

SQUAW VALLEY SKI RESORT

SQUAW VALLEY SKI RESORT

Box 2007
Olympic Valley, CA 96146
Tel. 916/583–6985

STATISTICALLY SPEAKING

Base elevation: 6,200 feet

Summit elevation: 9,050 feet

Vertical drop: 2,850 feet

Skiable terrain: 4,000 acres

Longest run: 3½ miles

Lifts and capacity: 1 cable car, 1 gondola, 4 high-speed quads, 1 quad, 7 triples, 11 doubles, 3 surface; 49,000 skiers per hour

Daily lift ticket: $46

Average annual snowfall: 450 inches

Number of skiing days 1995–96: 192

Snowmaking: 300 acres; 8%

Terrain mix: N 25%, I 45%, E 30%

Snowboarding: yes

Cross-country skiing: 30 kilometers

Squaw Valley is a big brute of a resort, its 4,000 lift-served acres out of a total of 8,000 skiable acres competing well with its megasize California neighbors: Mammoth at 3,500 acres and Heavenly at 4,800. Still, Squaw seems more intimidating than even Heavenly, more daunting, more in-your-face, with arguably the toughest skiing of any of the 19 ski resorts that ring the cobalt blue waters of Lake Tahoe. In part, Squaw gained such notoriety from the famous Warren Miller films featuring extreme skiers taking on the chutes, cliffs, and steeps, including the infamous KT-22 Peak. Squaw's ferociousness has been oversold, though, for despite all its serious terrain, 45% of the mountain is considered intermediate, and 25% is novice.

The resort, which sits high in the Sierra Nevada on the north shore of Lake Tahoe, began in 1949 as a modest single chairlift. In 1960 it attracted the world's attention as the site of the Winter Olympic Games, the first of the games to be televised daily. They were dubbed the "games of simplicity," reflecting Squaw's modest, close-knit community. From these humble beginnings, Squaw Valley has developed into a six-mountain colossus, with one of the largest ski-lift networks in North America. The lift system's chairs, cable car, and 150-passenger gondola can move 49,000 skiers an hour over 4,000 acres of open bowls in a layout of interconnected peaks and valleys similar to the broad resort expanses found in the Swiss Alps.

At the core of the resort is the Olympic Village (built for the games), some condominiums in the immediate vicinity, and two remarkable midmountain villages. One of the villages, the High Camp Bath and Tennis Club, at 8,200 feet, includes restaurants, bars, boutiques, and a recreation complex with an Olympic-size ice pavilion, a swimming pool, a health spa, tennis courts, and a bungee-jumping tower. Adjacent is the Gold Coast complex, with a fine, but smaller, collection of restaurants and bars.

Despite all its development, Squaw remains isolated, interacting little with the surrounding towns and hamlets. In this way, it is similar to its Olympic brother, Whiteface Mountain in New York state, existing to a large degree on its Olympian reputation, as

USEFUL NUMBERS
Area code: 916 (CA);
702 (NV)

Children's services: day care,
instruction, tel. 916/581–7280

Snow phone:
tel. 916/583–6955

Police: tel. 911

Hospital: Tahoe Forest Hospital, tel. 916/587–6011

North Tahoe Resort Association: tel. 916/581–6900 or
800/824–6348

Cross-country skiing:
tel. 916/583–6300

Road conditions:
tel. 916/445–1534

Towing: Dependable Tow,
Truckee, tel. 916/587–5292;
Lakeside Towing, Tahoe, tel.
916/587–6000

FIVE-STAR FAVORITES
Best run for vertical: West
face of KT-22 and Headwall

Best run overall:
Mountain Run

Best bar/nightclub: Bar One

Best hotel: Resort at
Squaw Creek

Best restaurant: Glissandi

aloof as the august members of the International Olympic Committee.

Tahoe City is a pretty lakefront town just 5 miles from the resort; the smaller Truckee, just 7 miles away, is similarly charming. Both are lively, with an abundance of restaurants, bars, shops, and services. Along a 10-mile stretch around the north end of the lake are strung the smaller residential communities of Tahoe Vista, Kings Beach, and Crystal Bay. The latter abuts the Nevada border, where the casino action lies. For more gaming, check out Incline Village—22 miles east of Squaw, just inside the Nevada state line—a tony enclave of high-priced homes and condos. These nearby towns provide choices for those Squaw visitors looking for accommodations within a short and straightforward drive from the mountain. There's lots of day parking at the resort as well as quick dispersion of skier traffic from the base area on the dizzying lift network.

The gondola and the cable car move intermediates and novices up to most of the green and blue slopes, while a pair of chairs sends experts to their proper terrain. The beginner/intermediate and expert terrains are in separate parts of the resort, which means that people with different skiing abilities don't see much of each other on the slopes. Since the only on-mountain lunch spot is the Gold Coast complex in a valley between two of Squaw's six peaks, meeting up midday with your whole group may not be feasible. The complex is a long way from other parts of the resort, such as the expert skiing on KT-22, and even farther from the mostly intermediate runs of Snow King Peak, which is reached directly from the self-contained Resort at Squaw Creek, about a mile outside the Olympic Village area.

HOW TO GET THERE

By Plane
Reno-Tahoe International Airport (*see* Getting to Nevada Resorts, *above*), in Reno, Nevada, is 42 miles (about 60 minutes by car) from Squaw Valley.

By Shuttle
The once-a-day **Sierra Nevada Grey Line ski shuttle** (tel. 916/542–5930 for South Lake Tahoe,

916/583–5585 or 800/822–6009 for Reno) serves South Lake Tahoe hotels to Squaw Valley starting at 7 AM; the return shuttle bus leaves Squaw Valley at 4:30 PM for Reno. There is no charge with a lift ticket, otherwise it costs $20 round-trip. The Reno shuttle departs for Squaw Valley starting at 6:50 AM from Reno hotels; the return shuttle bus leaves Squaw Valley at 4:30 PM for Reno. Fare is $20 round-trip.

By Car

From Reno-Tahoe International Airport, take 395 north for about 5 miles to I–80 west. At Truckee, about 30 miles along I–80, take Route 89 for about 8 miles to Squaw Valley Road. From Sacramento, 96 miles away, take I–80 east for 88 miles to Truckee, then take Route 89 to Squaw Valley Road. From San Francisco, 196 miles from Squaw, take I–80 east for 188 miles to Truckee, then take Route 89 to Squaw Valley Road. From Los Angeles, 450 miles away, take Route 14 235 miles to Lone Pine, then take Route 395 to the Carson Valley. Take Route 50 out of Carson City and pick up Route 28 for 60 miles into Tahoe City. Take Route 89 to Squaw Valley Road.

By Ferry

If you're staying on the south shore, you can take the *Tahoe Queen* (tel. 916/541–3364 or 800/238–2463) across the lake to Squaw. The boat departs the dock at the Ski Run Marina, at the bottom of Ski Run Boulevard (weekdays at 8 AM) and reaches the Homewood dock at 10 AM; you can buy breakfast on board. The $18 round-trip fare includes a shuttle bus up to the Squaw Valley Resort.

GETTING AROUND

A car is essential whether you are staying at the mountain or in the neighboring communities because it's the only way to explore the environs that contribute so much to the overall experience of skiing and vacationing here. Parking can be a nightmare on weekends; plan on leaving your car at your hotel and take a shuttle to ski areas.

By Shuttle

Shuttle bus service from **TART** (Tahoe Area Rapid Transit; tel. 916/581–6365 or 800/325–8278) is available between the major hotels and the resort, as well as scheduled service from Truckee, Reno, and the south shore. The free **Resort at Squaw Creek shuttle** (tel. 916/583–6300) runs every half hour from 7 to 6:30 seven days a week. The driver will drop you pretty much anywhere you like. The **Squaw Valley Ski Corporation Shuttle** (tel. 916/583–6985) runs twice a day to and from a number of stops in the North Lake Tahoe area and is also free.

By Taxi

North Shore Taxi (tel. 916/546–9090), **Sierra Taxi** (tel. 916/577–8888), and **Yellow Cabs** (tel. 916/546–3181), all based nearby, cover the Squaw Valley area.

THE SKIING

Most of the skiing at Squaw is in wide, open bowls, glades, and chutes above tree line, with very few defined and marked trails. Instead of trails, you count ski lifts or mountains—six of the latter and 33 of the former. The centerpiece of this mountain terrain is Squaw Peak, at 8,900 feet. It's flanked to the west by Broken Arrow, at 8,200 feet; Emigrant, at 8,700 feet; and Granite Chief, at 9,050 feet. To the east are KT-22, at 8,200 feet and Snow King, at 7,550 feet.

Each mountain offers distinct levels of terrain. Snow King is all intermediate and has most of the below-tree-line skiing found at the resort. KT-22 is the radical peak, with its legendary chutes, steeps, and extreme skiing. Squaw Peak, Broken Arrow, and Emigrant also have intermediate terrain, with a unique high-altitude novice area that starts at High Camp and gives beginners and early intermediates a chance to experience the breathtaking views that advanced skiers usually have more opportunity to see.

More than 70% of the terrain is free-form: It's find-your-own-way-down skiing, most of it beginning above the tree line. Although the layout might seem disconcerting at first, you'll quickly feel liberated at not having to abide by designated trails while skiing on the more than 450 inches (annual average snowfall) of snow cover. Take the skier's guide map with you as you explore the resort, but don't expect to find individual runs: It's simply a general mountain map identifying lifts as green, blue, or black and offering landmarks to help you get your bearings.

The big news for snowboarders is the addition of lights to the Central Park snowboard terrain park, meaning that snowboarders can ride the half pipe 12 hours a day. The terrain park is one of the largest in the Sierra. Squaw Valley hosts the annual Off the Wall Snowboarding Festival, featuring live music, product demos, and snowboarding exhibitions.

Novices
Nine of the 33 lifts at Squaw are designated green, with the majority at the High Camp area, although four are surface lifts (one at the base of Snow King, three at Olympic Village base) for never-evers to get started on. From the main base area, you can take either the gondola or the cable car to the green chairs off the High Camp lift (East Broadway, Belmont, Links, Bailey's Beach, or Riviera) and ski the wide-open expanse of gentle and groomed high-altitude slopes that are seldom visited by advanced skiers. You can play on these all day and then some, or take blue lifts, such as Gold Coast or High Camp, for more sustained pitch and length.

Intermediates
Squaw has a lot to offer intermediates, with 13 lifts serving the designated blue terrain, which includes all of Snow King Peak, the entire face of Broken Arrow, and the upper part of Emigrant. If you're ready to step up to black terrain, take the Headwall chair to the advanced but groomed slopes on the upper part of Squaw Peak or head over to Granite Chief for similar terrain. At the end of the day, ski the open terrain off the Mainline and Gold Coast lifts, then follow the broad, groomed Mountain Run (the route of the Olympic men's downhill race) or the parallel Home Run from the Gold Coast to the base village.

Experts
Only eight of Squaw's lifts are designated black, with the majority serving the wild, untamed terrain of KT-22 or

the upper limits of Squaw Peak. You can warm up on the steeps under the Cornice II or Headwall lifts—mostly ungroomed, pure fall-line adrenaline boosts with enough bowls, couloirs, and drops to tire you out. The real test, though, is KT-22, with its super-advanced west faces. It's in this area that you'll find the cliffs, the gulp-and-go chutes, the curled cornice lips, and the biggest bumps. If you venture out in this wild upper alpine terrain, it's best to ski it in the company of a guide (tel. 916/583–6985).

WHERE TO STAY

Squaw Mountain Village has about 2,000 beds, most of them expensive, and several good restaurants, bars, and shops. At the Gold Coast (at the top of the gondola; open until midnight) there are more bars, restaurants, bakeries, retail shops, and lockers, not to mention a full-fledged recreation center.

An alternative to the higher-end village hotels is Truckee, a 7-mile drive south of the mountain. It's a small Sierra town with a variety of moderate and inexpensive inns, lodges, motels, and hotels. Five miles north is Tahoe City, a small lakeside community with more moderately priced accommodations plus the best choice of restaurants and nightlife. In addition, a number of small residential lakefront communities lie within a 20- to 25-minute drive from the mountain, including the upscale Incline Village, on the Nevada side of the state line. You can also stay on the South Shore (see Heavenly, above), with its well-established casino life. The drive takes about an hour, or you can take the ferry boat across the

lake, but South Shore is only recommended as an overnight spot if you have a casino itch that you are desperate to scratch.

Expensive

Cal-Neva Lodge

One of the most storied of all the Tahoe lodges, this is also one of the oldest. Built in 1927 as a luxury retreat for celebrities and other high rollers, Cal-Neva prospered during Prohibition and thrived into the '50s. Frank Sinatra owned it in the 1960s, during which time it hosted gatherings for Hollywood moguls, the Mafia, and the upper-class elite. It began its decline in the late '60s and was closed from 1983 until 1986, when it was renovated and reopened. Reincarnated, it's a marvelous place—a grand and striking nine-story log-and-stone facade at the edge of Crystal Bay and precisely on the state line dividing California and Nevada. The vaulted Indian Room, still intact after the refurbishing of the lodge, has massive exposed beams, an enormous fireplace, stone floors, and a score of big-game trophies. Adjacent is the mesmerizing Crystal Bar, a circular extravaganza of wood paneling and mirrors topped by a cut-crystal dome overhead. You can choose a room, a suite with a balcony, a cottage with a small porch, or a chalet with a wraparound deck and a fireplace. All are decorated in French country style and offer views of the lake. *2 Stateline Rd., Box 368, Crystal Bay, NV 89402, tel. 702/832–4000 or 800/225–6382, fax 702/831–9007. 162 rooms with bath, 18 suites, 20 chalets and cottages. Facilities: restaurant, spa, sauna, steam room, massage, casino. AE, D, DC, MC, V. $69–$279.*

Olympic Village Inn

This gorgeous replica of a Swiss A-frame mountain lodge, with stucco walls, towers, and wooden balconies, is a quarter mile from the main lift area. Built as part of the original Olympic Village, the inn stresses simple elegance but has the added appeal of being family oriented and slightly more relaxed than some other luxury accommodations. Some suites come with a fireplace; reserve these early. The decor is sophisticated Swiss/French country, with delicate floral-print wall coverings and curtains, light-amber furnishings, and wood trim. All come with a queen-size bed, a queen-size sleeper sofa, and a kitchenette. Extra touches include eider-down comforters and terry-cloth robes. These units are comfortable and spacious enough for four people and a good choice for families. *1909 Chamonix Pl., Olympic Valley, CA 96146, tel. 916/581–6000 or 800/845–5243, fax 916/583–3135. 90 units. Facilities: lounge, library/game room, 5 outdoor hot tubs. AE, MC, V. $165–$275.*

Resort at Squaw Creek

This vast, 650-acre resort-within-a-resort is the class act at Squaw: It's a self-contained luxury emporium featuring everything from penthouse suites to a towering man-made waterfall. The rooms and suites, impeccably turned out in modern West Coast decor, are bright, window-dominated aeries, with exceptional views, sleek and stylish furnishings, original artwork, plants, and just about every finishing touch imaginable. The most deluxe units are the 18 penthouse suites, each with two levels of sleekly stylish living in individual owner–decorated plush palaces. Smooth and velvety couch coverings, striking broadloom and rugs, high-quality furnishings, and tasteful personal touches give each a unique feel. The standard rooms and suites, though smaller, are also well decorated and well furnished, and all come with a king- or two queen-size beds. It sits on the perimeter of Squaw Valley, with direct access to the slopes from its own chairlift. *400 Squaw Creek Rd., Olympic Valley, CA 96146, tel. 916/583–6300 or 800/327–3353, fax 916/581–6647. 200 rooms, 205 suites. Facilities: 4 restaurants, deli, health club, heated outdoor pool, sand beach pool, ski lift, ski rentals, ski shop, cross-country ski lessons, ski storage, 3 hot tubs, children's programs, baby-sitting, laundry service, shuttle to slopes, skating pavilion. AE, D, DC, MC, V. $209–$950.*

Squaw Valley Lodge

Here's an upscale ski-in/ski-out condo hotel, excellently situated in the mountain village at the base of the Squaw 1 express lift and near many others. It has personal touches such as goose-down comforters and sensible amenities including a coffeemaker and other small kitchen appliances. The stylish three-building enclave offers resort hotel facilities (fitness and health center, maid service, concierge, and bell staff) with practical additions such as kitchenettes and sleeper sofas. An all-suite hotel might be a better description of the lodge, but each unit is individually owned and styled. Decor ranges from contemporary European to Southwestern. The smallest is the deluxe studio, which has a queen-size bed separated from the living area and kitchenette by a bookcase or sliding doors. One-bedroom suites sleep four but offer more space and privacy. In addition to the separate bedroom, they have a full kitchen and a larger bathroom with two privacy doors. Oddly, the units best suited for families have only a kitchenette rather than a full kitchen. *201 Squaw Peak Rd., Box 2364, Olympic Village, CA 96146, tel. 916/583–5500 or 800/922–9970, fax 916/583–0326. 85 units. Facilities: health club, outdoor pool, 5 hot tubs, laundry, ski shop. AE, DC, MC, V. $160–$310.*

Moderate

Hyatt Regency Lake Tahoe

In striking contrast to the serene, wooded setting near the waters of Lake Tahoe, the Hyatt is a large, sprawling casino hotel that looks like a transplant from the South Shore (*see* Heavenly, *above*), with round-the-clock opportunities to chance fate. There are all-you-can-eat buffet specials, discounted lift tickets, and complimentary drinks. Rooms have California mountain-lodge decor—big wooden beds, pine armoires, and overstuffed furniture—and large bathrooms. One-bedroom and two-bedroom suites are spacious enough for four adults or a family. The cottages are lakeside and come with either a kitchen or a wet bar/kitchenette. In addition to the nonstop action in the casino, there's a multitude of other facilities to keep everyone occupied. A complimentary shuttle service runs to and from the resort. *Country Club Dr. and Lake Shore, Box 3239, Incline Village, NV 89450, tel. 702/832–1234 or 800/553–3288, fax 702/832–3222. 434 rooms, 24 suites/cottages. Facilities: 3 restaurants, 2 lounges, health spa, outdoor heated pool. AE, D, DC, MC, V. $135–$445.*

Mayfield House

This delightful stone-and-wood house was built in the 1930s by Norman Mayfield, one of the original development tycoons to work the Lake Tahoe area. It's a classic example of Tahoe architectural style from that era, and after a refurbishing in 1979 it was turned into this fine bed-and-breakfast. All bedrooms are decorated in English Tudor style and brim with extras such as fresh flowers, lots of books, and down comforters. Each room has its own nook for eating breakfast or relaxing with a book, and all have either a queen- or a king-size bed; one master suite has a king-size bed and a sitting area. There's also a large living room with a fireplace, and a full breakfast is served in the dining room. *236 Grove St., Box 5999, Tahoe City, CA 96145, tel. 916/583–1001. 5 rooms, 1 suite. Facilities: dining room. AE, MC, V. $85–$180.*

Richardson House

This Victorian-era house was built in 1881 and has mostly been maintained in its original style. It's a warm B&B, and despite its intimate size and friendly atmosphere, guests don't feel suffocated or imposed upon. Marvelous antiques decorate the rooms; there's also a lounge with a wood-burning stove where guests can compare notes on the day's ski adventures. *10154 High St., at Spring St., 11 mi from resort, Box*

2011, Truckee, CA 96160, tel. 916/
587–5388. 8 rooms, 6 with bath.
Facilities: outdoor hot tub. AE, MC, V.
$85–$135, including full breakfast.

River Ranch Lodge

This marvelous period property sits
serenely on a fat curve in the scenic
Truckee River, just 3 miles from the
Squaw Resort Village. The rustic timbered structure built in the 1950s
replaced the original inn built in
1888, which was a fashionable watering hole for people traveling by train.
Updated in 1960, it housed Olympic
dignitaries. The rooms meticulously
re-create an Early American pioneer
motif, with antiques and hand-crafted
period furnishings. They are comfortable, woodsy, and cozy and big
enough for four people on two queen-
size beds. There are no fireplaces or
hot tubs in the guest quarters, but
there's a sweet fireside room and a
dramatic lounge and restaurant sitting cantilevered over the rapids of
the river. Rte. 89 and Alpine Meadows
Rd., Box 197, Tahoe City, CA 96145,
tel. 916/583–4264 or 800/535–9900
in CA, fax 916/583–7237. 19 rooms.
Facilities: restaurant, lounge. AE, MC,
V. $55–$125, including Continental
breakfast.

Sunnyside Resort

This pretty little lakeside mountain
lodge is 3 miles south of Tahoe City,
on the west shore of Lake Tahoe. The
wood-and-rock structure is nestled
amid tall pines that dot the shoreline.
All rooms have a view of the lake and
a rustic, elegant decor, with locally
crafted wooden furnishings and bold,
textured country-style fabrics. Rooms
come in several sizes; some have a

fireplace and wet bar, and most can
accommodate four people comfortably. Sunnyside is a quiet spot that's
good for couples but a little too low-
key for families. 1850 W. Lake Blvd.,
Box 5969, Tahoe City, CA 96145, tel.
916/583–7200 or 800/822–2754, fax
916/583–2251. 23 rooms. Facilities:
restaurant, lounge. AE, MC, V. $100–
$165.

Inexpensive

Hostel at Squaw Valley

Bring your own sleeping bag if you
stay at this standard old-fashioned dormitory-style hostel, with 100 bunk-
style single beds split into male-only
and female-only units. It was used to
house Olympic athletes in 1960. Bathrooms (segregated by gender) are
shared, but the accommodations are
clean and reasonably quiet, even
though they're usually filled with singles. The biggest bonus here is the
two-minute walk from the lifts. There
is a community microwave and refrigerator. 1900 Squaw Valley Rd., Box
6655, Tahoe City, CA 96146, tel. 916/
583–7771 or 800/544–4723. 100 beds.
$22–$27 per person; cash only.

Tahoe City Travelodge

On the north shore of Lake Tahoe in
Tahoe City, this excellent motel is a
cut above many others around the
lake. Meticulously maintained, its
rooms are in color-coordinated soft
pastel tones, with brass fixtures and
quilted bedspreads. All rooms are
larger than average and have either
double or king-size beds, large bathrooms with massage showers and hair
dryers, and coffeemakers. There's also
a marvelous lake-view deck with a
hot tub and a sauna. A good family

spot, it has rooms large enough for four and is fairly quiet. *455 N. Lake Blvd., Box 84, Tahoe City, CA 96145, tel. 916/583–3766 or 800/578–7878. 47 rooms with bath. Facilities: hot tub, sauna. AE, D, DC, MC, V. $72–$97.*

Tahoma Lodge

A quiet little nest of mountain cabins, duplexes, and apartments about 15 miles from Squaw, this is an excellent choice for families or groups. The nine rustic cabins have wooden furnishings and touches like wainscoting, high-beamed ceilings, oak-panel trim, and a wood stove. With one or two double beds and a small but complete kitchen, the cabins are comfortable, clean, cozy, and romantic. The lodge is a three-minute walk from cross-country skiing trails. *7018 W. Lake Blvd., Box 72, Tahoma, CA 96142, tel. 916/525–7721. 9 units. Facilities: hot tub. MC, V. $70–$210.*

WHERE TO EAT

Restaurants and bars in Squaw are spread over a 10-mile radius within the valley. There are select spots in Tahoe City, Truckee, Incline Village, and Squaw and at a host of small lakeside communities. If you are staying at the resort, several places are noteworthy, but after more than a few days, you may want to explore a little farther afield.

On the Mountain

Alexander's

The red-and-white-checked tablecloths and cafélike awnings give a warm, charming ambience to this spot. Alexander's has casual dining, offering chili, burgers, goulash, and sandwiches for lunch. The more expansive evening menu includes pizzas and

daily specials such as lemon catfish and chicken Parmesan. At 8,200 feet, the dining room has an awe-inspiring view of Lake Tahoe through the big picture windows—it's definitely worth the trip. *High Camp Bldg., top of cable car, tel. 916/583–2555. Reservations essential. AE, MC, V.*

Expensive

Christy-Hill

The stark, minimalist decor here enables you to appreciate the stunning view of the peaks across the lake, a good reason in itself to enjoy an early dinner and, if you can, secure a table by the large picture window. The room is dominated by the river-rock fireplace with blond-wood trim that provides a foil for the white-washed walls. The menu offers northern California cuisine with Southwestern influences: baked Fanny Bay oysters are served with fresh salsa; a Southwestern chowder (containing clams, mussels, shrimp, and sometimes smoked salmon) has a spicy chili-based broth. There are also game dishes on the menu, such as corn-fed beef tenderloin sautéed with mushrooms and roasted shallots or elk broiled with green peppers, roasted red bell peppers, and shiitake mushrooms. For dessert, try the crème brûlée. *115 Grove St., Tahoe City, tel. 916/583–8551. MC, V.*

Glissandi

A spectacularly spacious and formal dining room with soaring picture windows and elegant tuxedoed waitstaff makes this place to go for a special evening. The Scandinavian decor includes sleek lines, buffed and polished blond wood, and lots of granite surfaces. The contemporary French and Californian menu may include such appetizers as baby bay scallops with shiitake mushrooms and leeks and entrées like roast wild boar with fresh morels and celery root, breast of duck with chipotle sauce, and tenderloin of beef with onion confit and Roquefort cheese. It's creative cooking, beautifully presented in a sophisticated atmosphere. For dessert, try the sweet squash flan with ginger and caramel. *Resort at Squaw Creek, 400 Squaw Creek Rd., Olympic Valley, tel. 916/583–6621. AE, D, DC, MC, V.*

Graham's of Squaw Valley
This is a pleasant, semiformal dining room with sophisticated rustic decor based on light-color walls, subtle wood trim, formal table settings, and two fireplaces. The mostly Mediterranean menu changes often and offers traditional dishes from Spain, such as seafood paella with saffron rice; from France, cassoulet de Toulouse (white beans, duck confit, lamb and garlic sausages, and tomatoes); and from Italy, *farfalle alla Norma* (sautéed eggplant, olives, hot peppers, garlic, tomato, and fresh basil). Other entrées include sea bass wrapped in parchment paper. *Christy Inn Lodge, 1650 Squaw Valley Rd., Olympic Village, tel. 916/581–0454. MC, V.*

Wolfdale's
Owner and chef Douglas Dale has created a casually elegant atmosphere inside the oldest building in Tahoe City (built on the South Shore in 1889, then barged across the lake to its present site in 1901), with a cross section of Japanese and American art, smart ceramic plates and bowls on crisp white linen, fresh flowers in hand-thrown vases, and black lacquer chopsticks. In this East-meets-West decor, each small table is gently illuminated by discreet track lighting, and the walls are in subtle tones of peach and off-white. The menu is ever evolving and eternally interesting. A unique appetizer is the tepee of grape leaves stuffed with dilled rice and smoked trout. The salads intrigue with such creations as a marvelous blossomlike presentation of butter lettuce, radishes, and whole wheat noodle threads in a ginger-tamari-sesame dressing. Entrées focus heavily on fish and may include grilled swordfish with Thai tamarind lobster sauce or salmon with a glaze made from enoki mushrooms. Other entrées to expect are roast quail with fennel sausage over kale and foie gras risotto or a fiery Thai stew with shrimp and scallops, snow peas, and shiitake mushrooms. Dessert choices include homemade coffee and cinnamon ice cream, pear and huckleberry strudel, or a sinful blackberry buttermilk torte with a pepper-spiked cherry sauce. *640 N. Lake Blvd., Tahoe City, tel. 916/583–5700. Reservations essential. MC, V.*

Moderate

Montagna Ristorante
Northern Italian cuisine is the specialty at this restaurant in the Resort at Squaw Creek. The casual decor focuses on the large, open kitchen with its brick ovens and walls and includes beamed ceilings, white walls, and light classical music playing in the background. The extensive menu offers four varieties of brick-oven

pizza (try the pesto and wild mushroom pie), unique pasta dishes such as linguine *di Gamberi* (shrimp and scallops with garlic, parsley, white wine sauce, and lemon butter) and rotisserie specialties including rosemary chicken and herb-marinated lamb loin with wild mushrooms. There's also a good selection of fish dishes, as well as fresh clams steamed with zucchini, onions, basil, and white wine and served over fettuccine. *400 Squaw Creek Rd., Olympic Valley, tel. 916/583–6300. AE, D, DC, MC, V.*

Pfeifer House
This is a quaint Alpine-style restaurant with a woodsy Tyrolean stucco exterior and a cozy fireplace-warmed interior filled with dark wood, heavy Germanic and Austrian furniture, and Alpine bric-a-brac and art. The European menu borrows from Austria, Switzerland, Hungary, and Germany. Schnitzels and sauerbraten, Swiss bratwurst and Hungarian goulash, roast duckling and steak tartare are all served with rich sauces and a choice of egg noodles, potato pancakes, or *rösti* potatoes. Also available is standard American and English fare, such as generous portions of succulent meats, including beef Wellington and rack of lamb, as well as fish and lobster. *760 River Rd., off Rte. 89, ¼ mi north of Tahoe City, Tahoe City, tel. 916/583–3102. Reservations essential. AE, DC, MC, V.*

River Ranch Restaurant
There are two quiet and cozy dining rooms in this classic Tahoe resort lodge. One overlooks the Truckee River through a large picture window, and the other has a large stone fireplace. Both have rustic log walls, sturdy pine tables and chairs, local art, and candlelighted place settings. The menu is straightforward American, with a mix of seafood and grill specialties. From the grill there's citrus-marinated chicken breast and a selection of corn-fed Kansas beef, including pepper steak with a delicious pepper-brandy sauce. Fish entrées include Idaho rainbow trout done with almonds and shiitake mushrooms, and game items include fresh elk loin. *Rte. 89 and Alpine Meadows Rd., Tahoe City, tel. 916/583–4264. AE, MC, V.*

Sunnyside Resort
The deck at Sunnyside is a Tahoe institution for breakfast, lunch, and dinner because of its location—as the name implies—on the sunny side of the lake. If weather doesn't permit this, move inside to the nautically themed Chris Craft dining room. Nibble on deep-fried zucchini and then choose from daily fish, pasta, and steak specials, all served with fisherman's chowder and San Francisco sourdough bread. *1850 W. Lake Blvd., Tahoe City, tel. 916/583–7200. AE, MC, V.*

Inexpensive
Hacienda del Lago
You'll get first-rate Mexican grub with second-rate Mexican decor, but it's a great spot with excellent prices for large portions of burritos, enchiladas, tacos, fajitas, and other standards. There's also a wild happy hour (4–6) with marvelous multiflavored margaritas, drink specials, and free nachos and other Mexican munchies. *760 N.*

Lake Blvd., upstairs in Boatworks Mall, Tahoe City, tel. 916/583–0358. Reservations not accepted. MC, V.

Lanza's

When you're ready for that Italian food fix, this is the place to visit. Classic country Italian style is presented—not too fancy, just well priced and well prepared. Pasta is plentiful, including manicotti, cannelloni, lasagna, and fettuccine. Veal comes Parmesan, *piccata*, and Milanese. Also try the calamari, and leave room for the homemade spumoni ice cream. *7739 N. Lake Blvd., next to Safeway, Kings Beach, tel. 916/546–2434. Reservations not accepted. MC, V.*

Rosie's Café

An institution in the Tahoe area, Rosie's has a charming atmosphere (with bicycles, skis, and snowshoes providing much of the funky decor, as well as deer antlers serving as lamps), après-ski appeal, and good, old-fashioned American food. For entrées, which come with home-baked sourdough bread, soup or salad, and vegetables, you can have Southern fried chicken with mashed potatoes and gravy, baby-back ribs, fish-and-chips, New York cut steak, stir-fry dishes, or a healthy choice of pastas. It's a cheerful, folksy place with live entertainment on Tuesday night. *571 N. Lake Blvd., Tahoe City, tel. 916/583–8504. Reservations not accepted. AE, D, DC, MC, V.*

Sweet Potatoes Deli

This bright and lively pick-and-snack deli emporium is a good spot if you don't feel like having a full meal. Its large windows, sparkling white walls, and tile floors are softened by wooden shelves filled with books for browsing or buying. The excellent assortment of deli dishes includes gourmet sandwiches, homemade soups, chili, quiche, and baked goods, as well as pasta salads, cheeses, and meats. If you just want to have a cup of coffee and some good conversation, there's also an espresso bar, liqueur coffees, yogurts, fresh fruits, and cheeses. You can eat at one of a dozen tables or take out. *400 Squaw Creek Rd., Resort at Squaw complex, base of Squaw Creek chairlift, Olympic Valley, tel. 916/583–6300, ext. 6935. AE, MC, V.*

Best Bets for Breakfast

Firesign

There's almost always a wait, but it's worth it. All the standard cholesterol fests including pancakes, waffles, and lots of different baked goods are offered. Fancier dishes such as eggs Benedict and Cape Cod Benedict (the traditional egg dish served with spinach and smoked salmon). There is also a popular blueberry coffee cake available. You can eye the dogsled in the rafters while you wait for your morning repast. *1785 W. Lake Blvd., Tahoe City, tel. 916/583–0871. DC, MC, V.*

Rosie's Café

This is an all-day café, but breakfast is where it really shines, with a lineup of omelets, scrambled egg dishes, muesli, and espresso drinks. Try the famous *huevos rancheros* or the All-American: two eggs, two slices of bacon, two pancakes, and home fries. *571 N. Lake Blvd., Tahoe City, tel. 916/583–8504. AE, D, DC, MC, V.*

NIGHTLIFE AND ENTERTAINMENT
Après-Ski
Bar One
This classic après-ski microbrew pub has a roaring fire and live music and dancing. It's a moving and grooving place, popular with an older crowd that is beyond the hard-belly stage, but the dance floor still rocks. *Olympic House, base of mountain, tel. 916/583–1777. AE, MC, V.*

Plaza Bar
At this sports bar, skiers swap tall tales with colorful local characters while they soak up big-screen TV sports. The cheerful bar is decorated with sporting memorabilia from the 1960 Winter Olympics. You can choose from a tremendous variety of beers, as well as among a repertory of hot, sweet cocktails. *Base village, Squaw Mountain, tel. 916/583–1588. AE, MC, V.*

Loud and Lively/Dancing
Crystal Bay Club
The classiest gambling place in Incline Village is also the center of most of the action. Locals claim it also has the best food deals of all the casinos. The real attractions are the gaming and the lounge acts. It's full-blown glitz and cash, some occasional headline acts, and in general, a place to have fun watching other people lose money. *Rte. 28, Crystal Bay, NV, tel. 702/831–0512. AE, D, DC, MC, V.*

Humpty's
At this spot you can hear live bands nightly, ranging from rock to blues to reggae. The quality and tempo are high, inspiring patrons to dance up a storm. Despite all the action, Humpty's has a neighborhood pub atmosphere, with an affable crowd of 20- and 30-somethings. *877 N. Lake Blvd., Tahoe City, tel. 916/583–4867. MC, V.*

Naughty Dawg
At this classic saloon with a neosurf "arf-deco" decor, you'll find one of the best selections of specialty beers in the area. It's a funky place with daily special events and good finger food. Generally an under-30 crowd hangs out here. *255 N. Lake Blvd., Tahoe City, tel. 916/581–3294. AE, D, DC, MC, V.*

More Mellow
Bullwhacker's Pub
This sports bar has multiple TVs, billiards, shuffleboard, and live entertainment, such as an acoustic guitarist or blues bands, six nights a week. The Old West theme adds some coziness; the copper bar counter and light fixtures contrast with dark woodwork. Generally, a 30-something-plus group makes up the nighttime clientele. *Resort at Squaw Creek, 400 Squaw Creek Rd., Olympic Valley, tel. 916/581–6617. AE, D, DC, MC, V.*

Few regions of America conjure up images of skiing as does Colorado, the Rocky Mountain State, which has traded in its mining heritage for one of outdoor recreation. In many ways it is the epicenter of the American ski experience.

Sliced north to south by the mountains of the Continental Divide, Colorado is a spectacular blend of high peaks, deep canyons, and vast, open plains so visually stunning that former U.S. president Teddy Roosevelt once remarked on looking at it: "The scenery bankrupts the English language." Dominating that scenery are the Rocky Mountains, three times as large in area as the Swiss Alps and home to 1,140 peaks over 10,000 feet, with 54 topping out at more than 14,000 feet.

This monumental barrier to east–west travel forces prevailing westerly winds from the Pacific to rise high up into the stratosphere and then release the moisture as the white gold now mined by more than 28 ski resorts across the state. These range in size and stature from the storied and world-renowned Aspen to the vastness of Vail to the quiet isolation of Steamboat. Regardless of size or stature, all of Colorado's ski resorts share the common bounty of frequent and intense snowfalls and the gateway city of Denver.

Closest to Denver is the Fraser Valley, a narrow slash of land cutting north from the Berthoud Pass (50 miles from Denver) and flanked on the east by the towering Continental Divide and to the west by the rugged Vasquez Ridge. In this valley lies Winter Park, a resort created by recreation-seeking Denverites and considered by many to be their own backyard ski area. Seventy-five miles west of Denver is Summit County, a four-resort (Copper Mountain, Keystone, Arapahoe Basin, and Breckenridge), four-town (Frisco, Silverthorne, Dillon, and Breckenridge) swath of the Arapaho National Forest, where the Ten Mile and Gore ranges clash in a marvelous display of 45 13,000-foot peaks. Just 20 miles farther west is the Vail Valley, a narrow aspen-draped mountain dip that cuts deep into the Gore Range and is home to America's largest single ski resort, Vail, and its neighbor, Beaver Creek.

In central Colorado is the Roaring Fork Valley, sandwiched between the Sawatch Range on the east and the Elk Mountains to the south and west, and Aspen, possibly America's best-known ski resort. This 50-mile-long valley is crowned by more than 500 peaks more than 12,000 feet, including Mt. Elbert, at 14,400 feet the Continental Divide's highest peak.

Southwestern Colorado is home to two more resorts, Crested Butte, in the Elk Mountains, and Telluride, in the San Juan Mountains. Both have endured the boom-and-bust cycle of mining, and now the well-preserved Victorian towns are a comfortable counterpoint to the modern resorts that have developed on their outskirts. Finally, northwestern Colorado is where you'll find Steamboat (the resort and the town), in a wide river valley of ranch land and steaming thermal springs.

GETTING TO COLORADO RESORTS

By Plane
Denver International Airport (DIA; tel. 303/342–2000), about 25 miles east of downtown Denver, is served by **American** (tel. 800/433–7300), **America West** (tel. 800/235–9292), **Continental** (tel. 303/925–4350 or 800/525–0280), **Delta** (tel. 800/221–1212), **Frontier** (tel. 800/432–1359), **Mesa** (tel. 800/637–2247), **Midwest Express** (tel. 800/452–2022), **Northwest** (tel. 800/225–2525), **TWA** (tel. 800/221–2000), **United** and **United Express** (tel. 800/241–6522), and **US Airways** (tel. 800/428–4322).

Car Rental
Alamo (tel. 800/327–9633), **Avis** (tel. 800/331–1212), **Budget** (tel. 303/949–6012), **Dollar** (tel. 303/398–2323), **Hertz** (tel. 303/524–7177), **National** (tel. 303/476–6634), **Payless** (tel. 303/399–2608), and **Thrifty** (tel. 303/949–7787) have offices at Denver's airport.

By Bus
Greyhound Lines (tel. 303/476–5137 or 800/231–2222) has a station in downtown Denver and offers daily service to most Colorado resorts.

By Train
Amtrak's *California Zephyr* (tel. 800/872–7245) has daily service with sleeping accommodations into Denver from the West Coast and Chicago.

ASPEN MOUNTAIN

Box 1248
Aspen, CO 81612
Tel. 970/925–1220 or
800/525–6200

STATISTICALLY SPEAKING

Base elevation: 7,945 feet

Summit elevation: 11,212 feet

Vertical drop: 3,267 feet

Skiable terrain: 631 acres

Number of trails: 76

Longest run: 3 miles

Lifts and capacity: 1 gondola,
1 high-speed quad, 2 quads, 4
doubles; 10,775 skiers per
hour

Daily lift ticket: $56 (valid in
Snowmass, Aspen Highlands,
and Buttermilk areas as well)

Average annual snowfall:
300 inches

Number of skiing days
1995–96: 133

Snowmaking: 210 acres, 33%

Terrain mix: N 0%, I 35%,
E 65%

Snowboarding: no
(see Snowmass, below)

Cross-country skiing:
80 kilometers of groomed
cross-country terrain in
Aspen and Snowmass areas

Aspen sits in the Roaring Fork Valley, a wide, U-shape cut of land created by glacial activity that lies in the heart of central Colorado's 2-million-acre White River National Forest. The valley stretches for nearly 50 miles northwest, from the town of Aspen to the community of Glenwood Springs, and is sandwiched between the Sawatch Range to the east and the Elk Mountains on the south and west. Among the more than 500 towering peaks reaching from 12,000 feet to higher than 14,000 feet is Mt. Elbert (14,400 feet), the highest peak along the Continental Divide. These strapping glacier-topped mountains created more than 15 million years ago provide the melt that feeds the restless Roaring Fork River, which rushes northeast until it merges near Glenwood Springs with the mighty Colorado River.

The valley's original inhabitants, the Ute Indians, were supplanted in the mid-1800s by prospectors and miners who came to reap the region's bounty of lead, zinc, copper, silver, and gold. By 1884 Aspen was a thriving frontier boomtown with more than 3,500 hardy souls; after the railroad was extended west over the Continental Divide, the once-obscure mining town flourished, and by 1892 it had become the third-largest city in the state, behind only Leadville and Ashcroft. Unfortunately, the mining mother lode that had financed the boom also ultimately created the bust when silver was demonetized in 1893 and prices hit rock bottom. Within just 30 days every mine in the area was forced to close.

For the next 40-odd years the once-splendid brick and sandstone buildings lay virtually dormant, and by the early 1920s the population reached its nadir of just 350. In 1937, however, the town was resuscitated when a small ski area and winter sports center opened on Aspen Mountain. Later, during World War II, the illustrious 10th Mountain Division—America's fighting skiers—trained here. Among those storied soldiers of the snow was Friedl Pfeifer, an Austrian-born, naturalized-American U.S. ski instructor who foresaw the skiing mecca that Aspen was to become. In partnership with Chicago industrialist Walter Paepke, Pfeifer formed the Aspen Skiing Corporation and in 1947 on Aspen Mountain opened the world's longest ski lift.

USEFUL NUMBERS

Area code: 970

Children's services: Powder Pandas at Buttermilk, tel. 970/925-6336

Snow phone: tel. 970/925-1221 or 888/277-3676

Aspen Valley police: tel. 970/920-5400

Eagle County sheriff: tel. 970/963-0375

Aspen Valley Hospital: tel. 970/925-1120

Aspen Central Reservations: tel. 970/925-9000 or 800/290-1325

Aspen Chamber Resort Association: tel. 970/925-1940

Aspen Visitor Center: tel. 970/925-5656

Avalanche hot line: tel. 970/920-1664

Road conditions: tel. 970/920-5454

Highway conditions: tel. 970/639-1234

Towing: Al's Towing and Recovery, tel. 970/920-0428; Tom's Mobile Assistance, tel. 970/923-6741

FIVE-STAR FAVORITES

Best run for vertical: North Star

Best run overall: Spar Gulch

Best bar/nightclub: Ajax Tavern

Best hotel: Hotel Jerome

Best restaurant: Piñons

The evolution from abandoned mining town to thriving ski resort had begun, and in 1950 the staging of the Federation Internationale du Ski (FIS) World Alpine Championships thrust Aspen into the skiing spotlight. Success begat expansion, and other ski areas opened, including Snowmass Resort (*see* Snowmass, *below*), 12 miles away, and the smaller Buttermilk, 2 miles away. Although Aspen Mountain dominates the town with its rugged presence, Snowmass nestles comfortably into the outskirts.

To its credit, the big banana of American ski resorts has survived with its soul relatively intact and its position in the pantheon of big-time ski resorts mostly unshaken. That's not to say that Aspen has not felt pressure from challengers jockeying for its number one position: The resorts of the '90s are definitely out to unseat the resort of the century. It won't be easy, though, for to call Aspen merely a ski resort is to call the *Queen Elizabeth II* merely a boat or the Grand Canyon just another hole in the ground. In addition to being a resort, Aspen is so many other things. It is a town rich in history that's laced with style and yet marvelously complete as a community. When you look beyond the soap opera lifestyle of the glitterati and the media bombardment of the paparazzi, what you find is a diverse and exciting combination of frills and substance.

The entire town of Aspen—which can be explored on foot—is compacted into a square mile between the banks of the Roaring Fork River on one side and Castle Creek on the other. Within a four-block cobblestone pedestrian mall beats the heart of the community: shops, boutiques, restaurants, galleries, and bars housed in perfectly preserved historic buildings.

A car is not necessary here, not only because of Aspen's size but also because this mountain community has one of the most efficient—and free—public transportation systems anywhere. The system, in turn, is supplemented by numerous private shuttles that ferry people from the airport to hotels and from there to either Aspen Mountain or to the Rubey Park Transportation Center, where buses leave for Snowmass Village, Aspen Highlands, and Buttermilk.

The efficient transportation system makes it convenient to stay at a reasonably priced accommodation outside the pricey downtown hub yet still participate in downtown activities. It also makes it easy to socialize and lodge in town but ski the considerably larger and more varied terrain of Snowmass, just 20 minutes away by shuttle.

HOW TO GET THERE

By Plane

Denver International Airport is about 200 miles from Aspen (*see* Getting to Colorado Resorts, *above*). United, United Express, and Western Pacific have daily flights into **Aspen Airport,** between Aspen and Snowmass. Grand Junction's **Walker Field,** 130 miles west of Aspen, also has service via America West, Skywest, and United Express.

Colorado Mountain Express (tel. 970/949–4227 or 800/525–6353) runs trips from Denver and Vail. **High Mountain Taxi** (tel. 970/925–8294 or 800/528–8294) provides prepaid charter service to and from Denver International Airport for groups of up to seven people ($550).

By Car

Aspen is a four-hour, 200-mile drive from Denver. From DIA follow Peña Boulevard toward Denver for 12 miles to I–70. Take I–70 west for about 3½ hours to CO 82 in Glenwood Springs. Follow CO 82 south for about one hour, passing Snowmass Village and the airport. CO 82 will become Main Street in Aspen.

Aspen Airport is served by **Avis** (tel. 800/331–1212), **Budget** (tel. 800/527–0700), **Hertz** (tel. 800/654–3131), and **Thrifty** (tel. 800/367–2277). Other car-rental companies in Aspen include **Alamo** (tel. 800/327–9633) and **Rocky Mountain Rent-A-Car** (tel. 970/925–2880).

By Bus

Greyhound Lines/Trailways (tel. 970/945–8501 or 800/231–2222) runs three trips daily from Denver to Glenwood Springs, 40 miles from Aspen. A round-trip ticket costs $35. **Aspen Limousine Service** (tel. 970/925–2400 or 800/222–2112) runs vans from the Glenwood Springs Station to Aspen for $40 round-trip.

By Train

Amtrak's *California Zephyr* (tel. 970/925–9563 in Glenwood Springs or 800/872–7245) makes weekly runs from Denver to Glenwood Springs, 40 miles from Aspen.

GETTING AROUND

High Mountain Taxi (tel. 970/925–8294) provides taxi service around Aspen. There is also regular shuttle bus service around Aspen and between Aspen and Snowmass, leaving from Aspen's Rubey Park Transportation Center (tel. 970/925–8484).

THE SKIING

Two things initially surprise first-time visitors to Aspen Mountain: The first is its size, just 631 acres—less than one-quarter the acreage of nearby Snowmass; the second is the absence of any novice runs. Those curiosities aside, this is a magnificent, rippling mountain whose peaks thrust high above its namesake town, its steep chutes, mogul-rich pitches, and gladed ridges tucked in the folds of its granite apron.

What you see from the base area is only the tip of this multifaceted mountain, but the hidden treasures are relatively easy to discover. From the top you can reach any of the three main ridges that comprise the mountain's skiing network. To your left as you look down (the west) is Ruthie's Ridge, the site of most of the straight-ahead giant slalom cruising runs; from Ruthie's you can also reach the area known as the Dumps, a series of double-black-diamond gladed chutes. On the far west extreme of Ruthie's is Aztec, site of one of the toughest World Cup downhill courses in the world.

The middle ridge is actually a separate peak called Bell Mountain, and its three sides—Face, Ridge, and Back—offer a series of snow-packed mogul pitches and some outstanding tree skiing. The uppermost part of the mountain, on the eastern fringe, is Gentleman's Ridge, with both the easiest intermediate runs and the tough, mean, and unrelenting far-eastern pitches of Walsh's Gulch.

In between Gentleman's Ridge and Bell Mountain Ridge are Spar and Copper gulches, which funnel skier traffic to the gondola base. Spar has the steepest sides as it cuts a distinct V-shaped groove through the heart of the mountain, but it's also well groomed and begs to be skied fast. Copper is wider and gentler, with a ripple of moguls just smooth and round enough to provide exhilaration without acceleration.

Getting up the mountain is a snap, as the entire town serves as a base area. In the center of town is the Silver Queen gondola, a six-passenger bullet that shoots to the summit in just 15 minutes—how long you'll have to wait for this varies from 5 to 10 minutes, depending on time of year, traffic, and weather. Although this is the fastest way to be transported up the mountain, it's also the most crowded; during weekends and holidays savvy skiers head over to the slower but less busy Lift 1A, a few blocks west of the gondola. Lift 1A begins a two-lift ride that lets you off at either the lower mountain, Ruthie's Ridge and the Dumps or at the summit runs. The three-leg journey all the way to the top takes about 25 minutes.

Aspen Mountain's simple layout and lift system make it easy to reach all sectors. There are no terminally tedious traverses, few flat spots, no endless cat tracks—just an honest, straightforward ski area best characterized by the 3-mile descent down 3,300 vertical feet from the summit to the base area at the bottom of the gondola.

Novices

There are no novice trails on Aspen Mountain. Even the most modest intermediate runs—of which there are precious few—are beyond the capability of beginners and even wanna-be intermediates. Beginners and borderline intermediates should head for either Snowmass, with its vast variety of novice and intermediate runs, or better still to Buttermilk's superb novice terrain.

Intermediates

If you can't handle bumps or are unable to link together strong, precise turns on unforgiving terrain, you may be overestimating your ability to handle—and, more importantly, to enjoy—

Aspen Mountain. For the steady, strong intermediate skier, however, Aspen Mountain has a tremendous mix of steep giant-slalom cruising and even steeper bump skiing.

The Silver Queen gondola is the fastest route to the summit, where most of the tamest intermediate runs are found. You can stick to the upper part of the mountain by riding Lift 3, the high-speed quad, which serves the runs to the left (looking down); or Lift 7, which gives access to the runs off Gents Ridge to the right. Keep in mind that this moderate terrain can be the most crowded part of the mountain. From the summit try 1&2 Leaf, a wide, well-groomed trail that's one of the easiest on the mountain. Next to that is Copper Cutoff, which is slightly steeper but still consistently maintained.

Another good, well-groomed cruiser is Dipsy Doodle, which cuts under Lift 3 and winds across to Bonnie's Restaurant. Stay to the right on the upper part of the run if you don't like bumps. Buckhorn is still another good cruiser, although it becomes heavily traveled and as a result develops icy and bare spots. Silver Bell and Silver Dip are a pair of smooth trails that feed you back to the bottom of Lift 3; after skiing on either you can try Blondies, a slightly steeper and shorter run that sometimes develops small moguls. A good combination for a mixture of some steep cruising, a little more wide-open bowl-type skiing, and a few bumps is Buckhorn to Ruthie's Road to North American.

When the crowds start to build on the upper mountain, head for Bell Mountain—the middle peak—which tends to be much less crowded than the runs served by the gondola. If you're heading over from the summit, take 1&2 Leaf, staying to the right of the gondola, then follow one of the traverses that go to either side of Bell. You can also get to Bell Mountain runs from the base area by taking Lift 4, skiing across Little Nell to the bottom of Lift 5, and then cruising down Deer Park.

If you want a little challenge, try the Face of Bell, which is not a single run but a broad area of glade skiing that holds the snow well. It occasionally develops a good crop of moguls that tend to be well rounded and fairly easy to pick through. You can spend several hours exploring the Face, taking different routes through the trees and riding Lifts 3 and 6 for shorter runs or Lift 5 for longer runs. Although the Face is considered an expert area, a strong intermediate can handle most of the terrain—and avoid the rest. It's a good place to head after you've warmed up on some of the more traditional blue runs.

Spar Gulch is a good warm-up run if you start the day on Bell, but as it's the main thoroughfare down the mountain, it gets crowded, especially in the afternoon. You can pick up the tempo on Spar by skiing up and down the Face.

Another good way to avoid the crowds is to start your day on Lift 1A, at the west end of town. This takes you halfway up the western ridge, Aztec, and from there you can ski down to Lift 8, which takes you to the top of the area known as Ruthie's. Ruthie's Run is a fantastic high-speed cruiser that forms part of the World Cup downhill course. For the full measure of this run, take Ruthie's, which is fairly flat; veer left on Summer Road to the top of Aztec, which is steep but smooth; and then pick up Spring Pitch to Strawpile to 5th Avenue, heading back to the bottom of Lift 1A. Keep in mind that while Ruthie's side of the mountain is less crowded than other areas, it's best to ski it in the morning before the sun turns the snow heavy and the moguls develop.

Don't overlook the lower part of the mountain—to the west side— served by Lift 1A. Magnifico Cutoff/ Lower Magnifico is a smooth, groomed cruiser; or try Strawpile, a wide giant-slalom cruiser with good pitch. You can add some zest to Strawpile by cutting right just below the La Baita restaurant and hammering down the small, well-rounded moguls on Corkscrew.

Experts

In the morning before the snow gets junky, head up Lift 1A (at the west end of town), then shoot up Lift 8 to the area known as the Dumps (from the gondola you can reach the Dumps by skiing down Buckhorn to Ruthie's Run and staying left all the way over to the top of Lift 6). Immediately to the left of Lift 6 is Bear Paw Glade, a steep section with monster moguls and deep snow that will really wake up your knees. When you reach the end of Bear Paw, keep right to reach Lift 6 again. If you stay left, you'll shoot into Spar Gulch for a faster and longer run down to the bottom of Lift 5. Zaugg Dump, Perry's Prowl, and Last Dollar are other bump runs in the Dumps; all tend to have good snow, fat but well-shaped moguls, and not much skier traffic. These trails are for

those who can launch a turn anytime on any bump. All these short, steep bumpers are reached from International, which is a fairly tame, wide boulevard from which most experts cut away as soon as possible. However, if you stick it out past Last Dollar to Silver Queen, you'll be rewarded: This is an outrageous deep-powder power run that begins with a mogul field and then plunges down toward the Elevator Shaft, a precipitous pitch that's one of the steepest on the mountain. From the Elevator you can go down one of two steep, narrow, and mogul-packed runs: Either cut right down Niagara over to Lift 5 or go left via Tower Ten Road to Franklin Dump.

In late morning take Lift 5 to the Face of Bell Mountain, where you can dance in the glades; or from the top of Lift 5, follow the Ridge of Bell to Shoulder for the longest ride on Bell Mountain. Just before Tower 19 cut left onto the Shoulder of Bell—a steeper, more heavily moguled run than the Face. The Ridge and the Shoulder usually have the best mogul runs on the mountain, and you better be prepared to handle the terrain because everyone in the gondola gets a "bump's-eye" view of your talent, especially when you're on the Ridge. Both the Shoulder and the Ridge feed back down to the bottom of Lift 5, but skier traffic can become heavy at lunchtime and at the end of the day, especially through the Grand Junction area. You can avoid the crowds by keeping right (looking down) through the trees.

If you have a hankering for supersteep and deep trails, head for the Walsh's Gulch area, on the east side of the mountain. Be warned, though, that this is tough, ungroomed terrain, so don't overestimate your ability. Take the gondola to the summit and ski across 1&2 Leaf to North Star for a good, steep bump run. Take the same route to a trio of runs that drop like elevator shafts down toward the Roaring Fork River. These three runs were opened in 1985, along with a number of unnamed, unpatrolled, and officially unrecommended alternatives. Before that they were the private preserve of the daring. Sadly, during the 1970s three local skiers were killed as they attempted to take on the 500 vertical feet of the most sustained steeps and avalanche-prone runs on Aspen Mountain.

These days active patrolling and steady traffic reduce the avalanche danger, but they're still the sort of runs that can beat you to death with their relentless 35- to 40-degree pitch and primo moguls. The first run you'll encounter is Walsh's, where—unless there was a good dump the night before—the first 100 yards or so is too steep to hold a lot of snow. Going into Walsh's straight over the top can be disastrous, so if there isn't much snow, it's best to cut left by the trees for a few turns and head back to the main chute to Hyrup's. This run merges into Walsh's halfway down, then into Kristi. Both are as mean and unrelenting as Walsh's, with the same penalty for the adrenaline-challenged: Whichever route you choose, there's only one way back to the Gent's Ridge chair, and that's via Lud's Lane—a terminally tedious flat (even a bit uphill) that requires a lot of momentum to overcome.

WHERE TO STAY

Accommodations in Aspen range from the laughably expensive to the moderately inexpensive, from ultraluxurious hotels and condos to small lodges, inns, and more modest hotels. Whether you plan to ski at Aspen Mountain or Snowmass (which has its own centralized village), your lodging decision for the most part will be based on price not location. The public transportation system for the mountains is excellent, and both resorts are accessible from almost anywhere in the Roaring Fork Valley. Aspen Central Reservations (tel. 800/ 262–7736) books accommodations.

Expensive

Hotel Jerome
The Jerome is everything a great ski hotel should be: steeped in tradition, ideally situated between the town and the mountain, and luxurious to the point of decadence. It opened in sumptuous style in 1889 and has been the physical and social heart of Aspen ever since. Victorian grandeur oozes from a dazzling array of vintage furnishings, crystal chandeliers, intricate woodwork, and gold-laced floor tiling. All rooms are large, with high ceilings and such ultraluxurious touches as oversize beds, antique armoires and chests, huge bathtubs, and hot tubs. *330 E. Main St., 81611, tel. 970/920–1000 or 800/331–7213, fax 970/544–0260. 93 rooms, 49 suites. Facilities: 2 restaurants, bar, lounge, hot tubs, heated outdoor pool, health club, 24-hr desk service, 24-hr room service, shuttle, ski valet, ski storage, ski shop, laundry. AE, DC, MC, V. $160–$1,300.*

Little Nell Hotel

An Aspen institution, Little Nell scores high on the pampering scale. This hotel offers European elegance with its open, airy spaces, stone walls, soft earth tones, hanging tapestries, Belgian wool carpets, and large, overstuffed down couches around the massive lobby fireplace. The luxurious rooms have a fireplace, one king-size or two queen-size beds with down comforters, a plush down couch and chair, and a large marble bathroom. Just 17 steps from the Silver Queen gondola, the Little Nell is technically the only ski-in/ski-out accommodation in Aspen. *675 E. Durant Ave., 81611, tel. 970/920–4600 or 800/525–6200, fax 970/920–4670. 86 rooms, 11 suites. Facilities: 2 restaurants, bar, lounge, hot tubs, heated outdoor pool, health club, spa facilities, 24-hr desk service, 24-hr room service, shuttle service, ski valet, ski storage, laundry. AE, D, DC, MC, V. $425–$4,000.*

The Residence

For exclusivity, luxury, and charm all in one tiny money-is-no-object package, this is the place. In the historic Aspen Block Building in the center of Aspen, the hotel contains just five individually designed one- and two-bedroom apartments. The apartments feature French and English antiques, marble bathrooms, Persian rugs, crystal chandeliers, and fireplaces. Each also has a fully equipped kitchen and dining room stocked with crystal, china, and silver. *305 S. Galena St., 81611, tel. 970/920–6532, fax 970/925–1125. 5 apartments. Facilities: concierge, health club and spa privileges. AE, DC, MC, V. $550–$2,250, including Continental breakfast.*

Ritz-Carlton

At the foot of Aspen Mountain, just a block and a half from the gondola and stretching across almost an entire block of downtown, this striking massive château comes complete with turrets and pitched arches. Customized furnishings, original art, plush carpets, and polished stone and marble decorate the public spaces inside; details such as king-size beds, oversize bathrooms, and Ritz mainstay items such as terry-cloth robes, down comforters, humidifiers, and deluxe toiletries make the guest rooms unforgettable. *315 E. Dean St., 81611, tel. 970/920–3434 or 800/241–3333, fax 970/920–7353. 195 rooms, 27 suites. Facilities: 2 restaurants, bar, lounge, hot tubs, outdoor pool, health club, spa facilities, beauty salon, 24-hr desk service, 24-hr room service, shuttle, ski valet, ski storage, laundry. AE, D, DC, MC, V. $339–$4,000.*

Sardy House

This 1892 Victorian treasure was one of the country's first homes to be built with indoor plumbing, central heating, and electricity. Guest rooms are elegantly decorated with cherry-wood furnishings, Laura Ashley comforters, custom-print wallpaper, oversize beds, and in all but two rooms, whirlpool baths. Breakfast is served either in your room or in the exquisite dining room. *128 E. Main St., 81611, tel. 970/920–2525 or 800/321–3457, fax 970/920–4478. 14 rooms, 6 suites. Facilities: restaurant, bar, parlor, hot tub, heated outdoor pool, ski valet, ski storage. AE, DC, MC, V. $265–$750.*

Moderate

Boomerang Lodge

This comfortable, functional property offers a wide range of accommodations, from somewhat drab standard hotel rooms to smartly appointed studios and deluxe rooms to three-bedroom apartments. There's even a log cabin. The nicest lodgings are the deluxe units, decorated in earth tones and with a Southwestern flair, each with a balcony, an enormous marble bath, a fireplace, and a wet bar. The staff is most hospitable. *500 W. Hopkins Ave., 81611, tel. 970/925–3416 or 800/992–8852, fax 970/925–3314. 34 rooms. Facilities: pool, hot tub, sauna, ski storage, daily maid service, laundry. AE, MC, V. $119–$532, including Continental breakfast.*

The Gant

This condominium complex at the base of the mountain on 5 acres of prime downtown Aspen real estate is a great find for families or groups who want a little luxury, more than the standard amount of space, and proximity to the action without breaking the bank. The Gant is not cheap, but it's reasonable compared to other properties that provide the same services. The one- to four-bedroom units are comfortably and individually furnished by independent owners, and although decor varies wildly from rental to rental, amenities are consistent: Each has a fireplace, a full kitchen, multiple bathrooms, and a balcony. When reserving a room, ask for one of the upper-floor units, as noise travels among lower-floor rooms at night. *610 West End St., 81611, tel. 970/925–5000 or 800/ 345–1471, fax 970/925–6891. 141*

units. *Facilities: 2 outdoor pools, 3 Jacuzzis, 2 saunas, shuttle service, ski storage, laundry. AE, D, DC, MC, V. $175–$835.*

Hotel Aspen

This hotel is a good find, especially considering its great location on Main Street, just a few minutes from the mall and the mountain. The modern exterior features huge windows to take full advantage of the view; inside reveals a Southwestern influence. Most rooms have a balcony or terrace and are comfortable, if not luxurious. Four guest rooms have hot tubs. *110 W. Main St., 81611, tel. 970/925– 3441 or 800/527–7369, fax 970/920– 1379. 45 rooms. Facilities: heated outdoor pool, 2 hot tubs, 24-hr desk service, ski storage. AE, D, DC, MC, V. $99–$329, including Continental breakfast and après-ski buffet.*

Limelite Lodge

In the early '50s this Aspen institution was a nightclub, but in 1958 it was converted to an inn by its present owners. Today it is a good value, particularly because of its prime location, just two blocks from the mall and three blocks from Lift 1A on Aspen Mountain. The guest rooms are furnished with brass or cherry-wood beds and wooden furniture. All are accessible from the outside, motel style, which makes the lodge convenient for families. *228 E. Cooper St., 81611, tel. 970/925–3025 or 800/ 433–0832, fax 970/925–5120. 63 rooms. Facilities: lounge, 2 outdoor pools, sauna, 2 outdoor whirlpools, 24-hr desk service, ski storage, laundry. AE, D, DC, MC, V. $79–$200, including Continental breakfast.*

Molly Gibson Lodge

Rooms in this funky, laid-back lodge three blocks from the mountain may have Jacuzzis, fireplaces, or both. There are also six two-bedroom suites with full kitchens. The lodge's romantic atmosphere is suitable for couples, though families can make good use of the suites. *101 W. Main St., 81611, tel. 970/925–3434 or 800/356–6559, fax 970/925–2582. 44 rooms, 6 suites. Facilities: bar, 2 outdoor Jacuzzis, outdoor pool, shuttle service, ski storage. AE, D, DC, MC, V. $89–$369, including Continental breakfast.*

Inexpensive

Aspen Manor Lodge

This lodge, built in the '60s, retains its unpretentious ski-lodge appeal. The interior is done in dark woods, and the guest rooms are simple and small, with mini-refrigerators. Just a couple of blocks from the Silver Queen gondola, the lodge is ideal for families and small groups who want comfort and convenience without extra trappings and higher cost. *411 S. Monarch St., 81611, tel. 970/925–3001 or 800/372–7736, fax 970/925–4213. 22 rooms. Facilities: lounge, outdoor hot tub, heated outdoor pool, sundeck, ski storage. AE, MC, V. $79–$199, including Continental breakfast.*

Le Clairvaux Condominiums

For condo space without the frills and steep prices, these individually owned two- and three-bedroom units are an excellent deal. There's nothing fancy here, just plain units with childproof furnishings, fireplaces, and fully equipped kitchens; there is twice-weekly maid service, however. Just two blocks from the Silver Queen gondola and close to the town's nightlife, this place is especially good for groups. *803 E. Durant Ave., 81611, tel. 970/925–1100 or 800/642–4210, fax 970/925–1101. 4 units. Facilities: ski storage. AE, MC, V. $175–$500.*

Little Red Ski Haus

Built in 1888 and filled with antiques, this inn occupies the site of one of Aspen's most notorious brothels. The rooms are spartan and in some cases only big enough for a single bed. Cheaper still are beds in the bunk room, which sleeps four. Only a few units have private bathrooms; everyone else shares a bath with one or two others. The friendly atmosphere is buoyed by a diverse guest list—this spot is particularly favored by Australian visitors—and an effusive staff. *118 E. Cooper St., 81611, tel. 970/925–3333, fax 970/925–4873. 21 rooms, 4 with bath; 50 beds. Facilities: lounge, ski storage. MC, V. $39–$122 per person, including full breakfast (Continental on Sat.).*

Mountain Chalet

Since 1955 the same couple has owned and operated this property, providing clean, comfortable, and affordable accommodations in the heart of Aspen. The two-bedroom units have simple decor, basic furnishings, and small bathrooms. The chalet's folksy, friendly atmosphere overcomes the absence of designer trappings. Two or three bunk rooms that sleep four in each are available, as well as four apartments with full kitchens that accommodate six. The chalet is a block from the Silver Queen gondola. *333 E. Durant St., 81611, tel.*

970/925–7797 or 800/321–7813, fax 970/925–7811. 47 rooms, 4 units. Facilities: hot tub, outdoor pool, health club, spa facilities, ski storage, laundry, game room. D, DC, MC, V. $80–$360, including full breakfast.

Skier's Chalet

This is arguably Aspen's best bargain. The location—100 feet from the ticket office and Chairlift 1A—can't be beat. Basic but snug rooms all have cable TV, private bath, and phone, and the staff and fellow clientele are unfailingly congenial. *233 Gilbert St., 81611, tel. 970/920–2037 or 800/262–7736. 20 rooms. Facilities: restaurant, pool. MC, V. $85–$130, including Continental breakfast.*

WHERE TO EAT

As you might expect, there's no shortage of restaurants in Aspen. There's also no shortage of extravagance, which translates into an exorbitant dinner bill at the end of the evening. Fortunately, though, moderately and inexpensively priced eateries abound as well.

On the Mountain

La Baita

At the only on-mountain restaurant with table service, standard Italian fare is spruced up with daily specials; try the penne with fresh chopped tomatoes or the veal chop with roast potatoes. There's also cafeteria service; enjoy the wraparound dining deck when weather allows. *Top of Lift 1A, tel. 970/920–0728. AE, MC, V.*

Sundeck

Friends meet here for lunch because it's easy to reach regardless of which side of the mountain you're skiing on. There are the usual mountain munchies: sandwiches, burgers, soups, salads, and top-class bagels with lox. The Sundeck, with its fireplace, is a great place to warm up. *Top of Silver Queen gondola. tel. 970/920–6335. AE, MC, V.*

Expensive

L'Hostaria

This latest entry vying for Aspen's northern Italian restaurant-of-the-moment is the brainchild of Dante Medri, who also manages La Baita (*see above*). He and his wife, Cristina, brought over all the furniture and fixtures from Italy to create a sophisticated yet rustic look, with an open-beamed farmhouse ceiling, sleek blond-wood chairs, contemporary art, and a floor-to-ceiling glass wine cooler in the center of the room. The menu relies on simple, subtle flavors in specialties such as goat cheese flan on mixed greens, gnocchi with duck ragout, risotto with veal sauce, and grilled veal filet mignon wrapped in bacon with fava beans and sweet baby corn. *620 E. Hyman Ave., tel. 970/925–9022. AE, DC, MC, V.*

Piñons

Piñons adheres to an understated image, with Southwestern ranch-style decor including leather-wrapped railings, a teal green ceiling, and upholstered walls. The American-style menu scores high on creativity: For an appetizer, try the lobster strudel or seared beef strips with spicy Thai peanut sauce and watercress on the side. As entrées go, the ahi coated in macadamia nuts is sensuously superb, and the elk tournedos with pink peppercorns are sensational. Still, simplicity rules, especially with side dishes such as honey-roasted yams or the truffled mashed potatoes. Wrap up a perfect meal with the decadent chocolate and macadamia nut tart or the fresh fruit gratin. *105 S. Mill St., tel. 970/920–2021. Reservations essential. AE, MC, V.*

Renaissance
This small, understated, but elegant French restaurant has clearly scaled the culinary peak. The entrance is unobtrusive, and its interior matches, with a subdued minimalist style that makes use of soft colors and lighting and combines rough granite and smooth pastel silks draped from the ceiling. Owner/master chef Charles Dale keeps the 50-seat operation intimate so that each dish can be prepared with personal touches and served with the occasional table-side chat. The menu is French modern—succulently light dishes that rely on fresh herbs, complex marinades, and international spices. Notable specialties include the roast magret and confit of duck with Thai glass noodles, roast Colorado pheasant with pear compote, and rack of lamb with couscous and cucumber-mint salsa. Upstairs, the R Bistro offers a taste of the kitchen's splendors at down-to-earth prices. *304 E. Hopkins Ave., tel. 970/925–2402. Reservations essential. AE, D, DC, MC, V.*

Syzygy
The tongue-twisting name of this restaurant means "the alignment of three or more heavenly bodies within the solar system that form a nearly straight line." Well, there's nothing straight about Syzygy's eclectic menu. The food is crisply flavored and sen-suously textured, floating from French to Asian to Southwestern influences without skipping a beat. Among the unusual entrées are seared salmon with sweet soy; grilled ahi with flash-fried vegetables; and angel-hair pasta with a delicious ginger-garlic sauce. Even the appetizers have their interesting twists, such as pheasant spring rolls. For dessert try the walnut pie, filled with caramel and topped with maple syrup ice cream. *520 E. Hyman Ave., tel. 970/925–3700. Reservations essential. AE, D, DC, MC, V.*

Wabi Sabi
This little jewel of a restaurant resembles a tiny Japanese teahouse. With only 12 tables and no reservations, you have to get in early to get a spot. The menu is Pacific Rim fusion cuisine—Thai meets Vietnamese meets Japanese—a kind of upscale noodle shop. Noodle dishes include buckwheat soba noodles in citrus miso broth with baby bok choy, wontons and seared scallops. Standout appetizers are the crabsticks over rice noodles and barbecue shrimp spring rolls with sweet mango dipping sauce; entrées range from marinated duck with red chili and plum puree to Szechuan pepper-crusted tenderloin with coconut sticky-rice cakes and asparagus tempura. Hearty appetites be forewarned: Portions are small, and prices are not. *315 E. Hyman Ave., tel. 970/920–2955. Reservations not accepted. AE, DC, MC, V.*

Moderate
Ajax Tavern
The brains behind two of Napa Valley's finest eateries have created this bright, pleasant restaurant in the Lit-

tle Nell Hotel (*see* Where to Stay, *above*), with its mahogany paneling, diamond-patterned floors, leather banquettes, open kitchen, and an eager, unpretentious waitstaff. Nick Morfogen's creative, healthful dishes take advantage of the region's bountiful produce whenever possible and are reasonably priced. You might begin with house-cured Colorado lamb prosciutto with pecorino and arugula, then opt for cedar-planked rare tuna and sweet potato chips in roasted pepper vinaigrette or a chicken breast slow-roasted in its own juices and served on a bed of wild mushrooms and house-smoked bacon. A typical sinful dessert might be poached pear cheesecake with pistachio phyllo crisp. The wine list, showcasing Napa's best, is almost matched by the fine selection of microbrews. *685 E. Durant Ave., tel. 970/920–9333. Reservations essential. AE, D, DC, MC, V.*

Cache Cache
Chef Mike Barry is a practitioner of cuisine *minceur*—no butter or cream is used in his preparations. But the sunny flavors of Provence explode on the palate thanks to the master's savvy use of garlic, tomato, eggplant, fennel, and rosemary. The lamb loin sandwiched between crisp potato *galettes* (pancakes) on a bed of spinach and ratatouille is sublime; salads and rotisserie items are sensational. *205 S. Mill St., tel. 970/925–3835. AE, D, DC, MC, V.*

Century Room
Everything about the Hotel Jerome (*see* Where to Stay, *above*) is exquisite, and dinner in the Century Room is no exception. With its high vaulted ceilings, massive stone-and-marble fireplace, designer wall coverings, and comfortable wingback chairs, it is at once both impressive and intimate. The menu mixes familiar items with innovative twists: the lacquered ahi on stir-fried baby bok choy with a gingery, garlicky butter sauce; or salmon crusted with mustard and served with basmati rice and saffron caper sauce. Another excellent choice is the venison chops, served with parsnip pancakes, roasted winter vegetables, and huckleberry sauce. To finish off a fine meal, indulge in the chocolate-chunk crème brûlée with raspberry compote. *Hotel Jerome, 330 E. Main St., tel. 970/920–1000. Reservations essential. AE, DC, MC, V.*

Smuggler Land Office Ltd.
In 1894 this building, which actually *was* once the Smuggler Mining Company's land office, processed the largest hunk of silver ever mined—a one-ton monster that was 90% pure. Mementos and documentation from that period decorate the interior of what is now a restaurant, where culinary nuggets such as Cajun and creole dishes are produced. The Cajun seafood gumbo, also with chicken and andouille, is excellent—and spicy. Rave reviews also come in for the wild game specials, lobster and asparagus penne, and blackened rack of lamb with jalapeño mint jelly. For dessert sink into the Mississippi mud pie. *415 E. Hopkins St., tel. 970/925–8624. AE, DC, MC, V.*

Takah Sushi
This is the older and smaller of the two sushi restaurants in Aspen; if you

want to sit at the 16-seat sushi bar, you'll have to get here either very early or very late in the evening because it fills up nightly. The excellent Japanese fare offered in the 60-seat dining room includes teriyaki steak and chicken, lightly battered tempura, seared and blackened tuna, and, of course, sushi. *420 E. Hyman Ave., tel. 970/925–8588. AE, D, DC, MC, V.*

Inexpensive

Boogie's Diner
This cheerful spot is filled with diner memorabilia and an outrageous waitstaff and resounds with rock-and-roll faves from the '50s and '60s. The menu has true diner range—from vegetarian specialties to grilled cheese and half-pound burgers (including turkey). Other items are excellent milk shakes, a monster chef salad, meat loaf and mashed potatoes, and a hot turkey sandwich. *534 E. Cooper St., tel. 970/925–6610. AE, MC, V.*

Flying Dog Brew Pub and Grille
Cheap and cheery, Aspen's only brew pub has a good selection of outstanding beers that you can try one at a time or as a four-glass sampler. A substantial selection of pub grub is available, too, from ribs to sandwiches to burgers and other assorted finger foods. *424 E. Cooper Ave., tel. 970/925–7464. AE, MC, V.*

La Cocina
For good inexpensive eats, follow the locals, and they'll lead you to this small Mexican restaurant, which they've been frequenting for more than 20 years. Almost every night the house is packed full. If the wait is too long, you'll likely cop a complimentary salsa dip or margarita for your trouble. *308 E. Hopkins Ave., tel. 970/925–9714. No credit cards.*

Red Onion
This lively century-old saloon may have the best burgers in town in addition to comfort food ranging from meat loaf to gigantic sandwiches, wings, ribs, and chicken. There's also a Mexican menu, with a lineup of tacos, burritos, and enchiladas. *420 E. Cooper St., tel. 970/925–9043. MC, V.*

Silver City Grille
Here's a classic American grill with all the traditional lunch-counter favorites—malteds, milk shakes, and the like. Excellent burgers are the mainstay, but there's also a good selection of sandwiches, soups, homemade desserts, and finger food, including awesome Cajun-spiced fries. The house specialty, however, is barbecued baby-back ribs. *308 S. Hunter St., tel. 970/925–6698. D, MC, V.*

Best Bets for Breakfast

Jour de Fete
If you're making an early morning run for the gondola, this café, just one block west, is a convenient stop for buns, berry muffins, scrumptious cinnamon rolls, and cappuccino to go. *710 E. Durant Ave., tel. 970/925–8691. MC, V.*

Main Street Bakery & Café
Perfectly brewed coffee and hot breakfast buns and pastries are served at this café along with a full breakfast menu including eggs and homemade granola. During late season when the sun is out, head out back to the deck for the mountain views. As locals will attest, this is also a good spot for

lunch and dinner. *201 E. Main St., tel. 970/925–6446. AE, D, MC, V.*

NIGHTLIFE AND ENTERTAINMENT
Après-Ski
Ajax Tavern
At the bottom of Aspen Mountain adjacent to the gondola, it offers bigger-than-life views of the mountain scene and golden rays from the setting sun. By 4 PM it's standing room only. Of course, no one wants to sit when the live band starts to play. *Little Nell Hotel, 685 E. Durant Ave., tel. 970/920–9333. AE, D, DC, MC, V.*

The Tippler
There's another wild deck scene going on here, just a stone's throw from the Ajax. This one attracts 35- to 45-year-olds looking to party. Music, mayhem, and mid-life crises are all on one packed deck. *535 E. Dean St., west of gondola, tel. 970/925–4977. AE, MC, V.*

Loud and Lively/Dancing
Double Diamond
Thirty-somethings who act like twenty-somethings come here for high-energy cruising and dancing to either live entertainment or a DJ. *450 S. Galena St., tel. 970/920–6905. AE, MC, V.*

J Bar
This is the unofficial site of Hunter Thompson's mayoral campaign and the place where hard-drinking philosophers gather to spread their wisdom. Locals used to take up permanent residence here, but now most have moved on, making way for tourists. *Hotel Jerome, 330 E. Main St., tel. 970/920–1000. AE, DC, MC, V.*

Woody Creek Tavern
A visit to Aspen isn't complete without the pilgrimage out of town to Woody's. By its own admission this bar "has no redeeming features." Maybe so, but Woody's is a great hangout, with a grungy atmosphere, assorted bar games, and notable visitors, such as Don Johnson and Hunter Thompson, who come because it's just like Aspen was 30 years ago. *0002 Woody Creek Plaza; 6 mi north of town on Rte. 82, make first right; tel. 970/923–4585. No credit cards.*

More Mellow
The Bar
The Bar offers live jazz and dancing nightly in a sophisticated but comfortable setting with a huge central fireplace and original Western artwork. *Ritz-Carlton, 315 E. Dean St., tel. 970/920–3300. AE, DC, MC, V.*

Italian Caviar
Kick back and relax in overstuffed chairs and couches in front of the requisite crackling fire. There's live piano music nightly. *535 E. Dean St., tel. 970/925–3151. AE, MC, V.*

BEAVER CREEK SKI RESORT

BEAVER CREEK SKI RESORT

Box 915
Avon, CO 81620
Tel. 970/949-5750 or
800/525-2257

STATISTICALLY SPEAKING

Base elevation: 7,400 feet

Summit elevation: 11,440 feet

Vertical drop: 4,040 feet

Skiable terrain: 1,529 acres

Number of trails: 85

Longest run: 2.75 miles

Lifts and capacity: 5 high-speed quads, 4 triples, 4 doubles; 23,739 skiers per hour

Daily lift ticket: $52

Average annual snowfall: 330 inches

Number of skiing days 1995–96: 142

Snowmaking: 375 acres, 25%

Terrain mix: N 19%, I 43%, E 38%

Snowboarding: yes

Nordic ski trails: 32 kilometers

Beaver Creek, sister resort to Vail, is 10 miles down the valley, built into a plateau just above the small town of Avon. This ultraluxurious enclave for those who like to be pampered is a distinct contrast to the vastness of Vail, but that's the way its creators (Vail Associates) wanted it: a resort experience that swaddles you in luxury and self-indulgence with everything from Ralph Lauren furnishings to slope valets who help you in and out of your skis; it's a resort for guests who want to go that extra step in convenience and luxury.

Created by big money, designed with computers, and crafted by environmentalists, it is an elegant, self-contained pedestrian-oriented village where service is the guiding philosophy. It's quieter than Vail, more geared toward families with comfortable elegance in mind and the pocketbook with which to indulge their whims. Yet at the same time, you can still get a taste of Vail—a shuttle bus connects the two resorts. If you spend a week at Beaver Creek, you would be remiss in not spending at least a day sampling the outstanding bowls of Vail or indulging in the more uptown nightlife and dining that the larger resort provides. Likewise, many's the day when savvy Vail locals, noting the peak-period crowds in town, head for Beaver Creek, where you can always count on shorter lift lines. (Multiday lift tickets at both resorts are interchangeable and are also honored at their two new sister resorts in Summit County: Keystone and Breckenridge.)

The village, which sits in terraced layers on either side of a small, scenic, and secluded valley, has won numerous awards for its architecture and design, eschewing the Tyrol styling of Vail for a more contemporary modern American feel, with lots of granite walls, slate roofs, sturdy timbers, and natural colors. The main village square, right at the bottom of the Centennial Express chair, is two levels of cobblestone walkways linking large hotels and condos, small lodges, stores, restaurants and bars, and other assorted elements of a chic alpine village. The new Market Square pedestrian plaza adds even more shops and restaurants, an ice-skating rink, the Beaver Creek Center for the Arts, and—the height of skier luxury—three alpine skier escalators. Above and

Children's services: day care
and Small World Play School
Nursery, tel. 970/845–5325;
instruction, tel. 970/476–3239
or 800/475–4543

Snow phone:
tel. 970/476–4888

Avon police:
tel. 970/949–5312

Beaver Creek Village Medical
Center: tel. 970/949–0800

Beaver Creek Resort Association: tel. 970/476–5601

Road conditions:
tel. 970/479–2226

Towing: Avon Towing,
tel. 970/827–5553

FIVE-STAR FAVORITES
Best run for vertical:
Golden Eagle

Best run overall: Centennial

Best bar/nightclub:
Coyote Café

Best hotel:
Lodge at Cordillera

Best restaurant: Mirabelle

below the village center are the rest of the accommodation clusters—condos, town houses, private villas—the exposed timber and stone architecture
nestled among trees and the natural contours of the
land, their decidedly upscale interior decor rich with
museum-quality collectibles, designer fixtures, and
luxury touches that range from heated towel racks to
handmade Persian carpets. It's all very elegant, very
civilized, and very exclusive.

You enter Beaver Creek through security gates on
the outskirts of Avon, a mile down the road, and
once inside, you feel like you're in a private club.
Bellpersons, doorpersons, and just about any other
person who can lift, tote, carry, or generally do your
bidding are at your disposal. There are more subtle
touches such as full-time fire tenders who maintain
outdoor fire pits in the village square, drivers of Sub-
urbans who chauffeur you around, bartenders who
remember your name and how you like your Manhattan, and hosts who serve cookies and hot beverages
in the morning lift lines. This is a resort for those
who want service and more service. It's also a
secluded retreat that offers direct access to the slopes
from more than 40% of the accommodations. In sum,
Beaver Creek is a resort that is seldom crowded,
where lift lines are rare, and where everything is
done with the skier's comfort and convenience in
mind.

HOW TO GET THERE
By Plane
Beaver Creek is about 2½ hours by car from **Denver
International Airport.** Vail's **Eagle County Air-
port** is 25 miles west of Beaver Creek, and American
and Delta have direct flights from Atlanta, Chicago,
Salt Lake City, Newark, New York's La Guardia Air-
port, Miami, and Dallas/Fort Worth. Northwest has
nonstops from Detroit and Minneapolis. United and
American fly daily nonstops from Los Angeles. United
Express and Delta offer connecting flights to
Vail–Eagle County from DIA.

By Car
From Denver International Airport take I–70 west
110 miles to Beaver Creek. Take Exit 167 for Avon

and Beaver Creek. A word of caution to those in a hurry to hit the slopes: I–70 is one of the most heavily patrolled stretches of highway in the country. Drive with a light foot.

By Bus

Regularly scheduled nonstop shuttle service is available from Denver to Beaver Creek. For times and fares contact **Vans to Vail** (tel. 303/476–4467 or 800/222–2212) or **Colorado Mountain Express** (tel. 303/949–4227 or 800/525–6353).

THE SKIING

The skiing at Beaver Creek is precisely laid out on a semicircular ridge and the double dome peaks of Grouse Mountain, with the new lower-elevation areas of Bachelor Gulch and Arrowhead, to the west of the main village, reserved strictly for novices and intermediates. To the east of the main village is the higher of the two peaks (11,440 feet), where there's a marvelous high-altitude novice area. Below that, off a saddle that yields a midmountain day area, is an entire face of blue runs, intersected by a snaking green run that brings novices safely from the upper green runs.

Grouse Mountain's second peak (10,688 feet) is where the toughest runs are found, but again they are intersected by a long, snaking blue run. Farther still to the west, where the western ridge begins to drop in elevation, is a small below-tree-line intermediate bowl area and a section of mainstream blue runs.

The well-designed layout includes an excellent lift system that starts with three lifts from the village. The Centennial Express goes to mid-

mountain at the Spruce Saddle day area; from there you can take either the Stump Park lift to the novice area or ski down to the Grouse Mountain Express lift, which gets you up to the black and double-black-diamond runs. The Strawberry Park Express goes from the village up the west ridge, where the moderate blue runs are good early morning warm-ups. From the top of the Strawberry Park chair you can also ski down the Larkspur Bowl to the bottom of Grouse Mountain. The new Elkhorn lift takes you over to Bachelor Gulch and Arrowhead. It's easy to move from one area to another, even for skiers of different abilities. One of the features that designers and environmentalists have considered when awarding the resort laurels for slope and trail design is that the trails have been carved from the heavily treed flanks of the mountain, not gouged out in wide swaths. The narrower, more natural cut of the trails at Beaver Creek may be a product of modern design, but they are also retro—a return to the more interesting twists and turns of trails cut around trees, not through them. Such trails have been shunned by most new resorts in favor of sweeping boulevards that can cater to the hordes delivered by quad chairs.

This is a well-groomed mountain, with virtually all trails except those in the Birds of Prey and Larkspur Bowl areas manicured daily by a fleet of state-of-the-art snow cats, all part of the pampering process for the well-heeled guests and part of the reason Beaver Creek is regarded as an intermediate's resort—a place to cruise and look good (despite the steeps of Birds of Prey).

For snowboarders, Beaver Creek's tree-lined slopes are full of natural glades and gullies to play in. Head to the Stickline terrain park and the Moonshine half pipe as well as many gladed tree runs designated for 'boarders. A snowboarder's trail map indicates where to go for the best ride.

Novices

Most mountains are designed with beginner trails situated on the mid- and lower mountain areas, but Beaver Creek's layout encourages novices to head to the top on the Centennial Express lift to Spruce Saddle at mid-mountain and then a quick scoot across to the Stump Park lift, which goes to the eastern summit. You can ski the runs under the Stump—Sheephorn, Centennial, and Flat Top—or head to the right side (looking down the mountain) of the ridge and try some turns on Red Buffalo, Booth Gardens, and Powell. This excellent novice area gets the early morning sun. Its well-laid-out trails provide steady pitch as well as terrain variety. Booth Gardens and Powell are wide smoothies, with a series of rolls and stands of trees; West Buffalo and Flat Top are narrower and feature more turns as they curve left and right around the ridge lines.

The Drink of Water lift, which can be reached from the bottom of the above-mentioned trails by way of Cinch, will take you back up to the top. When skiing in this area, however, make sure you don't turn off downhill from the long, winding Cinch run because you'll find yourself in black-diamond territory. For a really long run, zigzag along Cinch to the bottom of Centennial lift. Cinch is a bit of a snaking traverse, but it gives you an easy way down to the village, and along the way you can check out some of the blue trails that run down the front face of the lower mountain. You can also connect from Cinch to Dally, another long connector trail that takes you over to the Red Tail Camp (a good place for novices and intermediates to meet up with experts who have been skiing Birds of Prey) day area where you can either try some of the blue runs in the Larkspur Bowl area or carry on (by way of Dally) down to the base of the Strawberry Park Express and its moderate blue terrain on the west ridge.

Intermediates

Larkspur Bowl is a good place to start the day; you reach it either by taking the Centennial Express (to Spruce Saddle) and then skiing Red Tail to the Larkspur lift, which you ride up, or by taking the Strawberry Park Express to the top. From Larkspur Bowl you have a choice of some intermediate skiing down the middle—on Larkspur, Bluebell, or Paintbrush—or some steeper stuff down either side. Lupine and Loco (on the right side of the bowl) develop substantial moguls; and Yarrow, to the left, is seldom groomed and is best skied on a day following a fresh snowfall so you can make the most of the bowl's free-form shape and pitch before funneling down through the lower marked trails. This is a good intermediate area that gives strong intermediates a chance to step up to those steeper, although short, black pitches without committing to the Birds of Prey.

Directly under the Strawberry Park Express are Pitchfork and Stacker, a pair of high-end blue runs with some tough, steep sections. On the eastern side, take the Centennial and Stump Park lifts to the summit for excellent cruising, specifically down the Latigo, Gold Dust, and Gold Rush trails. Latigo is a wonderful twisting high-speed cruiser with some tight turns and hidden drops. Gold Dust tends to run to bumps down the right side before smoothing out through the lower Gold Rush section. The Centennial Trail, which begins at the summit as a green run, is a long top-to-bottom cruiser that turns blue shortly after its junction with Cinch. Another option from Centennial is Red Tail, which veers left under the Stump Park lift and feeds into the base of the Grouse Mountain Express. Ride the Grouse Mountain Express to the top and come down the steep but wide high-speed cruiser called Raven Ridge. If you're feeling particularly daring, consider trying Ptarmigan or the black-diamond section of Raven Ridge—both are short, steep chutes that will give you a little adrenaline rush.

Another option is to take the Elkhorn lift up and follow Maverick and Sawbuck to the base of the new Bachelor Gulch area. You have several blue options off this lift, or you can take the Primrose catwalk to the top of the Arrowbahn Express lift at Arrowhead. This is a prime intermediate skiing area, and the lower elevation means it can be up to 10 degrees warmer—a boon on cold days. Just remember to start heading back before 3:30 PM if you don't want to end up at the Arrowhead base area at the end of the day. There is no public transportation back from Bachelor Gulch.

Experts

The Birds of Prey area, accessible from the Centennial Express to the Westfall lifts, is your domain. From the summit, cut down the western flank on either Peregrine, Goshawk, or Golden Eagle. All three trails are designated as double black diamonds, and you can count on their being packed with moguls. Golden Eagle is the toughest of the three and also the hardest to find. Look for the starting point just to the left of the top of the Westfall lift. All three of these chutes will spit you out at the bottom of the Grouse Mountain Express, which you can ride to the top for a crack at some more steep stuff.

Screech Owl, to the left as you get off the lift, starts out steep and moguled but becomes intermediate about halfway down. Turn right off the lift for a choice of Bald Eagle, Falcon Peak, or Osprey. These are all double-black-diamond runs, and most of the time they're covered with massive moguls. If you get your fill of the tough stuff halfway down, bail out by taking Camp Robber Road under the chair and picking up the slightly tamer Ruffed Grouse. For a real challenge, head to the Royal Elk Glades, off Grouse Mountain. This is rugged, exposed off-piste terrain, so be sure you're up for it.

WHERE TO STAY

The Beaver Creek Village area offers a plethora of ski-in/ski-out hotel and condo facilities, almost all within the moderate to high-end range. Nearby Avon (2½ miles down the road) is where you'll find most of the more modestly priced accommodations: If price rather than convenience is a factor, Avon is your best bet. Vail, with its 30,000 beds, is just 10 miles down the highway, giving you another option. A convenient $2 shuttle runs every 20–30 minutes from either Avon or Vail. All lodging can be booked through Vail–Beaver Creek Central Reservations (Box 7, Vail 81658, tel. 800/525–2257).

Expensive

Hyatt Regency Beaver Creek

This grand full-service hotel is at the center of Beaver Creek. It has ski-in/ski-out access to the slopes and valet service that ensures your boots are warmed and your skis carried to the snow. Included in a standard hotel room with knotty-pine furnishings are niceties such as bathrobes. Suites—appropriately sized for larger groups—also have a fireplace and a kitchen in some. *Box 1595, Beaver Creek Resort, Avon 81620, tel. 970/949–1234 or 800/233–1234, fax 970/949–4164. 290 rooms, 5 suites, 26 units. Facilities: 3 restaurants, 2 bars, 8 hot tubs, outdoor pool, health club, spa, 24-hr desk service, shuttle, ski valet, ski storage, laundry, game room. AE, D, DC, MC, V. $390–$675.*

Lodge at Cordillera

A stunning château perched on 3,000 acres of pristine mountain wilderness above the Squaw Creek Valley, the lodge is just 20 minutes from Beaver Creek. The stone-and-stucco building, with its steep, sloping tile roof is styled in the tradition of the Spanish Pyrenees and includes one of the most exotic spa facilities in ski country. Inside are wood and wrought-iron furnishings and walls bedecked with original lithographs by Picasso, Miró, and Dali. The rooms are sumptuously comfortable, with polished wood, marble trim, and stunning views of the surrounding Gore and Sawatch mountain ranges. *Box 1110, Edwards, Vail Valley 81632, tel. 970/926–2200 or 800/877–3529, fax 970/926–2486. 20 rooms, 3 suites, 5 lofts. Facilities: restaurant, bar, hot tub, indoor-outdoor pool, health club, spa, 24-hr desk service, cross-country skiing, ski storage, shuttle. AE, MC, V. $150–$700.*

The Pines

This small ski-in/ski-out Beaver Creek winner combines posh digs with unpretentious atmosphere—and prices. The rooms are spacious, light, and airy, with blond-wood furnishings, pale pink ceilings, and fabrics in dusty rose, mint, and white. Each room has a TV/VCR (tapes are free), mini-refrigerator, and coffeemaker; several rooms have balconies overlooking the ski area and mountain range. The air of quiet pampering is furthered by little extras like a ski concierge who arranges complimentary guided mountain tours and a free wax for your skis. The Grouse Mountain Grill serves up superb new American cuisine in an unparalleled setting with huge picture windows and wrought-iron chandeliers. *Box 18450, Avon 81620, tel. 970/845–7900 or 800/859–8242, fax 970/845–7809. 60 rooms, 12 units. Facilities: restaurant, bar, pool, hot tub, spa, exercise room, laundry service. AE, D, MC, V. $150–$1,800.*

St. James Place

This marvelously stylish condo, in the heart of Beaver Creek Village, offers a variety of large one-, two-, and three-bedroom units. Each is individually owned—many on a time-share basis—so furnishings and designs vary. In general, each unit is a complete living environment, with a gas fireplace and a deck. *Box 1593, Avon 81620, tel. 970/845–9300 or 800/626–7100, fax 970/845–0099. 54 units. Facilities: restaurant, bar, 3 hot tubs, sauna, steam room, indoor pool, health club, 24-hr desk service, ski storage, laundry. AE, MC, V. $350–$1,200.*

Moderate

Beaver Creek Lodge

This all-suite hotel is only a few hundred yards from the lifts. The suites, with kitchenettes, gas fireplaces, large bedrooms, and living rooms with pullout sofas, are large enough for a group of four. You'll also find robes, slippers, and bottled water in every room. The one- to three-bedroom condos are individually owned, with decorating schemes ranging from Bavarian style done in lots of blue and burgundy, with vaulted ceilings and deep-mahogany wood trim, to Ralph Lauren style, with green-and-blue plaids and forest green carpeting. All the condos have outside decks and mountain views. *26 Avondale La., Box 2578, Beaver Creek 81620, tel. 970/845–9800 or 800/732–6777, fax 970/845–8242. 71 suites, 6 units. Facilities: restaurant, bar, lounge, hot tub, steam room, indoor pool, outdoor pool, health club, 24-hr desk service, ski valet, ski storage, laundry. AE, D, DC, MC, V. $145–$1,400.*

The Centennial

The bright and modern lodge rooms and one- to three-bedroom apartments in this seven-story complex all have plush carpeting and floral-print-covered furnishings. The large lodge rooms can easily accommodate four. The larger apartments, which have full kitchens, fireplaces, and washers and dryers, offer good value for families and groups; the multilevel layout gives everyone a little more privacy. *Box 348, Avon 81620, tel. 970/845–7600 or 800/845–7060, fax 970/845–7677. 3 lodge rooms, 23 units. Facilities: lounge, hot tubs, outdoor pool, ski storage, laundry, ski-in/walk-out. AE, MC, V. $120–$1,195.*

The Charter

This resort offers accommodations ranging from a standard lodge room for two to four guests to five-bedroom units that can comfortably house 12. The condos are furnished with plenty of big comfortable couches and easy chairs and have large windows, fireplaces, and balconies. *120 Offerson Rd., Box 5310, Avon 81620, tel. 970/949–6660 or 800/525–6660, fax 970/949–4667. 65 lodge rooms, 115 units. Facilities: restaurant, bar, hot tubs, steam room, indoor and outdoor pools, health club, spa, 24-hr desk service, shuttle, ski valet, ski-in/walk-out, ski storage, laundry. AE, MC, V. $150–$1,650.*

Inn At Beaver Creek

With a lift just 5 yards from its back entrance, this inn is a truly convenient ski-in/ski-out facility. It's a small, elegant lodge with a European feel. The public spaces are exquisite, with some handcrafted furnishings, plants, a stone fireplace, and a grand piano. The rooms are all large, bright, and decorated with colonial-style furnishings, striped or floral wall coverings and curtains, and coordinated eiderdowns and pillows. *10 Elk Track La., Beaver Creek 81620, tel. 970/ 845–7800, fax 970/845–5279. 37 rooms, 8 suites. Facilities: bar, lounge, hot tub, sauna, steam room, outdoor pool, 24-hr desk service, shuttle, ski storage, laundry, 24-hr concierge, intervillage limousine. AE, MC, V. $140–$760.*

Poste Montane
This is a small European-style lodge. Rooms are elegantly decorated in deep, rich colors and flowery wallpaper. The lodge rooms and deluxe rooms are large enough for four guests; the suites (two bedrooms, three baths) can easily accommodate six people. All deluxe rooms and suites have fireplaces. The lobby is a popular meeting spot, with dark wood paneling, forest green carpets, and comfy leather couches. In the afternoon there's a wine and cheese party in the lobby. *Box 5480, Avon 81620, tel. 970/845–7500 or 800/497–9238, fax 970/845–5012. 7 deluxe rooms, 4 studios, 13 suites. Facilities: restaurant, bar, pool, hot tub, sauna, steam room, shuttle, ski storage, ski shop, laundry. AE, MC, V. $195–$790, including full breakfast and après-ski buffet.*

Inexpensive
Christie Lodge
The Christie isn't much to look at with its prosaic gray-siding exterior, but this property is an affordable deal. It's in Avon (2½ miles down the road

from the resort) and offers one- and three-bedroom suites housed in seven buildings connected by an atrium. Clean and comfortable, the suites are decorated in relaxing pastel colors and come complete with a kitchenette, a fireplace, a balcony, and mountain views. Families and foursomes tend to lodge here. *Box 1196, Avon 81620, tel. 970/949–7700 or 800/551–4326, fax 970/845–4535. 280 suites. Facilities: restaurant, bar, lounge, hot tubs, sauna, indoor pool, health club, 24-hr desk service, shuttle service, laundry, game room. AE, D, DC, MC, V. $139–$399.*

Lodge at Avon Center
On the banks of the Eagle River, tucked amid a thicket of evergreens, stand these modestly priced one- to four-bedroom condos—an excellent deal for families. Each unit is individually owned and decorated and contains a full kitchen, a fireplace, and a balcony. *100 W. Beaver Creek Blvd., Box 964, Avon 81620, tel. 970/949–6202 or 800/441–4718, fax 970/949–7757. 52 units. Facilities: restaurant, bar, ski storage, laundry, shuttle. AE, MC, V. $110–$515.*

The Seasons
About 2 miles from the entrance to Beaver Creek, on the edge of a golf course, you'll find this attractive, modern three-story stone building with a distinctive old-world porte cochere. The lodge rooms and one-, two-, and three-bedroom condo units are delightful blends of European alpine and Southwestern influences. The decor is a mix of exposed beams and dark wood furnishings, stone fireplaces, and brightly colored Navajo-

style drapes and coverings. *Box 1370, Edwards 81632, tel. 970/926–8300 or 800/846–0233, fax 970/926–2390. 30 units. Facilities: hot tub, outdoor pool, lounge, ski-in/ski-out. AE, D, DC, MC, V. $25–$525.*

WHERE TO EAT

There is an ample if not overwhelming number of restaurants at Beaver Creek, with some additional inexpensive eateries in nearby Avon—and of course Vail is just 20 minutes away, with its excellent variety in all price categories.

On the Mountain

McCoy's

This breakfast and lunch spot is at the base of the Centennial Express lift. Although the lunch fare is traditional—soups, salads, and sandwiches—the breakfast menu is a notch above the others. The pancakes are excellent, and there's a good selection of other morning staples. *Tel. 970/949–1234. AE, D, MC, V.*

Spruce Saddle

You have two choices for dining at this midmountain restaurant at the top of the Centennial lift. On the lower level is a large, bright dining court with a good selection of American heritage cuisine: buffalo burgers, spicy duck pizza, wild beans, and chilies, along with a pasta station. The upper level houses Rafters, the fine-dining section. *Spruce Saddle, tel. 970/845–5520. AE, D, MC, V. Rafters, tel. 970/845–5528. AE, D, MC, V.*

Expensive

Beano's Cabin

Everything about Beano's is fantastic: the name, the history, and the food. You begin your journey at the Rendezvous Cabin, west of the Centennial lift, at the base of the mountain. There a sled host meets you, checks you in, and whisks you off by sleigh. During your 2-mile ride, the sled host fills you in on some mountain history. Your destination is a midmountain Montana pine-log cabin, warmed inside by a crackling fire and live dinner music. Here, a six-course meal of homemade soup, freshly baked bread, salad, and a choice of entrée is served. Take your pick from salmon, roast duck, grilled venison, loin of lamb, or the special of the day, but save room for dessert—especially the crème brûlée. *Meet at Centennial lift, tel. 970/949–9090. Reservations essential. AE, MC, V. No smoking.*

Mirabelle

Inside a restored century-old farmhouse just down the road from the Beaver Creek Resort, this excellent French restaurant is owned by the folks who brought the Left Bank (*see* Where to Eat *in* Vail) to Vail. The decor is particularly fetching, with a French-country-cottage style based on rough whitewashed walls with exposed beams, bright floral-print curtains, and elegant color-coordinated table settings. The wide-ranging menu offers fish, fowl, and game, with especially good veal and breast of duck entrées. *55 Village Rd., tel. 970/949–7728. AE, D, MC, V.*

Patina

The Southwestern/Pacific Rim menu here offers something for just about everyone, from Southwestern Caesar salad to wood-fired pizzas to sizzling

Thai snapper to duck with wild plum sauce and scallion pancakes. There are even a tapas bar and a sushi bar. Some specialties are light on calories. *Hyatt Regency Beaver Creek, tel. 970/ 845–2825. AE, D, DC, MC, V.*

Restaurant Picasso

Though this stylish French restaurant offers amazing views of Vail Valley from its 8,500-foot vantage point, the main attraction is an extraordinary collection of original Picasso lithographs. In addition to all the visual stimulation, Picasso's serves an impressive menu including roast lamb rack served with goat cheese gnocchi and semolina. A lighter spa menu is also available. *Lodge at Cordillera, tel. 970/926–2200. AE, DC, MC, V.*

Splendido

This ultraposh eatery is the height of decadence, with marble columns and statuary and custom-made Italian linens adorning the tables. Chef David Walford, who apprenticed at northern California's Auberge du Soleil and Masa's, is a master of new American cuisine, borrowing merrily from several different traditions. He is equally adept at turning out grouper baked with Moroccan spices, couscous, and fennel as he is at preparing lobster and white-bean chili with potato tortillas or elk chop in black pepper and pinot noir sauce with parsnip and sweet potato pancakes and chanterelles. Pastry chef Matt Olehy excels both at standards like crème brûlée and at such imaginative offerings as caramel-pumpkin *crostata* (puff pastry) with eggnog ice cream. *17 Chateau La., Beaver Creek, tel. 970/ 845–8808. AE, DC, MC, V.*

Moderate

Beaver Trap Tavern

Families frequent this restaurant because the menu is familiar and the prices reasonable. The lineup of fish, fowl, pasta, and beef—New York strip, porterhouse, and T-bone— makes it easy to please everyone. The steaks are charbroiled, and pasta dishes are offered with either Alfredo, white clam, Bolognese, marinara, or *fra diavolo* sauce. *St. James Place, tel. 970/845–8930. AE, MC, V.*

Fiesta's Café & Cantina

Authentic Mexican fare includes enchiladas, tacos, tostadas, and burritos in addition to daily specials such as chicken, beef, or shrimp fajitas or shrimp-filled chile relleños. The burrito *carne adovada* (pork marinated in hot red chilies) is a house specialty. *Edwards Plaza Bldg., 4 mi west of Beaver Creek, Edwards, tel. 970/926– 3048. AE, D, DC, MC, V.*

Golden Eagle

The mixed menu offers selections of seafood, pasta, and game. Try the game pâté as an appetizer, and if you're eager for more game, order either the loin of elk or the medallions of venison. Another interesting combination is the lobster and eggplant bisque, followed by the excellent roast duckling with a port wine sauce. More mainstream items include grilled salmon with fusilli, Southwestern-style shrimp scampi served with roasted red peppers, and grilled rainbow trout with wild rice. *Village Hall, tel. 970/949–1940. AE, MC, V.*

TraMonti

This breezy trattoria in the Charter at Beaver Creek showcases the vibrant progressive cuisine of chef Cynde Arnold. She loves experimenting with bold juxtapositions of flavors and is most successful with her gourmet pizzas (such as shrimp, goat cheese, braised scallions, and black olives) and pastas (penne with wild boar and veal Bolognese; ravioli stuffed with lobster, mascarpone, sun-dried tomatoes, and basil in saffron cream). *The Charter, tel. 970/949–5552. AE, MC, V.*

Inexpensive

Brass Parrot

There's no pretense here: It's good, basic pub grub in a sports bar atmosphere. You can chow down on chicken, prime rib, fish-and-chips, and spaghetti. *Avon Centre, tel. 970/ 949–7770. AE, D, MC, V.*

Cassidy's Hole in the Wall

If you're looking for the burger, you're in the right place: The Big-Bob one-pounder should sate you. Sandwiches, Mexican fare, and specialties such as chicken-fried steak and a 2-foot-long rack of ribs head the menu in this Western saloon that spans two floors. Looking for the action? Stay at ground zero. If you're partial to watching rather than participating, you'll want to be upstairs. *82 E. Beaver Creek Blvd., Avon, tel. 970/ 949–9449. Reservations essential for 8 or more. AE, D, MC, V.*

China Garden

Here you can eat Mandarin and Szechuan dishes as well as traditional egg rolls, barbecued spare ribs, and wonton soup. The take-out service is fast, and the eat-in restaurant is a cut above most area Chinese restaurants. *Avon Centre, tel. 970/949–4986. AE, D, DC, MC, V.*

The Gashouse

This classic local hangout, in a 50-year-old log cabin with trophy-covered walls, draws up-valley crowds who swear by the steaks, delicious ribs, and sautéed rock shrimp with chili-pesto pasta. Stop in for a brew and some heavenly jalapeño chips and watch how the Vail Valley kicks back. *Rte. 6, Edwards, tel. 970/926–2896. AE, DC, MC, V.*

Best Bets for Breakfast

Coffee Gallery

Come here for the best coffee in Beaver Creek, and you'll also get a good selection of muffins and pastries. *Beaver Creek Mall, tel. 970/ 949–1273. AE, MC, V.*

Terrace Restaurant

Favorite early morning eats include the omelets and the biscuits and gravy, especially on a cold day. If you want something lighter, try a cinnamon roll from the assortment of baked goods. *The Charter, tel. 970/ 949–6660. AE, MC, V.*

NIGHTLIFE AND ENTERTAINMENT

Although there are several good spots in Beaver Creek Village and in nearby Avon, the evening activities tend to be fairly subdued: hot tub soaking and fireside lounging. Remember, however, that Vail, only 20 minutes away, has a much greater variety of entertainment (*see* Nightlife and Entertainment *in* Vail). If partying is on your mind, leave the car here and take the shuttle bus.

Après-Ski

Coyote Café

This is a popular après-ski hangout because the atmosphere is lively and fun—with impromptu dancing, entertainment, and happy-hour surprises. *Village Hall, tel. 970/949-5001. AE, D, MC, V.*

Crooked Hearth Tavern

For a subdued if not romantic après-ski atmosphere, head for the Tavern in the Hyatt Regency. The large lobby bar offers live piano music and a warm, blazing fire maintained by a full-time fire tender. Complimentary munchies and happy-hour specials are provided. *Hyatt Regency Beaver Creek, tel. 970/949-1234. AE, MC, V.*

Loud and Lively/Dancing

Beaver Trap Tavern

The scene at the bar is festive, with the emphasis on ale quaffing, mingling, and carousing. The après-ski crowd tends to be on the young side, but forty-somethings won't feel out of place either. *St. James Place, tel. 970/845-8930. AE, MC, V.*

Paddy's Sports Bar & Grill

Thirteen TV screens join five large-screen monitors and one superscreen here. Children can easily occupy themselves in the playroom and games arcade, while adults watch the day's big game or sports videos. *40801 Rte. 6, at Rte. 24, tel. 970/949-6093. AE, D, MC, V.*

More Mellow

TraMonti

If you've boogied till you're beat or just want a pleasant piano-bar environment and a nightcap, this may be your prescription. *The Charter, tel. 970/949-5552. AE, MC, V.*

COPPER MOUNTAIN SKI RESORT

COPPER MOUNTAIN SKI RESORT

Box 3001
Copper Mountain, CO 80443
Tel. 970/968–2882 or
800/458–8386

STATISTICALLY SPEAKING

Base elevation: 9,712 feet

Summit elevation: 12,313 feet

Vertical drop: 2,601 feet

Skiable terrain: 2,433 acres

Number of trails: 117

Longest run: 2.8 miles

Lifts and capacity: 3 high-speed quads, 6 triples, 8 doubles, 4 surface; 29,190 skiers per hour

Daily lift ticket: $45

Average annual snowfall: 280 inches

Number of skiing days 1995–96: 180

Snowmaking: 270 acres, 20%

Terrain mix: N 21%, I 25%, E 54% (advanced 36%, extreme 18%)

Snowboarding: yes

Cross-country skiing: 25 kilometers of set tracks and skating lanes in Arapaho National Forest

One of the leading resorts in Summit—Colorado's prime skiing country—Copper Mountain shares the terrain of the Ten Mile Range with Keystone, Breckenridge, and Arapahoe Basin. In spite of a mix-and-match condo village and a homogenized approach to the hotels and restaurants, this resort feels pleasant and offers an abundance of good skiing on trails that are among the best laid out in the country.

A recent merger with Intrawest—the company that developed the Blackcomb resort in British Columbia—should finally give Copper a village worthy of this great ski mountain. Over the next 10 years more than $300 million will be invested in the village, adding 1,000 residential units and commercial space and with an additional $25 million creating improvements on the mountain.

For now, the Village Square—the main hub—is anything but unique, with its circa-'70s collection of functional condo buildings organized in three distinct areas along the serpentine banks of the Ten Mile Creek. The rather ordinary architecture does, however, play second fiddle to the soaring peaks of the Ten Mile Range and the stunning scenery of the Arapaho National Forest.

Two high-speed quads converge here to provide fast access to mid-mountain and any of Copper's three distinct levels of terrain. The square is a good location for families with teens because most of the shops, restaurants, and other facilities are within strolling distance. It's also the hub of Copper's nightlife, so it tends to stay busy into the night. Weigh both sides of this feature: There will be plenty of action, but it can also be noisier than the other clusters of accommodations.

To the west is the Union Creek base area, with standard condos and town homes, plus immediate access to the tremendous novice ski slopes on this part of the mountain. It's an ideal (and quieter) location. Though a bit of a hike from the Village Square, the Copper shuttle bus is an efficient alternative.

At the east end of the resort is the B Lift base area, which tends to draw a younger, crash-and-burn crowd that wants fast access to Copper's steepest and bumpiest terrain and a place to party at the end of the day.

Children's services: day care, tel. 970/968–2882, ext. 6345; instruction, tel. 970/968–2882, ext. 6330

Snow phone:
tel. 970/968–2100

Summit County Sheriff's Dept.: tel. 970/453–2232

Hospital: Colorado Mountain Medical Center, tel. 970/968–2330; Summit Medical Center (Frisco), tel. 970/468–6936

Resort Association:
tel. 970/968–6477

Avalanche hot line:
tel. 970/668–0600

Road conditions:
tel. 970/453–1090

Towing: Paul's Towing,
tel. 970/968–6311

FIVE-STAR FAVORITES
Best run for vertical:
Formidable

Best run overall:
Drainpipe to Far East

Best bar/nightclub: O'Shea's

Best hotel: Club Med

Best restaurant: Pesce Fresco

HOW TO GET THERE

By Plane
Copper Mountain is 95 miles west of **Denver International Airport.**

By Car
Copper Mountain is 75 miles, or 1½–2 hours, west of Denver, off I–70 Exit 195.

By Bus
From the Denver airport, buses and vans leave almost every hour for Copper Mountain. Call **Resort Express** (tel. 800/334–7433) for times. Round-trip fare from the airport is $78.

GETTING AROUND
A car can be useful in Summit County if you plan to do any exploring or ski more than one resort. However, the **Summit County Stage** (tel. 970/453–1339, no charge) is an efficient public-transit alternative. Buses leave Copper Mountain, Keystone, or Breckenridge at the top of the hour and meet at the Frisco Transfer Center on the half hour for connections to each resort. There are other stops along the route.

There's ample day parking at each of Copper's three base areas, although the only time you bother with a car at Copper is when you are heading to the nearby towns for a change of scenery.

THE SKIING
Just like the well-organized village complex at Copper, the skiing is neatly subdivided into three distinct areas. Copper Peak at 12,441 feet and adjacent Union Peak at 12,313 feet combine for 117 runs that are primarily north facing (which means they tend to hold onto their snow longer) and run west to east with increasing degrees of difficulty. Novices and never-evers tend to stick to the Union Creek area to the west; the center of the complex serves intermediates with a pair of high-speed quad chairs; and the toughest terrain is found on the eastern flank of Copper Peak, including the splendid bowl skiing found off the top of the Storm King surface lift.

The surface lift—a quirky throwback in lift technology—is necessary because high winds occasionally sweep the summit, but elsewhere the mountain is well served by a fleet of 21 chairlifts that cover the two peaks with the great efficiency that is typical of this resort. It's easy to get around Copper. The runs are well marked, cross-mountain lift transit is remarkably free from long catwalks or flats, and it's easy for groups to split up, chase their own level, yet still occasionally rendezvous with each other.

The hub of the mountain, and its busiest area, is where the American Flyer and the American Eagle quads converge, at the edge of the Village Center. It's always busy first thing in the morning, but the two quads nicely split the mountain: Upper intermediates, experts, and thrill seekers head up the Eagle to the bowls and steeps of Copper Peak; more temperate intermediates choose the subtle cruisers and demibowl skiers access them from the Flyer. Novices have their own area, which can also be reached via the Flyer or from the less busy Union Creek base area.

Skiers heading for the first tracks in the bowl areas tend to avoid lineups by taking the B lift at the east end of the resort, but unless you are staying in that area, you'll have to take a shuttle bus.

A snowboard terrain park opened in early 1997, and a snowboard-specific trail map is available. For beginning snowboarders, Copper offers one of the best deals in the state: Access to the K and L lifts, serving over 50 acres of beginner terrain, is free in January and April. Copper has long appealed to serious shredders because it hosts the longest-running amateur snowboard race series in the country and is the only area in the state to sponsor the training of a professional snowboarding team.

Novices
Beginners will want to start off at the Union Creek area (to the left, looking down the mountain), where you won't get into trouble on the mix of blue and green runs. The base chair (K) serves a trio of gradual green runs, and for a little more gusto, the Timberline Express quad takes you farther up the mountain for more novice/intermediate runs. You can also take the American Flyer quad from the Village Square, but make sure you turn right when you get off the lift. This is a superb beginners' area that neither overwhelms nor bores the novice. And for an added bonus, lift tickets good in this area only are free in January and April for novice skiers or those who want to try snowboarding. High Point, which begins just below the steeper slopes of the upper Union Bowl, is a wonderful wide cruising run that cuts in smooth easy curves back and forth across this part of the mountain. It tends to be the busiest run in this area because it's the first trail you come to after turning right off the lift. However, you can also cut right (looking down) at a Y junction and take Coppertone, a slightly narrower, well-groomed run that incorporates a few more dips and rolls.

The H chair will take you to a pair of beautiful, wide, and winding green runs called Easy Feeling and Scooter. If you're skiing Scooter, cut left (looking down the mountain) toward the bottom of the run, to Hidden Vein; if you veer right, you'll end up at the base of the American Flyer lift. As you gain confidence, you can move over to the west side of the ridge (left, looking down) by taking the H chair to a connector trail called Minor Matter, then taking the Timberline Express quad to a point just below the tree line (you can also access this point from the American Flyer lift). From here take High Point, a moderately steep but wide and speed-controlled slope that connects to Scooter about halfway down, for a long, easy, but interesting novice cruiser.

From the top of the Timberline Express quad, turn left to Roundabout, a long, looping catwalk that will take you to the bottom of the L chair, which serves the shortest and tamest of Copper's terrain. Or cut right on Soliloquy when it merges with Roundabout, then scoot back over to the Timberline Express lift. If you want to ski with your buddies off the American Flyer lift, you can play on Coppertone and High Point, but be prepared for more traffic than you've encountered on the western runs.

Intermediates

Your fastest way up to mid-mountain is on either the American Flyer or American Eagle high-speed quad. The Flyer serves part of the green/blue terrain on the lower flanks of Union Peak but also gives access to the two chairs that serve the above-tree-line steeps of Union Bowl. It's steep up here, but there's a nice mix of wide-open bowl skiing and some spirited glade dancing. For steep—and occasionally deep—terrain, try Southern Star or Union Peak; for some fun with

the firs, try Timberidge, a long multi-faceted run that combines pitch and trees in equal amounts.

For more variation, consider skiing Copper Peak, on the east side of the mountain. To reach it, take the American Eagle to mid-station and ski down to the E triple and ride it to the top. From here, you can access the challenging Collage and Andy's Encore—almost 2,000 vertical feet of some groomed terrain and some moguls. When you're ready to head back, take Copperopolis to Bouncer for a long and fast cruiser with good drop-offs, pitches, and turns.

Experts

There's no doubt about it—Copper Peak is your playground. Ride the American Eagle to the E lift, and the E lift to the Storm King poma, where you'll have your choice of the Hallelujah Ridge or Hallelujah Bowl, or the even steeper Spalding and Resolution bowls. This is above-tree-line skiing, with some excellent vertical and a good place to play in the powder. The steep chutes of the Spalding Bowl spit you out into the Spalding Glades for a high-speed giant-slalom run to the bottom of the Resolution lift. Pick your own chute down the bowl, do it all over again from the Resolution lift, and when the snow cruds up, head out of the bowls and go for a good high-speed top-to-bottom cruise on Andy's Encore. Just make sure you cut right on Ore Deal near the bottom, rather than left to the winding Skid Road, which is tediously tame and long.

From the A lift you can take Formidable for a fast, undulating steep or Far East for a good, steep mogul run. A great overall run is Drainpipe, a chute off the B lift, to Far East.

For a backcountry experience, you can ski Copper Bowl, an advanced-only area open since 1996. From the top of the Storm King poma or R or S lifts, drop into this south-facing bowl—wide open at the top and tree-gladed lower down. For even more challenge, hike into the in-bounds Tucker Mountain extreme area.

WHERE TO STAY

For convenience, and in most cases good value, it makes sense to stay on the mountain. Virtually all the 900 on-mountain properties are owned and operated by the resort, which gives you convenient one-stop shopping through Copper Mountain Lodging Services (tel. 800/458–8386) but doesn't offer much in the way of variety. Most on-mountain hotels and condos run from moderate to expensive, while the best budget choices are found in nearby Frisco, Dillon, and Breckenridge. Nearly every unit is within walking distance of one of the lift areas; for those that are not, an excellent free shuttle system serves the entire Copper complex. Even if you stay in the surrounding towns, the Summit County shuttle bus system is just as efficient and just as free. Summit County Central Reservations (Box 446, Dillon, CO 80435, tel. 970/468–6222 or 800/365–6365) covers the entire region and can find you anything from a humble bed-and-breakfast to a four-bedroom condo.

Expensive

Club Mediterranée
Copper Mountain's Club Med is the first and only North American opera-
tion of the famed French fun club. Ski or snowboard instruction with an international staff of instructors is included in the rate. The rooms were recently redone in neutral tones with Southwestern art and remain small but comfortable. A preferred place to relax is the country-inn-style lobby on the first floor, with a big fireplace, comfortable armchairs, and floor-to-ceiling windows overlooking the slopes. The international buffet and disco are open to nonguests when the club isn't full—call ahead for availability. *50 Beeler Pl., Copper Mountain 80443, tel. 970/968–2161 or 800/258–2633, fax 970/968–2216. 236 rooms. Facilities: 2 restaurants, bar, disco, piano bar, 4 Jacuzzis, 2 saunas, twice-daily aerobics and stretch classes, maid service, ski storage, laundry, game room. AE, MC, V. $1,000–$1,500 per person for 7 nights, including all meals, lift tickets, and instruction.*

Copper Mountain's Central Village

Most accommodations at Copper are predictably practical. The condo-based Central Village complex is the most convenient, within easy walking distance of the lifts, and the most favored by families. Units range in size from one to four bedrooms, with two- and three-bedroom penthouses also available; most have a fireplace and a balcony. Most of the 14 buildings have saunas and laundry facilities, some have hot tubs and underground parking, and one has an outdoor pool. All include use of the Copper Mountain Racquet and Athletic Club. *Box 3001, 0209 Ten Mile Circle, Copper Mountain 80443, tel. 970/968–2882 or 800/458–8386, fax*

970/968–6227. 600 units. Facilities: indoor hot tub (most), use of health club, sauna, 24-hr room service, 24-hr desk service, shuttle, maid service, ski storage, laundry (most). AE, D, DC, MC, V. $135–$725.

The Woods and Legends Town Homes

These units are definitely the class of Copper. The two small subdivisions of town homes have some of the largest and most upscale properties at the resort. Units have either three or four bedrooms, with full kitchens, dining areas, patios, garages, and in some cases, private hot tubs. Suitable for a large family or for two or three couples, they are spacious, comfortable, and beautifully decorated, many in country florals. *Box 3001, Copper Mountain Resort, 0209 Ten Mile Circle, Copper Mountain 80443, tel. 970/ 968–2882 or 800/458–8386, fax 970/ 968–6227. 54 units. Facilities: use of Copper Mountain Health Club, 24-hr desk service, shuttle, maid service, ski storage, laundry. AE, D, DC, MC, V. $240–$705.*

Moderate

Galena Street Mountain Inn

This pink-stuccoed inn is in nearby Frisco, 6½ miles from Copper Mountain. The reproduction mission furniture is simple but stylish, with square lines softened by light-colored paint. Rooms have curved moldings, washed-oak window trim, and down comforters. *106 Galena St., Frisco 80443, tel. 970/668–3224 or 800/248–9138, fax 970/668–5291. 15 rooms. Facilities: hot tub, sauna, shuttle, ski storage. AE, D, DC, MC. $85–$165, including full breakfast.*

Holiday Inn

A major renovation, scheduled for completion in late '97, will give this Holiday Inn more of a ski lodge atmosphere, with lots of natural wood furniture. The rooms accommodate groups of four, and the Frisco location is convenient, via a free shuttle or by an easy drive, to Keystone, Copper Mountain, and Breckenridge. Families may find it a bit noisy. *1129 N. Summit Blvd., Frisco 80443, tel. 970/668–5000 or 800/782–7669, fax 970/668–0718. 216 rooms. Facilities: restaurant, bar, indoor hot tub, indoor pool, exercise machines, sauna, 24-hr desk service, shuttle service, maid service, laundry, game room. AE, D, DC, MC, V. $135–$225.*

Lake Dillon Condotel

Its scenic location overlooking Lake Dillon gives this otherwise uninteresting stucco block building a touch of style. The one-, two-, and three-bedroom units are a good value. All come with a kitchenette, a fireplace, and a balcony, and each has an unobstructed view of the lake and the Ten Mile Range. *Box 308, 401 W. Lodgepole St., Dillon 80435, tel. 970/468–2409 or 800/323–7792, fax 970/468–2556. 30 units. Facilities: indoor hot tub, ski storage, laundry, game room. $110–$265.*

Ten Mile Creek Condominiums

In Frisco, this pleasant and comfortable condo complex is the most moderately priced in the area for the level of luxury it offers. Its two-, three-, and four-bedroom units are well maintained and well equipped, each with a full kitchen, a balcony, and a fireplace. *200 Granite St., Frisco 80443, tel. 970/668–3100 or 800/530–3070, fax 970/668–5733. 40 units. Facilities: indoor*

*hot tub, indoor pool, sauna, laundry.
AE, D, MC, V. $137–$326.*

Inexpensive

Continental Divide Lodge
This is a cute but not fancy Western-style lodge, comfortable and quiet without a lot of frills, just a half block from Frisco's Main Street. The lodge unit sleeps two to four, and the larger unit handles up to 10, with a small kitchen and fireplace. *Box 1919, 520 Galena St., Frisco 80443, tel. 970/ 668–0373. 2 units. Facilities: outdoor hot tub, ski storage, laundry. MC, V. $65–$450.*

Frisco Lodge B & B
Built in 1885, this is a classic period house, with relatively small rooms and a nice, comfortable feel. The rooms are rustic, some with a shared bath, but all are more than adequate for couples, and several can be connected to accommodate small families. There's a common living room with a fireplace. A full breakfast, featuring eggs, cereal, and pastry, is part of the price. *Box 1325, 321 Main St., Frisco 80443, tel. 970/ 668–0195 or 800/279–6000, fax 970/ 668–0149. 19 rooms, 10 with bath. AE, D, MC, V. Facilities: outdoor hot tub. $35–$125, including full breakfast.*

Sky Vue Motel
You'll find clean and comfortable rooms with sturdy bleached-oak furnishings, beige wallpaper with teal- and mauve-colored paintbrush strokes, and teal drapes and bedspreads. About half the rooms have small efficiency kitchens. *305 S. 2nd St., Frisco 80443, tel. 970/668–3311 or 800/672–3311. 26 rooms. Facilities: indoor hot tub, indoor pool, maid service, laundry. D, MC, V. $51–$114.*

WHERE TO EAT
On the Mountain
The Commons
This market-style cafeteria offers chili, burgers, and an expansive pasta, salad, and fruit bar, as well as pizza that's been voted the county's best. It tends to be the busiest spot on the mountain, but an efficient layout gets you in and out fast. On sunny days the outdoor patio is the perfect place to munch. *Copper Commons Bldg., base of American Eagle lift, Copper Mountain, tel. 970/968–2318, ext. 6574. AE, D, DC, MC, V.*

Solitude Station
The Solitude Station is a good place to go to avoid the really heavy lunchtime crowds, and it's a convenient rendezvous spot. The food is basic cafeteria fare, with your best bets—such as the hamburgers and chicken sandwiches—coming off the outdoor grill. *Solitude Station Bldg., top of American Eagle lift, Copper Mountain, tel. 970/968–2882, ext. 6522. AE, D, DC, MC, V.*

Expensive
Blue Spruce Inn
In a historic Rocky Mountain log cabin, the Blue Spruce serves Continental cuisine, including lamb chops sautéed in pesto and bread crumbs and served with a demiglace, veal scallopini with wild mushrooms, and trout sautéed with cracked peppercorn with saga blue cheese in lemon-butter sauce. All are done with a deft touch, and the atmosphere is pure romance. *20 Main St., Frisco, tel. 970/668–5900. AE, D, MC, V.*

Dining in the Woods

Take a horse-drawn sleigh ride to a heated miners' tent in the woods, enjoy live performances of country and folk music, and settle in for a gourmet repast, including smoked trout appetizers, broiled flank steak or mesquite smoked chicken, with bread pudding for dessert. *Departures 5:30 PM–8 PM from Copper Commons Bldg., Copper Mountain, tel. 970/968–2882, ext. 6320. Reservations essential. AE, D, DC, MC, V.*

Pesce Fresco

Pesce Fresco is *the* spot at Copper for hearty breakfasts, a surprisingly affordable sit-down lunch, après-ski hors d'oeuvres, evening nightcaps, and dinner. The menu is mainly fish, with some solid if uninspired pastas. Among the best entrées are pesto tortellini with broccoli, tomatoes, mushrooms, and cheese and veal *piccata.* Other highlights are grilled salmon, Rocky Mountain trout, and lasagna with roasted chicken. The understated decor, good service, and jazz entertainment make it a popular gathering place. *Mountain Plaza Bldg., Copper Mountain, tel. 970/968–2882, ext. 6505. AE, D, DC, MC, V.*

Poirrier's Cajun Cafe

No matter where you are staying, it's worth the drive to Breckenridge to eat here. The main attraction is a Cajun cuisine that you can make as hot as you like. The entrée list relies heavily on catfish, fried, grilled, and blackened in a variety of dishes; but the crawfish delicacies, Cajun sausage platter, and the gumbo are also excellent. On dark teal walls above wood wainscoting, the dining room mixes portraits of 19th-century figures with paintings of bayou scenes and Mardi Gras. *224 S. Main St., Breckenridge, tel. 970/453–1877. AE, D, DC, MC, V.*

Rackets

Rackets offers the best food in Copper, although its location next to an aerobics studio in the Athletic and Racquet Club makes it feel more like a health club café than a fine dining establishment. Among the entrées on the Southwestern menu are lamb with roasted garlic and shiitake mushrooms; tortilla-encrusted salmon with red-chili sweet-and-sour sauce; and Taos chicken with black bean bacon sauce and avocado-zucchini salsa. A variety of healthy, hearty soups can be ordered à la carte, and there is an excellent, less expensive salad bar with fresh vegetables and pasta and vegetable salads. *Copper Mountain Athletic and Racquet Club, Copper Mountain, tel. 970/968–2882, ext. 6386. AE, D, DC, MC, V.*

Moderate

Barkley's Margaritaville

Prime rib, fajitas, and burritos are the staples. There's a children's menu and plenty of meal-size appetizers, which go for half price during the bar's happy hour, 3:30–6:30 PM. The bar and the dining room rub shoulders and are decked out with strings of chili peppers and Mexican hats. Together they bring in a good mix of locals and tourists. *620 S. Main St., Frisco, tel. 970/668–3694. AE, MC, V.*

Double Diamond Restaurant

Pizza, pasta, and ribs are the bill of fare here. The food is hearty and basic, and the atmosphere befits a ski area, with rustic log cabin decor and ski videos on the big-screen TV. The slope-side deck is a gathering spot après-ski, with happy hour from 3 to 5 PM. *East Village's Foxpine Inn, 154 Wheeler Pl., Copper Mountain, tel. 970/968–2880. AE, D, MC, V.*

O'Shea's

This all-purpose restaurant sets the standard for hearty, family-style fare for all three meals. Its Central Village convenience makes it busy and a little rowdy every night. The menu emphasizes buffalo, with buffalo burgers, ribs, nachos—even a buffalo Caesar salad. Children under 12 eat free with their parents. *206 Ten Mile Circle, Copper Junction Bldg., Copper Mountain, tel. 970/968–2882, ext. 6504. AE, D, MC, V.*

Inexpensive

Blue Moon Bakery

In addition to its excellent bagels, this stylish local deli in Silverthorne has some excellent soups and pastas and a good selection of cold cuts and cheeses. Breakfast features homemade granola, scones, muffins, and turnovers. The Blue Moon's take on casual café style includes dried flowers hanging side by side with watercolors painted by a local artist. You can eat in or take out, but just get there before closing, at 6 PM. *253 Summit, Summit Plaza Shopping Center, Silverthorne, tel. 970/468–1472. No credit cards.*

Claimjumper

The Claimjumper serves good, basic dinner fare, with various daily specials. The owner does his own hickory smoking out back, which gives a nice bite to the meat and fish items (try the smoked buffalo burgers). For lighter appetites the smoked trout is a good bet. Also available are Mexican and vegetarian dishes, pasta, and salads. Large windows and hanging plants brighten the dining area, which has counter seating and comfortable oak booths. *805 N. Summit, Frisco, tel. 970/668–3617. AE, D, MC, V.*

Frisco Bar & Grill

Burgers, ribs, and red meat are presented in myriad forms at prices that even locals can afford. Daily specials and appetizers are an even cheaper alternative, while Tex-Mex, pasta, and seafood round out the offerings. More bar than grill, the F.B.&G.—as it's known in the area—is a Frisco tradition. *Boardwalk Bldg., 720 Granite St., Frisco, tel. 970/668–5051. Reservations not accepted. AE, MC, V.*

Imperial Palace

This is a good spot to satisfy the urge for egg rolls, fried rice, wok-cooked vegetables, and sweet-and-sour anything. It's not adventurous Chinese cooking, but it's reliable, familiar, and tasty. Spicy Szechuan and Hunan dishes are also on the menu. *Village Square, Copper Mountain, tel. 970/968–6688. MC, V.*

Best Bet for Breakfast

Lizzie's Bagelry and Coffeehouse

At Lizzie's you can grab a cup of coffee and a bagel on the run as you head for the American Flyer lift. Or you can sit, enjoy a cappuccino, and chat with locals about the best places to ski. Fresh-baked bagels, espresso drinks, and fresh-squeezed juices make up the bill of fare. *Village Square West Bldg., Copper Mountain, tel. 970/968–2036. No credit cards.*

NIGHTLIFE AND ENTERTAINMENT

Après-Ski

B-Lift Pub
This pub in the East Village features a daily happy hour from 4 to 6 PM, attracting a boisterous younger crowd, including many locals. Cheap shots, dollar beers, and some good music keep things lively, along with a pool table and a large-screen TV. *Snowflake Bldg., base of B lift, 104 Wheeler Pl., Copper Mountain, tel. 970/968–2525. MC, V.*

Kokomo's Bar
Kokomo's really cooks, with live entertainment, drink specials, and a formula après-ski approach that's big on special events and audience participation. *Copper Commons Bldg., base of America Eagle lift, Copper Mountain, tel. 970/968–2318. AE, D, DC, MC, V.*

Loud and Lively/Dancing

Moose Jaw
This is definitely a locals' hangout. Pool tables beckon the unwary, and a plethora of old photographs, trophies, and newspaper articles makes the barn's wooden walls all but invisible. *208 Main St., Frisco, tel. 970/668–3931. D, MC, V.*

O'Shea's
At the bar the theme is sports, and the entertainment is nonstop. TV screens compete for attention in the background, while the large, fun, noisy crowd holds its own front and center. *206 Ten Mile Circle, Copper Junction Bldg., Copper Mountain, tel. 970/968–2882, ext. 6504. AE, D, MC, V.*

More Mellow

The Pub
If you enjoy a taste other than that of the dry/light beer mania sweeping the nation's beer market, the Pub's selection of English ales, lagers, and bitters will appeal. There's also a good selection of single malt and specialty scotches, as well as cigars to savor. *Copper Commons Bldg., base of American Eagle lift, Copper Mountain, tel. 970/968–2318. AE, D, DC, MC, V.*

CRESTED BUTTE MOUNTAIN RESORT

Box A, 500 Gothic Rd.
Mt. Crested Butte, CO 81225
Tel. 970/349–2333

STATISTICALLY SPEAKING

Base elevation: 9,375 feet

Summit elevation: 12,162 feet

Vertical drop: 3,062 feet

Skiable terrain: 1,160 acres

Number of trails: 85

Longest run: 2.6 miles

Lifts and capacity: 2 high-speed quads, 3 triples, 4 doubles, 4 surface; 16,010 skiers per hour

Daily lift ticket: $44

Average annual snowfall: 290 inches

Number of skiing days 1995–96: 159

Snowmaking: 238 acres; 21%

Terrain mix: N 13%, I 40%, E 47%

Snowboarding: yes

Crested Butte takes you back in time: Not necessarily back to the mining era, when settlers were just staking their claims to this rugged and beautiful corner of the Elk Mountains, but back to the 1960s, when life seemed less pretentious. They march to the beat of a different drummer in Crested Butte: not the bell-bottomed, pony-tailed Woodstock beat that characterizes the expatriate hippies in Telluride, but a rhythm that's a little more square. A little more straight-on. A little more neighborly. Even the shuttle bus driver bringing you from nearby Gunnison Airport will offer to make stops at the liquor and grocery stores if you want to stock up. And local residents say hello when passing you on the street.

Elk Avenue, a 1,000-yard stretch of immaculately preserved Victoriana, is the main thoroughfare and one of the largest National Historic Districts in the country. What were once the bordellos, saloons, feed stores, and public buildings of a coal-mining town are now the restaurants, bars, shops, and boutiques of a resort. But the basic character remains unchanged: The clapboard and log structures have been renovated but not altered, leaving an atmosphere that is still true grit, not true glitz. Folks chat, stop, and linger a while, creating an atmosphere as natural as the wilderness of the West Elks and the Ruby Range, which surround this 150-year-old Colorado community.

Three miles from town is a single, soaring broad-hipped butte crowned with a distinctive arrowhead of a peak that at 12,162 feet traps nearly 300 inches of snow annually and yields some of the best in-bounds expert terrain in the state, maybe even the country. This is Mt. Crested Butte, a marvelous modern extension of the town, with its comfortable—not flashy—condo village whose attitude is as friendly and unaffected as the town's. This is a resort that actually offers *free* skiing at the beginning and end of the season (usually November 27–December 21 and April 7–20). This town and resort have a symbiotic relationship that is as unique as any you'll find in American ski country; in few other places are the pleasures of the mountain and treasures of the town so closely interwoven.

Children's services: day care, tel. 970/349–2259; instruction, tel. 970/346–2209

Snow phone: tel. 970/349–2323

Police: tel. 970/349–5231

Hospital: Crested Butte Medical Clinic, tel. 970/349–6651; Gunnison Valley Hospital, tel. 970/641–1456

Crested Butte Chamber of Commerce: tel. 970/349–6438

Resort association: tel. 970/349–4600

Road conditions: tel. 970/249–9363

Towing: C.B. Road Service and Recovery, tel. 970/349–7333; C.B. Auto Repair, tel. 970/349–5251

FIVE-STAR FAVORITES

Best run for vertical: Banana Funnel

Best run overall: Paradise Bowl to Treasury

Best bar/nightclub: Rafters

Best hotel: Grande Butte Hotel

Best restaurant: Soupçon

HOW TO GET THERE

By Plane

Flights from major cities land at **Denver International Airport** (*see* Getting to Colorado Resorts, *above*), 250 miles away. **Gunnison Airport** (tel. 970/641–2304) is 30 miles from the resort and has daily **United Express/Mesa** flights coming from Denver. In addition, **Western Pacific** flies to Gunnison through Colorado Springs, from about 15 cities nationwide. **American** goes direct from Dallas/Fort Worth, and **Delta** has three flights a week from Atlanta into Gunnison.

By Car

Crested Butte is 230 miles from Denver. Take Route 285 south to Poncha Springs; head west on Route 50 to Gunnison; then take Route 135 north into Crested Butte.

By Bus

Greyhound Lines (tel. 800/237–8211) has regularly scheduled service from Denver, Colorado Springs, and Grand Junction into Gunnison.

GETTING AROUND

By Shuttle

A shuttle bus, **Mountain Express** (tel. 970/349–5616), travels every 20 minutes between town and resort, making it easy to stay slope-side.

By Taxi

Alpine Express (tel. 970/641–5074) provides service between the town and the resort, as well as from Gunnison Airport.

THE SKIING

Just as the town of Crested Butte has eschewed the slinky status symbols that drive other remodeled ski towns, so, too, has the resort bucked the middle-of-the-road tendency that other liability-cautious resorts have adopted when it comes to the skiing. These days most ski areas don't promote extreme skiing for fear of lawsuits and even higher insurance premiums, but not Crested Butte.

The resort is unique because it hasn't tamed the radical stuff. I'm talking about the double-black-diamond dares of the Extreme Limits—gonzoid, out-of-bounds, take-your-life-in-your-own-hands terrain that few want and even fewer can handle. After all, this is where the U.S. Extreme Skiing Championships are held annually.

A legacy from an earlier time, this resort's extreme side goes back to the days when test pilots and air jockeys came to "the Butte" to tempt fate, to carve and twist and spin in reckless and radical abandon. Though it has been mellowed some by increased common sense and modern ski patrolling, that attitude is still here.

Oh, don't misunderstand, this is an all-around ski mountain, with a well-balanced mix of terrain from novice to advanced. The lower flanks of this intimidating-looking spire of a mountain provide a mellow novice area, while the midsection is mostly heads-up intermediate skiing with some advanced options that give you a taste of the Butte's wild side without committing you to the resort's 500-plus acres in the Extreme Limits—some of the steepest, gnarliest, most untamed in-bounds skiing in America.

Fanatics and families alike can seek their own level, and whether you're experiencing the thrill of those first linked turns on a mile-long novice run, stoking your way down an ego-stroking intermediate boulevard, or driving your skis down a 50-degree pitch, you're still pushing your own limits as far as you dare.

As you look up the mountain, the shoulders to the left and right are for adrenaline junkies and other experts—tough, steep, untamed double-black-diamond territory. The middle section of the mountain is mostly intermediate, with groomed, steep high-speed cruisers and some good but less extreme black runs; beginners have a section with long, meandering trails of the lower part of the mountain all to themselves.

All lift traffic starts with the Keystone or Silver Queen lifts, which terminate at the village base area. The Queen shoots straight up to a point just below the summit, where you can take the High lift for the extreme chutes or come back down the middle of the mountain on intermediate trails. The Keystone lift from the village cuts left to a mid-mountain ridge and gives novices access to the majority of the green runs; intermediates can ski from it down the lower part of the North Face and ride the Paradise or Teocalli lifts.

Although the overall layout appears to favor experts (47% of the terrain), other levels can be comfortable here because of the number of transition runs that encourage a novice to tackle a modest blue run and intermediates to try a groomed black run.

Snowboarders can also practice their skills here in a controlled environment or test their mettle on some of the most radical terrain in the country. A snowboarders-only terrain park on Smith Hill Run, expanded in 1996, contains log slides, quarter pipes, and other obstacles. But what Crested Butte is really becoming known for is adventure snowboarding: the steep, adventurous, no-holds-barred terrain in the Extreme Limits area. As testament to this reputation, the U.S. Extreme Snowboarding

Championships have been held here three years in a row.

Novices

Crested Butte's excellent novice terrain is well contained on the lower shoulder of the mountain, and there's little chance of inadvertent interaction with more advanced skiers. There are long, well-groomed green runs plus a smaller area of shorter runs for those first-ever turns. The Peachtree lift, which starts from the village center, serves those gentle slopes, and once you can turn your skis comfortably in either direction, you can head for the Keystone lift, which gives you a larger and slightly more challenging choice. If you go to the left as you get off the lift, pick up Houston, a mile-long extrawide boulevard that lets you carry your speed with security. Or take a sharp left onto Peanut, a gently undulating carpet where you can practice linking turns. From Peanut pick up Roller Coaster, which gives you a taste of some short, slightly steeper pitches; or Smith Hill, with its scattering of island glades.

Once you've gained confidence, head down to the Painter Boy and Gold Link lifts by taking Keystone to the top and coming down Houston. Here's a secluded mini–mountain network of blue/green runs that lets you open the envelope of experience a little wider. These are all groomed runs, with a slightly steeper pitch than you will have been used to, but their width and smooth cut makes them skiable for novices with basic ski control and a little ambition to improve. They are seldom crowded and contain no surprises like drop-offs, but you

can get your first taste of smooth, well-rounded moguls on Cascade.

Intermediates

Like all levels at Crested Butte, intermediates have a chance to push their experience meter a notch higher if they take advantage of the full range of terrain. You can start the day by taking either the Keystone or Silver Queen lifts from the base village.

If you take the Silver Queen, turn left off the lift and head for Keystone (the run), then Silver Queen Road; you can catch the early morning sun in the Paradise Bowl area. This wide-open bowl is a leg warmer that leads to the narrower intermediate runs of the lower Paradise.

From the Keystone lift, go right, into the network of blue runs that encompass the lower two-thirds of the mountain's north face. Drop down Meander through some trees and a steep at the end for a little adrenaline booster, then cut right onto the wide, tree-surrounded boulevard known as Bushwacker to the bottom of the Teocalli lift. Ride it to the top back to your original starting point.

Head right down Bushwacker again and take Paradise off to the right to Paradise lift, which takes you up to the wide and well-groomed Paradise Bowl area. Ski into the bowl and work your way down, staying right so you can pick up Canaan, a narrow (but not too narrow) and lightly trafficked twister that leads to Upper Treasury, a straight shot that pitches and dips through the trees to the bottom of the East River lift. From the top of this lift, on this lower hip of the mountain, there are a couple of steep cruisers such as Black

Eagle and Lower Treasury, or if you feel you can handle a black run, try the show-me-what-you-can-do bumps on Resurrection under the chair.

When you're ready to try some more challenging trails off the already-visited Paradise lift, take the East River lift to the top and turn right to Daisy, which you'll stay on all the way to the Paradise lift. Ride Paradise to the top and turn right onto Ruby Road, a steep, wide powder field that narrows as it cuts over to the Silver Queen lift and turns into the superlong and steep International. This leg burner—often ungroomed—takes you to the bottom of the Silver Queen lift. From the top of this lift, turn left onto Keystone for some well-rounded moguls. To avoid the slew of greens that lie below, take a sharp right onto lower Ruby Chief and cruise down to the bottom of Paradise lift. An alternative to this route is to take Silver Queen Road from the top of Silver Queen lift and move into the Paradise Bowl.

Experts

Do you want radical, untamed vertical chutes and eyeball-high moguls? To reach such challenges, ride the Silver Queen lift and go left on upper Keystone to the steep and bumpy Jokerville, Twister, and Crystal runs. When you're ready to move on, ski International or Silvanite down to the Silver Queen lift and take Keystone down a short stretch to the High lift to reach the Headwall, a vast, steep bowl dotted with glades that is ungroomed, untamed, and out of this world for those who can handle it.

Ski down the Headwall to the North Face lift and take it to the top to reach the Extreme Limits, the steepest and largest lift-served terrain in North America. (A typical black diamond slope at other American resorts averages between 27 and 33 degrees. By comparison, Crested Butte's extreme terrain averages 39 to 44 degrees.) Before tackling North Face, Spellbound Bowl, Phoenix Bowl, and Third Bowl—all high on the mountain's shoulders—remember that you're taking on the wilderness and all that goes with it: wide, steep couloirs, exposed rocks, heart-stopping cliffs, thick timber, and deep, ungroomed snow.

Another area for such extremism is the Banana Funnel, reached on the Silver Queen lift; turn left and then left again under the lift to explore the steep, narrow chutes of Upper Forest, Upper Peel, and Hot Rocks.

A good way to determine whether you're up to these extreme areas is to ski the Tower 11 chutes. To reach them, just ski down the right side of Paradise Bowl until you reach a marked gate in the boundary rope—then traverse a short distance to the edge of the chutes. They are steep, forested runs filled with deep snow that cross under the Paradise chair. If that feels comfortable, you can push your envelope by progressing your way across the North Face into steeper and more radical terrain.

You should note that the resort's staunch promotion of its extreme skiing does not suggest laxness toward irresponsible or reckless pursuit of the radical. If you are unsure, don't get in over your head. There are free guided tours of the Extreme Limits by the Crested Butte Resort guides twice daily, or you can arrange to join one of the extreme-skiing workshops that include lessons and guided tours.

WHERE TO STAY

The modern mountain village is mostly condos stacked on the hills around the base of the ski area. In the town of Crested Butte, small inns and B&Bs are part of the flavor of Colorado's largest National Historic District. A shuttle bus system links the two. Families and groups tend to stick to the on-mountain accommodation, while couples tend to feel more at home in the more personalized in-town lodgings. All accommodations can be booked through Crested Butte Central Reservations, tel. 800/544–8448.

Expensive

Crested Butte Club

The beautifully restored circa-1880 Croatian Miners' Hall in the town of Crested Butte is the epitome of Victorian elegance, enhanced by all the modern touches. The rooms are designer-decorated with period cherry furnishings, four-poster or canopy beds, fireplaces, and huge copper bathtubs. The lounge and piano bar are soothing oases of dark wood and brass trim. It's definitely a place for romantics. *512 2nd St., Crested Butte 81224, tel. 970/349–6655 or 800/ 815–2582, fax 970/349–7580. 6 rooms, 1 suite. Facilities: indoor lap pool, steam bath, hot tub, weight-lifting gym, aerobics room, climbing wall, massage, spa. MC, V. $150–$225, including Continental breakfast.*

Crested Mountain Village

This modern-looking condo complex stands slope side in the mountain village and comprises five different buildings—the Buttes, Crested Mountain, Crested Mountain North, the Penthouses, and Crested Butte Lodge. All but the lodge have multiroom units ranging from one to three bedrooms, with fireplaces and balconies. The condos are decorated with modern, comfortable, practical furnishings whose styles depend on the owner— anything from Southwestern with its requisite gentle earth tones to contemporary minimalist decor with lots of smooth surfaces and gray tones. *500 Gothic Rd., Mt. Crested Butte 81225, tel. 970/349–4700 or 800/ 544–8448, fax 970/349–2304. 22 rooms, 66 units. Facilities: indoor pool, hot tub, sauna, daily housekeeping. AE, D, MC, V. $54–$684.*

Gateway at Crested Butte

These ski-in/ski-out condos next to the Peach Tree lift are some of Crested Butte's nicest. The one- to three-bedroom units accommodate up to eight people. All have a full kitchen, fireplace, washer and dryer, and two balconies—most overlooking the slopes. A hot tub and sauna will soothe your muscles after a hard day on the steeps. If you don't mind being out of town a little—but want to be right in the middle of the ski action—this is the place to stay. *400 Gothic Rd., Mt. Crested Butte 81225, tel. 970/349– 5705 or 800/451–5699. 17 units. Facilities: sauna, hot tub. AE, D, MC, V. $185–$510.*

Grande Butte Hotel

This six-story, horseshoe-shape, off-white stucco building only 35 yards from the lifts is the only full-size, full-service ski-in/ski-out hotel on the mountain. The public areas are spacious, with deep carpets of maroon and dark green. Each of its standard rooms is large, with a sitting area with a sleeper couch and several comfortable chairs. The suites are twice as large. Both the rooms and the suites are finished in green and beige and come with a balcony, a wet bar, and a whirlpool tub. Some of the king-size suites have a fireplace. *500 Gothic Rd., Mt. Crested Butte 81225, tel. 970/349–4060 or 800/544–8448, fax 970/349–4466. 210 rooms, 52 suites. Facilities: 2 restaurants, lounge, indoor pool, sauna, 3 hot tubs, exercise room, recreation room, laundry. AE, D, DC, MC, V. $102–$281.*

Village Center Condominiums

These three condo buildings, about 50 feet from the lifts, are an excellent slope-side deal, with a combination of one-, two-, three- and four-bedroom units. The decor is ultramodern, with high ceilings, white walls, and contemporary furnishings. The individual units are not overly large, but they are well laid out to maximize space. Each comes with a fireplace and a balcony. *Box 5200, Mt. Crested Butte 81225, tel. 970/349–2111 or 800/521–6593, fax 970/349–6370. 30 units. Facilities: outdoor hot tub, ski storage. D, MC, V. $130–$485.*

Moderate

Elk Mountain Lodge

The miners who originally stayed in this turn-of-the-century hotel in the town of Crested Butte certainly never enjoyed the kind of luxury it now offers. The elegant lobby with its chintz-covered furnishings and grand piano sets the tone, and the peerless good taste continues in the individu-

ally decorated rooms. Room occupancy is limited to two guests, but children can be accommodated in an adjoining room—there are three sets of these. *129 Gothic Ave., Box 148, Crested Butte 81224, tel. 970/349–7533 or 800/374–6521, fax 970/349–5114. 19 rooms. Facilities: bar, hot tub, library. AE, D, MC, V. $88–$118, including full breakfast.*

Nordic Inn

If you prefer slope-side small-inn accommodations, this family-owned Norwegian-style lodge about 300 yards from the lifts is a good choice. The decor in the rooms and suites is Scandinavian simplicity, with lots of wood and mountain antiques. The rooms are not huge; if you need a little extra space, pick one of the suites or one of the adjacent chalets. *14 Treasury Rd., Mt. Crested Butte 81225, tel. 970/349–5542, fax 970/349–6487. 24 rooms, 2 suites, 2 chalets. Facilities: hot tub, sundeck. AE, MC, V. $107–$315.*

Inexpensive

Claim Jumper

This entire B&B is filled with a truly outrageous collection of memorabilia and antiques. Each of the rooms is themed to the hilt and could be a museum in its own right. One is a complete replica of a service station, gas pump and all; another is wall-to-wall Coca-Cola trinkets, including a soda machine, while yet another is bow-to-stern nautical gear. Rooms are equipped with a queen-size bed; suites have a queen and two twins, making them a good choice for families. Gourmet breakfast is included. *704 Whiterock Ave., Crested Butte*

*81224, tel. 970/349–6471. 5 rooms, 2
suites. Facilities: hot tub, sauna. MC, V.
$89–$129, including full breakfast.*

Cristiana Guesthaus
This cozy Euro-style lodge in the
town of Crested Butte combines B&B
friendliness with the privacy of an
inn. Some of the simple, homey, individually decorated rooms will handle
up to four people. Smoking is not
permitted. *621 Maroon Ave., Box 427,
Crested Butte 81224, tel. 970/349–
5326 or 800/824–7899, fax 970/
349–1962. 21 rooms. Facilities: sauna,
hot tub. AE, D, MC, V. $65–$87,
including Continental breakfast.*

Last Resort
This delightfully unpretentious B&B
in downtown Crested Butte has wood,
stucco, and brick decor. The best
room is the Miner's Cabin, the original cabin around which the rest of the
house is built. All rooms and suites
are equipped with skylights and balconies; the suites also have Jacuzzis.
Despite the luxuries, the mood is rustic and homey, as reflected in dark
woods, overstuffed furniture, and
simple pastel colors. Breakfast is
served in either the solarium or your
room. *213 3rd St., Box 722, Crested
Butte 81224, tel. 970/349–0445 or
800/349–0445. 4 rooms, 2 suites.
Facilities: solarium, steam room,
library. MC, V. $95–$105, including
full breakfast.*

Manor Lodge
The European-style Manor Lodge,
about 250 yards from the lifts, is an
alternative to condo living on the
mountain. The rooms are fairly large;
some have a fireplace. The wood-and-
brick decor creates a cozy mountain

ambience. *650 Gothic Rd., Mt. Crested
Butte 81225, tel. 970/349–5365 or
800/826–3210, fax 970/349–5360.
53 rooms, 4 suites. Facilities: restaurant, bar, hot tub, laundry, indoor ski
storage. AE, MC, V. $73–$135, including Continental breakfast.*

WHERE TO EAT
Expensive
Giovanni's Grande Café
You can enjoy sitting amid the linen
place settings and pink Italian marble
while taking in views of the Rocky
Mountains. Italian cuisine, northern
style, is the specialty; the menu
includes a new ravioli dish daily, such
as eggplant, shiitake mushrooms, and
ricotta cheese wrapped in roasted red-
pepper ravioli and topped with vegetable pasta sauce. You can also order
a game dish such as seared scallopini
of boar with pearl onions and fresh
tarragon. On the fish side, the
salmone in crosta salata (salmon fillet
baked in parchment paper and a salt
meringue crust) is a good choice.
*Grande Butte Hotel, Mt. Crested Butte,
tel. 970/349–4999. AE, D, MC, V.*

Soupçon
This is my favorite high-end dining
experience in town, mostly because it
serves innovative French cuisine in an
atmosphere that is reminiscent of a
small country inn in the heart of
France. It's tiny and tucked away off
the main street in a minuscule log
cabin built at the turn of the century.
The menu changes daily and is posted
on a chalkboard. Some exceptional
dishes that are always available are
swordfish with béarnaise sauce and
roast duckling with plum sauce. The
menu has been modified recently to

emphasize lighter fare, using less butter and cream. *Just off 2nd St. behind the Forest Queen, 127A Elk Ave., Crested Butte, tel. 970/349–5448. Reservations essential; 2 seatings nightly. AE, MC, V.*

Timberline Restaurant
This restored miner's cabin characterized by clean lines and light woods offers an intimate dining experience upstairs and something a bit more lively below. The menu is Continental, and the twists are pure Rocky Mountain. You'll rarely see the same menu twice. Entrées may include venison with wild mushrooms or pheasant braised with a ginger sauce. The crisp-skinned whitefish is deliciously different. *21 Elk Ave., Crested Butte, tel. 970/349–9831. AE, MC, V.*

Moderate

The Bacchanale
This small house turned restaurant—complete with antique tables, stained-glass windows and light fixtures, and the good old red and green found in so many houses of Italian cuisine—has a lineup of northern Italian dishes that includes the requisite pasta choices but also excellent veal and seafood dishes. The seafood *fra diavolo*, a blend of shrimp and scallops in a tomato and jalapeño pepper sauce, certainly lives up to expectations. You can have the same sauce with a boneless chicken breast or with a combination of the two. *208 Elk Ave., Crested Butte, tel. 970/349–5257. AE, D, MC, V.*

Idle Spur Brewery and Pub
Crested Butte's first microbrewery is a rollicking spot, with massive log beams and a huge stone fireplace—half bar and half restaurant—and serves the best steaks in town, all aged Colorado beef. The portions are huge and cooked precisely as ordered. There's also a choice of ribs and prime rib. I recommend chasing these down with Gary's custom-brewed ales. *226 Elk Ave., Crested Butte, tel. 970/349–5026. AE, MC, V.*

Penelope's Restaurant Bar & Market
This charming restaurant is in a greenhouse in the back of an 1879 house. The menu emphasizes fresh, seasonal food at affordable prices. Typical offerings might include venison chili or pan-seared Rocky Mountain trout with artichoke hearts and capers. The gourmet market offers sandwiches and treats, and upstairs is Crested Butte's only cigar bar, serving port, cognac, and grappa. *120 Elk Ave., Crested Butte, tel. 970/349–5178. AE, D, DC, MC, V.*

Swiss Chalet
At this wood-trimmed, chalet-style mountain restaurant with dark green and red decor and low ceilings, you can sample cheese and meat fondues, plus raclette in two varieties—one with traditional *Buendnerfleisch* and another with beef tenderloin. There are also some good German specialties, such as schnitzel, smoked pork loin chops, and a particularly good dish of grilled venison medallions served with lingonberry sauce. *620 Gothic Rd., Mt. Crested Butte, tel. 970/349–5917. AE, MC, V.*

Inexpensive

Donita's Cantina
Among the attractions here are monster margaritas, great salsa served with a mountain of nacho chips, and

fajitas in superlarge portions, sizzling and spicy. Olé! Watch out for long lines, however. *330 Elk Ave., Crested Butte, tel. 970/349–6674. Reservations not accepted. AE, D, MC, V.*

Karolina's Kitchen
The menu here is simple but extensive, with a series of daily blue plate specials ranging from meat loaf to fresh fish, plus other items, including enormous sandwiches, hamburgers, fish-and-chips, cajun chicken, kielbasa and sauerkraut, and beef bourguignonne. There's nothing if not variety here, and no entrée costs more than $10. *127 Elk Ave., Crested Butte, tel. 970/349–6756. MC, V.*

Roaring Elk Restaurant
Entrées here include ginger chicken penne, rib-eye steak, and even hand-tossed pizza, plus an extensive soup and salad bar. The chili lunch buffet is great, too, as is the more than ample breakfast offering called the Silver Queen buffet. *Grand Butte Hotel, Mt. Crested Butte, tel. 970/349–4042. AE, D, MC, V.*

The Slogar
This is another creation of Mac and Maura Bailey (who also own Soupçon, *above*), and on the surface you might think that a one-dish menu is nothing to rave about. But you'll quickly change your mind when you try the skillet-fried chicken, the centerpiece of the meal, served with all-you-can-eat helpings of delicious sweet-and-sour coleslaw, mashed potatoes, fresh-baked biscuits, and sweet corn. Ice cream tops off the meal. If you are totally antichicken, you can switch to steak, accompanied by the same dishes. It's in a great setting—a totally

renovated 1882 Victorian restaurant. *517 2nd St., Mt. Crested Butte, tel. 970/349–5765. MC, V.*

Wooden Nickel
This saloon-restaurant, which has dark wood decor, artwork portraying local scenes, and a 100-year-old back bar, offers a late-night menu and a happy hour from 3 to 6 daily. It serves fast food, done well, in a lively hive. The menu covers a wide range of tastes, including steaks, ribs, sandwiches, burgers, steamed clams, fresh fish, and lots of other staples. *222 Elk Ave., Mt. Crested Butte, tel. 970/349–6350. AE, D, DC, MC, V.*

Best Bets for Breakfast
Bakery at Mount Crested Butte
Here you can drink the best coffee on the mountain and enjoy an awesome lineup of muffins, breads, nut bars, cookies, and pastries, as well as the Bierox, a veggie pocket. *Opposite bus center, Mountain Village, tel. 970/349–1419. No credit cards.*

Bakery Café
In the center of town, this café has a full range of baked goods including croissants with different fillings and bagels, breads, and breakfast pastries. Specialty coffees and fresh-squeezed orange juice are available. *302 Elk Ave., tel. 970/349–7280. MC, V.*

NIGHTLIFE AND ENTERTAINMENT
Après-Ski
The Artichoke
They've got your favorite light rock or reggae playing while you munch on spicy fries, wings, nachos, and artichokes—artichoke hearts, artichoke dips, and whole artichokes. *Treasury*

Center, Mt. Crested Butte, tel. 970/ 349–6688. AE, D, MC, V.

Rafters

Right at the bottom of the lifts, Rafters is a natural after-ski watering hole. Count on it being crowded and noisy. It always has music. The beer is cheap, and the margaritas strong. *Gothic Bldg., Ski Village, tel. 970/349– 2298. AE, D, MC, V.*

Loud and Lively/Dancing

Kochevars Saloon and Gaming Hall

This saloon has been around for almost a century, and not a lot has changed. It's still the original log building that Butch Cassidy once vacated in a hurry, and the games are still the main theme—shuffleboard, pool, darts, and sports on TV. *127 Elk Ave., Crested Butte, tel. 970/349– 6745. MC, V.*

More Mellow

Crested Butte Club Pub

Complete with its wood-and-brass decor (including a back bar from 1886) and log fire, this is just the spot to sip some suds or enjoy a late night-cap. It has comfortable wingback chairs, an easy pace, and a dart board. There are TVs for sporting events. *Crested Butte Club, 512 2nd St., Crested Butte, tel. 970/349–6655. D, MC, V.*

KEYSTONE RESORT

Box 38
Keystone, CO 80435
Tel. 970/468–2316 or
800/222–0188

STATISTICALLY SPEAKING
Base elevation: 9,300 feet

Summit elevation: 12,200 feet

Vertical drop: 2,900 feet

Skiable terrain: 1,749 acres

Number of trails: 91

Longest run: 3 miles

Lifts and capacity: 2 high-speed gondolas, 3 high-speed quads, 1 quad, 3 triple chairlifts, 6 doubles, 5 surface; 26,582 skiers per hour

Daily lift ticket: $45

Average annual snowfall: 230 inches

Number of skiing days 1995–96: 210

Snowmaking: 851 acres; 49%

Terrain mix: N 51%, I 36%, E 13%

Snowboarding: yes

Among Summit County's four ski resorts, Keystone competes with Copper Mountain for size and variety of terrain. A merger of Keystone and Breckenridge with Vail Resorts (Vail and Beaver Creek), announced in early 1997, makes Keystone part of the world's largest ski company. For Keystone it should eventually mean an interchangeable lift ticket with the other three resorts as well as deep pockets to fund additional capital improvements.

Keystone has long been known for good, all-around skiing on three peaks and a well-run resort area, but overall it has lacked the spirit of Colorado ski areas that have grown up around established local communities, such as Breckenridge. Instead of a discernible resort center, the area was basically a string of suburban islands linked by shuttle bus. A scheme is afoot, however, to change all this. Intrawest—the folks who developed the award-winning Blackcomb resort in Canada and recently bought Copper Mountain—began a $700 million 20-year village upgrade in 1995 to create a pedestrian village at the heart of Keystone. Already several new stone-and-timber ski-in/ski-out lodges, along with taverns, brew pubs, cafés, and upscale shops, have revitalized the River Run base area. Plans eventually call for a performing arts theater, an expanded cross-country center at the golf course, and bike paths and boardwalks linking the resort's several neighborhoods.

Even before the completion of that plan, Keystone still has lots to recommend it: an enviable range of terrain spread over a vast skiable area, an ample variety of accommodations, arguably the best grooming outside Utah's Deer Valley or nearby Beaver Creek, the largest night-skiing operation in the country, and a superb shuttle bus system. It also draws more than a million skiers a year, most of them executive family types with cash to spare—the very folks Keystone's corporate honchos most want to impress with their impeccable attention to detail and their no-hassle, leave-everything-to-us approach to ski vacations.

That well-heeled crowd doesn't seem to mind the absence of a central village area, as most tend to think of nightlife as a quiet skate on the ice rink or an early night in front of the VCR. However, the opening

USEFUL NUMBERS
Area code: 970

Children's services:
tel. 970/468–2316

Snow phone: tel. 970/468–
4111 or 970/733–0191

Police: Summit County sheriff's dept., tel. 970/453–2232

Medical center:
Snake River Health Services,
tel. 970/468–1440

Hospital: Summit Medical
Center, tel. 970/668–3300

Summit County Chamber of
Commerce: tel. 970/668–5800

Ski the Summit:
tel. 970/468–6607

Avalanche hot line:
tel. 970/668–0600

Taxi: Around Town Taxi,
tel. 970/453–8294

Road conditions:
tel. 970/453–1090

Towing: Paul's Towing,
tel. 970/468–6936

FIVE-STAR FAVORITES
Best run for vertical: Ambush

Best run overall: Geronimo

Best bar/nightclub:
Snake River Saloon

Best hotel: Ski Tip Lodge

Best restaurant:
Keystone Ranch

of Keystone's slopes to snowboarders in 1996 is bringing a youthful energy to the resort, and several new après-ski spots should keep both skiers and locals around after the slopes close. If you're in need of more action, head over to nearby Frisco, which has some good and funky nightspots. If you crave action on the slopes, the Outback area should satisfy all but the most manic.

Most of the ski-in/ski-out accommodations are now at the River Run base area, where the Skyway gondola provides quick access to the summit and the more challenging runs on North Peak and Outback. The Mountain Village base area at the bottom of the Peru Express, on the west end of Keystone Mountain, also has slope-side condominiums.

Outside the ski area boundaries, about a mile down the highway toward Frisco, is the Keystone Village center, with the Keystone Lodge (the resort's flagship hotel), a restaurant and shopping arcade, and the largest outdoor skating rink in North America. This is a nice alternative to the River Run base area, but as it's not within walking distance of most area hotels, it tends to be a quiet spot, frequented mostly by guests of the Keystone Lodge. Shuttle buses connect guests from any of the resort's lodging properties with the lifts.

If you value privacy, efficiency, and moderately upscale pampering, this is a terrific place to ski.

HOW TO GET THERE

By Plane
Denver International Airport (*see* Getting to Colorado Resorts, *above*) is 75 miles away.

Shuttle Service
Resort Express (tel. 970/468–7600) runs an hourly shuttle from Denver International Airport between 9 AM and 11 PM and to the airport between 6 AM and 8 PM. The trip costs $39 one-way and $71 round-trip.

By Car
From Denver International Airport take I–70 west to Exit 205 and go 6 miles north on U.S. 6 to the Keystone Resort.

All major car-rental companies have offices at Denver International Airport (*see* Getting to Colorado Resorts, *above*).

By Bus
Greyhound Lines (tel. 800/231–2222) runs three trips daily from Denver to Silverthorne, 6 miles west of Keystone. The round-trip fare is $19.

By Train
See Getting to Colorado Resorts, *above*.

GETTING AROUND
Keystone is small enough so that you don't need a car. The Keystone Shuttle (tel. 970/468–4200) is a free regular bus service that stops at all points throughout Keystone and also connects the resort to the neighboring slopes at Breckenridge. Buses run between 7 AM and 2 AM. For Arapahoe Basin, take the **KAB Express** (tel. 970/468–4200). For the rest of Summit County, take the **Summit Stage** (tel. 970/453–1339).

THE SKIING
The skiing at Keystone actually runs over three mountain peaks: 11,640-foot Keystone Mountain, North Peak at 11,660 feet, and the Outback at 12,200 feet. You get to the backside peaks from the summit of Keystone Mountain, either by skiing down to the foot of North Peak or by riding the Outpost gondola from the top of Keystone Mountain to the top of North Peak.

The three peaks and four faces have a predictable mix of runs. Keystone Mountain provides the majority of the novice and intermediate slopes; North Peak caters to the upper inter-

mediates and quasi-experts; and the Outback, where the runs are seldom groomed, serves up the most consistently challenging terrain, including 633 acres of above-timberline bowl skiing for aggressive intermediate and strong expert skiers.

Snowboarders have long coveted the powder stashes and wide-open bowls on Keystone's Outback, but until 1996 the resort was one of the few holdouts that banned 'boarders. Now they're wooing them aggressively, with $2.5 million in snowboarder-friendly improvements. Enhancements include a 20-acre terrain garden and multiple half pipes in Packsaddle Bowl, with additional lighting to make it the largest night-snowboarding area in the state. In addition, a new 4,000-square-foot snowboard rental shop—one of the largest in North America—opened in 1996. Keystone's innovative Quick Carve learning system enables skiers to make a smooth transition to snowboarding by using a special learning board, ski poles, and a technique based on skiing theory.

Novices
You should start your day at the Mountain House base area, where the Peru Express quad will take you to a nest of green trails on the front side of Keystone Mountain. The beginners' area and the children's bunny slopes are also adjacent to the Peru Express. It's best to keep to the right (looking down) of the quad on your way down, picking up runs like Silver Spoon, Gold Rush Alley, or Gassy Thompson, all of which are smooth, groomed, and wide. Just make sure you stay right where all three of these

runs converge at the base of the Ida Belle lift; from here you can take the long, winding Schoolmarm back to the Peru Express.

When you're ready to ascend to the summit, take the Peru Express, ski down Silver Spoon, and ride the Saints John lift to the top. From there you can ski a scenic green wave across the mountain's shoulder before turning down Gold Rush Alley, for a taste of slightly steeper green, or Pack Saddle Bowl, for some wide-open slopes. If you feel you're up to some well-groomed blue runs, HooDoo, off the Peru Express, is a good start, or try Paymaster, via the Saints John lift with a short scoot down Schoolmarm.

For a change of scenery, ride the Outpost gondola from the Keystone summit to the North Peak summit, enjoy lunch at the Outpost Lodge, then take Fox Trot and Anticipation down to the Nordic Skiway, which will take you back to the Ruby lift, at the base of Keystone Mountain.

Intermediates

It really doesn't matter where you start, because eventually you are going to head to the backside of Keystone Mountain and then explore North Peak and the Outback. From the Mountain House base area take the Argentine double and then the Montezuma Express quad to the summit. From the River Run Plaza end of the resort, it's a straight shot on the Skyway gondola. There's a series of tempting intermediate runs down the face of Keystone Mountain that you can use for warm-ups, but don't go below the base of the Montezuma quad because you'll run a speed-controlled green all the way back to the crowds at the bottom. For some good heads-up speed and groomed snow, your best choices here are the Flying Dutchman, Frenchman, and the Wild Irishman.

When you're ready to move on, head over the backside and take a good cruise down Mozart, a sprightly blue run and a good way to get to the bottom of North Peak. Here you can push the envelope a little bit with some steeper, bumpier runs such as Star Fire or Last Alamo. Want to move up another notch? Try the ungroomed bumps on Ambush or Powder Cap, or practice your turns-on-demand in the partially gladed runs of Geronimo and Cat Dancer.

To move over to the Outback, take Anticipation, on the backside of North Peak, all the way down to the base of the Outback Express quad. From its top you'll find just about anything in the intermediate spectrum: the extrasteep Oh Bob and Elk Run; heads-up glade skiing on Wolverine and Wildfire; and the wild, ungroomed bumps of Big Horn and Porcupine. Try them all, and when you're ready to go that one extra step, head over to the heavily wooded Black Forest section of the Outback for some of the deepest snow and thickest woods on the mountain.

When you are ready to leave the Outback, there is a long, flat ski-out back to the base of North Peak, so carry a good head of speed as you pass the base of the Outback Express.

Experts

Head immediately for the Keystone Mountain summit on the Skyway gondola at the River Run Plaza. From the top get warmed up on either

Mineshaft or Diamond Back, two groomed, but wild, high-speed giant-slalom runs down the backside of Keystone Mountain. Grab the Santiago triple to the top of North Peak, and if the crowds are not too bad, try a run down Geronimo—steep, treed, and bumpy—or Cat Dancer—steeper and often bumpier—before heading back up on the Santiago lift. From here take a run down the intermediate Anticipation to the base of the Outback Express quad.

Your steepest and most challenging terrain on the Outback is a quartet of high-speed slashes through the woods—the Grizz, Badger, Bushwacker, and Timberwolf, where the snow is never groomed and turn-on-demand is your key to survival.

You can make turns through the trees all day here, but when it's time to leave, it can be a tedious glide on the endless Nordic Skiway to get back to the lift on Keystone Mountain. Leave early, before the track gets crowded, and spend the last few runs of the day on either North Peak or the front side of Keystone Mountain.

When you're ready to turn things up a notch, your best bet is to head for nearby Arapahoe Basin, where you will find some of the steepest, highest skiing in the state. Due to its elevation and wind-buffeted exposure, Arapahoe doesn't usually get enough snow to cover its gullies, steeps, and chutes until January. The compensation is that it often keeps operating until the beginning of July. At its best, A Basin will test almost any expert's mettle with its unpredictable weather, high winds, and supersteep terrain, including the legendary East Wall,

where snow-choked chutes and gullies attract the best and the bravest.

WHERE TO STAY

Keystone has some impressive new lodges at the River Run base area, within walking distance of the Skyway Gondola, as well as well-built new condominiums in the Ski Tip Ranch neighborhood, a short shuttle bus ride from the slopes, and the slope-side Chateaux d'Mont units at the base of Keystone Mountain. Most properties are owned and operated by Keystone. These usually upscale accommodations are consistent in price and quality; units closest to the lifts tend to be the most expensive, while taking a shuttle ride if you stay at those farther away can save you considerable money. Most units have access to Keystone Fitness Center (pool, health club, and spa). Keystone Central Reservations (tel. 800/222–0188) handles the bookings for all their properties. To explore the options in nearby Frisco, Dillon, and Breckenridge, call Summit County Central Reservations (tel. 800/365–6365). In these communities you'll find smaller inns, lodges, motels, and bed-and-breakfasts, most within an easy walk of dining and nightlife options. Dillon is 6 miles from Keystone, Frisco is 12 miles, and Breckenridge 20 miles. A shuttle bus network links all three communities with Keystone.

Expensive

Chateaux d'Mont
This is a classy ski-in/ski-out condo complex that has fine views overlooking the slopes. The suites—with two or three bedrooms—have tasteful fur-

nishings ranging from French provincial to Colorado Southwest and are loaded with extras, including complimentary snacks and beverages, a pair of terry-cloth bathrobes, turndown service, complimentary Continental breakfast and après-ski hors d'oeuvres, and fresh flowers. A balcony or terrace, a fireplace, a hot tub, a washer and dryer, and a whirlpool bath are part of every unit, and guests have access to Keystone Fitness Center. *Bldg. 21996, U.S. 6, Keystone 80435, tel. 970/468–2316 or 800/222–0188, fax 970/496–4343. 14 units. Facilities: 24-hr desk service, maid service, ski storage. $700–$1,300.*

The Inn at Keystone
The seven-story towerlike redbrick building, built in 1990, houses a modern full-service hotel with comfortable but not overly luxurious rooms and suites. Outdoor hot tubs overlook a spectacular view of Keystone Mountain, and guests have access to the health club at Keystone Lodge. All rooms are equipped with mini-refrigerator and coffeemakers, and two suites have hot tubs. Throughout the hotel a shiny, modern Art Deco theme prevails, with an emphasis on turquoise, pink, and black. *23044 U.S. 6, Keystone 80435, tel. 970/468–1334 or 800/222–0188, fax 970/496–4343. 86 rooms, 17 suites. Facilities: restaurant, bar, 3 outdoor hot tubs, 24-hr desk service, shuttle, maid service, ski storage. AE, D, DC, MC, V. $140–$240.*

Keystone Condominiums
You'll find all shapes and sizes of condo convenience at the scattered properties managed by Keystone, ranging from studios to five-bedroom houses. Most are fully equipped, with a kitchen, a fireplace, 24-hour switchboard service, daily housekeeping, and either a sauna, a Jacuzzi, or a pool. All have access to Keystone Fitness Center. Price for the most part is determined by proximity to the mountain, so taking a 10-minute shuttle bus ride can save you hundreds of dollars. Mountain Premium is the priciest group, with all its units slope side, followed by Village, Resort II, and the earliest condos in Keystone, Resort I. *U.S. 6, Keystone 80435, tel. 970/468–2316 or 800/222–0188, fax 970/496–4343. 1,300 units. Facilities: restaurant, bar, hot tub, 24-hr desk service, shuttle, maid service, ski storage, laundry. AE, D, DC, MC, V. $120–$1025, including Continental breakfast.*

Keystone Lodge
This is a large, modern, sprawling hotel bordered by Keystone Lake on one side and U.S. 6 on the other. Midway along the length of the resort area, it's a five-minute shuttle bus ride from the lifts. The standard double rooms and suites are luxurious, though not overly large, and are decorated with Western motifs. Try for one with a balcony lakeside. *U.S. 6, Keystone 80435, tel. 970/468–2316 or 800/222–0188. 152 rooms. Facilities: restaurant, bar, hot tub, pool, 2 tennis courts, health club, spa, 24-hr desk service, shuttle, maid service, ski storage, laundry. AE, D, DC, MC, V. $200–$280.*

Moderate
Allaire Timbers Inn
Nestled in a wooded area at the south end of Main Street in the charming

town of Breckenridge, this stone-and-timber log cabin inn has a great room anchored by a huge stone fireplace, as well as a reading loft and sunroom with a green slate floor and lots of wicker furniture. The main deck and hot tub offer spectacular views of the Ten-Mile Range. *9511 S. Main St., Breckenridge 80424, tel. 970/453–7530 or 800/624–4904, fax 970/453–8699. 8 rooms, 2 suites. Facilities: outdoor hot tub, shuttle, maid service, ski storage. AE, D, MC, V. $130–$245, including full breakfast.*

Ski Tip Lodge

This painstakingly preserved 1860s stagecoach stop converted into an idyllic bed-and-breakfast has a variety of cozy rooms filled with antiques; uneven floors, bent beams, and a massive stone fireplace complement the period decor. Guests have access to Keystone Fitness Center. A full buffet breakfast is included in the price, and the restaurant also serves a fine four-course dinner. *0764 Montezuma Rd., 1 mi off U.S. 6, Dillon 80435, tel. 970/468–4202 or 800/222–0188. 9 rooms, 7 with bath, 2 suites. Facilities: restaurant, bar, shuttle service, maid service, ski storage. AE, D, DC, MC, V. $71–$199, including full breakfast.*

Twilight Inn

The three-story log structure was built in 1987, but the owners based their design on neighboring historic buildings in downtown Frisco. The guest rooms are filled with antiques; no two rooms look alike, but all share a casual country feel. The extraordinary selection of beds includes an antique mission-style sleigh bed, a Shaker-style four-poster, an iron-and-brass

bed, and most delightful of all, Aspen log bunk beds. The common areas include a library, a TV room, and a living room in which a Continental breakfast is served each morning. *308 Main St., Frisco 80443, tel. 970/668–5009 or 800/262–1002. 12 rooms, 8 with bath. Facilities: indoor hot tub, steam room, maid service, ski storage, laundry. AE, D, MC, V. $90–$128, including Continental breakfast.*

Woods Inn

In 1994 a new two-story log lodge was constructed right next to an authentic log cabin B&B in the heart of Frisco's historic district, about a block from Main Street. The B&B is comfortably rustic, with a variety of room choices from single to queen-size with bunk bed; there are two sitting rooms, a reading room, and spa facilities. The hotel has a flexible configuration of rooms and studios that can be opened up to produce large suites, complete with spacious living room areas. The brightly colored rooms in both buildings have lodgepole pine furniture. *205 S. 2nd Ave., Frisco 80443, tel. 970/668–3389 or 800/668–4448. 7 rooms share 2 baths (B&B); 12 rooms (hotel). Facilities: outdoor hot tub, ski storage. AE, D, MC, V. $45–$120, including full breakfast (in B&B only).*

Inexpensive

Dillon Super 8 Motel

This inexpensive standard motel is mostly frequented by college students; expect a lively and sometimes noisy atmosphere. Rooms are large and clean and have the basic amenities, some with two double beds, others with one queen-size bed. *808 Little Beaver Trail,*

Dillon 80435, tel. 970/468–8888 or 800/800–8000, fax 970/468–2086. 61 rooms. Facilities: 24-hr desk service, shuttle, maid service, ski storage. AE, D, DC, MC, V. $75–$115, including Continental breakfast.

Luxury Inn

This affordable hotel in the middle of nearby Silverthorne has a log exterior. Rooms range in size from standard to king, most with multiple beds. Guests gravitate toward the hot tub room, where a large window overlooks the mountains. 540 Silverthorne Ln., Silverthorne 80498, tel. 970/468–0800 or 800/742–1972, fax 970/267–0797. 59 rooms. Facilities: indoor hot tub, 24-hr desk service, shuttle, maid service. AE, D, DC, MC, V. $50–$120, including Continental breakfast.

Snowshoe Motel

Groups may enjoy this funky, old-style ski motor lodge, although families may find it a little too noisy. Its tidy two-story gray cedar exterior has balconies looking onto the street. Some rooms have kitchenettes, and there is a two-room suite with a kitchen and a whirlpool tub. All rooms have a private entrance, and some connect. 521 Main St., Frisco 80443, tel. 970/668–3444 or 800/445–8658, fax 970/668–3883. 36 rooms, 1 suite. Facilities: indoor hot tub, sauna, 24-hr desk service, shuttle, maid service. AE, D, DC, MC, V. $38–$130.

WHERE TO EAT

Keystone boasts the finest dining establishments in Summit County, with several AAA four-diamond restaurants, while Breckenridge is an up-and-coming epicurean center. Keystone and the nearby towns of Silverthorne and Frisco also offer a good range of medium-price family eateries.

On the Mountain

The Outpost

This magnificent log-and-glass structure on the top of North Peak has views as lofty as the ceiling beams that support it. The upscale ski cafeteria serves pasta, meat, and poultry favorites. The deck barbecue is a favorite on warm days. (See also Alpenglow Stube and Fondue Chessel, below). Outpost Lodge, top of North Peak, Keystone, tel. 970/468–4386. AE, D, DC, MC, V.

Expensive

Alpenglow Stube

This is the finest on-mountain restaurant in Colorado. The decor is warmly elegant, with exposed wood beams, a stone fireplace, antler chandeliers, and floral upholstery. At night the gondola ride you take to get here is itself worth the price of a meal. Dinner is a six-course extravaganza featuring such Stube specialties as smoked saddle of rabbit in tricolor peppercorn sauce or rack of boar in Poire William sauce. At lunch plush slippers are provided when you remove your ski boots. Outpost Lodge, top of North Peak, Keystone, tel. 970/ 468–4386. Reservations essential. AE, D, DC, MC, V.

Keystone Ranch

A former working cattle ranch house, this handsome 1930s log building is nestled in the trees at the Keystone Golf Course. Contrasting with the woody exterior, the dining room's Oriental rugs, antiques, and fine china create an elegantly rustic ambience. The outstanding six-course prix fixe meal may include Muscovy duck over foie gras, veal medallions, and peppered trout. *Keystone Golf Course, Soda Ridge Rd., Keystone, tel. 970/ 468–4386. Reservations essential. AE, D, DC, MC, V.*

Ski Tip Lodge

You could cut the ambience in this 1860s stagecoach station with a steak knife, and almost everything on the menu will melt in your mouth. The four-course prix fixe dinner is a favorite in the area for its American cuisine with a Colorado twist. The main course may be a hickory-smoked tenderloin, braised Ringneck pheasant, or red trout paupiettes with crab, shrimp, and spinach. The delicious homemade bread and soup offered in the first course are a meal in themselves. Quilts, antiques, and a stone fireplace make the lodge's Old West charm irresistible. *0764 Montezuma Rd., 1 mi off U.S. 6, Keystone, tel. 970/ 468–4202. AE, D, DC, MC, V.*

Moderate

Cafe Alpine

The eclectic menu at this cozy house offers Continental fare with Asian and Southwestern flair. Try the grilled yellowfin tuna with pink guava and mango sauce and green papaya slaw or the chili-rubbed Rocky Mountain chicken with pico de gallo, ravioli, and ancho posole broth. At the tapas bar (served after 4) you can sample small plates of food from around the world. The moderately priced wine list is particularly well thought out, with several Australian and Chilean selections. *106 E. Adams Ave., Breck-*enridge, tel. 970/453–8218. AE, D, DC, MC, V.*

Fondue Chessel

It's a worthwhile experience, complete with a great view, excellent fondues, and the requisite live Bavarian music. The menu consists of a prix fixe four-course traditional Swiss fondue meal, including cheeses, salad, and chocolate fondue for dessert. The raclette cheese comes with your choice of scallops, shrimp, breast of chicken, veal sausage, or tenderloin of beef. A crusty French bread, apples, and crisp vegetables are provided for dipping in the fondue, a blend of Gruyère and Emmental Swiss cheeses accented with white wine. *Timber Ridge Room, Outpost Lodge, top of North Peak, Keystone, tel. 970/468–4386. Reservations essential. AE, D, DC, MC, V.*

Historic Mint

Built in 1862, this raucous eatery originally served as a bar and brothel. The old days are still evident in the bar's brass handles and hand-carved wood, as well as in the antiques and vintage photographs covering the walls of the dining area. Red meat and fish are the specialty here; you cook your own on lava rocks sizzling at 1,100 degrees. A well-stocked salad bar complements your entrée. If you prefer to leave the cooking to the chef, there's a prime rib special. *347 Blue River Pkwy., Silverthorne, tel. 970/468–5247. MC, V.*

Ida Belle's Bar and Grill

In keeping with its previous incarnation as a gold mine, this restaurant has a dining room that is reached through the old mineshaft entrance and is supported by hardwood pillars and decorated with gold pans, picks, and photographs from mining days. The cuisine is mild but tasty Tex-Mex, with highlights such as chili and fajitas; the ribs and half-pound burgers are also good. For dessert, it has to be the Mal Brown sundae: a chocolate brownie with three scoops of vanilla ice cream, topped with hot fudge, whipped cream, nuts, and a cherry. *Lakeside Condominiums, next to skating pond, Keystone Village, tel. 970/468–4289. AE, D, DC, MC, V.*

Inexpensive

Gassy Thompson's
This restaurant, named for a miner who lived in town in the late 1800s and said to have made his living by swindling other miners, serves hearty American fare in generous portions. Pork barbecue is the specialty, with burgers and extralarge sandwiches vying for second place. Memorabilia from Colorado's mining days—picks, buckets, lamps, and drawings—keeps Gassy's spirit alive despite the now-honest dealings. *Mountain House, base of Keystone Mountain, Keystone Rd., Keystone Village, tel. 970/468–4130. AE, D, DC, MC, V.*

Kickapoo Tavern
This rustic bar and grill features Colorado microbrews on tap and big portions of home-style American food like chili, hearty sandwiches and "a chicken in every pot" pie. The central location, outdoor patio, and TVs tuned to favorite sporting events keep the place hopping day and night. *Jackpine Lodge, River Run Plaza, Keystone, tel. 970/468–4601. AE, D, DC, MC, V.*

Best Bet for Breakfast

Razzberries at the Inn
Fill up on steak, eggs, hash browns, pancakes, and fruit at the all-you-can-eat breakfast bar overlooking the mountain before you head out to ski. *The Inn, 23044 U.S. 6, Keystone, tel. 970/468–1334. AE, D, DC, MC, V.*

NIGHTLIFE AND ENTERTAINMENT
Après-Ski

Keysters
A good place for avoiding the end-of-the-day shuttle gridlock, this place is loud and made even louder by the performers on the karaoke machine. The lone big-screen TV is tuned to sports every hour of the day and evening. *River Run Plaza, base of gondola, Keystone, tel. 970/468–4022. AE, D, MC, V.*

Last Lift
Another end-of-the-day refuge from the bus exodus, the Last Lift features live swing music between 3 PM and 6 PM daily. Good specials from the bar prompt occasional dancing. *Mountain House, base of Keystone Mountain, Keystone Rd., Keystone, tel. 970/468–4148. AE, D, DC, MC, V.*

Loud and Lively/Dancing

Breckenridge Brewery and Pub
The "Breck Brew Pub" has not only a great selection of homemade beers but also occasional top-quality live blues, Motown, and other R&B bands. This is a bar with all the right ingredients; just ask the locals. *600 S. Main St., Breckenridge, tel. 970/453–1550. D, MC, V.*

Salt Creek Saloon

For a boot-scootin' good time, head for this country-and-western bar in Breckenridge. Occasionally live bands perform, and line-dancing lessons are offered several nights a week. *110 E. Lincoln Ave., Breckenridge, tel. 970/453–4959. AE, D, DC, MC, V.*

Snake River Saloon

Live music with rockabilly leanings makes this a good spot to drink beer if you like a loud, music-driven environment. The crowd is generally under 30, but the occasional over-30 "senior" slips in. *23074 U.S. 6, 1 mi east of Keystone, tel. 970/468–2788. AE, DC, MC, V.*

More Mellow

Inxpot

After skiing or dinner sink into an overstuffed armchair in front of the fire, grab a book or a Hollywood script from the library shelves, play a board game, and enjoy espresso drinks, spirits, cheese and crackers, and desserts. *Black Bear Lodge, River Run Plaza, Keystone, tel. 970/496–4627. AE, D, DC, MC, V.*

Ski Tip Lodge

Sipping a brandy by the fireside at this old Western lodge filled with antiques is a good way to cap an evening. *0764 Montezuma Rd., 1 mi off Rte. 6, Dillon, tel. 970/468–4202. AE, D, DC, MC, V.*

SNOWMASS SKI RESORT

SNOWMASS SKI RESORT

Box 1248
Aspen, CO 81612
Tel. 970/925–1220 or
800/525–6200

STATISTICALLY SPEAKING
Base elevation: 8,104 feet

Summit elevation: 12,310 feet

Vertical drop: 4,206 feet

Skiable terrain: 2,655 acres

Number of trails: 79

Longest run: 4⅕ miles

Lifts and capacity: 7 high-speed quads, 1 triple, 7 doubles, 2 platter pulls; 23,979 skiers per hour

Daily lift ticket: $56

Average annual snowfall:
300 inches

Number of skiing days
1995–96: 133

Snowmaking: 115 acres, 4%

Terrain mix: N 10%, I 52%,
E 38%

Snowboarding: yes

Cross-country skiing:
48 miles of trails

Snowmass is almost always considered part of Aspen. However, this immense self-contained resort is larger than the combined acreage of the other three areas (Aspen Highlands, Aspen Mountain, and Buttermilk) that make up the Aspen scene. Snowmass is large enough to be ranked among the five largest resorts in America, yet it's difficult to be considered an entity separate from Aspen. Most people who visit Snowmass Resort spend at least some time in the town of Aspen, and visitors to Aspen—even those addicted to Aspen Mountain—would be remiss in not spending a day or two at Snowmass.

But make no mistake: One could visit Snowmass for a week and still not experience the entire Brobdingnagian mass of its five mountain sections. All levels of skiers can be challenged here and, although Snowmass is often marketed as a complete family destination because 52% of its terrain is designated intermediate, it features enough curl-your-toes steeps to keep hard-core extremists happy.

At the base of this massive mountain is the Snowmass Village and shopping mall—the pedestrian epicenter of the resort—with a rapidly expanding selection of shops, restaurants, bars, hotels, and condominiums. The most appealing feature of the Snowmass complex is that virtually all of the accommodations are considered ski-in/ski-out, with pocket-size developments nestled on the mountain's lower flanks amid the cedars and aspens.

HOW TO GET THERE
By Car
Snowmass is 200 miles from Denver International Airport. Follow I–70 west for 3½ hours to Glenwood Springs. Follow Route 82 for 45 minutes to the Snowmass Village exit. Turn right on Brush Creek Road and follow signs to the village.

GETTING AROUND
Everything is within easy walking distance in Snowmass Village, and the Snowmass–Aspen shuttle bus (tel. 970/925–8484) runs constantly from 8 to 10 and 3 to 6. At other times it runs every 15 minutes. Shuttle buses take you just about anywhere in Snowmass.

Children's services: day care, tel. 970/923–1220; nighttime baby-sitting, tel. 970/923–6080 or 800/215–7669; instruction, tel. 970/923–0570 or 800/525–6200

Snow phone: tel. 970/925–1221 or 888/277–3676

Police: tel. 970/923–5330

Aspen Valley Hospital: tel. 970/925–1120

Snowmass central reservations: tel. 970/923–2000 or 800/215–7669

Resort association: tel. 970/923–2000

Aspen Valley Hospital: tel. 970/925–1120

Road conditions: tel. 970/920–5454

Towing: Al's Towing, tel. 970/925–2265

FIVE-STAR FAVORITES

Best run for vertical: Baby Ruth

Best run overall: Hanging Valley Wall

Best bar/nightclub: Mountain Dragon

Best hotel: Silvertree Hotel

Best restaurant: La Boheme

THE SKIING

Snowmass is an elongated ridge of peaks and valleys that for the most part lack the knee-pounding precipitousness of the unforgiving Aspen Mountain—a vertical peak that ripples and folds into itself. That's not to say that Snowmass is all easy skiing, but it does have some of the longest, widest, most meticulously groomed intermediate slopes in Colorado. Despite its sprawling acreage it's remarkably easy to move around the mountain, picking your favorite runs from the five distinct sectors: Elk Camp, High Alpine/Alpine Springs, Big Burn, Sam's Knob, and Campground. Except for the latter, all sections funnel into the base area.

At the far eastern end of the Snowmass Ridge is Elk Camp, a mostly intermediate section that tops out just above the timberline and offers some of the easier intermediate runs on the mountain. Because of its exposure above the timberline, it can also be one of the coldest parts of the mountain, so you'd best head for it on sunny days or days when the wind is light. To the west of that easy cruising section is the High Alpine area (also above the timberline), with its tremendous variety of advanced and expert runs in the Hanging Valley Wall. Here you'll find steep, wide-open bowls and tree skiing in the slightly lower Hanging Valley Glades. When the light is flat or it's snowing, this is your best choice as long as you can manage the steeps; the lower portion turns into some easy-to-handle intermediate terrain.

The Big Burn and the wide-open intermediate and upper-intermediate boulevards, for which the resort is best known, crisscross the middle of Snowmass. On clear, sunny days this is generally the busiest part of the mountain, but on windy or snowy days visibility becomes a major problem, and you're better off heading to another area, such as Sam's Knob, which is about 1,200 feet lower and protected somewhat by the thick stands of trees. It's directly above the village, near the west end of the ridge, and has a collection of mostly advanced-intermediate runs, with a few long, winding beginner trails cutting a circuitous, gentle path down to the village. At the far west side is the Campground area, with some of the longest concentrated advanced-intermediate trails on the mountain. This area is usually one of the least crowded sections of Snowmass, and because of its lower elevation it tends to be the best choice on cold or windy days.

Each of the individual Snowmass areas is easily reached from the central base village. Early morning traffic tends to spread out quickly; the only notable traffic jam usually occurs at the Burlingame lift, which takes you up to the Sam's Knob lift. From the top of Sam's Knob you can ski down to the Big Burn lift or head down into the Campground area. To avoid this crush, you can go to the Alpine Springs or Naked Lady lifts (via the Wood Run chair from the lower village area) or take the Funnel chair up to the Elk Camp lift.

For snowboarders, Snowmass has a terrain park at Elk Camp as well as the longest half pipe in the country. Many of the gladed runs are ideal for snowboarders. Another nice thing about the mountain is that there aren't a lot of traverses between runs.

Novices

Absolute beginners or extremely timid novices will probably want to start out on Assay Hill, the easiest beginner slope at the resort, or Fanny Hill, a slightly longer but similarly easy green run. Both have their own lifts and are immediately above the village area, making the chairs easy to reach from the mall. This setup is also fairly unintimidating for beginners, as more advanced skiers don't join you on the chairs—a first-time experience that's often more frightening than going down the mountain.

When you're ready to tackle something a little longer, take the Funnel lift along the east side of the mountain and try a long, easy cruise on the wide and flat Funnel Bypass. You can also ride the Burlingame lift up the middle of the mountain to the Sam's Knob chair, which you can take to the top of Sam's Knob. As you get off the lift, turn left and head for the wide-open Max Park for an introduction to skiing bowls. Take note: This green run is a little steeper than those previously mentioned, and it can also become quite crowded with more-advanced skiers heading for the Knob's intermediate trails or those heading down to the Big Burn lift.

To avoid the crowds, don't take the chair to the summit; instead, begin from the top of the Burlingame lift, where you can move easily over to Lunchline, a bit of a catwalk; to Scooper, which is slightly steeper than Lunchline but much less crowded; and to Dawdler, for a long, winding run back to the village.

Intermediates

When you're ready to move up to gentle intermediates, your best bet is to head for the Elk Camp area on the eastern side of the resort. The mostly blue runs in this area are wide and well groomed and provide an excellent place to work on turns and enjoy gentle cruising. The cut of the runs is graceful and gradual, and if you continue past the bottom of the Elk Camp lift you can enjoy a long top-to-bottom intermediate cruise of more than 2 miles on smooth Adam's Avenue. If the weather isn't suitable for the exposed Elk Camp, head for the top of

Big Burn but keep in mind that the easiest runs from the top are those to the left (looking down); the runs get more difficult as you go to the right. The easiest way from the top is via Sneaky's (to the far left, looking down) or Mick's Gully, which, although it has a slight gully shape, doesn't have the steepness or walls usually found in similar gully runs. It has a steady, easy pitch, and like Sneaky's, brings you back to the green Max Park.

Experts

The best area for experts is the High Alpine; the fastest route is on the Wood Run and Alpine Springs chairs, then up the High Alpine double chair. If you feel like taking a long cruising run just to get the legs warmed up, turn right off the High Alpine chair and follow the narrow traverse (a little uphill pushing is required) that leads to Green Cabin. From the top, Green Cabin—which is usually groomed—drops to rolling, wide-open terrain, then narrows slightly as it cuts through the trees above Gwyn's High Alpine restaurant, then dips and rolls to the right before widening at a broad speed-control section. Make sure you turn right just below this and head back to the Alpine Springs chair; if you go left, it's a long, flat meander down to the village. On the next run head for Reiders, which starts out as a wide-open cruiser with the occasional tree patch, then turns bumpy. If you don't like the moguls, head to the side in the trees, where there's usually good powder. Another good, but short, cruiser is Showcase, which runs directly under the High Alpine chair. It's fairly tame at the top, but be care-

ful if you're carrying too much speed because the run drops off about midway down, when it becomes much steeper. The Edge—just to the right (looking down) of Showcase is another good combo run, with fast, groomed cruising up top, then a steeper mogul section—interspersed with clutches of trees—on the bottom half. All three of these runs take you to the bottom of the High Alpine chair, but if you drop any lower, you are in mostly blue territory back to the bottom of the Alice Springs lift.

For a spectacular steep, turn left off the High Alpine chair to Baby Ruth. When you feel sufficiently warmed up, head for the Hanging Valley Wall. Turn left off the High Alpine chair for a short traverse; then you'll have to take your skis off for a five-minute hike up to a control gate. From here you can turn right to the Headwall or left to Roberto's. Most regulars take Headwall because it usually has better snow thanks to better exposure, is protected from the prevailing winds, and generally draws lighter traffic. Many people end up taking Roberto's because it has the most obvious entrance. Roberto's is narrower and cut between high rock faces, and big bumps build up through the middle section. Below Roberto's and the Headwall, which converge in a fairly flat area, you have three choices. Stick to the left-hand boundary line, and you'll enter the Union area, which is usually not crowded. It's a pretty, gladed route, not too steep, and generally has good powder. Staying with the main trail on the flats will take you to the Wall, which is wide open and has the most vertical drop of any run on the mountain, but it also tends to be the most crowded. Another option is to head for the Ladder, on the right side of the flats, which is a narrower run and because of its northeast exposure tends to have better snow.

Another area where you can get your adrenaline fix is the Big Burn, which is served by the Big Burn and Sheer Bliss chairs. To the left (looking down) it's mostly intermediate territory, but to the right is a good selection of black runs. For bumps try West Face or Free Fall, and for good speed cruising try the steady, even pitch of KT Gully.

WHERE TO STAY

Virtually all the accommodations at Snowmass Village are condominiums, with most buildings dating from 1967, when the resort opened. Many have been renovated in recent years, but there remains a sameness about them. About 90% of the accommodations are ski-in/ski-out, so if slope-side convenience is your preference, it makes sense for you to stay at Snowmass. For one-stop booking, contact Snowmass central reservations (tel. 800/215–7669). See also Where to Stay in Aspen for alternatives.

Expensive

The Crestwood

These condos are comfortable, practically furnished with couches and plenty of chairs, and well designed for families and small groups. The units range in size from spacious studios to one-, two-, and three-bedroom units, each with a fireplace. The decor is a pleasant mix of wood and stucco, with wheat-color furnishings and broadloom carpeting. *400 Wood Rd.,*

Box 5460, Snowmass Village, 81615, tel. 970/923–2450 or 800/356–5949, fax 970/923–5018. 122 units. Facilities: heated outdoor pool, 2 Jacuzzis, sauna, exercise room, complimentary airport shuttle, laundry, ski storage. AE, D, DC, MC, V. $131–$999.

Silvertree Hotel

The only full-service ski-in/ski-out hotel at Snowmass is definitely a class act. Although the rooms aren't especially large, they are comfortable and beautifully decorated with oak furniture. About half have balconies facing the surrounding mountains or the mall. If you think you may need extra space, consider a suite, designed for four or more, with such luxurious appointments as extralarge bathrooms and mountain-facing balconies. There are also condos, from studio to five-bedroom in size, all with a kitchen, and some with a fireplace and a balcony. *100 Elbert La., Box 5009, Snowmass Village, 81615, tel. 970/923–3520 or 800/525–9402, fax 970/923–5192. 262 rooms, 15 suites, 200 units. Facilities: 4 restaurants, bar, lounge, 2 heated outdoor pools, 2 hot tubs, 2 saunas, health club, steam room, 24-hr desk service, shuttle, ski valet, ski shop, laundry, game room. AE, D, DC, MC, V. $115–$1,535.*

Snowmass Lodge & Club

This upscale lodge and villa complex is one of Snowmass's most complete facilities, with a selection of standard, premium, and deluxe rooms and one-, two-, and three-bedroom villas. Although it's not a ski-in/ski-out property, it is only about five minutes from the lifts by shuttle bus. The spacious, ultramodern lodge rooms include pine antiques and have a balcony overlooking the mountain or the golf course. The villas—better suited to families or small groups—are equally well appointed, with plush furniture and a fireplace. The lodge building is cozy, with a fireplace, plush couches, and hardwood floors. *0239 Snowmass Club Circle, Box G-2, 81615, tel. 970/ 923–5600 or 800/525–0710, fax 970/ 923–6944. 76 rooms, 54 villas. Facilities: restaurant, 2 snack bars, bar, health club, 3 outdoor pools (1 heated), 3 hot tubs (1 outdoor), saunas, steam room, 2 indoor tennis courts, weight room, aerobics gym, massage center, golf, cross-country center, 24-hr desk service, shuttle, ski concierge, ski storage, baby-sitting, laundry, dry cleaning. AE, D, DC, MC, V. $131–$415.*

Woodrun V Townhouses

These ultraluxurious town houses have a multilevel layout that provides lots of space, as well as some privacy. The complex is across Fanny Hill from the mall, so you can just click into your bindings and catch a lift up the mountain; in the evening you'll have only a five-minute walk to the Snowmass Mall. The units are exceptionally well furnished in a Southwestern motif and are remarkably complete, with luxury extras such as a hot tub, stone fireplace, private balcony, wet bar, multiple TVs, oversize master bathroom, and laundry facilities. There are two-bedroom units with various bed configurations. *Wood Rd., Box 5550, 81615, tel. 970/923–4350 or 800/525–9402, fax 970/923–5494. 3 units. Access to facilities at Silvertree Hotel (see above). AE, D, DC, MC, V. $305–$1,535.*

Moderate

Laurelwood

These studio-size condos, two levels above the Village Mall and a 20-yard walk from the slope, have a sensible layout that makes them a cost-efficient option for four people. It's not often that you find condo convenience in pint-size packages, but Laurelwood has put them together nicely without the added cost of multibedroom units. These are well-designed quarters with high ceilings, lots of light to give the illusion of space, and little extras such as a full kitchen, a fireplace, and a balcony with a view of the mountain or the valley. *Snowmass Resort, Box 5600, 81615, tel. 970/923–3110 or 800/ 356–7893, fax 970/923–5314. 52 units. Facilities: outdoor pool, hot tub, sauna, daily maid service, ski storage, laundry. AE, MC, V. $100–$290.*

Stonebridge Inn

The boxy, industrial exterior does little to reveal Stonebridge's true character: This mountain inn is an excellent hotel option in a village gone condo crazy. The inn's rooms and suites are not loaded with frills, but they're roomy and comfortable: Room decor is functional and homey and follows an alpine theme. Rooms are equipped with a coffeemaker and mini-refrigerator. *300 Carriage Way, Box 5008, 81615, tel. 970/923–2420 or 800/922–7242, fax 970/923–5889. 90 rooms, 5 suites. Facilities: restaurant, bar, lounge, heated outdoor pool, outdoor hot tub, sauna, 24-hr desk service, room service, complimentary airport shuttle, ski storage, laundry. AE, D, MC, V. $150–$965, including Continental breakfast.*

Top of the Village

These are good-size two-, three-, and four-bedroom condos tucked into the side of the hill just above the Village Mall. The trade-off for ski-in/ski-out convenience is the 450-yard trek up from the village. These condos appeal mostly to families who want to be close to the slopes yet far enough away from the commotion in the mall. The units are family-friendly—not designer decorated—and each has a fireplace and a private balcony. *855 Carriage Way, Box 5629, 81615, tel. 970/923–3673 or 800/525–4200, fax 970/923–4420. 86 units. Facilities: heated outdoor pool, Jacuzzi, exercise room, sauna, daily maid service, ski lockers, shuttle. No credit cards. $220–$825.*

Wildwood Lodge

If you prefer hotel accommodations to condos, this hotel on the Snowmass Village Shopping Plaza, 400 yards from the slopes, is a good choice because of the friendly staff. The contemporary, comfortable decor evokes a rustic Western-lodge feeling, and rooms have practical extras such as mini-refrigerators and coffeemakers. Many have a balcony overlooking the mountain. *40 Elbert La., Box 5037, 81615, tel. 970/923–3550 or 800/525–9402, fax 970/923–4844. 150 rooms. Facilities: restaurant, bar, hot tub, heated outdoor pool, sauna, health club, 24-hr desk service, shuttle, ski valet, ski storage, laundry. AE, D, DC, MC, V. $69–$249, including Continental breakfast.*

Inexpensive

Pokolodi Lodge

This friendly, no-frills motel-style lodge in the center of the Village Mall provides all of the basics at a basic price. Comfortable, clean rooms can accommodate four close friends or a small family. Units are furnished with a coffeemaker, mini-refrigerator, and TV. Newspapers are provided daily. *25 Daly La., Box 5640, 81615, tel. 970/923–4310 or 800/666–4556, fax 970/923–2819. 50 rooms. Facilities: outdoor hot tub, heated outdoor pool, 24-hr desk service, shuttle, ski storage, laundry. D, MC, V. $60–$188, including Continental breakfast.*

Snowmass Inn

This is one of the original properties at Snowmass and so commands a prime location in the middle of the Village Mall, a short stroll from the slopes. Guest rooms are spacious and comfortable, although slightly outdated and beginning to show signs of wear. Each unit has a queen-size bed and a queen-size sofa bed, plus basic creature comforts such as a refrigerator and coffeemaker. *67 Daly La., Box 5640, 81615, tel. 970/923–4202, fax 970/923–2819. 39 rooms. Facilities: outdoor pool, Jacuzzi, sauna, 24-hr desk service, shuttle, ski storage, laundry. MC, V. $65–$160.*

Tamarack Townhouses

There are only three buildings with six units each in two- or four-bedroom layouts in this small but well-designed complex of town houses. All units have multiple bathrooms and fireplaces. Each is decorated according to the owner's taste. Tamarack is just a few minutes' walk from the main Snowmass Village area and an even shorter distance from Lift 18. *135 Carriage Way, Box 5550, 81615, tel. 970/923–2420 or 800/525–9402.*

18 units. *Facilities: outdoor pool, Jacuzzi, sauna, ski storage. AE, D, DC, MC, V. $110–$490.*

The Willows

This is another comfortable but not deluxe group of town houses a short walk from the village mall. The four dark-wood structures are built like steps up the side of the hill. Available in studio and two-bedroom sizes, units are individually owned and decorated. Some have undergone a recent face-lift, but others are a bit dated. In general, all are well maintained and well equipped, with a fireplace, a laundry room, and a full-size kitchen. *Village Mall, Box 5550, 81615, tel. 970/923–4350 or 800/525–9402. 280 units. AE, D, DC, MC, V. $75–$465.*

WHERE TO EAT

You have the option of taking the 20-minute drive or shuttle bus to Aspen (*see* Where to Eat *in* Aspen), but don't overlook the expanding selection of restaurants in Snowmass.

On the Mountain

Gwyn's High Alpine Restaurant

Both cafeteria-style and full-service breakfast and lunch are offered here. If you go the cafeteria route, choose from a menu of veggie burgers and other sandwiches, fajitas, salads, and excellent soups. In the sit-down area you can order entrées such as grilled salmon and a variety of pastas. To be sure of a seat, make reservations for 11:30 AM; seating at other times is first-come, first-served. *Center of mountain, top of Alpine Springs and Naked Lady lifts, tel. 970/923–5188. AE, MC, V.*

Ullrhof

The most popular restaurant on the mountain has long lines, but the cafeteria setup moves things along. In addition to burgers, soups, stews, chili, and sandwiches, some healthier salads have been added to the menu. On sunny days the deck sees a lot of action. *Snowmass Mountain, base of Big Burn lift, tel. 970/923–5143. Reservations not accepted. AE, MC, V.*

Expensive

La Boheme

Snowmass's flagship restaurant consists of two rooms separated by a large bar; the understated decor emphasizes calm pastel tones, modern beech furnishings, plenty of windows, and Impressionist paintings. Nightly live music sets the tone for haute French cuisine hallmarked by subtle spices and fresh herbs. Try roast pheasant with raspberry *poivrade* (peppercorn sauce with peppers and port); other favorites are striped bass baked in parchment, smoked Norwegian salmon fillet, and a mixed grill of red deer and caribou. When you make your reservation, ask for a table next to the picture window that overlooks the village. *315 Gateway Bldg., upper level of mall, tel. 970/923–6804. AE, DC, MC, V.*

Cowboys Restaurant & Bar

Don't let the rustic ranch-house decor and Western memorabilia fool you. This is a fine-dining spot with a lineup of Southwestern-style entrées that lean heavily toward fresh game. Consider the Muscovy duck crepe with spinach and buffalo mozzarella or perhaps the tournedos with green peppercorn sauce and sweet-potato straw. Also commanding high praise are the prime Colorado beef and fresh river fish. After dinner the cowboy atmosphere continues with live country-and-western entertainment and dancing. *78 Elbert La., Silvertree Complex, tel. 970/923–5249. AE, MC, V.*

Krabloonik

Owner Dan MacEachen has a penchant for dogsled racing and Krabloonik (Eskimo for "big eyebrows," the name of Dan's first lead dog) helps subsidize his expensive hobby. The restaurant is in a rustic log cabin where a woodstove provides the only heat and light comes via propane lanterns. The menu is primarily game, and although some domestic meat and poultry dishes are available for the timid, you'll do best if you stay on the wilder side. Moose loin, mesquite-grilled caribou, wild boar, and roasted breast of pheasant lead the list of favorites. No matter what you choose as an entrée, order wild-mushroom soup as an appetizer. *4250 Divide Rd., tel. 970/923–3953. Reserve 2 wks in advance for dogsled ride. MC, V.*

Moderate

Brothers' Grille

Chef Dave Brillhart, who oversees the kitchen of this American grill, proudly boasts his usual first-place position in the Snowmass Village Chili Shoot-Out, and his white-bean chicken chili also hits the spot on a cold day. Other selections are blackened prime rib sandwich and a variety of burgers, salads, and pastas. *100 Fall La., Silvertree Hotel, tel. 970/923–3520. AE, D, DC, MC, V.*

La Piñata

For Mexican or traditional Southwestern fare this restaurant, with its casual, convivial atmosphere and pleasant, subdued decor (light brick and wood walls offset by brightly colored wall hangings), is a good choice. The menu includes such oddities as ahi fajitas marinated in orange tarragon and served with melon salsa, smoked seafood enchiladas, and grilled pork crown glazed with Southwestern cranberry chutney. *65 Daly La., lower level of mall, tel. 970/923–2153. Reservations essential for 6 or more. AE, MC, V.*

Il Poggio

This slick Italian eatery eschews traditional checkered tablecloths and Chianti-bottle candleholders for marble-and-granite minimalism. Excellent pasta dishes are served, including capellini with shrimp and prosciutto, ravioli with herbed ricotta, and fettuccine with wild mushrooms and sun-dried tomatoes. Specialty pizzas come with an eclectic variety of toppings. *54 Elbert La., Snowmass Mall, tel. 970/923–4292. MC, V.*

Sage Restaurant

The bistro food served here ranges from appetizers and pizzas to salads and sandwiches. Among the favorites are oven-roasted chicken with roasted garlic and mashed potatoes and lightly smoked pan-roasted brook trout with creamed corn. Decor is comfortably casual, with sandstone-color brick complimented by blond-wood trim and Southwestern art and wall hangings. *Snowmass Lodge & Club, 0239 Snowmass Circle, 81615, tel. 970/923–0923. AE, D, DC, MC, V.*

StoneBridge Restaurant

In the Stonebridge Inn, just a stone's throw from the mall, kick back to live bluegrass music on Saturday evenings around the stone fireplace in the bar. The upstairs dining room, done in rustic Southwestern decor with log chairs, has views from every vantage point. The menu offers something for everyone, from chicken potpie to pepper-crusted elk medallions to ruby red Rocky Mountain trout. *300 Carriage Way, tel. 970/923–2420. AE, D, DC, MC, V.*

Wildcat Cafe

This cheerful, lively spot has a bright atmosphere complimented by stylish, modern furnishings, colorful table settings, and lots of windows with views over the mountain. Worthwhile dishes here include eggs Benedict, grilled salmon, steak, and Far East chicken. There's also a children's menu. Outdoor seating is available. *Snowmass Center, tel. 970/923–5990. MC, V.*

Inexpensive

Snowmass Pizza

For a fast, cheap, good pie—the best on the mountain—stop here. You can also get basic fast foods such as tacos, soups, chili, hot dogs, and heroes. Make your choice at the walk-up window, then grab a picnic table outside—or call for delivery. *35 Village Sq., Snowmass Mall, tel. 970/923–5711. Reservations not accepted. No credit cards.*

The Stewpot

There's a lot more than stew on the menu here, but stick to the namesake dish—a hearty bowl served with homemade bread. Beef and chicken are the standard ingredients, but there's also a stew of the day that sometimes includes other meats. Daily soup specials—tomato cheddar, chicken vegetable barley—and a selection of sandwiches are also offered. The two-story restaurant has a casual atmosphere enlivened by windows overlooking the mall and by the photography of local artists that hangs on the walls. *62 Snowmass Village Mall, tel. 970/923–2263. Reservations essential for 6 or more. MC, V.*

Best Bets for Breakfast

Paradise Bakery

Stop here on your way to the slopes for a great selection of fresh-baked breads, muffins, cinnamon rolls, stuffed croissants, and yogurt. Paradise also has the best coffee on the mountain: Try the cappuccino, espresso, or latte. *100 Elbert La., Silvertree Plaza, tel. 970/923–4712. No credit cards.*

NIGHTLIFE AND ENTERTAINMENT

Snowmass is a quiet spot after dark. The après-ski scene cooks for a while, but when it cools down, Aspen is the place for action.

Après-Ski

The Conservatory

Live music and impromptu dancing draw the thirty-something crowd in this otherwise family-oriented resort. The scene at the Conservatory isn't as crazy as in other major après-ski spots, so you can feel comfortable without feeling old. *100 Elbert La., Silvertree Hotel, tel. 970/923–3520. AE, D, DC, MC, V.*

The Timbermill

This place rocks with nonstop dancing and happy-hour prices. From the deck to the cavernous bar (with live music), the Timbermill is always packed, usually with an under-30 crowd. *105 Village Sq., Timbermill Bldg., tel. 970/923–4774. AE, D, DC, MC, V.*

Loud and Lively/Dancing

Cowboy's

In this down-home place you can stomp and hop to the hottest C&W sounds, performed live. The dance floor really heats up with timid two-steppers and wild whirlers wearing Stetson hats and boots. *78 Elbert La., Silvertree Plaza, tel. 970/923–5249. AE, MC, V.*

The Tower

Magicians-cum-bartenders bring magic to this cheerful spot. Local and imported talent performs comedy routines regularly for an audience filled with people of all ages. *45 Village Sq., Snowmass Village Mall, tel. 970/923–4650. AE, DC, MC, V.*

More Mellow

La Boheme

The live jazz in this low-key spot attracts couples and parents who have just tucked the kids into bed. *315 Gateway Bldg., upper level of mall, tel. 970/923–6804. AE, DC, MC, V.*

Mountain Dragon

This usually quiet spot is the hangout of choice for many of the resort's ski instructors. Sometimes there's live entertainment, but the place is most often filled with small talk. *22 Elbert La., Village Mall, tel. 970/923–3576. AE, MC, V.*

STEAMBOAT SKI RESORT

STEAMBOAT SKI RESORT

2305 Mt. Werner Circle
Steamboat Springs, CO 80487
Tel. 970/879–6111 or
800/922–2722

STATISTICALLY SPEAKING

Base elevation: 6,900 feet

Summit elevation: 10,568 feet

Vertical drop: 3,668 feet

Skiable terrain: 2,500 acres

Number of trails: 107

Longest run: 3 miles

Lifts and capacity: 1 gondola, 3 express quads, 1 quad, 6 triples, 6 doubles, 1 ski-school chair, 3 surface lifts; capacity 30,581 skiers per hour

Daily lift ticket: $41 weekdays, $46 weekends

Average annual snowfall: 300 inches

Number of skiing days 1995–96: 142

Snowmaking: 375 acres; 15%

Terrain mix: N 15%, I 54%, E 31%

Cross-country skiing: 30 kilometers

Snowboarding: yes

In the northwest corner of Colorado, where the Continental Divide veers east, merging with Rabbit Ears Pass, there's the Yampa River Valley. Here, ruggedly timbered slopes of the Park Range, to the east, and the Elkhead Range, to the north, yield to the scattered sagebrush and grassy meadows of the largest river valley in this part of the state.

Once a summer hunting ground for the wandering Ute tribe, the region is blessed with hundreds of thermal hot springs. Among the towns that established themselves around these waters was Steamboat Springs, a ranching community on the banks of the Yampa River. Besides the ranchers from Utah, Texas, and Wyoming who raised cattle and horses, there were Norwegian immigrants who brought with them their masonry and ski-jumping skills and were ultimately responsible for the onset of the ski industry in this part of the state. These Scandinavians blazed ski trails as a means of delivering the mail and built ski jumps to entertain themselves in their spare time, much as they had done at home. In particular, a young Norwegian, Carl Howelsen, already a champion jumper in his home country when he arrived in Steamboat in 1912, dazzled everyone with his jumping exploits and went on to introduce local residents to ski jumping and cross-country racing. In 1914 he established the Winter Carnival and the first jumping competitions. Skiing continued to be a big part of the community through the next five decades, as numerous national championships were staged, and skiing became part of the curriculum in local schools. Between 1950 and the mid-1960s, 74 Steamboat skiers competed in Junior National teams, and 11 made the National and Olympic teams. Since the early days Steamboat has produced more than 35 Olympic athletes.

In 1962 the resort that was to become Steamboat's centerpiece was opened on nearby Storm Mountain by a group of local businesspeople led by Jim Temple, son of an early ranching family. The mountain was renamed Mt. Werner in 1964 in honor of Wallace "Buddy" Werner, who began skiing in Steamboat at age two and during the '50s and '60s led America's Olympic challenge to European skiers. Buddy was killed in an avalanche in Switzerland that same year,

USEFUL NUMBERS

Area code: 970

Children's services: day care, tel. 970/879-6111, ext. 218

Snow phone: tel. 970/879-7300

Police: tel. 970/879-1144

Routt County Search and Rescue: tel. 970/879-1090

Medical center: Routt Memorial Hospital, tel. 970/879-1322

Resort association: tel. 970/879-0880

Steamboat Central Reservations: tel. 800/525-2628

Road conditions: tel. 970/639-1234

Towing: A-Towing, tel. 970/879-1951

FIVE-STAR FAVORITES

Best run for vertical: Dropout

Best run overall: Shadows

Best bar/nightclub: Heavenly Daze Brewery

Best hotel: Torian Plum

Best restaurant: La Montana

but his legacy can be seen everywhere at today's Steamboat resort.

When you think of modern-day Steamboat, two images come to mind: One is a leather-faced cowboy in chaps and a Stetson hat astride a horse galloping in knee-deep snow, and the other is light champagne-color powder star-bursting in a delicate spray against a cobalt blue sky as skiers cut first tracks in the morning sun. Both images are authentic, which is one reason for Steamboat's enduring popularity as both a ski destination and a resort town.

Steamboat Springs has retained some of its treasures from the Old West, including its cow-town facade and locals who are proud to be descendants of some of the original ranchers who settled here. The streets, lined with hotels, restaurants, and shops, are extrawide, a legacy from the days when ranchers pushed thousands of head of cattle through town en route to the rail yards on the Wyoming border.

Although one complements the other in a comfortable way that is only matched by, say, Crested Butte or Telluride, the resort and the town are self-contained entities, and you can be comfortable staying in either place. In town, small hotels, lodges, and inns offer a moderately priced alternative to the posh resort, with its cluster of classy condos and stylish hotels. Perhaps the primary difference between staying in town and lodging in the ski village is that life is so convenient at the latter. If you stay there, expect instant access to the lifts; a built-in village plaza with shops, restaurants, and watering holes; and generally larger, more luxurious accommodations. Also expect resort accommodations to be significantly more expensive. The resort tends to be a bit quieter at night than town, a trait that families with children, or couples looking for a private, romantic getaway find appealing. Unfortunately, the resort village is suffering from development blight as a result of its increasing popularity.

In town, however, you can still find European-style lodgings—typically small, owner-operated inns with fewer than 75 rooms. You'll have to shuttle to and from the mountain, but the regular service can whisk you back and forth in about 10 minutes. The town offers varied architecture and a slightly rambunctious nightlife. Lincoln Avenue is the strip to stroll: a mile-long stretch of restaurants, bars, boutiques, and other diversions housed in a mix of Victorian, cowboy-funk, and ski-town chic buildings.

There's an earthy realism to the town, even as it succumbs to the demands of tourists; real ranchers still stroll the town's sidewalks, and there's an earnest friendliness between cowboys and skiers that goes right to the heart of Steamboat's origins.

HOW TO GET THERE

By Plane
There are connecting flights from **Denver International Airport** (tel. 303/342–2000; see Getting to Colorado Resorts, above) via Continental Express Maverick Airways (tel. 800/435–9628) into **Steamboat Springs Airport** (5 miles from the resort) and United Express (tel. 800/241–6522) into the **Yampa Valley Regional Airport** (tel. 970/276–3669), at Hayden, 22 miles from the resort.

By Shuttle
Steamboat Express (tel. 800/525–6050; $60 one-way) has shuttle service that leaves twice daily from Denver International Airport for Steamboat. From either Yampa Valley Regional Airport or Steamboat Springs Airport, the following shuttle services are available: **Alpine Luxury Limo** (tel. 970/879–2800), **Steamboat Taxi** (tel. 970/879–3335), and **Steamboat Express** (tel. 970/879–3400). **Steamboat Central Reservations** (tel. 800/922–2722) can help make car-rental

reservations and other ground transportation arrangements.

By Car
Steamboat Springs is 157 miles, or a three-hour drive, northwest of Denver. From Denver International Airport, take Pena Boulevard for 15 miles to I–70W. Once you're through the Eisenhower Tunnel, take the Silverthorne exit onto Route 9 north to Kremmling, then take U.S. 40 west over Rabbit Ears Pass and on to Steamboat Springs.

For car rentals from Denver International Airport, see Getting to Colorado Resorts, above. Car-rental companies available at Yampa Valley Regional Airport and Steamboat Springs Airport are **Budget, Hertz, and National.**

By Bus
Greyhound Lines (tel. 800/231–2222) offers bus service from Denver twice daily.

GETTING AROUND
A car is not necessary at Steamboat because the town and the resort are only 3 miles apart, and most major properties provide a free shuttle between the resort and the town. There's also a free town shuttle. Even if you miss the shuttle bus, there are a number of taxi services that will do the run for about $10. The Steamboat Springs Transit shuttle (tel. 970/879–5585) is your best way, though; it's fast (about 10 minutes from resort to town), convenient (roughly every 20 minutes with stops along the route), and cheap (50¢ each way). If you must take a taxi, the following are available: **Steamboat Taxi** (tel.

970/879–3335) and **Alpine Taxi** (tel. 970/879–2800 or 800/343–7433).

THE SKIING

The four peaks that make up Steamboat Resort provide a big, broad-faced mountain ridge that sucks in the ultralight snow dropped from storms as they race across the desert lands to the west. When the powder lies deep and untouched, the forested flanks of the four peaks provide nature's most demanding slalom course. For sheer lump-in-your-throat thrills there's nothing quite like dancing through thigh-deep powder in a grove of aspens.

For the most part, though, Steamboat's 2,500 acres are a near-perfect cruising playground for intermediates and upper intermediates. Of course, there's considerable novice terrain, and the experts will find their share of thrills, but for the majority of skiers this is the place to let loose, try some ego cruising, then back off into your comfort zone. The lack of congestion is a nice feature here. You won't find too many people skiing in your way; Steamboat doesn't draw a huge day-skier crowd, and the relatively small number of destination skiers seldom makes a dent in the resort's uphill capacity, so lineups are rare except for the early morning traffic on the Silver Bullet gondola, which you can avoid by taking the Christie lifts to the Thunderhead/Arrowhead combo and then the Burgess Creek chair, which will give you access to the Sundown Express and the summit of Sunshine Peak.

The skiing on Mt. Werner's four peaks is well divided into abilities, so everyone can ski at his/her own level but won't get hopelessly separated from the gang. The key here is the Thunderhead Peak area, which serves as a midmountain rendezvous accessible to skiers of all abilities. It's an excellent place for lunch, with its three restaurants, and lifts and trails from all parts of the resort converge here. Below Thunderhead are mostly novice and easy intermediate trails, and above that (on Mt. Werner, Storm Peak, and Sunshine Peak) are mostly intermediate and expert trails.

Storm Peak, at 10,372 feet, is where most of the upper-intermediate and advanced skiers go for steep powder fields and the densely packed glades. From this point you can also ski down the backside into the Morningside Park area, which is a mix of intermediate and moderately expert slopes, and more important, give you access to the top of Mt. Werner and its black-diamond runs, which are a mix of steep glades, couloirs, and narrow chutes.

Sunshine Peak, at 10,385 feet, is mostly intermediate cruising with a good variety of short, steep pitches and slightly more open glades, and long, smooth, wide-open cruisers. At the very bottom of the resort is the Christie Peak area, with its collection of beginner novice slopes served by the Christie chairs.

Intermediates and up should consider skiing the mountain the way the locals do, by following the sun. Start at the Morningside Park area in the early morning, tackle Mt. Werner closer to noon (and stop for lunch at the Four Points Hut midway down Storm Peak), and then in the afternoon move over to the aptly named

One O'Clock, Two O'Clock, and Three O'Clock runs, on Sunshine Peak.

Snowboarders have access to the entire mountain and to all lifts. There's also a terrain park on the lower part of Storm Peak, just above Thunderhead.

Novices

For absolute beginners or even second-timers, there are four lifts serving the gentlest terrain on the mountain. These start just to the left of the gondola base and take you up increasing distances, which you can opt for as you gain confidence. The shortest, the Preview, is a free lift so beginners can get their taste of terror before buying a pass. The South Face, Headwall, and Pony lifts let you work your way down a smooth, wide, slow-skiing zone until you're ready to move on to more challenging runs. When you want to ski some longer distances, head for the Christie II and III lifts and play around on some lengthier, winding trails called Boulevard, Giggle Gulch, and Yoo Hoo. Your next step up would be on the Silver Bullet gondola to Thunderhead Peak, the point on the mountain from which you can reach all other peaks.

Thunderhead is a good spot for lunch and a convenient place for novices to meet up with their more advanced skiing friends. You can do a little safe exploring from Thunderhead: Turn left off the gondola and take Why Not to So What, a green/blue combo that will test but not terrify you. To the right off the gondola, there's Spur Run, which will take you down to the chairs that serve Sunshine Peak. Head up here if you feel like moving things up a notch and try-ing a long blue cruising run such as Tomahawk.

Intermediates

Although more than 50% of Steamboat's runs are designated intermediate, a good steady blue skier will quickly graduate to some of the mountain's black runs. It's the snow that will test your mettle with its dry, light consistency, which helps put a bite in your edge, a spring in your step, and a brake on the vertical. From the base area take the Silver Bullet gondola to Thunderhead, then ski down Huffman to the Sundown Express lift, which will take you to the top of Sunshine Peak. Head right as you get off the chair for some sweet cruising runs that wind around the trees. If you stay high on the ridge and take Tomahawk, you'll be able to pick from a half-dozen short but steep straight shots through the trees and shoot down to either Flintlock or Quick Draw. Either of these will bring you out to the bottom of the Sunshine chair, which you can take back up to the Sunshine Peak; here you'll find a mixture of good blue cruising runs to the right and steeper, more direct blacks to the left. For nonstop giant-slalom cruising, in the Sunshine Peak area, try High Noon, Flintlock, or Quickdraw for a few runs.

By riding the Storm Peak Express, you get a chance to ski the Upper Storm Peak snowfields—steep, wide bowl-like areas that are sprinkled with stands of aspens and firs. It's up-tempo intermediate skiing best done after a fresh overnight snowfall. Below the snowfields are a trio of serious, narrow, mogul-studded black runs—Twister, Nelson's Run, and Hurricane—that you may want to avoid. Instead, opt for Sunset or Rainbow, running under the Burgess Creek chair and down to the bottom of the Storm Peak Express.

Experts

If you think you have the right stuff, then there's some stuff here to keep you honest. The trails may not be as tough and unrelenting as some you'll find at Crested Butte or Jackson Hole, but when the snows run deep and the moguls grow steep, all but the most manic group of renegade extreme skiers will find that edge on the wild side. Ride Silver Bullet gondola, and then take a quick warm-up scoot down Rudi's Run to Ego to catch the Storm Peak Express. The Storm Peak snowfield is high-speed yahoo cruising around the trees, especially after a good snow; when coupled with one of the three drop-off trails—Nelson's Run, Twister, or Hurricane—either one will send your excitement meter into the red zone.

For a dance in the steep and snow-packed glades that are among the finest in Colorado, slide to the right as you get off Storm Peak Express down to the heavily treed flank of Sunshine Peak. Pine, fir, and aspen are more densely packed here than a Manhattan parking lot. Although there are only three or four officially designated runs, your particular route down may be more a result of survival tactics than topography. Closet and Shadows are the steepest and densest trails; there are also some steep chutes, which are called Three O'Clock, Two O'Clock and One O'Clock. In between Two and Three is Twilight, a run that the truly deranged use as their own treed slalom run. This is not a place for the tree-timid.

The upper runs off Mt. Werner are where you'll find the steepest, snowiest, and in some cases, the best glade runs on the mountain. To access the top of Werner (which until recently was only available to those willing to hike a little), take the runs down Morningside, reached from either the top of the Sundown, Storm Peak, or Bar-UE lifts, then come back up the Morningside lift to the summit of Mt. Werner. Try Chutes 1, 2, 3, or the Ridge, and Crow Track—which will shunt and bump you down to the wider Flying Z snowfield with its tree clusters, then down into the high-speed Dropout. This route follows the northern perimeter of the resort, and traffic is usually light. If you do find a lot of skiers on the Storm Express, stop at the bottom of the Flying Z, where it meets the Bar UE chair, and take it back up to the top.

WHERE TO STAY

Most of the accommodations at the resort are condos, with precious few smaller hotels or lodges, especially if you want to stay on the mountain. The old town of Steamboat is only a 10-minute shuttle bus ride away, and it has a good selection of moderately priced traditional ski-country-style accommodations. Although condos are run by different condo companies, all lodging (even those in town) can be booked through Steamboat Central Reservations (Box 774728, Steamboat Springs 80477, tel. 970/879–0740 or 800/922–2722).

Expensive

Bear Claw Condominiums

These slope-side brick-and-wood condos with red-iron balconies and great views of the mountain are ski-in/ski-out accommodations. The units range in size from studios to four bedrooms, each decorated in earth tones, with woodwork and the occasional Western collectible. Studios are relatively spacious, and the four-bedroom unit (with a loft) is so huge that 10 people could stay here without tripping over each other. Each unit has a balcony, a fireplace, a full kitchen with high-tech appliances, and a TV/VCR. *2420 Ski Trail La., Steamboat Springs 80487, tel. 970/879–6100 or 800/232–7252, fax 970/879–8306. 67 units. Facilities: pool, sauna, health spa, game room, laundry, housekeeping. AE, MC, V. $115–$1,205.*

Dulany Condominiums

Brick fireplaces, light-wood cabinetry, polished tiles, and Tiffany-style lamps give these two- and three-bedroom wood-and-stucco condos a warmer touch than any other accommodation in Steamboat. All units have complete kitchen facilities with upscale appliances, a washer-dryer, and a balcony. Although there's lots of space in all the units, the curl-up-in-front-of-the-fire ambience is not sacrificed. Best of all, the condos are just 50 yards from the gondola. *Steamboat Resorts, Box 2995, Steamboat Springs 80477, tel. 970/879–6007 or 800/525–5502, fax 970/879–2353. 24 units. Facilities: outdoor hot tub. AE, MC, V. $205–$755.*

Sheraton Steamboat Hotel and Conference Center

This is not the prettiest building at the resort, but it is a full-service hotel with dependable Sheraton service and amenities. It's also a ski-in/ski-out property, just steps from the gondola right in the heart of Ski Time Square. There is a combination of standard hotel rooms plus some larger suites, and an adjacent building has some additional moderately priced apartment units. It also has major conference facilities that attract large groups. *2200 Village Inn Ct., Box 774808, Steamboat Springs 80477, tel. 970/879–2220 or 800/848–8878, fax 970/879–7322. 273 rooms, 3 suites, 12 units, 16 apartments. Facilities: 2 restaurants, 2 lounges, heated outdoor pool, 2 hot tubs, sauna. AE, D, DC, MC, V. $99–$799.*

Waterford Townhomes

These rustically designed dark brown wooden town houses have timber-beamed ceilings, a massive stone fireplace, a separate dining area that seats 10, and a kitchen large enough to whip up a meal for every trail hand in the valley. All the units are large, with three or four bedrooms and are suitable for families or groups who like their creature comforts and lots of room. Other touches include a washer-dryer, a private hot tub, and a sauna. Each house also has a two-car garage, although you won't need it to drive to the gondola, just 400 yards away. *Steamboat Resorts, Box 2015, 2025 Walton Creek Rd., Steamboat Springs 80477, tel. 970/879–7000 or 800/525–5502, fax 970/879–7263. 28 units. Facilities: heated outdoor pool. AE, MC, V. $185–$645.*

Moderate

Ptarmigan Inn

Steamboat should have a few more places like the Ptarmigan, a small tan-stucco European-style lodge with ski-in/ski-out access to the lifts. The emphasis at this Best Western property is on hotel-style service without sacrificing personalized pampering. The spacious, comfortable rooms come with queen- or king-size beds; most have a balcony and a refrigerator. This is a friendly and intimate spot that's good for couples and families. *2304 Après Ski Way, Box 773240, Steamboat Springs 80477, tel. 970/879–1730 or 800/538–7519, fax 970/879–6044. 77 rooms. Facilities: restaurant, lounge, heated outdoor pool, hot tub, sauna. AE, D, DC, MC, V. $99–$225.*

Ranch at Steamboat

These two-, three-, and four-bedroom town houses are 1½ miles from the slopes (a complimentary shuttle gets you there), and for that minor inconvenience you get one of the best deals in full-size accommodations found at the resort. The ranch-style timber-and-stone town houses are deluxe if not designer and perfect for families who want to be in a quiet location. Each unit is spacious, with a balcony overlooking the mountains and a private bathroom for each bedroom. There's a full-size kitchen plus an electric barbecue on the balcony, a fireplace, and a washer-dryer. *1 Ranch Rd., Steamboat Springs, 80487, tel. 970/879–3000 or 800/525–2002, fax 970/879–5409. 88 units. Facilities: heated outdoor pool, 2 hot tubs, sauna, housekeeping. AE, MC, V. $120–$660.*

Torian Plum

One of my favorite properties at the resort, the Torian Plum is opposite the gondola, with easy ski-in/ski-out access, and the full-size lobby and 24-hour service make it feel more like a hotel than a condo complex. There are 47 units, ranging in size from one to three bedrooms, and all come with well-equipped kitchens. They are well decorated and, more importantly, well maintained—with modern furnishings, imaginative decorations, and pine trim and cabinetry. Each unit also has a fireplace, a whirlpool bath, a balcony, a washer-dryer, a TV, and a VCR. *1855 Ski Time Square Dr., Steamboat Springs 80487, tel. 970/897–8811 or 800/228–2458, fax 970/879–5381. 47 units. Facilities: outdoor pool, sauna, ski storage, daily housekeeping, laundry, underground parking, concierge. AE, MC, V. $265–$585.*

Trappeur's Crossing

This ranch-style wooden condo complex with cathedral windows has well-designed units that can accommodate the extra bodies who sometimes tag along with groups or families. The one-bedroom unit (750 square feet), for instance, has one queen-size bed in the main bedroom, a second in a small den, a third in a small loft, and a full-size sofa bed in the living room. The larger units are similarly laid out, with up to four bedrooms that can easily sleep 10. There are full kitchen facilities, a fireplace, a balcony, and a TV/VCR in all units. The only drawback here is the five- to seven-minute two-block walk to the gondola. *1855 Ski Time Square Dr., Steamboat Springs 80487, tel. 970/879–8811 or 800/228–2458, fax 970/*

879–5381. *34 units. Facilities: indoor-outdoor pool, 2 hot tubs, sauna, laundry. AE, MC, V. $145–$695.*

Inexpensive

Harbor Hotel

One of the oldest hotels in Steamboat, the cream-color stucco-and-brick Harbor is bedecked with English antique furnishings, dark woods, and stonework. In addition to the original section, there's a newer, less baroque annex, as well as condos. All offer that Euro-lodge ambience. Whether you choose a room, a suite, or a condo, these are among the best deals in town. *703 Lincoln Ave., Box 774109, Steamboat Springs 80477, tel. 970/879–1522 or 800/543–8888, fax 970/879–1737. 86 rooms, 3 suites, 24 units. Facilities: Jacuzzi, sauna, steam room. AE, D, DC, MC, V. $60–$200.*

Inn at Steamboat

This pale-yellow-and-blue inn, larger than average, is a delightful spot that retains a cozy, home-style feeling. The large rooms are decorated in earth tones, and most have a great view of either the ski mountain or the surrounding Yampa Valley. The great stone fireplace in the lobby warms comfortable couches. *3070 Columbine Dr., Box 775084, Steamboat Springs 80477, tel. 970/879–2600 or 800/872–2601. 32 rooms. Facilities: heated outdoor pool, bar. AE, D, MC, V. $69–$139, including Continental breakfast.*

Rabbit Ears Motel

As motels go, this dark-wood structure with a flat roof is clean, comfortable, and affordable, in addition to being in the center of old Steamboat and just across the road from the community-run hot springs. Some rooms are oversize, and most have two double or queen-size beds. There are also suites with lovely riverfront views. Rabbit Ears is a friendly, family-run operation with such in-room extras as coffeemakers, refrigerators, and microwaves. *201 Lincoln Ave., Box 573, Steamboat Springs 80477, tel. 970/879–1150 or 800/828–7702, fax 970/870–0483. 32 rooms, 33 suites. AE, D, DC, MC, V. $79–$109, including Continental breakfast.*

Steamboat Bed and Breakfast

This is a pretty little tin-roofed colonial-style house set in the middle of Steamboat Springs's historic section. Its rooms are all individually decorated and have private baths. There is also a TV with VCR in the conservatory room. Coffee and tea are served throughout the day. *442 Pine St., Steamboat Springs 80477, tel. and fax 970/879–5724. 7 rooms. Facilities: Jacuzzi. AE, D, MC, V. $105–$125, including full breakfast.*

WHERE TO EAT

Combined, the resort area and the town of Steamboat have a large and varied selection of restaurants, cafés, and bars, and as there are only 3 miles between mountain and town, it's easy to try many no matter where you are staying.

On the Mountain

Hazie's

Delicious sit-down lunch fare is served in an elegant, uncrowded two-level dining room that offers a spectacular view of the mountain. Expect a great lineup of light-bite salads, such as grilled chicken Caesar or vegetarian pasta, plus a selection of monstrous sandwiches and assorted entrées, including Hazie's own crab cakes. *Top of Silver Bullet gondola, tel. 970/879–6111, ext. 465. Reservations essential. AE, D, DC, MC, V.*

Ragnars

The look is Norwegian with cream-color and flowered walls and antique ski photos. You get big portions of Scandinavian specialties among other fare. Try the *fiske suppe* (fish soup) for starters and the chicken breast Lillehammer over linguine with morels, chanterelles, scallions, garlic, tomatoes, and green beans. *Rendezvous Saddle, halfway down High Noon run, tel. 970/879–6111, ext. 465. Reservations essential. D, DC, MC, V.*

Expensive

Hazie's

Named for a woman who moved to Steamboat so her children could ski, this beautiful mountaintop restaurant offers a view that takes in the entire Yampa Valley with its twinkling lights and endless skies. The menu is Continental, the atmosphere is romantic but comfortable, and the mood is mountain high. There is a four-course daily special ($49); other entrées are a mix of fish such as salmon with roasted bell pepper sauce, game, including charbroiled venison with lingonberry sauce, and meat featuring chateaubriand with béarnaise sauce and rack of Colorado lamb. Diners can also enjoy live piano music nightly. *Top of Silver Bullet gondola, tel. 970/879–6111, ext. 465. Reservations essential. AE, D, DC, MC, V.*

L'apogée

This is an intimate, candlelighted French restaurant filled with wildlife art and stained glass. Chef Richard Billingham changes the menu often to keep things interesting and fresh and to be able to use seasonal ingredients. The focus is on game such as medallions of Texas Nilgai antelope and seafood such as Chesapeake Bay softshell crabs when they're in season, Beluga caviar from the Caspian Sea, and fresh ahi. There are also Rocky Mountain specialties such as elk and buffalo. Regardless of what specials come out of the kitchen, you can count on fine dining, great service, and choosing from one of the largest wine cellars in town. *911 Lincoln Ave., tel. 970/879–1919. Reservations essential. AE, MC, V.*

Mattie Silks

Mattie Silks made a reputation for herself as one of Denver's most colorful turn-of-the-century madams, and her namesake restaurant is keeping her name and style alive some seven decades after she passed from the scene. The interior is ornate, with velvet curtains and decorative lamps, and is perfectly matched to the fine dining found here. It's a Continental menu with some interesting variations and some traditional dishes. For your entrée consider the linguine paella, a twist using pasta instead of rice on the traditional Spanish dish of fresh shrimp, calamari, mussels, and clams. If you prefer meat, try the filet mignon prepared with a Gorgonzola cheese crust or the Jamaican jerk mixed grill that features boar, pheasant, and elk marinated in island spices. For dessert choose between the blackberry pie or the raspberry crème brûlée with chocolate sauce. *1890 Mt. Werner Rd., tel. 970/879–2441. Reservations essential. AE, D, MC, V.*

Moderate

Antares Restaurant
In a restored 1908 livery stable with a stone-and-wood decor, this upscale bistro has a menu that can best be described as eclectic international. It offers an exotic array of dishes with a Pacific Rim influence and flavored with fresh herbs. The napa cabbage stuffed with Asian-style vegetables, cellophane noodles, and topped with a spicy tomato sauce is a good choice, as is the three-mushroom sauté or the Thai chili-sautéed prawns. For a light dessert try the iced vanilla coffee or the *Frangelico,* frothed with steamed milk. *57½ 8th St., tel. 970/879–9939. Reservations essential. AE, MC, V.*

Coral Grill
This warm and woodsy restaurant offers spectacular views of the mountain. Fresh seafood is flown in daily, and the menu changes according to what's available. Oysters on ice or oysters Rockefeller are good starters. Some reliable favorite entrées include panfried Rocky Mountain trout, Cajun-style broiled red snapper, and baked salmon. There's also a hearty selection of meat and poultry dishes, including veal, beef, chicken, duckling, and a mixed grill. *Sundance Plaza, Anglers Dr., halfway between town and resort, tel. 970/879–6858. Reservations essential. AE, MC, V.*

La Montana
This restaurant's Southwestern style is enhanced with local artworks and the owner's photography. The sizzling-good fajitas are the house specialty, and there are six versions from which to choose (including elk). Another popular special is the blend of elk, lamb, and chorizo sausages, braided and then grilled over a mesquite fire. Other noteworthy entrées include elk loin with pecans and bourbon cream sauce; red chili pasta; and jumbo shrimp stuffed with crabmeat, Monterey jack cheese, and *pico de gallo* (a hot salsa mix), and then wrapped in bacon and smothered in Hollandaise sauce. For the more timid there are the standard Tex-Mex favorites such as burritos, enchiladas, and tacos. *Après Ski Way at 25 Village Dr., tel. 970/879–5800. Reservations essential. AE, D, MC, V.*

Ore House at the Pine Grove
In a 100-year-old barn, this rustic restaurant, decorated with ranch memorabilia and Western art, is an institution in Steamboat. Not-to-miss appetizers include coyote shrimp with Cajun spices and mesquite teriyaki steak bits. Although the focus is on meat such as prime rib—which comes in three cuts, from 8 to 16 ounces, plus a blackened version done with roasted garlic sauce—don't overlook the fresh fish, which is flown in daily and can include swordfish, mahimahi or salmon. Game is big on the menu, too, including buffalo steak in a peppercorn sauce or elk loin in a lingonberry sauce. There is occasional dinner entertainment in the upstairs loft. *1465 Pine Grove Rd., Pine Grove Ctr., tel. 970/879–1190. AE, D, MC, V.*

Riggio's Fine Italian Food
The tone here is set by ceiling fans and a handcrafted wooden bar.

Besides excellent pasta dishes, including manicotti, lasagna, and several spaghetti variations, veal, chicken, and seafood are creatively prepared and served. The veal *piccata* is delightfully light, and the saltimbocca is a full-flavored scallopini smothered in eggplant, prosciutto, cheese, and Bardolino sauce. Vegetarians will enjoy the stir-fry *Italiano,* with vegetables sautéed in olive oil and tossed with pasta *al pesto. 1151 Lincoln Ave., tel. 970/879–9010. Reservations essential. D, DC, MC, V.*

Inexpensive

Cat House Café
This Victorian-style restaurant with a turn-of-the-century antique bar was once the bar for Mattie Silks (*see above*) but was turned into a café with a separate menu. Come here for a fast fix: a salad—black bean and chicken, perhaps—followed by pasta or a sandwich. If you go with the former, try the angel-hair variety with grilled chicken; if you want a sandwich, the open-face steak Diane is juicy, and the club sandwich is hefty and filling. For dessert try the key lime pie. *Ski Time Sq., tel. 970/879–2441. AE, D, DC, MC, V.*

Dos Amigos
The decor is traditional Mexican, with hats, pottery, and blankets covering the walls. Good Tex-Mex is offered here, with the usual à la carte menu of tacos, burritos, enchiladas, and tortillas, as well as steak, chicken, and seafood. It's perfect for families or groups with divided food preferences. *1910 Mt. Werner Rd., Ski Time Sq., tel. 970/879–4270. AE, DC, MC, V.*

Old Town Pub
The building that this restaurant occupies has been a hotel, a hospital, and a post office, but its latest tenant is probably the most popular. You'll find good family dining here, with three-course menus that run the gamut from shrimp scampi to prime rib to linguine *puttanesca.* There's a good selection of steaks and a terrific Sunday brunch that includes eggs Benedict and French toast made with croissants. *600 Lincoln Ave., tel. 970/879–2101. AE, D, MC, V.*

Steamboat Smokehouse
It's kind of like a deli, kind of like a barbecue pit—*and* kind of wacky here. The rustic rock walls sport mounted animal heads, and the floor is a sea of peanut shells. There's a mother lode of hickory-smoked meats from which to choose, as a sandwich or as an entrée. Sides such as fries, smokehouse rice, and Mr. B's smoked beans are necessary accoutrements. *Thiesen Mall, 912 Lincoln Ave., tel. 970/879–5570. AE, MC, V.*

Best Bets for Breakfast

Express Oh
If you're starting from the ski village, this is a necessary first stop before first tracks. You'll get the best coffee on the mountain and a good selection of pastries, muffins, and breakfast breads. *Gondola Bldg., tel. 970/879–6111, ext. 513. No credit cards.*

In Season Bakery–Deli Café
In this small brick-walled café, you'll find a great selection of coffees to enjoy, with classical music in the background and an awesome array of fresh-baked breakfast goodies, not to

mention the divine eggs Benedict. *131 11th St., tel. 970/879–1840. MC, V.*

NIGHTLIFE AND ENTERTAINMENT
Après-Ski

Slopeside Grill
This place is so close to the slopes you can practically ski in the front door. Inside it's a fun spot, with a four-sided bar, lots of locals, and a sports bar atmosphere. Happy hour starts late (9 PM) and features $2 pints and $5 pizzas. When the weather's right, there's also seating on the outdoor patio. *Torian Plum Plaza, tel. 970/ 879–2916. AE, D, MC, V.*

Loud and Lively/Dancing

Heavenly Daze Brewery
Steamboat's own log-cabin-style microbrewery gets up a good head of steam with live entertainment, daily specials, and a half-dozen local brews. The three floors are filled with action from après-ski until midnight, with some folks grabbing dinner in between. Check out the pool tables on the third floor. *1860 Ski Time Square Dr., tel. 970/879–8080. AE, MC, V.*

Inferno Restaurant & Bar
The decor here is urban industrial with a hint of neon disco and two old-style tin-topped bars. It's definitely the hippest place on the mountain,

with live rock music nightly, a large and well-used dance floor, plus an assortment of bar games and TVs. *Base of mountain in Gondola Sq., tel. 970/879–5111. AE, D, MC, V.*

The Tugboat Grill & Pub
This is one of the oldest spots on the mountain and attracts a mixed crowd, from families in the early evening to more aggressive partyers once the live entertainment and dancing kicks in. The music ranges from funky to plain old C&W, and depending on the act there's occasionally a cover charge. *Pine Grove Ctr., Mt. Werner Dr., Ski Time Sq., tel. 970/879–7070. AE, D, MC, V.*

More Mellow

Antares Restaurant
This is a pleasant late-evening spot, with wood-paneled walls, brass fittings, and bar or table seating. Live jazz is on tap nightly, and there's a cozy atmosphere that's unique in Steamboat. *57½ 8th St., tel. 970/879– 9939. AE, MC, V.*

Harwig's Bar
A soothingly mellow spot with warm, rustic decor and comfortable furniture, Harwig's has light music that's just right for conversation. *911 Lincoln Ave., tel. 970/879–1980. AE, MC, V.*

TELLURIDE SKI RESORT

TELLURIDE SKI RESORT

562 Mountain Village Blvd.
Box 11155
Telluride, CO 81435
Tel. 970/728-3856

STATISTICALLY SPEAKING
Base elevation: 8,725 feet

Summit elevation: 11,890 feet

Vertical drop: 3,522 feet

Skiable terrain: 1,050 acres

Number of trails: 64

Longest run: 2.85 mi

Lifts and capacity: 1 gondola, 2 high-speed quads, 2 triples, 5 doubles, 1 poma; 10,000 skiers per hour

Daily lift ticket: $45

Average annual snowfall: 300 inches

Number of skiing days 1995–96: 142

Snowmaking: 155 acres; 15%

Terrain mix: N 21%, I 47%, E 32%

Snowboarding: yes; all runs and terrain park

Cross-country skiing: 30 kilometers (10 kilometers groomed) of Nordic trails

At the headwaters of the San Miguel River, deep in the San Juan Mountains, is Telluride—a town and ski resort just far enough off the beaten path to serve as a hideout for fan-weary Hollywood types. In fact, this high-mountain hideaway has gained considerable cachet in recent years, as the counterculture crowd that gravitated here during the '60s and '70s ceded a slice of this spectacular mountain valley to such high rollers as Oprah Winfrey, Ralph Lauren, and Tom Cruise.

Historically the town has endured the boom and bust cycle so common to small isolated communities dependent on capricious gold and silver prices. During the boom things were fine, of course: Grand Victorian-style hotels were built, an opera house opened, and the population swelled from 100 to 5,000 or more. Come the bust, in the 1930s, the tiny town clung to life, much as it clings to two historical footnotes—the exploits of an extroverted bank robber and an introverted lawyer. A baby-face Butch Cassidy chose Telluride for the debut of his legendary bank-robbing career, and L. L. Nunn created the first practical application of AC electricity when he ran 8 miles of transmission line into the valley, and the small mountain town became the most brightly illuminated community in the world.

Telluride is still struggling, but these days the fight is to reconcile the values of the community with the growth of Mountain Village, 6 miles down the road. Some vocal locals decry the arrival of the glitz-and-spritzer ski set as the first step down the path to the Aspenization of their wholesome, whole-wheat, non-conformist, ecopacifist community.

Fortunately, the fundamental character of the town remains unchanged. It began life as an 80-acre tent city in 1878, grew into a thriving mining town at the turn of the century, and finally became a high-alpine recreation retreat during the 1960s and '70s. Organized skiing didn't appear until 1973, when Joseph T. Zoline, a businessman from California, decided that snow was a commodity that could be mined as surely as the ore and minerals that had sustained the town for more than a century. He envisioned a $100 million megaresort that would rival the best in the United States. Twenty years later that vision is becoming reality, especially since a gondola linking the town and the mountain was completed in the summer of 1996.

Although it has generally been conceded by even the most diehard locals that the gondola is an acceptable eco-friendly addition to the community, most are still on the alert for more offensive lifestyle intrusions. In sharp contrast to the century-old mining town, with its original brick and wooden buildings and street-loads of character and characters, is the ultramodern Telluride Ski Area, which, according to some, is spreading too quickly across the mountain.

The collection of condos on Telluride Mountain, known as Mountain Village, appears haphazard, with nondescript architecture and an atmosphere that's a far cry from the feeling of the old town. Nonetheless, it is perfect for families who enjoy the solitude and comfort of self-contained condo living plus easy access to the novice areas.

There are lots of alternative accommodations plus some good-spirited nightlife in and around town. The gondola now connects the two solitudes of Telluride to give visitors easy access to both the town and the resort, and as the mountain village continues to grow and as the town continues to adjust to growth, this man-made umbilical cord should help link even more intimately two sides of Telluride.

HOW TO GET THERE
By Plane
Denver International Airport (DIA), more than 300 miles (a day's drive) away, is the closest international airport (*see* Getting to Colorado Resorts, *above*).

Telluride Regional Airport (tel. 970/728–5313) is 5 miles from the resort. America West has several flights weekly from Phoenix, and Continental and United have daily flights from Denver.

Montrose Airport (tel. 970/249–3203) is 67 miles from Telluride; Continental and United fly here daily from Denver, America West has daily service from Phoenix, and Continental Express runs a direct flight from Houston on Saturday.

Grand Junction Airport (tel. 970/244–9100), 127 miles north of Telluride, has service from Denver on Continental and United Express and from Salt Lake City on Delta Connection.

Gunnison Airport (tel. 970/641–2304), 125 miles northeast of Telluride, has service from Dallas/Fort Worth on American, Saturday service from Houston on Continental, and thrice-weekly flights from Atlanta on Delta.

By Shuttle

Telluride Transit (tel. 970/728–6000 or 800/800–6228) runs pre-scheduled shuttle service from the Telluride Regional ($14), Montrose ($50), Gunnison ($80), Durango ($80), Grand Junction ($80) and Cortez ($80) airports. All prices are round-trip per person with a four- to five-person minimum.

By Car

Telluride Airport is an easy 5-mile drive down Route 145 into town. It's a different story if you're coming from DIA: The 330-mile journey goes through some tough but beautiful mountain areas. Allow at least a full day in each direction. From DIA follow I–70 west 200 miles to the Clifton exit; follow Route 141 south for 5 miles to Route 50; turn left and follow Route 50 south to Montrose, where it becomes Route 550; continue 27 miles south and turn right at Ridgeway onto Route 62W; follow it for 30 miles to Route 145S, which after 18 miles brings you to Telluride.

Hertz, Budget, and Dollar operate out of the Montrose and Telluride regional airports. Avis and Hertz have offices in Gunnison. (*See* Car Rental *in* Getting to Colorado Resorts, *above.*)

By Bus

Telluride Transit (tel. 970/728–6000) offers prearranged service from Montrose and Gunnison airports and also stops in Grand Junction.

By Train

Amtrak's (tel. 800/872–7245) daily *California Zephyr* service from the West Coast and Chicago stops in Denver and Grand Junction (120 miles north of Telluride).

GETTING AROUND

A car in Telluride can be useful for a little independence and freedom to explore the surrounding area, but there's also an excellent free shuttle service that runs between town and the resort every 15 minutes. The town is small, and almost everything is within walking distance. Three local taxi services, **Mountain Limo** (tel. 970/728–9606), **Skip's Taxi** (tel. 970/728–6667), and **Telluride Transit** (tel. 970/728–6000), provide transportation in town and between town and resort. They also serve neighboring towns.

THE SKIING

Telluride's reputation has preceded its emergence as an all-around destination resort, and although much of the beast has been cut, trimmed, and groomed out of the vertiginous, avalanche-prone slopes, most people still regard it as one of Colorado's toughest ski areas.

Although you'll still find some of the toe-curling, radical in-your-face runs that first attracted the on-the-fringe crowd in the '60s and '70s, the boomers of the '90s have sent their message. Wise to marketing ways, the resort has responded with winch-cat grooming and trail-widening plus the development of one of the best beginner areas and ski schools anywhere.

Another nice feature is the mountain's layout: It is broken into three distinct areas. The front face of the mountain, almost immediately above the old town, is where the hotshots and wanna-be experts gather for regular shots of adrenaline. Midarea on the mountain is directly above the ski village, and that's where most of the intermediate terrain is found. To the north is a marvelous novice area with meticulous grooming and some of the longest green runs in the state.

Snowboarders have access to the entire mountain and to all lifts. There's also a terrain park off Lifts 3 and 4 plus several half pipes elsewhere on the mountain.

Novices

Telluride has set aside a mountain just for you, and it has a quad chairlift to take you up to some of the finest beginner runs I've ever seen. They are long, meandering trails, alternately gentle and slightly pitched, that cascade easily from the 10,000-foot summit. From Lift 10 you can go left or right. If you choose to go left, take the blue Sundance to Double Cabin. Next time up, come off the chair to the right and follow Double Cabin the whole way to the base. For something slightly steeper but just as wide, pick up Bridges or Galloping Goose. The best part of this designated novice area is that all the runs head back to the Mountain Village, which means skiers at this level can easily meet up with friends skiing the more advanced runs at lunchtime or at the end of the day.

When you've built up your confidence, head over to Lifts 1, 2, and 3 for green-blue combinations such as Boomerang or the slightly more challenging Peek-a-Boo. From either of these runs you can ski directly back to the base of Lift 3 or take the Village Bypass cutoff to the bottom of Lift 10. If you're keen to explore without getting into trouble, try Telluride Trail, a long, easy green run that winds its way into town from the top of Lift 7. When you reach the bottom of the run, take Lift 7 to the top and pick up Boomerang, which will lead you to the village area.

Intermediates

Although Telluride's reputation is based on its ferocious expert terrain, surprisingly almost 50% of its runs are intermediate. That percentage has increased slightly over the past couple of years as the resort has taken to some serious grooming, causing a number of black runs to be downgraded to blue intermediates. There's a good mix of intermediate and upper-intermediate runs in the Gorrono Basin area, which is served by Lifts 2, 3, 4, and 5. The steeper stuff tends to be found off the top of Lift 6, while the longer runs are found off the top of Lift 9, which is good if you're starting your day from the town side of the mountain—where you can catch the early sun. From the top of Lift 9 try the moderately steep combination of Upper See Forever, Upper Lookout, and Lower Lookout, a stiff intermediate challenge that starts off steep through a gladed area, narrows slightly while maintaining good pitch, then widens as it curves to the bottom of Lift 9 (take this back to the top rather than continuing down to the base of Lift 8). Your other choice on this side of the mountain is the tame version of the Plunge, the famed black diamond drop that helps give Telluride its expert reputation. The groomed-down intermediate version is actually marked double blue, which tells you that it's just a little tougher than your average blue run. It's steep, narrow, and when groomed, a high-speed joyride for upper intermediates and experts. The Gorrono Basin is your next-best bet; you can reach the crossover trail to the left of Upper See Forever about a third of the way down from the top. There are about a dozen runs in this area, including Lower See Forever, Misty Maiden, and Peek-a-Boo for cruising or Hermit for some solid bumps. Although they are medium-length runs, they sustain good pitch; if they offered a longer, more sustained challenge, they might be considered black runs. Grooming has mellowed them, and it can be fun tripping up Lift 4 and ripping down the pitch of Humboldt Draw, Pick and Gad, or Peek-a-Boo. It's heads-up skiing, and there's enough variety to keep you coming back for more. When you are ready to move up a notch, the black diamond runs off the top of Lift 6 (reached from the top of Lift 9) are a good intermediate challenge because they are steeper but also well groomed. Silver Glade, Zulu Queen, and Chongos are supersteep and supergroomed runs that are per-

fect for pushing the intermediate envelope.

Experts

Although winch-cat grooming has taken the edge off some of Telluride's supersteep expert terrain, the core runs of its fearsome reputation remain intact, and double-black-diamond addicts will love the combination of steep, unrelenting terrain and power-packed bump runs. The Plunge—Telluride's signature run—and Spiral Stairs (both reached by Lifts 8 and 9 from the town side) are two of the most intense sustained mogul runs anywhere; from Lift 11 you can challenge some sublimely steep, powder-stuffed chutes like Electra and Dynamo. Most of the expert terrain is best reached from the town side; if you are starting from the resort village, it's a three- or four-lift ride that you should take into account when setting a time for meeting friends. If you don't want to plunge into the Plunge, try one of the good alternatives from the top of Lift 9. Bushwacker, Kant-Mak-M, and Mammoth are narrow, steep, unpredictable, twisting slashes with lots of drop-offs, tight turns, and patches of bumps. They are among the longest expert runs on the mountain, but you can start off with a little more pacing by turning right off Lift 9 and heading for the expert terrain on Gold Hill Ridge. Two lifts serve this area, where there are a dozen shorter (but no less steep) runs. The runs become steeper the farther along the ridge you go until you reach the Gold Hill summit, at 12,247 feet, and the insanely steep Little Rose beckons you. All the runs off this ridge are an exquisite mix of snow-filled chutes, eyes-over-your-ski-tips steepness, and tricky little glades. When you feel like stretching your runs out a little, you can always head back to the town side of the ridge and play on high-speed cruisers such as Power Line and East Drain.

WHERE TO STAY

I prefer to stay in the town of Telluride because I enjoy its Victorian character, the chance to interact with the locals, and the ability to walk to the restaurants and nightspots—in short, to be in the center of the action. Families, on the other hand, may place a higher premium on being away from the hubbub and closer to the beginner and intermediate terrain at the ski village. Many of the newer, more luxurious accommodations are centered around the ski village, whereas in-town lodgings are of the small-hotel, lodge, and B&B variety. This is not to say they are without luxury, but these more intimate places are geared to smaller groups, couples, and those for whom a curfew is not a problem. The gondola back up to Mountain Village shuts down at midnight. If you prefer ski-in/ski-out convenience, Mountain Village is your best choice, although most in-town accommodations are within a short walk of town lifts and the gondola.

The majority of accommodations in Telluride are managed by several different management companies. The Telluride Visitors Center (666 W. Colorado Ave., Box 653, Telluride 81435, tel. 970/728–6265 or 800/525–2717, fax 970/728–9054) represents all Telluride accommodations.

Expensive

Aspen Ridge

For large family groups or two or three couples, these town houses are just right. All units are three-bedroom, three-bathroom monsters loaded with such niceties as a fireplace, a sauna, a hot tub or jetted bathtub, a steam shower, and a garage. The kitchen is appliance packed with anything that plugs into a wall socket, and the overall decor is refined mountain elegance with modern, stylish furnishings, complementary local artwork, and subdued colors such as dusty rose and sandstone. Four units sit right on a ski run: Book early if you want this kind of ski-in/ski-out convenience. You can board the gondola just across the street from the front entrance. *100 Aspen Ridge Dr., Box 11165, Telluride Mountain Village, 81435, tel. 970/728–4217 or 800/324–6388, fax 970/728–6557. 13 units. Facilities: ski storage, laundry. MC, V. $600–$700.*

Hotel Columbia

The Columbia may be small in size, but it's big in style and stature, with a sumptuous elegance that is matched by few places in town. The spacious rooms and suites are decorated in rich tones and superbly appointed with a down comforter, overstuffed chairs, a fireplace, a large luxurious bathroom (with steam shower, bathrobes, and a six-foot claw-foot tub), original art, fresh flowers, and a balcony, which provides a superb view of the surrounding mountains and the San Miguel River. The penthouse suites also come with a kitchen and a Jacuzzi. This is a first-class establishment with an emphasis on service and substance. It's just a couple hundred feet from the gondola and two blocks from downtown. *300 W. San Juan Ave., Box 800, 81435, tel. 970/728–0660 or 800/201–9505, fax 970/728–9249. 19 rooms, 2 suites. Facilities: restaurant, lounge, library, rooftop hot tub, desk service (7 AM–midnight), daily maid service, ski storage, laundry. AE, MC, V. $205–$340.*

Ice House

No alpine import, this lodge, and particularly its condo units, are decorated in modern Southwestern style. Antique Navajo rugs on the raw-plaster walls, clay lighting fixtures, and a dark-maroon-and-green color scheme set the tone. The odd-shape building has a wooden exterior and a sky-lighted mezzanine on the third floor that can be viewed from a fourth-floor balcony. Service is unobtrusive but attentive, and there is the sense of quiet intimacy you would expect to find in a small inn. The hotel is one block from the gondola, with downtown only two blocks away. Rooms are appropriately sized for couples, and small families can manage in the suites; larger groups prefer the condos, which can sleep eight and are equipped with a full kitchen, a balcony, and a dining area. *310 S. Fir St., Box 2909, 81435, tel. 970/728–6300 or 800/544–3436, fax 970/728–6358. 20 rooms, 22 suites, 13 units. Facilities: bar, lounge, Jacuzzi, outdoor pool, steam room, 24-hr desk service, ski storage, ski valet, laundry. AE, D, DC, MC, V. $420–$460, including full breakfast.*

Peaks Resort & Spa

At this château in the mountains you'll find oversize rooms and every conceivable service, including an enormous four-level health spa whose use is complimentary for guests. The spa facilities are heavenly: indoor and outdoor swimming pools, saunas, steam rooms, Jacuzzis, weight rooms, aerobics classes, massages, and more. The Peaks, in the Mountain Village just a short schuss from the slopes, is the place to stay if money is no object and convenience is up there on your list of priorities. The rooms and suites are sumptuously furnished with plush couches and chairs and elegantly styled with rich draperies, area rugs, and wall coverings, all reflecting a Southwestern motif. They're loaded with touches such as terry robes and extralarge bathrooms with marble vanities. There's also a spectacular view from all rooms. *Telluride Mountain Village, 136 Country Club Rd., Box 2702, 81435, tel. 970/728–6800 or 800/789–2220, fax 970/728–6175. 149 rooms, 28 suites. Facilities: 2 restaurants, bar, spa, 24-hr desk service, ski storage, ski valet, shuttle to Telluride Airport, laundry. AE, DC, MC, V. $355–$1,550.*

Moderate

Alpine Inn B&B

If you enjoy the friendliness and homespun ambience of a B&B, this reincarnation of an original 1903 Telluride hotel will suit you fine. All but two of the rooms—each larger than the average B&B unit—have private baths, and all are beautifully decorated and furnished with period antiques and handmade quilts. The suite has a fireplace, a terrace, and a whirlpool. If you're interested in mingling with other guests, the glass solarium, where a full breakfast is served, is a good meeting place, as is the hot tub. Otherwise, this lodging allows for a lot of privacy, as rooms are comfortable enough to hide away in—a characteristic that couples love. The location, about two blocks from the Oak Street lift and gondola, is convenient. *440 W. Colorado Ave., Box 2398, 81435, tel. 970/728–6282 or 800/707–3344, fax 970/728–3424. 7 rooms, 1 suite. Facilities: hot tub, ski storage. MC, V. $75–$230.*

Pennington's Mountain Village Inn

This alpine inn, on the 12th fairway of a golf course halfway between Telluride and the ski village, is marvelously isolated. Under the many-peaked roof are sumptuously decorated rooms with cathedral ceilings and French-country decor. Guest rooms and the slightly larger suites, which have a separate sitting area, are outfitted with a king- or queen-size bed, a deck offering panoramic views of Sunshine Mountain and Mt. Wilson, and a small fridge packed with snacks and juices. Full breakfast is served to guests in their rooms or in the dining area. A daily happy hour takes place in the lounge. *100 Pennington Ct., Box 2428, 81435, tel. 970/728–5337 or 800/543–1437, fax 970/728–5338. 9 rooms, 3 suites. Facilities: lounge, library, billiards, Jacuzzi, steam room, ski storage, laundry. AE, D, MC, V. $140–$300, including full breakfast.*

Riverside Condominiums

This is a good condo deal, in downtown Telluride on the banks of the San Miguel River, just two blocks from the Oak Street lift and gondola. One-, two-, and three-bedroom units are available; the absence of four-bedroom mega-group units may account for Riverside's quiet atmosphere. At five blocks from the main drag, it's a little removed from the action but close enough to essential stores and services, making it a good choice for families. The units are well equipped with a kitchen, a fireplace, a washer-dryer, and a balcony. The only drawback for those with youngsters may be the absence of a pool, but adults appreciate the hot tub on the deck overlooking the mountains. *460 S. Pine St., Box 100, 81435, tel. 970/728–6621 or 800/538–7754, fax 970/728–6160. 25 units. Facilities: 2 hot tubs, ski storage, laundry. AE, D, MC, V. $95–$425.*

San Sophia B&B

This distinguished, comfortable, luxurious mountain inn is among the finest in Colorado. Snuggled up against its namesake mountains, the property is ideally located, one block from the Oak Street lift and gondola, in Old Telluride. Inside the turreted building are 16 distinctive rooms, each washed in pastels and named after a local mine. Furnishings include Victorian antiques and brass beds with handmade quilts. The bathrooms have double oval-shape tubs, terry robes, and a monster basket of toiletries. For an extramemorable experience try the upper-turret room, with its 360° view. Families with children should call ahead for restrictions. *330 W. Pacific Ave., Box 1825, 81435, tel. 970/728–3001 or 800/537–4781, fax 970/728–6228. 16 rooms. Facilities: library, observatory, Jacuzzi, ski storage, laundry service. AE, MC, V. $150–$275, including full breakfast and après-ski snacks.*

Inexpensive

Bear Creek B&B

Contemporary design and decor lend an all-American feel to this downtown inn, a change of pace from all the historical B&Bs in the area. Rooms are large, with natural-wood furnishings, brightly colored upholstery, and pastel wall coverings. Guests enjoy gathering around the fireplace in the living room or on the roof deck with its jetted spa and panoramic view. *21 E. Colorado Ave., Box 2369, 81435, tel. 970/728–6681 or 800/338–7064. 10 rooms. Facilities: sauna, steam room, ski storage, MC, V. $60–$165, including full breakfast and après-ski snacks.*

New Sheridan Hotel

Here's another of Telluride's small inns that gets high marks for its authentic style, reasonable prices, and good location—in the heart of downtown Telluride, just a block from the gondola. Built in 1892, it has recently been totally renovated. Rooms vary from small (with shared bathrooms) to suites with sitting areas. All are impeccably furnished with antiques and period pieces such as canopy beds and antique armoires and are decorated in soft tones of rose, beige, and off-white. It's a friendly spot with socializing revolving around the breakfast table, the après-ski munchies in the library, and the two rooftop hot tubs. A half block away there are six newer condos that sleep six. *231 W. Colorado Ave., Box 231, 81435, tel. 970/728–4351, fax 970/728–3233 or 800/200–1891. 10 rooms, 2 with bath, 8 suites, 6 units. Facilities: hot tub, fitness room. AE, D, DC, MC, V. $85–$225.*

Oak Street Inn

This clean, comfortable place is the cheapest accommodation in town and attracts a hard-partying crowd of budget skiers who would rather spend money in the saloon than on a room. No-frills guest rooms have double beds or bunks and can sleep as many as six. It's the sort of no-fuss, conveniently located place—only three blocks from the Oak Street lift—of which all ski resorts should have more. *134 N. Oak St., 81435, tel. 970/728–3383. 24 rooms, 2 with bath. Facilities: TV lounge, sauna. AE, D, MC, V. $58–$72; $14 each additional person.*

Telluride Lodge

These are deceptively luxurious condos, with the rather plain exterior yielding spacious, well-decorated, and well-equipped units that can sleep 10. The units range in size from studio to three bedrooms, with the latter spread over three floors. All come with a full kitchen, a fireplace, a TV, and distinctive decorating touches. The lodge is just 200 feet from the Coonskin lift and about a five-minute walk from downtown. *747 W. Pacific Ave., Box 127, 81435, tel. 970/728–4446 or 800/662–8747, fax 970/728–5228. 45 units. Facilities: hot tubs, steam room, ski lockers, laundry. AE, MC, V. $160–$425.*

WHERE TO EAT
On the Mountain

Giuseppe's

On a clear day 11,890 feet up (via Lift 9), you'll be able to see all the way to Utah. It gets crowded here at peak hours on sunny days. The menu includes Italian fare such as pizza and pasta and an excellent black bean, potato, and cheese stir-fry. *Top of Lift 9, tel. 970/728–7503. No credit cards.*

Gorrono Ranch Restaurant
Ranch-style dining and ranch-style portions are two sure bets at this restaurant in an original homestead at midmountain. A daily barbecue with burgers, chicken, and steaks is offered, as well as fresh lobster. *Misty Maiden run under Lift 4, tel. 970/728–7566. D, MC, V.*

Expensive
Campagna
If you want authentic Tuscan cuisine, there is no other place in Telluride to have such a meal. The cozy dining room of this Victorian house has great ambience. The decor is warm, and the antique tables, oak floor, and old photos of Italy promote the illusion of eating at an Italian home. Hallmark dishes include delicate pastas in unusually light sauces, as well as braised or grilled meats and fish. Try the New Zealand rack of lamb with rosemary and garlic or the whole roasted snapper stuffed with fennel. *435 W. Pacific Ave., tel. 970/728–6190. Reservations essential. MC, V.*

Evangelines
If you're craving Cajun, this is the place to go for dishes that conjure the soul of New Orleans. The restaurant is intimate, and the contemporary decor with white-linen service adds elegance. The menu features such classic Louisiana dishes as shrimp creole, as well as imaginative creations such as oysters Rockefeller ravioli. The chocolate bread pudding is a new twist on an old favorite. *646 Mountain Village Blvd., tel. 970/728–9717. Reservations essential. AE, D, DC, MC, V.*

Excelsior Café
This delightfully intimate restaurant is spread over two floors of a magnificently restored Victorian house. The Italian menu includes a fantastic Caesar salad, deli meats and imported cheeses, a delicious thin-crust pizza, and more traditional pasta and veal entrées. There's also an antipasto bar that will have you going back for seconds. The Excelsior is a good spot for a couple of romantics looking for a quiet, quaint place to break bread. *200 W. Colorado Ave., tel. 970/728–4250. AE, MC, V.*

La Marmotte
This restaurant, French to the core, rates as the best overall in town. Walk through the door of what was once an icehouse, and the brick walls, lace curtains, and fresh flowers greet you like a kiss on both cheeks. The menu is a mix of traditional- and nouvelle-French haute cuisine, with a range of entrées that include duck-leg confit and sautéed pink duck breast in a white bean and roasted garlic sauce, grilled veal chop with five-grain rice and tomato-coriander sauce, rack of venison, Colorado lamb, and Atlantic salmon. *150 San Juan St., tel. 970/728–6232. Reservations essential. AE, D, MC, V.*

Moderate
Bistro Nouveau
This hip, happening American bistro has stylish decor, with whitewashed walls splashed with color, sleek, modern furnishings, and exposed wood. The menu is as loose as the atmosphere, with a range of dishes includ-

ing lamb, fish, and pasta presented in Colorado ranch-lands style. There are also low-fat, spa-style Peaks Performance dishes like the herb-crusted chicken with roasted vegetable hash and grilled shrimp flavored with soy, sesame, and ginger. *115 W. Colorado Ave., tel. 970/728–1915. AE, MC, V.*

Leimgruber's Bierstube

Pronounce the name correctly (*lime-groob-ers*) so you won't sound like a tourist when you're asking for directions. It's a warm, friendly place with log walls, handcrafted furnishings, and lots of antiques. German specialties such as schnitzel (Wiener or Jager), sauerbraten, smoked pork, and bratwurst are all prepared in classic style. There's also an excellent selection of wines and German beers. *573 W. Pacific Ave., tel. 970/728–4663. AE, MC, V.*

Powder House

An American-bistro atmosphere combines with Rocky Mountain cuisine to make Powder House a casual, satisfying place for a meal. Roast duckling, elk tenderloin, buffalo sausage, fresh fettuccine, sautéed shrimp, scallops, crab, and roasted chicken head the list of entrées, but don't overlook the large lineup of appetizers, including a smoked-game platter and fried calamari. The food is dynamite—and, incidentally, the building in which Powder House resides was once used as an explosives storage shed. *226 W. Colorado Ave., tel. 970/728–3622. AE, MC, V.*

Swede-Finn Hall

Swedish and Finnish miners were some of the earliest settlers in Telluride, and although they rarely got together in those days, they eventually settled their differences around the turn of the century. The Swede-Finn Hall, a legacy of mining days, has also served as a church, a basketball court, and a storage shed. Today it's a cheerful restaurant with a bistro menu. The owners have tried to preserve the building's original 1890s look, with walnut wood floors, 12-foot ceilings, a large stage at one end for occasional music and comedy, and walls adorned with yellowing antique photographs of the early gold rush days of Telluride. There's even an old-fashioned billiards hall in the basement and a bar that serves beer from five Colorado microbreweries. On the menu you'll find such local delights as Rocky Mountain trout, quail, venison, and a variety of European dishes, including vegetarian shepherd's pie, bouillabaisse, and Athenian chicken pasta. *472 W. Pacific Ave., tel. 970/728–2085. Reservations essential. MC, V.*

Inexpensive

Eddie's

This is a classic American diner with a menu that Eddie describes as "ethnic American." It's part deli, part pizzeria, part pasta palace, and it's the place to get almost any comfort food you crave. The pizzas, with dozens of exotic toppings, are a rave; salads—of spinach, Cobb, and garden variety—are huge; and sandwiches include such homegrown faves as Philly cheese steaks, roast beef cheddar melt, and veggie pitas. There are also pasta and burgers. *300 W. Colorado Ave., tel. 970/728–6108. MC, V.*

Floradora

This great little restaurant qualifies as a Telluride institution: It's been around since 1978, when the current owners began as dishwasher and waitress. The straightforward menu, well-prepared family-style meals, and casual friendly attitude make this a local favorite. The menu is varied but not fancy, with prime cuts of beef, Southwestern specialties (like chicken fajitas), and great burgers. For greens grazers there's a humongous salad bar. *103 W. Colorado Ave., tel. 970/728–3888. AE, D, MC, V.*

Roma Café and Bar

During the 1890s the Roma was a lounge, and today the downstairs is still dominated by the marvelous original Brunswick bar with its 12-foot French mirrors. The decor is early American saloon, with lots of wood, brass, and mirrors; and the menu is resoundingly Italian, with a good selection of fresh, homemade pasta dishes, including penne, lasagna, ravioli, daily spaghetti specials, and a few popular items such as prime rib, barbecued ribs, veal parmigiana, and veal Oscar. While you're here, pick up a bottle of the homemade vinegar created by the chef's wife, Tito. *133 E. Colorado Ave., tel. 970/728–3669. MC, V.*

T-Ride Country Club

If you enjoy nothing more than the aroma of a sizzling backyard barbecue, you'll love the T-Ride Country Club. A large selection of meat, fowl, and fish is done to perfection on a giant mesquite grill, and there's a large salad bar. If you have to wait, there are 11 TVs and 14 beers on tap.

T-Ride is a loud, raucously happy place with huge windows that overlook the street. *333 W. Colorado Ave., tel. 970/728–6344. AE, D, MC, V.*

Best Bets for Breakfast

Sofío's Mexican Café

The best breakfasts in town are found here, including light, fluffy omelets, French waffles, pancakes, seafood Benedict, and Mexican specialties such as *huevos rancheros* (eggs with salsa). Fresh-squeezed juices and tasty, strong coffee will get you going in the morning. *110 E. Colorado Ave., tel. 970/728–4882. AE, MC, V.*

Steaming Bean

Get your java jolt here—you won't find better coffee in town—and try the soups, muffins, and pastries. A good selection of gentle wake-up blends plus an eye-opening espresso and designer flavors are available. *221 W. Colorado Ave., tel. 970/728–0793. MC, V.*

NIGHTLIFE AND ENTERTAINMENT

Après-Ski

The Cultured Pearl International Pub

Such a long name for a very small bar that's perfectly located at the bottom of Lifts 3 and 4 in Mountain Village. Its wooden walls and low ceilings lend a cozy, rustic ambience, and the tight confines make it seem like the center of après-ski action—which in fact it is. *565 Mountain Village Blvd., Mountain Village, tel. 970/728–5200. AE, MC, V.*

Leimgruber's Bierstube

This is definitely the place to be for après-ski. But get here early because it fills up fast with locals and in-the-know visitors. There are personalized beer mugs hanging over the bar, a half-dozen German beers on tap, and the ever-present challenge of the Boot, a monster beer glass that only the bold dare order. It's a fun, friendly spot that eventually turns into the more refined dining room mentioned above. *573 W. Pacific Ave., tel. 970/728–4663. AE, MC, V.*

Loud and Lively/Dancing

Fly Me to the Moon Saloon
If you want to shake some ache out of your legs, try the legendary spring-loaded dance floor here. The saloon hosts the hottest live bands in town most nights and packs in the crowds—especially the very hip under-30 set. *132 E. Colorado Ave., tel. 970/728–6666. No credit cards.*

Last Dollar Saloon
This main street bar is also known as the Buck by locals, and for my money has the best artificial gas fireplace that I've ever seen. Beyond that, it's a friendly, fun place, with wooden floors, brick walls, tin ceilings, and windows overlooking the street scene. There are also a hearty selection of some 40 beers, a multitude on tap, plus some good music. *100 E. Colorado Ave., no phone. No credit cards.*

New Sheridan Hotel Bar
This big, Western-style saloon in the revamped oldest hotel in town practically guarantees a good time. It's rough and ready, with wooden floors, walls loaded with antiques (or maybe just junk), and a huge bar. Tradition allows for local cowboy Roudy Roudebush to occasionally ride his horse right into the bar. Beer is the beverage of choice, and the bartenders keep it flowing as the crowd keeps on growing. Now and then there's live entertainment. *New Sheridan Hotel, 231 W. Colorado Ave., tel. 970/728–3911. MC, V.*

More Mellow

Eagles Bar
The first thing you notice about this stylish, modern bar is the collection of eagles carved from solid pieces of wood. This is a hip establishment done in soothing Southwestern colors and dominated by a large square bar adjacent to a stylish dining area. Lots of microbrews on tap provide the liquid refreshment, and the duck-stuffed spring rolls are the upscale bar munchies that match the trendy scene. *100 W. Colorado Ave., tel. 970/728–0886. AE, D, DC, MC, V.*

Powder House
This is a great place for your last stop of the night, where you can meet friends and enjoy the cozy atmosphere as you sip on a nightcap or indulge in a delicious dessert. This well-established Telluride institution has a pleasant feel and a soothing ambience. *226 W. Colorado Ave., tel. 970/728–3622. AE, MC, V.*

VAIL SKI RESORT

VAIL SKI RESORT

Vail Associates Inc.
Box 7
Vail, CO 81658
Tel. 970/845-5725 or
800/525-2257

STATISTICALLY SPEAKING
Base elevation: 8,120 feet

Summit elevation: 11,450 feet

Vertical drop: 3,330 feet

Skiable terrain: 4,112 acres

Number of trails: 121

Longest run: 4.5 miles

Lifts and capacity: 1 gondola, 1 enclosed high-speed quad, 10 high-speed quads, 2 fixed-grip quads, 3 triples, 6 doubles, 5 surface lifts; 45,213 skiers per hour

Daily lift ticket: $52

Average annual snowfall: 335 inches

Number of skiing days 1995–96: 163

Snowmaking: 332 acres, 8%

Terrain mix: N 32%, I 36%, E 32%

Snowboarding: yes

Cross-country skiing: Golden Peak and Vail Golf Course

When you first see Vail through the windshield of a moving car, it probably won't look like the largest ski resort in America. That's because there isn't really one Vail but several, spread over 7 miles of base area. Within the base are individual mountain centers (Golden Peak, Vail Village, Lionshead, Cascade Village) with pedestrians-only malls and modern Tyrolean/American-style architecture. Also keep in mind that what you see is not all you ski: More than 50% of Vail's vast, varied terrain is out of view, on the back side in the famed bowl areas.

The other remarkable feature of this sprawling ski complex is its accessibility, thanks to an efficient, free shuttle bus operation between centers and the mother of all lift systems, including 10 high-speed quads that make cross-mountain travel painless. There's a constant push by Vail's owners to maximize the efficiency of its existing services and introduce new skier-friendly services—all to ensure a supreme ski experience.

Despite a barrage of superlatives about its size, snow, sizzle, and illustrious citizenry, Vail offers something for everyone. Here, a person's castle can be a 10-bedroom designer home high on a hill, a modest motel room in the shadow of a service station, or anything in between. It's still possible for the ultra-moneyed set to short-circuit a platinum credit card in one week of unabashed frivolity. But there are ways and means for almost any self-respecting skier, regardless of income, to experience Vail. The skiing terrain shows no favorites, either. From in-your-face bowl bashing to hero cruising on autobahns of white to confidence-stroking novice runs from the summit, Vail does not skip a beat when sorting out the green brigade from the double-diamond headhunters.

HOW TO GET THERE
By Plane
Denver International Airport (DIA), 120 miles and two hours' drive away, is the closest international facility (*see* Getting to Colorado Resorts, *above*). American and Delta have direct flights to **Vail–Eagle County Airport** (33 miles from the resort, 30 minutes by car) from Atlanta, Chicago, Salt Lake City, Newark, New York's La Guardia Airport, Miami, and

Children's services: day care,
tel. 970/479–2044; instruction, tel. 970/476–3229 or
800/475–4543

Snow phone:
tel. 970/476–4888

Police: tel. 970/479–2200

Vail Valley Medical:
tel. 970/476–2452

Vail Valley Tourism and
Convention Bureau:
tel. 800/824–5737

Road conditions:
tel. 970/479–2226

Towing: Vail Amoco Service,
tel. 970/476–1810

FIVE-STAR FAVORITES
Best run for vertical:
Prima Cornice

Best run overall: Riva Ridge

Best bar/nightclub:
Club Chelsea

Best hotel: Sonnenalp Resort

Best restaurant: Sweet Basil

Dallas/Fort Worth. Northwest has nonstops from Detroit and Minneapolis. United and American fly daily nonstops from Los Angeles. United Express and Delta offer connecting flights to Vail–Eagle County from DIA.

From DIA **Vans to Vail** (tel. 970/476–4467 or 800/222–2212) and **Colorado Mountain Express** (tel. 970/949–4227 or 800/525–6353) offer regularly scheduled nonstop shuttle service.

By Car

Vail is 100 miles west of Denver, and for the most part it's an easy, scenic drive. From DIA follow I–70 west for two hours to the resort. There are three exits for Vail: Exit 180 into East Vail, Exit 176 for Vail Village, and Exit 173 for West Vail. If you're uncertain about the location of your accommodations, take the Vail Village exit. A word of caution about driving on I–70: Radar traps are more common here than on any other stretch of highway in ski country.

GETTING AROUND

No matter where you stay in Vail, you're never far from the action, be it superb skiing or lively nightlife and schmoozing. Because the efficient, free **Town of Vail bus system** (tel. 970/328–8143) travels everywhere from the Golden Peak area all the way over to Beaver Creek, you won't need a car here. **Vail Valley Taxi** (tel. 970/476–8294) provides transportation in town and between town and resort.

THE SKIING

Vail Mountain is a rippling behemoth that stretches for nearly 7 miles above the Gore Valley, giving skiers 4,112 acres of terrain, 3,330 feet of vertical, and a network of 28 lifts. It's unprepossessing, without the craggy peaks and deep valleys of other Colorado mountains. In fact, so benign is the view from the valley that the original developers bypassed it many times in search of more dominant peaks. Just prior to opening day, December 15, 1962, in a *New York Times* article, historian Marshall Sprague described it as "a placid, oblong pile, nicely clad in aspen, spruce, and lodgepole pine."

But it's what you don't see from the valley that makes Vail special. The front face, or north slopes, provide immense variety of length and pitch; and the south-facing bowls offer some of the purest, wildest open-terrain skiing on the continent. The 11,450-foot summit is just below timberline, so the north face is protected from wind; yet the elevation helps produce an annual snowfall of more than 330 inches.

There are 121 marked trails, the longest of which runs 4½ miles down the face, but the 2,700 acres of back-bowl skiing—all of which are left ungroomed, providing the entire spectrum of snow conditions, from fresh powder to breakable crust—yield a virtually limitless number of routes down the mountain. You could ski Vail for a year and not discover all its virtues, but fortunately visitors vacationing for a week or so can benefit from the most extensive modern lift network in the country. The scope and immensity of the terrain may be staggering at first, but 10 detachable quad chairs are strategically situated to provide access to individual faces and bowls on the mountain.

Vail's size makes it the most egalitarian American ski resort, a place with something for every level of skier. It may lack the throat-gurgling steepness of Jackson Hole, Taos, or Snowbird, the primitive powder of Alta, the elite image of Deer Valley, and the remoteness of Big Sky, but in its Brobdingnagian mass it manages to provide as much or as little challenge as needed.

Vail offers as much for snowboarders as it does for skiers. A lighted terrain park with two half pipes for day and night riding and the Unvailed Park for expert 'boarders, with a 300-foot technical half pipe, both opened in 1996 at Adventure Ridge atop Lionshead. A special trail map for snowboarders indicates log slides, handrails, and other features on the mountain. Of course, the ultimate terrain for skiers or snowboarders is the back bowls on a powder day.

Novices

There are several well-defined novice areas at Vail. It's important to pay careful attention to trail markers because a wrong turn can lead to a serious misadventure. Never presume that because the base area is in sight, you can't get into trouble: There are some heady black diamond runs leading into Vail Village. First-time skiers should begin at the Gopher Hill lift, which is one of the Golden Peak lifts, on the far-eastern side of the resort. It serves a wide, well-groomed beginner run that allows you no opportunity to get in over your head. Once you've found your ski legs, take a ride on the Golden Peak lift to Fort Whipper Snapper and try the long cruising run called Mule Skinner.

Green runs are accessible from every lift on the front side of the mountain. When in doubt, you can follow many long, winding catwalks that will ease you down to ground zero. If you're starting from Vail Village, the Vista Bahn lift to Mid-Vail will give you access to Lion's Way or Gitalong Road. Lion's Way will take you to the Avanti Express, and Gitalong winds back to the Vista Bahn or Avanti lifts. These are all well-groomed runs protected from the wind by trees, so all maintain a good, firm base. With a little luck you'll catch some sun on these runs by early afternoon.

From the top of Avanti take Over Easy down to where the Mountaintop Express and Hunky Dory lifts meet. The Mountaintop Express will take you to the summit, where you can choose Ramshorn to the west or Swingsville to the east. From Hunky Dory head down Eagle's Nest Ridge and turn right just before the Avanti lift to the Meadows. This beautifully groomed wide-open trail bypasses several black runs, depositing you at the Mountaintop Express–Hunky Dory intersection.

If you start your day from the Lionshead Center and ride the gondola, take Cub's Way (a well-protected run with groomed snow that zigzags all the way down to Avanti Express lift) to stay out of harm's way or follow Owl's Roost (a wide run with packed, groomed snow that leads you through the trees) down to Ledges and then to Cub's Way. Pay special attention at this junction because this is where Ledges turns expert.

The Eagle's Nest beginner park, with five trails served by six lifts, is also ideal terrain on which to start out. The snow here is typically better than the base, and there's a wide variety of terrain.

Intermediates

There is arguably no other resort in America that offers as much variety for intermediates as Vail. Starting from Vail Village, take the Vista Bahn Express up to Mid-Vail, then the Mountaintop Express to the summit. From here you have a choice of Cappuccino, a fast, well-groomed cruising glade run; Espresso, which is slightly steeper and prone to substantial mogul development; or Whistle Pig, the steepest of the three, where the moguls tend to be the biggest.

If bumps are not your thing, head for Christmas, to the right (looking down) of Swingsville. It's a good, fast giant-slalom run that cuts through the trees and remains mostly mogul-free. Another challenging choice is the designated-black Riva Ridge, perhaps the best overall intermediate-to-advanced run on the mountain. Regardless of its color, a strong intermediate should be able to handle it. Those who want a real challenge should follow Riva Ridge to Tourist Trap—an extremely steep section just below Mid-Vail. Your other option, however, is to bail out on Compromise, then rejoin Riva Ridge all the way to the bottom.

If you take the Hunky Dory lift from Mid-Vail, take Race Track or Hunky Dory (both to the left as you get off the lift). Both are excellent wide-open, bowl-like runs that you can cruise down without getting into any trouble. From Mid-Vail you can travel east on the Gitalong Road catwalk to the Trans Montane catwalk and head up the Northwoods Express lift or go west along Lion's Way to the Avanti Express.

At the top of the Northwoods lift turn left onto the Timberline catwalk; you'll pass a couple of steep black diamond runs—First Step and North Star—that a strong intermediate could handle. Serious moguls grow on the top sections, but the rest is manageable. If you stay on Timberline past the black runs, you'll see Northwoods, a wide-open cruiser with a series of rolls, and Snag Park, a slightly steeper run that eventually merges with Northwoods. Another choice, especially on fresh-powder days, is Gandy Dancer, which can be reached by going right from the Northwoods Express lift, skiing Swingsville Ridge for a short time, and picking up Gandy Dancer on your right under the Northwoods Express lift. Although this is a black run, most strong intermediates can handle it because it is usually well groomed and virtually mogul-free.

The Avanti Express lift gives you access to Avanti, a blue-black cruiser that drops and pitches with consistency and is usually well groomed; and Picaroon, another intermediate-expert combination with some extremely steep pitches. Berries is a good choice, although it does get fairly difficult toward the bottom half. If you don't want to try the black portion, cut left on Ledges and pick up Lodge Pole or Columbine.

There is another excellent set of intermediate runs to the right (getting off the lift) of the Game Creek Express, at the west end of the mountain in the Game Creek Bowl. Except for the occasional mogul-shaving operation, the Woods and Baccarat are rarely groomed but are prime intermediate runs. Showboat, immediately under the lift, has a split personality: The right side offers fairly smooth, straightforward cruising, but the left side builds up with moguls. You can take Chair 7 to the top and ski Eagle's Nest Ridge to the Eagle's Nest area. From here Simba, Bawana, Safari, and Born Free, four fairly steady cruising runs, take you back to the Lionshead gondola.

For the most part, the back bowls of Vail are a cut above the intermediate rating, although the right conditions, plenty of snow, and a little work—and a workout—will get you down in one piece, even if you do a lot of traversing. If you want to give the bowls a try but don't want to damage your health or ego, start from the Two Elk Restaurant (on the eastern back side of the mountain) and tackle the designated-blue West and East Poppyfields (wide-open bowls with a little pitch but lots of room to maneuver). These runs will put you at the bottom of the Orient Express lift. Come off to your left, follow the short catwalk, and ski West and East Poppyfields for the second time.

Experts
Vail's back bowls beckon many expert skiers, especially after a good overnight snowfall. Go early, when the morning sun has begun to soften the snow, before the powder gets too chopped up; by midday the snow turns heavy and wet. To reach the back bowls and avoid crowded lift lines, go to the Golden Peak lift, at the east end of the resort. Connect with the Highline lift and ski down to Sourdough to reach the West Wall (surface) lift. Take the West Wall and—voilà—you'll be at the top of the China Bowl.

If you start early to beat the crowds, the journey from Golden Peak lift to the China Bowl can be done in less than 40 minutes. It's time well invested because this is where you'll spend most of the morning, enjoying the sublime skiing in this massive bowl area and riding the relatively uncrowded Orient Express quad. Try

Shangri-La, which takes you through the trees, or attempt the extreme steeps of Dragon's Teeth, Genghis Khan, and Emperor's Choice. Another option from the Orient Express lift is to skirt the top of the ridge toward the Siberia Bowl, where Red Square, Gorky Park, Rasputin's Revenge, and Orient Express offer steep, un-groomed terrain.

Serious expert skiers can head far-ther east to the Inner and Outer Mon-golia bowls. This is the wildest area at Vail—not in the radical sense, but because the terrain is so vast—and it should never be skied alone. Be espe-cially cautious when the light is flat or visibility low, because it's easy to become disoriented here. At times the snow can turn cruddy, but the experi-ence of being able to point your skis and not have boundaries is priceless. Keep in mind that the route back to the Orient Express lift is by way of the long Silk Road catwalk, so try to carry some speed as you reach the bottom of the bowl. This is primitive skiing at its best, with a wild variety of snow surfaces that can include deep soft stuff, chopped-up crud, sun-kissed crust, and wind-packed powder, all accented by the sheer steepness and isolation.

During late morning head west toward the Sundown Bowl and take a run down Forever, which has one of the longest sustained verticals on the back side. The runs in this vast bowl have the southernmost exposure and are therefore warmest.

Around lunchtime you'll want to take the Hunky Dory lift to the rela-tively uncrowded Wildwood Smoke-house, on the north-facing front side of the mountain. From Wildwood ski east along the Minturn Mile to the Skipper, then pick up Look Ma. Ride the Mountaintop Express lift and get ready for Prima, Prima Cornice, and Pronto—three mogul-studded brutes that are as steep as anything you will ever ski. Prima Cornice, for instance, slants as much as 43%.

WHERE TO STAY

There are four village areas along the length of the resort, and where you stay will be determined by how much money you want to spend, whether you want to be in the center of the action, and with whom you'll be trav-eling. The Golden Peak area, at the far-east end of Vail Resort, is suitable for families and those looking for a quiet atmosphere. Most of the accom-modations are in the upper moderate price range because you pay a pre-mium for access to the Golden Peak lifts. These two lifts serve the begin-ners' area and connect with the upper lifts and more difficult terrain.

The action is in Vail Village, at the center of the resort. You'll pay top dol-lar for most of the accommodations, which are European-style lodges. The emphasis is on design, service, and poshness. This village is the nightlife hub, and bars, bistros, and boogie spots line Bridge Street, a 150-yard stretch of entertainment. Most of the lodges, inns, and elegant condos in Vail Village are within walking dis-tance of the high-speed Vista Bahn lift, which takes you to midmountain in just nine minutes.

The Lionshead gondola area, the third village, is at the west end of the resort and is more condo than Tyrolean in its styling, but it offers the greatest variety of accommodations in terms of size and price. This village, too, has its own nightlife, but it leans toward sports bars rather than piano bars, and the crowd tends to be younger and more spirited.

Farther west is Cascade Village, the least developed of Vail's four village areas. It's served by the Cascade Village lift, which you must take to reach the main lift network at the Lionshead center. You can also take the Vail shuttle bus into Lionshead or Vail Village. At the end of the day you can ski back to Cascade on the green Cascade Way Trail.

For a less expensive option, move away from the resort proper and bunk down in one of the smaller, inexpensive motels and small lodges across the highway.

Vail has an astonishing number of condominiums, ranging from practical studios to sumptuous four- and five-bedroom units. When comparing prices, don't let the per-night rate mislead you: Do your math and divide the space by the number of occupants paying the freight. You can make your own arrangements by calling direct, or you can book virtually anything through Vail Central Reservations (tel. 800/525–2257). The Vail Valley Tourism and Convention Bureau (tel. 800/824–5737) may also be of assistance.

Expensive

Christiania at Vail
Bavarian styling makes this a Vail classic: Individually designed rooms and suites have wood-beam ceilings, rustic hand-carved furnishings, and fluffy eiderdown comforters. Public spaces are as cozy as the guest quarters and include an elegant but unpre-tentious lobby decorated with stone, wood, and stucco. In addition to the hotel's beauty, the location is superb—only 100 yards from the Vista Bahn lift. There are also 50 condos, most of which have kitchen facilities, a fireplace, and a Jacuzzi and/or steam bath. *356 E. Hanson Ranch Rd., 81657, tel. 970/476–5641 or 800/530–3999, fax 970/476–0470. 16 rooms, 6 suites, 50 units. Facilities: bar, heated outdoor pool, sauna, daily maid service, ski storage, ski valet. AE, MC, V. $220–$1150, including Continental breakfast.*

Lodge at Vail
This wonderful place—one of three hotels around which most of Vail Village was built in 1962—is at once elegant and informal. Styled after the famous Lodge at Sun Valley, the Lodge at Vail brings the same European elegance to Colorado. Although the quarters are not overly large, they are all beautifully appointed, with mahogany furnishings and customized fabrics throughout. Rooms are within a snowball's throw of the Vista Bahn lift. Rates, which vary according to the view outside your window, include a buffet breakfast that is one of the best morning meals in Vail. *174 E. Gore Creek Dr., 81657, tel. 970/476–5011 or 800/331–5634, fax 970/476–7425. 63 rooms, 40 units. Facilities: 2 restaurants, bar, outdoor lap pool, Jacuzzi, exercise room, sauna, 24-hr desk service, shuttle service, ski storage, ski valet, laundry. AE, DC, MC, V. $300–$1,600.*

Manor Vail
Young families enjoy the convenience of these condos close to the lifts and children's center. The lodge rooms

and studio, one-, and two-bedroom units are designed for comfort. Each is privately owned, and you may walk into Southwestern, early American, or colonial decor. There's a wood-burning fireplace and a private balcony in all units (except the lodge rooms). *595 E. Vail Valley Dr., 81657, tel. 970/ 476–5000 or 800/950–8245, fax 970/ 476–4982. 143 lodge rooms, 83 units. Facilities: restaurant, bar, 2 outdoor pools, 2 Jacuzzis, sauna, 24-hr desk service, shuttle, daily maid service, ski storage, ski valet, laundry. AE, D, DC, MC, V. $120–$1,450.*

Sonnenalp Resort

This family-owned-and-operated business is actually two separate lodges, both within Vail Village and minutes from the Vista Bahn lift. Austria Haus and Bavaria Haus are the quintessence of European style, with wood trim and detailing and comfortable well-decorated rooms. Units range from simple hotel rooms to two-bedroom units with a fireplace and a balcony. *20 Vail Rd., 81657, tel. 970/ 476–5656 or 800/654–8312, fax 970/ 476–1639. 57 rooms, 90 suites. Facilities: 4 restaurants, 3 bars, 4 Jacuzzis, heated outdoor pool, 2 indoor pools, 2 spas, 6 saunas, exercise room, 24-hr desk service, shuttle, ski storage, laundry, game room. D, DC, MC, V. $258– $1,456.*

Vail Cascade Hotel & Club

Although it looks like a château on the outside, this giant hotel in Cascade Village eschews traditional Tyrolean decor in favor of a more American, Ralph Lauren lodge style inside. Its luxurious guest quarters incorporate dark woods, deep jewel tones, balconies, and expansive views. The condo units have one to three bedrooms and a kitchen. *1300 Westhaven Dr., 81657, tel. 970/476–7111 or 800/ 453–7133, fax 970/479–7025. 289 rooms, 29 suites, 89 units. Facilities: 2 restaurants, bar, outdoor pool, beauty salon, 2 outdoor hot tubs, sauna, steam room, health club, cinema, 24-hr desk service, shuttle, ski storage, ski valet, laundry service, meeting rooms. AE, D, DC, MC, V. $199–$1,000.*

Moderate

Gasthof Gramshammer

At this small, personal, A-frame lodge in the heart of Vail Village each room is different in size and decor, but all have traditional Austrian carved-wood furnishings and accents, bright floral-print curtains and upholstery, folk art, and artifacts, as well as balconies. *231 E. Gore Creek Dr., 81657, tel. 970/476–5626 or 800/610–7374, fax 970/476–8816. 27 rooms, 5 apartment suites. Facilities: 2 restaurants, bar, ski storage, ski shop. AE, MC, V. $138–$610, including Continental breakfast.*

Simba Run

The large two-bedroom ivory, brown, and burgundy rooms at this modern condo complex about a mile and a half from the Lionshead gondola are filled with soft pillowy sofas and chairs, handsome drapes, and well-crafted accents. Each condo has a splendid view of the valley. *1100 N. Frontage Rd., 81657, tel. 970/476– 0344 or 800/746–2278, fax 970/476– 0888. 70 units. Facilities: indoor pool, Jacuzzi, saunas, steam rooms, exercise room, shuttle, laundry, game room. No credit cards. $180–$415.*

Sitzmark Lodge

For the money, this small, owner-operated European-style property is one of my favorites. It's in the center of the action, allowing you to walk to a variety of restaurants, shops, and bars, and you are one block from the slopes. All rooms have a balcony that overlooks Gore Creek or the mountain, as well as a refrigerator. The decor is European modern: Bright upholstery and sleekly designed furnishings of blond wood. *183 Gore Creek Dr., 81657, tel. 970/476–5001, fax 970/476–8702. 35 rooms. Facilities: restaurant-bar, outdoor whirlpool, sauna, outdoor pool, ski storage, laundry. D, MC, V. $116–$252, including Continental breakfast and après-ski refreshments.*

Vail Village Inn

The family-run inn's buildings are arranged around a quad, with three sides bordered by hotel buildings and a fourth by retail stores and restaurants. Bavarian-style architectural details are everywhere, from ceiling panels to room furnishings. Guest quarters range from basic to luxurious (a four-bedroom condo with a private elevator) and are priced accordingly. *100 E. Meadow Dr., 81657, tel. 970/476–5622 or 800/445–4014, fax 970/476–4661. 80 rooms, 40 units. Facilities: 3 restaurants, bar, lounge, heated outdoor pool, sauna, Jacuzzi, 24-hr desk service, shuttle, ski storage, laundry. AE, DC, MC, V. $130–$1,250, including full breakfast.*

The Willows

The traditional European-style exterior of this four-story lodge gives way to a Rocky Mountain–modern interior with plenty of wood and stone. The location, minutes from the Vista Bahn lift, makes this an exceptionally good deal. Condos have a good-size kitchen and fireplace. *74 Willow Rd., 81657, tel. 970/476–2233 or 800/826–1274, fax 970/476–5714. 4 rooms, 42 units. Facilities: whirlpool, steam room, ski storage, laundry. AE, MC, V. $140–$1,200, including Continental breakfast and après-ski refreshments.*

Inexpensive

Black Bear Inn

Inside this honey-bronze log building on the banks of Gore Creek is a cozy great room with a gas stove. The cabin rooms either have a sitting area by the bay window overlooking the mountain or one with a sleep sofa flanked by carved trunks. Down comforters cover handcrafted queen-size or twin beds, and local artists' watercolors decorate the log walls. You won't find a TV or radio in your room. *2405 Elliott Rd., West Vail 81657, tel. 970/476–1304, fax 970/476–0433. 12 rooms. Facilities: ski storage, laundry, TV in common room. MC, V. $115–$195, including full breakfast and après-ski snacks.*

Minturn Inn

This 1915 three-story home is older than the town of Vail itself. The three owners, all originally from New England, have painstakingly restored it into a charming inn with 10 theme rooms. The Angler, for example, has carved wooden fish and fly-fishing paraphernalia, while the 10th Mountain Division sports skis and snowshoes on the walls. The beds are handmade of logs, with quilt coverings. Most rooms have views of the red cliffs unique to the area and the river; some have Jacuzzis and steam showers. The only drawback is that you'll need a car to reach the ski slopes—Minturn lacks public transportation. *442 N. Main St., Box 186, Minturn 81645, tel. 970/827-9647 or 800/646-8876, fax 970/827-5590. 10 rooms, 8 with bath. Facilities: sauna. AE, D, MC, V. $79–$199, including full breakfast and après-ski snacks.*

Roost Lodge
This property should be high on any bargain hunter's list because it's one of the best deals in Vail. The rooms are very functional, with a variety of bed arrangements. The lobby invites guests to lounge and swap stories by the fire. The lodge is one block from the town bus stop. *1783 N. Frontage Rd. W, 81657, tel. 970/476-5451 or 800/873-3065, fax 970/476-9158. 70 rooms, 2 suites. Facilities: indoor pool, outdoor Jacuzzi, sauna, shuttle, ski storage. AE, D, DC, MC, V. $69–$179, including Continental breakfast and après-ski snacks.*

Tivoli Lodge
This family-run traditional Bavarian-style lodge sprang up in the heart of Vail during the village's early years. Guest rooms are bright and spacious, decorated with stucco, floral fabrics, and dusty rose carpeting and furnished with light-oak furniture and small refrigerators. The room rate is determined by the view: If you can live without seeing the peaks from your window, you can save dollars. Most units have more than one bed and can comfortably sleep three or four people, which is one reason the Tivoli is popular with families. There is a bus stop across the street. *386*

Hanson Ranch Rd., 81657, tel. 970/476-5615 or 800/451-4756, fax 970/476-6601. 50 rooms. Facilities: bar, lounge, heated outdoor pool, 2 outdoor Jacuzzis, sauna, ski storage, laundry. AE, D, DC, MC, V. $139–$225, including Continental breakfast.

Westwind at Vail
A convenient location and a variety of sleeping arrangements make this a good choice for families and groups. Choose from standard hotel rooms and condos ranging in size from one to three bedrooms. Each condo unit is decorated by its owners with functional rather than fashionable furnishings, but all have a kitchen, a fireplace, a balcony, and a TV/VCR. It's one block from two bus stops. *1031-D S. Frontage Rd., 81657, tel. 970/476-5031 or 800/852-9378, fax 970/476-9152. 12 rooms, 25 units. Facilities: 2 outdoor Jacuzzis, heated outdoor pool, sauna, ski storage, laundry, daily maid service. AE, MC, V. $99–$745.*

WHERE TO EAT
Aside from Aspen, Vail has the largest number of dining options of any U.S. ski resort, running the gamut from fancy to frugal.

On the Mountain
Cook Shack
Its mid-Vail location makes this full-service lunch restaurant one of the busiest spots on the mountain. The mostly Southwestern menu includes fajitas and black bean chili as well as such items as pesto chicken. *Top of Vista Bahn lift, tel. 970/479-4570. Reservations essential. AE, D, MC, V.*

Two Elk Restaurant

If you're on the China, Teacup, or Sun bowls on the back of the mountain, stop at this log cabin east of the Orient Express lift. The serve-yourself gourmet restaurant offers everything from pizzas and salads to pastas but is best known for its magnificent view. *Top of China Bowl, tel. 970/479–4560. AE, D, MC, V.*

Expensive

Game Creek Club

Vail's exclusive on-mountain lunch club is now open to the public for dinner. Your evening begins in a heated gondola that whisks you up Lionshead to Eagle's Nest. From here you catch an open snowcat (covered in inclement weather) for the short ride to the Bavarian-style lodge. Be prepared to linger over a five-course prix fixe meal. Entrées are Continental with an Asian flair—dishes like seared ahi served sushi style with cucumbers and sesame vinaigrette or a more traditional beef tenderloin with blue cheese crust served with lyonnaise potatoes and green peppercorn sauce. *600 Lionshead Circle, tel. 970/479–4275. Reservations essential. AE, D, DC, MC, V.*

La Tour

The two carpeted dining rooms, decorated with French paintings and pictures of the owners' friends, draw families as well as the business crowd. Try the duck with pepper sauce, roasted breast of pheasant with sautéed mushrooms, or quail's breast stuffed with foie gras. *122 E. Meadow Dr., tel. 970/476–4403. Reservations essential. AE, MC, V.*

Left Bank

The tone in this elegant dining room is defined by tasteful artwork and china table settings, but the mood is friendly and comfortable. Start your meal with the tomato surprise (a bowl of soup with a puff-pastry topping), then try fresh loin of elk sautéed in elk stock or pepper steak served with a cream-and-brandy sauce. Reserve a table by the window, where you'll be lulled by classical music as you look out over Gore Creek. *Sitzmark Lodge, 183 Gore Creek Dr., tel. 970/476–3696. No credit cards.*

Montauk Seafood Grill

Alaskan bass, Florida grouper, Maine lobster, swordfish, halibut, mahimahi, and crab are here for the picking in this nautically decorated restaurant. Pair your seafood choice with one of the three daily sauces served. There's also a raw bar with a variety of oysters, clams, and other shellfish. If you don't like fish, you can also get steak or pasta. For dessert try the signature Sand Pie. *549 Lionshead Circle (in mall), tel. 970/476–2601. AE, MC, V.*

Tyrolean Inn

The antlers and other hunting trophies adorning the walls should clue you in to the specialty of this Bavarian-style inn: game, much of it raised on owner Pepi Langegger's ranch. The menu includes elk, caribou, buffalo, wild boar, salmon, duck, pheasant, and trout, among others. Try mandarin-orange pepper duck or pheasant *kroatzbeere* (boneless breast marinated in apple wine and sautéed in blackberry glaze, shallots, and cognac). The apple strudel will satisfy your sweet tooth. *400 E. Meadow Dr., tel. 970/476–2204. AE, MC, V.*

Moderate

Blu's

You have to love a restaurant that offers dishes such as Kick Ass California Chicken Relleño (a whole poblano pepper packed with jack cheese and wrapped in a chicken breast) and Cowboy Steak (a 14-ounce bone-in rib eye with chili sauce and fried squash ravioli). The rest of the menu is similarly diverse, with a little of everything from fish to fowl, including pasta and blackened tuna. Blu's is a lively spot, more bistro than restaurant, and enjoys a great location in the heart of Vail Village. *193 E. Gore Creek, tel. 970/476–3113. AE, DC, MC, V.*

Michael's American Bistro

This very sleek, stylish boîte overlooks the atrium of the Gateway Mall, but the space is dramatic: fancifully carved wood columns, lacquered black tables, and striking photographs and art. The hip atmosphere is further accentuated by the cool jazz and the slinky waitstaff garbed entirely in black. You could make a meal of the openers alone: grilled smoked quail with orange chutney, gourmet spicy shrimp pizza with roasted onion sauce, and a vegetable terrine with three pestos. If you can't decide, order the tapas plate, an assortment of three appetizers that changes daily. The fine extensive wine list has several bargains under $25. *12 S. Frontage Rd., tel. 970/476–5353. AE, D, DC, MC, V.*

Ore House

Known for its steaks, the Ore House also offers all sorts of other meaty specials, such as pepper steak, beef kebabs, and prime rib, as well as chicken, seafood and vegetarian entrées. Start things off right with an order of popcorn shrimp and finish with the key lime pie. Decor is true to the Western mining theme, with mining carts converted into tables and Western art and stock certificates hanging on the walls. *232 Bridge St., tel. 970/476–5100. Reservations essential for 8 or more. AE, DC, MC, V.*

Sweet Basil

The understated decor—blond-wood chairs and muted teal-and-buff walls—is enlivened by towering floral arrangements and abstract art, and the Pacific Rim–influenced Mediterranean cuisine is intensely flavored and beautifully presented. Standouts include sesame seared tuna on a bed of crisp Asian vegetables, a meaty Portobello and goat cheese tart drizzled with basil-pepper and balsamic vinaigrettes, almond-crusted rack of lamb with shiitake pot stickers, and a honey-baked pork chop with wild rice pancakes and ruby grapefruit sauce. The menu changes seasonally, and the daily specials are invariably brilliant. *193 E. Gore Creek Dr., tel. 970/476–0125. AE, MC, V.*

Up the Creek

This casual restaurant a rod's length from Gore Creek is decorated with soft pastel-colored walls, whimsical watercolors, and small, intimate table settings suited to groups of two or four. The menu is heavy on fish: cedar-plank salmon, catfish, mahimahi, Colorado trout, plus daily fish specials. If you're interested in something from the field rather than the stream, try the rack of lamb or the roasted herb free-range chicken served over polenta. *223 Gore Creek Dr., tel. 970/476–8141. AE, D, DC, MC, V.*

Inexpensive
Bully Ranch
This saloon is pure Western—complete with wooden floor, beamed ceiling, large bar, and cowboy memorabilia on the walls. Menu selections range from build-your-own barbecue platters of chicken, ribs, and kielbasa to Southwestern lasagna (tortillas layered with three cheeses, roasted peppers, and chorizo in a spicy green-chili sauce). *Sonnenalp Resort, 20 Vail Rd., tel. 970/476–5656. D, DC, MC, V.*

Clancy's Windy City Irish Pub
Clancy's is a self-styled Chicago diner with a menu of hearty entrées as well as finger-food favorites such as chicken fingers, onion rings, and chicken wings. Locals frequent Clancy's for its high activity level and low prices, and the many TV screens appeal to fans of "da Bulls and da Bears." *1300 Westhaven Dr., tel. 970/ 476–3886. AE, D, MC, V.*

Hubcap Brew Pub
Vail's only brew pub is the locals' favorite hangout for intense cheek-to-jowl ambience, an excellent selection of beer (ale and amber, wheat, and golden stout), and off-the-wall munchies. The rotisserie chicken, steamed mussels, meat loaf, and chicken potpie are big hits. *143 E. Meadow Dr., tel. 970/476–5757. AE, MC, V.*

The Saloon
Skiers in the know do the "Minturn Mile" at the end of the day, bushwhacking out the bottom of Game Creek Bowl and ending up a few steps from this venerable gathering place. (Warning: this is not ski-area-maintained terrain, and there is no transportation back. Of course, you can always drive here.) The reward is margaritas made with real lime juice, serve-yourself chips and homemade salsa, specialties like chili *relleños* and the steak and quail plate, and a bar that's always packed with locals. *146 N. Main St., Minturn, tel. 970/827–5954. Reservations not accepted. AE, MC, V.*

Best Bets for Breakfast
Daily Grind
This is a great place to catch a cappuccino or other specialty coffee or a quick conversation with locals heading out to find the untracked powder. There's a selection of baked goodies and deli sandwiches. *288 Bridge St., tel. 970/476–5856. MC, V.*

DJ McCadam's Diner
If you're heading up the mountain on the gondola at Lionshead, DJ's is the place to fuel up with a hearty breakfast. The French toast is the toast of the town, and breakfast blintzes get glowing reviews. Omelets and other egg dishes are available, too. *616 W. Lionshead Circle, Concert Hall Plaza, Lionshead Mall, tel. 970/476–2336. No credit cards.*

NIGHTLIFE AND ENTERTAINMENT
Après-Ski
Red Lion
This is the après-ski gathering spot, just down the hill from the gondola. The deck is wildly popular, and later on there is mellow live entertainment.

Try the heaping mound of nachos as an appetizer. *304 Bridge St., tel. 970/476-7676. AE, D, MC, V.*

Loud and Lively/Dancing

Garfinkel's

Garfinkel's is a ski-school hangout, predictably popular with the younger set—especially snowboarders. *536 W. Lionshead Mall, tel. 970/476-3789. AE, MC, V.*

Garton's

You can find everything from rock to reggae, from Cajun to country in this big barnlike structure. *Crossroads Shopping Center, tel. 970/476-0607. AE, MC, V.*

More Mellow

Club Chelsea

Club Chelsea has it all: a quiet piano bar that feels like a speakeasy, a raucous disco and a room for cigar smoking complete with leopard-skin couches around the fire. *304 Bridge St., tel. 970/476-5600. AE, D, DC, MC, V.*

Palmo's

This is Vail's coolest hangout, with eye-catching decor that was designed and carved by local artist Menzel, who utilizes gorgeously textured 200-year-old wormwood (visible throughout the mall; notice the wild stairways) to dazzling effect. The tables alone reputedly cost $3,000 each. There's a selection of hot drinks, brandies, and single malts. *Gateway Plaza, tel. 970/476-7767. AE, MC, V.*

Pepi's Bar

Relax to live music in this piano bar with one of your favorite people. *Gasthof Gramshammer, 231 E. Gore Creek Dr., tel. 970/476-5626. AE, DC, MC, V.*

WINTER PARK RESORT

WINTER PARK RESORT

Box 36
Winter Park, CO 80482
Tel. 970/726–5514

STATISTICALLY SPEAKING

Base elevation: 9,000 feet

Summit elevation: 12,060 feet

Vertical drop: 3,060 feet

Skiable terrain: 1,358 acres

Number of trails: 121

Longest run: 5.1 miles

Lifts and capacity: 7 high-speed quads, 8 doubles, 5 triples; 34,023 skiers per hour

Daily lift ticket: $45

Average annual snowfall: 355 inches

Number of skiing days 1995–96: 158

Snowmaking: 280 acres, 20%

Terrain mix: N 19%, I 61%, E 20%

Snowboarding: yes

Winter Park is the most visited ski area in Colorado, and although it doesn't attract the glitterati that flock to Aspen or the CEO-type crowd that migrates to Vail, it's a reliable all-around resort, with excellent skiing, a good choice of reasonably priced accommodations, and one of the country's finest ski programs for people with disabilities. What Winter Park lacks, however, is a ski-town image that can be captured in a visual vignette. The town itself—2 miles from the resort and its three mountains—is spread out along 2 miles of Route 40 in a series of prosaic, interconnected shopping plazas.

First-time visitors could easily drive past the resort—barely visible from the highway—and not realize it. That Winter Park's physical style is unmemorable is not a problem for day skiers from Denver, as most of them seldom venture beyond the slopes before heading back to the bright lights of the city. For destination skiers scanning brochures, however, the resort seems disjointed and unglamorous.

Although the resort is physically nondescript, it has personality. Here the locals shuffle rather than bustle, the train still brings skiers into Winter Park, and there's even a youth hostel in the middle of town where a bed can be had for $15.

There are a few things that could be improved. The parking at the resort is chaotic, and the alternative, shuttle bus service, could be better—although its fleet of cramped school buses does get the job done. There is only one on-slope condo complex, and even that property stretches the definition a bit, as it is somewhat of a hike to the slopes. Also, it would behoove area developers to build alternatives to the strip-mall parade that stretches down the valley.

But these are minor inconveniences when you consider that this is one of the most reasonably priced, unpretentious resorts in the country. There are no $1,000-a-night hotel rooms here, but there is an assortment of modestly priced accommodations that make a weeklong family ski vacation as affordable as a weekend is at many other areas. It's not just a family affair, either. Singles and groups can enjoy the same relatively inexpensive benefits, and although nightlife options are not endless, there's

more than enough variety to satisfy all but the most
torrid party animals.

HOW TO GET THERE

By Plane
Denver International Airport (*see* Getting to
Colorado Resorts, *above*) is 75 miles from Winter
Park.

By Car
From the airport take I–70 west for about 50 miles to
Exit 232 (U.S. 40) and continue north for 25 miles
over the Berthoud Pass and into Winter Park.

By Bus
Gray Line of Denver (tel. 800/348–6877) provides daily round-trip service from several locations
in Denver.

By Train
The **Ski Train** (tel. 303/296–4754) leaves Denver's
Union Station weekends at 7:15 AM and departs from
Winter Park at 4:15 PM, arriving in Denver at 6:15 PM.
Amtrak's *California Zephyr* (tel. 800/453–2525)
serves Winter Park daily from Los Angeles, San Fran-
cisco, Seattle, and Chicago. The train has sleeping
accommodations.

By Shuttle
The **Home James** (tel. 970/726–5060 or 800/451–
4844) shuttle service has regularly scheduled round-
trip service between Denver and Winter Park. The
one-way rate is $34 per person, round-trip $68.
Reservations are advised. Private charter service
through Home James is also available and costs $285
for 10 people, $305 for 14.

THE SKIING
For many years the skiing at Winter Park was considered terminally tame: It was thought of as a great
place for families and groups of modest intermediates
but one that lacked the steep, challenging runs found
in other Rocky Mountain resorts. This misleading reputation had developed in part because the resort
emphasizes its enormous innovative teaching programs rather than Mary Jane's steeps, which pack

enough punch to keep all but the most manic experts happy. Winter Park offers a well-rounded, complete ski experience with some of the deepest, most consistent snow coverage in the entire state.

The terrain is divided into four neatly defined areas, which allows skiers to pick their niche without getting in over their heads or becoming bored. Winter Park Mountain is an excellent area for novices and fledgling intermediates; Vasquez Ridge turns things up a notch with solid intermediate trails; Mary Jane pulls no punches with some of the steepest, heaviest mogul runs in Colorado; and the Parsenn Bowl gives intermediates 200 acres of above-treeline bowl skiing without the prohibitive challenges of expert bowls.

There are two main base areas: the village at the bottom of Winter Park mountain and the Mary Jane base area. Both have parking, but slots fill quickly with the day-skier traffic from Denver, so it's better to avail yourself of the shuttle bus that runs between most accommodations and the two base areas. Although this setup allows novices and intermediates to explore their own limits without interfering with each other, it makes meeting up at the end of the day a bit difficult, especially for beginners, who might have trouble finding a safe route to Mary Jane. Intermediates and experts can more readily scoot back from Mary Jane to Winter Park. Consider this when making arrangements to meet, and put the onus on better skiers to make the trek. (The other option is for novices to hop on the free shuttle bus that connects the two base areas.)

Moving from mountain to mountain is fairly easy, with very few flat sections except for the extremely long runoff from the Vasquez Ridge area (the Big Valley). To avoid this as you head from Vasquez to Winter Park, take Buckaroo, a medium-pitch, groomed blue run that will take you to the bottom of the Olympia chair, which goes to the top of Winter Park. From the top of Vasquez Ridge you can also take the green Gunbarrel Run (turn left off the Pioneer Express) over to the High Lonesome Express, which goes to the top of Mary Jane, where novices will find a half-dozen green runs and intermediates and experts can access the steeper blue and black runs of the Parsenn Bowl area. From the top of Mary Jane you can make your way back to the Winter Park base area by skiing down Whistle Stop to Allan Phipps or Cranmer Cutoff, which is also green. Those who are intermediate and better can avoid the novice area by taking Cranmer (blue) or one of a half-dozen blue/black runs.

Snowboarders have three different terrain parks to choose from, all of which underwent major improvements in 1996–97. Two terrain parks on the Winter Park side feature rail slides, quarter pipes, and a series of jumps, and a new half pipe on Jabberwocky is open to snowboarders only. On the Mary Jane side, Stone Grove is a favorite for 'boarders who like to ride the glades. For beginners, the enclosed Discovery Park 30-acre learn-to-ski and -snowboard area is a good place to practice, with several gladed adventure trails and rolled terrain with banked turns. Special events for snowboarders throughout the season include a SuperCarve clinic to help skiers make the transition to snowboarding, the Bump Jamboree, and a freestyle snowboard camp.

Novices

Nearly half the trails at Winter Park mountain are green, and most are easy to reach from the far right (facing the mountain) of the base area. The Gemini Express lift takes you about a third of the way up the mountain to Discovery Park, a 30-acre enclosed learn-to-ski area. Here you can practice on the gentle, rolling, well-groomed terrain of Porcupine, Bobcat, and Marmot Flats. When you are ready to leave this area, Parkway will ease you back down to the bottom of the Gemini lift, or you can scoot to the left looking down the mountain and feed to the bottom of Marmot Flats, where three lifts converge. Any of these chairs will take you higher up the mountain to the gently undulating, meticulously groomed Allan Phipps or March Hare trails. The Cranmer Cutoff intersects both and carries you back down to Parkway and Larry Sale. If you aren't ready for such long runs, either stay on Allan Phipps all the way to the bottom (where the three lifts meet) or hop the Discovery lift, which serves a shorter green run called Bill Wilson's Way.

Aggressive novices may want to take the Zephyr Express lift from the Winter Park base to the summit at Winter Park and then follow an easy catwalk to the High Lonesome Express lift, which climbs to the top of Mary Jane. What's nice about Mary Jane is its modest beginner area at the base, which lets first-timers stay on the same mountain as their more advanced friends. From the summit there are a half-dozen green runs that wind down through the trees to the bottom of High Lonesome. Switchyard is a wide boulevard that follows the ski-area boundary (left, looking down); it includes some interesting dips and rolls and also tends to be busy. Hobo Alley and Whistle Stop (to the right, looking down) are much narrower trails that cut through the trees and tend to be less exposed if it's windy. You can either continue to the bottom of Winter Park on March Hare or Allan Phipps or ride the lift back to the higher elevation.

Intermediates

If you start from the Winter Park base area, take the Zephyr Express lift to the summit and turn right off the lift for the steady pitch and groomed terrain of the Hughes, Bradley's Bash, or Cranmer runs. Upper and Lower Hughes and Bradley's Bash are most consistently groomed and more suited to cruising, and Cranmer is groomed on one side and left ungroomed on the other, making it an excellent run to practice a few mogul turns with an easy escape route.

In general the runs on the left or backside of Mary Jane are mid- to upper intermediate, and the middle and right-side runs are considerably steeper and bumpier. Take the Summit Express lift to the Mary Jane summit, from which you can reach more than a dozen intermediate runs on the back side of Mary Jane or on the Parsenn Bowl farther up. The Parsenn Bowl beckons from the top of Mary Jane, but watch the weather. If it's clear, head down to the Timberline lift and play in the bowl with its wide, swooping, treeless terrain. On bad-weather days when visibility is low or the light is flat, it's best to stick to the below-tree-line runs. If you've never experienced the freedom of a wide-open bowl, skiing the Parsenn is a perfect introduction because it's not toe-curling steep yet is precipitous enough to let you carry the speed to handle deep snow. Although it's mostly ungroomed, it is usually well mannered enough not to inhibit first-time powder hounds; the more than 200 acres offer lots of space for wide, sweeping turns and no areas where you can get into trouble. A few new gladed runs allow for some challenging but not too threatening tree skiing.

Vasquez Ridge, at the far west end of the resort, is another great intermediate playground. From Mary Jane take Lonesome Whistle to Wagon Train, which will take you to the bottom of the Pioneer Express lift; if you're coming from Winter Park, take Jabberwocky to Wagon Train for some quality cruising on groomed terrain. The majority of runs on Vasquez Ridge are solid high-speed cruisers with good pitch and roll. Stagecoach, Sundance, and Quickdraw are good choices for steady pitch and groomed snow, but all eventually feed into Big Valley, a tediously long ski-out that winds back to the bottom of the lift. To avoid the hassle, pick up Buckaroo from Sundance about halfway down.

Once you're comfortable, move up a notch: Gambler and Aces and Eights are two short, steep mogul runs that are worth a try. Toward the end of the day make sure you take Gunbarrel from the top of the Pioneer Express, as it will take you back to the High Lonesome Express lift and to runs leading to Winter Park.

Experts

The Mary Jane section of the resort has gained a reputation for some of the steepest, most sustained mogul runs in the West. From the Winter Park base area the Zephyr Express is your fastest way to the top: Plunge into things with a sharp turn to the left to access a mean bump chute called Outhouse, which takes you back down to the Mary Jane base. The Summit Express lift gives you a fast trip to the top and a number of solidly advanced bump or glade runs. For steep glades try Sluice Box or Pine Cliff, and for bumps take either Gandy Dancer or Drunken Frenchman.

The truly hard-core have a good selection of mostly ungroomed, wildly steep runs down the right side of Mary Jane. Try the precipitous quartet Hole-in-the-Wall, Awe Chute, Baldy's Chute, or Jeff's Chute to really drive your knees into your chest. These runs are among the steepest on the mountain and accessible only through control gates, but they'll give any steep-freak a good ride, especially after a good dump, when they become choked with snow and stay that way long after other runs have been skied off. Take Phantom Ridge for a high-speed mix of bumps, drop-offs, and rolls. Derailer is similarly mixed but has a few twisting turns through the trees. And don't ignore the Winter Park side: Mulligans, Retta's, and Engledive offer some steep thrills.

WHERE TO STAY

The town of Winter Park and the Fraser Valley have some of the best-value accommodations in Colorado. The emphasis is on practical condo units, with small mountain inns and a number of standard motels also available. There are a dozen or so bed-and-breakfasts. Most accommodations are on either side of U.S. 40 between the resort and the town of Fraser, about 4 miles down the valley from the slopes. Slope-side accommodations are limited to one condo complex, but a shuttle bus system connects virtually every place to the mountain. All accommodations can be booked through **Winter Park Central Reservations** (tel. 970/726–5587 or 800/729–5183).

Expensive

Crestview Place

This condo complex in the middle of the town of Winter Park, 2 miles from the slopes, is a good choice if you want to be within walking distance of the stores, restaurants, and nightlife. The units are large, with high ceilings, multiple bathrooms, and full kitchens. All have a unified design scheme of mauve, lavender, and teal. Unfortunately, the building and the individual units are starting to show signs of wear. Still, large groups, families, and even groups of families will find them comfortable and convenient. Amenities are spartan, with laundry rooms on alternating floors and two hot tubs. The Winter Park shuttle bus stops at the front door. *78737 U.S. 40, Box 3095, Winter Park 80482, tel. 970/726–9421 or 800/228–1025. 19 units. Facilities: 2 indoor hot tubs, shuttle, maid service, ski storage, laundry. AE, D, MC, V. $92–$440.*

Gasthaus Eichler

This traditional stone, stucco, and wood Bavarian-style mountain lodge is a warm, woodsy, homey place in the middle of town. Guest rooms have whirlpool tubs and are individually decorated with such nice touches as lace curtains, down comforters, and complimentary toiletries. There's a pleasant fireside lounge and a German restaurant (*see* Where to Eat, *below*). Its five-course dinner is included in the cost of a room. *78786 U.S. 40, Box 430, Winter Park 80482, tel. 970/726–5133 or 800/543–3899, fax 970/726–5175. 15 rooms. Facilities: restaurant, bar, lounge, shuttle, maid service, ski storage. AE, MC, V. $100–$140, including dinner.*

Iron Horse Resort Retreat

If the convenience of ski-in/ski-out accommodation is your preference, the Iron Horse is your only choice at Winter Park. This large condo complex at the Mary Jane end of the resort has rooms, studios, and suites and is a good spot for families and large groups looking for extra space and the convenience of hotel-type service and amenities. The condos are well appointed, with a fireplace and full kitchen facilities. The smaller lodge rooms are good for couples. *257 Winter Park Dr., Box 1286, Winter Park 80482, tel. 970/726–8851 or 800/621–8190, fax 970/726–2321. 133 units. Facilities: restaurant, lounge, 4 outdoor hot tubs, indoor-outdoor pool, health club, steam room, 24-hr desk service, maid service, ski shop, ski storage, laundry, game room. AE, DC, MC, V. $150–$535.*

Vintage Hotel

This is the only traditional full-service hotel in Winter Park, and its rooms and suites are among the resort's most luxurious. Smaller studio and one-bedroom units have a kitchenette and a fireplace; larger penthouse suites give you more space to spread out in front of the fire and full-size kitchens for preparing meals. The hotel is temptingly close to the slopes (although it is not ski-in/ski-out), with a spectacular view from the rooms facing the mountain. Reproduction Victorian furniture and wallpaper adorn the guest rooms and the comfortable library, where easy chairs and sofas surround the fireplace. The hotel's isolation makes it more suitable for couples than for those looking to socialize in town. *100 Winter Park Dr., Box 1369, Winter Park 80482, tel. 970/726–8801 or 800/ 472–7017, fax 970/726–9250. 112 rooms, 6 suites. Facilities: restaurant, bar, deli, outdoor hot tub, outdoor pool, exercise room, sauna, 24-hr desk service, shuttle, maid service, ski shop, ski storage, laundry, game room. AE, D, DC, MC, V. $85–$525.*

Moderate

The Anna Leah

You'll feel like you're staying at a good friend's house at this B&B, thanks to the congenial owner, Patricia Handel, who will accommodate almost any request. The inn is just past the town of Fraser, about 5 miles from the ski area. With balconies overlooking the national forest and the Continental Divide, it has a wonderfully serene feel. *1001 County Rd. 8, Fraser 80442, tel. 970/726–4414 or 800/237–9913. 5 rooms. Facilities: maid service, ski storage. V. $85–$165, including full breakfast.*

Beaver Village Condos

These accommodations are deluxe for the money and range in size, from studio to three bedrooms, all with a kitchen and a fireplace. The decor suggests upscale Southwestern, with Native American patterns meeting pastel greens and blues. The one-bedroom units are good for couples or for two or three friends who aren't fussy about privacy. Families and groups, especially those who want to be slightly removed from the main-street action of Winter Park, may like the larger units. *50 Village Dr., Box 349, Winter Park 80482, tel. 970/ 726–8813 or 800/824–8438. 130 units. Facilities: 3 indoor hot tubs, indoor pool, sauna, shuttle, ski storage, laundry. AE, D, MC, V. $40–$460.*

Grand Victorian

This luxury B&B is a three-story neo-Victorian in downtown Winter Park. Amenities include robes, slippers, and potpourri sachets in the rooms and an afternoon happy hour featuring Colorado wines and beers. The huge gourmet breakfast may include potato pancakes, quiches, or delectable macadamia nut waffles. *78542 Fraser Valley Parkway, Winter Park 80482, tel. 970/726–5881 or 800/204–1170. 10 rooms. Facilities: whirlpool baths, shuttle, maid service, ski storage, meeting room. AE, D, DC, MC, V. $65– $175, including full breakfast.*

High Country Haus Condominiums

These large, well-maintained units are great for families, are within walking distance of town, and contain a recreation complex complete with hot tubs, a heated pool, a sauna, and a game room. Units are spread among 24 buildings surrounding the recreation complex and range in size from one to three bedrooms. Each has a full-size kitchen, a fireplace, multiple bathrooms, and extra sleeping space for unexpected guests. *78415 U.S. 40, Box 3095, Winter Park 80482, tel. 970/726–9421 or 800/228–1025, fax 970/726–8004. 145 units. Facilities: 4 indoor hot tubs, indoor pool, sauna, shuttle, ski storage, laundry, game room. AE, D, MC, V. $86–$408.*

Inexpensive

Morningstar Ranch Sports Lodge

This no-frills lodge is on the trails at the Devil's Thumb cross-country ski area and about a 10-minute drive to Winter Park. *County Road 8, Box 930, Fraser 80482, tel. 970/726–4895 or 800/875–9739. 8 rooms share 4 baths. Facilities: ski storage. MC, V. $39–$79, including Continental breakfast.*

Sundowner Motel

At this motel in downtown Winter Park, the larger-than-average rooms have one queen-size or two double beds and a good-size bathroom. Two guests will be more than comfortable, four a comfortable squeeze in the regular rooms. Some larger rooms sleep six. Rooms have a refrigerator, a microwave, and a coffeemaker, and there's an outdoor hot tub in a gazebo. *78869 U.S. 40, Box 221, Winter Park 80482, tel. 970/726–9451 or 800/521–8279. 22 rooms. AE, D, MC, V. $54–$118.*

Viking Lodge

A location in the middle of Winter Park makes this a good bet if you want easy access to dinner and nightlife. The units come in a variety of sizes, from small economy rooms to deluxe suites. Walls are wood pan-eled, floors are carpeted, and the furniture is virtually damageproof—not fancy, but not fragile either. *U.S. 40 and Vasquez Rd., Box 89, Winter Park 80482, tel. 970/726–8885 or 800/421–4013. 22 rooms, 3 units. Facilities: indoor hot tub, sauna, shuttle, maid service, ski shop, ski storage, game room. AE, D, MC, V. $39–$239, including Continental breakfast.*

Winter Park Hostel International

Several inveterate hostelers I spoke with declared this the cleanest, safest hostel they had ever stayed in. Eight of the rooms sleep two; the remaining rooms sleep one, four, or six. There are five kitchens and five small living rooms with couches, coffee tables, books, and games. The hours from 10 PM to 7 AM are designated as quiet time inside the hostel, but step out, and you'll find a wide range of nearby activities, starting with 100 kilometers of groomed cross-country trails just outside the door. *29 Wanderer's Way, Box 3323, Winter Park 80482, tel. 970/726–5356. 15 rooms share 5 baths. Facilities: shuttle service, ski storage. MC, V. $15.50–$18.50 per person.*

Woodspur Lodge

This classic log-cabin lodge is on the edge of the Arapaho National Forest, about 1½ miles from town. The small rooms are more rustic than posh, with furnishings handmade from local lodgepole pines, and the emphasis is on mingling in the common areas. Breakfast, dinner, and après-ski hors d'oeuvres are included in the room rate and are served in a dining area with a giant fireplace and a soaring roof. Many rooms have adjoining access. *111 Van Anderson Dr., Box 249,*

Winter Park 80482, tel. 970/726–8417
or 800/626–6562, fax 970/726–8553.
32 rooms. Facilities: private bar (guests
only), 2 outdoor hot tubs, sauna, shuttle, maid service, ski storage, laundry,
game room. D, MC, V. $48–$92, including full breakfast and dinner.

WHERE TO EAT
On the Mountain
Lodge at Sunspot
This striking log-and-glass structure
on the summit of Winter Park Mountain has two excellent places to eat.
The Sunspot dining room (see below)
is an upscale sit-down restaurant with
a diverse lunch menu that includes
everything from soups and sandwiches to full meals. The Provisioner
is a serve-yourself deli-marketplace
with fresh baked goods, soups, salads,
bratwurst, fast food, and a panoramic
view. Both restaurants get busy
between noon and 2, so be prepared
to wait. Top of Zephyr Express lift,
Winter Park, tel. 970/726–8155. AE,
D, DC, MC, V.

Sundance Cafe
This is a good choice on busy days
because it's in what is generally the
least crowded area of the resort. The
best dishes are the beef stew or chili
in a bread bowl. Top of Pioneer
Express, Winter Park, tel. 800/453–
2525. No credit cards.

Expensive
Alpeggio's
You won't go away hungry from the
traditional four-course Italian meal
served here: soup, pasta or other
entrée, salad, and fruit and cheese.
The vitello alpeggio—veal scallopini

with fresh spinach and shrimp—is
delicious, as is the penne fantasia—
pasta with grilled chicken, walnuts,
and grapes in a Gorgonzola cream
sauce. The rooms upstairs rent by the
night. U.S. 40, Winter Park, tel. 970/
726–5402. AE, D, DC, MC, V.

Gasthaus Eichler
This is Winter Park's most romantic
dining spot, with quaint Bavarian
decor, antler chandeliers, and Strauss
playing softly in the background. Veal
is the specialty here, done in a variety
of ways, including veal Parmesan,
veal dumplings, and a sublime veal
schnitzel. Meats are cooked with a
Black Forest twist, as are such traditional German staples as sauerkraut,
bratwurst, and goulash. The dining
room, of white stucco and natural
wood, overlooks woods and a mountain stream. 78786 U.S. 40, Winter
Park, tel. 970/726–5133. AE, MC, V.

Sunspot Dining Room
The Lodge at Sunspot is a magnificent
log-and-stone complex at the top of
the Zephyr lift. Rough-hewn log
beams and furniture are accented
with Southwestern rugs hung on the
walls. You should visit for lunch to
enjoy the view, but be sure to return
by gondola for an evening meal. The
prix fixe menu offers game and fish
paired with interesting side dishes
such as wild rice from Minnesota and
Idaho red potatoes roasted in olive oil
and herbs. The restaurant is open for
dinner on Thursday, Friday, and Saturday only, so plan accordingly. Top of
Zephyr Express lift, Winter Park, tel.
970/726–1446. Reservations essential.
AE, D, DC, MC, V.

Winston's at the Vintage

This classy but casual restaurant and pub was built around a massive 19th-century English bar, transported from what was reportedly Winston Churchill's favorite watering hole in London. Wood wainscoting and a collection of paintings depicting Churchill complete the mood. The menu is a bit of Britain and a bit of everything else, with a deservedly renowned flagship beef Wellington (carved at the table) and a good selection of meat, fish, and pasta dishes. The *cappellini d'Angelo* (shrimp sautéed in lobster sauce, with angel-hair pasta and pine nuts) is exceptional. *Vintage Hotel, 100 Winter Park Dr., Winter Park, tel. 970/726–8801. Reservations essential on weekends. AE, D, DC, MC, V.*

Moderate

Deno's Mountain Bistro

Deno's is my favorite all-purpose place at Winter Park because it truly does it all. It doesn't look like much from the outside, but it serves huge lunches, is positively jammed with people for après-ski, and has a great dinner menu with some of the largest portions you'll ever confront. The food is American bistro, with a little of everything from angel-hair *pomodoro* (in tomato sauce) with rock shrimp to grilled Rocky Mountain trout and the best burgers in town. The downstairs is a more refined dining area, with tablecloths and candlelight, a dark-wood bar, and skiing pictures on the walls. *78911 U.S. 40, Winter Park, tel. 970/726–5332. AE, D, DC, MC, V.*

Divide Grill

This cheerful, informal family-dining spot is named for the Continental Divide. The grill is airy, well lighted, and decorated in burgundies, greens, and traditional brass trim. Menu favorites include elk medallions, grilled jerk swordfish, and mix-and-match pastas and sauces. *Cooper Creek Sq., Suite 305, Cooper Way, Winter Park, tel. 970/726–4900. AE, DC, MC, V.*

Fontenot's Cajun Cafe

The only spot in town for Cajun has become known for its fresh fish. Favorites include blackened catfish, crawfish étouffée, and of course, gumbo and jambalaya. The atmosphere at this shopping center restaurant is just a step up from a coffee shop, but the food is authentic and the service friendly. *78521 U.S. 40, Winter Park, tel. 970/726–4021. D, MC, V.*

The Last Waltz

This homey place was supposed to be the last of seven restaurants for owner-chef Nancy Waltz, who later changed her mind and opened Alpeggio's (*see above*). The huge menu jumps from bagels and lox to burritos without missing a beat. The south-of-the-border dishes are best: zesty *calientitas* (fried jalapeños filled with cream cheese and served with a devilish salsa) and black bean tostadas are especially noteworthy. *U.S. 40, Winter Park, tel. 970/726–4877. Reservations not accepted. AE, D, DC, MC, V.*

Inexpensive

Crooked Creek Saloon

An interesting selection of meal-size sandwiches—a chicken breast, grilled cheese, and grilled vegetables, for example—and a daily fish special are among the inexpensive, filling choices here. Steak, ribs, pasta, and chicken complete the menu. An extension of the Grand County Historical Society, the saloon is filled with photographs documenting the settling of Fraser and Winter Park. The adjacent bar is a Stetson-and-checked-shirt kind of place, with live rockabilly music and a home-on-the-range atmosphere. If you're the two-stepping type, you'll want to strut your stuff on the dance floor. *401 Zerex (U.S. 40), 2 mi from Winter Park, Fraser, tel. 970/726–9250. MC, V.*

Hernando's Pizza Pub

Here the specialties are pizzas and pastas, with a respectable selection to eat in or take out. Try the Roma pizza, with a layer of olive oil, fresh basil, and minced garlic covered with Roma tomatoes and the toppings of your choice. The most popular pasta is the vegetarian lasagna (a meat variety is also available). Long wooden tables and benches, along with a crackling fireplace and a busy bar area, create a rustic, casual atmosphere. *78199 U.S. 40, Winter Park, tel. 970/726–5409. AE, MC, V.*

Rudi's Deli

The only true deli-style eatery in Winter Park, Rudi's has such deli delights as soups, chili, stews, and some excellent home-baked bread to eat in or take home. *Park Plaza Center, Winter Park, tel. 970/726–8955. No credit cards.*

Smokin' Mo's

For Texas- and Oklahoma-style barbecue, Smokin' Mo's is a recent addition to the Winter Park culinary scene. Meats are smoked with hickory imported from Osage County, Oklahoma, and there are plenty of side orders from which to choose. The rough-hewn log walls are festooned with rusty farm tools, and on each table there's a generous roll of paper towels for cleaning up after the ribs. *Cooper Creek Square, Winter Park, tel. 970/726–4600. AE, DC, MC, V.*

Best Bets for Breakfast

Carver's Bakery Café

Carver's is a delightfully bright and breezy breakfast spot with lots of natural light to get the sleep out of your eyes. There's an ample selection of baked goods—muffins, croissants, and pastries—plus excellent omelets with a variety of fillings. *93 Cooper Creek Way, behind Cooper Creek Square, Winter Park, tel. 970/726–8202. AE, D, MC, V.*

Moffat Bagel Station

For one of the better bagels this side of New York, plus coffee that will jump-start you, this is the place. There are also fresh muffins and scones for those who eschew bagels. *U.S. 40, Winter Park, tel. 970/726–5530. No credit cards.*

NIGHTLIFE AND ENTERTAINMENT

Après-Ski

Derailer Bar

In the West Portal Station at the Winter Park base area, the Derailer packs them in early with après-ski prices, live entertainment, and great pizza by the pan. Near the site of the historic Moffat Tunnel, opened in 1926, the bar has a railroad theme: a mural on railroad history covers one wall. Several TVs turn the place into a sports bar during games, and the view of the slopes provides close-up live action. The crowd is mostly young. *West Portal Station, Winter Park, tel. 970/726–5514, ext. 1957. AE, D, V.*

The Slope
Hot bands and a happy hour from 2 to 7 ensure nonstop action at the bar that's been voted the number one après-ski bar by the *Rocky Mountain News*. For those more inclined to play than to dance, there's a giant game room. The action continues well into the night, an easy quarter mile from the Winter Park base area. *1161 Winter Park Dr., Winter Park, tel. 970/726–5727. MC, V.*

Loud and Lively/Dancing

Deno's Mountain Bistro
Upstairs the atmosphere is high-octane and happening, with occa-sional live music and a good mixture of locals and visitors watching sports on the pub's 11 TV sets (*see* Where to Eat, *above*).

Rome on the Range
Dance downstairs, shoot pool upstairs, or just pull up a cowhide-covered stool to the bar. Line-dancing lessons are offered once a week. *78941 Hwy. 40, Winter Park, tel. 970/726–1111. AE, V.*

More Mellow

The Rails
A large fireplace dominates this laid-back spot where relaxing in comfy chairs and couches is the name of the game. The decor is modern, and train prints line the walls. Things liven up every other Wednesday, when comedy troupes perform. *Iron Horse Resort, 275 Winter Park Dr., Winter Park, tel. 970/726–8851. AE, DC, MC, V.*

T here is a certain irony that the state of Idaho, with its spectacular wilderness carved by geologic activities that created mountains as high as 12,000 feet and valleys as deep as 800 feet, should be best known to outsiders for the lowly potato. For beyond that ubiquitous tuber are some 83,000 square miles of recreational wilderness that includes more than 2,000 lakes, 200 mountain peaks above the 12,000-foot mark, America's deepest gorge (Hell's Canyon), petrified lava fields, and dense forests that cover 40% of the state.

Wedged between Wyoming to the east and Oregon and Washington state to the west, Idaho is bisected by the northernmost range of the Rocky Mountains before they continue across the Canadian border. Snuggled in among these towering peaks and reaping the benefits of moisture-laden storms from the West Coast are 18 ski resorts, including the state's best-known natural commodity after the potato—Sun Valley.

Discovered by Austrian count Felix Schaffgotsch, who remarked that "among the many attractive spots I have visited [during a six-week tour through the mountains of California, Wyoming, Utah, and Colorado], this combines more delightful features than any place I have seen in the U.S., Switzerland, or Austria for a winter sports resort." Built by a millionaire railroad tycoon and visited by movie stars, royalty, presidents, and literary luminaries, Sun Valley is arguably the most storied and enduring of all U.S. ski resorts.

The physical attributes of Idaho's Sawtooth Mountains are not overshadowed by the glitterati that give the resort its luster. The sharp peaks provide a craggy crown for skiing's royal resort, and the perfectly shaped Mt. Baldy is the skiing jewel in this regal setting. The low-lying Wood River valley is a verdant, wildlife-rich counterpoint to the jagged peaks, with its ranches and small communities providing an amiable mix of longtime residents and seasonal escapees from urban life.

SUN VALLEY SKI RESORT

SUN VALLEY SKI RESORT

Sun Valley, Idaho 83353
Tel. 208/622–4111 or
800/786–8259

STATISTICALLY SPEAKING

Base elevation: 5,750 feet

Summit elevation: 9,150 feet

Vertical drop: 3,400 feet

Skiable terrain: 2,054 acres

Number of trails: 60

Longest run: 3 miles

Lifts and capacity: 7 high-speed quads, 5 triples, 5 doubles; 28,180 skiers per hour

Daily lift ticket: $50

Average annual snowfall: 175 inches

Number of skiing days 1995–96: 134

Snowmaking: 630 acres, 31%

Terrain mix: N 36%, I 42%, E 22%

Snowboarding: yes

When railroad tycoon Averell Harriman made Sun Valley America's first destination resort in 1936, the place sparkled with glamour like fresh powder in the moonlight. Gary Cooper, Darryl Zanuck, Judy Garland, Clark Gable, and Bing Crosby led the charge from Hollywood, and later ice queen Sonja Henie and Marilyn Monroe followed in their footsteps. The Sun Valley of the '40s and '50s was a mecca for moguls, a hangout for celebs, and the seasonal home of Ernest Hemingway, who wrote parts of *For Whom the Bell Tolls* in his room at the Sun Valley Lodge. Hundreds of visits by presidents and royalty, millionaires and movie stars, entertainers and athletes have given Sun Valley a unique star-studded aura, a halo of fame now tinged by nostalgia.

For the glory days did not last forever. In the late '60s Aspen and Vail began siphoning away the chic and sleek, and for more than a decade Sun Valley lapsed into a development coma while other major resorts were indulging in a building orgy. The resort didn't so much lose its luster as get dusted by the winds of change gusting through the modern destination resort industry. In short, cash had replaced cachet as the defining quality of a ski resort, and Sun Valley was slow to jump on the bandwagon. This was probably a blessing in the long run. The resort weathered its decline with considerable dignity, keeping its original style intact; and when the modernization spending spree did get underway at the start of the '90s, Sun Valley was ready to embrace it without being swallowed up by it. A mountainwide lift rejuvenation gave Sun Valley the second-largest number of detachable quads in America, after Vail, and one of the biggest automated snowmaking systems in the world. The glamour that Harriman created blended easily with the new, expanded accommodations. By 1995 Sun Valley was once again regarded as one of the country's preeminent ski resorts.

Tucked into the end of the Wood River valley and surrounded by the jagged peaks of Idaho's Sawtooth Range, Sun Valley is actually a fairly diversified area made up of several distinct parts. The original Sun Valley Village is a self-contained community centered around the Sun Valley Lodge, a complex consisting of a conference center, condos, town houses, and

USEFUL NUMBERS
Area code: 208

Children's services: day care, Sun Valley Resort, tel. 208/622-2288; instruction, tel. 208/622-2248

Snow phone: tel. 208/622-2095 or 800/635-4150

Police: Ketchum, tel. 208/726-7833; Sun Valley, tel. 208/622-5345

Hospital: Wood River Medical Center, Sun Valley, tel. 208/622-3333; Wood River Medical Center, Hailey, tel. 208/788-2222

Chamber of Commerce: tel. 208/726-3423 or 800/634-3347

Road conditions: tel. 208/886-2266

Towing: AAA, tel. 208/726-3955; Dick York Auto, tel. 208/726-4583

FIVE-STAR FAVORITES
Best run for vertical: Inhibition

Best run overall: Limelight

Best bar/nightclub: Whiskey Jacques'

Best hotel: Sun Valley Lodge

Best restaurant: Ketchum Grill

assorted shops. One mile away, linked by a walking path/bike trail and the free KART shuttle bus, is Ketchum, the former cattle-ranching and mining town that has changed little in the 60 years since it was the end of the line for Harriman's Union Pacific Railroad. Today Ketchum is still without sidewalks, it still has a permanent population of only about 3,000, and although Range Rovers are now more common than pickup trucks, it still retains a funky, rustic appearance, with older wood-sided and log homes scattered among the newer brick buildings and plazas. It's the heart of Sun Valley's nighttime action, with a comfortable mix of restaurants, bars, galleries, and coffee shops. The newest development at Sun Valley is the Elkhorn Village area, about 1½ miles from Ketchum and a mile from Sun Valley Village. It's a hillside development of large private houses and condominium buildings, with the Elkhorn Radisson Plaza at its center. It, too, is linked to Ketchum, the Village, and the two mountains by the KART shuttle system.

Two mountains? That's right. Although the dominant 9,150-foot Bald Mountain (known as Baldy) is the main mountain at Sun Valley, there's also Dollar Mountain, Sun Valley's original ski hill and the site of the world's first chairlift. At 6,638 feet, it's a tiny knob of a mountain by today's ski resort standards, but it's the hill of choice for never-evers, novices, and kids. Both mountains are linked to the three main accommodation centers by the KART shuttle, with Dollar just a minute's ride from Sun Valley and Elkhorn and about five minutes from Ketchum. The big one, Baldy, is about a five-minute shuttle ride from Sun Valley, Elkhorn, and Ketchum. The shuttle bus is definitely the way to go because parking is limited almost everywhere, especially at the Warm Springs base area (there is more parking at the River Run base area).

This remarkable mix of the old and the new works well, giving Sun Valley a unique blend of historical tradition and contemporary development, rough, woodsy texture, and high style. It also continues to attract the rich and famous; celebs such as Brooke Shields, Clint Eastwood, and Bruce Willis and Demi

Moore are among the many who have houses in the new Sun Valley.

HOW TO GET THERE

By Plane

Friedman Memorial Airport (tel. 208/788–9511), in Hailey, is served by Skywest Airlines/Delta (tel. 800/453–9417) with connections through Salt Lake City and Horizon Airlines/Alaska (tel. 800/547–9308) from Boise, Portland, and Seattle.

By Car

From Boise (160 miles away), take I–84 to South Mountain Home, then Route 20 east to Route 75N to Hailey, Ketchum, and Sun Valley. From Salt Lake City, Utah (292 miles away), follow I–15 north to Tremonton, Utah, then I–84 west to Twin Falls, and then take Route 75 north to Hailey, Ketchum, and Sun Valley.

All major car-rental companies are available at Salt Lake City Airport, and the following are available at Boise Airport: **Avis** (tel. 208/383–3350); **Budget** (tel. 208/383–3090); **Hertz** (tel. 208/383–3100); **National** (tel. 208/383–3210); **U Save** (tel. 208/322–2751). Cars from Avis, Budget, Hertz, and National may be dropped off in Sun Valley; all others must be booked round-trip.

By Bus

Sun Valley Stages (tel. 800/821–9064) departs Boise Airport daily at 2:30 PM and arrives at the Sun Valley Inn at 5:30 PM. Return buses depart the Sun Valley Inn daily at 8 AM and arrive at Boise Airport at 11 AM.

By Train

Amtrak (tel. 800/872–7245) has service three times weekly from Chicago and Seattle to Shoshone, Idaho, 40 miles from Sun Valley. Tours include transfers from the station to the resort, but if you're on your own, make arrangements for pickup ahead of time with **Practical Rent-a-Car** (tel. 800/437–7136), **U Save** (tel. 800/995–9707), or **Town and Country Tours** (tel. 800/234–1569; $125 one-way).

GETTING AROUND

Sun Valley Resort, Elkhorn Village, Ketchum, and the base lodge areas at both mountains are all connected by the scheduled **KART bus service** (tel. 208/726–7140), which runs from 7:30 AM to midnight. It's a good idea to use it because parking is limited at the base areas of Baldy and in and around Ketchum. Pick up a schedule when you arrive and keep it with you. Taxi service is also available from **A-1 Taxi** (tel. 208/726–9351).

THE SKIING

The skiing at Sun Valley takes place on two mountains, the relatively modest Dollar Mountain, with its gentle novice terrain, and Bald Mountain (known as Baldy), a perfectly pitched, broad-shouldered beast that I think is the finest single ski mountain in America. The reason I believe this (and I'm far from alone) is consistency. Unlike those at so many other ski areas, the runs on Baldy streak from top to bottom with near-perfect fall-line precision, no flat spots, no run-outs, no bailouts, just a steep, straight-up peak that lets you kick into your first turn from the get-go and never lets up for 3,400 vertical feet. It's straight-shot skiing, with mile-long runs leading to a clutch of intermediate and expert bowls; the thickly timbered lower slopes cut through with well-groomed and extra-wide cruising trails. Also, the infinite variety on three faces lets you follow the sun throughout the day.

Although snowboarders are allowed everywhere on the mountain except Christin's Silver and Southern Comfort, under the Seattle Ridge chair, there are no special grooming features specifically for them. But the mountain's consistent pitch, efficient lift system, and lack of long catwalks make it very snowboard-friendly.

Novices

The place for you is Dollar Mountain. With four lifts carrying you up to several different elevations (the highest at 6,638 feet), Dollar gives you variety and some challenge but not too much. Lessons are always on the go, and you will notice that all ages are enrolled. Lessons, by the way, are an especially rewarding experience here, for Sun Valley has one of the best ski schools in the country; you'll advance faster and gain more control than you will by trying to master technique solo.

To ski Dollar, start by going up Poverty Flats, taking the Quarter Dollar lift. If you find yourself skating, then you have passed the test and are ready to progress to Half Dollar. This lift gives you access to four runs (Hidden Valley, Graduation, Half Dollar Bowl, and Cabin Practice Slope), where you can make some turns and get comfortable before taking Dollar lift to the top. All the runs are groomed extremely well, so you don't have to worry about moguls, powder, or ice.

When you have conquered Dollar Mountain, go over to Elkhorn by taking Dollar lift to the top and skiing off to your left onto the cat track that leads past Sepp's Bowl and Sheepherder to the Elkhorn area. You can then take Joint Venture to the base of the Elkhorn lift, which gives you access to two green runs, Elkhorn Bowl and Joint Venture, as well as some intermediate trails. From the top you can ski back down on another cat track to the base of Dollar and to wide, gentle Sepp's Bowl.

Intermediates

The place for you is Bald Mountain, and I suggest starting at the River Run base to catch the morning sun. Take the combined nine-minute ride on River Run and Lookout Express and go off to your right to ski Upper College to Lower College, cutting back to the right at the bottom to catch Lookout Express again. To follow the sun, take Challenger to the top again, ski down Ridge to Blue Grouse or Cutoff, and then pick up Roundhouse Lane to Gun Tower Lane to catch the Seattle Ridge lift on the south side of the mountain.

On Seattle Ridge you'll catch the sun from early morning to midafternoon as you ski Gretchen's Gold, Southern Comfort, Christin's Silver, Byron's Park, Seattle Ridge, or Broadway. Don't be fooled by the novice designation of these runs: They are challenging. Remember, the pitch at Sun Valley is probably more than you are used to. When you're ready to step it up a little, head for the intermediate bowls reached from the top of Baldy. Mayday, Lefty, Farout, and Sigi's all have good, sustained pitch, and they start out wide open at the top, gradually tapering down to narrower tree-surrounded sections. The Mayday lift is the most direct access to the summit—a seven-minute ride that will put you in bowl heaven. If you find these bowls a little too steep, you can head for the Christmas bowl area, which starts at the top of the Christmas lift. These are moderately pitched bowls that give you a good feel for skiing the wide-open spaces without pushing your fear meter into the red zone. When you feel like returning to groomed terrain, all the bowls in this area feed back to the confluence of the Exhibition, the Christmas, and the Cold Springs lifts, which give you access to groomed cruisers.

From the top of the Christmas lift, you can start to move over to the Warm Springs side of the mountain by taking the Warm Springs Face, an invigorating, groomed, and wide cruiser that lets you carry speed with confidence yet provides enough surprise to keep you heads-up. Here, you have the choice of returning to the Warm Springs base area or heading for the Flying Squirrel lift, where you'll find some good intermediate bump runs.

Experts
From the River Run base area, ride the River Run and Lookout Express chairs up, turn right (looking up), and take Limelight, a wonderfully wide and pure fall-line cruiser that will get your legs warmed up. Run this a few times before the crowds start to build

up, then ski under the chair on Upper River Run, where you'll usually find some good medium-size moguls, especially down the left-hand side of the run. Avoid going right down to the River Run base area; instead pick up the Exhibition chair where the Lookout Express, Sunnyside, and Exhibition chairs all converge. From here you can ski down Lower Christmas Bowl to Inhibition for a super-steep vertical. Ride the Cold Springs chair back up to the top of Exhibition chair. Underneath the Exhibition chair is Exhibition, another steep mogul run; it's short but gnarly, with large moguls. Beat yourself up on that for a little while, then take the Lookout Express and head for the bowls. You can try a few blue bowl runs from the top of the Lookout chair, or you can take the second Lookout Express across the top of the bowls and over to the summit of Baldy. From here you have a choice of three of Sun Valley's meanest bowls—Little Easter (steep); Easter (steeper); and Lookout (steepest). If you want the max in steepness, stick close to the right-hand side (looking down) and ski Lookout, then ride Mayday chair back to the summit. This is just a seven-minute ride, and it's your best and least crowded access to the bowl area. Although there are only eight named bowls, this is actually a wide and wild area, with wind-sculpted chutes, ridges, and gullies, wide-open swaths of steepness, and some tantalizing glade areas midway down the Lookout Bowl.

WHERE TO STAY
Accommodations in Sun Valley cluster in three main areas—Sun Valley Resort, Elkhorn Village, and down-

town Ketchum. All are connected by the KART shuttle service and are no more than a 10-minute ride from the ski area. The resort is a self-contained village center, and along with Elkhorn Village, generally has the most expensive and upscale accommodations. Ketchum has more of a price mix, but it also has some properties in the expensive range. If you are price conscious or prefer to be within walking distance of the town's nightlife, Ketchum is your best choice.

Expensive

Idaho Country Inn

This magnificent 9,000-square-foot mountain house, standing on a knoll halfway between Ketchum and Sun Valley, is a peeled log and river rock dwelling that is practically a museum of the area's natural heritage. The large, individually designed and themed rooms, all boasting views of the mountains and each reflecting a slice of Idaho life, are decorated with willow canopied beds, wagon-wheel headboards, handmade armoires, log and pine chairs, and wildlife art. There's a library with an excellent collection of natural history books about the area, a living room where afternoon appetizers are served next to a massive rock-faced fireplace, and an adjacent dining room where you get a full Idaho breakfast. *134 Latigo La., Box 2355, Sun Valley 83353, tel. 208/ 726–1019 or 800/250–8341, fax 208/ 726–5718. 11 rooms. Facilities: outdoor hot tub, library. AE, MC, V. $125– $185, including full breakfast and après-ski snacks.*

Knob Hill Inn

This large, sprawling, ultradeluxe European-style lodge, 2 miles from the River Run base area, is wonderfully soothing for romantics. From its steeply sloping roof and carved balconies to its brick walkways and courtyard, the inn displays the clean lines of modern mountain chalet design. Inside it continues the theme with softly rounded doorways and windows, brick and stucco walls, light-color wood trim, Southwestern rugs, and beams and tiled floors in creamy peach tones. The rooms and suites are all spacious and have balconies; the decor is modern, with soft pastel tones of jade and peach, modern art on the walls, and large marble-tile bathrooms with oversize tubs and separate showers. *960 N. Main St., Box 800, Ketchum 83340, tel. 208/726–8010 or 800/526–8010, fax 208/726–2712. 20 rooms, 4 suites. Facilities: restaurant, café-bakery, indoor lap pool, indoor-outdoor hot tub, exercise area, sauna. AE, MC, V. $175–$350.*

Pennay's at River Run

At the River Run base area, just five minutes from Ketchum, the 19 one- and two-bedroom units are housed in three separate buildings next to a picturesque stream and within ski-in/ ski-out distance of the River Run lift (along a flat, groomed path). The stucco and brown-stained clapboard buildings blend in pleasantly with the trees. The furnishings are modern in style and muted in tone; there is a fireplace and washer-dryer in each unit, and each bedroom has a private bath. *Box 1298, Sun Valley 83353, tel. 208/726–9086 or 800/736–7503, fax*

208/726-4541. 19 units. MC, V. $160– $300.

Sun Valley Resort

At the Sun Valley Resort you have a choice of three distinct accommodation types: the lodge, the inn, and the surrounding condominiums and cottages. They are all part of a 4,200-acre wooded estate village that wraps around a small lake just a mile from Ketchum. Every manner of recreation and service lies within the confines of this classy resort.

The Sun Valley Lodge may be the most famous resort lodge in America, the very famous have cavorted here, as the photos lining the walls and hallways attest. The concrete exterior is stained and textured to look like a wooden mountain lodge. Its rooms have a country-floral motif, with Laura Ashley drapes, Oriental rugs, and handsome French provincial furniture in rich, dark woods. As comfortable as the rooms are, the real ambience of the lodge can only be savored in the common areas: the high-ceilinged sunroom with a grand piano, the glass-enclosed circular pool, the Duchin Bar with its leather couches, the dining room with its crystal chandeliers and polished dance floor, and the outdoor rink shimmering with a thousand tiny lights.

The inn was built in 1937 to handle the overflow from the instantly popular lodge, and aside from its Tyrolean styling, it offers the same rustic Western grandeur as the lodge and the same luxury in its guest rooms.

The log, stone, and board-and-batten cottages were the houses of the original founders of the resort, which have been totally renovated and decorated in the same style as the lodge and inn. They all have two bedrooms, each with a queen-size bed, a marble bathroom, and a brick fireplace. The condos, scattered in tree-shrouded clusters around the fringe of the property, are more modern in furnishings, with warm earth tones and pastel hues and fireplaces.

Guests at the resort have access to all facilities; a shuttle bus makes scheduled runs around the property as well as to Dollar Mountain (less than two minutes away) and Mt. Baldy (about 10 minutes away). *1 Sun Valley Rd., Sun Valley 83353, tel. 208/622-4111 or 800/786–8259, fax 208/622–2030. 148 lodge rooms, 113 inn rooms, 200 units, 6 cottages. Facilities: 7 restaurants, lounge, indoor lap pool, 2 outdoor lap pools, exercise room, games room, bowling alley, ice rink, sauna, massage room. AE, D, DC, MC, V. $99–$1,000.*

Moderate

Elkhorn Resort and Golf Club

The centerpiece of the Elkhorn Village area combines a full-service four-story stucco hotel with a cluster of upscale condominium units set around the central village plaza area and alongside the fairways of a golf course designed by Robert Trent Jones, Jr. The rooms and public areas are badly in need of refurbishing, but the new ownership plans to spruce up the rooms and add a full-service spa by 1998. Hotel rooms vary in size from standard to spacious two-bedroom suites, all decorated in earth tones with modern furnishings. The larger suites have fireplaces, full kitchens, and whirlpool tubs. The adjacent condominiums range from studio to four bedrooms and have the same modern decor, although individual owners have added their personal touches. All guests have access to the facilities in the complex. The KART bus makes regular stops to shuttle you to the mountain or to Ketchum, or you can catch the Elkhorn lift to the top of Dollar Mountain. *1 Elkhorn Rd., Sun Valley 83354, tel. 208/622–4511 or 800/333–3333, fax 208/622–3261. 125 rooms, 7 suites, 44 units. Facilities: 3 restaurants, lounge, bakery-coffee shop, hot tub, sauna, exercise room, ice-skating, post office, general store. AE, D, DC, MC, V. $114–$295.*

Kentwood Lodge

You can't beat the location of this new lodge in the center of Ketchum. The playful Western decor includes custom-made log furniture, steel cowboy-cutout fire screens, and Indian rugs on the walls. There's a large glassed-in pool and Jacuzzi off the lobby and a café serving breakfast and lunch. The rooms all have either a king- or two queen-size beds, a microwave and refrigerator, and either a fireplace or a balcony; some also have a full kitchen, sleeper sofa, and a Jacuzzi. The best part is the amiable owners. *180 S. Main St., Ketchum 83340, tel. 208/726–4114 or 800/805–1001, fax 208/726–2417. 57 rooms. Facilities: café, indoor pool, hot tub, weight room, coin laundry, meeting rooms. AE, D, DC, MC, V. $75–$145.*

Premier Resorts at Sun Valley

This property management company handles the bulk of the condominium rentals in the area, ranging from one-bedrooms to luxurious private homes. Properties are located throughout the valley—in Elkhorn, Ketchum, and Sun Valley. *Box 659, Sun Valley 83354, tel. 208/721–4000 or 800/635–4444, fax 208/727–4040. 350 units, 235 homes. AE, D, MC, V. $65–$6,000.*

Tamarack Lodge

The Tamarack is conveniently located in downtown Ketchum. The guest rooms are spacious, with basic motel furnishings. Room layouts range from a standard hotel room to a king-size suite with a separate bedroom and a living room. All rooms have a microwave, a refrigerator, and a coffee-maker, and the larger units come with a wet bar. *Box 2000, Sun Valley 83353, tel. 208/726–3344 or 800/521–5379, fax 208/727–4040. 21 rooms, 5 suites. Facilities: indoor pool, outdoor hot tub. AE, D, DC, MC, V. $92–$134.*

Tyrolean Lodge

This pretty little lodge sits in the heart of Ketchum just 400 yards from the lifts at the River Run base area. The style is classic Austrian both inside and out—a steep roof, barn-board wood paneling, stucco walls with hand-painted crests and flowers, a large stone fireplace in the common room, and heavy wood beams. The rooms, which come in various configurations but are all large enough for at least four, are decorated in shades of Wedgwood blue and rose pink, with hand-painted headboards and other Austrian folk art touches. All rooms have balconies. *Box 202, Sun Valley 83353, tel. 208/726–5336 or 800/333–7912, fax 208/726–2081. 56 rooms. Facilities: 2 indoor hot tubs,* *exercise room, laundry, game room. AE, D, DC, MC, V. $95–$150, including Continental breakfast.*

Inexpensive

Bald Mountain Lodge

This 1920s log-cabin motel covers the basics well, with small but comfortable rooms and some slightly larger family units with a small sitting area and modest kitchen facilities. The decor is of the knotty pine rec room period, with carpeted floors and a mix of single, double, and queen-size beds. The lodge is just a few blocks from the center of Ketchum. *151 S. Main St., Box 2000, Sun Valley 83353, tel. 208/726–9963 or 800/892–7407, fax 208/726–1854. 8 rooms, 10 units. AE, D, DC, MC, V. $45–$115.*

Christiania Lodge

The location of this U-shape gray-wood Best Western in the middle of Ketchum is hard to beat, and so is the price of the large, clean rooms with two queen-size or double beds (10 suites also have a king-size bed), fold-away kitchenettes, and entrances overlooking a central courtyard. The slightly larger king suites have fireplaces and more ample kitchens. The KART shuttle bus stops right outside the door. *Box 2196, 651 Sun Valley Rd., Ketchum 83340, tel. 208/726–3351 or 800/535–3241, fax 208/726–3055. 28 rooms, 10 suites. Facilities: outdoor hot tub. AE, D, DC, MC, V. $59–$82, including Continental breakfast.*

Ketchum Korral Motor Lodge

This cozy little complex tucked away on a side street two blocks from the center of Ketchum offers log cabins and one large motel-type building with an additional nine rooms. The log cabins, which were built in a grove of trees in the '30s and were a preferred hangout of Hemingway, are rustic, with wood-burning stone fireplaces, rough barn-board walls, and full kitchens. There is one large cabin with two queen-size beds, one queen-size sleeper sofa, and one twin bed. The smaller units come with one queen-size bed and a queen-size sofa bed. The motel rooms are slightly more contemporary in decor and furnishings. *310 S. Main St., Box 2241, Ketchum 83340, tel. 208/726–3510 or 800/657–2657. 9 rooms, 8 cabins. Facilities: outdoor hot tub. AE, D, MC, V. $45–$125.*

Ski View Lodge

These gingerbread-style log cabins with brightly painted window and door frames are right out of the '40s, and it's just the sort of place you might find if you were stumbling around in the woods. In fact, they are just a few blocks from downtown Ketchum and a good choice if you're looking for basic rustic accommodations on the cheap side. There are no cooking facilities, just two double beds and a comfortable, woodsy ambience. And the best part is that your pet is welcome. *409 South St., Box 2254, Ketchum 83340, tel. 208/ 726–3441. 8 units. MC, V. $45–$125.*

WHERE TO EAT

There's a tremendous variety of dining options in Sun Valley, Elkhorn Village, and downtown Ketchum, ranging from high-end gourmet to specialty cuisine and Western staples.

On the Mountain

River Run Lodge

This two-story timber-and-rock master-piece has turned River Run into the main base area at Sun Valley. Besides gourmet food, you can also get ski rentals, lockers, and lift tickets here. Plush carpets, leather chairs, marble tabletops, and towering fresh-flower arrangements give it the feel of a four-star hotel rather than a ski area base lodge. The food is as elegant as the setting, featuring brick-oven pizzas, fresh roasts, made-to-order wok specialties, and the crèpe of the day. A jazz trio or pianist plays après-ski. *River Run base area, Sun Valley, tel. 208/622–4111. AE, MC, V.*

Seattle Ridge Lodge

When it comes to style, this on-mountain restaurant rivals America's best, and it is without a doubt the champion in the quality of the food. The massive cathedral-size log cabin is imbued with so much luxury and elegance that you almost feel you should take your ski boots off on entering. Polished pine beams, marble floors, Oriental rugs, leather chairs and couches, magnificent chandeliers, and Ralph Lauren antiques set the tone. You can lunch in the dining room in front of numerous fireplaces, including a central one with three sides, or you can wander outside to the glass-enclosed cobblestone patio kept snow-free by hot underground springs. The full menu includes everything from giant baked Idaho potatoes with a choice of more than 20 toppings to perfectly cooked roast beef cut from a massive hip by the chef. *Top of Seattle Ridge chairlift, Sun Valley, tel. 208/622–4111. AE, MC, V.*

Expensive

Chandler's

This cozy, intimate house in downtown Ketchum features several small dining rooms. The menu emphasizes American cuisine using fresh Idaho ingredients, with specialties such as elk loin in a red wine reduction with caramelized shallots or grilled fresh salmon on garlic potato purée and sautéed spinach with basil and sun-dried tomato sauce. The best deal is the prix fixe American dinner menu for $16.95, including a soup or salad, a choice of six entrées, and dessert. *200 S. Main St., Ketchum, tel. 208/ 726–1776. Reservations essential. AE, MC, V.*

Evergreen Bistro

This eclectic, upscale bistro is a slice of Montparnasse in the mountains. The seven dining rooms make up a kind of Franco-American collectibles museum, with Moulin Rouge posters; reproduction Renaissance paintings and tapestries; a mix of pine and French provincial chairs, corner cupboards, and pedestal tables; steamer trunks; and a massive copper bistro bar in the main foyer. The menu is a mélange of French, Asian, and Southwestern influences. The Provençal-style bouillabaisse is exceptional, with a generous mix of shellfish in a fennel, garlic, and saffron broth. There's also grilled Idaho trout served Cajun style; New York–cut steak served with watercress, Stilton butter, and Belgian endive; and something called Vegetable Chaos, a medley of seasonal vegetables with a stuffed chili-and-mushroom bundle. Preferred tables are next to the fire or in an alcove in the Fireplace Room. *171 1st Ave.,*

Ketchum, tel. 208/726–3888. Reservations essential. AE, MC, V.

Lodge Dining Room
The elegance of this oval-shaped dining room with high-back leather chairs and immaculate crystal and linen place settings evokes memories of the rich and famous who have dined and danced here. This is one of the last bastions of such a crowd; the softly lighted polished dance floor still lures many. The menu is primarily Continental, with some local specialties such as Rocky Mountain trout or Idaho beef. The entrées change daily but may include pan-seared elk medallions and ahi with citrus fruit compote. *Sun Valley Lodge, 2nd floor, Sun Valley, tel. 208/622–2150. Reservations essential. AE, D, DC, MC, V.*

Trail Creek Cabin
This is a meat-and-potatoes experience that includes a scenic sleigh ride to a rustic 1938 log-and-rock cabin. It might look rough, but notables like Hemingway, Gary Cooper, and Ava Gardner used to come here for New Year's Eve dinner. The horse-drawn sleigh leaves at 6, 7, and 8 PM from Tuesday through Saturday and takes about a half hour. The atmosphere is casual and bustling, with table-side entertainment. The specialty of the house is the barbecued ribs, but there's also a good selection of grilled steak, chicken, duck, trout, and lamb. *Sun Valley Resort, Sun Valley, tel. 208/ 622–2135. Reservations essential. AE, D, DC, MC, V.*

Moderate
China Pepper
This hip, modern Thai restaurant is in a colonnaded building just off Ketchum's main street. It's an airy, wide-open space with stone-tile floors, large tropical trees, chrome-and-glass tables, and large abstract art canvases on the walls. The menu is Thai and Chinese—hot and spicy but light. Entrées include Thai shrimp, tiger prawns poached and served with coconut-peanut sauce on a bed of spinach; Thai-style barbecued duck, charbroiled and smothered in a spicy orange barbecue sauce; and crisp pork—flash-fried strips of pork tossed with bell peppers, water chestnuts, and bamboo shoots in a hoisin sauce. There's also a sushi bar. *511 Leadville St., Ketchum, tel. 208/726–0959. MC, V.*

Ketchum Grill
Built in 1856 out of barn board, this is a Ketchum classic. With wooden floors, original brass lighting, and a gallery of photo stills of classic cowboy movies starring the likes of Roy Rogers, Tom Mix, and Gene Autry, it has a casual, cheerful atmosphere. You'll find great entrées such as grilled homemade fennel sausages, braised rabbit with pancetta and fresh herbs, or warm spinach salad with bacon and grilled chicken breast. The pizzas are unique; among available toppings are rock shrimp, pesto, pine nuts, and fontina cheese. *520 East Ave., Ketchum, tel. 208/726–4660. Reservations essential. AE, MC, V.*

Pioneer Saloon
This is the place to go when you have a craving for extralarge portions of red meat. It's small—just 30 tables or so—but it attracts a loud and lively crowd that spills over from the bar up front. The barn-board walls are

decked with fishing and hunting collectibles and period firearms. The prime rib comes in four sizes; the largest, called the full cut, weighs in at about 32 ounces, while the thick, red, and juicy steaks are either sirloin, rib eye, or New York–cut, a monster at 14 ounces. Ribs are also available occasionally. *308 N. Main St., Ketchum, tel. 208/726–3149. Reservations not accepted. AE, MC, V.*

Sawtooth Club

It's not because I sat next to Michael Keaton or bumped into Clint Eastwood as I was leaving that I have such a fondness for this place. Rather, it's because this is a first-rate restaurant with a great casual bistro ambience, a cheerful, lively feel, and a creative Southwestern-style menu. The restaurant above the main-floor bar is richly decorated with wood-paneled walls and ceiling, brass wall lamps, and white and maroon table settings. The ambitious menu encompasses mesquite-grilled dishes such as rack of lamb or Southwestern-style ribs, some original pasta creations, and several varieties of poultry, including a delicious rotisserie-roasted free-range chicken done in a Jamaican citrus marinade. Seafood offerings include a Southwestern version of scampi using olive oil, cilantro, lime, tequila, and other seasonings. *231 Main St., Ketchum, tel. 208/726–5233. AE, MC, V.*

Inexpensive

Bob Dog Pizza

Bob Dog is top dog for pizza with more than two dozen designer varieties, plus you can create your own from a list of more than 30 ingredients such as pine nuts, snow peas, smoked oysters, fresh cilantro, caramelized red onions, and smoked chicken. Cheese choices include gouda, feta, brie, and fontina. The crusts are crisp and thin with an herb flavoring, and there's a huge salad bar that will more than satisfy the non-pizza eaters. It's a lively, busy spot with big-screen TV entertainment. *200 6th St., Ketchum, tel. 208/726–2358. MC, V.*

Desperados

This is a good spot for fresh, health-conscious Mexican dishes, with some novel variations on the most popular themes. The white walls are decorated with bright posters, paintings, and signs. Try the fish taco, filled with lightly breaded cod, or the *carne asada* burrito, filled with charbroiled steak and feta cheese. There's also an excellent selection of house salsas, including a blindingly hot jalapeño and carrot version. *211 4th St., Ketchum, tel. 208/726–3068. AE, D, MC, V.*

Konditorei

The Konditorei, which has been a Sun Valley institution since the early 1960s, is renowned for its fine freshly baked goods. The menu includes a variety of light meals, salads, and sandwiches. It has a cozy, informal European ambience, with exposed brick walls decorated with Austrian antiques and artifacts, a warming fire burning in the copper-faced fireplace, and light classical music playing in the background. Try the Idaho smoked trout salad, the quiche of the day, or a daily soup special served with hot homemade bread. Be sure to save room for the pastry or something from the big selection of Continental cakes and tarts. *Sun Valley Resort, Sun Valley, tel. 208/622–2235. AE, D, DC, MC, V.*

Smoky Mountain Pizza and Pasta
This is a classic Italian eatery with wood-slat chairs, pine walls, and red-and-white-checked tablecloths. The food is strictly mainstream—homemade pasta (try the spicy chicken linguine) or pizza—and the atmosphere is warm and homey. *200 Sun Valley Rd., Ketchum, tel. 208/622–5625. D, MC, V.*

Best Bets for Breakfast

Java Coffee and Café
This is a good spot for a cup of joe to go in various designer flavors or just strong and fresh *café ordinaire*. There's also a daily lineup of fresh-baked muffins, scones, and cookies along with the standard breakfast and lunch specials, which change daily. *191 4th St., Ketchum, (other locations at the Warm Springs base area and in Hailey), tel. 208/726–2882. No credit cards.*

Kneadery
For a traditional home-style breakfast in a rustic atmosphere with fireplaces and wooden floors, get here early or endure the wait. It's well worth it. The egg dishes come with a mound of hash browns, sliced tomatoes, and a muffin of your choice. For a special treat, try the Idaho smoked trout and eggs. Waffles, pancakes, and various homemade breads round out the hearty, belly-filling menu. *260 Leadville Ave., Ketchum, tel. 208/726–9462. AE, MC, V.*

NIGHTLIFE AND ENTERTAINMENT

Après-Ski

Apples
A bustling hangout for the chic and the cheeky, it has good, thumping music, happy-hour munchies, and an outside patio. *215 Picabo St., Sun Valley, tel. 208/726–7067. No credit cards.*

Bald Base Club
Better known as the BBC, this is definitely the hottest après-ski spot in town—it's *the* place to be seen. It hums with live bands and loud crowds and lots of impromptu dancing. *Opposite Warm Springs base area, 106 Lloyd Dr., Sun Valley, tel. 208/726–3838. AE, MC, V.*

Loud and Lively/Dancing

Grumpy's
This locals' hangout just outside Ketchum's downtown core is popular for its cheap beer—a 32-ounce bowl of Schooner for just $2.75. The decor is early beer can, with hundreds of them hanging from the ceiling, along with an eclectic collection of tin trays. The crowd is mostly male and under 30. *860 Warm Springs Rd., Ketchum, tel. 208/726–7452. No credit cards.*

Pioneer Saloon
Its rough barn-board walls are decked with dozens of trophy heads of buffalo, moose, elk, and lynx plus a collection of antique hunting rifles, including a massive 8-foot-long buffalo gun. Wrought iron, Tiffany lamps, hardwood floors, and a long oak bar give it the classic American saloon atmosphere: It's the genuine article, the locals' favorite watering hole, and attracts visitors of all ages.

308 N. Main St., Ketchum, tel. 208/726–3149. AE, MC, V.

Whiskey Jacques'

This is the only place in town featuring live music almost nightly. Things start hopping at 4 PM, with a happy hour weeknights and a lively après-ski show at 5:30 PM on weekends. There are also big-screen TVs and a good munchie menu of burgers, hand-tossed pizzas, and calzone. *271 Main St., Ketchum, tel. 208/726–5297. MC, V.*

More Mellow

Atrium Lounge

The Elkhorn's quiet lobby bar has a rich, woody ambience, lots of comfortable chairs, and live entertainment in the form of a solo pianist or guitarist. *1 Elkhorn Rd., Sun Valley, tel. 208/622–4511, ext. 1044. AE, D, DC, MC, V.*

Duchin Lounge

Ah, to savor a quiet cocktail at the Duchin is to savor the elegance of the original Sun Valley. Leather couches, dark-wood wainscoting, rich brocade upholstery, and a long mahogany bar with a dozen seats give it a clubby Ivy League feel. There are also a live light-jazz trio and a small dance floor. *Sun Valley Lodge, Sun Valley, tel. 208/622–2145. AE, D, DC, MC, V.*

In case you want to see the world.

At American Express, we're here to make your journey a smooth one. So we have over 1,700 travel service locations in over 120 countries ready to help. What else would you expect from the world's largest travel agency?

do more ®

http://www.americanexpress.com/travel

Travel

In case you want to be welcomed there.

We're here to see that you're always welcomed at establishments everywhere. That's why millions of people carry the American Express® Card — for peace of mind, confidence, and security, around the world or just around the corner.

do more

AMERICAN EXPRESS

Cards

In case you're running low.

We're here to help with more than 118,000 Express Cash locations around the world. In order to enroll, just call American Express before you start your vacation.

do more

Express Cash

T he state of Maine is a land of striking contrasts. Between its eastern 3,478-mile-long shoreline of rocky coves and white-sand beaches and the mountains on the west side of the state, it enjoys some of the richest geographic diversity in the northeastern United States. At 33,000-plus square miles, it is larger than all the other New England states combined, and it is dotted with some 6,000 lakes, 32,000 miles of rivers and streams, and 17 million acres of dense forest. It yields a cornucopia of wildlife from moose to puffins, and a population of just over 1 million leaves its natural wonders wide open for year-round recreation, including skiing.

The mountains that contain the state's ski resorts are an extension of the Appalachians called the White Mountains and are on the western edge of Maine, at the New Hampshire border. With some peaks topping the 4,000-foot mark, they receive steady, plentiful snowfalls, thanks to the drift of moist Atlantic air pushed inland from the coast, and with their heavily forested flanks and rugged outcroppings they remind many people of the craggy scenery found in the Pacific Northwest.

This section of the state is also known as the Western Lakes and Mountains Region. Its forests are speckled with thousands of lakes and rivers strung like pearls across 200 miles of wilderness, from the Sebago Lakes, just outside Portland, to the Rangeley Lakes, near the Canadian border.

There are about a dozen ski resorts throughout the state, but the only true destination areas are two: Sunday River, near Bethel, and Sugarloaf/USA, at the north end of Carrabassett Valley. Sugarloaf, which occupies a striking peak that is distinctive for its above-tree-line summit, has long been the main resort in the state, but more recently Sunday River has emerged as one of the fastest-growing, largest resorts in the Northeast.

GETTING TO MAINE RESORTS

By Plane

Portland Airport is served by Business Express (tel. 800/345–3400), Continental (tel. 800/525–0280), Delta (tel. 800/221–1212), United (tel. 800/241–6522), and US Airways (tel. 800/428–4322), with connections from other major centers. **Bangor International Airport** is served by Business Express (tel. 800/345–3400), Continental (tel. 800/525–0280), Delta (tel. 800/221–1212), Northwest (tel. 800/225–2525), and US Airways Express (tel. 800 428–4322). Boston's **Logan International Airport** is served by all major carriers.

Car Rental

Portland's airport has car-rental service from **Avis** (tel. 800/331–1212), **Budget** (tel. 800/527–0700), **Hertz** (tel. 800/654–3131) and **National** (tel. 800/328–4567). Bangor Airport has Avis, Budget, and Hertz.

By Bus

Greyhound Lines (tel. 800/231–2222) has scheduled service into either Portland or Bangor.

By Train

Amtrak (tel. 800/872–7245) has regularly scheduled service into Portland.

SUGARLOAF/USA

SUGARLOAF/USA

R.R. 1, Box 5000
Carrabassett Valley, ME 04947
Tel. 207/237-2000 or
800/843-5623

STATISTICALLY SPEAKING

Base elevation: 1,400 feet

Summit elevation: 4,237 feet

Vertical drop: 2,820 feet

Skiable terrain: 505 acres

Number of trails: 105

Longest run: 3 miles

Lifts and capacity: 1 gondola, 3 quads, 1 triple, 8 doubles; 19,400 skiers per hour

Daily lift ticket: $43 weekdays; $46 weekends and holidays

Average annual snowfall: 175 inches

Number of skiing days 1995–96: 189

Snowmaking: 454 acres, 90%

Terrain mix: N 33%, I 35%, E 32%

Snowboarding: yes

The locals call it Ohmygosh Corner, and it's easy to see why. Sugarloaf/USA is way up there in Maine (50% of the clientele is from the state). After driving hours, perhaps even seeing a moose, you suddenly see it around a bend of Route 27—the 'Loaf. On a clear day it is a triangular jewel, white-capped and waiting with both above-tree-line skiing in the Snowfields and scores of challenges snaking down from its cap. In the Carrabassett Valley near the town of Kingfield, Sugarloaf retains the wildness of its Maine logging heritage. You can see it as you look at the Bigelow Mountain range from the summit, where live the highest concentration of 4,000-foot mountains in the Pine Tree State, or nearby, where the Appalachian Trail winds. You can hear it in the trail names—Skidder, Tote Road, Moose Alley. This is one big mountain that presents challenges for all.

There are more than 900 condominiums from which to choose at the resort, plus rooms with mountain views, 21 restaurants, and a village center with a grocery, shops, and lots of après-ski activities. Sugarloaf also turns part of its base lodge into a concert hall, attracting big-name rockers and country crooners during the ski season.

At night streetlights show a path up to the base lodge. A stream rushes by. Bridges are perfect places for a quiet chat or more. The ski-in/ski-out aspect of Sugarloaf lets you put on your boots at the foot of your bed if you want to. Two lifts run up and down above the accommodations, giving skiers a bird's-eye view of it all.

HOW TO GET THERE

By Plane

Portland Airport is 2½ hours from Sugarloaf, and Bangor International Airport is about two hours away. Boston's **Logan International Airport** is four hours from Sugarloaf. (*See* Getting to Maine Resorts, *above.*)

By Car

From the south take the Maine Turnpike from Portland to Auburn, Exit 12, and follow Route 4 north through Farmington. Then pick up Route 27 north to Kingfield and follow the road to the resort. From the west, including Montreal and elsewhere in Quebec, head east on Route 10 to the U.S. border. From northern Maine take I–95 south to Newport, then take Route 2 west to Skowhegan. Pick up Route 201 north to Route 148, then west through Madison to Route 201A, and north to North Anson. Then take Route 16 west to Kingfield and Route 27 north to Sugarloaf.

Portland and Bangor International airports are served by major car-rental firms (*see* Getting to Maine Resorts, *above*).

By Bus
Riverbend Express (tel. 207/628–2877) has regularly scheduled shuttle bus service from Portland and Bangor to Sugarloaf.

GETTING AROUND

Sugarloaf is self-contained; once you get here, you won't need the car. Free **Carrabasset Valley shuttle buses** (tel. 207/235–2645) make their way four times every hour around the Loaf. Depending on the season and where you are staying, the front desk can also radio one in for you. However, if you are staying in nearby Kingfield or the even smaller village of Stratton, a car is essential because there is no shuttle service linking either community to the mountain.

THE SKIING

The state of Maine's (or state o' Maine's, if you're a native) only gondolas are here—one going from about midway up the mountain to the summit and the other, built in 1994, a high-speed, detachable quad chair, going from the base area to the summit in just over six minutes. The summit is above tree line and exposed to the elements; it can get downright cold and windy here. Because it's so far north, nearly hugging the Canadian border, the snow can come early and stay late here, making spring skiing a pleasure.

Experts can find their steeps and bumps; intermediates have cruisers to explore, and beginners can experience wide, mellow slopes of white. Lift lines can grow a bit long on busy days, as there are only three quads on the mountain.

There is a secret to Sugarloaf—it is called West Mountain. Underutilized, this is where to park to avoid the rush. The West Mountain double lift goes to Bullwinkle's, a mountain lodge with hot food—a good place to sneak into for an early or late snack or lunch. Beginners can warm up on Horseshoe to the West Mountain Trail, under the lift. Intermediates and experts can head down the Bucksaw Crosscut to Tote Road to the base and to the rest of the Loaf. West is also where the sun first hits.

Snowboarders have access to the entire mountain and to all lifts. There are also as many as six terrain parks (depending on snow conditions) and the largest half pipe in the country.

Novices

Never-ever skiers start on the Birches Slope, between Sugarloaf Inn and the base lodge. It is very gentle and wide. Once you've progressed past beginner, you owe it to yourself to continue down Snowbrook Trail to the rest of the accommodations. There's a tunnel, and kids (both young and old) just love to ski through it.

The Skidway lift, a short double chair, gives green circle skiers access to the Landing. From there the Double Chair East is your ticket to Boardwalk (nice and wide, but everyone is there) and Lower Winter's Way, narrower but fun. The first blue run you may want to try can be reached from the Whiffletree quad: Buckboard. Remember, there are always West Mountain and Lower Tote Road, too.

Intermediates

Go to the King Pine Bowl and stay there. Don't be fooled by the single black diamonds. Strong intermediates will love the wide, steep, well-groomed pitches of Haulbeck (half bumped up) and Rip Saw. Blue square Ramdown and Boomauger are pleasures. Take the Whiffletree quad, ski down Tohaul, and ride the King Pine quad.

The central corridor of the mountain (Double and Spillway chairs) fills up fast. Hit it early. Double Chair West takes you to Lower Narrow Gauge, a good warm-up. Then take Spillway West to Tote Road and cruise. From the summit to the base, Tote Road is 3 miles of wide, ear-to-ear-grinning turns. Off the Spillway West chair, Spillway, Lower Narrow Gauge, and Competition Hill are black diamond zippers for advanced intermediates and experts. Get to Competition Hill early to avoid the Carrabasset Valley Academy racers. From the top of Spillway West, for variety the Spillway Crosscut goes east to King Pine Bowl. Test your nerves by looking down. Choker is the place for first bumps.

Experts

The summit beckons. The Snowfields are the only lift-served above-tree-line skiing in the East. The gondola will get you there. The supersteeps are here in the form of double black diamonds. White Nitro (groomed), Bubble Cuffer (narrow and bumpy), and Powder Keg will teach you respect. The gondola summit building has topographical maps of the area so you can see where you are.

During seasons of abundant natural snow, experts can reach what's known as the backside, where there's no snowmaking. Hike up past the radio antenna and schuss down chutes, through trees, and over rocks.

It's for experts only. Good bump runs are Skidder and those under the gondola line when they don't groom it.

WHERE TO STAY

Accommodations at Sugarloaf are concentrated in three distinct areas. In and around the resort are some of the most architecturally pleasing, well-built, and stylish condos found at any eastern resort. Fourteen miles south on Route 27 is the pleasant little town of Kingfield, with a collection of smaller inns, motels, and B&Bs, while 7 miles north on Route 27 is the even smaller village of Stratton, where most of the inexpensive options are found. In general, you pay a premium for staying at the mountain, so if price is a consideration, the drive in either direction is worth the effort.

Expensive

Inn on Winters Hill

This hilltop mansion overlooks the quaint community of Kingfield and is a great alternative to staying at Sugarloaf. The turn-of-the-century Georgian Revival house has large rooms in the main building as well as in the attached carriage barn. The rooms are individually styled, with soft tones, period antiques, and vibrant quilts and curtains, plus grand furnishings such as bird's-eye maple beds, armoires, chests, and side tables. The entire establishment, including the magnificent wood-paneled, antique-laden lobby–lounge area and restaurant, has a warm and hospitable ambience. *R.R. 1, Box 1272, Kingfield 04947, tel. 207/265–5421 or 800/233–9687, fax 207/265–5424. 4 rooms in main house, 16 rooms in carriage barn. Facilities: din-*

ing room, lounge, indoor hot tub and pool, recreation room, cross-country skiing, dogsled rides. AE, MC, V. $76–$135.

Sugarloaf Mountain Hotel

This six-story polychrome-brick hotel is the flagship of the resort. The building dominates the mountainside area with its gabled roof and stylish alpine look. Inside, the rooms have wood trim, pastel tones and accents, solid furnishings, and large windows. If you have a choice, go for the slope-side up-mountain views. Most are well equipped with a queen-size bed, a sleeper sofa, a microwave, a wet bar, and a mini-refrigerator. *R.R. 1, Box 2299, Carrabassett Valley 04947, tel. 207/237–2222 or 800/527–9879, fax 207/237–2874. 119 rooms. Facilities: restaurant, lounge, sauna, steam room, 2 indoor hot tubs, library. AE, D, DC, MC, V. $100–$270.*

Sugarloaf Condominiums

The hundreds of condos here have been tastefully designed and are situated out of view of the access road so you don't even realize the extent of the clusters until you drive to the north and east of the slopes. The condos to the east of the access road are served by the Snubber chairlift. Most units are similar in style, size, and furnishings. The only exceptions to this more-than-acceptable standard are the slightly more upscale units at the Village on the Green.

All of the following rooms, condos, town houses, and duplexes are privately owned and managed by several different rental agencies. The dominant one is the Sugarloaf Mountain Corporation; by renting through it you gain free access to the Sugarloaf

Sports and Fitness Center, on Mountainside Road in the midst of the condos. Facilities there include an indoor pool, indoor and outdoor hot tubs, sauna, steam room, Jacuzzi, and a 25-station fitness center. Adult ski lessons are also included in the price. *Sugarloaf Mountain Corp., R.R. 1, Box 5000, Carrabasset Valley 04947, tel. 207/237–2000 or 800/843–5623, fax 207/237–3052. 912 units. MC, V. $110–$680.*

If the sports center is not important to you or you don't mind paying $10 per day to use it, the alternate rental group, Mountain Valley Property, claims up to 30% savings for the same units. *Mountain Valley Property, Box 281, Carrabassett Valley 04947, tel. 207/235–2560 or 800/435–7162, fax 207/235–2584. 100 units. AE, D, MC, V. $95–$453.*

Bigelows

These four-, five-, and six-bedroom units are five minutes from the Whiffletree quad. They are among the most spacious and luxurious units on the mountain. Each comes with a full kitchen, a fireplace, and a minimum of two baths.

The Commons

These units feature a selection of three-, four-, and five-bedroom triplex units, each with two or three full bathrooms, a completely equipped full-size kitchen, living and dining areas, a fireplace, and a deck. All have access to the slopes from the Snubber chair midstation.

Gondola Village

This is a four-story apartment building with a combination of standard hotel-size rooms with two queen-size beds and larger two-bedroom units with two bathrooms and a full kitchen. There are also one-bedroom and one-bedroom-with-loft units available. It's just behind the Whiffletree lift.

Snowbrook Village

By the Snubber chair, these one- and two-bedroom units (also available with loft) are furnished in a no-frills but comfortable manner. There is a full kitchen in all units, and some come with a fireplace.

Village on the Green

These duplexes are among the nicest units on the mountain. Their luxurious furnishings and stylish decor complement a spectacular view of the mountain from their private location just off West Mountain Road. They come with either three or four bedrooms, two or three bathrooms, a full kitchen with high-quality appliances, a fireplace, and an attached garage.

Moderate

Herbert Hotel

This handsome three-story restored Beaux Arts–style building, constructed in 1918, is in historic downtown Kingfield. The rooms are furnished with antiques, some of which are the hotel's originals, and bright-colored quilts, area rugs, and drapes. All rooms come with private baths equipped with whirlpool tubs, and there's a variety of bed options, including double, twins, queen, and king. The lobby is a comfortable hangout, with a roaring fireplace, stuffed moose heads, and several laid-back dogs. *Main St., Kingfield 04947, tel. 207/265–2000 or 800/843–4372, fax 207/265–4594. 33 rooms. Facili-*

ties: dining room, bar, hot tub, sauna. *AE, D, DC, MC, V. $80–$150, including Continental breakfast.*

Spillover Motel
This modern two-story gray-wash motel is on the outskirts of Stratton some 10 minutes north of the mountain. Each unit has two double beds and enough space so four won't feel overly crowded. Rooms are tastefully decorated with no-nonsense furnishings and pleasing earth-tone colors. *Rte. 27, Box 427, Stratton 04982, tel. 207/246–6571. 20 units. AE, MC, V. $58–$68, including Continental breakfast.*

Sugarloaf Inn
This inn was the first structure, built in 1960, to house skiers overnight on the mountain. Well located behind the Sawduster chair, it is just far enough away from the noise of the village. The rooms are not overly large, but guests have privileges at the Sugartree Sports and Fitness Center. Also in the hotel is a large, comfortable lounge dominated by a giant brick fireplace and the slope-view Season's Restaurant. *Sugarloaf Mountain Corp., R.R. 1, Box 5000, Carrabassett Valley 04947, tel. 207/237–2000 or 800/843–5623, fax 207/237–2000. 42 rooms. Facilities: restaurant, lounge. AE, MC, V. $120–$188.*

Three Stanley Avenue
This early 19th-century farmhouse is today a bed-and-breakfast run by the same folks who own one of the area's best restaurants—One Stanley Avenue—right next door. The rooms are cozy, comfortable, and decorated in a country Victorian motif, with period furnishings and collectibles, floral print curtains, and bright-colored handmade quilts. There is no TV or telephone in the rooms. *Box 169, Kingfield 04947, tel. 207/265–5541. 6 rooms, 3 with bath. Facilities: restaurant, lounge. AE, MC, V. $35–$60, including full breakfast.*

Inexpensive

Putts Place
Jim and Elaine Poitras are your hosts at this small but charming B&B, about 10 minutes from the mountain in nearby Stratton. The four rooms, all on the second floor, are cozy and snug, with plump featherbeds, colorful quilts, and handmade crafts and antiques. Rooms have either a double bed or two or three twins. Breakfast, which varies daily, features such homemade goodies as pumpkin-raisin or walnut bread, orange-flavor cream cheese, and French toast. After dinner there's a comfortable fireplace lounge, where you'll find assorted games and Elaine's ever-present jigsaw puzzle, which needs your contribution for its completion. *Rte. 27, 8 Main St., Stratton 04982, tel. 207/246–4181. 4 rooms. MC, V. $50–$75, including full breakfast.*

Stratton Motel
This modest small motel is operated by Bill Flynn, the author of *Meditations of a Christian Martial Artist.* The rooms are basic, with two double beds and cable TV. There is also a condo that sleeps eight, with a full kitchen, a full bath, a living room, and a small dining room. *Main St., Rte. 27, Box 284, Stratton 04982, tel. 207/246–4171. 5 rooms, 1 condo. Facilities: cross-country skiing. AE, D, MC, V. $40–$95.*

Stratton Plaza Hotel

This small, three-story turn-of-the-century hotel has rooms with private baths, double and queen-size beds, and a forest of wood paneling. There's also a restaurant and lounge with live country-and-western entertainment on weekends. It's a funky, folksy place with no pretensions, despite its lofty-sounding name. *Main St., Box P, Stratton 04982, tel. 207/246–2000, fax 207/246–6593. 12 rooms. Facilities: restaurant, lounge. AE, D, MC, V. $40.*

Widow's Walk

This rambling Victorian bed-and-breakfast is on the National Register of Historic Places. Living up to its name, the hotel has a widow's walk on its three-story tower. Each room is artfully decorated with simple furnishings and bright bed covers and curtains. The comfortable living room has a fireplace and lots of plush, comfy chairs. Breakfast and a hearty dinner are served family style. *171 Main St., Box 150, Stratton 04982, tel. 207/246–6901 or 800/943–6995. 6 rooms share 3 baths. Facilities: dining room, ski storage room, recreation room. MC, V. $46, including full breakfast; $5 per person additional for dinner.*

WHERE TO EAT

The resort and the nearby Kingfield and Stratton villages offer a small but varied assortment of restaurants. Overall, this is a fairly quiet night scene, with a lot of condo cooking and stay-at-home entertainment.

Expensive

Diamanti's

Before you head into the dining room, check out the spacious bar replete with antique sports equipment including sleighs, toboggans, golf clubs, and hockey gear. It's in contrast to the sumptuous, candlelighted, and carpeted dining room, with a menu that features baked salmon, pork teriyaki sirloin, pork chops stuffed with sausage and rice, and balsamic chicken in a medley of tomatoes, onions, garlic, and basil. *Mountain Village, Sugarloaf, tel. 207/237–2222. Reservations essential. D, MC, V.*

Julia's at the Inn on Winters Hill

This delightfully formal dining room is part of the Georgian Revival mansion that is now an inn. There are two dining rooms here, the Pink and Green rooms, both small and intimate. The Pink Room has a massive brick fireplace with a mirrored cherry-wood mantel and cherry and birch flooring. A set of wood-and-glass pocket doors separate it from the Green Room, which has the same exceptional woodwork and trim. The menu is a mix of Continental and contemporary New England: beef Wellington, lobster and shrimp en croûte, and Cornish game hen marinated in a sherry-sesame blend. For dessert try Dessert Julia, a raspberry and Grand Marnier compote over homemade ice cream. *Inn on Winters Hill, Winters Hill Rd., Kingfield, tel. 207/265–5421. Reservations essential. AE, D, MC, V.*

One Stanley Avenue

Set in a picturesque Victorian house, One Stanley Avenue offers what chef and owner Dan Davis calls classic Maine cuisine. The menu includes Maine mussels with dill dressing; roast duck with rhubarb, red wine, cinnamon, and lemon glaze; chicken with fiddlehead ferns and hemlock needles, and roasted rabbit smothered in raspberry sauce with sage butter. For dessert, try the blueberry and raspberry cream. *1 Stanley Ave., Kingfield, tel. 207/265–5541. Reservations essential. AE, MC, V. Closed Mon.*

Shucks

Check out the bar first at this restaurant because you won't find a more appealing view of adjacent Bigelow Range than through the full-size windows in the wide-open lounge. Then head for the private and more sedate dining room with its stylish wine-color and dark-wood ambience. Oysters are the order of the day, in every style, flavor, and fashion you can imagine. Go for the rack of lamb encrusted in baked rosemary and served with garlic-mashed potatoes. *Mountain Village West, Sugarloaf, tel. 207/237–2040. AE, MC, V.*

Moderate

Carrabassett Yacht Club

This is a lively, casual restaurant done in a nautical theme complete with portholes, flags, life rings, and marine colors of white and blue. The menu offers a bit of everything: several seafood choices, including grilled blackened tuna and West Coast haddock; meat options such as prime rib, barbecued ribs, and sirloin steak; and chicken stir-fry and fajitas. There's also pizza, burgers, and an extensive appetizer list. Desserts include Bailey's chocolate-chip cheesecake. *Rte. 27, Carrabassett Valley, tel. 207/235–2730. AE, D, MC, V.*

Gepetto's

At this casual and lively spot, a large, U-shape bar separates the dining area from the lounge, and warm, woodsy decor welcomes you. The menu is large and varied, featuring classic American favorites served in hearty portions. There are spare ribs, pork tenderloin, and teriyaki sirloin on the meat side of the menu; on the seafood side is fresh lobster, with several other fish specials nightly. There's also a choice of three stir-fry dishes—veggie, chicken, or shrimp—as well as pastas and pizza. *Mountain Village West, Sugarloaf, tel. 207/237–2192. AE, MC, V.*

Hug's

This intimate Italian restaurant has simple country-cottage decor, with candlelight and historic photographs of Sugarloaf over the years on the walls. The menu reflects a careful home-cooked approach that goes with the familial ambience. For an appetizer try the artichoke hearts with fresh basil and romano. Pasta specialties include fettuccine with pink Alfredo sauce, *agnolotti* (rolled half-moon-shaped pasta filled with Romano cheese, pesto, and pink Alfredo sauce), and wild mushroom ravioli in walnut pesto or Alfredo sauce. Nightly veal specials include those cooked marsala, *francese,* and *piccata* styles. *Rte. 27, 1 mi from access road, Carrabassett Valley, tel. 207/237–2392. MC, V.*

Longfellow's

In a classic 1860s post-and-beam building on Main Street in Kingfield and filled with antiques of that era, this is a rustic and comfortable dining spot with a large and varied menu. There's a heavy emphasis on chicken, with such choices as chicken Longfellow (a boneless breast with herb stuffing, topped with a sour cream sauce) or Cajun chicken (with sautéed onions and hot red peppers). There's an equally large list of fish entrées, including haddock Longfellow (with a creamy celery and cheese sauce), baked stuffed scallops, and a shrimp stir-fry. Pasta is not overlooked either, with a half-dozen choices including linguine Parmesan and lasagna. *Main St., Kingfield, tel. 207/265–4394. AE, MC, V.*

Inexpensive
Bag and Kettle
A convenient location in the middle of the village makes this pub-restaurant a popular spot, but it's also a good dinner choice because of its prices and standard family faves from chicken to "bag burgers" (that is, takeout) to wood-fired brick-oven pizza. The busy, bustling atmosphere is cheerful and friendly, and how many places offer a chance to read antique sheet music (which decorates the walls) while awaiting your meal? *Mountain Village, Sugarloaf, tel. 207/ 237–2451. MC, V.*

Nostalgia Tavern
Busy and lively, this place is popular with locals for its hearty portions and thrifty prices. With an adjacent bar, including pool tables and video games, it's a tad on the noisy side as well. You go here for the family dining favorites, which include daily specials such as meat loaf or baked haddock, monster portions of grilled steak or chicken, and a peerless 16-ounce prime rib. *Rte. 27, Kingfield, tel. 207/265–2559. D, MC, V.*

White Wolf Inn Cafe
Good, standard Maine fare is served up here with reasonable prices, drawing a strong local clientele. A live white wolf (her name is Luna) greets diners, and a collection of wasps' nests (no longer active) decorates the wall. There's always a fish special and usually a game dish or two on the evolving menu, plus all the traditional standards from steak to pasta. It's a funky spot with a lot of character. *Main St., Stratton, tel. 207/246–2922. D, MC, V.*

Best Bets for Breakfast
Mainely Yours
At this classic diner, standard breakfast fare in hearty portions for a good price includes two eggs, bacon, home fries, and toast. On the healthier side are a fresh fruit bowl and some great homemade breads (try the pumpkin) and muffins. *9 Main St., Stratton, tel. 207/246–2999. MC.*

Narrow Gauge Food Court
For a slope-side grab-and-go breakfast, this cafeteria is a good choice. The coffee is strong and varied, and there's a good lineup of muffins, sweet breads, and bagels. *Main base lodge, Sugarloaf, tel. 207/237–2000. MC, V.*

NIGHTLIFE AND ENTERTAINMENT
Après-Ski
Widowmaker Lounge
This is the hottest après-ski spot on the mountain, with a giant U-shaped bar, live entertainment, lots of promotional themes and giveaways, and a spirited crowd that thrives on the action. There are pool tables and a deck. *Main base lodge, Sugarloaf, tel. 207/237–2000. MC, V.*

Loud and Lively/Dancing

Judson's

This is a locals' bar where visiting skiers are also quite welcome. The old-fashioned decor includes skis and boots hanging on the walls and displays of bar mugs dating from the '20s. There are also TVs for sports fans and games for the action-oriented. *Rte. 27, Carrabassett Valley, tel. 207/235–2641. AE, MC, V.*

Shucks

A great view of the Bigelow Range makes this a must for an early end of the day; when the sun goes down, the appeal is in the multiple TVs that dominate this sports bar. *Mountain Village West, Sugarloaf, tel. 207/237–2040. AE, D, V.*

More Mellow

Bag and Kettle

This mellow tavern offers live entertainment on Monday night, usually in the form of local blues bands. The full bar has a wide selection of beers from local microbreweries. *Mountain Village, Sugarloaf, tel. 207/237–2451. MC, V.*

Truffle Hound

This quaint country-style pub offers plenty of beer, drink specials, sports on the tube, and jazz piano. *Mountain Village West, Carrabassett Valley, tel. 207/237–2355. AE, D, MC, V.*

SUNDAY RIVER SKI RESORT

SUNDAY RIVER SKI RESORT

Box 450
Bethel, ME 04217
Tel. 207/824-3000

STATISTICALLY SPEAKING

Base elevation: 800 feet

Summit elevation: 3,100 feet

Vertical drop: 2,300 feet

Skiable terrain: 602 acres

Number of trails: 102

Longest run: 3 miles

Lifts and capacity: 3 high-speed quads, 4 fixed quads, 5 triples, 2 doubles; 28,000 skiers per hour

Daily lift ticket: $43 weekdays, $46 weekend

Average annual snowfall: 150 inches

Number of skiing days 1995–96: 191

Snowmaking: 491 acres, 91%

Terrain mix: N 24%, I 41%, E 35%

Snowboarding: 10 snowboarding playgrounds

Good snow and short lift lines—this simple philosophy has made Sunday River, a self-contained destination ski resort outside Bethel, Maine, a major force in eastern skiing. Moreover, there doesn't seem to be a year when Sunday River doesn't offer a major improvement. In 1993–94, for example, it started a ski train to shuttle passengers from Portland, Maine, to Bethel. For the 1994–95 season it opened a seventh mountain for skiing—Jordan Bowl. The resort holds permits for six additional lifts and more than 200 acres of skiing. Plans also call for more lodging and base areas. All this development is well thought out. Whenever the resort adds a new lift, it cuts new, wide trails. It's also adding a train station, shopping, a movie theater, and more to the town of Bethel.

Commercial skiing at Sunday River started in 1958 on Barker Mountain; it was then a local area with about 70 acres of skiing. Innovation, progressive thinking, and good fortune contributed to its success, and since it was purchased by Les Otten in 1980 for $840,000, Sunday River has had a streak of record ski seasons and expanded to more than 602 acres. It now encompasses seven peaks, three base lodges, one mountain lodge, 14 chairlifts, a conference center, slope-side condominiums, a ski dorm, and town houses.

The resort has no main center of shopping, restaurants, and glitz. The three base lodges—Barker, White Cap, and South Ridge—provide all that skiers need. South is the hub, with guest services, the ski school, food, and rental shops. Barker has ticket sales, pay phones, more guest services, a lounge, and a ski shop, while White Cap has tickets, rentals, a cafeteria, and a pub.

That good snow mentioned earlier comes from one of the most powerful snowmaking systems in the country. More than a thousand snow guns blanket the slopes, meaning snow comes early and stays late. It stays so late, in fact, that every May 1 is a free ski day at the mountain.

Area code: 207

Children's services: day care, tel. 207/824–3000; instruction, tel. 207/824–3000

Snow phone: tel. 207/824–6400

Medical center: Bethel Area Health Center, tel. 207/824–2193

Hospital: Stephens Memorial Hospital, tel. 207/743–5933

Police: tel. 207/743–8934

Chamber of Commerce: tel. 207/824–2282

Road conditions: tel. 207/774–8866

Towing: Autotech, tel. 207/824–3363; Gaudreau's Repair, tel. 207/824–2807

FIVE-STAR FAVORITES
Best run for vertical: White Heat

Best run overall: Shockwave

Best bar/nightclub: Sud's Pub

Best hotel: Bethel Inn and Country Club

Best restaurant: L'Auberge

HOW TO GET THERE

By Plane

Portland International Airport (tel. 207/774–7301) is 75 minutes from the resort by car, and Boston's **Logan International Airport** is three hours away by car. (*See* Getting to Maine Resorts, *above.*)

By Car

From Boston take I–95 north to the Maine Turnpike; from Portland follow the turnpike north to Exit 11, Gray. Follow Route 26 north to the exit for Bethel and Sunday River. Sunday River Ski Resort is 6 miles north of Bethel, Maine, off U.S. Route 2E, in the town of Newry.

By Train

The Sunday River **Silver Bullet ski express** (tel. 207/824–7245) has scheduled daily service from Portland, Maine, to Sunday River. The train departs Portland at 6:50 AM and arrives in Bethel at 9 AM (shuttle buses take you up to the resort); it leaves Bethel for Portland at 4:30 PM; round-trip fare is $17.

GETTING AROUND

A free shuttle, the **Trolley** (tel. 207/824–3000), makes the rounds through the resort every 20 minutes. **Bethel Express** (tel. 207/824–4646) provides taxi service.

THE SKIING

With seven peaks from which to choose (White Cap, Locke, Barker, Spruce, North, Aurora, and Jordan Bowl), this is a cruiser's delight. A relative newcomer to eastern skiing, Sunday River has had the luxury of carefully considering the way it cuts new trails. The result: Many are wide, between 100 and 200 feet across, providing more space for skiers who don't like to be too close to the woods. Yet there are also classic steep and winding trails for experts, zingers for intermediates, and slow, gentle slopes for fledgling snow lovers.

Each peak has its own lift and trail network of at least four major runs, totaling 14 lifts and 102 trails. More advanced skiers should start from the less-congested Barker and White Cap lodges. Most families and beginners will head to the South Ridge Lodge. At the South Ridge Learning Center, beginners learn to ride the lifts and glide down the hill. Sunday River believes so strongly in its learn-to-ski program that if it doesn't work for you, you get your money back.

Snowboarders have access to the entire mountain and to all lifts. There are also a terrain park on each of its mountains and a lighted half pipe above the Whitecap base lodge that operates from 5 PM to 10 PM.

Novices

The learning area at South Ridge is served by three lifts—the South Ridge Express detachable quad, the Fall Line double, and the South Ridge triple. Once up, beginners can choose from about a dozen ways down on such trails as Broadway, Double Dipper, and Sundance.

You can then take the South Ridge Express to Lower Lazy River and catch the Sunday River Express lift to the top of Barker Mountain for a mellow time winding around the mountain on Three Mile Trail. Spruce Peak also offers a beginner run: The Spruce Peak triple takes you up to the playful Sirius, Aludra, and Light's Out combo. North Peak offers a pair of delights: Dreammaker itself eases down to the South Ridge base area, or you can take it to Ridge Run for a 1¼-mile run that will help you find muscles you didn't know you had.

Often overlooked on White Cap is the green cruiser Moonstruck, off the White Cap quad. From the White Cap you can also take a good first blue run on Starlight.

Intermediates

A good, strong intermediate can attack every peak here. The Sunday River Express detachable quad, at the base of Barker Mountain, will be your focus. Get there at 8:30, avoid it at noon, and come back after 1:30. Barker Mountain is a blue-square delight, with the winding Lazy River and Ecstasy and the slightly steeper Sunday Punch. For some fun take Ecstasy to steep, slanting Cascades, on Locke Mountain. Off Cascades is a little-known but great trail—very consistent in pitch with nice rolls and turns—called Wildfire, in the Lower White Cap area. Although it says black diamond, Right Stuff, on Barker, is one of the easier of the difficult run, which most strong intermediate skiers can handle.

Two premiere blue runs are the wide-cruising Risky Business and the long, wide American Express, on Spruce Peak, accessible from the Spruce Peak triple. North Peak, reached from the North Peak triple, has several good intermediate runs: 3-D has bumps and a fairly steep upper section, while Grand Rapids is gentle. Don't forget Aurora's Northern Lights—a scenic trail with continually changing pitches and rolls. To get to them, ski down Paradigm from the top of North Peak.

Experts

It's called the longest and steepest in the East and it's on White Cap: It is White Heat, a double black diamond with the White Heat quad overhead, making the embarrassment potential high if you don't know your stuff. The right side is groomed, and a strong advanced skier can make his or her way down. This is also a place to bail out, but be careful—it gets skied off toward the end of the day. The left side has huge bumps—experts only. Also on White Cap, Obsession is a more playful expert trail with curves and sweeps. Another White Cap special is Shockwave, a double black that twists and widens out to a sudden drop. White Cap is also home to a pair of glades for experts—Chutzpah and Hard Ball.

Steep pitches mark a trio of trails at Barker Mountain—Right Stuff, Top Gun, and Agony—which you reach on the Sunday River Express detachable quad. For a challenge try Vortex, on Aurora. It's cut for southpaws, so right-handed skiers should make sure they know their stuff. Locke Mountain's T-2 was an old racing trail and goes right down the face of the hill. Between Barker and Spruce are some new glades known collectively as Last Tango.

WHERE TO STAY

Sunday River is fortunate. Although the rapid growth of the ski area has produced its share of condominium sprawl, it has been tempered by the presence of Bethel, Maine, just 7 miles from the resort. Despite its classic picture-postcard collection of quaint and tasteful Colonial architecture, Bethel is also a sturdy working town. It's here you'll find the real accommodation gems, plus a good selection of after-dark options. There are classic colonial resort hotels, historic lodges, small inns, bed-and-breakfasts, and a variety of interesting independently owned hotels and motels within the town and its environs and along the highway between the town and the resort.

Most of the on-mountain accommodations are condos of indistinguishable appeal and among the higher priced in the area. If slope-side convenience is your choice (particularly for larger groups or families who want kitchen facilities), the prices vary according to ski-in/ski-out access and the newer units' frills, such as pools and hot tubs. You can make most arrangements through Sunday River Central Reservations (tel. 800/543–2854).

Expensive

Bethel Inn and Country Club
The inn, the social high-water mark of the town, is smack in the middle of historic Bethel. Opened in 1913, it is a perfect rendering of the elegant Colonial, a white-and-yellow three-story mansion—clapboard, columns, and all. The traditional inn has been augmented by a small, stylish collection of new town houses, but the 200-acre property has softened the modern intrusion. The rooms in the inn come in three sizes, including suites, all tastefully done with country florals and calico prints, handmade quilts, and antique furnishings; some rooms and suites also have fireplaces. Standard rooms are quite small, but each has its cozy elegance. The condos are all two-bedroom layouts, complete with a full kitchen, a fireplace, and a washer-dryer. Furnishings are mostly well-crafted colonial reproductions. *The Common, Bethel 04217, tel. 207/824–2175 or 800/654–0125, fax 207/824–2233. 57 rooms, 40 units. Facilities: dining room, pub, outdoor pool, hot tub, sauna, library. AE, D,*

*DC, MC, V. $65–$180 per person,
including full breakfast and dinner
(in rooms).*

Holidae House

Designed and built more than 100
years ago by a local lumber baron as
his showcase, this Victorian house
was the first in town to be electrified.
Most of the first floor is common
space, with a living room and a family
room heated with a wood-burning
stove; both rooms are furnished with
antiques, Oriental rugs, and lace curtains. Wood abounds—flooring, wainscoting, staircases—and the rooms are
filled with an astonishing collection of
period antiques and well-crafted
reproductions. The larger-than-average rooms come with a queen-size
four-poster. *Main St., Bethel 04217,
tel. 207/824–3400 or 800/442–5826.
9 rooms. Facilities: breakfast room,
whirlpools. AE, MC, V. $45–$150,
including Continental breakfast.*

Sunday River Condos

At Sunday River the eight buildings of
slope-side wood-stained condos are
virtually indistinguishable in their
barrackslike uniformity. Though aesthetically unappealing, they nonetheless provide good value for families
and groups, are functional and comfortable, and eliminate the drive to
and from the slopes each morning.
Several of the buildings have their own
built-in water-sport facilities, others
have shared access, and most have
ski-in/ski-out lift or slope access. The
studio, one-, two-, and three-bedroom
condos are all well maintained, clean,
well equipped (with a kitchen), and
functional in design and decor. If you
have a choice when booking, note
that condos on the South Ridge side
have access to the novice trails, while
those on the Whitecap side access
only the intermediate and advanced
trails. *Sunday River Ski Resort, Box
450, Bethel 04217, tel. 207/824–3000
or 800/543–2754, fax 207/824–2111.
402 units. Facilities: restaurant, 3 outdoor pools, 2 indoor pools, 7 saunas, 6
hot tubs, laundry facilities. AE, D, DC,
MC, V. $110–$400.*

Telemark Inn

Ten miles down a dirt road outside
Bethel lies the secluded Telemark
Inn, a gloriously restored Adiron-
dack-style lodge nestled at the foot
of Caribou Mountain. Inside it's a
remarkable example of what money
and fine carpenters and cabinetmak-
ers could achieve at the turn of the
century. The inn is filled with wood-
paneled walls, Norway pine plank
floors, and a trove of handcrafted
furnishings carefully restored by
owner Steve Crone. The rooms, filled
with antiques and paintings, sleep
four on beds piled high with handmade quilts. Dining is family style at
the 7-foot-diameter cherry-wood dining table, and further relaxing is
possible in the outdoor wood-fired
hot tub, on the natural skating rink,
or swaddled in blankets on a sleigh
pulled by Belgian draft horses. The
Telemark offers 22 kilometers of
groomed cross-country skiing trails.
Its only drawback for serious alpine
skiers might be the 15-mile drive
to the resort, but for families or
groups who want both alpine and
cross-country skiing, it's a wonderful
compromise. *R.D. 2, Box 800,
Bethel 04217, tel. 207/836–2703.
6 rooms. Facilities: dining room, hot*

tub, ice skating. AE, MC, V. $110 per person, including full breakfast and dinner.

Moderate

L'Auberge Country Inn

This century-old building that was a barn, a theater, and a carriage house seems best suited to its present incarnation—as an intimate and elegant country inn. The rooms are large and light filled, done in pastel tones with coordinated wall coverings and pine, beech, and birch antique furnishings. Guests can relax in the lobby common space, where there's a fireplace, a baby grand Steinway, and lots of reading material. *Mill Hill Rd., Box 21, Bethel 04217, tel. 207/824–2774 or 800/760–2774. 5 rooms, 2 suites. Facilities: dining room. AE, D, MC, V. $75–$125.*

Norseman Inn and Motel

Just 5 miles from the ski area, the Norseman is a pleasantly comfortable and remarkably restored 200-year-old farmhouse and 100-year-old barn. The tasteful conversion from working farm to skier accommodations resulted in the creation in the old farmhouse of 10 B&B rooms (no TVs, some with shared baths) outfitted with antiques, while the barn has 22 more modern rooms, with private bath, queen-size beds, and cable TV. The rooms are bright and decorated in fresh, soft colors. There's also lots of comfortable common space, including a rug-strewn woody lobby with a fireplace, a piano, and a large-screen TV, where wine and cheese are served après-ski. *Rte. 2, 134 Mayville Rd., Bethel 04217, tel. 207/824–2002. 32 rooms. MC, V. $58–$98.*

Snow Cap Inn

They could do with a few more places like the Snow Cap Inn up at the mountain. It's a warm, rustic traditional ski lodge: nothing fancy, but aesthetically pleasing and a good alternative to the condo ghettos. This is a substantial log building with a large, woody lobby centered on a hand-carved tree trunk and a massive stone fireplace. The rooms are clean and comfortably decorated; each has two queen-size beds. The inn is a good spot for couples rather than families, and it tends to draw a good number of forty-somethings. *Sunday River Rd., Box 450 R, Bethel 04217, tel. 207/824–7669 or 800/543–2754, fax 207/824–2111. 32 rooms. Facilities: games room, outdoor hot tub, Jacuzzi. AE, D, MC, V. $64–$69 per person, including Continental breakfast.*

Sudbury Inn

This all-purpose hospitality emporium is probably the best-known spot in town—thanks to the efforts of owners Cheri and Fuzzy Thurston and its location in the middle of Bethel. Built at the turn of the century when the railroad hit town, it's a stylish Victorian mansion and carriage house with rooms and suites, an excellent restaurant, and Sud's Pub, the hottest nightspot in town. The interior is a genuine study in Victoriana. The lobby is awash in chintz and floral wall coverings, Oriental rugs, velvet wingback chairs, original art, and fresh flowers; the rooms are filled with the antiques and fussy knick-knacks of the period. The main house has rooms and suites, and the carriage house has rooms only. It's a lively, friendly, well-run place with appeal for both families and couples. *151 Lower Main St., Bethel 04217, tel. 207/824–2174 or 800/395–7837, fax 207/824–2329. 17 rooms, 5 suites. Facilities: restaurant, pub. AE, D, MC, V. $50–$150 per person.*

Inexpensive

Chapman Inn

On the edge of the Bethel Common in one of the town's oldest buildings, with an odd collection of rooms, bunk beds, and efficiency apartments. The main house, with white-wood clapboard and black shutters, built around 1865, has decent-size rooms that are clean, comfortable, and furnished with catchall collectibles that might remind you of your grandmother's house. Next door the former barn has sleeping space for 21 in three sets of bunk beds, dormitory style. Guests share two floors plus a common area with a game room, a TV, cooking facilities, and saunas. Also available in an adjacent building are suites in a one-, two-, or three-bedroom layout. *1 Mill Hill Rd., Box 206, Bethel 04217, tel. 207/824–2657. 6 rooms, 2 with bath, 3 suites, 1 dorm. Facilities: 2 saunas. AE, MC, V. $25–$85 per person, including full breakfast.*

Douglass Place

The little gray-haired lady with a twinkle in her eye is exactly the type of proprietor you would expect to find at this homey traditional-style B&B. Barbara Douglass started the business in 1982. The cozy confines of this green-trimmed white colonial- and Victorian-style house, built in the early 1800s, seem unchanged since the Douglass offspring occupied what are now the four guest rooms. The neat-as-a-pin house is filled with family antiques, memories, and memorabilia, and each room has little touches like handmade quilts, unique pieces of furniture, and colorful throw rugs. The rooms range in size from small, with single or twin beds, to larger, with one queen-size bed and a sofa; all are bright and cheery. Downstairs there are a dining room, an indoor Jacuzzi, a pool table, a Ping-Pong table, and a piano where the occasional sing-along will break out. This quiet spot is about 4 miles from the resort. *162 Mayville Rd., Bethel 04217, tel. 207/824–2229. 4 rooms share 2 baths. AE. $55, including Continental breakfast.*

Pleasant River Motel

This is a delightful little no fuss/no frills motel with bright, spacious standard rooms plus a clutch of condo apartments in a newer building. The exterior of the motel is white wood siding with pink doors. Inside, the rooms come with two double beds; four are efficiencies and include a small sitting area plus minikitchen. The condos, gray with red shutters, are large enough for six people in the two bedrooms and a foldout couch in the living area. Like the motel rooms, they are clean, spacious, and bright with a great view from the large balcony. There is also a three-bedroom house that sleeps 12. *Rte. 2, West Bethel, Bethel 04286, tel. 207/836–3575, fax 207/836–3575. 22 rooms, 10 units. Facilities: restaurant, game room, laundry. D, MC, V. $75–$289.*

Snow Cap Lodge and Ski Dorm

This excellent modern dormitory facility, simple and with a stained-wood exterior, has 200 bunk beds in rooms that sleep eight. The good-size rooms come with two separate bathroom facilities. Technically they are sex segregated, but four cozy couples can request their own mixed unit. The best room in the building is the more private Bus Drivers room, which has just one double bed. Common space is bright and clean, with three TVs, Ping-Pong tables, and laundry facilities. It stands about 500 yards from the South Ridge base lodge. Call well in advance as groups love this place. *Sunday River Ski Area, Box 450, Bethel 04217, tel. 207/824–2187 ext. 225 or 800/543–2754, fax 207/824–2111. 200 beds. Facilities: games room, laundry. AE, D, MC, V. $35 per person.*

WHERE TO EAT

There are numerous dining spots at the resort that will prove to be filling and adequate if you don't feel like taking the drive into Bethel, but the town itself has a much greater variety of restaurants, and it's well worth the effort to check them out.

Expensive

Bethel Inn Restaurant

This enormous formal dining room has a comfortable country feeling to it even though it's filled with elegant trappings such as brass chandeliers, a large fireplace, white linen tablecloths, fresh flowers, tabletop candles, and hand-painted plates. In the center a pianist plays soft classical music while you dine. The menu combines New England favorites—broiled lobster and broiled fresh swordfish—with Continental dishes such as scampi Milanaise (jumbo shrimp sautéed in garlic, chives, and white wine) and roast duckling glazed with a sweet and sour sauce. Other exceptional entrées include a 16-ounce portion of prime rib, broiled haddock with lemon-pepper seasoning, and Cajun-style broiled swordfish. *Bethel Inn, Broad St., the Commons, Bethel, tel. 207/824–2175 or 800/654–0125. Reservations essential. AE, D, DC, MC, V.*

L'Auberge Fine Dining

The three small rooms that comprise the restaurant at L'Auberge are cozy, intimate, and casual, with small table groupings, soft lighting, and a European café ambience. The menu is mainly Continental, including pecan chicken (a boneless breast sautéed in a butter sauce with pecans) and the fettuccine *fruits de mer* (fresh lobster, shrimp, scallops, and crabmeat sautéed with shallots and roasted hazelnuts, in a lobster sauce over fettuccine). It was here that I enjoyed one of the finest duck dishes ever: a boneless moist-on-the-inside/crisp-on-the-outside duckling smothered in a mushroom-peppercorn cream sauce. Other entrées to consider are the rack of lamb or the broiled swordfish. *L'Auberge Country Inn, just off Bethel Common, tel. 207/824–2774. Reservations essential. AE, D, MC, V.*

Sudbury Inn Restaurant

Just down the road from the Bethel Inn is the smaller but livelier Sudbury Inn, with its three-room restaurant. In true country-inn style, you'll find table linens, crystal and silver place settings, a crackling fireplace, and intimate table arrangements. The menu is a mixture of New England specialties, Continental favorites, and lighter bites such as stir-fries and even pizza. Try the roasted Maine lobster Sudbury, a shelled lobster roasted and served on a bed of fettuccine with cream sauce or an excellent scallopini of veal done with fresh spinach, sautéed shrimp, and béarnaise sauce. For dessert try any of the supremely decadent homemade desserts. *151 Lower Main St., Bethel, tel. 207/824–2174 or 800/395–7837. Reservations essential. AE, D, MC, V.*

Moderate

Madison

The Madison is some 14 miles east of the ski area, but it's worth the drive for some fine food and a delightful atmosphere. The dining room is built of modern mortise-and-tenon beams with intricate exposed trusses supporting the roof. The high end of the dining room is all glass and provides a serene view of the river and the snow-dappled trees, and the entire space is a trophy room documenting the owner's successful hunting ventures. The Madison is definitely noted for its meat—try the prime rib with all the trimmings or the rack of lamb baked with fresh rosemary and Dijon mustard. *Rte. 2, Rumford, tel. 207/364–7973 or 800/258–6234. Reservations essential. AE, D, DC, MC, V.*

Moose's Tale at the Sunday River Brewing Company

At the intersection of Route 2 and the Sunday River Access Road stands a shrine to brew pubs, with stainless steel tanks displayed behind a glass wall and back-reflected by mirrors. The huge bilevel space has interior trusses, no shortage of windows, a large moose head over the fieldstone fireplace, and a lively bistro atmosphere that spills over from the bar into the dining area. It's definitely casual, and so is the menu, with a sterling lineup of hearty fare that runs the gamut from straightforward bar and finger food, such as wings, burgers, potato skins, and interesting sandwich combos, to entrées that include sirloin steak rubbed in hot Texas spices, boilermaker chicken (marinated and baked in bourbon and beer), and an excellent seafood platter, plus pasta and the catch of the day. It's a cheerful spot, perfect for families. *29 Sunday River Rd., Bethel, tel. 207/824–3541. MC, V.*

Mother's

Mother's is a community standby; the menu quotes aptly from the 1665 restaurant review by Samuel Pepys: "Strange to see how a good dinner and feasting reconciles everybody." It certainly applies in this casual restaurant where good food is served in four small dining rooms filled with eclectic collectibles such as a full-size mannequin in a Victorian gown. The menu is equally eclectic, ranging from fondue (a good choice) to vegetarian and scallop stir-fries to several pasta dishes. The Maine crab cakes are also a good choice, as is whatever comes from the daily Stew Pot. *Upper Main St., Bethel, tel. 207/824–2589. MC, V.*

Walsh and Hill Trading Company Restaurant

This Western lobster house, as legend would have us believe, was the creation of J. P. Walsh, a Montana cattleman, and Lillian Hill, a teacher from the woods of Maine. Evidently, as the menu explains, their torrid affair got them thrown out of Montana, where Lillian had gone to teach in a territory school. With her cowboy in tow, she returned to Maine, where they took up lobstering and cattle raising. Apocryphal or not, the story gives a raison d'être to this steak and seafood emporium with its brass fixtures, dark wood, and gold-and-green decor. The menu offers a variety of steak cuts plus a large selection of seafood including fresh Maine lobster and grilled marinated shrimp. It's a cheerful, casual place and one of the few restaurants with a two-sided fireplace. *Fall Line Condominium Bldg., Sunday River Rd., Bethel, tel. 207/824–5067, ext. 396. Reservations essential. AE, D, DC, MC, V.*

Inexpensive

Bottle and Bag

This all-purpose restaurant and take-out deli is on Route 2 about halfway between the mountain and Bethel. The exterior is red barn-board siding, while inside is basic wood paneling with pine and oak fixtures. You can stop for pasta dishes or sandwich-and-soup combos, or pick up beer, wine, cold cuts, bread, and cheese to take home. This place opens at 5:30 for breakfast, and it's worth a stop just for their red flannel hash (cooked in beet juice). *Rte. 2, Bethel, tel. 207/ 824–3673. D, DC, MC, V.*

Breau's Pizza & Subs

You can't miss this pizza/ice cream parlor as you drive down Route 2 because the neon sign advertising the daily special will blind you. A jukebox blares while you await your food. The pizzas come with a thick or thin crust and a wide variety of toppings; if

you're really hungry, try the five-meat pizza: ground beef, pepperoni, ham, barbecued chicken, and salami, topped with two different cheeses. *Rte. 2 , Bethel, tel. 207/824–3192. No credit cards.*

Rhea Lu's

When you need a fast fix of Chinese food, Rhea Lu's is the place to go. Originally a house converted into a restaurant, the interior is natural wood, with a red-and-white theme and Chinese ornaments for decoration. It has a full menu of traditional Asian favorites, including an excellent General Tso's chicken as well as some specialty lobster dishes. Overall the quality and cooking are good and the portions large. It also has a delivery service. *Rte. 2, Bethel, tel. 207/824– 2249. AE, MC, V.*

Sud's Pub

This is my favorite low-budget eatery in town because of its lively atmosphere and friendly, woody, pubby decor. The menu is huge, with a selection of bar and finger foods ranging from calamari to nachos to peel-and-eat shrimp, plus a good lineup of interesting soups and salads such as lobster gazpacho, shrimp and tomato salad, and tortellini and chicken salad. It also has huge hamburger and sandwich plates plus the best pizza in town. There's also a great selection of microbrewed beer. *Sudbury Inn, Lower Main St., Bethel, tel. 207/824–6558. AE, D, MC, V.*

Best Bet for Breakfast

Bethel Inn and Country Club

If you like to start your day with an elegant and refined breakfast, head here. There's white linen and crystal service in a serene environment with the full range of breakfast options, including standard egg dishes, fresh fruit, waffles, pancakes, and a great selection of fresh pastries and sweet breads. *The Common, Bethel, tel. 207/ 824–2175 or 800/654–0125. AE, D, MC, V.*

NIGHTLIFE AND ENTERTAINMENT
Après-Ski
Sunday River Brewing Company
This shrine to brew pubs has no shortage of windows, a large moose head over the fieldstone fireplace, and a lively bistro atmosphere. It's definitely casual. *1 Sunday River Rd., Bethel, tel. 207/824–4253. AE, MC, V.*

Loud and Lively/Dancing
Sud's Pub
In this cheerful pub there's live entertainment nightly, including acoustic groups and rock bands. *Sudbury Inn, Lower Main St., Bethel, tel. 207/824–6558. AE, D, MC, V.*

Sunday River Brewing Company
On weekends you can dance to live band music on the small dance floor. *1 Sunday River Rd., Bethel, tel. 207/ 824–4253. AE, MC, V.*

T he sweeping ranchland, the broad river-washed valleys, the thick, rich forests, and the string of crowning mountain ranges of Montana all have one thing in common: lack of people. This least-populated state in the United States is a vast, expansive tableau of natural attributes made all the more dramatic by the absence of a smothering population. Wildlife is still the master of this domain—deer, elk, moose, bears, eagles, and buffalo all comfortably thrive on millions of acres of protected wilderness, including the ecosystem of the greater Yellowstone Park area. The state is sliced by an extension of the Canadian Rockies from north to south. More than 50 mountain ranges form this rugged wall, with the tallest peaks topping 12,000 feet.

This is also, along with Wyoming, the classic cowboy state, with the touch and easy independence of the American cowboy manifesting itself in the pure and empty wilderness of a state that some call "the last best place." The images reinforce this. Ranches outnumber shopping malls, horses are more common than four-wheel-drive vehicles, Stetsons are more functional than decorative, and cows outnumber people 4 to 1. You make your mark here with substance not sizzle; and the stoicism inherent in individualism is tempered by an effusive enjoyment of the state's most precious resource—the land.

The modern counterpoint to all this is the state's ski resorts. Isolated peaks that hum with modernity, they are beacons of commerce that rely on the resources of nature to attract skiers who prefer the northern lights dancing in the night sky to the light show of a trendy nightspot. The largest of these resorts is Big Sky, in the southwest corner of the state adjacent to the 3-million-acre Spanish Peaks Wilderness area. Big Sky's long-standing appeal lies in its unhurried pace and uncrowded skiing, but it also has taken bold steps in development. A single-span tram lift to the top of 11,160-foot Lone Mountain, opened in 1995, gives Big Sky the greatest vertical drop in the United States—4,180 feet.

BIG SKY RESORT

Box 160001
1 Lone Mountain Trail
Big Sky, MT 59716
Tel. 406/995–5000 or
800/548–4486

STATISTICALLY SPEAKING

Base elevation: 6,970 feet

Summit elevation: 11,150 feet

Vertical drop: 4,180 feet

Skiable terrain: 3,500 acres

Number of trails: 75

Longest run: 6 miles

Lifts and capacity: 1 tram,
1 gondola, 1 quad, 3 high-
speed quads, 3 doubles,
3 triples, 3 surface; 18,000
skiers per hour

Daily lift ticket: $46

Average annual snowfall:
400 inches

Number of skiing days
1995–96: 150

Snowmaking: 315 acres, 10%

Terrain mix: N 10%, I 47%,
E 43%

Snowboarding: yes

It's hard to compare Big Sky with any of the other 29 resorts in this book. It is indeed unique—as unique as the state of Montana itself, which has been called the "last best place," in tribute to its natural wonders and relatively unhurried pace. Big Sky is an unaffected major-league resort perched at the base of Lone Mountain, a perfect pyramid of a peak halfway between Bozeman and Yellowstone National Park— in the middle of nowhere.

Of course, that's part of its uniqueness. Surrounded by 10,000 acres of spectacular wilderness acquired in the early '70s by the late NBC newscaster Chet Huntley and his partners, Big Sky is a wide-open and gloriously scenic resort where spotting a golden eagle in flight is more exciting than catching a fleeting glimpse of a celebrity. Notwithstanding the 170,000-acre spread owned by Ted Turner and Jane Fonda over in the next valley, there's considerably more wildlife than star life at Big Sky. Buffalo still roam in the wild valleys, elk and moose slide easily through the woods, horses outnumber pickup trucks, and ranches are more common than alpine chalets.

You roll up to Big Sky through a broad plateau gently rising from the Gallatin Canyon that slices through the Madison Range of the Rocky Mountains. Immediately to the north is the Spanish Peaks Wilderness Area; just to the south lies the western border of Yellowstone National Park. Combined, these two vast areas surround the resort of Big Sky with more than 3 million acres of pristine wilderness dramatically accented with a parade of peaks that top the 11,000-foot mark.

This riveting tableau of mountains and sky reduces the resort to a speck in the distance, and when you arrive, you see that the mountain village stands in harmonious balance with the surrounding wilderness, rolling ranch lands, and rugged forested foothills. It's an American classic, with clean lines and simple designs, free of both the Swiss and Austrian kitsch and the fake cowboy facades that crop up in so many other Western resorts. There's no need to import a back-to-nature wilderness theme either, for Big Sky is surrounded by the real thing.

The mountainside development, though prosaic in patches, is reasonably well laid out, its sturdy stone-

Area code: 406

Children's services: day care,
tel. 406/995–3332; instruction, tel. 406/995–5000,
ext. 5743

Snow phone:
tel. 406/995–5900

Police: tel. 406/582–2100

Hospital: Bozeman Deaconess
Hospital, tel. 406/586–8511

Road conditions:
tel. 800/525–5555

Towing: Canyon Towing,
tel. 406/995–4577

FIVE-STAR FAVORITES

Best run for vertical:
Little Rock Tongue

Best run overall:
Elk Park Ridge

Best bar/nightclub:
Half Moon Saloon

Best hotel: Buck's T-4

Best restaurant: Rocco's

and-beam buildings tucked into knolls, perched on the edge of streams, or surrounded by trees. The heart of the Mountain Village is the combination of Huntley Lodge, Yellowstone Conference Center, and Shoshone condominiums, all adjacent to the Mountain Mall complex, an open, double-deck structure with elaborate ironwork that gives it a galleria feeling. It's the center of activity during the day, and after dark the numerous restaurants and bars—including those in the adjacent Huntley Lodge—are about the only nightlife happening at the ski-base area of Big Sky.

Spread out around this are the various condominium complexes. Although the first wave of condos built in the '70s look a bit dated and blandly uniform now, the new ones, such as Arrowhead and Shoshone, are striking stone-and-wood structures that should set the standard for future building.

The Mountain Village offers a total of about 1,300 beds, most within walking distance of the Village Mall and the base-area lifts. Six miles away at the bottom of Big Sky Road is Meadow Village, a subdivision with private homes, condominium buildings, restaurants, and shops. It's much more spread out than the Mountain Village, so you really need a car to get around, but the accommodations here are also considerably less expensive. There is another patchwork collection of small hotels and motels north of Meadow Village and down the Gallatin Canyon, and you'll also find some more nightlife options here.

Unlike Steamboat or Crested Butte, Big Sky has no quaint restored Victorian town to focus it: There's just the Mountain Village, the lower Meadow Village, and the scattering of hotels and restaurants down the Gallatin Canyon. This is a quiet resort, more a place where you come to get away from it all than to end up in the middle of it all (though it does have some entertaining diversions and knock-'em-down bars).

This is not a resort that attracts an uptown crowd with attitude. It's a resort for those who want a low-key wilderness experience and who like the pace and price of a mountainside village that has not become smothered in glitz.

HOW TO GET THERE

By Plane

Gallatin Field, in Bozeman, Montana, 45 miles north of Big Sky, is the nearest airport. **Delta** and **Skywest** (tel. 406/388–6591 or 800/221–1212), **Northwest** (tel. 406/388–4202 or 800/692–700) and **Horizon** (tel. 406/388–1733 or 800/547–9308) have daily scheduled flights from Salt Lake City, Minneapolis/St. Paul, and Seattle, respectively.

Shuttle Service

4 × 4 Stage (tel. 406/388–6404 or 800/517–8243) has a shuttle bus meeting all flights into Bozeman; the one-hour drive to Big Sky costs $35 round-trip. **City Taxi** (tel. 406/586–2341) and **Mountain Taxi** (tel. 406/995–4895) run cabs between the airport and the resort for about $110 round-trip.

By Car

From Bozeman take Route 191 south 45 miles to the turnoff to Big Sky. The resort is 45 miles north of West Yellowstone on Route 191.

The following major car-rental companies have outlets at Gallatin Field, in Bozeman: **Avis** (tel. 406/388–6414), **Budget** (tel. 406/388–4091), **Hertz** (tel. 406/388–6939), and **National** (tel. 406/388–6694).

By Bus

The nearest **Greyhound Lines** (tel. 406/587–3110 or 800/822–6009) bus station is in Bozeman.

By Helicopter

Helicopter landing areas are available in the Mountain Village (upper) and Meadow Village (lower) areas of the resort. You must obtain prior permission if you want to do any helicopter skiing on Lone Mountain.

GETTING AROUND

A car is definitely an asset at Big Sky because it allows you the flexibility and freedom to move back and forth from the mountain to the valley and the surrounding environs. If, however, you plan to bunk down in the village and make only the occasional foray down to the valley (5 miles), you can use the free **Snow Express** (tel. 406/995–5000) shuttle bus, which runs in several loops (around the village, the meadow, and the valley) and includes stops at individual accommodations, restaurants, resorts, and nightspots. The service runs from 7 AM (9 AM if the overnight temperature goes below –20°) to 11 PM, so even if you have a car, it's a good alternative if you plan to sip a few suds. If you miss the last bus or are feeling flush, taxi service is available (*see* How to Get There, *above*).

THE SKIING

The skiing at Big Sky takes place on two peaks. To the left of the base area is Andesite Mountain, an 8,800-foot three-sided peak of mostly intermediate terrain; to the right is Lone Mountain, the 11,166-foot Fuji-like cone that has both some of the toughest and some of the easiest runs at the resort. Whichever mountain you choose, you won't lack for long, wide-open cruising. That's the hallmark of Big Sky, and the abundance of these runs has given the area a reputation as strictly an intermediate mountain. In fact, there's plenty of steep and rugged skiing in the above–tree line bowls off the Lone Peak triple chair, and the immense amount of terrain serviced by the new Lone Peak tram is a playground for experts only. The Challenger chair serves some gulp-and-go double-black pitches as well as some outrageous glade skiing. For even more challenge, check out the ultrasteep wide-open bowl of the South Wall area and the ridge of the Pinnacles area, which has some of the steepest terrain on the mountain.

Still, intermediates *are* the core group at Big Sky, and the runs are groomed to reflect that sit-back-and-let-them-run comfort zone. You can't get much closer to intermediate heaven than on the middle section of the massive upper bowl, served by the Lone Peak Triple. This is a wondrous expanse of intermediate bowl skiing with a combination of marked runs and seek-a-way-down options.

The major lifts, including the gondola, all originate from the Mountain Village, so it's easy to move back and forth between the two mountains to meet up with friends as well as follow the sun as it moves from Lone Mountain to Andesite Mountain. With short lift lines and fast lifts, it's easy to rack up impressive vertical. You may be cruising, but you'll also be working.

Snowboarders are welcome on all trails. Natural features for snowboarders are indicated on the trail map.

Novices

If you are a never-ever or raw novice, you'll need to start on your own lift, the Explorer, a double chair that serves the green runs on the lower part of Lone Mountain. It's just a short shuffle from the Mountain Mall area and away from the more heavily trafficked gondola loading areas.

White's Wing is a good place to start. Turn right off the chair, and you'll find this deliciously wide, smooth carpet curving naturally back down to the bottom of the lift. There are no cutoffs and no surprises.

Warm up on that for a few runs and then turn left off the chair and head for Mr. K., a slightly narrower, teensy bit steeper run with the occasional roll and swell. Your third choice off this lift is Lone Wolf, directly under the chair, a relatively straight shot that will let you experiment with some speed. When you are ready for a longer run, take Gondola 1 to the top. Lower Morning Star and Mr. K are the only green runs down from this point. Turn right off the chair and follow the sign for the upper part of Mr. K. It starts out a little narrower and slightly steeper than the lower runs, but with some steady snow plow turns you should be able to work your way through this and then spread out a little about a third of the way down.

If you are heading back to the gondola and want to try a short stretch of blue terrain, cut right on Marmot Meadows, which starts out green, then turns blue for a short stretch as it leads back to the base.

The other exclusively green area at the resort is the series of long runs on the south face of Andesite Mountain. To get to them, take the Ramcharger quad and then ski down toward the top of the Southern Comfort triple chair. Three runs snake down this flank with a moderate pitch that incorporates some interesting rolls and modest drop-offs. Deep South and Sacajawea are the narrowest, curving gracefully through the trees, while El Dorado runs wider and steeper right under the chair.

From here you can also take a stab at some blue runs when you are ready. Ponderosa, to the right off the Southern Comfort triple, is a medium-grade intermediate, steeper than you might be used to, but wide, groomed, and smooth, with a long green runoff section near the bottom. Keep in mind that if you want to return to the main base area from the top of Andesite, you'll be on moderately intermediate terrain all the way. Africa is the most direct, but I don't recommend it because it is narrow and steep. Hangmans is not quite as steep, and it's definitely wider. The easiest route back is on Pacifier, a wide, gentle trail that meets up with Africa close to the bottom, past most of its pitch.

Intermediates

This is really your mountain. Almost 50% of the runs are marked blue, and if you enjoy wide-open Giant Slalom–style cruising on well-groomed slopes, Big Sky is ideal. Start the day by riding either Gondola 1 and then skiing down Crazy Horse or the Swift Current Express chair (twice as fast as the gondola) and skiing Lobo Meadows. Both are well-pitched warm-up runs with some good pace and lots of rolls; true, you'll hit some moguls if you ski down the left side of Lobo, but overall these are a good taste of the resort's renowned cruising runs.

Calamity Jane, reached from either gondola, is another good blue challenge, a little steeper, with some mellow bumps to warm the legs and a steep optional cutoff called Huntley Hollow. If you want to try the bowls, it's best to get up there around mid-

morning on a sunny day. The Lone Peak triple, down and to the right of the gondolas, takes you up to about 1,000 feet below the 11,150-foot summit, and from up there a vast expanse of steep intermediate bowl skiing lies before you. The two marked trails, Never Sweat and Upper Morning Star, are the easiest ways down the bowl because they tend to be well traveled, but once you gain some confidence, experiment a little. Slide across the bowl, pick fresh snow, or tackle a steep pitch: This is free-form bowl skiing, and the routes down are limited only by your imagination.

After lunch the sun moves over to Andesite Mountain, and you can rack up some impressive mileage by riding the Ramcharger quad and skiing the long, blue cruisers on that face. Hangmans is a good place to start (see Novices, above). By turning left off the chair, you can head down upper Silverknife, a long cruiser to the bottom that offers several options, such as the steep mogul pitches of south and north Ambush or the lightly gladed Meadows area. You can also split to the right at the intersection with Elk Park Ridge about halfway down and head for the Elk Park Meadows, a wide expanse of ungroomed glades that takes you to the bottom of the Thunder Wolf quad.

If you still have spring in your legs and want to try a few black runs, there's a half-dozen short, steep shots on either side of the chair. Broken Arrow and Mad Wolf are never groomed and are great leg-burning mogul runs that never seem to end. Crazy Raven and Snakepit are shorter but steeper. You can also continue with wide-open cruising from the top of the Thunder Wolf chair by heading down Big Horn, a long, looping boulevard, or by heading back over to the blue runs served by the Ramcharger chair.

Experts

The trail map identifies 43% of Big Sky's 3,500 acres as expert terrain, so you won't lack for excitement. Although there are a number of challenging bump runs and steep pitches on Andesite Mountain and on the lower half of Lone Mountain, the real action is at the top of the 11,150-foot Lone Peak Tram. Riding the tram to Lone Peak is itself breathtaking. Once at the top, skiers who aren't up for double-black-diamond terrain can opt to ride the tram down to the midway point. Experts can choose from the terrain offered by the south face and slopes above the bowl, including the Big Couloir, a steep, narrow chute directly under the tram. This is serious stuff: You are required to ski with a partner, have an avalanche transceiver and shovel, and sign in with the ski patrol.

For less hair-raising but still keep-on-your-toes skiing, stick to the bowl on either side of the Lone Peak triple. To the left of this lift is the South Wall, an ultrasteep, craggy expanse that combines vertical thrill with heads-up skiing. To the far right of the Lone Peak chair is the Challenger chair, an experts-only lift that rises to a sharp ridge in the midst of double-black territory. Immediately under the lift are Little Rock Tongue and Big Rock Tongue, two tough couloirs that are brutally steep and gloriously wild, with narrow chutes, scattered glades, deep snow, and cliffs. On the far side

of the same ridge is the Nashville Basin, a natural north-facing snow trap where the mode is full-bore powder blasting in the open areas and in the patches of glades.

At the top of the Challenger lift is a rope tow up to the craggy area known as the Pinnacles (note that the tow, used by the ski patrol to reach areas for avalanche blasting, is not always open). Here you'll find some steep, narrow, and tree-stuffed chutes; or if that's not good enough, you can hike (for about 15 minutes) farther up the ridge to the A–Z Chutes, a collection of radical pitches—narrow and rocky—that attract the resort's extreme-skier brigade. If this sounds tempting, try to take a local skier along for company.

WHERE TO STAY

Most skiers at Big Sky stay in condos in one of three distinct areas. The units at the Mountain Village tend to be the newest and the most expensive, while the lower Meadow Village, 15 minutes from the slopes, offers more moderate (in price and decor) units. There is a range of smaller and/or more unusual accommodations down the Gallatin Canyon, between the entrance to the resort and a point about 7 miles down the highway. When you're weighing the options, keep in mind that a regular shuttle bus links the lower Meadow Village and environs to the mountain. Almost all condos are individually owned, which has two effects on the accommodation available: First, only a portion of units at a complex may be for rent at any given time, and second, interior design in adjoining units can vary from Art Deco to rustic Southwestern to drab and dreary. Two companies manage most of the condominium properties: Golden Eagle Property Management (Box 160008, Big Sky 59716, tel. 406/995–4800 or 800/548–4488) handles the majority of the properties in the Meadow Village area, while Triple Creek Realty & Management (Box 160219, Big Sky 59716, tel. 406/995–4848 or 800/548–4632) deals with the Mountain Village properties. Another local property management company is Blue Grouse Real Estate (Box 160318, Big Sky 59716, tel. 406/995–2318 or 800/799–2919).

Expensive

Arrowhead

These freestanding chalets at the bottom of the Silver Knife Run are all three-level luxury dwellings, each with three or four bedrooms, on a pleasant, tree-surrounded hillside. The pastel-and-wheat-colored Southwestern furnishings are not quite as elegant or distinctive as those in the Beaverhead condominiums (*see below*), but you do get lots of space: large bedrooms, including a master bedroom with a king-size bed and Jacuzzi, and more than ample living and dining areas. The kitchen is both big and well equipped, and the living room has a stone fireplace. Guests can use the health spa facilities at the Huntley Lodge (*see below*). *1 Lone Mountain Trail, Box 160001, Big Sky 59716, tel. 406/995–5000 or 800/548–4486, fax 406/995–5001. 23 units. AE, D, DC, MC, V. $370–$545.*

Beaverhead

These large, luxurious two- to four-bedroom units in a private little townhouse-style enclave are among the nicest on the mountain, with the added bonus of ski-in/ski-out access on the White Wing beginner run. They all have vaulted cedar-lined ceilings, large floor-to-ceiling stone fireplaces, and a split-level living room/dining room area. You can really spread out in the full-size kitchen and breakfast nook. Guests have access to the Huntley Lodge facilities. *1 Lone Mountain Trail, Box 160001, Big Sky 59716, tel. 406/995–5000 or 800/548–4486, fax 406/995–5001. 23 units. Facilities: washer-dryer, private garage. AE, D, DC, MC, V. $341–$755.*

Lone Mountain Ranch

This marvelously preserved slice of Americana is a self-contained cross-country skiing resort with a 65-kilometer trail network. It's only 5 miles from Big Sky, with a regular shuttle to and from the mountain. Though the heritage of a 1915 working ranch is lovingly preserved, the resort brims with luxury and hums with service. The log cabins, nestled in the pines on either side of a brook, accommodate from 2 to 10 people amid the rustic elegance of polished wood, bright Native American fabrics, antiques, and eiderdown. All that's lacking are telephones, TVs, and radios. In 1994 the Ridgetop Lodge was completed, with six guest rooms, each with a king-size and a single bed and decorated in traditional lodgepole pine furniture and handmade quilts. There is a saloon and restaurant (*see* Where to Eat, *below*) that serves outstanding food. There is usually a seven-night minimum, and the package price includes all meals plus a sleigh-ride dinner, cross-country or two days of downhill skiing, and evening programs. *Lone Mountain*

Access Rd., Box 160069, Big Sky 59716, tel. 406/995–4644 or 800/514–4644, fax 406/995–4670. 24 cabins, 6 rooms with bath. Facilities: restaurant, bar, 2 outdoor hot tubs, rental shop, massage service. D, MC, V. $863–$1,482 (per 7-day week, MAP).

Shoshone Condominiums
These condos, connected to the Huntley Lodge, are among the newest on the mountain. It's a great ski-in/ski-out location, and the units, with one bedroom or one bedroom with loft, are smart, upscale, and well designed, with first-class furnishings and a pleasant sand-and-wheat-color decor that includes lots of wood trim, textured wall coverings, Berber carpeting, and natural finishes. Spacious common areas have deep couches and a gas fireplace, and the kitchens are full-size. Guests have full privileges at the Shoshone Health Center (heated outdoor pool, saunas, hot tubs, and exercise gym). 1 Lone Mountain Trail, Box 160001, Big Sky 59716, tel. 406/995–5000 or 800/548–4486, fax 406/995–5001. 94 units. AE, D, DC, MC, V. $242–$512.

Moderate

Big Horn Condominiums
These duplex condos have ski-in/ski-out access on their own poma lift to the Silver Knife trail. The units all have three bedrooms, so they are perfect for large groups. They are bright, with contemporary furnishings and muted tones—not upscale-designer fancy but more than comfortable, with a large central stone fireplace, a full kitchen, a dining room, and three bathrooms. 1 Lone Mountain Trail, Box 160001, Big Sky 59716, tel. 406/

995–5000 or 800/548–4486, fax 406/995–5001. 48 units. Facilities: washer-dryer, private garage. AE, D, DC, MC, V. $355–$526.

Buck's T-4
Despite the Best Western sign over the front entrance, Buck's is an authentic Big Sky institution, offering big rooms, two restaurants, a lounge, and one of the best deals in the area. Originally built as a lodge for local hunters, it has expanded into a sprawling hospitality complex. The three-story main building is finished in light-brown log siding with a dark-brown trim. A picturesque wooded hill rises directly behind the hotel, and to one side there's an equestrian center where horses graze on open pastures. Room decor runs to rich colors, country floral bedcovers, and solid, well-made furnishings. U.S. 191, 1½ mi south of Big Sky entrance, Box 160279, Big Sky 59716, tel. 406/995–4111 or 800/822–4484, fax 406/995–2191. 73 rooms, 2 suites. Facilities: 2 restaurants, bar, 2 outdoor hot tubs. AE, D, DC, MC, V. $87–$328, including daily lift tickets.

Huntley Lodge
This is the only full-service hotel at the resort, and it's right in the heart of the Mountain Village, with ski-in/ski-out access to the slopes and direct connection to the Shoshone condominium complex and the Yellowstone Conference Center. The large multi-story building has a stone-and-wood lobby with big game trophies, elk antler chandeliers, and numerous fireplaces and sitting areas. The rooms are freshly decorated in peach and wheat tones, with colonial reproduc-

Pick up the phone.
Pick up the miles.

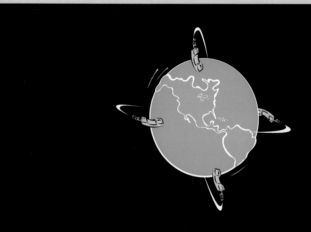

1-800-FLY-FREE

Is this a great time, or what? :-)

Now when you sign up with MCI you can receive up to 8,000 bonus frequent flyer miles on one of seven major airlines.

Then earn another 5 miles for every dollar you spend on a variety of MCI services, including MCI Card® calls from virtually anywhere in the world.*

You're going to use these services anyway. Why not rack up the miles while you're doing it?

tions and a small wet bar/fridge; the larger rooms have sleeping lofts and accommodate up to six. *1 Lone Mountain Trail, Box 160001, Big Sky 59716, tel. 406/995–5000 or 800/548–4486, fax 406/995–5001. 204 rooms. Facilities: restaurant, bar, pool, 2 outdoor hot tubs, exercise room, sauna. AE, D, DC, MC, V. $149–$325.*

Sky Crest Condominiums

The Sky Crest is a good on-mountain complex with large units. The extra-large three-bedroom with loft accommodates 14. The interior decor is fairly utilitarian, with durable and sensible furnishings in dirtproof earth and wheat tones, but stone and wood accents contribute a little mountain character. You get a large kitchen and dining room, a fireplace, a sun room, a Jacuzzi, and a bathroom for each bedroom. The mountain is just a half mile away. *1 Lone Mountain Trail, Box 160001, Big Sky 59716, tel. 406/995–5000 or 800/548–4486, fax 406/995–5001. 35 units. Facilities: laundry, shuttle, underground parking. AE, D, DC, MC, V. $290–$492.*

Inexpensive

Corral Motel

Five miles south of Big Sky, you'll run across the Corral, a straight-up roadside motel with straightforward motel rooms that are among the cheapest in the area. Each room has two or three queen-size beds and not much else except cleanliness and comfort. If you crave TV, duck into the adjoining restaurant and bar. The shuttle bus to Big Sky stops outside three times a day from either direction. *42895 Gallatin Rd., U.S. 191, Gallatin Gateway 59730, tel. 406/995–4249. 8 rooms.*

Facilities: restaurant, bar, hot tub. AE, D, MC, V. $40–$70.

Golden Eagle Lodge

The heart shapes carved in the railings that surround this quaint Bavarian-style three-story wood-and-stucco lodge are pretty much the extent of the frills at this place. But it's great for groups on a budget; dormitory-style rooms sleep up to eight in a variety of bedding arrangements. You won't find much in the way of extras, but it's a good, clean, and comfortable economy lodging with a bright, cheery interior of blue-painted and stained-wood trim. This is a quiet and well-run spot suitable for families. There are also standard double rooms without phones. *Little Coyote Rd., Box 160008, Meadow Village, Big Sky 59716, tel. 406/995–4800 or 800/548–4488, fax 406/995–2447. 6 rooms, 9 dormitories. D, MC, V. $45 double room; $65 dormitory (up to 4 people), $8 each additional person.*

Hidden Village

This "village" of isolated condo town house–style buildings is indeed hidden in 40 wooded acres on the side of a hill, with stunning views of the Spanish Peaks Wilderness Area to the north and Lone Mountain to the west. As is often the case in Big Sky, the individual condos can have very different interiors, and although many of the units at Hidden Village are extremely modern and trendy, there remain a good number that suffer from a drab decor of dark wood and institutional fabrics. But this is more than compensated for by the excellent size, price, and location of all the accommodations. The units, ranging from two to five bedrooms, are among the largest of the Meadow Village rental properties. They have full-size kitchens, separate dining and living rooms, and striking rough-stone fireplaces. *Off Andesite Rd., Box 160008, 6 mi from slopes, Big Sky 59716, tel. 406/995–4800 or 800/548–4488, fax 406/995–2447. 140 units. Facilities: outdoor hot tub. D, MC, V. $160–$500.*

Silverbow
This neat gathering of condos is built in the classic Meadow Village style: rustic chalets with cedar siding and sloping cedar-shake roofs. Try for one of the units with more modern furnishings, but even if you end up in one with tacky circa-'60s decor, you'll appreciate the value of these large, versatile one- to three-bedroom condos next to a golf course 6 miles from the slopes. The smallest unit sleeps four with space to spare, and the largest will handle eight. Each unit has a fireplace and a full kitchen. *Black Otter Rd., Box 160008, Big Sky 59716, tel. 406/995–4800 or 800/548–4488, fax 406/995–2447. 30 units. Facilities: sauna, whirlpool. D, MC, V. $110–$235.*

WHERE TO EAT
Mountain Village dining at Big Sky is pretty limited and mostly mainstream. It is, however, convenient if you don't feel like driving or hopping the shuttle bus into the valley area, where there is considerably more variety as well as some entertaining nightlife options.

Expensive

Buck's T-4 Restaurant
Busy, bustling, casual, and friendly, Buck's serves up first-rate meals with an emphasis on wild game dishes in two dining rooms with wooden booths, stucco walls, and wagon-wheel chandeliers. The New Zealand red deer, sautéed in port wine, shallots, thyme, and butter sauce and garnished with artichoke hearts, is the best I've ever tasted. Other winners include fillet of panfried rainbow trout topped with pecans and wild boar sautéed and served on a bed of sweet vermouth cream sauce with huckleberries. For dessert, try either the Russian cream with fresh raspberries or the apple dumpling with homemade cinnamon ice cream. *U.S. 191, 1½ mi south of Big Sky entrance, Big Sky, tel. 406/995–4111 or 800/822–4484. AE, D, DC, MC, V.*

Café Edelweiss
"An Irishman from Miami in Montana cooking German food," is how John Kelly, the owner of this tiny Tirol look-alike, sums up his place in the Big Sky culinary scene. The restaurant's interior is a monument to wooden curlicues, with storybook characters and endless scrollwork carved into every post, beam, and panel. The Continental menu emphasizes traditional Austrian dishes (schnitzels, excellent bratwurst and knockwurst sausages, and *Schweine braten,* a pork roast with homemade sauerkraut), and the quiet, low-key ambience attracts a steady crowd of couples and other romantics. *Meadow Village, U.S. 191, Big Sky, tel. 406/995–4665. AE, D, MC, V.*

First Place
A wall of windows overlooks the Gallatin Valley, and massive fieldstones

and square-cut ceiling beams harmonize with the subdued lighting and soft apricot tones of the table settings. The house specialty is pheasant with port sauce and mushrooms, or try the rack of lamb, charbroiled with rosemary and garlic. The small, snug wood-walled lounge, decorated with hunting trophies, is a nice place for an aperitif or nightcap by the fire. *Meadow Village, Big Sky, tel. 406/ 995–4244. AE, D, MC, V.*

Lone Mountain Guest Ranch Dining Room

The dining room alone is a good reason to visit this guest ranch. In the massive log building at the center of the ranch property, it's a bright, amber-hued room with 30-foot vaulted ceilings, massive beam work, a large stone fireplace, three elk antler chandeliers, a collection of Native American artifacts, and tables glowing with linen and crystal. The menu has an unmistakable Western theme, with entrées such as Montana bison medallions done with rosemary, garlic, and lingonberry and Montana trout baked with spinach and brie and served in lemon-butter sauce. A changing selection of vegetarian dishes includes a vegetable strudel (fresh country vegetables baked in pastry and served with baked polenta and Gorgonzola). *Lone Mountain Ranch, Big Sky, tel. 406/995–2782. Reservations essential. D, MC, V.*

Moderate

All Goods

At this pleasantly casual restaurant, the ambience is mountain rustic and the menu straightforward Montana barbecue. The decor is dull, clean, and modern, but a selection of old photos of the early days at Big Sky Resort adds a certain color. The baby-back ribs, hickory smoked and charbroiled with an excellent sauce, are a good example of what the place does best. The bar serves more than 40 beers, including a multitude of local microbrews. *West Fork Plaza, Meadow Village, Big Sky, tel. 406/995–2750. AE, D, DC, MC, V.*

Dante's Inferno

This is a large, barnlike structure with posts, pillars, beams, and a curious mix of decorations including trophy heads and a pair of model World War I–vintage biplanes. The food is authentic Italian, with the buffalo mozzarella and pancetta imported from Italy. There are five different pastas nightly; pizzas and calzones are made with a cornmeal crust; and focaccia sandwiches come with pasta chips. Meals can be served family style for larger groups. The wine list contains affordable selections from Italy and California. An après-ski happy hour from 3 to 6 features live entertainment and drink specials. *Mountain Mall, Big Sky, tel. 406/995– 3999. AE, MC, V.*

Rocco's

This large barn of a restaurant with Wedgwood blue walls and a big stone fireplace at the center can't decide whether to specialize in Italian or Mexican cuisine—so it does both superbly. The homemade salsa, in three styles, is as distinctive as the rich marinara sauce used in the pasta dishes. The Mexican side of the menu has the favorites—enchiladas, burritos, and fajitas, plus excellent chili relleños. Italian fare is represented by a variety of pasta dishes including lasagna and by mainstay items such as chicken parmigiana, veal marsala, and scampi. *Golden Eagle Lodge, Meadow Village, Big Sky, tel. 406/925–4200. MC, V.*

Twin Panda

The bright and cheerful Twin Panda features old favorites—chow mein and egg rolls, with a few Szechuan dishes thrown in—and the clientele consists mostly of families or groups of young people. *Arrowhead Mall, 3rd floor, Mountain Village, Big Sky, tel. 406/995–2425. MC, V.*

Inexpensive

Buck's Grill

If Mom and Dad prefer the dining room at the other end of Buck's T-4 complex (*see* Expensive, *above*), this is a good place for the kids to come to feast on deep-pan pizza, hero sandwiches, charbroiled burgers, or a first-rate homemade chili. The decor is kid-proof, with green tiles on the floor, solid wood tables, and inexpensive Western prints on the walls. *Buck's T-4, U.S. 191, 1½ mi south of Big Sky entrance, Big Sky, tel. 406/995–4811. AE, D, DC, MC, V.*

The Corral

Have you ever had a buffalo burger? If not, you should seriously consider sinking your teeth into one at this kitschy, funky, friendly locals' hangout. The fainter of heart can stick with the sandwiches, regular burgers, and daily specials such as fresh seafood and a delicious Italian marinated beef kebab. The atmosphere is as much of a draw as the food: The log walls are awash in collectibles and

there's an old wood stove, a jukebox, gambling machines, and four TVs. *42895 Gallatin Rd., U.S. 191, 5 mi south of Big Sky entrance, Gallatin Gateway, tel. 406/995–4249. AE, D, MC, V.*

Mountain Top Pizza

Good, hearty pizza is the bill of fare here—choose from traditional varieties as well as specialty toppings like black bean salsa. Skiing and snowboarding photos and old skis dot the walls. *Mountain Mall, Big Sky, tel. 406/995–4646. AE, MC, V.*

Scissorbills Bar and Grill

This lively, youthful little place serves basic burgers, sandwiches, soup, salads, and chili in a brass- and fern-filled space. *Arrowhead Mall, upstairs, Big Sky, tel. 406/995–4933. MC, V.*

Best Bets for Breakfast

The Corral

Here you can get trucker-size portions of everything from pancakes, classic Western steak and eggs, and scrumptious hash browns to egg dishes in every form, including standout deep omelets. *42895 Gallatin Rd., U.S. 191, 5 mi south of Big Sky entrance, Gallatin Gateway, tel. 406/995–4249. AE, D, MC, V.*

Huntley Lodge Dining Room

Up in the Mountain Village, the Huntley Lodge dining room serves an excellent two-part buffet breakfast. On one side there are hot dishes—eggs, crepes, French toast—and on the other side a fruit, cereal, yogurt, and muffin selections. *Huntley Lodge, 1 Lone Mountain Trail, Big Sky, tel. 406/995–5783 or 800/548–4486. AE, MC, V.*

NIGHTLIFE AND ENTERTAINMENT

Nightlife action is spread out between the Mountain Village and the surrounding valley. Most immediate après-ski action is in the village and is followed by early evening trips to the valley's more eclectic bars.

Après Ski

Saloon

Unlike the exuberant Chet's, the Saloon at Lone Mountain Ranch is relatively mellow. A long copper bar with log stools is perfect for lounging, or you can settle in front of the copper corner fireplace. Occasionally a solo guitarist entertains. *Lone Mountain Ranch, Big Sky, tel. 406/995–4644. D, MC, V.*

Loud and Lively/Dancing

Half Moon Saloon

This big barn of a saloon has wide-planked hardwood floors, a long bar, three pool tables, shuffleboard, and multiple TVs. If you don't like what's showing on the screen, you can always watch moose and elk out the back door. This is a cheerful, friendly place where locals hold court, but visitors also feel welcome. *45130 Gallatin Rd., Gallatin Gateway, tel. 406/ 995–4533. MC, V.*

Lolo's Saloon

This loud, lively bar is downstairs from Mountain Top Pizza. The nightly rock and jazz attract mainly an under-30 crowd. There's live entertainment on weekends beginning at 9 PM and a good-size dance floor. *Mountain Mall, Big Sky, tel. 406/995–3455. MC, V.*

Rocco's

This hybrid bar/restaurant occasionally turns into an all-out dancing nightclub when the owner, Larry, decides to perform with his group, the Piranha Brothers—a raunchy rock-and-roll group that can shake the rafters of the large barnlike structure. *Golden Eagle Lodge, Meadow Village, Big Sky, tel. 406/995–4200. MC, V.*

Scissorbills Bar and Grill

Scissorbills attracts a younger crowd. It's a classic fern-bar atmosphere: bright, lots of brass and wood, plus good, loud recorded music. *Arrowhead Mall, Big Sky Mountain Village, Big Sky, tel. 406/995–4933. MC, V.*

More Mellow

Buck's Lounge

There has been a bar here continuously since 1945, and the wooden floor and walls still have the original planks. It's small and comfortable, with light country-and-western music playing in the background and some gambling machines in a small alcove. *Buck's T-4, U.S. 191, 1½ mi south of Big Sky entrance, Big Sky, tel. 406/ 995–4111. AE, D, DC, MC, V.*

Chet's

Chet's mellows out with a solo guitarist or duet on one side and live poker on the other. *Huntley Lodge, 1 Lone Mountain Trail, Big Sky, tel. 406/ 995–5784. AE, MC. V.*

Skiing in New Hampshire often gets short shrift in the realm of eastern skiing, mostly because the more storied resorts of Vermont, and to a lesser extent Maine, attract the most publicity and the biggest crowds.

Such anonymity mirrors the character of this unique slice of New England, a state whose license plates sport the phrase LIVE FREE OR DIE. For generations this quiet independence has forged a character as tough as the granite peaks that form some of the most dramatic mountain landscapes in the eastern United States.

The White Mountains' Presidential Range—a wall of high peaks and outcrops that cuts a dazzling northeast–southwest swath through the state—includes more than 40 peaks that top the 4,000-foot mark, among them Mt. Washington, at 6,288 feet, the highest mountain in New England.

Almost a dozen ski resorts within the 730,000 square miles of White Mountain National Forest stake their claim in New Hampshire's beautiful wilderness. Some, such as Wildcat and Cannon mountains, have achieved cult status for their steep, straight-ahead narrow trails; another, Tuckerman's Ravine on Mt. Washington, offers the last stand against conformity with its absence of lifts and its 2-mile hike to its steep snowfields. For the most part, however, these remain secret places, known best by locals and only slowly being discovered by visitors from out of state.

Curiously, although the world may not be beating a path to New Hampshire resorts, the World Cup is, and in its wake more and more people are discovering Waterville Valley, the state's largest and most modern resort. This self-contained community doesn't have the steepest or toughest runs in New Hampshire (nearby Loon Mountain can arguably stake that claim) but has hosted more World Cup races than any other resort in the country except Vail.

WATERVILLE VALLEY SKI RESORT

WATERVILLE VALLEY SKI RESORT

Waterville Valley,
New Hampshire 03215
Tel. 603/236–8311 or
800/468–2553

STATISTICALLY SPEAKING
Base elevation: 1,984 feet

Summit elevation: 4,004 feet

Vertical drop: 2,020 feet

Skiable terrain: 286 acres

Number of trails: 53

Longest run: 3 miles

Lifts and capacity: 1 high-speed detachable quad, 3 triples, 5 doubles, 1 T-bar, 1 J-bar, 1 platter, 1 handle tow; 15,500 skiers per hour

Daily lift ticket: $37 weekdays; $43 weekends

Average annual snowfall: 140 inches

Number of skiing days 1995–96: 165

Snowmaking: 255 acres, 96%

Terrain mix: N 20%, I 60%, E 20%

Snowboarding: yes

This tidy resort and town offers parking lot–to–mountaintop coddling, which amounts to a ski experience that's both sanitized and ultimately satisfying.

When former U.S. ski team star Tom Corcoran—the resort's founder—first cut these trails in the '60s, most New England resorts featured narrow, twisting trails. Today almost every resort worth its boomer business has moved to wider, highly groomed boulevards similar to those Corcoran created for Waterville Valley. The broad, well-groomed trails of Mt. Tecumseh and the neatly maintained condos of the adjacent village were created with families in mind. And with weekly packages costing less than $300 (including lift tickets) it's affordable for groups and couples to pack up and get away, too.

Although the main village is about a mile from the slopes, the efficient shuttle makes the commute painless and a car unnecessary. At first the village—the focus of Waterville Valley's less-than-torrid nightlife—seems sterile, with a two-level collection of small specialty stores, restaurants, and bars. But the normally taciturn New Hampshire locals become positively garrulous when dealing with visitors from out of state. The character of the village will come, but it already has the characters to compensate.

HOW TO GET THERE

By Plane
Boston's Logan International Airport is served by most major carriers, with connections from many major cities. United and Delta Business Express fly direct from Pittsburgh and Plattsburgh into Manchester Airport, about 70 miles from the resort. Continental, Delta, and US Airways also fly into Manchester from Boston with connections from other major cities.

By Car
From Boston it's 130 miles and about 2½ hours to the resort. Take I–93 north to Exit 28, then follow Route 49 11 miles east to Waterville Valley. From New York, 325 miles away, it's about six hours; take I–95 to I–91 to I–84 to the Massachusetts Turnpike; then pick up I–290 to I–495 to Route 3N to I–93 north to Exit 28. From Manchester, 70 miles away, about 1½ hours,

Area code: 603

Children's services: day care, instruction, tel. 603/236–8311, ext. 3136.

Snow phone: tel. 603/236–4144

Police: tel. 911 or 603/236–8809

Medical center and ambulance: tel. 603/524–1545

Waterville Valley Chamber of Commerce: tel. 800/237–2307

Road conditions: 603/485–3806

Towing: Mobil station, tel. 603/236–8604

FIVE-STAR FAVORITES
Best run for vertical: Gema

Best run overall: Upper Bobby/Lower Bobby

Best bar/nightclub: Legends 1291

Best hotel: Golden Eagle Lodge

Best restaurant: Valley Inn

take I–293 to I–93 north to Exit 28. All major rental agencies are represented at both airports.

By Bus
Concord Trailways (tel. 603/536–4430) has daily scheduled trips from Logan Airport to Plymouth ($26 one-way), 25 minutes from the resort. From there you can take a $23 cab ride or arrange with your hotel for a shuttle pickup.

GETTING AROUND
Park the car at your accommodation and leave it. Even if you're among the first arrivals of the day at Waterville Valley, it's still a fair hike to the lifts from the parking lots. Shuttle service is efficient, and Waterville Valley and environs are best explored on foot anyway.

By Shuttle
The Waterville Valley shuttle bus (tel. 603/236–8311) runs between the village and the mountain and in and around the village area at 10-minute intervals daily 7:30–4:30 from December through March.

By Taxi
It's unlikely you'll need a cab in Waterville Valley, but if that occasion arises, there are two services: Fred Gall's Town Taxi (tel. 603/536–4649) and McGill and Sons Taxi Service (tel. 603/536–2435).

THE SKIING
The Waterville Valley ski area comprises two peaks: 4,000-foot Mt. Tecumseh and the more modest Snow's Mountain. The latter, open only when skier traffic warrants, is primarily a novice area, with gently rolling terrain. It's a great spot for families to picnic and get away from the bustle of the big mountain.

Most real skiing is on Mt. Tecumseh, where there's a good mix of mostly wide, well-groomed giant slalom cruising runs. What you won't find here is buckle-your-knees, in-your-face skiing. Overall, the skiing rates as solid intermediate, with the High Country quad followed by the Valley Run triple providing the speed to get you up and down as fast and often as your legs can handle.

Waterville Valley's lifts open at 8 (9 on nonholiday weekdays), so really ambitious skiers can get an earlier-than-usual start. The locals' tried-and-true strategy is to hit the slopes for first tracks and call it a day at about 11 AM, when the crowds arrive.

Snowboarders have access to the entire mountain and to all lifts. There's also Boneyard Snowboard Park, with a half pipe, on Exhibition.

Novices

Snow's Mountain is your best bet for runs that are generally uncrowded and novice-friendly. However, because it does not have snowmaking and the lifts run only when the crowds max out, you'll most likely have to stick to beginner areas on Mt. Tecumseh.

Lower Meadows has three ultra-wide, smooth trails leading from its double chairlift and is a good place to get started. There is little variety among these three, however, so eventually you'll want to spread your wings and try Valley Run, which although designated blue, is suitable for novices with the basics under their belts. You can take Valley Run double chair about three-quarters of the way up or grab the Valley Run triple chair if you want to go higher up the mountain. From either point you'll be able to enjoy one of the nicest lower-intermediate trails in New England. In addition to its flawlessly groomed terrain, Valley Run tends to be warmer than other runs because it's protected from the wind and exposed to the morning sun.

When skiing Mt. Tecumseh, if you're at all nervous, stay on the right side (looking down the mountain) because it's straightforward and predictable; for a bit more challenge and some dips and rolls, ski the left side.

Intermediates

If you're a reasonably strong intermediate skier, there are probably only a few testy little bump runs on the mountain that may be out of your domain. The rest of Waterville Valley's runs are pure intermediate cruisers, and by linking several you can enjoy some excellent top-to-bottom skiing. Start by taking the High Country express quad and the Valley Run double to the summit, then go to the left (looking down the mountain) to the rolling Tree Line Trail to White Caps, just below the High Country double. This is one of my favorite routes because although White Caps periodically offers a few bumps, overall it allows you to maintain good speed to the point just above the top of the World Cup triple chair. From there you can either continue straight down the chute on steeper, bumpier terrain designated black or cut left to the more forgiving Sel's Choice. Although Sel's is also marked black, it is actually a first-rate upper-level intermediate cruiser that skis like a good giant slalom course, with several pitch variances and banked turns. If you enjoy Sel's Choice, you can reach it directly by riding the World Cup triple chair and staying in this area for a while. By not taking the High Country quad and the High Country double to the summit, you escape some of the crowds.

Another high-speed cruiser is Express (to the far right, looking down the mountain), reached from the High Country express quad to

Oblivion and then to Upper Valley. This is especially good early in the day, when you can catch the morning sun. Also try Tree Line to Upper Bobby's to Psyched to Exhibition—a series of runs that streaks straight down the face of the mountain but tends to be well traveled and prone to icy patches.

To really steer clear of the crowds, you can take the Northside double lift—the least busy lift on the mountain—to Waterville Valley's northern flank. From there you can ski Tippecanoe and Tyler Too, a pair of standard, wide-open Waterville Valley cruisers; or Tangent and Periphery, a pair of narrower though slightly more tedious blue trails.

Experts

Let's be frank: If you're looking for true challenge, you'll find Waterville Valley lacking, especially on the north face of the mountain, where Sel's Choice is your only choice. But while you're there, start by taking a few warm-up runs on this first-rate giant slalom cruiser. Then head over to the Sunnyside triple chair, which serves Ciao, Gema, and True Grit—three short, steep mogul runs. The latter is the toughest and bumpiest on the mountain. The bumps are biggest on the left side of the trail, but when they get too big and too hard, the right side is the better alternative. Gema, which runs parallel, has about the same pitch as True Grit, but it's skied less, hence the moguls are smaller. Ciao is wider than the other two and a little less bumpy.

Bobby's Run is the other expert trail to head for, especially after a decent snowfall. It can be reached from either the Sunnyside triple chair or the High Country quad. Bobby's seems to be the favorite of patrollers, who frequently close it off when the snow is sparse (there's no snowmaking here), prompting some local wags to suggest that they are keeping it for themselves. But when there's a foot of fresh powder, it's a great cruiser with good pitch, few bumps (because it's skied so little), and a nice sweeping curve that takes you to the bottom of the chair.

WHERE TO STAY

The accommodations at Waterville Valley are low-key—about 80% of the 6,500 beds are in nests of condos, town houses, and private chalets built into the hillside between the village and the resort. There are also a few hotels, inns, lodges, and B&Bs for those who want to eschew the take-care-of-yourself approach of condo living. None of these are flashy pamper palaces, just solid, unpretentious living spaces, strong on quality and value. Virtually all accommodations are within 1½ miles of the mountain or within walking distance of the town square, and many of the more distant ones are served by the shuttle, which goes to the slopes. Accommodations in town can be booked through Waterville Valley Central Reservations (tel. 800/468–2553). If you're looking for cheaper, motel-style accommodations, you may have to commute from the nearby towns of Plymouth or Campton.

Expensive

Resort Condominium Rental
This organization rents some of the largest condo and town house units in the valley, ranging in size from one to

four bedrooms and most within walking distance of the town square. The exteriors are stained in different colors, and on the inside the units are generally bright and well furnished in a mountain-modern style that includes white walls and a lot of wood. All come equipped with full kitchens including dishwasher and microwave, plus a woodstove or fireplace and usually a washer-dryer. *Valley Rd., Box 379, Waterville Valley 03215, tel. 603/236–4101 or 800/556–6522, fax 603/236–4890. 50 units. Facilities: sports center, shuttle service, ski storage, game room. AE, D, DC, MC, V. $189–$369.*

Town Square Resort
These huge village-square condo apartments are a great bargain, mainly because of their uniform white exteriors and that they show a little more wear and tear than some other buildings. Each unit has three bedrooms on a two- or three-floor layout. The comfortably furnished common areas include a large kitchen, a dining area, and two bathrooms. *Village Rd., Waterville Valley 03215, tel. 603/236–4071 or 800/468–2553. 33 units. Facilities: sports center, shuttle service, maid service, ski storage, laundry, game room. AE, DC, MC, V. $279.*

Village Condominium
These one- and two-story clapboard condos have from one to five bedrooms and are fully equipped, with a kitchen, a fireplace, a living/dining room, and laundry facilities, making them popular with families and groups. Some have access to the sports center; ask when booking. *Rte. 49, Waterville Valley 03215, tel. 603/*

236–8301 or 800/468–2553, fax 603/236–3363. 25 units. Facilities: sauna, maid service, shuttle, ski storage, laundry, game room. D, MC, V. $270–$500.

Windsor Hill Condominiums
These one-, two-, and three-bedroom redwood-clapboard condos and town houses are among the closest to the slopes. Each has a kitchen or kitchenette, a fireplace, and laundry facilities. The decor is standard modern, with functional, not fancy, furnishings. *Jennings Peak Rd., Box 440, Waterville Valley 03215, tel. 603/236–8321 or 800/343–1286. 132 units. Facilities: ski storage, laundry. MC, V. $140–$355.*

Moderate
Black Bear Lodge
Known as a condo hotel, this rambling six-story clapboard lodge is dominated by families drawn to the large, functional, comfortable suites that can easily sleep six people. Each unit has one or two bedrooms, a large living area with a Murphy bed, a kitchen, and a dining area. The suites are well maintained, and the furnishings are unremarkable but definitely childproof. *Village Rd., Box 357, Waterville Valley 03215, tel. 603/236–4501 or 800/349–2327, fax 603/236–4114, ext 232. 98 suites. Facilities: whirlpool, sauna, steam room, laundry, indoor-outdoor heated pool, maid service, ski storage, 24-hr desk service, shuttle, game room. AE, D, DC, MC, V. $189–$239.*

Golden Eagle Lodge
The peaked roofs and corner turrets of this large hotel next to the village square proudly announce that it was built in the grand style of earlier New

Hampshire resorts. The one- and two-bedroom suites can easily handle six people. Each has a separate living and dining area, a complete kitchen, and one or two full bathrooms. The furnishings are above average, with big couches, comfy chairs, and modern appliances. In the morning there is complimentary coffee in the impressive wood-and-stone lobby. *Snowbrook Rd., Box 495, Waterville Valley 03215, tel. 603/236–4551 or 800/910–4499, fax 603/263–4947. 139 suites. Facilities: lounge, indoor pool, whirlpool, sauna, 24-hr desk service, shuttle service, maid service, laundry, game room. AE, D, DC, MC, V. $279–$319.*

Snowy Owl Inn

Small enough to be charming yet large enough to provide all the amenities, this inn is just off the village square, and there is a crisp, rustic cleanliness to the whole place. There is a soaring atrium lobby, amber-hued wood finishings, antiques, and massive fieldstone fireplaces. The Snowy Owl draws equal numbers of families (thanks to its unique bunk-bed rooms) and couples searching for a little low-key privacy. *Village Rd., Box 379, Waterville Valley 03215, tel. 603/236–8383 or 800/766–9969, fax 603/236–4890. 83 rooms. Facilities: indoor pool, whirlpool, shuttle, 24-hr desk service, maid service, ski storage, game room. AE, D, DC, MC, V. $169–$209, including full breakfast and après-ski refreshments.*

Valley Inn

A wood exterior gives this attractive alternative to a hotel an innlike feeling. There is a variety of rooms, ranging from standard (with two full-size beds) to larger, more luxurious suites. There are also a half-dozen extra-large two-story apartment suites that have more of a designer's touch. *Tecumseh Rd., Box 1, Waterville Valley 03215, tel. 603/236–8336 or 800/343–0969, fax 603/236–4294. 47 rooms, 5 suites. Facilities: restaurant, bar, lounge, heated indoor-outdoor pool, whirlpool, sauna, shuttle, 24-hr desk service, maid service, ski storage. AE, D, DC, MC, V. $75–$275.*

Inexpensive

Best Western White Mountains

This motel on the edge of Campton, 15 minutes south of Waterville Valley, has a chalet-style exterior, but the room decor is pure modern American, with basic pine furnishings and one king-size or two double beds. *Rte. 3, Exit 27 off I–93, R.R. 1, Box 355, Plymouth 03264, tel. 603/536–3520 or 800/370–8666, fax 603/536–8114. 101 rooms. Facilities: restaurant, lounge, indoor pool, Jacuzzi, sauna, steam room, 24-hr desk service, laundry, game room. AE, D, DC, MC, V. $76–$83.*

Susse Chalet Hotel

In Plymouth, 20 minutes south of Waterville Valley, you'll find this two-story chain hotel with a misty-mauve-and-beige concrete exterior. There's nothing flashy about the comfortable wallpapered rooms. The color scheme is off-white, and furnishings are light wood. *Rte. 3, R.F.D. 1, Box 4, Plymouth 03264, tel. 603/536–2330 or 800/524–2538, fax 603/536–2686. 38 rooms. Facilities: outdoor pool, 24-hr desk service, laundry. AE, D, DC, MC, V. $40–$80, including Continental breakfast.*

WHERE TO EAT

The selection of food in Waterville Valley, with a couple of notable exceptions, is limited, with the emphasis on traditional dishes prepared in traditional ways.

On the Mountain

Sunnyside Up Lodge

To find the lodge, keep tight to the left side of the upper valley run and turn uphill just past the bottom of the Sunnyside triple chair, about a third of the way down the mountain. This striking log structure has a standard repertoire of good, wholesome lunchtime fare, from burgers and sandwiches to soups, chili, stew, and salads served cafeteria style. It tends to be less crowded than other places on the mountain because it's so easy to miss. *Beside Valley Run, tel. 603/ 236–8311, ext. 3292. No credit cards.*

Schwendi Hutte

Just below the summit of the mountain, on a plateau where the High Country double chairlift begins, this restaurant has a cafeteria and table service with white cloths and real cutlery. Start with Daphne's lobster bisque and then choose among German sausages and sauerkraut, large sandwiches with dips, salads, and side dishes such as sweet and sour braised red cabbage. *Top of mountain, tel. 603/ 236–8330, ext. 3144. AE, D, DC, MC, V.*

Expensive

Valley Inn

For a somewhat formal (and candle-lighted) dining experience, visit the Valley Inn, where the menu includes seafood, beef, pork, chicken, and pasta. Popular dishes are steak Hora-

tio (twin tournedos of beef sautéed with wild mushrooms and smothered in a port, cognac, and heavy cream sauce) and duckling with maple sauce and cranberry-pecan fritter. Service is fairly slow, so relax and enjoy the ambience. *Tecumseh Rd., Waterville Valley, tel. 603/236–8336. AE, D, DC, MC, V.*

William Tell

It's worth a 7-mile drive west to find this small country restaurant with stucco and wood-beam construction, two small dining rooms that are quiet and romantic, and taped classical music in the front room. If you like traditional Bavarian, Austrian, and Swiss dishes such as schnitzel, sauerbraten, fondue, and fresh venison, you'll get your fill here. *Rte. 49, Thornton, tel. 603/726–3618. AE, MC, V.*

Moderate

Chile Peppers

Antique barbed wire and Southwestern prints hang on the walls of this eatery, where Tex-Mex staples are featured. Chile Peppers caters to skiers with its hearty selection of fajitas, tacos, and enchiladas. The food here may not be authentic Mexican, but it's well priced and filling. A margarita tops off everything nicely. If you prefer Tex to Mex, there's a lineup of standards such as ribs, steak, seafood, and chicken. *Town Square, Waterville Valley, tel. 603/236–4646. AE, DC, MC, V.*

Common Man Restaurant and Bar

Antique lanterns, a fireplace, and a woodstove help create a rustic atmosphere at this seafood restaurant that offers an abundance of fresh fish. The shellfish stew is a must, with shrimp, scallops, mussels, and king crabs in a spicy tomato broth served over linguine. *Town Square, Waterville Valley, tel. 603/236–8885. Reservations not accepted. AE, D, MC, V.*

Inexpensive

Alpine Pizza

Pizza in this town-square eatery is pretty good, with a medium-thick crust and a selection of toppings. They also have pastas, salads, hot and cold subs, soups, and hamburgers. *Town Square, Waterville Valley, tel. 603/236–4173. No credit cards.*

Jugtown Deli

You can stock up here for a do-it-yourself dinner back at the condo or sit down at the tables. A good selection of deli food—cold cuts, fancy breads and buns, cheeses, and other snacks—is available. *Town Square, Waterville Valley, tel. 603/236–8662. AE, MC, V.*

Best Bet for Breakfast

Coffee Emporium

If you like to take your time and smell the coffee, then this is where you'll find the best selection in town. The bright dining room is filled with coffee paraphernalia and cookbooks. Full breakfast is also served, including Belgian waffles, egg dishes, and a large selection of breakfast pastries and muffins. *Town Square, Waterville Valley, tel. 603/236–4021. No credit cards.*

NIGHTLIFE AND ENTERTAINMENT

Après-Ski

World Cup Bar & Grill

The A-frame loft bar is always packed for après-ski, when there's often live entertainment and sports action on the big-screen TV. World Cup flags hang on the walls, and a large picture window lets in the sunset. *Upstairs at Waterville Valley base lodge, tel. 603/236–8311, ext. 3142. AE, D, DC, MC, V.*

Loud and Lively/Dancing

Common Man Restaurant and Bar

The rustic atmosphere makes it easy to curl up in front of the fireplace with a few bar munchies; or if you've got energy to spare, you can shake it loose on the dance floor to a live band on weekends. *Town Square, Waterville Valley, tel. 603/236–8885. AE, D, MC, V.*

Legends 1291

A DJ delivering delirium and a crowd as high-octane as it gets in Waterville Valley make this the best place to shake it loose on the dance floor. You may find guitar music, a live band, or a DJ, depending on what night you're there. *Town Square, Waterville Valley, tel. 603/236–4678. AE, MC, V.*

Many aspects of New Mexico surprise and enchant visitors—1,000-year-old Pueblo villages, sweeping desert vistas, a lively artistic and creative community—but the biggest surprise of all is the skiing. For here in the land of adobe dwellings, tumbling sagebrush, and ocher-colored buttes, are the Sangre de Cristo Mountains, sun-kissed peaks that soar high above the desert floor reaping the benefits of climatic clashes between the dry air of the lowlands and the moist air traveling from the west.

There are just four ski resorts in these mountains, and of these the best known and largest is Taos Ski Valley, the southernmost resort in the United States and one that has gained a worldwide reputation for its steep, challenging slopes, consistent snowfall, and extraordinarily sunny days.

Taos is a magical, mystical place, a physical and spiritual Shangri-la surrounded by the stunning peaks of the Sangre de Cristo Mountains, bathed in pure desert air, and steeped in history and culture. Native Americans have inhabited the Taos pueblo for 1,000 years, creating an intricate multitiered adobe structure that stands today as the world's oldest apartment building. The centuries have brought little change to Taos—the pueblo is still without electricity or running water—although large-scale tourism has introduced a commercial element.

The Taos pueblo stands near the town of Taos, a community of traditional adobe buildings surrounding cobblestone courtyards, plazas, and quiet side streets with nary a strip mall or shopping center in sight. This old, compact town is also home to one of the largest concentrations of art galleries and Native American crafts shops found anywhere in America. It has long been the adopted home of assorted writers, artists, and musicians, all drawn by its serene isolation and the mystique of its ancient culture. The stark Southwestern canvases of Georgia O'Keeffe, who lived in New Mexico for decades, are world famous. D. H. Lawrence was also a devotee.

TAOS SKI VALLEY

Box 90
Taos Ski Valley, NM 87525
Tel. 505/776–2291

STATISTICALLY SPEAKING

Base elevation: 9,207 feet

Summit elevation: 11,819 feet

Vertical drop: 2,612 feet

Skiable terrain: 1,094 acres

Number of trails: 72

Longest run: 5¼ miles

Lifts and capacity: 4 quads, 1 triple, 5 doubles, 1 surface; 15,000 skiers per hour

Daily lift ticket: $39

Average annual snowfall: 302 inches

Number of skiing days 1995–96: 129

Snowmaking: 95% of beginner and intermediate slopes only

Terrain mix: N 24%, I 25%, E 51%

Snowboarding: no

If I had just one ski trip left in my legs, bank account, or life, I think I would return to Taos. Taos Ski Valley is 18 miles from the town of Taos and 2,000 feet higher, at the fringe of the Carson National Forest, where the sage and piñon of the desert give way to the tall pines of the mountains. To get here, you drive through flat desert scrubland bathed in the surreal Southwestern light and up a slash of a valley called the Rio Grande Gorge. The resort is the offspring of the late Ernie Blake, a native of Switzerland, who scratched and clawed to make his dream of a European-style alpine village and ski mountain into a reality. Everything about Taos Ski Valley reflects the vision and single-minded determination of this extraordinary man.

The mountain village itself is a tiny, pedestrian-oriented enclave of a dozen small lodges and a modest number of condominiums nestled on either side of the Rio Hondo Creek, all connected by a network of walkways and bridges and all within easy walking distance of the base area lifts. It could easily have been transported lock, stock, and chalet from the mountains of Europe, and you are just as likely to hear French and German spoken as you are Spanish and English. Many of the early entrepreneurs came here from the classic resort centers in Europe and brought with them the concept of packaged ski weeks including lessons, meals, lift tickets, and accommodations for an all-inclusive single price. Most of the original hotels and lodges at the mountain still offer this arrangement, and it is not a bad way to take your first week at Taos (although there are other alternatives). The lessons are excellent (two hours each morning), it's a good way to get to know the mountain, the food packages are generous, and the price at an average of about $1,300–$1,500 per person per week is a good deal.

Besides, the togetherness approach produces a spirited camaraderie that compensates for the decided lack of nightlife at the mountain village. If you are staying in the village, a car is not required, but if you stay in town, it's a must. A car is useful in either case because there is so much else to see and do in the area.

Anytime is the right time to visit Taos, but Christmas is particularly magical. The Pueblo tribe make bonfires of piñon wood, and masked dancers stage traditional torchlighted parades. The town glows softly from the thousands of *farolitas* (lights made from candles inside sand-filled paper bags), and up on the slopes skiers search for *porrones* (hand-blown glass flasks filled with gin and buried in the snow).

Whenever I am here I am mesmerized by the contrast of a high mountain hamlet and a centuries-old desert community; the towering peaks of the Sangre de Christo Mountains, including Mt. Wheeler, New Mexico's highest peak, at 13,161 feet, yield to the flat sun-scorched earth of the New Mexican mesa. It is this quality of majesty and mystery that will always draw me back to Taos.

HOW TO GET THERE

By Plane
Albuquerque International Airport (tel. 505/ 842–4366), 135 miles south of Taos, is the major airport closest to the resort. It is served with regularly scheduled flights by America West (tel. 800/235–9292), American (tel. 800/433–7300), Continental (tel. 800/525–0280), Delta (tel. 800/221–1212), Mesa Air (tel. 800/637–2247), Northwest (tel. 800/ 225–2525), Reno Air (tel. 800/736–6247), Southwest (tel. 800/435–9792), TWA (tel. 800/221–2000), United (tel. 800/241–6522), US Airways (tel. 800/ 428–4322), and Western Pacific (tel. 800/930–3030).

By Car
From the Albuquerque airport, take I–25 to Santa Fe, then pick up Route 84 heading north to Espanola, and then follow Route 68 into Taos. This is a marvelously picturesque drive on snow-free roads, and a stop in Santa Fe is a perfect halfway break.

At the Albuquerque airport the following car rentals are available: **Advantage** (tel. 800/777–5500), **Alamo** (tel. 800/327–9633), **All American** (tel. 800/242–7743), **Budget** (tel. 800/527–0700), **Dollar** (tel. 800/421–6868), **Enterprise** (tel. 800/ 325–8007), **Hertz** (tel. 800/654–3131), **National** (tel. 800/328–4567), **Payless** (tel. 800/541–1566), and **Thrifty** (tel. 800/367–2277).

By Bus

Frequent daily and weekly shuttle buses operate between the Albuquerque airport and Taos and Taos Ski Resort. Check with either of the following for rates and schedules: **The Pride of Taos** (tel. 505/758–8340 or 800/273–8340) or **Faust's Transportation** (tel. 505/758–3410).

By Train

Amtrak (tel. 800/872–7245) provides service into Lamy or Raton (90 miles east of Taos on Route 64).

GETTING AROUND

A car is useful in Taos because of the distance between the resort and the town, the myriad side trips you can take, and because the shuttle service (**Faust's Transportation,** tel. 505/758–3410, $10 round-trip) between the slopes and the nightlife of Taos is infrequent—just three runs each way daily. Faust's also operates a taxi service (tel. 505/758–7359) between the ski valley and town; it costs $35 one-way for the first two passengers.

THE SKIING

If there is one ski resort in America or, perhaps, in the entire world that can truly be said to bear the personal stamp of one man, it is Taos Ski Valley. It's impossible to ski this marvelous sun-drenched, north-facing mountain without constant reminders of its creator, Ernie Blake. In the 1950s Ernie sought a mountain that would provide challenge, and when he spotted this isolated peak while flying over the area, he knew he had found his mountain. From then until his death in 1989, he worked tirelessly to realize his vision of the perfect American ski resort.

Ernie's legacy is evident in little touches, like the witty sign at the bottom of the fiercely steep and mogul-studded Al's Run that reads: "Don't panic. You're looking at only 1/30th of Taos Ski Valley. We have many easy runs, too!" Although there's truth in that statement, it's also equally true that Taos is a mountain of supreme challenge, where 51% of the runs are black diamond and 19 of those 36 runs are double black diamond. Ernie personally named the toughest runs—after Greek gods, Mexican revolutionaries, and German generals who died in their attempts to assassinate Adolf Hitler.

Ernie knew what he wanted in a ski resort, and the broad-shouldered north-facing mountain ridge has it all. Its high altitude and southerly latitude provide a perfect combination of sun and snow—desert-dried snow that Blake described as "fluffy as egg whites and dependable as a Swiss watch." Ernie believed that challenge was essential to the total skiing experience, and he made sure that challenge was built in by personally supervising the cutting of every trail in the early years, insisting on runs that others claimed were too steep to be skied. He resolutely resisted running a lift to the summit of the mountain, 12,481-foot Kachina Peak, where some of the steepest and most outrageous skiing is found. "Americans are too lazy," he said. "The hike is good for them."

And hike they do, for up to an hour to reach the Kachina Peak with its free-fall chutes or for 15–20 minutes to the Highline and West Basin ridges. Those areas are the true taste of Taos, but even visiting experts should tackle them only in the company of a guide—or at least a knowledgeable local. Challenge may be the keynote of Taos, but there's plenty of variety here, too. The part of the mountain served by lifts is surprisingly compact and easy to move around on. No matter what your ski level, you can follow the sun across its breadth.

Novices

Despite Taos's fearsome reputation, novice skiers can find a good range of green runs sprinkled around the mountain—in fact, there's a green run down from the top of all the lifts. I recommend starting off in the company of the ski school. If you want to go it alone, your best bet is to start by taking the Lift 1 to the top and following White Feather, a long, perfectly groomed run that cruises in and around the trees all the way down.

With your legs warmed up, take Lift 1 again, but this time follow White Feather to the base of Lift 6, and at the top go off to the left to hook up with Honeysuckle. There are black runs all around you, but Honeysuckle is your sanctuary. You'll find the occasional steep pitch, but overall this is a mellow cruise that alternately widens and narrows before snaking back to the bottom of Lift 7. You can also make a sharp left turn at the top of Lower Totemoff, a consistently wide pitch that tends to be less busy than Honeysuckle. This is good because it's also slightly steeper as it shoots down to Lift 7. Take this lift, follow Honeysuckle again, but instead of turning left at the bottom, cut right

down Winkleried, a fairly flat runoff that takes you over to the base of the Kachina lift. If you go left off the Kachina lift, you'll find Easy Trip, a tight, winding run through the trees that connects up with Japanese Flag, which in turn leads you back to Honeysuckle.

If you want to head back to village center, pick up Rubezahl at the base of the Kachina lift. You can ride this extremely mellow and scenic run for nearly 2 miles, letting your skis run here because there are several flat spots. Keep moving at a steady pace, especially as you come within sight of the village. You can play with this circuit for several days, exploring some of the short cutoff runs that link this green route. When you are ready to try something a little more challenging, head for Porcupine, to the right off Lift 1. This is a well-groomed, wide, and friendly blue run, with enough rolls and pitches to give you some challenge and some easier sections where you can take a breather before pressing on. You can also get to Porcupine via Lift 5, but it operates only when the mountain is busy. At the bottom of Porcupine you can connect with White Feather again and follow this long, flat lower section back to the village center.

Intermediates

Although only 25% of the runs at Taos are blue, you won't lack for challenge or variety.

Start your day by heading up Lift 1 from the village, and ski down White Feather until you reach Powderhorn, a good medium-grade blue run that has a variety of rolls and dips to warm your legs. It's always groomed and wide enough to get some good, wide giant-slalom turns working. Near the bottom cut a hard left onto Whitefeather and follow it to the bottom of Lift 8. This lift will take you up to Lower Stauffenberg, a steeper, not always groomed roller-coaster run with a good sustained pitch; it connects up with Don't Tell, then Willy Tell back to the bottom of Lift 8.

Take this back up again and turn left onto Mucho Gusto, a short, fairly steep pitch that carries you to the bottom of Lifts 2 and 6. From the top of either you can turn left and follow Bambi, a moderate blue run that's wide and groomed and fairly easy cruising. Just make sure you don't drop over onto Zagava, a nasty black pitch that starts just above the top of Lift 5. Instead, turn left onto Upper Powderhorn, a gentle speed-controlled pitch that goes back to Lifts 2 and 6. From the top of either you can head down Honeysuckle until you connect with Baby Bear, which will take you to the bottom of the Kachina chair. You can also cut off Honeysuckle onto either Upper Totemoff, with its medium-size moguls on the upper part, or Lone Star, a steep but bump-free pitch. Both will take you to the bottom of Lift 7; or if you turn right onto Winkleried, you can get over to the Kachina chair.

The top of Kachina puts you on Shalako, one of my favorite blue runs on that mountain. It starts out as a minibowl, a steep and wide extension of the seriously steep chutes off the top of the Kachina Ridge, and then narrows slightly as it dips and rolls through some trees before linking up to Baby Bear; here it mellows out as it heads down to Winkleried and back

to the base of the chair. You can skip Baby Bear by cutting left onto Papa Bear for a short taste of some decent-size bumps. Keep in mind that to return to the village from this part of the mountain, you either have to take the long run out Rubezahl or head back up Kachina and follow Shalako to Japanese Flag to Honeysuckle (both green runs) to the base of Lift 7, and from its top take the short Seventh Heaven lift, which deposits you at the top of Bambi. Check your watch and make sure you have time to do this.

Experts

You may as well plunge right in and tackle the precipitous and demanding Al's Run by taking Lift 1. This is a tough, bumpy first-run challenge that will get the legs pumping. You can avoid some of the bumps by staying to the left (looking down), but don't expect much reprieve. Another, less bumpy alternative from the top of Lift 1 is the combination of Rhoda's, Inferno, and Snakedance, three connected runs that are just as steep as Al's Run but not as heavily moguled. Next head for Lift 2 or 6, and as you get off, turn right and take the High Traverse into the steep bowl runs of the West Basin Ridge. Stauffenberg is the most popular choice from here, although as a result it also tends to be the busiest. Less crowded alternatives are Reforma, Blitz, and West Blitz, which are steep and wide and provide some high-speed giant-slalom cruising. Narrower pitches with straight-shot verticals for speed junkies are Spitfire, Oster, and Fabian. You can take an extended hike—about 15 minutes—to the West Basin Ridge, where you'll find the wide-open bowl terrain of St. Bernard, Thunderbird, Hondo, and Wonder Bowl. These are real snow traps and, because of the effort required to get there, are seldom, if ever, busy. The only downside is the need to take the blue Lower Stauffenberg (which connects to Don't Tell and Willy Tell) down to the bottom of Lift 8; take it to the top and then ski down another blue run (Mucho Gusto) to the bottom of Lift 6 to get back up to the High Traverse. From there you can stay in the West Ridge Basin or turn left off the lift and head for the gladed runs of the Walkyries Bowl. Walkyries Chute, Sir Arnold Lunn, and Lorelei Trees are all steep and deep snow runs with tightly packed thickets of trees and sudden and unpredictable drop-offs.

When you are ready for Taos's ultimate test, it's time to head for Kachina Peak. You ride Lift 6 to the beginning of a 60- to 75-minute hike up to the Highline Ridge, and for obvious reasons this route is not for the faint of heart or weak of legs. Never, under any circumstances, attempt to tackle this alone; all skiers are required to check into the patrol shack before starting out. It's a strenuous hike, but the effort will be rewarded by the runs that give Taos its fearsome reputation. Everything from the Highline Ridge is ultrasteep, double-black-diamond stuff, and if the patrollers have any suspicion that you can't handle this, they'll send you back down. You can have another, less demanding steep bowl experience in the Hunziker Bowl, which is a five-minute hike to the right (looking down) of Lift 4. The Hunziker Bowl looks innocent enough when you start out on its mellow, concave upper part, but it quickly turns ultrasteep and narrow, forcing you into quick, short, precise turns. If you really want to experience the full measure of the Taos mystique, try to hook up with a local or an area guide and always keep a trail map in your pocket.

WHERE TO STAY
Eighteen miles separate the town of Taos from the mountain village; where you choose to stay depends on your priorities. Mountainside accommodations tend to be slightly more expensive but obviously more convenient. It's also fairly quiet in the evenings, with a limited number of dining spots. This is not necessarily a problem, as many lodges offer package deals with meals included. The town of Taos is wonderfully rich in history, culture, dining, and entertainment options, and if you want to take full advantage of them, your best bet is to choose a hotel in town. There are also numerous accommodations on Ski Valley Road, but at any of them a car is essential.

Reservations and other arrangements can be booked through the Taos Valley Resort Association (Box 85, Taos 87525, tel. 505/776–2233 or 800/776–1111). There's also the Taos Bed & Breakfast Association (Box 2772, Taos 87571, tel. 505/758–4747 or 800/876–7857), which can book you into any of the numerous B&Bs in the area.

Expensive
Chalet Montesano
Unlike most accommodations at the Taos mountain village, this secluded and stylish retreat is tucked away in

the woods, a short walk from the ski village. It's a large Swiss-alpine-style chalet with studios, a one-bedroom, and suites. The decor in all units is mountain elegance, with rich honey-colored and pine-paneled walls, bright and vibrant fabric accents, large comfortable couches, modern appliances, and lots of tasteful art. Except for the minisuites, all units have fireplaces and full kitchens. Units have an outside entrance for additional privacy. There's a marvelous light-filled, cedar-lined spa with an indoor lap pool and a Jacuzzi, plus exercise equipment. Serene and romantic, this place does not accommodate children under 14. *Box 77, Taos Ski Valley 87525, tel. 505/776–8226 or 800/723–9104, fax 505/776–8760. 5 units. Facilities: health spa, Jacuzzi, indoor lap pool. MC, V. $110–$260.*

St. Bernard Condominiums

These excellent modern condominiums are among the most upscale at the resort. The two-bedroom, two-bathroom units sleep six people. The decor is modern Southwestern, with soft pastel tones, well-crafted furniture, and lots of colorful accents. Each unit comes with a fully equipped kitchen and a fireplace. They usually rent by the week, though exceptions are sometimes made. *Box 676, Taos Ski Valley 87525, tel. 505/776–8506 or 888/306–4135. 12 units. Facilities: hot tub. AE, MC, V. $975–$1,320 per week, including dinner nightly at the St. Bernard Hotel (see below), 6 days' skiing, and lessons.*

St. Bernard Hotel

When you stay at the St. Bernard, you don't just get a room, you get an experience: a symphony of lodging, dining, ski lessons, entertainment, and skiing orchestrated by Jean Mayer, owner of the lodge, technical director of the Taos Ski School, and one of the pioneers of Taos Ski Valley. The rustic log-and-cedar lodge is a marvelous European-style hostelry with cozy accommodations. The lodge, just steps from the lifts, comprises three buildings. Exposed beams, flagstone floors, and countless antiques give the place a wonderfully warm and woody atmosphere. The rooms are actually quite small but not lacking for anything (except TV, telephone, and fireplace) with their quaintness enhanced by white wood-trimmed walls, handmade wooden furniture, bright quilts, and tapestries. Meals at the St. Bernard are equally satisfying, with variety and imagination in the breakfast and lunch offerings and a seven-course dinner that changes daily but leans heavily toward Continental dishes rich with sauces or toward more traditional local accents. *Box 88, Taos Ski Valley 87525, tel. 505/776–2251. 28 rooms. Facilities: restaurant, lounge, indoor hot tub, workout room, massage, ski shop. No credit cards. $1,170–$1,370 per person, including 3 meals daily, 6 days' skiing, and lessons.*

Salsa del Salto

About halfway between the mountain village and the town of Taos, this elegant bed-and-breakfast is a stunning hacienda, designed and built out of native adobe by architect Antoine Predock as his private residence. The interior is anchored by an enormous two-story four-sided stone fireplace, and local touches include a vaulted pine-paneled ceiling, terra-cotta floor tiles, textured plaster walls, a gently sloping atrium wall, handcrafted furniture including sumptuous soft leather couches, and lots of original New Mexican art in bright, bold colors. Each of the individually designed rooms has a spectacular view of the surrounding mountains. Bedroom decor extends the New Mexican theme with soft pastel shades of turquoise and peach accented by vivid artwork and striking Navajo-print goose eiderdowns and sheets, splashy area rugs, and handmade furniture in bleached and painted woods. *Box 1468, El Prado 87529, tel. 505/776–2422. 7 rooms. Facilities: library, outdoor pool and hot tub, tennis court. MC, V. $95–$160, including full breakfast and après-ski snacks.*

Taos Inn

This marvelous genuine adobe inn, my favorite place in town, is both the physical and cultural heart of Taos. The lobby—with its soaring *vigas* (projecting wooden roof beams), polished wood floors, arched walls, wrought-iron fixtures, and central fountain (once the town well)—is a local institution. Artists have gathered here for a century. The rooms, like the lobby, are decorated with local art and pottery and filled with handmade furniture and bright rugs, bed covers, and tapestries. Thirty of the rooms have a wood-burning kiva fireplace. Be sure to eat at the restaurant Doc Martin's. *125 Paseo del Pueblo Norte, Taos 87571, tel. 505/758–2233 or 800/826–7466, fax 505/758–5776. 37 rooms. Facilities: restaurant, bar, pool, indoor Jacuzzi. AE, DC, MC, V. $75–$195.*

Moderate

Austing Haus

The Austing Haus is the creation of Paul Austing, the whirling dervish owner, who started in 1982 with just four rooms and now commands an empire that includes the main A-frame-style motel building, the nearby Columbine Lodge, a riverfront building, and several private homes that he oversees for absentee owners. He built the lodge, just a mile from the mountain, from scratch, using mortise and tenon joinery and not a single nail. He's also the chef in the Austing Haus dining room, always on hand to chat with diners and dispense advice. The rooms at the main lodge and the Columbine are all large and comfortable, with stucco walls, exposed beams, wood trim, and colonial-style furnishings; many have fireplaces. The riverfront suites, with queen-size beds plus a loft bedroom in the upper units, all have a kitchen and a fireplace. The private houses have three bedrooms. *Box 8, Taos Ski Valley 87525, tel. 505/776–2649 or 800/748–2932, fax 505/776–2649. 36 rooms, 8 suites, 4 houses. Facilities: indoor hot tub, meeting rooms. D, DC, MC, V. $110–$220, including Continental breakfast.*

Inn at Snakedance

Previously known as the Hondo Lodge, this was the first accommodation at Taos, originally built as a hunting lodge before the resort opened and now totally renovated and smack in the middle of the mountain village just 10 yards from the quad lift. It's a magnificent structure made of massive pine timbers cut during a copper-mining operation in the 1890s; the renovation added stucco and brick and a gabled roof true to its hunting-lodge heritage. Inside, it's all exposed beams and stone floors, with a large stone fireplace dominating the lobby area. The rooms are decorated in contemporary mountain style and range in size from standard to deluxe fireplace rooms. Two adjoining units can handle seven persons. *Box 89, Taos Ski Valley 87525, tel. 505/776–2277 or 800/322–9815, fax 505/776–1410. 60 rooms. Facilities: restaurant, lounge, library, health spa with indoor hot tub, sauna, exercise room, massage. MC, V. $125–$330.*

Kandahar Condominiums

The Kandahar overlooks the mountain village from the edge of Strawberry Hill, a beginners' run that gives you ski-in/ski-out access to the lifts. The building itself is an unremarkable elongated chalet-style structure, but the studios and one- and two-bedroom units are comfortable and spacious, if a little dated in decor. The style is Southwestern rec room, with white walls, dark-wood trim, and earth- or wheat-toned carpets and couches. All the units come with a separate living room, a full kitchen, a fireplace, and two bathrooms. These are good value for slope-side accommodations. *Box 72, Taos Ski Valley 87525, tel. 505/776–2226 or 800/ 756–2226, fax 505/776–2481. 27 units. Facilities: indoor hot tub, steam room, laundry. AE, MC, V. $150–$350.*

Taos Mountain Lodge

This adobe-style lodge nestles amid the pines and aspens about a mile from the mountain village. The suites are decorated in contemporary South-western style, with handmade furnishings, bright handwoven rugs, original art, and polished wood trim. The standard loft suites have a main-floor bedroom with a queen-size bed and a spacious loft bedroom, as well as a living room and a small kitchenette; two larger, deluxe loft suites add a full kitchen and a fireplace. All suites are ideal for families or two couples. The inviting central lobby has a *saltillo* tile floor, a viga ceiling, and a large stone fireplace. *Box 698, Taos Ski Valley 87525, tel. 505/776–2229 or 800/ 530–8098, fax 505/776–2229. 10 units. Facilities: indoor and outdoor hot tubs. AE, D, MC, V. $138–$205.*

Inexpensive

El Pueblo Lodge

I think this is one of the best bargains in the area, ideal for families, groups, and even budget-minded couples. It is well located, just a few minutes' walk from the Taos Plaza on a quiet, secluded side street surrounded by shrubbery and towering cottonwoods and pines. A complex of six traditional adobe-style buildings surrounds a landscaped courtyard. The rooms and condos are all spacious, clean, and well decorated with traditional Southwestern furnishings, exposed beams, *latilla* (shaved strips of wood) ceilings, and colorful area rugs. The standard rooms come with two double beds, the efficiency units have a kiva fireplace and a kitchenette, and the condos have either one, two, or three bedrooms, each with a private bath, a full kitchen, a separate living room with a large stone fireplace, and a dining area. *412 Paseo del Pueblo Norte, Box 92, Taos 87571, tel. 505/ 758–8700 or 800/433–9612, fax 505/*

758–7321. 57 rooms, 3 units. Facilities: heated outdoor pool, hot tub, laundry. AE, D, MC, V. $63–$215, including Continental breakfast.

Kachina Lodge de Taos
According to the Hopi, kachinas are spirits that cause clouds to form, rain to fall, and good things to happen. The Kachina Lodge, standing within walking distance of the Taos Plaza, is a large courtyard-style hotel filled with Southwestern art and traditional Hopi kachina masks and dolls. This is a good, affordable choice for families. The spacious and comfortable rooms are decorated in a Southwestern motif, with hand-carved furnishings in dark wood. *413 N. Pueblo Rd., Box NN, Taos 87571, tel. 505/758–2275 or 800/522–4462, fax 505/758–9207. 113 rooms, 5 suites. Facilities: restaurant, lounge, heated outdoor pool, hot tub, shuttle to mountain. AE, D, DC, MC, V. $85–$125.*

Old Taos Guest House
This 150-year-old hacienda of traditional adobe construction is nestled in a secluded grove of trees on a 7½-acre rise just 2 miles from the Taos Plaza. It has been converted into a quiet and cozy bed-and-breakfast with rooms and suites around a picturesque stone courtyard. Each room is decorated in Southwestern style, with vigas and beams, red oak floors, and handmade wooden furnishings all accented with bright Navajo rugs and bedcovers. All rooms and suites have outside entrances on the courtyard. This is an ideal choice for couples. *1028 Witt Rd., Box 6552, Taos, 87571, tel. 505/758–5448 or 800/758–5448. 7 rooms, 2 suites. Facilities: outdoor hot tub.*

MC, V. $70–$115, including Continental breakfast.

Sagebrush Inn
This 1929-vintage pueblo mission-style inn 3 miles from downtown Taos was originally an upscale stopover for well-heeled guests from the East Coast, and the painter Georgia O'Keeffe actually lived here for a while during the 1940s. Today it's a lively hotel, a striking example of classic Southwest architecture, with graceful portals, intimate patios, adobe construction, and a near-priceless collection of rugs, pottery, antiques, and paintings. All the rooms and suites have hand-carved furniture, terra-cotta-tiled bathrooms, Navajo-style rugs and bedcovers, pottery lamps, vigas, and tin light fixtures. *S. Santa Fe Rd., Box 557, Taos 87571, tel. 505/758–2254 or 800/428–3626, fax 505/758–5077. 47 rooms, 32 suites. Facilities: 2 restaurants, lounge, 2 indoor hot tubs. AE, D, DC, MC, V. $60–$140.*

WHERE TO EAT
Because many of the on-mountain lodges offer only all-inclusive meal packages, the mountain village does not have a lot of dining options. However, Taos has an extensive variety, ranging from small local diners to upscale restaurants. There's also much emphasis on traditional Southwestern cuisine, with spicy chili, salsa, and cilantro the most common taste enhancers.

On the Mountain
Phoenix Restaurant
If you want beer or wine with your food, this is the place. It has a number

of daily specials, plus sandwiches and burgers cooked on the outdoor barbecue. *Base of Lift 4, tel. 505/776–2291. No credit cards.*

Whistlestop

This is a basic on-mountain eatery featuring a fairly standard lineup of pizzas, sandwiches, soups, and chilis. *Base of Lift 6, tel. 505/776–2291. No credit cards.*

Expensive

Casa Cordova

You enter this 150-year-old classic hacienda-style adobe building through a cobblestone courtyard, and you dine in a setting that blends traditional Southwestern decor (terracotta tile floors, *latilla* ceilings, gaily painted lavender walls, large kiva fireplaces) with local art. It's a cheerful place with a bustling bistro atmosphere. The mainstay items are Continental—baked quail with raspberry sauce, baked stuffed pork with a two-wine sauce, tournedos with béarnaise sauce, and broiled scallops with chardonnay butter. The stone-walled lounge is an inviting place to have a drink before or after dinner. *Rte. 150, 8 mi north of Taos, Arroyo Seco, tel. 505/776–2500. AE, D, MC, V.*

Doc Martin's

This is the historic home of Doc Martin, Taos's first doctor, who bought this house (now part of the Taos Inn) in the 1890s. It later became the headquarters for the Taos Society of Artists. Today it is one of Taos's best restaurants, under the able supervision of chef Patrick Lambert, who trained at Napa's Mustard Grill, among other places. His blending of Asian ingredients with Southwestern flavors, using locally grown organic produce, results in such signature dishes as pomegranate venison chop with mashed yams, chard, pomegranate sauce, and fried onions or braised Spanish lamb with a coffee, honey, and port broth. Even the desserts are out of the ordinary, like the blue corn crepe with white chocolate mousse in apricot coulis. The best deal is a $14.95 prix fixe meal, with a choice of five entrées, offered nightly. The restaurant's extensive wine list has won numerous awards. *Taos Inn, 125 Paseo del Pueblo Norte, tel. 505/758–1977. AE, DC, MC, V. Reservations essential.*

Lambert's of Taos

This is the class act in Taos—a refined, clean-lined restaurant with white-on-white decor, soft lighting, marble-top tables, blond hardwood floors, and crystal and linen place settings. The main dining room is the largest, with tables for about 40, but you can also dine in one of three smaller rooms. The menu of contemporary American grill cuisine changes weekly according to the chef's whim. Entrées might include broiled halibut and asparagus stew served on linguine, pepper-crusted lamb served with a garlic pasta, grilled pheasant with port wine sauce and squash soufflé, or grilled pork tenderloin with chipotle sauce and warm potato salad. *309 Paseo del Pueblo Sur, Taos, tel. 505/758–1009. AE, D, DC, MC, V.*

Villa Fontana

Carlo Gislimberti, the co-owner and chef of this intimate and formal Italian restaurant housed in a traditional adobe building, has won high praise for his innovative northern Italian cooking. Carlo is also a preeminent mycophagist (mushroom epicure), and his wild mushroom soup is to die for. The entrée list, with many daily specials, includes osso buco (succulent veal shanks braised in wine and herbs) and medallions of red deer with a wild mushroom and brandy sauce. Among his fish dishes are whole Dover sole and grilled salmon. *Rte. 522, 5 mi north of Taos, tel. 505/758–5800. AE, D, DC, MC, V.*

Moderate

Glass Dining Room

The atrium-style room is festooned with plants, paintings, and antiques and built with the same nail-free craftsmanship for which the Austing Haus is renowned. It's a bright, cheery room; if you prefer a little intimacy, ask for a table in the raised alcove near the fireplace. The menu offers a little of everything—medallions of beef bordelaise and traditional steaks; scampi, orange roughy, and sea kabobs; and a selection of chicken and pasta dishes. For dessert, the homemade apple strudel is one of the best I've ever tasted. *Austing Haus, Taos Ski Valley, tel. 505/776–2649. DC, MC, V.*

Inn at Snakedance Dining Room

The dining room here is large and formal without being too fussy—a vaulted ceiling with exposed beams, picture windows, hand-plastered walls decorated with old black-and-white photographs of the region and local artwork, and a large stone fireplace. The menu offers traditional Southwestern fare such as organic chicken chipotle with barbecue sauce

or prawns sautéed in white wine and basil served over spinach noodles with a grilled red pepper sauce, as well as broiled New York strip steak with grilled roasted green chili butter. *Inn at Snakedance, Taos Ski Valley, tel. 505/776–2277. MC, V.*

Rhoda's Restaurant

Rhoda's, named for the late Ernie Blake's wife, is a bright, friendly family dining spot in the mountain village with modern Southwestern decor of blond-wood beams, wood trim, and an avocado-and-pink color scheme. Tapestries, Navajo blankets, and vintage photos of the area decorate the walls. The menu is a mixture of conventional American favorites such as prime rib, New York strip steak, rack of lamb, and a daily fish special, plus grilled Cajun kabobs with scallops and shrimp, Wiener schnitzel, and pastas. *Resort center, Taos Ski Valley, tel. 505/776–2005. AE, MC, V.*

Stakeout Grill and Bar

The Stakeout, about 8 miles south of town, has a spectacular setting high atop Outlaw Hill with a 360-degree panorama of the surrounding countryside. The restaurant, in an old adobe building, has Wild West artifacts and collectibles that add to its rustic and casual atmosphere. Steaks are a mainstay, big and charbroiled in various forms and sizes up to 18 ounces. Seafood options include grilled salmon, Alaskan king crab legs, and baked rainbow trout, and there are veal scallopini sautéed with marsala wine and artichokes and chicken roll wrapped in goat cheese and sun-dried tomatoes. *Rte. 68, Outlaw Hill, 4 mi south of Ranchos de*

Taos, Taos, tel. 505/758–2042. AE, D, DC, MC, V.

Inexpensive

El Pueblo Café

This is a classic diner with a lunch counter, lots of cheap chrome, fake wood tables, and a delightful greasy-spoon atmosphere. The menu has two sides—standard comfort food, such as fried chicken, pork chops, burgers, sandwiches, and breakfast all day, and traditional Mexican dishes including fajitas, red or green chili *relleños,* burritos, tacos, and enchiladas. It's fast, friendly, virtually unknown by visitors, and has the best Mexican grub in town. *625 Paseo del Pueblo Norte, Rte. 522, Taos, tel. 505/758–2053. D, DC, MC, V.*

Outback

This is a wonderful, rough place, with wooden floors and walls and a noisy, steamy atmosphere. The restaurant is warmed by a giant antique woodstove and is redolent with the aromas emanating from the large open kitchen. It's not fancy and can get awfully crowded, but it serves the best pizza in town—thin crusted with more than a dozen choices of toppings. There's also an excellent selection of salads served with fresh-baked pita bread, daily soup specials, pastas, and calzones (rolled pizza, like a turnover). *Paseo del Pueblo Norte, Rte. 522, Taos, tel. 505/758–3112. MC, V.*

Tim's Stray Dog Cantina

This is a loud and lively spot on the mountain much favored by a young local crowd for its good, inexpensive northern New Mexican dishes. In addition to enchiladas, burritos, tacos, and tortillas, there is an excellent chili relleño, as well as cilantro chicken, panfried trout, and tequila shrimp. Tim's, though, is best known for its green chilis; amateurs beware—these are real sizzlers. *Taos Ski Valley mountain village, tel. 505/776–2894. AE, MC, V.*

Wild and Natural Café

This quaint, lively vegetarian restaurant serves up huge portions of ultra-healthy foods including veggie burgers, a steamed vegetable platter, blue corn enchiladas, green chili, homemade soups, organic salads, sandwiches, stuffed squash, and a selection of healthy desserts such as fruit smoothies. The decor features the art of local artists. *812 Paseo del Pueblo Norte, south of Cid's Food Market, Taos, tel. 505/751–0480. D, MC, V.*

Best Bets for Breakfast

Casa Fresen Bakery

In the heart of Arroyo Seco, a small village on the Ski Valley Road up to the mountain, this is a good place to stop for fresh-baked breads, muffins, pastries, and cakes. It also has the best coffee in the area. *482 State Rd., Rte. 150, Arroyo Seco, tel. 505/776–2969. MC, V.*

Kiva Coffee Shop

Breakfast is served from 6 AM to 5 PM. It has all the traditional American breakfast favorites—eggs and bacon, ham, or sausages with home fries or grits, pancakes, waffles, and French toast—along with Mexican specialties such as *huevos rancheros* and burritos. *Paseo del Pueblo Norte, Taos, tel. 505/758–2275. AE, D, DC, MC, V.*

NIGHTLIFE

If you come to Taos for the nightlife and entertainment, you're sure to be disappointed, especially up in the mountain village, where the action is severely limited after the après-ski period. The town of Taos is a little livelier, but it still doesn't have the action-oriented bar and nightclub scene found at some other resorts.

Après-Ski

Martini Tree

In the main base lodge building, this busy, hustling spot has live entertainment, high-decibel conversations, dancing, and a large sundeck. It tends to attract a younger crowd. *Taos Ski Valley Mountain Village, tel. 505/776–2291. AE, MC, V.*

Rathskeller

When the sun is shining, the Cheeseburgers in Paradise Sun Deck is the place to hang out, but when the weather turns foul, step inside to this woody bar filled with antiques, atmosphere, dancing, and live entertainment—reggae, rock, jazz, and blues. *Hotel St. Bernard, Taos Ski Valley, tel. 505/776–2251. No credit cards.*

Loud and Lively/Dancing

Eske's Brew Pub

This is something a little different for Taos—a British-style pub. Eske's features a sterling lineup of well-crafted brews, including a novel and delicious green chili variety. It's a friendly, comfortable place in a 70-year-old flat-roofed adobe building renovated by members of the Taos ski patrol. Live entertainment—jazz or folk—happens at least four nights a week, and you can graze on an eclectic mixture of pub grub. *106 Desgeorges La., near Taos Plaza, Taos, tel. 505/758–1517. MC, V.*

Sagebrush Inn

Live country-and-western entertainment is the ticket here, and the place really jumps even though it's 2 miles outside town. The lounge actually spills out into the lobby, giving it a free-form kind of atmosphere, and there's a steady stream of dancers roaming the dance floor. It's definitely one of the livelier spots in town. *1508 Paseo del Pueblo Sur, Taos, tel. 505/758–2254. AE, D, DC, MC, V.*

More Mellow

Casa Cordova

The small separate bar area has light music and lots of comfortable chairs. The terra-cotta tile floor is occasionally used for dancing, and the adobe walls decorated with local art give it a nice romantic feel. *Rte. 150, 8 mi north of Taos, Arroyo Seco, tel. 505/776–2500. AE, D, MC, V.*

No state in the United States, and indeed few regions in the world, can count as many individual ski resorts as New York. From the Catskills in the southern part of the state to the rugged Adirondacks in the north, there are more than 100 individual ski areas ranging in size from tiny two-lift mom-and-pop local areas to the storied Olympic region of Lake Placid with towering Whiteface Mountain.

Although the well-rounded mountains of the lesser ranges provide 99% of the state's well-run, highly popular resorts, it is the mighty Adirondacks that provide the best skiing. In the northeast corner of the state, within a day's drive of more than 35 million people, they encompass an area slightly larger than the state of Connecticut and run north to the Canadian border.

In all, this rugged range has 44 peaks that top the 4,000-foot mark, including Mt. Marcy, at 5,344 feet, where the northern source of the Hudson River is, at Tear-of-the-Clouds Lake. Although none of the peaks—there are some 500 individual mountains—top the lofty summits found in the nearby White Mountains of New Hampshire or the Black Mountains of North Carolina, their general elevation is higher than that of any range east of the Rockies.

The 6-million-acre Adirondack Wilderness—2.3 million acres of which are under the jurisdiction of the New York State Forest Preserve and must remain "forever wild"—is spectacular not only for its prodigious peaks but also for its vast tracts of dense forest, its countless lakes and gushing trout streams, and its impressive gorges and waterfalls.

The resort town of Lake Placid is a marvelous place whose character has been shaped by the surrounding rugged Adirondack wilderness, the money of the rich, and the sweat of Olympic athletes. It is a town full of memories of a gilded age: During the 1930s and '40s legendary millionaires—leaders of the day—built their luxury camps here as retreats from the cities and their powerful businesses. Their mansions still dot the shorelines of the lakes, their luster somewhat dimmed but their style still a fond memory.

Then there are the Olympic memories. If ever a town is inexorably linked with the five rings of the Winter Games, it is this tiny mountain village. In the 1932 and 1980 Olympics the athletes created images and memories of snow and ice that are at least as enduring as the camps of the rich and reclusive.

WHITEFACE MOUNTAIN SKI CENTER

Wilmington, New York
Tel. 518/946–2223

Olympic Regional
Development Authority
Olympic Center
Lake Placid, New York 12946
tel. 518/523–1655 or
800/462–6236

STATISTICALLY SPEAKING
Base elevation: 1,200 feet

Summit elevation: 4,867 feet

Vertical drop: 3,216 feet

Skiable terrain: 153 acres

Number of trails: 65

Longest run: 3 miles

Lifts and capacity: 2 triples, 7
doubles, 1 handle tow; 10,385
skiers per hour

Lift ticket: $34 weekdays,
$39 weekends

Average annual snowfall:
191 inches

Number of skiing days
1995–96: 145

Snowmaking: 142 acres, 93%

Terrain mix: N 35%, I 37%,
E 28%

Snowboarding: yes

Cross-country skiing: 31 miles

Lake Placid is no longer a playground of the rich and storied but is rather an egalitarian winter-sports center with a plethora of medium-price accommodations. Families and groups of college students with varied interests and conservative budgets take advantage of the diverse options available within close range. Evidence of Olympic influence is everywhere, from the unsurpassed Olympic winter-sports facilities to the extensive services in town. You could easily spend a couple of days in Lake Placid and stay entertained even if you never hit the Olympic slopes on Whiteface Mountain. Shops, restaurants, bars, cafés, and hotels line Main Street, and within a 5-mile drive there's virtually unlimited winter-sports excitement. Ride the Olympic bobsled or luge runs; ski the meticulous trails of the Mt. Van Hoevenburg Olympic Cross-Country Center; take a spin around the 400-meter Olympic speed-skating oval; or simply stand in the Olympic arena and recall the improbable victory of an overachieving U.S. team in the gold medal game of the 1980 Olympic hockey tournament.

The town itself is actually on Mirror Lake, separated from Lake Placid by a narrow isthmus. It is quite compact, with action-packed Main Street running the length of Mirror Lake. The majority of the stores, restaurants, bars, and accommodations are strung between the Olympic speed-skating oval at one end of town and the venerable Mirror Lake Inn at the other. The south end of Saranac Avenue (heading west away from the lake) is being developed, but for most visitors Main Street is the main track.

The Olympic Regional Development Authority (ORDA) manages the facilities leftover from the Olympics and develops innovative programs to ensure maximum usage. The area would benefit from an efficient shuttle system, which would eliminate traffic jams between town and the mountain and help Lake Placid match the developments taking place at other ski areas.

HOW TO GET THERE
By Plane
Logan International Airport (tel. 617/567–5400), in Boston, is the closest international airport to Lake Placid/Whiteface, which is a 5½-hour drive

EFUL NUMBERS
ea code: 518

ildren's services: instruc-
n, tel. 518/946-2223

ow phone:
l. 800/462-6236

olice: tel. 518/523-3306

Medical center:
el. 518/523-3311

ake Placid Visitors Bureau:
el. 518/523-2445

Vhiteface Mountain
Regional Visitors Bureau:
el. 518/946-2255

Road conditions:
tel. 800/429-7623

Towing: Central Garage,
tel. 518/523-3378

FIVE-STAR FAVORITES

Best run for vertical:
Cloudspin

Best run overall: Cloudspin to
Broadway to Ladies Bridge to
Upper Boreen to Lower Valley

Best bar/nightclub:
R.F. McDougall's Saloon

Best hotel: Mirror Lake Inn

Best restaurant:
Lake Placid Lodge

away. Fifty-two airlines serve the airport, among them American Airlines (tel. 800/433–7300), Continental and Continental Express (tel. 800/525–0280), Delta (tel. 800/221–1212), Northwest (tel. 800/225–2525), Trans World Express (tel. 800/221–2000), United (tel. 800/241–6522), and US Airways (tel. 800/428–4322).

The **Lake Placid Airport** (tel. 518/523–2473) is a mile south of the village on Route 73. It serves chartered aircraft.

The **Adirondack Airport** (tel. 518/891–4600) is northwest of Saranac Lake, 16 miles from Lake Placid on Route 86. US Airways flies here from eastern locations.

Albany County Airport (tel. 518/869–3021), a 2½-hour drive from Lake Placid, is the closest major airport. American Airlines, Continental Express, Delta, Northwest, United, and US Airways have flights here from all major U.S. cities.

By Car

From the metropolitan New York City area and northern New Jersey, take the New York State Thruway (I–87) north to Exit 24 (Albany) then the Northway (I–87) to Exit 30. Follow Route 9 north 2 miles to Route 73 and continue 28 miles to Lake Placid.

From Buffalo, Rochester, Syracuse, and points west, take I–90 (the west section of the New York State Thruway) east to Exit 36 (Syracuse) and pick up I–81N to Watertown. At Route 3 go east to Saranac Lake, then take Route 86 east to Lake Placid.

From Boston, Springfield, and Hartford, take I–90 west (here it's the Massachusetts Turnpike) to Albany, then I–787 north to Cohoes. Connect with Route 7W and then take I–87 north. Follow I–87 to Exit 30 and pick up Route 9N for 2 miles to Route 73. Continue for 28 miles to Lake Placid.

Avis (249 Main St., tel. 518/563–4120 or 800/331–1212) and **Hertz** (69 Saranac Ave., tel. 518/523–3158 or 800/654–3131) have offices in Lake Placid.

By Bus

Adirondack Trailways (tel. 800/225–6815) has regularly scheduled service from Albany and New York City and its suburbs.

By Train

Amtrak (tel. 800/872–7245) has a line from New York City with a stop in Westport, New York (40 minutes from Lake Placid). Shuttle bus service to Lake Placid is available through **Lake Placid Sightseeing Tours** (tel. 518/523–4431) and **Adirondack Trailways** (*see above*).

GETTING AROUND

A car is indispensable in Lake Placid, both because of the absence of an efficient shuttle bus system and because it's 9 miles from the town to the mountain, which is in the hamlet of Wilmington. At Whiteface there's parking by the mountain and a free pickup and drop-off service to take you from your car to the base lodge and back if you don't get a parking space close enough to walk.

Lake Placid Sightseeing (tel. 518/523–4431) has scheduled runs between the major hotels in the village and the mountain for $5 per person (one-way or round-trip). Call for times. The downtown area is small enough to walk everywhere, but if you want to take a taxi, try **Gene's Taxi** (tel. 518/523–3161).

THE SKIING

Whiteface Mountain is not the highest peak in the Adirondacks, but its Olympian reputation overshadows others in the region. Whiteface sits alone, 9 miles from Lake Placid, exposed on all sides and occasionally buffeted by cold winds from Canada or shrouded in low clouds produced by warm and cold fronts clashing in the sky above.

Because it's in the Adirondack Forest Preserve, the mountain is not excessively built up. You won't have to navigate condos or souvenir shops on these slopes—the trails, the lifts, a base lodge, a midstation lodge, and other skiers are all you'll see besides what's there naturally.

The mountain has taken its share of knocks from skiers who complain about the frigid weather, the windswept slopes, and the relatively antiquated lift network that runs to the summit of Whiteface and its shoulder peak of Little Whiteface. There's truth in all three complaints: Whiteface can be brutally cold and windy, and despite the nearly 100% snowmaking, many of the exposed runs on the upper mountain can be rock-hard and icy. But almost every ski mountain in the East can be battered by the hand of winter, and on a good skiing day Whiteface's 3,216 vertical feet (the greatest of any mountain in the East) can be as good as it gets.

More annoying than the capriciousness of winter weather, however, is the tediously slow collection of triple and double chairlifts that pale in comparison to the fast, modern quads that most resorts now provide. It takes almost 30 minutes to ride the two chairs to the summit, a situation that could easily be remedied by the installation of a top-to-bottom quad. Whiteface needs an upgrade.

Another anomaly of this Olympic mountain is that it has more to offer experts and beginners than true intermediates. Experts will relish the steep challenge of the upper mountain, and novices won't get into any trouble from midmountain on down, but intermediates will find themselves caught between the two areas. They must either put up with reasonably tame cruising or push themselves into tackling some of the black trails on Little Whiteface.

Those problems aside, Whiteface can be an exhilarating experience, a true northeastern in-your-face clash with nature. It's certainly one of the most challenging mountains east of the Rockies. Its temperament is tempered by the top-to-bottom snowmaking that is just one of the region's Olympic legacies.

Novices

Beginners at Whiteface have their own secluded section to the left and right of the main base area. Never-evers should start at the Bunny Hutch lift (to your right, as you look up the mountain) and try the Bronze, Silver, or Gold runs—a trio of smooth, wide, gentle trails that meander down the slope. Main Street, Runner Up, and Medalist, on the same side, also give a good, smooth ride. To the far left of the base area is the Bear lift, which serves a trio of wider, softly falling novice runs called Wolf, Bear, and Deer.

When you're ready for something a little longer, take the Valley triple chair to midmountain, turn right off the lift and enjoy the long way down on Easy Way to Upper Boreen. From here take Ladies Bridge to Boreen, then link up with Bronze, Silver, or Gold to the bottom. This series of trails starts out a bit steep at Easy Way but quickly turns to gentle slopes.

Intermediates

Steady intermediates may be a little frustrated when skiing Whiteface because their share of the terrain is considerably less than that at more modern resorts. For instance, there are only two blue trails that come down from the summit, Paron's Run and Ridge Runner, so if you want to enjoy upper-elevation skiing, you may have to push your limits by taking on some of the steeper black runs. Start by riding the Valley triple lift and the Summit triple lift to Paron's Run, a 3-mile reasonably wide giant-slalom cruiser that winds its way down to the shoulder of Little Whiteface. Here it connects with the shorter, steeper pitches of Lower Northway, Excelsior, and Lower Cloudspin. All three take you back to the base of the summit triple, where you can fast track it back to the summit without getting caught up in the lower mountain traffic. If you find the upper part of Paron's Run a little too steep, look for the Follies, a slightly less steep alternative that lets you skirt the advanced intermediate section off the summit and reconnects with Paron's Run a little farther down the mountain.

Ridge Runner is another good intermediate track from the summit, although you will have to watch the trail signs to pick up blue extensions such as Upper and Lower Switchback, Crossover Loop, or Glen. You can stretch out your summit run by getting on Broadway, just below the Summit triple lift, then connecting with River Run for a long cruise to the valley. The only problem with this route is that you are forced to take the generally busy Valley triple lift back up to midmountain, then the Summit triple lift back to the top. You won't get into any real trouble on any of these blue runs: All are good, wide cruisers with the occasional drop-off and slightly steeper pitch, and they have the most consistent grooming on the mountain.

Your other option for a little more steepness and challenge or to warm up for the black runs is to ride the Little Whiteface triple lift from the top of the midstation shuttle lift or to ski down Upper Valley from the top of Valley triple and take a crack at Parkway and Thruway, a pair of short black-to-blue high-speed cruisers that were the courses for the 1980 Olympic giant slalom and slalom events. For a bit more challenge, try the moguls on Mountain Run and Wilderness, both black trails reached by the same lift.

On good snow days strong intermediates can enjoy the steep, occasionally bumpy Empire and McKenzie runs, also accessible from the top of Little Whiteface. Although they're designated black, they're definitely manageable. When you're ready to push the thrill meter up a notch, take the Summit triple to the top of Whiteface and take a run down either Upper Cloudspin or Skyward, the men's and women's Olympic downhill course. They may be steep and twisting, but they're generally bump-free.

Experts

Head straight for the summit and get your legs warmed up on either the Skyward—the women's Olympic downhill—or Cloudspin, the men's Olympic downhill. Both are high-speed giant-slalom runs with plenty of pitch, tight turns, drop-offs, and even the occasional bumpy section. Unless you're heading over to Little Whiteface triple lift, don't drop below the base of the Summit triple lift: The run-out to the lower base area is a tame blue

cruise. It's here, to the right (looking down) off the Summit triple, that you'll find a half dozen of the steepest runs in the east: Mountain Run and Wilderness are where the bumps grow largest, especially where they cross under the lift and pop up through stands of sturdy Adirondack timber; Upper Parkway and Upper Thruway—the Olympic giant-slalom and slalom courses—give you as much pitch without the bumps; or you can opt for the high-speed, generally well-groomed Empire or Upper McKenzie.

Snowboarders have access to the entire mountain and to all lifts. There's also a snowboard park with half pipe off the Lower Valley run.

WHERE TO STAY

One of the more practical legacies of the 1980 Olympics is the ample supply of medium-price accommodations that were built to handle the crowds. Around every corner downtown and immediately off the main thoroughfares, small motel and cabin developments with vacancy signs push their way to the road. Many of the nicer places are less visible. Accommodations can also be found in the surrounding area, including Saranac Lake, about 10 miles west on Highway 86, and all lodgings can be booked through the Lake Placid Visitors' Bureau (tel. 518/523–2445 or 800/462–6236).

Expensive

Holiday Inn SunSpree Resort
This plain blockhouse-style structure, built in 1969, occupies a high point overlooking the Olympic Arena and contains an unexpected variety of large, modern, brightly decorated

rooms, suites, chalets, and condos. Extensive on-site amenities make this place suitable for families. *1 Olympic Dr., Lake Placid 12946, tel. 518/523–2556 or 800/974–1980, fax 518/523–9410. 192 rooms, 13 suites, 2 chalets, 3 units. Facilities: 2 restaurants, bar, lounge, hot tub, indoor pool, health club, 24-hr desk service, maid service, shuttle, ski storage, laundry, game room. AE, D, DC, MC, V. $109–$325.*

Lake Placid Lodge

Built in 1882, this vestige of the age of Great Camps is on the shore of Lake Placid, about 5 miles west of town. Its rooms combine rustic opulence with modern conveniences. All are woody and warm, with twig and birch-bark furnishings, antiques, Oriental rugs, fireplaces (in most rooms), and a great view of the lake. The location is pure romance. *Whiteface Inn Rd., Box 550, Lake Placid 12946, tel. 518/523–2573, fax 518/523–1124. 36 rooms. Facilities: restaurant, pub, lounge, library, games room, maid service, ski storage, cross-country skiing. AE, D, DC, MC, V. $175–$450.*

Mirror Lake Inn

This resort hotel on a terraced rise at the south end of Mirror Lake is a complex of seven buildings anchored by the early 1920s main lodge, which was destroyed by fire in 1988 and carefully restored to its original neocolonial splendor, complete with white exterior, large windows, and high pillars. Inside, the grand style continues, with walnut floors, mahogany wall trim, and comfortable lounge areas full of plush furnishings and antique fixtures. Even the smallest rooms are large enough to be comfortable, with marble and mahogany bathrooms, pastel rugs and wall coverings, and plenty of wood trim. *5 Mirror Lake Dr., Lake Placid 12946, tel. 518/523–2544, fax 518/523–2871. 110 rooms, 18 suites. Facilities: 2 restaurants, 2 bars, sauna, Jacuzzi, indoor pool, health club, massage, library, 24-hr desk service, maid service, shuttle, ski storage, skating rink, planned fitness activities. AE, D, DC, MC, V. $94–$310.*

The Point

About 30 miles west of Lake Placid, this exclusive lodge was once the home of multimillionaire William Rockefeller. It is a picture of rustic elegance—set in a rugged woodland beside a lake—with a magnificent log main lodge plus four outbuildings with guest quarters that are spectacularly decorated in deep wine tones and much wood. Each has a massive stone fireplace, Oriental carpets, original art, and Adirondack furnishings and antiques. Dinner is served family style in the 30-foot-by-50-foot Great Hall, and the formal attire (black tie two nights a week) is a fitting salute to haute cuisine. If the snow is good, you can cross-country ski nearby, and when the small lake freezes over, it's ideal for ice skating. *Star Rte., HCR 1, Box 65, Saranac Lake 12983, tel. 518/891–5674 or 800/255-3530, fax 518/891–1152. 11 rooms. Facilities: bar, pub, maid service, shuttle, ski storage, snowshoeing, ice skating, ice fishing, cross-country skiing. AE. $825–$1300, including all meals and activities.*

Moderate

Highland House Hideaways

A few minutes' walk from Main Street you'll find a series of five cottages that are ideal for families as they sleep eight people. The rooms are decorated in a rough-hewed but charming fashion, with antique furniture. Each cottage has a wood-burning fireplace, a wraparound deck, separate bedrooms with private baths, a pullout couch, and a full kitchen. *3 Highland Pl., Lake Placid 12946, tel. 518/523–2377, fax 518/523–1863. 5 cottages. Facilities: TV, VCR, stereo, outdoor hot tub, maid service, laundry facilities, ski storage. MC, V. $90–$300.*

Hungry Trout Motor Inn

This motel on 10 acres in Wilmington, about a half mile from the ski area, is one of the accommodations closest to Whiteface Mountain. That the Hungry Trout is tucked away in the trees overlooking the Flume Falls section of the Ausable River more than compensates for its prosaic appearance. Each of the cozy, practical rooms has two double beds, a TV, and a coffeemaker. The two-room suites are a good choice for families or groups who want to be on the quieter side of Lake Placid. *Rte. 86, Wilmington 12997, tel. 518/946–2217 or 800/766–9137, fax 518/946–7418. 18 rooms, 2 suites. Facilities: restaurant, bar. AE, DC, MC, V. $49–$129.*

Interlaken Inn

You won't have to look hard to find this fully restored 1906 Victorian inn in a stand of trees overlooking Mirror Lake. The Interlaken is three stories high, and its clapboard exterior is painted a gay colonial blue with cream trim. The rooms range in size from small and cozy to large and spacious, but each has a private bath and is a trove of antiques and reproduc-

tions, with four-poster, canopy, brass, and other period beds plus touches like bird's-eye-maple dressers, Lincoln rockers, and handmade quilts. *15 Interlaken Ave., Lake Placid 12946, tel. 518/523–3180 or 800/428–4369. 11 rooms. Facilities: restaurant, bar, lounge, shuttle service, ski storage, maid service, laundry. AE, MC, V. $120–$180, including all meals.*

Stagecoach Inn

Built in 1833 as a stopover for coaches, this is the oldest hotel—and probably the oldest building—in Lake Placid. It still presents a striking portrait of the 19th century, with its wraparound front porch, Georgia pine wainscoting, antique furniture, lace curtains, and fireplaces. There are only nine rooms, each individually furnished with a brass-and-iron bed, a handmade quilt, Native American art, and antiques. Two of the larger rooms have fireplaces. *370 Old Military Rd., Lake Placid 12946, tel. 518/523–9474 or 800/520–9474. 9 rooms. Facilities: maid service. MC, V. $60–$85.*

Inexpensive

Adirondack Inn

This two-story stone-frame building opposite the Olympic Arena has straightforward hotel-type accommodations and is favored by ski groups and families. Rooms are comfortable, with two double beds and a bathroom, and the decor is cheerful, with floral print spreads, a table for two, and sliding glass doors that access a balcony. *217 Main St., Lake Placid 12946, tel. 518/523–2424 or 800/556–2424, fax 518/523–2425. 50 rooms. Facilities: 2 restaurants, bar, lounge, indoor pool, sauna, Jacuzzi,* exercise facilities, 24-hr desk service, maid service, ski storage, game room. AE, MC, V. $60–$120.

Budget Host Town & Country Motor Inn

A clean, simple, centrally located motel-type lodge, it has a variety of modern rooms in sizes that can accommodate from two to six people. The Town & Country is attractive to those on a budget as you get full value for your money. *65–67 Saranac Ave., Lake Placid 12946, tel. 518/523–9268 or 800/283–4678, fax 518/523–8058. 24 rooms, 1 suite, 1 cottage. Facilities: maid service. AE, D, MC, V. $95–$120, including full breakfast.*

Mt. Van Hoevenberg Bed & Breakfast and Cottages

This pleasant natural-wood farmhouse—with just four rooms in the main building plus a half-dozen small cabins on the 5-acre property—is next to the Olympic recreation facility, home to cross-country skiing, luging, and bobsledding. The rooms are basic, with either a double bed, two twins, or one double and bunks. Cabins are different sizes, with beds for as many as six, but all have complete kitchen facilities. *Rte. 73, HCR 1 Box 37, Lake Placid 12946, tel. 518/523–9572, fax 518/523–2956. 4 rooms share 2 baths, 6 cabins. Facilities: ski-waxing room, sauna. MC, V. $50–$150, including full breakfast (in rooms).*

WHERE TO EAT

Although there is no shortage of places to eat, Lake Placid is basically a meat-and-potatoes town, and there's little in the way of creative cuisine. Steaks and other standard meat dishes top most menus, but with a little effort it's possible to uncover a smattering of more adventurous offerings. You'll find the majority of eateries on and around Main Street, with a select few off the main drag.

Expensive

Averil Conwell Dining Room

This elegant but casual restaurant at the Mirror Lake Inn has a mahogany-trimmed fireplace, candlelight, a floral-print burgundy carpet, mahogany accents, murals and paintings by Lake Placid artist Averil Courtney Conwell, and best of all, a superb view of Mirror Lake. The menu is Continental, with regional touches like home-smoked items and the liberal use of real Adirondack maple syrup. There are excellent meat and fish entrées, such as succulent venison and pan-seared salmon fillet. For dessert indulge in sinful banana bread pudding with a warm caramel sauce. *5 Mirror Lake Dr., Lake Placid, tel. 518/523–2544. Reservations essential. AE, D, DC, MC, V.*

Charcoal Pit Restaurant

A pleasant roadhouse atmosphere, simple wooden decor, white tablecloths, and a central location make this a good family spot. Although it's primarily a steak emporium—with the main attraction cooked to order over a real charcoal fire—it does have plenty of alternatives, such as Greek shrimp served with an olive-and-feta sauce, veal marsala, or veal Angela (with broccoli). *Saranac Ave., Rte. 86W, Lake Placid, tel. 518/523–3050. AE, D, DC, MC, V. Closed Tues.–Wed. in Jan.*

Hungry Trout

Antique fishing equipment and mounted trout decorate the walls of this secluded eatery next to the west branch of the fecund Ausable River. The mainstay of the menu is trout—rainbow trout, specifically—personally selected by owner Jerry Botcher, an aficionado of fly-fishing. The restaurant serves trout four ways: baked with lemon butter, blackened with Cajun spices, with a shallot and Grand Marnier butter sauce, and Rocky Mountain style, in a crisp seasoned crust. The menu includes other fish dishes, game, and daily specials, plus several varieties of steak. You also get a great view of Whiteface Mountain. *Rte. 86, Wilmington, tel. 518/946–2217. Reservations essential. AE, DC, MC, V.*

Lake Placid Lodge

If you have any questions about Adirondack style, look around in this elegant dining room for answers—every detail, down to the birch-bark bread baskets, has been carefully considered. The Adirondack-American offerings here are creative. The roast loin of New Zealand venison with huckleberry sauce is delicious, and every dish tastes even better than it looks. The strawberry cheesecake is surprisingly light. *Whiteface Inn Rd., Lake Placid, tel. 518/523–2573. Reservations essential. AE, D, DC, MC, V.*

Moderate

Alpine Cellar

The beamed ceiling, stucco finish, antique plates, and European landscape paintings might lead you to surmise that this is an eatery modeled after the classic inns of Switzerland and Bavaria—and you'd be right. Schnitzel is the big item and is served four ways. There are other Black Forest favorites, too, including sauer-

braten and bratwurst. *Alpine Motor Inn, 50 Wilmington Rd., Lake Placid, tel. 518/523–2180. AE, D, DC, MC, V. Closed Mon.–Tues.*

Fireside Steak House

This Bavarian-style wood-and-stucco building houses three dining areas and an upstairs lounge with oversize couches and a fireplace. The menu doesn't stray far from tried-and-true Placid favorites: Steaks are the big item, along with excellent prime rib and variations on the kebab theme. Veal, chicken, and pasta are also available, and all are served in generous proportions. *229 Main St., Lake Placid 12946, tel. 518/523–2682. AE, DC, MC, V.*

Great Adirondack Steak & Seafood

Here a display of Adirondack antiques and other collectibles (old skis, fishing poles, model trains, and so on) fills the walls. The emphasis is on large portions of popular standards, including monster T-bone steaks, prime rib, lobster, and shrimp. *34 Main St., Lake Placid, tel. 518/523–1629. AE, D, DC, MC, V.*

Thirsty Moose

The stylish ambience of this restaurant with its forest green and burgundy tones and light maple-wood trim belies its casual nature. There's an open bar in the middle of the dining area, and the walls are covered with classic Adirondack photography. The menu includes shrimp tequila, rock shrimp served in a tangy cream sauce, and steak au poivre, a hearty sirloin smothered in a peppercorn and brandy cream sauce. *57 Saranac Ave., Lake Placid, tel. 518/523–3222. Reservations not accepted. AE, MC, V.*

Inexpensive

Artist's Cafe

This is not a big place—only 45 seats—but it combines a view of Mirror Lake and barn-board decor heavy on wood and stone with well-prepared food and friendly service. There's a wide variety of steaks, seafood, salads, and microbrewed beers. Try my all-time favorite: a pound of steamed fresh shrimp. The place is always busy, but if you have to wait, you can hang out in the cozy bar. *1 Main St., Lake Placid, tel. 518/ 523–9493. Reservations not accepted. AE, D, DC, MC, V.*

Black Bear Restaurant

A lively, casual spot with rough-hewed log beams, birch paneling, and a small bar up front, this is the perfect place to concoct a dinner of appetizers: Pick your way through chicken fingers, potato skins, Cajun fries, crab cakes, deep-fried mozzarella, nachos, and wings. Portions are huge, but if you insist on having an entrée, there is a huge selection of burgers plus a little of everything from the four basic fast-food groups—steak, chicken, seafood, and pasta. *157 Main St., Lake Placid, tel. 518/523–9886. Reservations not accepted. AE, D, DC, MC, V.*

Cottage Cafe

A young, fashionable crowd frequents this café on the shore of Mirror Lake. The place is warm and woody, with a large stand-up bar and a fire in the hearth. The menu consists of designer sandwiches with fillings such as artichoke hearts, provolone, tomatoes, and onions with cayenne mayonnaise. Salad options include feta, taco, and spinach, and there's also an excellent

daily quiche, homemade soup, and delicacies like baked brie and peel-your-own shrimp. *Mirror Lake Inn, 5 Mirror Lake Dr., Lake Placid, tel. 518/ 523–9845. Reservations not accepted. AE, D, MC, V.*

Downtown Diner and Bakery

This is a diner in the classic tradition, with a long counter, faux Tiffany lamps, and blue-checked tablecloths. The lunch menu's mainstays are good soups and burgers and staples like grilled cheese, chef's salad, and hot roast beef or turkey sandwiches, plus a daily special. *330 Main St., Lake Placid, tel. 518/523–1429. No credit cards. No dinner.*

Best Bets for Breakfast

Upper Crust Bakery

This is your best bet for a great selection of baked breakfast goodies, plus the best oatmeal since Mom used to make it. You can choose from the corned beef hash, fresh bagels, and home-baked breads. The Upper Crust gets busy, and service can be slow. *315 Main St., Lake Placid, tel. 518/523– 2269. No credit cards. Closed Tues.*

NIGHTLIFE AND ENTERTAINMENT

Après-Ski

Cloudspin Lounge

You'll find this place in the main ski lodge at Whiteface. From about 3 PM to 5:30 PM it's packed, and the young singles crowd feasts on drinks and music daily, with a DJ on the weekends. *Rte. 86, Wilmington, tel. 518/ 946–2223.*

Dancing Bears Lounge

Cheap drinks and the best complimentary munchies in town draw a huge crowd to this bar in the Hilton. It's big, with a crackling fireplace and pictures of bears everywhere. There's also a dance floor, and live music that starts at 9 PM and goes till 1 AM on weekends. *Lake Placid Hilton, 1 Mirror Lake Dr., tel. 518/523–4411. AE, D, DC, MC, V.*

Loud and Lively/Dancing

Lake Placid Pub & Brewery
Something of a local hangout—mainly because it's tucked away, off Main Street at the south end of the lake—this rustic stone-and-wood pub-cum-sports-bar offers happy-hour specials and countless TVs in action at all times. *14 Shore Dr., tel. 518/523–4913. MC, V.*

R.F. McDougall's Saloon

This wonderfully warm, woody neighborhood pub has oak floors, spruce and cherry trim, and authentic prints and paintings from the Adirondacks. The twin centerpieces are the 17-foot handcrafted solid-cherry Victorian bar and the massive stone fireplace. *Hungry Trout Restaurant, Rte. 86, Wilmington, tel. 518/946–2217.*

More Mellow

Dakotas
This pub serves everything from burgers to hand-cut steaks. Its casual atmosphere is enhanced by the '50s and '60s oldies playing in the background. Every Sunday night there's live jazz. *Quality Inn, 124 Main St., tel. 518/523–2337 AE, MC, V.*

Nowhere else in the world of skiing is there a place as unique as Utah, with more than a dozen ski resorts within an hour's drive of a major metropolitan area. That's Salt Lake City, the delightful urban center started by the Mormons in the 18th century and today a hub of high-tech activity as dozens of modern industries relocate here to take advantage of a favorable tax base and an equally favorable climate.

Beyond its business appeal, Salt Lake City deserves special mention because it would be a mistake to ski any of the Utah resorts described here and not savor the city. The city center is rich in attractions and dining, with a surprising diversity of restaurants, nightspots, and hotels, and its neat grid layout is a breeze to get around in by bus, by car, or on foot.

Ultimately, though, all roads lead to Temple Square—metaphorically, if not physically—and this Mormon showcase, with its Tabernacle Choir, museum, and Genealogy Center, is Utah's most famous attraction. If you travel here during the Christmas period, the appeal is even greater, with millions of lights decorating the square and carolers in full Christmas song.

To the north, beyond the towering wall of the Wasatch Range, is the Great Salt Lake Desert, which wrings dry the moist air moving from the west and blesses the resorts that lie within sight of the city with prodigious amounts of some of the driest and lightest snow found anywhere. It's here that resorts like the ultramodern Snowbird, the bustling Park City, the tony Deer Valley, and anachronistic Alta coexist and share the snowy bounty. All four are within a 40-minute drive of Salt Lake City, and shuttle buses connect them to each other. Each offers its own kind of mountain charm; if you come to ski one, you should take a day to ski one of the others.

These resorts are so close to Salt Lake that staying in the city is an alternative to slope-side accommodations, and for travelers flying in from distant points it means being able to ski the afternoon you arrive.

GETTING TO UTAH RESORTS

By Plane

The closest major facility, **Salt Lake City International Airport** (tel. 801/575–2400), is served by the following airlines, all of which make connections from most major cities: American Airlines (tel. 800/433–7300), America West (tel. 800/228–7862), Continental Airlines (tel. 800/525–0280), Delta Airlines (tel. 800/221–1212), Frontier Airlines (tel. 800/432–1359), Northwest (tel. 800/225–2525), Southwest Airlines (tel. 800/466–7747), Skywest (tel. 800/453–9417), TWA (tel. 800/221–2000), and United Airlines (tel. 800/241–6522).

Car Rental

The following car rental firms have desks at Salt Lake City International Airport: **Alamo** (tel. 800/327–9633), **Avis** (tel. 800/331–1212), **Budget** (tel. 800/527–0700), **Dollar** (tel. 800/800–4000), **Hertz** (tel. 800/654–3131), **National** (tel. 800/328–4567), and **Payless** (tel. 800/729–5377).

By Train

Amtrak's *Zephyr Express* (tel. 800/872–7245) serves Salt Lake City's downtown Rio Grande rail station (tel. 801/531–0188) daily from Chicago and Emeryville (near Oakland), California.

By Bus

The **Greyhound Lines** (tel. 801/355–9579 or 800/231–2222) terminal is on South Temple in downtown Salt Lake City and has regularly scheduled service from all major cities.

GETTING AROUND

UTA City Transit (tel. 801/287–4636) runs regularly scheduled bus service to the ski areas for $9 round-trip from various locations in the city. **Lewis Brothers Stages** (tel. 801/649–2256 or 800/826–5844) makes regular stops at most downtown hotels for a fare of $17 round-trip to and from the ski areas.

ALTA SKI RESORT

ALTA SKI RESORT

Box 8007
Alta, UT 84092
Tel. 801/742–3333
Fax 801/742–3333, ext. 411

STATISTICALLY SPEAKING

Base elevation: 8,550 feet

Summit elevation: 10,650 feet

Vertical drop: 2,100 feet

Skiable terrain: 2,200 acres

Number of trails: 39 marked runs

Longest run: 3½ miles

Lifts and capacity: 2 triples, 6 doubles, 4 surface; 9,100 skiers per hour

Daily lift ticket: $27

Average annual snowfall: 500 inches

Number of skiing days 1995–96: 149

Snowmaking: 50 acres, 2%

Terrain mix: N 25%, I 40%, E 35%

Snowboarding: no

Alta is an old-fashioned, unpretentious resort that has resisted change and is proud of it. Unlike almost every other ski destination in the country, this one has eschewed the mania for high-speed quad chairs and trams, thus limiting the number of skiers on the mountain at any one time. Lift-ticket prices are about half those at most other resorts, so locals can still afford to ski here. Most important to ski purists, the management grooms terrain for all skiing abilities, allowing the mountain to retain its rustic beauty instead of becoming a sanitized highway of glossy white runs. This is why some people stay loyal to Alta and its simple beauty while others choose to go elsewhere.

At first glance there doesn't seem to be much to Alta, tucked away at the end of Little Cottonwood Canyon. The former mining town reached its zenith in 1883, when it had a population of 8,000 and nearly 200 buildings including a courthouse, a jail, and 26 saloons. In those days it was a raucous, rollicking town that recorded an average of one murder a day. But when the silver ran out it took with it the town's fortunes.

It wasn't until the 1930s that Alta emerged as a ski destination, when the first chairlift was constructed and the Alta Lodge opened for business. Skiing became the lifeblood of the new Alta and remains its most important industry. Visitors might feel as though they've stepped back in time, for Alta's base area is only a long, narrow wedge of modest development sandwiched between the high walls of the canyon. Within the canyon are five ski lodges, a handful of small businesses, and the ski area itself. It's one of the few privately owned ski resorts in the country. The decidedly more modern Snowbird lies less than a mile away, just over the ridge.

Alta has two base areas: the Albion day lodge, which serves the novice, intermediate, and expert terrain at the eastern edge of 11,000-foot Mt. Baldy; and the Goldminer's Daughter day lodge, which serves intermediate and expert terrain on the western edge. In between are Alta's accommodations, linked to each other by a unique rope tow. With a giant vertical bow wheel at each end, this tow moves skiers from one end of the resort to the other, passing the shorter, more conventional uphill rope tows that

ALTA SKI RESORT **255**

Children's services: day care,
tel. 801/742–3042; instruction, tel. 801/742–2600

Snow phone:
tel. 801/572–3939

Police: tel. 901/572–1211

Ski Finder: tel. 801/943–6244;
for pager, 801/533–1377

Medical Center: Snowbird Ski
Resort, tel. 801/742–2222

Hospital: Alta View Hospital,
Sandy, tel. 801/576–2600

Resort Association:
tel. 801/942–0404

Road conditions:
tel. 801/742–3333

Towing: AAA,
tel. 801/364–5610

FIVE-STAR FAVORITES
Best run for vertical:
Alf's High Rustler

Best run overall: Mambo

Best bar/nightclub:
Alta Peruvian Bar

Best hotel: Alta Lodge

Best restaurant: Shallow Shaft

carry skiers to the lodges built into the canyon's
northern sides. This unorthodox means of transportation perfectly reflects Alta's charming personality—so
simple, yet so efficient.

That's all there is to Alta: no mountain malls, no
condo villages, no true epicenter, and little in the
way of nightlife. It's just a resort with lots of character and lots of characters who like things more or less
the way they have been for more than a half century.

HOW TO GET THERE

Shuttle Service

Several shuttle vans make the run between the Salt
Lake City Airport and Alta/Snowbird. **Canyon
Transport** (tel. 801/255–1841 or 800/255–1841)
is the largest service, with regularly scheduled runs
on the hour between Alta, the airport, and the SLC
downtown area. The charge is $17 per person, one-
way, from the airport or downtown SLC. **Lewis
Brothers Stages** (tel. 801/649–2256 or 800/826–
5844) has daily scheduled motor-coach service to
Alta and all other SLC ski areas. The fare is $17
round-trip from downtown hotels.

By Car

From the airport in Salt Lake City follow I–80 east to
I–215 south (also known as the Belt Route) to Route
210, and follow signs to Little Cottonwood Canyon.
From the SLC downtown area take I–15 south to
I–215 to Route 210, then follow signs to Little Cottonwood Canyon. The drive from the airport or city
center is about 25 miles, or 45 minutes, depending
on weather conditions. Little Cottonwood Canyon is
a high avalanche area, and driving is often tricky—or
prohibited—due to a fall or the threat of one. Call
801/964–6000 for road conditions.

By Bus

The Utah Transit Authority (UTA, tel. 801/287–
4636) serves Little Cottonwood Canyon from downtown SLC, making stops in the city center and at
various locations throughout the valley. Fares are
$4.50 one-way from downtown to Canyon area and
$1.75 one-way for the Alta/Snowbird shuttle. *See
also* Snowbird, *below*.

GETTING AROUND

A car is definitely not necessary at Alta. The entire length of the resort community can be walked in 10 minutes, and efficient UTA shuttle-bus service (tel. 801/287–4636) runs between Alta and Snowbird (1 mile away), with stops at each lodge in both resorts. You'll pay $1 per ride, and buses run daily, every 15 minutes 9–5. **Canyon Transportation** (tel. 800/255–1841) runs a shuttle daily 5 AM–11 PM between Alta and Snowbird, with stops at the lodges. Dial 7433 from any lodge in Snowbird or Alta for a pickup; the fare is $2 for a one-way ride. **Yellow Cab** (tel. 801/521–2100) is a third alternative if you want to travel outside the resort area.

THE SKIING

Like the resort itself, the skiing at Alta is quirky. Mt. Baldy is a broad, sloping giant that ripples and unfolds across Alta's front facade, providing a series of crests and valleys that have to be explored rather than just skied. At the western end of the Alta ridge the mountain reaches its maximum height of 11,068 feet, its wide face concealing steep pitches, chutes, and gullies that harbor challenging, mostly ungroomed runs.

The Alta trail map lists only 39 runs, but hundreds of routes lead down the mountain. You'll have to work to find them by taking the many traverses and cat tracks that link the sectors until you find your favorite way down. The owners of the resort haven't homogenized the base area with neatly organized condo satellites, nor have they cannibalized the mountain with wide boulevards or an indulgent, highfalutin lift system. Only eight lifts serve the 2,200 acres of skiable terrain, and like the features of the mountain itself, they effectively separate the green and blue terrain from the black.

The Albion, Sunnyside, and Cecret lifts serve the novice and easier intermediate trails, and primarily intermediates and experts ride the other five chairs. The system works well, providing all levels with distinct territory to explore, and limited parking guarantees the area will not be overrun. Alta caters to skiers without pampering them.

Although its vertical drop is 1,000 feet less than the 3,100 feet of neighboring Snowbird, Alta's terrain is still challenging. The front face of Peruvian Ridge is uncompromisingly steep, with chutes, gullies, and heavily wooded areas; the western face yields a series of wide, steep bowls filled with the famous Utah powder; and the northern flank has exceptional tree skiing. To get the best of Alta, you must be willing to explore off the beaten track and take some remarkably long but ultimately satisfying traverses.

Of course, one of the primary ingredients in Alta's success is the snow. Like other Utah resorts, Alta receives an average of 500 inches a year. For the most part, it's the dry, desert-brushed powder that the state is justifiably famous for, and the resort—displaying the same policy of restraint that it applies to development—doesn't let its grooming machines run amok. Although there are plenty of groomed trails, there are lots of untouched runs for die-hard powder skiers. Alta does not permit snowboarding on any trails, and there are no current plans to allow it.

Novices

Beginners should stick to the east side (to the left looking up) of the mountain, known as the Albion Basin, where the Sunnyside, Albion, and Cecret lifts are located. Practice linking your turns on Crooked Mile or Sunnyside, two deliciously long runs that wind down the meadowy terrain on Peruvian Ridge's lower flanks. On a snowy day when the trail is groomed, you'll be able to pick up speed and practice big, swooping giant slalom turns here. When you want a change of scenery, take another ride up the Sunnyside or Albion lifts, but stay to your left to get to the Cecret chairlift. Eventually Sweet and Easy connects to Sunnyside for another long cruise down to the base area.

Once you've gained some confidence on those long green runs, ride Sunnyside or Albion to the Supreme lift via Cecret lift. At the top of the chair take Big Dipper, a moderate blue run that will give you a taste of the trees to whet your appetite for the glade skiing that will come with experience. Don't worry, though, the trees aren't so tight that you need panic; they're just tight enough to challenge you. Next try Rock and Roll, another long, winding blue run with enough moderately steep pitches to make you work your edges, plus some broad sweeping stretches around islands of trees. These runs are mostly groomed, although you can find some loose powder off to the sides, especially if you skirt the trees. These marvelous intermediate blue trails are some of

the most mellow cruisers in Utah: They're tame enough not to terrify but spicy enough to put some thrill into your skiing.

Intermediates

First thing in the morning ride the renovated Wildcat lift to the top and follow the narrow cat track to the left to the top of Aggie's Alley, a long, wide, groomed leg warmer with pitches and rolls and enough steepness to make things interesting. Run it top-to-bottom a couple of times before heading over to the base of the Germania lift, which gives you access to the higher elevations of the West Rustler face. Here there are two excellent blue runs, giving you the choice of solid steeps with some bumps (Mambo) or a long, wide bowl area (Ballroom)—both connect to Main Street, a long, usually groomed run back to the base of the Germania lift. From the top take the traverse over the Germania Pass to Devil's Elbow, a beautifully long run that starts out steep in the trees, mellows slightly as it widens into meadows, goes through a series of rolls, then becomes a full-bore cruiser all the way to the bottom of the Sugarloaf and Cecret lifts. From the top of the Cecret lift, ski down to the Supreme lift, where you'll find some of the best tree skiing on the mountain. Get yourself in the mood to dance with the pines by taking either Challenger or Big Dipper, both of which have good glade sections and wide-open terrain. These two runs connect with the longer, well-groomed Rock and Roll, which takes you back to the bottom of the Supreme lift. At this point you can pick up the pace. The area served by the Supreme lift is a vast series of treed bowls with few marked trails but many routes down. Although this area, called Piney Glade and White Squaw, is considered black diamond, an intrepid intermediate can selectively pick one's way through the trees, gullies, bowls, and chutes for an adventure as varied as it is gratifying.

Experts

This mountain begs to be explored beyond the 18 trails designated black diamond, because for every marked trail there are dozens of unmarked alternatives. If you're really keen to discover Alta's wild side, hook up with a local who's been up and down the mountain a zillion times and knows where to find the hidden treasures. (The bar at the Alta Peruvian Lodge is a good place to shop for local knowledge.) For your introduction to the mountain, however, ride the Wildcat lift to the top of the front face and take Warmup, a top-to-bottom, mostly groomed screamer that starts wide just above the tree line then narrows as it follows the fall line almost immediately under the Wildcat lift. From the top again take Peruvian Ridge, another ultrasteep run that skirts the eastern ridge then cuts into the middle, where you have a choice of the steeper Rock Gulley, the even steeper Wildcat Face, or the untamed wilderness of the Wildcat area.

Next take the Germania lift to Alf's High Rustler for a fast vertical run that starts off a cliff and shoots through some trees onto a wide hump slope. When you've had enough of the front face, take the Germania lift again to explore the unmarked bowl and backcountry skiing designated as

Glory Hole, Yellow Trail, East Greeley, and Greeley Bowl. This is where you'll find the deepest, purest snow, and it's where you can experience free-form, break-the-rules skiing at its best. It's the best way to ski Alta: Where the snow lies untouched, jump in with both feet. Follow your instincts or those of skiers who look like they know where to go, but don't assume you've found the ultimate run, because eventually you'll discover one that's just a little sweeter.

WHERE TO STAY

Because there are only five lodges in the base area, accommodations at Alta are straightforward. All properties connect with a rope tow that moves skiers across the resort, so all accommodations are considered ski-in/ski-out. All operate on the Modified American Plan (MAP), so your daily or weekly rate includes meals. This plan is stipulated by the town because constant avalanche threats often force guests to remain inside for extended periods. Some properties don't take credit cards, but they do accept personal checks. An alternative to Alta's on-mountain lodges is nearby Snowbird (*see* Snowbird, *below*), just a mile down Little Cottonwood Canyon, or Salt Lake City, about a 45-minute drive away. If you're more interested in staying at a resort town, Park City (*see* *below*), about one hour from Alta, is another possibility.

Expensive

Alta Lodge

This Swiss-style log building has been expanded several times since it was first built as a lodge in 1939. From the roadside entrance you descend three flights of stairs (the entrance is a little below the level of the road because the lodge is built into the side of a hill) to the main lobby, with its warm, rustic decor, where you'll get a truer sense of the coziness the lodge offers. Old-fashioned comfortable chairs, books, magazines, and parlor games are scattered about the common areas, and guests mingle as though at a family reunion. Rooms have different sizes and configurations, but some corner rooms have a private balcony and a fireplace. None of the Alta Lodge rooms is large, but all are comfortable and well furnished. *Little Cottonwood Canyon Rd., Alta 84092, tel. 801/742–3500 or 800/707–2582, fax 801/742–3504. 54 rooms, 48 with bath, 2 dorms. Facilities: TV room, lounge, 2 indoor hot tubs, 2 saunas, game room. No credit cards. $96–$301 per person.*

Alta Peruvian Lodge

You'll first enter the plant-filled lobby, where a large stone fireplace dominates a room filled with handcrafted blond-wood furniture, books, and hotel guests relaxing after an intense day on the slopes. A picture window overlooks the outdoor swimming pool and hot tub, with the mountain in the background. This is the quintessential unpretentious classic ski lodge where après ski means hot chocolate, apple cider, and brownies set out on tables around the room. The family-style dining room and the bar upstairs are equally cozy, but the rooms can be tiny, and more than half have shared bathrooms down the hall. Room styles vary from dorms to two-bedroom suites. The dorms have 24 bunks for men and four for women. At times the Peruvian

seems a bit disheveled, as though there had been a big pajama party here the night before, but this is part of its simplicity and charm. *Little Cottonwood Canyon Rd., Box 8017, Alta 84092, tel. 801/742–3000 or 800/453–8488, fax 801/742–3007. 97 rooms, 3 dorms. Facilities: heated outdoor pool, outdoor hot tub, sauna, bar, laundry, ski shop, gift shop, game room. $127–$219 per person, including lift ticket and 3 meals. AE, D, MC, V.*

Goldminer's Daughter

Although its quarry-rock walls and large atrium front give it a slightly grand appearance, Goldminer's is more of a motel than the other properties in the canyon. The narrow hallways in rough-cut wood and the low lighting make this place feel as though it's underground. Rooms are either large or small, the former equipped with a king-size or two double beds and a full bathroom, the latter with one double bed and a shower (no bath). All have vintage '60s decor and an orange, brown, and green color scheme. Guest quarters are clean and comfortable, albeit cheerless. There are also four suites, one of which sleeps six, and one relatively inexpensive dorm with four twin beds. *Little Cottonwood Canyon, Box 8055, Alta 84092, tel. 801/742–2300 or 800/453–4573. 81 rooms, 4 suites, 1 dorm. Facilities: bar-lounge, 2 saunas, exercise room, indoor hot tub, laundry, game room, ski shop. $99–$163 per person. MC, V.*

Rustler Lodge

The fanciest lodge in Alta most resembles a traditional full-service hotel. The interior is decidedly upscale, with dark wood paneling, burgundy chairs and couches, handsome wooden backgammon tables, and a grand piano dominating a small sitting room off the main lobby. Rooms range in size and configuration from dorms to deluxe suites, the latter the largest and most posh, with a king-size bed and two pullout sofas. Sitting areas have comfortable armchairs, a coffee table, a wet bar, and a balcony. Most units have a private bathroom, but several share facilities. Guest quarters are handsomely decorated with dark woods, white brick walls, and richly colorful coverings and drapes. *Little Cottonwood Canyon, Box 8030, Alta 84092, tel. 801/742–2200 or 800/451–5223, fax 801/742–3832. 56 rooms, 49 with bath, 1 dorm. Facilities: restaurant, bar-lounge, outdoor pool, indoor hot tub, 2 saunas, ski shop, laundry facilities, game room. No credit cards. $95–$235 per person ($85 dorm).*

Moderate

Snowpine Lodge

Built in 1938 as a hostel for area workers, this is the oldest lodge in Little Cottonwood Canyon, the smallest, and possibly the friendliest. The original hand-carved granite walls and wide-plank wooden floors have been exposed, giving Snowpine the feel of a cozy cottage. There are just 16 rooms and two dorms (the women's sleeps four, the men's sleeps 12). None of the rooms is large, but all are spotless and tastefully appointed with coordinated rugs and bedcovers. *Little Cottonwood Canyon, Box 8062, Alta 84092, tel. 801/742–2000. 16 rooms, 8 with bath, 2 dorms. Facilities: outdoor hot tub, sauna. No credit cards.*

$99–$163 per person, including breakfast and dinner.

WHERE TO EAT

All of Alta's lodges operate on the Modified American Plan, and only one independent restaurant supplements the dining rooms in the lodges and the on-mountain eateries. Nearby Snowbird (1 mile away; *see* Snowbird, *below*) and Salt Lake City (about 25 miles away) offer countless alternatives. Space can be a problem at some lodge dining rooms—especially in high season—but all accommodate outside guests as space permits. Call for reservations. Credit cards may not be accepted in all places.

On the Mountain

Alpenglow

A distinct counterpoint to Chic's Place (*see below*), this on-mountain eatery serves the requisite stick-to-the-ribs, belly-warming skier's lunches: good stews and chili, hearty sandwiches, and grilled burgers. The large stucco building lacks charm, but the huge windows with great views down the mountain offer some compensation. *Bottom of Cecret and Sugarloaf lifts (access on Sunnyside or Sweet and Easy), tel. 801/742–2424. MC, V.*

Chic's Place

It's funny to see an ultrachic restaurant at a ski resort, much less a resort as laid-back as Alta. Toasty sheepskin booties are stacked neatly by the door so you can slip into them on the way to your linen-, crystal-, and silverware-dressed table. A fireside sitting area, warm pink carpeting, and blond-wood-paneled walls enhance the serene ambience. You may want to start with the smoked Norwegian salmon and caviar or the broiled oysters. The Continental menu lists an array of pastas, filet mignon, and designer sandwiches, and there's always a catch of the day, Caesar salad, New York strip steak, and numerous chef's specials. If you're a sweets fanatic, top off your meal with chocolate-avalanche cake, homemade custard flan, or apple strudel with hot brandy sauce. *Bottom of Germania lift (access via Aggies from Top of Wildcat or Collins lift, or Mambo, Main Street, and Ballroom from top of Germania lift), tel. 801/742–3037. AE, MC, V.*

Moderate

Alta Lodge Dining Room
When space permits, you can get a reservation at this simple, wood-paneled room decorated with Middle Eastern weavings and paintings. Each table has fresh flowers, candles, and sweet floral-print napkins. Seating is family style. The menu changes daily and usually offers a choice of three entrées (perhaps steak or grilled tuna smothered in a delicious salsa), and there's always a choice of soup or salad, homemade bread, and a dessert, such as apple pie with homemade ice cream. *Alta Lodge, tel. 801/742–3500. Reservations essential. No credit cards.*

Rustler Lodge Dining Room
This baroque dining spot surrounds you with dark wood and deep-colored accents and is warmed by a huge round fireplace. The menu changes daily, and the emphasis is on regional American fare: well-prepared steaks and wild game. The pepper steak is especially good, as is the rack of lamb

with gratin potatoes or the basil fettuccine with fresh seafood. *Rustler Lodge, tel. 801/742–2200. Reservations essential. AE, MC, V.*

Shallow Shaft
This is the only non-lodge-affiliated restaurant in Alta, and it's definitely worth a visit, if only to get you out of whatever lodge you've been eating and sleeping in for a week. The small interior is cozy and decorated in funky Southwestern style with a sandy color scheme and walls adorned with 19th-century mining tools found on the mountain. The menu is also Southwestern, with adventurous specials including lamb chops grilled and served in ancho-chili sauce and pork medallions braised in apple cider. The restaurant makes its own ice cream daily. *Alta Rd., tel. 801/742–2177. Reservations essential on weekends. AE, D, MC, V.*

Inexpensive

Goldminer's Daughter Cafeteria
This cafeteria is open only during the daytime—primarily for the skiing crowd. The offerings are decidedly American, with burgers, soups, and chili leading the way. This is a casual spot with a young crowd. *Goldminer's Daughter Cafeteria, Level 2, tel. 801/ 742–2300. No credit cards.*

Best Bets for Breakfast

Alta Lodge or Rustler Lodge
Both serve an ample breakfast buffet with made-to-order dishes such as omelets, eggs any style, and pancakes, as well as a selection of cold cereals and breads. *Alta Lodge, tel. 801/742–3500; Rustler Lodge, tel. 801/742–2200. No credit cards.*

NIGHTLIFE AND ENTERTAINMENT

Nightlife at Alta is limited. Four of the five lodges have a bar or lounge, all open to outside guests who have a club card, per Utah's oddball liquor regulations. This pseudomembership allows you to drink unfettered and in some cases is transferable. Credit cards are not accepted at hotel lounges.

Alta Peruvian Bar

Mostly a locals' hangout, this is a good place to head if you want to pick up tips on powder stashes or other insider information. Walls adorned with hunting trophies and a large fireplace surrounded by well-worn couches suit the casual atmosphere. *Tel. 801/742–3000.*

Goldminer's Daughter Lounge

The liveliest of Alta's beer bars, this spot attracts a young crowd. The large, rough-hewn sports bar has lots of wood and lots of hustle (at least on an Alta scale). There's a Tex-Mex menu, recorded music, games, and a large-screen TV. *Tel. 801/742–2300.*

Rustler Club

You'll feel like you're in a British pub at the Rustler, with its long, highly polished oak bar, lounge chairs, large fireplace, and Tudor-style stucco-and-wood decor. It's mostly mellow, a place where people stop to sip a nightcap around the fire or play a game of darts. *Tel. 801/742–2200.*

Sitzmark Club

You'll find this small, dark bar upstairs at the Alta Lodge. It has a rustic, woodsy feeling, and the walls are decorated with period photographs from the early days of the resort. The small bar is in one corner, and the fireplace is the focus around which friends curl up to chat. *Tel. 801/742–3500.*

DEER VALLEY SKI RESORT

**DEER VALLEY
SKI RESORT**

Box 1525
Park City, UT 84060
Tel. 801/649-1000 or
800/424-3337
Fax 801/645-6939

STATISTICALLY SPEAKING

Base elevation: 7,200 feet

Summit elevation: 9,400 feet

Vertical drop: 2,200 feet

Skiable terrain: 1,100 acres

Number of trails: 67

Longest run: 3 miles

Lifts and capacity: 3 quads,
8 triples, 2 doubles; 22,800
skiers per hour

Daily lift ticket: $52

Average annual snowfall:
300 inches

Number of skiing days
1995-96: 128

Snowmaking: 325 acres, 29%

Terrain mix: N 15%, I 50%,
E 35%

Snowboarding: no

Deer Valley lies on the other side of the ridge from the Park City ski area and is just 1 mile from historic Main Street in the bustling former mining town of Park City. The two resorts, however, could not be more different. Park City is a proletarian playground for the masses; Deer Valley is a patrician preserve for the few. Park City hums with a youthful vibrancy, Deer Valley is soothingly serene. They are not entirely incompatible, however, this odd couple of Utah skiing. You can stay in Park City and ski at Deer Valley, or you can reside in the upscale pamper palaces of the latter and still ski the more expansive and varied terrain of the former. A free, efficient, and regularly scheduled shuttle service lets you easily explore both worlds.

This juxtaposition of two decidedly different resort experiences is somewhat akin to the dual personalities of Vail and its upscale neighbor Beaver Creek. In fact, of any resort in the United States—or indeed North America—Beaver Creek comes closest to matching Deer Valley's intimacy, service, and style. That's the way Edgar Stern, the multimillionaire entrepreneur and founder of Deer Valley, wanted it when he carved America's most civilized resort out of 2,000 acres of Wasatch wilderness. Unlike most western resorts, which are built on land leased from the U.S. Forest Service, Deer Valley is actually owned by Stern and his partner, Roger Penske of Indy 500 fame. Stern envisioned this as a blue-chip enclave for blue bloods and Fortune 500 captains, a resort built and run like a luxury hotel with as much attention lavished on the atmosphere, comfort, food, and service as on the skiing. His success is evident everywhere, from the cheerful attendants in dark green uniforms to the discreet architectural development of chalets and condominiums amid the aspens and firs to the ultimate luxury of them all—uncrowded and flawlessly groomed slopes, kept that way by the strict limit placed on the number of skiers and by the most meticulous grooming program found anywhere. Every night one-third to one-half of the mountain is groomed, and the rest is left in its natural state to challenge even the best of skiers.

Deer Valley has another unique feature. Because it is all built on private land, the lavish, upscale condominiums and private residences are up on the moun-

Area code: 801

Children's services: day care, tel. 801/649–1000, ext. 6612; instruction, tel. 801/645–6648

Snow phone: tel. 801/649–2000

Police: tel. 801/645–5050

Medical center: Park City Care, tel. 801/649–7640

Resort-office services: tel. 801/534–1779 or 800/754–8824

Road conditions: tel. 800/492–2400

Towing: tel. 801/645–7775

FIVE-STAR FAVORITES
Best run for vertical: Ruins of Pompeii

Best run overall: Birdseye

Best bar/nightclub: Troll Hallen Lounge

Best hotel: Stein Eriksen Lodge

Best restaurant: Glitretind

tain, not in the valley below; vacation retreats dot the knolls and valleys, the ridges, and the forested slopes of Bald Eagle Mountain.

The resort itself encompasses three mountains and two base areas. The lower Snow Park Lodge base area is what at most resorts would be called the day lodge, but it is, in fact, a magnificent cedar-and-sandstone complex that houses several restaurants, upscale boutiques, and shops. The main Deer Valley lodging check-in center is conveniently nearby on the approach to Snow Park Lodge. A mile up Bald Eagle Mountain, linked by road and two chairlifts, is the decadently isolated Silver Lake Village, a self-contained mountain community consisting of a small shopping concourse and a nest of upscale accommodations such as the Stein Eriksen Lodge, a grand hotel created by the Norwegian former Olympic slalom champion, and the Goldener Hirsch, a smaller but no less elegant replica of the original in Salzburg, Austria. Silver Lake provides access to Deer Valley's two other peaks—9,400-foot Bald Mountain and 9,100-foot Flagstaff Mountain.

Accommodations are clustered in and around Snowpark and Silver Lake Village, most within a short distance of the lifts, and a shuttle service links the two areas around the clock. Luxury and attention to detail are the name of the game throughout the resort.

HOW TO GET THERE

Shuttle Services
The following companies provide regularly scheduled and prebooked shuttle service between the Salt Lake City airport and Deer Valley: **Canyon Transport** (tel. 801/255–1841 or 800/255–1841), **Classic Limousine & Airport Shuttle** (tel. 800/233–8201), **Lewis Brothers Stages** (tel. 801/649–2256 or 800/826–5844). All charge $17 per person each way. A free, regularly scheduled bus service runs between Deer Valley and nearby Park City, with about 20 stops along the 1-mile route.

By Car
Deer Valley is 25 miles east of downtown Salt Lake City and 3 miles east of downtown Park City. From Salt Lake City take I–80 east to the Park City exit,

Route 224, where it turns into Park Avenue. Turn left at Deer Valley Drive and continue 1 mile to the Deer Valley lodging center. It's about a 40-minute drive. For car-rental information, *see* Getting to Utah Resorts, *above.*

GETTING AROUND

A car is not necessary or particularly practical at Deer Valley. The two village areas and most of the individual accommodations are served by the Deer Valley Shuttle service. A shuttle-on-demand service is also available through the concierge or bell desk at most hotels. To visit nearby Park City, your best bet is to take the scheduled Park City shuttle bus service, especially in light of the lack of parking in Park City. The Park City shuttle bus also serves the Deer Valley resort. **Park City Transportation** (tel. 801/649–8567) also runs a taxi service around Deer Valley and between Deer Valley and Park City.

THE SKIING

The skiing at Deer Valley takes place on three distinct mountains—Bald Eagle Mountain, which has primarily novice and intermediate runs; Flagstaff Mountain, which is almost exclusively intermediate except for the double-diamond steeps of the Ontario Bowl; and Bald Mountain, which is split evenly between intermediate and expert terrain, including the Mayflower and Perseverance bowls. Two hundred more acres have been gladed on Bald and Flagstaff mountains in order to provide additional tree skiing.

Ordinarily you might think it difficult to move around in a three-peak resort, but the lift layout at Deer Val-

ley is as well planned as all other aspects of the resort. From the Snow Park lodge at the base of Bald Eagle Mountain, two lifts—the high-speed, detachable quad Carpenter and the Clipper—take you up to the Silver Lake Village. From there you can ski Bald Eagle Mountain or fan out and ride the Red Cloud and Northside lifts up Flagstaff Mountain or take the Sterling or the Wasatch (another new Garaventa CTEC high-speed detachable quad) lifts up to the summit of Bald Mountain. There are no flats, or endless traverses, no intersections cluttered with skiers of different abilities, and almost always no congestion on the lifts.

Most of Deer Valley's runs are north or northeast facing, and most follow the fall line with remarkable precision, running among and around the trees, which for the most part have been left intact. If you go to Deer Valley looking for extreme skiing or gulp-and-go verticals, you'll likely be disappointed; if you enjoy well-groomed runs with consistent pitch, wide-open bowl cruising, or dipsy-doodling your way through glades, you'll love it. It's a resort that makes novices feel like intermediates, intermediates feel like experts, and experts—well, if you're that much of an expert, you're probably better off at nearby Park City. But before you experts dismiss Deer Valley, check out the special experts-only trail map that not only highlights the named black diamond trails but also suggests off-piste routes down the mountains. At this time snowboarding is not permitted at Deer Valley. Future plans to include it are uncertain; an ongoing survey of guests will help decide the issue.

Novices

Your best place to start is Bald Eagle Mountain. From the Snow Park Lodge base area the Carpenter Express lift will take you to the top of Bald Eagle Mountain and Success, a wide, precisely groomed run that follows the fall line back to Carpenter Express. If this run seems too challenging, then stay on Wide West, a protected pure beginners' area that is served by the Burns and Snowflake chairlifts.

Once you're warmed up, head back up Success and experiment with some of the short, slightly steeper cutoffs that link with it. Little Bell, to the right just down from the top of Success, is still green but involves some gentle rolls; Little Kate, to your right near the bottom, gives you a taste of some trees; and if you want to try a cutoff that's blue just to see if you can handle the pitch, cut right onto White Owl about halfway down.

When you're ready to move on, ride Clipper to Silver Lake Village, turn left, and take McHenry. The trail map designates it as a blue run, but it is actually as mellow as the green runs you have skied to this point. At the bottom of McHenry, ride the Wasatch lift and get off to your right. Ski down Sunset to Sunset West, making sure you stay to your left so that you eventually pick up Ontario. This whole section is a gently rolling run that alternately widens and narrows, giving you a chance to work on your turns and let your skis run back down to the base of the Red Cloud lift.

By now you should be ready to try some blue runs. Take the Homestake lift to the top of Success, then stay to your left and catch either Last Chance or Dew Drop, a pair of wide, winding blue runs that have some steepness but also enough rolls and dips so that you can control your speed. Both eventually end up back on Success, where you can take a breather.

Intermediates

Bald Mountain and Flagstaff Mountain are your best choices. If you are coming from the Snow Park Lodge area, take the Carpenter Express high-speed detachable quad, a recently added lift, to Silver Lake Village, then head over to the Sterling lift, which goes to the summit of Bald Mountain. Start with a run on Birdseye, a long, winding cruiser that is usually groomed and perfect for high-speed giant slalom turns and that ends up back at the bottom of the Sterling chair. Next up should be Nabob, a slightly narrower and somewhat steeper run that combines a series of rolls and pure fall-line pitch.

This will take you back to the bottom of the Wasatch chair. From the top of Wasatch head down Keno, a straight-shot blast that lets you rack up lots of high-speed vertical without worrying about bumps. Ride Wasatch up again and head down Tycoon, which starts out steep and extrawide, narrows somewhat, then widens out for a long, smooth cruise down to the bottom of the Sultan lift.

From the top of the Sultan, turn left and head over to the Perseverance Bowl. This is marked as a black diamond, but if your legs are warm and your confidence buoyed, you should be able to handle it. The upper part is hardly ever groomed, so it does get bumpy, but because the skier traffic is always light at Deer Valley, the moguls remain smooth and well rounded—

perfect for working on your bump technique. If you want to avoid the worst of them, keep to the far right on Perseverance and follow its arcing course around the shoulder of the mountain until it cuts back into the trees. It narrows somewhat as it approaches an intersection. To the right is Stein's Way, a steep pitch down to the bottom of the Mayflower chair (which serves mostly black and double-black runs); if you stay to the left, you'll end up back at the bottom of the Sultan chair. Stein's is an especially good area to ski on Deer Valley's frequent powder days.

On Flagstaff Mountain there's a mixture of ungroomed bump runs (turn left off the Northside lift) and smoother, groomed cruisers (turn right off the lift), plus a number of glade runs.

Experts

Experts at Deer Valley have their own trail map, partly because the resort is trying to overcome its reputation for lacking challenging terrain and partly because there are some exquisite nuggets of advanced off-piste terrain that should be explored. Make sure you get a copy of the map—and use it.

Bald Mountain is where the majority of marked black and double-black runs are found. In fact, there are only two black runs on Bald Eagle Mountain—Know You Don't and Lucky Bill—which are hard-core, mogul-mashing ways back down to the Snow Park lodge. Flagstaff Mountain has only one marked black run, Square Deal, a short, wicked staircase of big bumps. But Flagstaff does give you access to the supersteep double-black glade skiing of the Ontario Bowl or

the more heavily timbered sections known as DT's Trees and the Gumby Glade. Both these areas are free-form expanses of open faces, gullies, and tree islands—definitely the place to ski during or after a storm, when the snow is deep, ungroomed, and undisturbed.

By now you'll be itching to tackle the black runs of Bald Mountain. Off the Sultain chair, Ruins of Pompeii offers a steep vertical drop that will grab your attention and help you understand why Deer Valley will host the 2002 Olympic slalom, mogul, and aerial events. For big-bump hounds, your two best bets are Rattler, under the Wasatch chair, or Narrow Gauge, under the Mayflower chair, where the bumps grow largest. The Mayflower Chutes—accessed through gates off the Mayflower Bowl—are a series of supersteep, narrow, rock-lined chutes that offer the kind of gulp-and-go challenge that Deer Valley is seldom given credit for. In fact, challenge abounds on the entire Mayflower Bowl: too steep to groom, the area has a good mix of steep, set-your-edges cruisers, glades, and bumps.

Another heads-up area is the Free Thinker Glade—reached from Stein's Way—or the Black Forest—reached from the top of Perseverance Bowl—where you'll find some of the heaviest and tightest timber on the mountain. If you yearn for excitement beyond warp-speed cruising on empty, pool-table-smooth fall-line crank-and-go runs, the key at Deer Valley is to explore a little. Scour the glades for untouched snow, play slalom in the heavy timbers, shoot the chutes—especially after a big dump—and use the fast and empty chairs to chalk up vertical.

WHERE TO STAY

Most of the lodging at Deer Valley is run by property management firms; it consists primarily of deluxe condominiums and luxury hotel suites in and around the two village areas of Snow Park and Silver Lake. Ultra-expensive and expensive are really the only two categories. Nearby Park City is the best bet if you're looking for more moderate prices or a more varied selection of small hotels, inns, and B&Bs. The following are some of the most impressive accommodations at Deer Valley; all rooms have concierge and daily maid service unless otherwise noted. If the facility is ski-in/ski-out, it is noted; all others are served by the Deer Valley shuttle service.

Most accommodations at the resort, as well as much of the less expensive lodging throughout Park City and select lodging in Salt Lake City, can be booked through Deer Valley Lodging (tel. 801/649–4040 or 800/453–3833).

Expensive

Daystar

The three-bedroom town house units of Daystar are as elegant and sumptuous as they are spacious, with 2,000 square feet spread over three floors. The decor includes high beamed ceilings, brass and polished wood trim, tiled entranceways, wood plank floors, handmade pine and bent twig furniture, dark, richly colored fabrics, and large atrium-style windows. All bedrooms have their own bathrooms, and the kitchens are, as you might expect, full size and fully equipped. It's a third of a mile from the Snowpark base area. *Deer Valley Lodging, Box 3000, Park City 84060, tel. 801/ 649–4040 or 800/453–3833, fax 801/ 645–8419. 18 units. AE, D, MC, V. $425–$695.*

Fawngrove

Divided among six stone-and-clapboard structures with deep slanting roof lines, these units run smaller than most other Deer Valley condos, but they are just as luxurious in decor and furnishings. The two- to four-bedroom units have stone and beam work, large fireplaces, deep plush couches and chairs in subtle pastels and floral earth tones, large windows, and tiled entrance foyers; some even have private spa facilities. All bedrooms have private bathrooms. The fully equipped kitchen is a marvel of space-compacting efficiency; and the dining area, though small by Deer Valley standards, is certainly comfortable enough for six diners. In the same league design-, style-, and pricewise are the Courchevel, Queen Esther, and Stonebridge condo clusters. All these, like Fawngrove, are within a half mile of the Snowpark base lodge. *Deer Valley Lodging, Box 3000, Park City 84060, tel. 801/649–4040 or 800/ 453–3833, fax 801/645–8419. 60 units. AE, D, MC, V. $270–$890.*

Goldener Hirsch

This is a full-service hotel in a small, Austrian-style chalet. It exudes a marvelous Old World atmosphere that envelops you the moment you enter through the massive wrought-iron and glass doors and set foot on the fieldstone floor of the stucco-walled lobby. Rooms here run the gamut from regular-size hotel rooms to a large penthouse suite with separate living room and bedroom. Regardless of size, all rooms have clean white lines, soft pastel color schemes accented with printed wall coverings, handmade down comforters, and individual Austrian furnishings that range from hand-painted four-poster beds to hand-carved armoires and chests. This splendid hotel re-creates the quiet elegance of its namesake in Salzburg, Austria—no small feat in the Utah Rockies. It stands about 300 yards from the lifts at Silver Lake Village. *7570 Royal St. E, Box 859, Deer Valley, Park City 84060, tel. 801/649–7770 or 800/252–3373, fax 801/649–7901. 19 rooms with bath, 1 suite. Facilities: restaurant, lounge, indoor and outdoor hot tubs, sauna, exercise room. AE, MC, V. 195–$750, including Continental breakfast.*

Mont Cervin

These condos are split between two handsome fieldstone and gray clapboard buildings in the Silver Lake Village area, just steps from the lifts. The classic and sturdy construction continues inside, with solid wood doors, solid oak and beech cabinetry, giant stone fireplaces, and contemporary furnishings. Opulence is the keynote throughout: Each bedroom has its own bath; the monster master suites have a large bathroom with a Jacuzzi and access to the balcony hot tub. *Deer Valley Lodging, Box 3000, Park City 84060, tel. 801/649–4040 or 800/453–3833, fax 801/645–8419. 20 units. AE, D, MC, V. $425–$1,365.*

Pinnacle

If you're into deluxe to the max, choose the Pinnacle town houses. Set into the hillside about a half mile from the Snowpark Village base lodge, these three- and four-bedroom town houses are among the largest at the resort. With their striking blond wood and black-roofed exteriors, these units contrast sharply with the more subtle style of surrounding buildings. Inside each unit the spacious living area rises three floors to an arched ceiling that towers over the massive central copper-faced fireplace, trimmed with marble. The overall decor is rich with colorful ceramic tiles, handmade wooden furniture, antiques, wall tapestries, and Native American art. In every bedroom you'll find handmade quilts and an en suite bathroom with a walk-in shower and tub. *Deer Valley Lodging, Box 3000, Park City 84060, tel. 801/649–4040 or 800/453–3833, fax 801/645–8419. 84 units. AE, D, MC, V. $575–$1,125.*

Powder Run

The Powder Run condos occupy three towering fieldstone and amber wood buildings 150 yards from Snowpark Lodge. The units, with either two or three bedrooms, have textured and hand-painted walls, floor-to-ceiling windows, plush couches and chairs, and myriad objets d'art. You get comfortable space and lots of luxury: a bathroom with a whirlpool tub connected to every bedroom, a huge stone fireplace in the immense living area, and a full-size kitchen equipped with every conceivable appliance. *Deer Valley Lodging, Box 3000, Park City 84060, tel. 801/649–4040 or 800/453–3833, fax 801/645–8419. 36 units. AE, D, MC, V. $465–$880.*

Stein Eriksen Lodge

Without a doubt this is the flagship property at Deer Valley. It combines grandeur with intimacy, service, and the convenience of a ski-in/ski-out location just 50 yards from the lifts. The lodge sits high on the hill at Silver Lake Village, its amber log-and-stone construction blending in perfectly with the surrounding pines and aspens. Inside, the hunter green and wine red carpeting and furniture, floral print fabrics, polished wood beams, paneled walls, and numerous floor-to-ceiling stone fireplaces create an atmosphere of rustic Norwegian elegance. All the guest rooms are lavishly decorated with imported fabrics, heavy brushed pine furnishings, hand-painted tiles, colorful down comforters, and accessories in brass, copper, and wood. *7700 Stein Way, Box 3177, Park City 84060, tel. 801/649–3700 or 800/ 453–1302, fax 801/649–5825. 81 rooms, 51 suites. Facilities: 2 restaurants, lounge, heated outdoor pool, hot tub, sauna, exercise room. AE, D, DC, MC, V. $400–$2,000.*

Sterlingwood

These three- and four-bedroom town houses have a choice ski-in/ski-out location up the mountain in the Silver Lake Village area. The living area on the main floor features a high wood-lined ceiling with soft-toned sandstone walls decked with vivid art and wall hangings, lots of polished blond wood trim, the requisite floor-to-ceiling fieldstone fireplace, a glossy tiled entrance foyer, and thick plush carpeting. The large master bedroom, sprawling over the third floor, comes with its own fireplace and a large bathroom with a steam shower and a

whirlpool tub. The remaining bedrooms are slightly smaller and simpler. Other amenities include a full-size kitchen, a dining area with seating for at least eight, a large outdoor deck with a hot tub, and a private garage for each unit. *Deer Valley Lodging, Box 3000, Park City 84060, tel. 801/649–4040 or 800/453–3833, fax 801/645–8419. 18 units. A, D, MC, V. $590–$1,365.*

WHERE TO EAT

The quality of food served in and around the resort is just what you'd expect from this opulent enclave. The dining is as important to the resort as its grooming. The resort's two day-lodge restaurants and other on-mountain locations and the remaining privately owned restaurants offer a uniformly excellent dining experience that lives up to its award-winning reputation for ski resort dining.

For the most part, dress is casually elegant (many men don jackets, but they are not required). Keep in mind also that Park City, just a mile away, is a more varied, lively, and less expensive alternative.

On the Mountain

Silver Lake Lodge Restaurant
This magnificent, almost baronial six-room (each with a fireplace) lodge is in the middle of Silver Lake Village. Built of logs and stone, it has the opulence of a fine hotel, with tile floors and brass fittings (even the faucets in the bathroom). The lunch buffet presents a legion of daily specials, thick hearty soups, main courses like New York strip steak, quiche, fluffy omelets, stew, carved roasts of beef,

turkey or pork, grilled salmon, and designer pizzas. The salad bar is a grazing ground of greens, vegetables, pastas, and fruits both common and exotic. It's open for breakfast and lunch. *Silver Lake Village, tel. 801/ 649–1000. AE, MC, V.*

Snow Park Lodge Restaurant
This dining room is identical in style and menu to the Silver Lake Lodge. *Snow Park Lodge, tel. 801/649–1000. AE, D, DC, MC, V.*

Expensive

Glitretind
The Glitretind is posh without being ostentatious, gracious without being overbearing, exemplary in service, and impeccable in decor, with softly colored textured walls, handsome wood trim, cranberry tablecloths, crystal glasses, hand-painted tableware, and fresh-cut flowers. It is, in a word, exquisite. The entrées include South Dakota buffalo tenderloin with root vegetable cakes and black truffle sauce; mustard-encrusted rack of Utah lamb with lentils and arugula strudel and mustard seed jus; and New Zealand red deer loin slices fanned with wild mushrooms and served with sweet potato cakes. *Stein Eriksen Lodge, Silver Lake Village, tel. 801/649–3700. AE, D, DC, MC, V.*

Goldener Hirsch Restaurant
The restaurant at the Goldener Hirsch is friendly and comfortable and unmistakably Austrian in style: The furniture was hand-carved in Austria, the waitstaff floats about in dirndls, and the tables are set with crisp white cloths. The menu consists of European standards such as Wiener schnitzel, as well as North American favorites such as rack of Utah lamb, served with spring vegetables; certified Angus beef; free-range chicken breast with sun-dried cherry stuffing; and a selection of wild game including New Zealand venison. *Goldener Hirsch, Silver Lake Village, tel. 801/ 649–7770. AE, MC, V.*

Olive Barrel Food Company
The Olive Barrel is a delightful spot with an Italian country-inn ambience of white stucco and brick walls decked with antiques and paintings, heavy wooden tables and chairs, wood-plank floors, a large brick wood-fired oven, and classical music in the background. The Italian soups and salads are excellent, and entrées include cherry- and aspen-wood-smoked salmon with pesto; brick-oven-grilled veal chops; and a marinated seafood platter that includes grilled octopus, squid, clams, and shrimp. *Silver Lake Village, tel. 801/647–7777. Reservations essential. AE, MC, V.*

Moderate

McHenry's
Casual in style (a rarity in swanky Deer Valley) but also chic, McHenry's bustles with an upbeat bistro atmosphere. It's a large restaurant with an open kitchen, lots of pine paneling, terra-cotta tile floors, and big overhead beams. The menu offers lighter fare including grilled turkey quesadilla, grilled chicken sandwich with eggplant, vegetarian burgers, or entrées such as chicken Santa Fe, a boneless breast in pepper, lime, and soy marinade; grilled salmon; or certified Angus beef steaks. *Silver Lake Lodge, tel. 801/645–6724. AE, D, DC, MC, V.*

Seafood Buffet

Plan to eat here at least once during your stay at Deer Valley. It's the talk of the mountain for its extensive selection of fresh seafood from both coasts (the choices vary nightly and seasonally) and its loose, casual atmosphere. You select your own hot and cold choices from the buffet table, which include oysters on the half shell, crab legs, and fresh Chilean sea bass, and then enjoy table service for beverages. *Snow Park Lodge, tel. 801/ 645–6632. Reservations essential. AE, D, DC, MC, V.*

Inexpensive

Stewpot

This is a good spot for some fast and inexpensive noshing on a variety of homemade stews and soups. They have two types of stew every day: the old-fashioned beef stew and another based on chicken, lamb, or pork. The menu also has all the predictables— burgers, salads, baked potatoes—plus a selection of home-baked breads. *1375 Deer Valley Plaza, tel. 801/645– 7839. AE, D, MC, V.*

Best Bets for Breakfast

Silver Lake Lodge or
Snow Park Lodge

Both serve a sumptuous buffet breakfast with custom-made items such as omelets, eggs Benedict, waffles with fresh fruit, and eggs any style. There's also an extraordinary fruit, yogurt, and natural cereal table, with grains and goodness from around the world. *Silver Lake Lodge, Snow Park Lodge, tel. 801/649–1000. AE, D, DC, MC, V.*

NIGHTLIFE AND ENTERTAINMENT

When the sun goes down and the lights go on, Deer Valley visitors and residents tend to turn inward toward the fireplace and the dining room table. There is no night scene to speak of at the resort, but if you want action, Park City is the place to head (*see* Park City, *below*). At the resort there are two places to gather for après-ski, and many guests choose to dine early and linger over liqueurs in the resort's sumptuous restaurants.

Après-Ski

Snow Park Lounge

The Lounge is a lively emporium with musical entertainment, radical ski videos, contests, and a young crowd; it stays open until about 6 PM. The handsome hewn-wood and stone bar area is warmed by a giant central fireplace. *Snow Park Lodge, tel. 801/649– 1000. AE, D, DC, MC, V.*

More Mellow

Troll Hallen Lounge

This is a marvelously serene scene, with live piano music setting the tone amid soft blond wood and polished brass decor. A fire crackles in the large stone fireplace; hors d'oeuvres and appetizers are served by a gracious and attentive staff. It's warm, slightly clubby, and a great people-watching spot. The lounge stays open for evening cocktails or a nightcap until midnight. *Stein Eriksen Lodge, Silver Lake Village, tel. 801/649–3700. AE, DC, MC, V.*

PARK CITY SKI RESORT

PARK CITY
SKI RESORT

Box 39
Park City, UT 84060
Tel. 801/649–8111
Fax 801/647–5374

STATISTICALLY SPEAKING

Base elevation: 6,900 feet

Summit elevation: 10,000 feet

Vertical drop: 3,100 feet

Skiable terrain: 2,200 acres

Number of trails: 89

Longest run: 3½ miles

Lifts and capacity: 1 gondola, 1 6-person chair, 2 quads, 6 triples, 4 doubles; 23,000 skiers per hour

Daily lift ticket: $49

Average annual snowfall: 350 inches

Number of skiing days 1995–96: 127

Snowmaking: 45%

Terrain mix: N 16%, I 45%, E 39%

Snowboarding: yes

Just over 125 years ago the town of Park City was the site of the largest silver-mining camp in the country. In those halcyon days its population swelled to nearly 10,000 fortune seekers, and its Main Street was a veritable sinners' den of bars, bordellos, and gambling houses. During the ensuing period of silver fever, hundreds of mines were opened, thousands of miles of tunnels were dug, $400 million worth of silver ore was mined, and 23 men became millionaires, including George Hearst, founder of the Hearst mining and newspaper empire.

The silver and the miners are long gone, but their legacy remains in the form of a busy, colorful resort town that combines the images of the past with the amenities of the present. In straitlaced Utah, Park City is still considered a veritable sin city. Most of the original buildings on Main Street have been so carefully preserved and restored that the entire district is now listed on the National Register of Historic Places. Most buildings house restaurants, bars, shops, galleries, museums, and hotels. Fanning out from this slice of history is modern Park City, a subdivision of contemporary hotels and condominiums spilling across the sage meadows, lining the high ridges, and filling the tiny canyon in and around the ski resort.

Some skiers prefer this to Alta or Snowbird because it has more après-ski and evening opportunities as well as somewhere to go on a day off the slopes. Park City, the resort, and the town cozy up to each other; indeed they even overlap, with the lower slopes of the resort descending to the edge of town. In fact, one lift—the Town triple—begins its journey up the mountain from the foot of Park Avenue, in the heart of town.

This natural merging of community and resort makes it easy to commute between the mountain and the town on the free transit system that shuttles skiers from more than 100 in-town stops to the slopes as well as to the adjacent resort of Deer Valley, just 3 miles away. If you find even the five-minute shuttle inconvenient, there's also a well-developed resort at the base of the gondola, with bars, restaurants, and shops. For total convenience, many condo units provide ski-in/ski-out access.

Park City may no longer be the bawdy, rollicking town of its youth, but in its reincarnation as a ski resort, it is spirited and zesty, with plenty of daytime and nighttime attractions to satisfy visitors.

HOW TO GET THERE

Shuttle Service
Several shuttle bus companies link the resort and the Salt Lake City airport and points in between. **Canyon Transport** (tel. 801/255–1841 or 800/255–1841), **Park City Transportation** (tel. 801/649–8567 or 800/637–3803), and **Lewis Brothers Stages** (tel. 801/359–8677 or 800/826–5844) all have scheduled shuttle service from the airport or downtown Salt Lake City. Rates range from $17 one-way in a motor coach to $25 one-way in a four-passenger limousine. All three have service desks at the Salt Lake City airport.

By Car
Park City is about 35 miles east of the Salt Lake City airport. From the airport take I–80 east to the Park City exit, Route 224, which turns into Park Avenue, and follow signs to Park City.

GETTING AROUND
As the shuttle bus system in Park City (Park City Transportation, tel. 801/645–5130 or 801/364–8472) is efficient and free, a car isn't absolutely necessary unless you want to visit neighboring ski resorts or towns. Buses run throughout Park City between 7:40 AM and 1:10 AM, making regular stops about every 15 minutes at more than 20 locations in and around the town and resort. The shuttle serves Deer Valley as well. There are also taxicab companies in the Park City area, including **Daytrips** (tel. 801/649–8294), **Park City Taxi** (tel. 801/649–8515), and **Snow Cab** (tel. 801/645–5867). Rates vary based on distance, and they'll go anywhere you're willing to pay.

THE SKIING
Park City is Utah's largest ski area. It's known mostly as an intermediate's cruising resort, but it also has more than 650 acres of upper-elevation bowl skiing

that includes some serious, super-steep stuff. The area is a crescent-shape ridge that runs north to south, and from the base elevation of just under 7,000 feet it's impossible to see the various faces and bowls off the top of Jupiter Peak, 4,000 feet above.

One of the unique aspects of the area is its terrain, which faces virtually every direction, making it easy to follow the sun around the mountain. The Pioneer, Crescent, and Ski Team ridge areas (served by the gondola and the Ski Team and Three Kings lifts) get the early morning rays; the Prospector area, on the west side of Crescent Ridge (served by King Con, the new six-passenger, high-speed detachable Silverlode and Motherlode lifts), is the place to head midmorning; and by early afternoon the Jupiter Bowl is sunnyside up. This is also a neatly divided mountain, with distinct areas for all levels. Experts love the high bowls, intermediates are usually happiest on the west face of Crescent Ridge, and novices can stick to the east side of Crescent Ridge.

Another of Park City's fine features is the lift layout, which provides options for reaching the top of the mountain. On busy days you can skip the gondola and take a combination of the Payday, Crescent, and Pioneer lifts to the summit, or opt for the shorter ride on the Ski Team lift to the top of Ski Team Ridge and ski down Claimjumper (green) or King Con (blue) to the Silverlode chair. If you want to avoid the base lodge area entirely, you can grab a shuttle bus to the Town lift, then take the Crescent, Pioneer, or Silverlode lift to the top. Trails of all levels are accessible from these alternate lifts.

Park City has opened its entire area to snowboarders. There are also rental facilities and lessons available. There are no plans to create snowboards-only terrain.

Novices
Unlike some ski resorts, Park City offers novice skiers trails from the top of the mountain that are easily reached from the gondola. There's a 3½-mile wide and ultraeasy combination of three groomed runs, beginning with Claimjumper. From Claimjumper, turn right on the cat track leading to Bonanza and follow that to Sidewinder, which you'll take all the way back to the base of the gondola. Even intermediates can enjoy this long run in the early morning sun. If you're feeling apprehensive about the length of the run, First Time and Three Kings lifts also serve the three easiest and shortest novice runs, Three Kings, King's Crown, and Pick and Shovel.

Once you've warmed up sufficiently and want to pick up the pace, take the Bonanza cat track and cut left down Claimjumper as it veers toward the Prospector area. You're still in the green here, but it's a bit steeper and leads to the bottom of the Silverlode lift, from which you can explore some of the easier blue runs. Hidden Splendor, for instance, is a beautiful wide-open, bowl-like run that is a bit steep but is always well groomed and should present no problems. Mel's Alley is a little narrower but has about the same pitch and is also always groomed. Both runs are reached directly from the top of the Silverlode lift, but if you want to eliminate the steeper upper part of the Prospector runs, you can follow

Claimjumper and cut left onto either Powder King or Assessment, both of which are shorter and narrower but give you a chance to work on your turns before making the commitment to the longer runs. Both cut back toward lower Claimjumper (so you'll get some relief from the pitch) and will feed you back to the bottom of the Silverlode lift.

If you're feeling comfortable on those runs and are looking for a little more blue action, head to the King Con lift on Broadway, at the bottom of the Silverlode lift. The King Con serves all blue runs, but at least half of them are always groomed and mogul-free, and you can't really get into any trouble if you have basic turns under control.

Intermediates

Whether you're starting from town on the Town triple or from the resort center on the Payday lift (the latter is less crowded than the gondola early in the morning), the Payday trail should be your first choice for a stirring warm-up cruise. From the top of the Town triple lift there's about 500 yards of gentle green before you hit Payday (the Payday lift deposits you right at the top of the run), which starts out fairly narrow and then widens into a groomed, well-pitched autobahn cruiser that curves around the eastern edge of the mountain and brings you back to the resort center. While the crowds are still lining up for the gondola, head for the Ski Team double lift (also less crowded because it requires a short walk), which takes you to Crescent Ridge, the heaviest concentration of blue runs on the mountain. The first run to take should

be the wide, groomed King Con Access, which takes you to the confluence of a dozen fairly steep but ultra-groomed blue runs that head down to the bottom of the King Con quad. This lift takes you to the summit of the ridge in less than six minutes, and in an hour or so (depending on the lift lines) you can explore each of these excellent intermediate trails: Sitka, Shamus, and Liberty have the steepest pitch and are the narrowest, while Courchevel, Chance, and High Card are wider and a little less steep. All these runs are fairly short, but they don't lack variety and have enough pitches, rolls, and drop-offs to keep things interesting; a moderate intermediate could easily spend an entire day in this area without getting bored.

When you're ready to fly, take the King Con Access, cutting left onto King Con, which will take you down to the bottom of the Silverlode lift. From the top of Prospector the blue runs get steeper but are still well groomed, with one or two occasionally allowed to grow some decent-size bumps. Start on Prospector, which begins fairly wide, allowing you to adjust to the increased pitch. About halfway down there's a short black section that can be avoided if you veer left at Parley's Park, which, if you stay right all the way down, will take you back to the bottom of the Silverlode lift. It then narrows considerably as it crosses under the quad chair. The next run you opt for should be Hidden Splendor, a glorious wide run through the meadows and one that is sometimes left with ungroomed snow after a recent fall. If you stay right on this, it will take you to the bottom portion of Claimjumper, a temperate green; if you want to skip Claimjumper, stay left and pick up Mel's Alley, a steep, narrow gully that cuts through the trees and back down to the bottom of the Silverlode six-passenger lift. For a long, groomed, steep cruise, take Sunnyside from the top of the Silverlode lift.

Also, from here you can take the Prospector run for about 500 yards and then swing left on to Single Jack, a steep, straight shot down to the bottom of the Motherlode lift. From the top of Motherlode there is a pair of usually ungroomed tree runs—Jupiter Access and Keystone—that cut through the woods, making you work a little harder. Next try either Double Jack or the Hoist, a pair of moderately steep blacks that are never groomed and grow some medium-size moguls.

Experts

Skip the gondola for the first runs of the day and walk the extra distance to the Ski Team lift, which you'll take to the top. From the lift, get in some early morning steeps and bumps on Silver Skis, which has megamoguls and apart from the bowls is among the steepest runs on the mountain. Once you've gotten warmed up, take the gondola to the top and try a few runs down either the Hoist or Thaynes, both of which are steep, narrow, and bumpy and will take you back down to the bottom of the Thaynes lift.

When you've had your fill of bumps, head for Blue Slip Bowl, a short, wide, and steep expanse of ungroomed snow from which you'll be able to judge if you're ready for more bowl action. If you're comfortable on this bowl, head across Jupiter Access to the bottom of the Jupiter lift, which serves the steepest and most demanding terrain on the mountain. As you get off the lift, the wide-open faces to your left are good tests, or if you're confident, drop into a radical collection of narrow chutes and gullies that plunge like elevator shafts through the densely packed evergreens. Try Silver Cliff, Six Bells, or Indicator for a real taste of gulp-and-go vertical, and keep in mind that trees are only your friends if you don't slam in to them. If you feel you aren't ready for these, try the wider, more open Fortune Teller or Shadow Ridge, both of which run directly under the lift. To the far left from the top of the Jupiter lift is Portuguese Gap, another staggeringly steep run through the trees, or you can opt to traverse over to Scotts Bowl, which is still ultra-steep but devoid of glades.

For another supersteep, head over to the east face of Jupiter Peak from Jupiter chair (requires about a 15-minute hike up the Pioneer Ridge), where you'll find the Puma Bowl and McConkey's Bowl. Because it takes extra effort to reach these bowls, they are the best places on the mountain to find untracked powder. Try to snag a local for a tour of this area.

WHERE TO STAY

Of all the resorts in Utah, Park City has the most varied accommodations. You can stay slope side in hotels or condo units or choose from in-town historic bed-and-breakfasts, small European-style hotels, contemporary resort lodges, and condominiums. In the surrounding region are the ultradeluxe hotels and condominiums of nearby Deer Valley (*see* Deer Valley, *above*) and the more mainstream hotels and motels in Salt Lake City, 35 miles away. Accommodations and/or packages can be booked through **Park City Reservations** (tel. 800/ 453–5789), **Park City Resort Lodging** (tel. 800/545–7669), **Park City Ski Holidays** (tel. 800/222– 7275), or **Deer Valley Central Reservations** (tel. 800/424–3337).

Expensive

All Seasons
These stylish, modern one- to three-bedroom condominiums are among the newest in Park City and also among the most upscale. The decor and furnishings are ultradeluxe, with hardwood floors, Berber carpeting, Laura Ashley–style wallpaper, flagstone fireplaces, and contemporary artwork. Each comes with an equally modern full kitchen with ceramic counters and state-of-the-art appliances. Each bedroom has an en suite bathroom; all units have a sleeper sofa. Deluxe touches include comfortable, well-made colonial-style chairs and couches and private decks. Next to the eighth green of the Park City Golf Course, it has a spectacular view of the mountain. *Park City Golf Course, 1485 Empire Ave., Park City, 84060, tel. 801/649–5500 or 800/ 331–8652, fax 801/649–6647. 16 units. Facilities: heated outdoor pool, hot tub, laundry facilities, 24-hr front desk service. AE, D, MC, V. $150–$590.*

Resort Center Lodge and Inn
Three buildings at the base of the Park City lifts make up this large wood-and-stone complex with a gabled roof that blends nicely with the environment. There's easy access among the three buildings, and all units are spacious, even the studios. The huge four-bedroom units spread over two levels and can sleep up to 12 people in privacy and comfort. The interior decor is modern, with natural-color Berber carpeting, tile accents, stucco walls, and floor-to-ceiling windows and cathedral ceilings in the larger suites. This should be your first choice if you are looking for ski-in/ski-out convenience, hotel service, and practical condo amenities. *Base of gondola, resort center, Box 3449, Park City, 84060, tel. 801/649– 0800 or 800/824–5331, fax 801/649– 1464. 140 units. Facilities: indoor-outdoor pool, sauna, steam room, indoor-outdoor whirlpool. AE, D, DC, MC, V. $130–$1,289.*

Silver King Hotel
Epitomizing the very best of modern mountain architecture, this ultrastylish condo hotel has soaring windows, exposed beams, and an atrium lobby. Guests can choose from four unit sizes: a studio, a one-bedroom, a two-bedroom, and larger penthouse suites. The decor in each is also modern but softened by handmade pine furnishings, peaceful colors, and little touches such as woven area rugs. Guests congregate in the expansive lobby, where a modern tile fireplace warms large sectional sofas. The condo is just steps from the lifts. *1485 Empire Ave., Box 2818, Park City, 84060, tel. 801/649–5500 or 800/331–8652, fax 801/649–6647. 62 units. Facilities: indoor-outdoor pool, sauna, whirlpool. AE, D, MC, V. $135– $610.*

Washington School Inn

Few schools are like this inn, a marvelous example of turn-of-the-century architecture, with huge windows and a distinctive bell tower. It was home to thousands of students during its heyday, but in the mid-1930s it closed and then fell into disrepair. It was reincarnated as an elegant country inn in the 1980s. The interior is spacious and designer-perfect, with high, vaulted ceilings, cherry-wood wainscoting, and a stunning center staircase leading to the bell tower. The large rooms and suites are elegant, with country-style wall coverings, handwoven area rugs, tile-and-stone flooring, and four-poster canopy beds. There's a large hand-carved lobby fireplace, twig furniture, flagstone flooring in the spa area, and a comfortable sitting area with wingback armchairs. The inn is in town on the upper road, about a half mile from the ski area. No children under 12. *543 Park Ave., Box 536, Park City, 84060, tel. 801/649–3800 or 800/824–1672, fax 801/649–3802. 12 rooms, 3 suites. Facilities: sauna, indoor hot tub, lounge. AE, MC, V. $190–$350, including full breakfast and après-ski refreshments.*

Moderate

Shadow Ridge Resort Hotel

Guests are drawn to the Shadow Ridge for its comfortable ambience. The decor includes dark-wood trim and furnishings, accented by white walls and heavy tapestrylike drapes and upholstery. It also has a remarkable selection of rooms, ranging from a standard twin to spacious one-, two-, or three-bedroom condo units—each featuring distinctive appointments and decor. All rooms come with a private balcony. Best of all, the hotel is just 100 yards from the Park City lifts, in front of the resort center. *50 Shadow Ridge Dr., Box 1820, Park City, 84060, tel. 801/649–4300 or 800/451–3031, fax 801/649–5951. 150 units. Facilities: heated outdoor pool, whirlpool, sauna, fitness center, lounge, billiard room, laundry facilities. AE, D, DC, MC, V. $69–$780.*

Silver Queen

Here's a classic, historic Park City structure right on Main Street in the heart of town. The wedge-shape building is solid brick, with intricate detailing, curved window tops, and a wraparound balcony that overhangs the sidewalk on two sides. Inside, the decor is period, with colonial-style wall coverings, archways, wainscoting, latticework, and thick, richly colored carpeting. The units, available with either one or two bedrooms, are individually designed and decorated with pine antiques, brass beds, wicker accessories, dark-wood trim, tile and brick accents, and large, comfortable chairs and couches. Modern amenities include a full kitchen, a Jacuzzi, a fireplace, and a washer/dryer. There's a delightful European feel here in both the ambience and the service, and if you enjoy luxury in a historic setting, it's a good choice. *632 Main St., Box 2391, Park City, 84060, tel. 801/649–5986 or 800/447–6423, fax 801/649–3572. 12 units. Facilities: ski lockers. D, MC, V. $250–$310.*

Snowed Inn

Although it's been around for only about 10 years, this charming Victorian-style country inn is perfectly suited for the turn-of-the-century atmosphere of the original Park City. High ceilings and large windows, distinctive antique furnishings such as pine hutches, brass beds, colorful wall coverings, and goose-down comforters give rooms an old-fashioned ambience. A sumptuous parlor with a towering mahogany-pillared fireplace encourages mingling. There is one family suite, with a wood-burning fireplace. The inn's award-winning Juniper restaurant serves delightful American cuisine in a cozy setting. Horse-drawn sleigh rides are available in the afternoon and before dinner. The inn is on the highway between Wolf Mountain and Park City. *3770 N. Rte. 224, Park City, 84060, tel. 801/649–5713 or 800/545–7669, fax 801/645–7672. 10 rooms. Facilities: outdoor hot tub. AE, D, MC, V. $150–$285, including Continental breakfast.*

The Yarrow

Looking as though it's been transplanted from Colonial Williamsburg, this distinctive complex has a neat brick facade, wood-trimmed peaked windows, and an ersatz clock tower. Inside, the rooms and suites come in a variety of configurations, including studios, standard and deluxe rooms, and suites. In general, rooms are large enough to accommodate four, but if you need extra space, there are also a number of one- and two-bedroom condo units with enough beds to sleep six, along with a full kitchen, a fireplace, and living and dining areas. The Yarrow is just a short walk from town and from the ski lifts. *1800 Park Ave., Box 1840, Park City, 84060, tel. 801/649–7000 or 800/327–2332, fax 801/645–7007. 159 rooms, 22 units. Facilities: restaurant, pub, heated out-door pool, sauna, exercise room, hot tub. AE, D, DC, MC, V. $99–$489.*

Inexpensive

Edelweiss Haus

This simple, unpretentious condo hotel is at the resort, just 1½ blocks from the lifts. The units range from standard hotel rooms to one- and two-bedroom condos, but all quarters are clean and comfortable. The larger condos have kitchen facilities. *1482 Empire Rd., Box 495, Park City, 84060, tel. 801/649–9342 or 800/438–3855, fax 801/649–4049. 16 rooms, 39 units. Facilities: heated outdoor pool, outdoor Jacuzzi, sauna. AE, D, MC, V. $90–$350.*

Inn at Prospector Square

This sprawling inn, just minutes from Park City's Main Street and only a five-minute shuttle bus ride from the resort, is actually six buildings centered around the Prospector Square Athletic Club (headquarters for the U.S. Olympic Ski Team). It offers a mix of standard hotel rooms, studios with and without lofts, and one-, two-, and three-bedroom condominiums. Most units are utilitarian with basic child- and group-proof decor, but all are comfortable and well equipped. All condos have a full kitchen and a gas fireplace. Included in the rate is daily membership at the Athletic Club, which has all sorts of exercise facilities and activities available. *2200 Sidewinder Dr., Box 1698, Park City, 84060, tel. 801/649–7100 or 800/453–3812, fax 801/649–8377. 235 units. Facilities: 8 indoor hot tubs. AE, D, DC, MC, V. $142–$400.*

Old Miner's Lodge

Built in 1889 as a miners' boarding-house, this lodge retains much of its original style, beginning with its exceptional length and grand position atop a hill high above town. In 1983 the lodge was renovated, with most of the original fittings, woodwork, and furnishings painstakingly restored. No two rooms are alike, but all are similar in the warmth and authenticity of furnishings, including such touches as claw-foot tubs, four-poster beds, willow chairs and headboards, and handmade pine furniture. All suites have small fridges, and all rooms come with terry-cloth robes and down comforters, but there are no TVs. *615 Woodside Ave., Park City, 84060, tel. 801/645–8068 or 800/648–8068, fax 801/645–7420. 9 rooms, 3 suites. Facilities: outdoor hot tub. AE, D, MC, V. $95–$205, including full breakfast.*

Snow Flower

This four-building wooden complex, wedged into the side of a hill, is not the most stylish design in town. But it does have a ski-in/ski-out location and an impressive collection of rooms and suites, the largest of which is a five-bedroom monster with space for at least a dozen close friends. Each unit is individually owned, so decor and furnishings vary considerably. All come with a kitchen (of varying sizes), a fireplace, and sensible furnishings. Guests are provided voice mailboxes. *400 Silver King Dr., Box 957, Park City, 84060, tel. 801/649–6400 or 800/852–3101, fax 801/649–6049. 142 units. Facilities: 2 heated outdoor pools, laundry, ski storage. AE, MC, V. $70–$750.*

WHERE TO EAT

Unlike neighboring Alta or Snowbird, Park City has a bustling and varied dining and nightlife scene. There are dozens of interesting spots, mostly along Main Street, ranging from the predictable to the avant-garde, with a lot of good old-fashioned Western ambience thrown in. To enjoy Park City's rollicking nightclub and bar scene, you'll have to abide by the Club Membership rule, which applies to all of Utah.

On the Mountain

Mid-Mountain Lodge

Although it's nearly a mile from its original site, this late-1800s lodge stands as the oldest mine building in Utah. Its three separate dining areas all have exceptional food. There's an excellent choice of daily specials—veggie lasagna, seafood casserole, and clam chowder—plus standards such as chili, sandwiches, burgers, and soups. *On Webster run in Pioneer lift area, tel. 801/649–3044. V.*

Summit House

The fairly standard selection of burgers, soups, salads, chili, and stews here gives you plenty to choose from. The crowds are smaller here than at Mid-Mountain. Diners can also sit on the outdoor deck and enjoy the spectacular 200-mile view. *Top of gondola, tel. 801/649–4333. No credit cards.*

Expensive

Chimayo

Southwestern cuisine is the name of the game at this lively restaurant. Its decor includes soft-brown stone walls, huge wooden ceiling trusses, terra-cotta tiles, dramatic lighting, and a hint of mesquite in the air. For starters try the toasted corn chowder. Follow that with the Farmer's Market salad, with marinated cactus and adobo vinaigrette. For entrées there's an equally off-the-wall selection of such things as crab-stuffed grouper steamed in a banana leaf and served with avocado slaw or the seared elk burrito with blackened tomato sauce and Mexican oregano. For dessert try the grilled banana sundae. *368 Main St., tel. 801/649–6222. AE, D, MC, V.*

Ichiban Sushi

Not only is the food here fresh and creatively prepared, but the dining room is comfortable, with an extra-large bar—appropriate for the extra-large selection of sushi choices. The decor is upbeat, with a slatted wood ceiling, a wall of personal chopsticks (organized by number) from which regulars just pick up their own, and a giant tropical fish tank. Apart from a good selection of traditional sushi, the chef also makes some excellent hand rolls. If you prefer, there's also tempura, teriyaki, sukiyaki, and *donburi. 586 Main St., tel. 801/649–2865. AE, MC, V.*

Riverhorse Café

The two large upper-level warehouse rooms that make up this café resemble an ultramodern big-city supper club, with exposed beams, polished hardwood floors, black and white furnishings, and walls adorned with huge portraits of such well-known Native Americans as Sitting Bull and Geronimo. House specialties are seared ahi tuna in a puff pastry tart with eggplant and citrus sauce and charred rack of Utah lamb in a caber-

net demiglace with goat cheese ravioli, roasted garlic, fresh herbs and the restaurant's signature mashed potatoes. *540 Main St., tel. 801/649–3536. Reservations essential. AE, D, MC, V.*

Moderate

Baja Cantina

For Mexican favorites, the Baja, at the base of the lifts in the resort center, is a good choice. It's a bright, busy greenhouse-style building with lots of tile and stucco and hand-painted bird-of-paradise art on the walls from floor to ceiling. The menu offers virtually anything you can think of from south of the border. Without exception, this is the best Mexican food in Park City. *1284 Empire Ave., resort center, tel. 801/649–2252. AE, D, MC, V.*

Claimjumper

The Claimjumper is a bustling place in the heart of the historic Old Town, with Americana decor including hardwood floors, brick walls, a large stone fireplace, hunter green curtains, and a menu printed on an empty wine bottle. The mainstay here is steak, ranging from an 8-ounce cut to a slab the size of your plate. It's all aged beef, cooked precisely as requested. There are variations on the steak theme, including prime rib, baby-back ribs, buffalo steaks, and monster burgers, plus a few nonbeef items. *573 Main St., tel. 801/649–8051. AE, D, MC, V.*

Coyote Grill

This bright, open Southwestern-style restaurant has exposed beams, lots of windows, hunter green tones, and potted cacti. The wildly varied menu includes pasta, fish, meat, and fowl with interesting twists and subtle flavorings. For pasta, try the penne *rigate* with smoked salmon, bell peppers, and dill cream. Fish fans should taste the grilled Atlantic swordfish on a lemon-caper cream with an herbed tomato relish. If you're a meat eater, don't pass up the New Zealand venison medallions sautéed with a sundried berry sauce and roasted pine nuts. If you're in the mood for fowl, order the three grilled quail on black bean cake with smoked tomato sauce and cilantro. *Resort Center Lodge, 1415 Lowell Ave., tel. 801/649–1180. AE, MC, V.*

Steakhouse on Wolf Mountain

The name of this restaurant provides more than just a clue as to what can be found on the menu. Certified Angus beef is featured in filet mignon, prime rib, and strip steaks. (There are also baby-back ribs, pork chops, barbecued chicken, salmon steak, and lobster tails.) All dinners include a 30-item salad bar, which can be a meal in itself. Dessert is simple but good; try the hot fudge brownie or cheesecake. The steakhouse is slightly off the beaten path, on the top floor of the main building at the Wolf Mountain ski area, and attracts locals even more than tourists. *400 Park West, at Wolf Mountain, tel. 801/649–2086. AE, D, MC, V.*

350 Main Seafood & Oyster Co.

This strikingly stylized Art Deco emporium has black lacquer tables, pearl-color walls, maple wood flooring, and a copper-tinted ceiling. The menu runs from cornmeal-crusted seabass, peppered ahi tuna, and lobster ravioli to filet mignon, herb-marinated chicken breast, and a grilled vegetable platter. If you're not very

hungry but just want to nibble, there's also a selection of fried catfish, barbecued shrimp, and an oyster bar that includes mussels, clams, and peel-and-eat shrimp. *350 Main St., tel. 801/649–3140. AE, MC, V.*

Inexpensive

Burgie's

What you'll find at this lively place are beef, lamb, turkey, buffalo, and vegetarian burgers with all sorts of combos, low prices, and a cheerful, diner-style atmosphere. An interesting side dish is the mound of crisp, batter-dipped fried onion rings served with a mildly hot sauce. *570 Main St., tel. 801/649–0011. AE, D, MC, V.*

Main Street Delicatessen

This deli is a good spot for a fast sandwich, eat in or take it out. It's pleasantly furnished with pine chairs and tables and offers a good selection of deli meats and innovative designer sandwich combinations on a variety of breads. *525 Main St., tel. 801/649–1110. No credit cards.*

Main Street Pizza & Noodle

This bright, modern pasta emporium with floor-to-ceiling windows makes California-style pizza as well as pastas and filling alternatives such as calzone and *stromboli* (pizza dough rolled over and filled with such items as Asian-style chicken, pepperoni, veggies, and cheese), soups, and salads. *530 Main St., tel. 801/645–8878. AE, MC, D, V.*

Mt. Air Café

Bring your appetite to this old-fashioned country diner serving comfort foods such as ground sirloin, liver and onions, roasted chicken, fish-and-chips, country-fried steak, and a variety of daily specials. Sit at the lunch counter or grab a booth. The café also serves breakfast all day. *Rtes. 248 and 224E, tel. 801/649–9868. AE, MC, V.*

Best Bets for Breakfast

Eating Establishment

Known as the Double E by locals, this is a good spot for hearty skillet breakfasts, including omelets, flapjacks, waffles, and ham and eggs. *317 Main St., tel. 801/649–7289; Plaza level at resort center near Payday lift, tel. 801/649–8284. AE, MC, V.*

Morning Ray Café & Bakery

This café-style restaurant has a good selection of pastries, muffins, cereals, and specialty breads for the continental crowd. Diners can also hunker down to some serious omelets, pancakes, and quiches, some prepared with organic ingredients. *268 Main St., tel. 801/649–5686. AE, MC, V.*

NIGHTLIFE AND ENTERTAINMENT

Après-Ski

Baja Cantina

A must on the après-ski list, this is a crowded bar with happy-hour munchies, schmoozing, and the best margaritas in town. *1284 Empire Ave., resort center, tel. 801/649–2252. AE, D, MC, V.*

Steeps

The place to go immediately after the lifts close, it fills up with people of all ages who come for dancing to live music, happy-hour munching, and large-screen TV watching. *1284 Empire Ave., at lower gondola building, tel. 801/647–7746. AE, MC, V.*

Loud and Lively/Dancing

The Alamo Saloon

A classic old-style saloon where you'll find the locals hanging out, this part–dance club, part–sports bar is raucous but not dangerous. The usually young crowd comes for the live rock music, billiards, pinball, darts, and lots of TVs. *447 Main St., tel. 801/649–2380. No credit cards.*

Lakota

Park City's only restaurant-cum-bar features live entertainment and a state-of-the-art audiovisual system that adds to the upbeat mood and convivial atmosphere. *751 Main St., in the Caledonian, tel. 801/658–3400. AE, DC, MC, V.*

More Mellow

Mileti's

This popular locals' hangout is colored in soft pinks and greens with lots of mahogany fixtures and giant mirrors. It's the place for conversation and socializing. *412 Main St., tel. 801/649–8211. MC, V.*

Sneaker's

This quiet, somewhat upscale sports lounge has soft lighting, comfortable chairs, and music that mostly appeals to the over-30 crowd. *1200 E. Little Kate Rd., Park City Racquet Club, tel. 801/649–7742. AE, MC, V.*

SNOWBIRD SUMMER AND SKI RESORT

Snowbird, UT 84092
Tel. 801/742–2222 or
800/453–3000
Fax 801/742–3300

STATISTICALLY SPEAKING

Base elevation: 7,760 feet

Summit elevation: 11,000 feet

Vertical drop: 3,240 feet

Skiable terrain: 2,000 acres

Number of trails: 66

Longest run: 2.5 miles

Lifts and capacity: 1 tram, 8 doubles; 9,200 skiers per hour

Daily lift ticket: $36, chairs; $45, tram

Average annual snowfall: 500 inches

Number of skiing days 1995–96: 149

Snowmaking: 25 acres

Terrain mix: N 25%, I 30%, E 45%

Snowboarding: yes

This is not a resort that relies on frills to make its point or to carve its place on the ski map. It's a resort for people who love to ski. In fact, there's a decided absence of frills at the minimalist base village area tucked near the end of Little Cottonwood Canyon just 30 miles from downtown Salt Lake City. The towering 10-story Cliff Lodge dominates the resort, and nearby are three slightly smaller condominium buildings, for a total on-mountain bed base of about 1,000. A hundred yards from this wall of granite is the base area plaza, which contains the three-story atrium-style Snowbird Center. Here you'll find a small selection of shops, including a deli-market, several sports stores, a liquor store, various resort-services offices, a base-area cafeteria, a nightclub, and three restaurants. A shuttle bus regularly circles the entire complex, but you can also cover the area on foot in under 30 minutes. That's it. Day one you can discover it all, and by day three if you yearn for more diversions, you'll be thinking about heading into Salt Lake City.

Above all this soars the 11,000-foot Hidden Peak, in a massively rugged part of the Wasatch Range. This, along with the legendary featherweight Utah powder, which averages more than 500 inches a year, is the main reason skiers come to Snowbird.

Powder. It defines Snowbird as much as the soaring granite peaks and the forests of Engelmann spruce, lodgepole pine, and Douglas fir. You come to Snowbird for the steep and deep—and no other reason. And that's the way builder Dick Bass envisioned his little slice of Cottonwood Canyon. Bass, an entrepreneurial adventurer—his other claim to fame is his ascent of the highest peaks on each of the seven continents—wanted a no-nonsense, purpose-built resort, and his sleek, steep, modernistic Snowbird fits the bill. The country's fastest tram takes seven minutes to get you to the top of 3,000 vertical feet of top-to-bottom skiing, and when the combination of snow-stuffed bowls, chutes, couloirs, and cirques have taken their toll, the village is right there.

Outside, the resort is a resilient buttress against the howling wind and snowstorms that sweep the canyon; inside, it's a comfortable, contemporary labyrinth of convenience. Like the mountain, this is a stern, stoic, and well-laid-out village. Towers of granite and glass engulf the canyon timber, buildings are linked by paved stone pathways, and the only bright lights are a thousand miles straight up, studding the coal black sky with a lonely luminescence.

HOW TO GET THERE
Shuttle Services
From Salt Lake City International Airport, **Canyon Transport** (tel. 801/255–1841 or 800/255–1841) and **Classic Limousine and Airport Shuttle** (tel. 800/233–8201) run regularly scheduled service. No advance booking is necessary. The cost is approximately $17 per person one-way. **Salt Lake Transit** (UTA; tel. 801/287–4636) runs a ski bus every 15 minutes from the city center to Snowbird. One-way fare is $4.50.

By Car
Snowbird is 20 miles, about a 30-minute drive, from the heart of Salt Lake City, up Little Cottonwood Canyon. Follow I–80 east to I–215 south, then take Exit 6 and follow signs to Little Cottonwood Canyon. For car-rental information, *see* Getting to Utah Resorts, *above.*

GETTING AROUND
A free ski shuttle bus runs between Gad Valley and Snowbird Center from 8 to 5. In the evening this shuttle runs every 30 minutes until 11 and will drop you at any accommodation. There's also regularly scheduled service ($1 each way) between Snowbird and Alta (about a mile away), with stops at various locations. **Canyon Transport** (*see* Shuttle Services, *above*) offers service to downtown Salt Lake City. **Yellow Cab** (tel. 801/521–2100 or 800/826–4746) offers taxi service in the area.

THE SKIING
To get the lay of the land of Snowbird, know that the 125-passenger Snowbird tram is the line that divides the mountain neatly in half. Directly underneath the tram are some of the best straight-shot black diamond plunges in the country; to the left (looking up) is the blue-black cruising and bowl skiing of the

Peruvian Gulch area; and to the right, the Little Cloud Bowl area with its steep black diamond cruising. Below the Little Cloud Bowl, where the timberline starts, is the Gad Valley area, with a half-dozen intermediate runs, and below that the minimal novice area. A long traverse called the Bass Highway links the Gad Valley with the tram side of the mountain. There's also a high-country traverse from the top of either the tram or the Little Cloud lift that is the highest ride on the Gad Valley side. The Baby Thunder area has seen the addition of a new run in the novice/intermediate terrain.

The skiing at Snowbird is tough. Many of the blue runs here would be rated black elsewhere. Experts and strong intermediates can ski from the tram and the Little Cloud lift, but less sturdy intermediates and novices are best advised to stick to the Wilbere, Gad, and Mid Gad lifts.

If you head over to the Peruvian Gulch from the Little Cloud lift, it's a fairly hard uphill slog that takes about five minutes. Coming from the top of the tram, there's a short uphill climb, then a tricky cat track to get over to the Little Cloud Bowl.

If you're a strong skier and want first crack at the early powder, head for the tram right away. If you are less dedicated, the sun warms the Gad Valley area in the morning and then moves to the Little Cloud Bowl by midday. It's a good way to warm up slowly and get comfortable before moving over to the Peruvian Gulch side of the mountain in the afternoon.

Overall, it's easy to get around at Snowbird, but if you feel intimidated by the unknown possibilities, the resort's free mountain host tour service is an excellent way to become familiar with the layout. Skiers meet at prearranged times, are sorted into ability groups, and then are led on a mountain tour.

Another thing to remember at Snowbird is the two-level ticket system: An all-inclusive ticket is $45, and a chairlift-only ticket is $36. If the tram terrain is beyond your ability, there's no point in paying the full fare. Snowboarders take note: The entire mountain is now open for 'boarding!

Novices
If you have never skied before and are considering a visit to Snowbird—don't bother. This is not the place to take up the sport, notwithstanding the first-rate Snowbird ski school. Never-evers will be restricted to two short teaching runs—Chickadee and Chickadee Loop, served by their own chair—which curiously are also the main footpath for anybody walking from Cliff Lodge to Snowbird Center. It's a layout flaw that not only puts hazards in the way of beginning skiers, but also saddles Cliff guests with a tricky and slippery walk.

Even experienced novices with a few days of skiing under their boots will find the green terrain extremely limited. There are just a half-dozen novice slopes on the Gad Valley side of the mountain. If you fit that category and you're already here, the best way to start the day is to take the Mid-Gad lift up to the Mid-Gad station. From there you have only one choice: Big Emma, a green run that weaves easily through a wooded area before spilling out on to a wider, well-groomed section that takes you back down to the bottom of Gad Valley. About midway down Big Emma, you can detour onto West Second South and West Second South On-Ramp, both fairly short and flat in sections.

If you feel you are ready to step up to some modest blue runs, your best bet is to take the Gad 1 lift, which runs parallel to the Mid-Gad lift but takes you slightly higher up, to the bottom of the Little Cloud lift. From there you can try Lunch Run (turn right as you get off the lift), a fairly steep but well-groomed extension of Big Emma. Or you can turn left and take Bassackwards, a longer, slightly more challenging blue run that winds around the middle of the Gad Valley. Here you'll find a moderately difficult section of trees, then a wider, groomed stretch that feeds into Lower Bassackwards. This is a nice rolling cruiser—with a few steep pitches—that feeds back to the Gad 1 and Mid-Gad lifts. From this run you can also take the Wilbere Cutoff—cut right as you cross under the two chairs—to the bottom of the Wilbere lift. The Wilbere will take you to the top of Wilbere Ridge (make sure you turn right off the chair), a short run that will give you a taste of some steep pitches plus some interesting rolls and dips.

Intermediates

Unless you are a strong intermediate skier, your best bet is to start out on the Gad Valley side of the mountain, which enjoys the early morning sun. Take the Gad 1 lift and warm up on Lunch Run, a good, wide cruiser. As it crosses under the lift, pick up Bassackwards and enjoy some good pitches and rolls on your way down to the bottom of the Gad 2 lift.

From the top of this lift, head for Bananas. On the upper part it's fairly steep and lightly treed, but once it curves under the Gad 2 lift, it widens out and is usually groomed, so you can carry good speed back down to the bottom of the Gad 2. Ride to the top of this lift again, turn left, and either take Election for some well-spaced bumps or head straight off the lift to the upper part of Bassackwards, which is steep and usually groomed. If you like a good, long cruising run without bumps or ungroomed stretches, stay on Bassackwards all the way back down to the bottom of the Gad 1 lift.

At the point where this crosses under the chair, you can also cut hard right and take Wilbere Cutoff down to the bottom of the Wilbere lift. This section can get a little bumpy, but it's short, and you can stay on the right side to avoid the biggest moguls. A short ride on the Wilbere chair takes you to the top of Wilbere Ridge, another well-groomed cruiser through some stands of trees.

More aggressive intermediates looking to step up should consider heading back up the Gad 1 lift to the Little Cloud lift. Signs here indicate that you are heading for black-diamond territory, but anyone with a strong parallel turn can ski this terrain. It's wide open—almost bowl-like—and throws some nice dips and rolls at you, especially on the upper part. This is pick-your-own-route skiing, but you'll want to stick to the area marked Regulator Johnson (on your right going down) and definitely avoid the Gad Chutes, which drop off to your right about halfway down. These are double-black monsters, steep, ungroomed, and with lots of trees.

If you feel comfortable on Regulator Johnson, get back on the Little Cloud lift, turn right when you get off, and take the Road to Provo. This can be a tricky little traverse, so stay in control. You soon arrive at a pair of black bowl runs called Shireen and Mark Malu Fork. Again, a strong intermediate should be able to handle either one because they are wide enough to allow long, sweeping, speed-checking turns.

The Peruvian Gulch side of Snowbird doesn't offer much for the intermediate. Chips is the only blue run here (the only blue run off the tram), and though it's almost 3 miles long, it's a bit of a cat track along the top section before it widens out into a broad meadow that is usually groomed. At the lower end of the meadow, you'll begin a long, circuitous run back to the bottom of the tram. Watch the signs carefully because at numerous points the trail intersects with some black runs that you may not want to tackle.

Experts
There's no doubt that this is the mountain for you. It's even possible to rack up more vertical here than you'd get in a day of helicopter skiing. So cut loose and have fun.

The tram, your fastest and most direct way to the top, is an eight-minute ride that unleashes almost 3,000 feet of vertical. Some locals play "beat the tram"—shooting down to the bottom fast enough to catch the same car back up to the top. The most direct and challenging route is Silver Fox, a vertiginous wall that shows little mercy to those not totally in control of their skis. From the top of the tram, you can also turn right and head over to the Little Cloud Bowl area or turn left and take High Baldy over to the West Baldy area. If there has been fresh snow overnight, expect a crowd in both areas.

If you prefer a more mellow start to your day, you might consider following the sun. Start on the Gad Valley side by taking the Gad 1 lift to the top and then enjoy some short, steep blacks that snap the knees awake. By midmorning head for the Little Cloud lift and pick up the pace on the steep, wide-open bowl. Little Cloud skirts along the top of the bowl for a twisting and spirited ride back down to the bottom of the Little Cloud lift; Regulator Johnson charts a steeper, more direct route down to the same spot. You'll catch the sun here and beat the traffic that arrives later in the day.

By early afternoon take the traverse over to the Peruvian Gulch side of the mountain, then follow the Cirque Traverse until you find a tantalizing way down. Great Scott and Upper Cirque are extreme steeps, more chutes than anything else and quite often require a leap of faith off a cornice. Farther along the traverse is the Peruvian Cirque, a more traditional and slightly less precipitous bowl. All three routes take you to the corner of the Cirque, where you can drop over the top of the ridge and tackle two double-black-diamond bump runs—Dalton's Draw and Mach Schnell—that combine steepness with monster moguls.

Remember, this is where you can really maximize the Snowbird vertical, running the full length of Hidden

Peak on everything from narrow, steep chutes to sweeping, banked giant slalom cuts to knees-to-your-chest moguls. By mid-afternoon head over to the Peruvian Gulch area on the High Baldy Traverse. Here you can go a little more free-form in the steep openness of this vast bowl. Primrose Path is unrelenting and made for high speed, High Baldy lets you carve larger slalom turns, and everything in between is strictly pick-your-own-route down.

WHERE TO STAY

Because lodging at Snowbird is limited to a single hotel, three condominium buildings, and a small number of privately owned and rented condo units, you might want to consider staying in nearby Salt Lake City, with its ample lineup of traditional chain hotels, bed-and-breakfasts, and numerous inexpensive motels. It's an easy 40-minute commute to the resort and gives you access to other activities besides skiing. The Alta resort, only a mile away, offers yet another range of alternatives (*see* Where to Stay *in* Alta, above). A free shuttle bus service connects the two resorts. All rooms at the resort can be booked through Snowbird Central Reservations (tel. 800/453–3000).

Expensive

Canyon Services Condo Rentals

About a half mile from Snowbird, on the bypass road to the Alta resort, is a small cluster of private homes, town houses, and condominium buildings, known as the Village at Sugar Plum, Sugar Plum Townhouses, Superior Point, and the Meadows at Sug-

arplum. Snowbird owner Dick Bass lives here. A very limited number are available for rental; the upscale units range from two to five bedrooms. If you want space, exclusivity, and privacy, it's worth investigating the available options here. *Canyon Services, Box 920025, Snowbird 84092, tel. 801/943–1842 or 800/562–2888, fax 801/943–4161. 37 units. A, D, MC, V. $325–$875.*

Cliff Lodge

This massive granite-and-glass structure is the only truly full-service hotel at the resort. It is something of an impersonal monster, with its unfinished granite walls (deliberately left that way to harmonize with the nearby mountain) and its confusing labyrinth of shops, restaurants, and facilities. The 500-plus rooms come in three basic configurations: the standard hotel room, the slightly larger suites, and the two-bedroom suites, which are actually a combination of the first two. Overall, furnishings and decor are fairly ordinary, with beige and earth tones predominating, but they are spacious and meticulously maintained. At press time, a 25-meter outdoor swimming pool and three outdoor hot tubs were under construction and scheduled for completion by late 1997. The lodge's location provides ski-in/ski-out access to the tram. There are also limited dormitory-style accommodations. *Box 929000, Snowbird 84092, tel. 801/742–2222 or 800/453–3000, fax 801/742–3204. 460 rooms, 47 suites. Facilities: 4 restaurants, 3 outdoor pools, health club, spa, ski rental, baby-sitting. A, D, DC, MC, V. $209–$879.*

Moderate

Iron Blosam

This time-share building has only a limited number of units available at any given time. The room configurations are similar to those at both the Lodge and the Inn at Snowbird (*see below*); the decor of each unit varies slightly according to the individual owner's taste. *Box 929000, Snowbird 84092, tel. 801/742–2222 or 800/453–3000, fax 801/742–2211. 34 rooms, 36 suites, 17 studios, 72 efficiencies. Facilities: restaurant, outdoor heated pool, whirlpool, exercise room. AE, D, DC, MC, V. $195–$615.*

Lodge at Snowbird and Inn at Snowbird

The lodge and the inn, two identical condo buildings situated next door to the Cliff Lodge, are remarkable only for their ordinariness. They both have the same unfinished granite construction as the Cliff and a dour, gray decor that starts in the hallways and extends into the rooms, which are decorated in a kind of Mormon minimalism. Room layouts range from studios to studio lofts to one-bedrooms with loft. Not fancy but less expensive than the Cliff, the lodges are about a five-minute walk from the lifts, and both are on the Snowbird Village shuttle bus loop. *Box 929000, Snowbird 84092, tel. 801/742–2222 or 800/453–3000, fax 801/742–3311 for lodge or 801/742–2211 for inn. 145 units in lodge, 42 units in inn. Facilities: restaurant, bar, heated outdoor pool, whirlpool spa. AE, D, DC, MC, V. $195–$615, lodge; $179–$593, inn.*

WHERE TO EAT

The resort has a limited number of unimaginative dining spots, but Salt Lake City is an alternative; so are the nearby hotel dining rooms of Alta (*see Alta, above*). Keep in mind that all purchases can be charged back to your room while you stay in Snowbird.

On the Mountain

Mid-Gad Restaurant

In Gad Valley at the top of the Gad lift, this is the only on-mountain cafeteria at Snowbird, and it serves the standard ski resort fare, including soups, stews, chili, sandwiches, burgers, pizza, and other snack-type lunches. *Tel. 801/742–2222, ext. 4167. AE, D, DC, MC, V.*

Expensive

The Aerie

This is Snowbird's most formal and most intimate dining room. The modern decor emphasizes glass, mountain views, polished black surfaces, and soft lighting, and a cocktail pianist adds a swanky, sophisticated touch. The menu is loosely Continental, with local specialties such as Colorado rack of lamb, prime rib with browned shallots, and medallions of elk, as well as the only sushi bar in the area. *Cliff Lodge, 10th floor, Snowbird, tel. 801/742–2222, ext. 5500. AE, D, DC, MC, V.*

La Caille

Ten miles from the resort near the bottom of Little Cottonwood Canyon, this stunning replica of a grand 17th-century French château is well worth the trip. You enter through wrought-iron gates and proceed along a cobblestone driveway. Inside, arched ceilings, carved-wood garlands, a winding staircase, and 17th-century antiques establish a regal Gallic tone.

You can feast on entrées such as *carré d'agneau* (broiled rack of New Zealand lamb with a Grand Marnier glaze and fresh rosemary), charbroiled filet mignon with crumbled Roquefort cheese and cognac *moutard,* or Norwegian salmon and leek pesto in a peppercorn crust with citron cream. *9565 Wasatch Blvd., Little Cottonwood Canyon, tel. 801/942–1751. AE, D, DC, MC, V.*

The Steak Pit

This is the oldest restaurant at Snowbird—an institution among regulars and popular with families. The dining room is casual and pleasant, with cedar tongue-and-groove walls, lots of plants, and wooden booths around the perimeter. The steak lineup, impressive in size but a bit uneven in quality, runs the gamut from filet mignon to top sirloin—with two sizes in each cut—plus combo plates such as steak and lobster. At this hearty-eater heaven, everything comes in large portions, including the all-you-can-eat salad. *Snowbird Center, Level 1, tel. 801/742–2222, ext. 4060. AE, D, DC, MC, V.*

Moderate

Lodge Club Bistro

This intimate spot has a glass atrium front wall that curls partway across the ceiling, adding a dramatic touch to the modern, minimalist decor of chrome furnishings, earth-tone walls, gray accents, modern art, white tablecloths, and subdued lighting. The menu includes a variety of light entrées, such as a daily pizza special and such pasta dishes as lemon-chicken ravioli, *capellini* with shrimp and calamari, and lemon-pepper fet-

tuccine. If you want something more substantial, try the excellent braised pork tenderloin done with sherry vinegar and roasted pine nuts. *Lodge at Snowbird, tel. 801/742–2222, ext. 3042. AE, D, DC, MC, V.*

Keyhole Junction

This restaurant has rough-hewn wood trim, Southwestern art, small table groupings, and a huge stone fireplace. The fare is standard Southwestern, with specialties such as fajitas, wild mushroom enchiladas, and wild trout tamales, plus steak and barbecued chicken. *Cliff Lodge, Level A, Snowbird, tel. 801/742–2222, ext. 5100. AE, D, DC, MC, V.*

Wildflower Ristorante

If you've a passion for Italian cooking, this bright, warm, and welcoming restaurant in the Iron Blosam is the perfect choice. You can order such appetizers as *calamaretti fritti alla arrabiata* (lightly breaded baby squid with a spicy tomato and black pepper sauce) and entrées such as duck ravioli, a house specialty, and cioppino (shrimp, calamari, fish, scallop, and clam stew). *Iron Blosam, Level 3, Snowbird, tel. 801/742–2222, ext. 1042. AE, D, DC, MC, V.*

Inexpensive

Pier 49 San Francisco Pizza

For a fast-food fix or an early dinner on the cheap, this is a good bet (it's open until 6 PM). Sourdough-crust pizza comes with a good selection of exotic toppings, available by the slice or pie. You can eat in or take out. *Snowbird Center, Level 2, tel. 801/742–2222, ext. 4076. AE, D, DC, MC, V.*

Best Bets for Breakfast

The Atrium

The Atrium is a bright, cheery breakfast spot that offers an excellent buffet breakfast of muffins, pastries, hot and cold cereals, eggs in all styles, bacon, and custom-made omelets. *Cliff Lodge, Level B, tel. 801/521–6040, ext. 5300. AE, D, DC, MC, V.*

Espress Stations

If you're itching to get on the slopes but need to eat breakfast first, this establishment is quick and easy. Pastries, muffins, gourmet coffees, and, of course, espresso, are the staples here. *Cliff Lodge, Level C; top and bottom of tram; outside Snowbird Center, Level 3; tel. 801/521–6040. AE, D, DC, MC, V.*

NIGHTLIFE AND ENTERTAINMENT

The best after-dark entertainment at Snowbird is gazing at the star-studded night sky, looking for wildlife as you ramble around the base area, or relaxing in the hot tub or pool. Snowbird after dark is, in a word, quiet. If you absolutely have to mingle, here is the lineup of choices.

Après-Ski

The Atrium

People come here for the après-ski munchies (of the nachos and buffalo wings variety), hot and cold beverages, and a mellow kind of atmosphere. You can sometimes catch some folksy live entertainment. *Cliff Lodge, Level B, tel. 801/521–6040, ext. 5300. AE, D, DC, MC, V.*

Forklift

The Forklift is a little livelier than the Atrium and tends to draw a younger crowd for a slightly more upbeat music scene, along with snacks. For entertainment there are three TVs and live guitarists weeknights during peak ski season. *Snowbird Center, Level 2, tel. 801/742–2222, ext. 4100. AE, D, DC, MC, V.*

Loud and Lively/Dancing

Tram Club

There's live music every night—rock, blues, reggae—and when there are no live bands taking center stage, there is a good-size dance floor for those whose legs haven't been sufficiently beaten up on the slopes. For more entertainment there are also 12 televisions, pinball, pool, a dart board, and a fireplace. *Snowbird Center, lower level, tel. 801/742–3010, ext. 4250. AE, D, DC, MC, V.*

More Mellow

Aerie Lounge

This comfortable lounge adjacent to the Aerie restaurant has a long two-sided bar plus a sitting area. Live entertainment—usually a folk guitarist or duo—starts at 9 PM. *Cliff Lodge, 10th floor, tel. 801/521–6040, ext. 5500. AE, D, DC, MC, V.*

F or East Coast Americans—and indeed many Canadians—Vermont is skiing, and skiing is Vermont. Perhaps nowhere else in America is the history of the sport so indelibly enshrined. This is where lift-served skiing in the United States began, with the installation of a rope tow near Woodstock in 1934. Many of the best ski areas in New England are in Vermont—Stowe, Killington, Mad River Glen—all saturated in the skiing tradition rich with famous skiers, famous events, and images of leather boots, spindly bamboo poles, and bear-trap bindings.

The state neatly divides itself geographically as far as the skiing is concerned. In the north the towns are small and isolated, the low-lying meadowlands yielding to fjordlike lakes and midsize mountains such as Stowe's Mt. Mansfield, which act as snow traps for weather systems moving across the Canadian border. Through the center of the state cut the western slope of the Green Mountains and the network of roads that connect larger communities such as Rutland and Woodstock and make it easy to get to resorts like Killington and Sugarbush from the urban centers of New York and Boston. Finally there is southern Vermont, the most heavily developed part of the state, where the rolling hills and occasional big mountain are dotted with a mix of original farms and homes and a collection of second-home developments created by urbanites seeking a pastoral alternative to city life. It's here that resorts like Stratton and Mt. Snow, two modernized mountains, cater to baby-boom cruisers who like the skiing predictable, the access easy, and the images of the past nicely renovated.

The variety and picturesque quality of the Vermont countryside is an overwhelming draw for New Englanders, many of whom have skied the same resorts for decades. The western states have sweeping panoramas and deep snow, but the skiing in Vermont has a special quality. From storied Stowe to teeming Killington, no other state presents the many faces of skiing in such a compact package, and the occasional deep freeze or period of flinty snow (two consistent knocks against Vermont skiing) should not deter even spoiled, warm-weather western skiers from sampling Vermont skiing.

GETTING TO VERMONT RESORTS

By Plane

Boston's **Logan International Airport** is served by most major carriers, including American Airlines (tel. 800/433–7300), Continental (tel. 800/525–0280), Delta (tel. 800/221–1212), TWA (tel. 800/221–2000), and United (tel. 800/241–6522). **Bradley International Airport,** in Hartford, Connecticut, is served by all major airlines. **Albany Airport,** Albany, New York, has service by American, Delta, and United. Other choices are the **Burlington,** Vermont, and **Lebanon,** New Hampshire, airports, served by commuter airlines from Boston and Albany.

Most major car-rental firms have desks at both the Boston and Burlington airports, including **Avis** (tel. 800/331–1212), **Budget** (tel. 800/527–0700), **Hertz** (tel. 800/654–3131), **National** (tel. 800/328–4567), and **Payless** (tel. 800/237–2804).

KILLINGTON SKI RESORT

KILLINGTON SKI RESORT

Killington Rd.
Killington, VT 05751
Tel. 802/422-3333

STATISTICALLY SPEAKING

Base elevation: 1,045 feet

Summit elevation: 4,241 feet

Vertical drop: 3,150 feet

Skiable terrain: 860 acres

Number of trails: 162

Longest run: 10.2 miles

Lifts and capacity: 1 gondola, 7 quads, 4 triples, 5 doubles, 2 surface lifts; 36,327 skiers per hour

Daily lift ticket: $48

Average annual snowfall: 252 inches

Number of skiing days: 1995–96: 248

Snowmaking: 552 acres; 65%

Terrain mix: N 49%, I 20%, E 31%

Snowboarding: yes

When you think Killington, you think big. It's the biggest area in Vermont, in the East, and by acreage and number of trails, among the biggest in the country. When Killington opened on December 13, 1958, it had four lifts and seven trails on one mountain. Today Killington has skiing on six mountains and nine separate skiing areas connected by 75 miles of alpine trails and served by 19 lifts. The lifts include the longest chairlift in the United States and a 2½-mile heated high-speed gondola, christened the Skyeship. The 10.2-mile Juggernaut is the longest alpine ski trail in the United States. It also has a staggering 17 on-mountain places to eat.

Killington operates from mid-October through late May or early June, the longest ski season in the East for more than 33 consecutive years. The extended season is made possible by one of the most extensive snowmaking systems in the world, covering 44 miles of trail. The area's snowmaking is matched only by its snow grooming—its 26 vehicles groom more than 135,000 miles of trails each season, roughly equivalent to 5½ times around the world.

Killington's trails range from Juggernaut, which meanders gently through three townships, to Outer Limits, a half mile of bumps the size of vans cascading down a 43% gradient that from the top looks like an egg carton stood nearly on end. The megaresort has a snowboarding half pipe at the bottom of Lower Highline Trail, in plain sight of the 3,000-square-foot viewing deck attached to the Killington base lodge. There is one gently sloping hill, Snow Slope, reserved strictly for beginners, with its own lift system and base lodge. Broad trails, narrow trails, vastly popular trails, and virtually unknown trails are scattered over the six separate peaks.

People love Killington Road because it houses skiing institutions—the Wobbly Barn and Pickle Barrel dance halls, Casey's Caboose and Mother Shapiro's restaurants, plus ski shops and clothing shops and just about every other commercial venture associated with snow. It's hated for much the same reason: too glitzy, too commercial, and too citified for a ski area in the middle of Vermont.

Actually, love and hate describe the way many skiers feel about Killington in general. You'll never

Children's services: day care, instruction, tel. 802/773–1330

Snow phone: tel. 802/422–3261

Police: tel. 802/773–9101

Hospital: Rutland Regional Medical Center, tel. 802/775–7111

Resort office services: tel. 802/422–3333, ext. 6228

Killington-Pico Area Association: tel. 802/773–4181

Road conditions: tel. 800/429–7623

Taxi: Killington Travel Service, tel. 800/372–2007

Towing: Habro, tel. 802/422–3434; Buxton's Sunoco, tel. 802/773–9747

FIVE-STAR FAVORITES
Best run for vertical: Devil's Fiddle

Best run overall: Chute

Best bar/nightclub: Wobbly Barn

Best hotel: Cortina Inn

Best restaurant: Hemingway's

hear more grumbling from more people, which makes you eventually ask why they keep coming back year after year after year. The answer is: Like Everest, it's there. It's loud, brash, commercial, fast-paced, over-adrenalized, too big, and impossible to ignore. It is the standard by which other areas in the eastern United States reluctantly measure themselves.

HOW TO GET THERE

By Car

Boston is 156 miles from Killington; the drive should take less than three hours. Take I–93 north to I–89, just south of Concord, New Hampshire. Follow that north to U.S. 4 at Rutland and take it to Killington Road. From Hartford (166 miles away) follow I–91 north to Exit 6 onto VT 103, north of Bellows Falls, Vermont; follow VT 103 to VT 100; take VT 100 north to U.S. 4 and follow that west to Killington. From Albany (110 miles away) take I–87 north to NY 149 and follow it east to U.S. 4; take that east to Killington. From Burlington (84 miles away) take U.S. 7 south to Rutland and U.S. 4 east to Killington. From Lebanon (39 miles away) take I–89 to U.S. 4 west to Killington. From New York (250 miles away) take the New York Thruway to Exit 24 in Albany and then follow the Albany instructions above.

By Bus

Vermont Transit Company (122 Merchants Row, Rutland, tel. 802/773–2774) offers daily service from Rutland to Killington with connections from most major centers.

By Train

Amtrak (tel. 800/872–7245) has scheduled service into Boston from most major centers, and connections are available to Rutland.

GETTING AROUND

Even though a free shuttle bus service, **the Bus** (tel. 802/773–3244), runs up and down Killington Road and between the resort and nearby Rutland, a car is really your best option. It gives you much more flexibility and a chance to explore the surrounding area or dine at some of the outlying restaurants. If you head out for a night of imbibing, a designated driver is a good idea because the police do patrol the road regularly, even setting up a spot check at the entrance to U.S. 4.

THE SKIING

The big ski resort at the end of a 5-mile access road off U.S. 4 is not the only Killington. The resort begins 6 miles east of Killington Road, where U.S. 4 meets Route 100 as it wanders up from the south. That's the Sunrise area, formerly called Northeast Passage. The advantage of Sunrise (elevation 2,456 feet)—besides the early morning sun—is that crowds are few, parking spaces many, and it has an exclusive, little-known, heavily discounted lift ticket. The disadvantage is that the lift, the Northeast Passage triple, takes 17 minutes to carry you from the base station to the top. The skiing at Sunrise is a mixture of beginners' slopes, wide intermediate terrain, and a couple of steep and bumpy expert trails. The slopes catch a lot of sun but are light on snowmaking and elevation.

One mile west of Sunrise along U.S. 4 is the next Killington entrance, the Skyeship base station. It used to take 28 minutes from bottom to top on the old gondola. Since the installation of a heated gondola, the trip is just 12½ minutes. The Skyeship reaches only to Skye Peak (elevation 3,800 feet), which has two faces—one steep, the other moderately gentle. The eight-passenger gondola runs this shortened route because winds on Killington often rendered its predecessor's final leg inoperable.

Right beside the Skyeship entrance is a winding road that offers a third access to Killington, this one to the Bear Mountain Base Lodge. Although Bear Mountain (elevation 3,295 feet) is far from the largest of Killington's mountains, it is by far the most celebrated, with some of the steepest terrain in the area and the mogul slope (some would say cliff) Outer Limits that has lighted more smiles and ruined more knees than any other in the country. The knees belong to the mogul maniacs who are drawn, like moths to a flame, to its steep face, but they share the smiles with those who gather on warm late-winter days at the Bear Mountain Base Lodge to watch these young heroes engage in their never-ending "battle of the bumps."

The next entrance off U.S. 4, on the other side of Skye Peak, is Killington Road, which takes you to the Killington base area, the center of the resort. Most of the trails down 4,241-foot Killington Peak's face are expert.

West of Killington Peak and reached from the main base area is Snowdon Mountain (elevation 3,592 feet), a good place for beginners and intermediates, though it has a few advanced trails thrown in. It's served by a triple and a quad chairlift and mainly for use by racers, a Poma lift.

Rams Head Mountain, also reached from Killington Road, is the resort's westernmost peak. It stands 3,610 feet and is served by the Rams Head double chair, a leisurely lift that takes 14 minutes from bottom to top. Its trails are, with two exceptions, all beginner and intermediate.

Across Killington Road from Rams Head Mountain lies the hill Killington devotes exclusively to learning, Snowshed. With three short chairlifts, including a high-speed quad and a Poma for the upper slopes and with its own ski school, children's center, cafeteria, restaurant, ski shop, rental shop, repair shop, ticket windows, and medical center, this is among the best equipped and busiest ski- and snowboard-learning centers in the country.

On busy weekends and holidays, you should seriously consider skipping Killington Road completely and driving to Bear Mountain, the Skyeship station, or Sunrise. There are tickets, rentals, and food at all of them. The one thing that's unavailable is lessons, which start at the Snowshed and Killington Peak base lodges. But you can take a lift to lessons (be sure to allow enough time—the Killington trail map indicates the number of minutes each lift takes), and you'll avoid snarled parking lots, long waits for tickets, and cold lift lines.

Killington's lifts, except the high-speed quads and the Skyeship, are free the first 45 minutes of every day. If you don't like the snow conditions (or are satisfied with less than an hour of skiing a day), you can simply quit after a couple of runs.

Killington's extralong season means that early in the ski year, in October and November, you should expect to ski with too many young men with too much testosterone who go faster than they should—they haven't seen snow in a few months. You have two choices: Put your baseball cap on backward and join them or wait until December to start your skiing/boarding season.

Late in the season—May and even early June—Killington has the only lift-served skiing in the East. The snow is soft, the sun is high, the mosquitoes are after you, and those same young men you met in October are still here. Only now they've mellowed out after a winter on snow and are much better company.

Should you get lost (which can happen even after reading this chapter, taking a tour, studying the trail map, and carrying a compass) and find yourself at the end of the day at one base area while your car is at another, Killington will shuttle you back to your car for a very small fee.

Snowboarders have access to the entire mountain and to all lifts. There are also a half pipe and a minipipe on Snowdon Mountain and six terrain parks with whales, rolls, quarter pipes, banks, and switchbacks on each of the six mountains.

Novices

Every one of Killington's six peaks can be skied from the top by beginners. Yes, surprisingly this megaresort with the fearsome reputation is entirely accessible to wedge-turning, steep-hating, snowplowing, speed-fearing novices. In fact, the very best way to get your bearings is to spend your first morning on a guided tour of the mountains. This is also the best deal. The tour—which leaves the Snowshed area on Monday at 9:45 AM and 12:45 PM; Tuesday, Friday, and Saturday at 9:45 AM—is free, and it's conducted entirely on beginner terrain. To take it, wait under the MEET THE MOUNTAINS TOUR sign in front of Snowshed Base Lodge.

When you graduate from Snowshed, the natural progression is up to Snowdon and Rams Head. Novices on

Rams Head will have the most luck on the gentle Caper, which leads to the base of the Snowdon chair, just below Killington's most vexing bottleneck. Be careful at the intersection of Mouse Trap, Mouse Run, Chute, and Racer's Edge—it's often a tangle of falling skiers and blasting snow guns. On busy days avoid it altogether.

The greatest indulgence for beginners, however, starts on Killington Peak. Here, at the top of the resort, is where the novice trail Juggernaut begins its 10-mile ramble. Most people assume they can do it in a half hour, but Killington advises leaving up to two hours to get through this meandering, level, sometimes uphill trail that ends up at the Skyeship base station.

The gentler side of Skye is accessible from the Skye Peak quad; if you're a confident learner, you should try your legs on Pipe Dream, 4-Mile Trail, and Wanderer. When you find yourself at the top of Bear Mountain, remember every peak at Killington has an easy way down, and Bear Mountain is no exception. Shagback leads novices back to Snowshed, and Falls Brook Trail heads slowly down to the Bear Mountain Base Lodge.

Just above the Sunrise Village area across from the base of Bear Mountain, you can pick up the amiable Juggernaut Too, which works its slow way down to the Sunrise Base Lodge. The less-used Sun Dog has a gradual pitch and no surprise steeps as it winds down this hill. These trails are at relatively low elevation and all do not have snowmaking, so check their snow conditions before you start down.

Intermediates

Many of Killington's most challenging trails start gently, and then after you've committed yourself, drop like an elevator shaft. But they are marked: If the sign says double diamond, you can safely assume it means just that.

Try starting on the least-known intermediate trail, Swirl, on Rams Head. This perfectly named trail twists, turns, and swirls down the mountain, and if you get there early enough in the morning, you'll find yourself cutting clean tracks through unmarked snow. The long Chute underneath the Snowden quad is a good, steep cruiser.

For high-mountain intermediate skiing, the Glades triple, on Killington, is relatively uncrowded in the morning, and the trails from it are often piled deep with natural powder. Incidentally, the Glades has a lot of nonglade skiing; try Rime, just below the triple chair. You can make a short eastward swing from the top on 4-Mile Trail to Skye Peak and take a long cruise on it down to the Skyeship base station.

Experts

For a little-used run, try Catwalk, on Killington Peak. To get there, you have to de-ski at the top of the lift and hike a few yards on a path through snowy woods on the way to the peak. When you come to the start of Catwalk, before pushing off, look down. If your stomach stays below your throat, if there's been a recent and heavy snowfall, and if you can link tight turns on a steep and narrow trail, by all means ski it. If, on the other hand, at least one of these criteria is not met, continue walking to the peak and enjoy one of the finest views in New England.

Choosing to skip Catwalk is by no means bailing out—some tough double-black-diamond expert trails like Downdraft and the broad (200 feet across) but steep (up to 54% gradient) Double Dipper start here, too. Killington's tree skiing is on the double-black Big Dipper Glade, served by the Canyon quad, which tends to be less crowded.

Ski these for a while, or branch off to the east on Great Eastern to link up with the expert trails on Skye Peak. On its more difficult face, Skye Lark, Skye Hawk, and Superstar will give you a shot of adrenaline as they drop precipitously toward the base of the Superstar detachable quad. Or head down the gentler side of the mountain on Skyeburst or Dream-Maker to the infamous Bear Mountain.

On Bear Mountain, besides the double-diamond egg carton that is Outer Limits, there's the steep, long, and devilishly difficult Devil's Fiddle. As the top half of the Fiddle is without snowmaking, ski it only after a snowfall. Each of these double-diamond trails has its own lift; when the crowds are up, head for the Fiddle, which gets much less traffic.

Sunrise, Snowdon, and Rams Head also have some strong stuff for strong skiers. Though short, Thunderball and the Judge, on Sunrise, can be white-knuckle runs when the bumps are up. On Rams Head, Upper Header and Lower Vagabond are both fairly steep and can be full of moguls.

Advanced skiers can arrange tailored tours on tougher terrain. Ask at the Snowshed Ski School desk for information about hiring a mountain guide.

WHERE TO STAY

This is condo country. There are more than three dozen complexes on Killington Road, which is the place to be for nightlife, and several more clusters on U.S. 4 toward nearby Rutland. The quality of individual units varies considerably; some are starting to show signs of wear and tear. A dozen properties are managed by Killington Resort—book those directly through the central reservations office (tel. 800/621–6867, fax 802/747–4419). There are also several noteworthy private lodges, inns, and large hotels within a few miles of the slopes, and Rutland, 15 miles away, has many chain motels.

Expensive

Cortina Inn

This rambling two-story stucco building with brick and wood facades and canopied terraces is a refreshing change in this condo-crazed area. The large, bright, high-ceilinged lobby, which connects the two main buildings, is filled with comfortable chairs and couches, Persian rugs, and local art (for sale, of course). Spacious rooms have handcrafted furnishings, queen-size four-poster beds, and colorful quilts; 12 have fireplaces. Kids are welcome—family suites have bunk beds—but overall this place is better for couples. You can even take a spin on the skating pond or a moonlighted sleigh ride. *HCR 34, Box 33, Killington 05751, tel. 802/773–3333 or 800/451–6108, fax 802/775–6948. 97 rooms. Facilities: 2 restaurants, bar, hot tub, indoor pool, spa, sauna, exer-*

cise room, skating pond, library, shuttle, game room, ski storage, 24-hr desk service. *AE, D, DC, MC, V. $129–$244, including full breakfast.*

Fall Line Condominiums
The tan clapboard town-house-style buildings are terraced on a hill above the access road and connected by cobblestone walkways, so the complex feels like a community. Wooden furnishings and comfortable couches, centered around a large brick fireplace, make the individual units cozy as well. Though the living area is small by condo standards, the bedrooms are extralarge, with high vaulted ceilings and large windows. There's a full kitchen in each unit, as well as a washer-dryer and a whirlpool. *Killington Resort Villages, Box 2460, Killington 05751, tel. 802/422–3101 or 800/343–0762, fax 802/422–6788. 40 units. Facilities: indoor pool, Jacuzzi, sauna, exercise room, game room, ski shuttle. AE, D, DC, MC, V. $125–$515.*

Highridge Condominiums
The units in this well-maintained complex, at the highest point of land in the main base area, have dark-stained wood and peaked roofs. Tastefully decorated, with especially large living areas that have high cedar-paneled ceilings and comfortable furnishings, they are bright and functional. Each unit has oak trim and a marble or slate fireplace. Light pours in through the windows, which also offer good views. The kitchens are compact but complete, and there's a good-size dining area. Every unit has a washer-dryer and an extralarge bathroom with a whirlpool and

sauna. *Killington Resort Villages, Box 2460, Killington 05751, tel. 802/422–3101 or 800/343–0762, fax 802/422–6788. 100 units. Facilities: indoor pool, health club, exercise room, sauna, outdoor hot tub, game room, ski shuttle. AE, D, MC, V. $125–$715.*

Inn of the Six Mountains
This attractive hotel has an Adirondack look, with stained wood shingles, a rippled gable roof, natural stonework, and finished wood beams. A floor-to-ceiling fireplace is the lobby centerpiece. The rooms have pleasant, modern mountain-inn decor—wood trim, handmade armoires, a small desk, overstuffed chairs, and tasteful art. *R.R. 1, Box 2900, Killington Rd., Killington 05751, tel. 802/422–4302 or 800/228–4676, fax 802/422–4321. 99 rooms, 4 suites. Facilities: restaurant, bar, indoor lap pool, sauna, whirlpool, game room, shuttle, ski storage. AE, D, DC, MC, V. $89–$269, including full breakfast.*

Woods at Killington
This is a self-contained complex of individually owned contemporary town houses and condos with gray wood siding and cedar shingled roofs. Although decor varies, most units are well appointed with quality furnishings, including queen-size beds and artistic touches. They are remarkably complete—with a fireplace, a washer-dryer, a Jacuzzi, and a full kitchen. *R.R. 1, Killington Rd., Box 2210, Killington 05751, tel. 802/422–3244, fax 802/422–3320. 57 units. Facilities: restaurant, lounge, indoor pool, sauna, steam room, spa, laundry, aerobics, yoga, ski shuttle. AE, MC, V. $615–$942 for 2 nights.*

Moderate

Glazebrook Townhouse Resort

For the roominess of a town house at a reasonable price, these cedar-shake, blond-stained units are a good bet. The two- and three-bedroom units can comfortably sleep six and eight, respectively, and all have large living areas and a wide brick fireplace. They come loaded with a fully equipped kitchen, a sauna, a whirlpool, a washer-dryer, and a private deck. A minimum two-night stay is required. *Box 505, Killington Rd., Killington 05751, tel. 802/422–4425, fax 802/422–2221. 27 units. Facilities: 2 restaurants, bar, sauna, ski shuttle. AE, MC, V. $642–$846 for first 2 days; $198–$264 per day thereafter.*

Killington Village Inn

This red clapboard barn-style inn has a genuine New England alpine feel, complete with knotty pine paneling, a huge fieldstone fireplace, and a cozy bar. The guest rooms are comfortable but spartan; the public spaces are more inviting. *Box 153, Killington Rd., Killington 05751, tel. 802/422–3301 or 800/451–4105, fax 802/422–3971. 20 rooms. Facilities: restaurant, indoor hot tub, game room, lounge. AE, D, DC, MC, V. $35–$58 per person, $14 each additional person, MAP.*

Red Rob Inn

This classic hillside New England inn is relaxed, pleasant, and unpretentious. Its facade is cedar, glass, and limestone, and the rooms are comfortable and bright, done in a white and woodsy minimalist style. Most come with a queen-size bed and a balcony or deck. *Box 2865, Killington Rd., Killington 05751, tel. 802/422–3303 or 800/451–4105. 33 rooms. Facilities: restaurant, lounge, indoor pool, outdoor hot tub, sauna, game room. AE, D, DC, MC, V. $78–$129, including full breakfast.*

Summit Lodge

You can't help noticing the dark rough-cut timber and cedar shingles of this hotel from the access road. Venture inside, and St. Bernards Henry and Heidi welcome you. Inside are exposed beams, stucco walls, and a trove of antiques from Calvin Coolidge's Plymouth, Vermont, home. Rooms are not fancy or especially large, but they are clean and woodsy, with antiques and handmade furniture, and they have great views. *Killington Rd., Box 119, Killington 05751, tel. 802/422–3535 or 800/635–6343, fax 802/422–3536. 45 rooms, 8 family suites, 2 suites. Facilities: restaurant, lounge, outdoor pool, Jacuzzi, sauna, massage, racquetball, laundry, game room, library, ski storage. AE, DC, MC, V. $45–$70 per person.*

Whiffle Tree Condominiums

These pine-stained condos with peaked wood-shake roofs are starting to show signs of age. They are, however, one of the few places in the area to which you can ski back at the end of the day. The roomy units range from one to four bedrooms and have contemporary decor and most creature comforts, including a full kitchen and laundry facilities. *Killington Resort Villages, Box 2460, Killington Rd., Killington 05751, tel. 802/422–3101 or 800/343–0762, fax 802/422–6788. 72 units. Facilities: ski shuttle. AE, D, DC, MC, V. $105–$519.*

Inexpensive

Butternut on the Mountain
You'll find tasteful contemporary rooms at this country inn. The exterior is New England contemporary clapboard in an ivory tone with deep mauve trim. The rooms are not large, but they are comfortable, and the library doubles as a cozy fireside lounge. *Box 306, Killington Rd., Killington 05751, tel. 802/422–2000 or 800/524–7654, fax 802/422–3937. 18 rooms. Facilities: restaurant, indoor pool, whirlpool, game room, laundry, ski-tuning room, library. AE, D, MC, V. $80–$110.*

Comfort Inn Killington Centre
This upscale Comfort Inn has a mountain chalet look. The standard rooms have two double beds; larger studio suites have a minikitchen, a dining area, and a whirlpool. *Box 493, Killington Rd., Killington 05751, tel. 802/422–4222 or 800/257–8664, fax 802/422–4226. 60 rooms, 20 suites. AE, D, DC, MC, V. $62–$206, including Continental breakfast.*

Little Buckhorn
This small chalet-style bed-and-breakfast is comfortable but spare. The top-floor rooms are wood-paneled and have high beamed ceilings. There are a quiet den area for reading or playing chess and an efficiency kitchen for making snacks. *Box 2318, Killington Rd., Box 2318, Killington 05751, tel. 802/422–3314 or 800/827–3314. 9 rooms. Facilities: indoor hot tub, sauna, ski locker. AE, MC, V. $32–$50, including full breakfast.*

Mountain Sports Inn
A traditional natural-cedar Austrian-style chalet, this inn provides clean, basic accommodations just 3 miles from the slopes. The rooms have light-oak furniture with rose and lavender accents. *R.R. 1, Box 2215, Killington Rd., Killington 05751, tel. 802/422–3315, fax 802/422–3315. 25 rooms. Facilities: ski tuning room, exercise room. AE, D, MC, V. $44–$140, including full breakfast.*

WHERE TO EAT

You don't have to drive far to find restaurants in the Killington area. There are more than two dozen clustered on the access road between U.S. 4 and the resort, and many of the hotels and lodges offer a MAP arrangement for guests. There is, however, a distinct lack of diversity—steak, seafood, and pasta emporiums seem to dominate Killington along with all other New England ski areas, and with just a few exceptions, most fall in the inexpensive to moderate range.

On the Mountain

Coyote's Restaurant
The modern stucco alpine-style building with brown decks is just off the Sun Dog and Juggernaut Too trails. A wide expanse of glass with views of the mountain, an oak-and-brass bar, and wooden tables covered with white cloths set the tone for the menu of burgers, soups, and salads in the daytime, and Black Angus steak, veal, and salmon at dinnertime. *Off Sun Dog Trail, Sunrise Village, tel. 802/ 422–8666. AE, MC, V.*

Summit Café
Atop Killington Peak, this lunch place combines spectacular views with designer sandwiches, soups, and sal-

ads. The fireplace completes the comfortable ambience. *Peak Lodge, Killington, tel. 802/422–3333. No credit cards.*

Expensive

Claude's

The intimate interior here is contemporary, done in mauve and gray with high-back chairs, candles, and fresh-cut flowers. A good choice is the breast of duck cassis, a marinated and medium-rare fowl dressed in a port and black-currant sauce. Other choices may include *coquille St. Jacques* and shrimp (scallops, mushrooms, wine, and duchess potatoes served gratiné, accompanied by shrimp Florentine) and breast of chicken saltimbocca, stuffed with prosciutto and feta cheese. *Glazebrook Center, Killington Rd., Killington, tel. 802/422–4030. Reservations essential. AE, MC, V.*

Hemingway's

This is truly one of the landmark dining establishments in eastern ski country. The atmosphere is set once you enter the front door of this modest 1860s farmhouse. Richly stained and polished panels encircle a high wainscoted bar and room divider, and the sitting room has a fine Bukhara rug in front of a blazing fieldstone fireplace. All around are splendid sculptures and objets d'art. Hemingway's offers three distinct dining areas—the largest, a formal dining room with clean pastel tones, high-vaulted ceilings, and elaborate chandeliers; the more cozy brick-walled garden room, with wrought-iron tables and chairs and a warming fireplace; and the intimate wine cellar,

with just a half-dozen tables and the original stone walls and low ceiling. Game birds are the specialty, but there are plenty of other wonderful options, including a wine-tasting menu. Popular entrées include Napoleon of beef tenderloin with Roquefort pastry and risotto with Maine lobster, shrimp, and grilled asparagus. There is also a four-course vegetarian menu that changes nightly. *Rte. 4, Killington, tel. 802/422–3886. Reservations essential. AE, DC, MC, V.*

Moderate

Casey's Caboose

Casey Jones's caboose has been replicated here as a restaurant, along with a 35-ton turn-of-the-century railroad snowplow car. It's a cheerful dining spot with lots of nooks and crannies—the best places to eat are up in or under the caboose observation compartment (two tables for two) or in the raised observation deck atop the old snowplow car (table for six). Casey's has a mainstream menu: If you're really hungry, go for the locomotive cut, 16 ounces of signature prime rib; if you can't handle that, the caboose cut is 4 ounces smaller. There are live Maine lobsters in tanks as well as a selection of steaks, ribs, pastas, seafood, and some outstanding buffalo wings. *Killington Rd., Killington, tel. 802/422–3795. AE, D, MC, V.*

Charity's

The centerpiece of this cathedral-shape barn-board building is the exquisite 1887 cherry-wood bar with handrail and pillars of Italian marble, moved here in 1971 from its original installation in Davis, West Virginia. In the dining room is a huge fieldstone fireplace, and above the numerous booths are lead-glass lamps and other antiques, giving the whole place a 19th-century saloon atmosphere. The menu offers steaks, fresh pasta dishes, a smattering of seafood choices, and even some Mexican favorites like fajitas. *Killington Rd., Killington, tel. 802/422-3800. AE, DC, MC, V.*

Grist Mill
Picturesquely situated on the edge of Summit Pond, this post-and-beam rendering of an early grist mill is complete with a waterwheel and a wraparound deck. Lively and cheerful, it is decorated in earth tones and has a gigantic fieldstone fireplace, a wood stove, antiques, a large moose head, and a busy dance floor. The hearty New England fare includes steak, seafood, poultry (such as berry-glazed chicken breast stuffed with artichoke hearts and cheese), pasta, and some excellent soup-and-salad combos. *Killington Rd., Killington, tel. 802/422-3970. AE, D, MC, V.*

Mother Shapiro's Restaurant
The interior has a Victorian decor overflowing with antiques, marble-top tables, beveled mirrors, and old church pews. There's a midnight breakfast menu called "Lox Around the Clock" that includes delicious French toast made with challah bread. At this loony place, shtick and marketing are as important as the food. The menu ranges from pot roast to pasta, from blooming onions to smoked mussels, from large portions of chicken to spaghetti. And mothers, despite the zaniness, you can bring your children here. *Killington Rd.,*

Killington, tel. 802/422-9933. AE, D, DC, MC, V.

Mrs. Brady's Restaurant
This low-key, contemporary dining room has a warm, intimate feeling. In addition to burgers, prime rib sandwiches, and chicken parmigiana on a poppy seed roll, there are also a large salad bar and a full dinner menu with steak cuts and a daily pasta special (such as fettuccine Alfredo with scallops) as well as baked stuffed lobster and stir-fries. *Butternut on the Mountain, Killington Rd., Killington, tel. 802/422-2020. AE, D, DC, MC, V.*

Six Mountain Grill
This casual American dining spot has a natural wainscoting interior with big picture windows overlooking the Vermont mountains. The two levels are eclectically decorated with flowered wall coverings. Entrées include black Angus steak, Vermont baby-back ribs with pure Vermont maple syrup, and sun-dried tomato and basil ravioli. *Inn of the Six Mountains, Killington Rd., Killington, tel. 802/422-4302. AE, D, DC, MC, V.*

Wobbly Barn Steakhouse
This cavernous barn with its red-wood interior doesn't actually wobble, but the ceiling and floors of the restaurant do shake from the nightclub on the floor above. Meat here comes in all forms, either barbecued or mesquite broiled. The cuts tend to be large and are cooked precisely to your specs. There is a smattering of seafood and chicken dishes, not to mention a bountiful soup, salad, and bread bar. Children are warmly welcomed. *Killington Rd., Killington, tel. 802/422-3392. AE, DC, MC, V.*

Zola's Grill

There's no shortage of oaky detail here, from the elaborate wood trim to the Windsor chairs. The menu features contemporary American food and changes regularly; for entrées, there is New England scrod with diced tomatoes and prosciutto or leg of lamb stuffed with goat cheese and served with a roasted garlic sauce. *Cortina Inn, Rte. 4, 3 mi west of Killington, tel. 802/773–3331. Reservations essential. AE, D, DC, MC, V.*

Inexpensive

Deli at Killington

Here you can get made-to-order sandwiches and subs piled high with toppings, plus there are soups and hot sandwiches such as turkey or roast beef. It's a quick-grab, no-fuss place, good for buying a lunch to enjoy on the mountain. *Killington Rd., Killington, tel. 802/775–1599. AE, MC, V.*

Kanpei Lounge at the Chinese Gourmet

On the go or on the table: Downstairs you'll find standard Chinese, with hand-painted, handcrafted tables and cathedral ceilings, and upstairs is Japanese fare, with a sushi bar, fish tanks, and a Japanese-style pillow room. Kanpei even delivers to your room, condo, town house, or chalet. *Killington Rd., Killington, tel. 802/ 422–4241. AE, MC, V.*

Outback Pizza

The Outback serves wood-fired pizza in a funky, eclectic environment that's pure Australian. Mock alligators cruise branches beneath the canvas-awning ceiling. Try the Vermont BLT pizza with cheddar, mozzarella, crumbled bacon, tomato slices, basil, and artichoke hearts. You can eat here or take it with you. *Killington Rd., Killington, tel. 802/422–9885. AE, MC, V.*

Peppers Bar and Grill

Amid Rube Goldberg gadgetry in a steel-and-wood environment reminiscent of a '40s diner, you can enjoy some of the most inexpensive dining on the mountain road—items like stir-fry chicken and broccoli over linguine with a mustard cream sauce, and grilled salmon. Look for the building with the stainless steel facade and neon portholes. *Killington Rd., Killington, tel. 802/422–3177. AE, D, MC, V.*

Powderhounds New World Restaurant

The skylighted dining room of this unusual brown-cedar-clapboard restaurant has light-wood booths built of horizontal wooden slats. The light and innovative cuisine here is a mix of Thai, European, and new American vegetarian dishes. Some favorites include the crabmeat and angel-hair fritters and *pahd phak* (Thai noodles with stir-fry vegetables, Thai basil, and chili peppers). *Killington Rd., Killington, tel. 802/422–4141. AE, DC, MC, V.*

Best Bets for Breakfast

Cortina Inn

The setting is formal—white linen and silver—but the style is buffet, with smoked Vermont ham, custom-cooked eggs, fresh fruit, waffles and pancakes, and omelets to order. *Rte. 4, 3 mi west of Killington, tel. 802/ 773–3333. AE, D, DC, MC, V.*

Mother Shapiro's Restaurant

Breakfast is served nearly around the clock at Mother's—monster-sized portions of good old-fashioned ham, eggs, home fries, pancakes, French toast, or bagels and lox. It's fast, fun, and friendly. *Killington Rd., Killington, tel. 802/422–9933. AE, D, DC, MC, V.*

NIGHTLIFE AND ENTERTAINMENT
Après-Ski
Avalanche Bar and Grill
The late-afternoon scene hops with live entertainment (either rock or more mellow guitar) and crowds of twenty- to thirty-something skiers, who sometimes dance between the small wooden tables. The look is rustic, with barn board and a large wooden bar. Munchies include veggie roll-ups, mountain bread, chicken wings, and pizzas. *Snowshed Base Lodge, tel. 802/422–3333, ext. 6428. AE, D, MC, V.*

Nightspot
Past the yellow awning on this '60s-vintage chalet-style wooden building, you find a relaxed dance club with oak and brass, as well as the Outback Pizza (*see above*), an enclosed deck where you can get pizza. *Killington Rd., 4½ mi from Rte. 4, Killington, tel. 802/422–9885. AE, MC, V.*

Loud and Lively/Dancing
Grist Mill
The lounge here jumps with rock bands during happy hour and after 9 PM ($3–$5 cover charge). The 30-plus crowd dances and samples

Goombay Smashes and other lubricants at the two bars. There's ice skating outside for kids, plus a bonfire and hot chocolate when the weather dictates. *Killington Rd., Killington, tel. 802/422–3970. AE, D, MC, V.*

Wobbly Barn
The upper two levels of this barn have been a nightclub since 1963. It's a high-energy place that grooves with duos and trios during happy hour and three or four rock bands nightly. It's filled with twenty- and thirty-somethings out for a good time on the dance floor. *Killington Rd., Killington, tel. 802/422–3392. AE, DC, MC, V.*

More Mellow
Mountain Inn
In this long blue-gray clapboard restaurant with dormers, the lounge has a casual country feel, with wood and carpeting, neutral colors, a large fieldstone fireplace, and small tables and chairs. A guitar duo plays easy music. *1 Killington Rd., 3½ mi from Rte. 4, Killington, tel. 802/422–3595. AE, D, MC, V.*

Summit Lodge
The lounge at this clapboard ski lodge is a good place to cool out after a hard day on the slopes. The carpeted room has small tables, couches, and a large fieldstone fireplace. One or two musicians play quiet music. *Killington Rd., Killington, tel. 802/422–3535.*

MOUNT SNOW RESORT

MOUNT SNOW RESORT

Mount Snow, VT 05356
Tel. 802/464-3333

STATISTICALLY SPEAKING

Base elevation: 1,900 feet

Summit elevation: 3,600 feet

Vertical drop: 1,700 feet

Skiable terrain: 767 acres

Number of trails: 130

Longest run: 2½ miles

Lifts and capacity: 3 quads, 9 triples, 8 doubles, 4 surface; 34,000 skiers per hour

Daily lift ticket: $47 weekends, $45 weekdays

Average annual snowfall: 153 inches

Number of skiing days 1995–96: 180

Snowmaking: 537 acres; 85%

Terrain mix: N 20%, I 60%, E 20%

Snowboarding: yes

Cross-country skiing: 3 miles

Mount Snow got its start in 1954 when colorful entrepreneur Walter Schoenknecht turned farmer Reuben Snow's upper pastures on Mt. Pisgah into Mount Snow Resort. It quickly became a mecca for serious skiers and for snow bunnies from all over the Northeast. Now under the American Skiing Company umbrella of seriously skier-minded resorts, Mount Snow is Vermont's second-largest ski resort, and it draws a huge variety of skiers, from locals to intense hotshots young and old, as well as families from Connecticut and the New York metropolitan area. There's equally varied skiing on 50 miles of trails on five mountains. You can ski the two peaks of Haystack (the second is called the Witches), then get on a shuttle bus to gentle Carinthia, from which you can wend your way northward to the slopes of the Main Mountain; from its summit you can tackle the terrifying steeps of the North Face or circle around the back of the mountain to sunny Sunbrook. Food and warmth can be found at five base lodges—the weatherboard-modern main base lodge as well as Carinthia (also known as Planet 9), Haystack Lower, Haystack Upper, and Sundance. Mount Snow attracts serious skiers and serious snowboarders, while Haystack is frequented by families, many with youngsters just learning to ski.

If you're renting skis or taking a lesson, you can buy your lift ticket at the rental shop or ski school without having to line up at ticket windows. On weekends, unless you're putting your kids in ski school, don't buy your tickets at the main lodge; instead, turn off Route 100 onto Handle Road and head for the still relatively undiscovered Carinthia. The parking lot is refreshingly compact, lines are short, and if all you need are lift tickets or rentals, you can take care of your business here.

On weekends, when you're ready for lunch, beware: All the cafeterias are crowded, and particularly on holiday weekends, it's nearly impossible to find a place to sit; the main base lodge is clogged with people eating standing up, eating in hallways, eating on stairwells—and paying high prices for the privilege. So eat early, BYO, or head for Carinthia or shuttle over to Haystack, whose lodge is also prettier.

Children's services: day care,
instruction, tel. 802/464-3333

Snow phone:
tel. 802/464-2151

Police: tel. 802/464-2020

Medical center: Deerfield
Valley Health Center,
tel. 802/464-5311

Hospital: Southwestern
Vermont Medical Center,
tel. 802/442-6361

Resort services:
tel. 802/464-8501

Cross-country skiing: Timber
Creek Cross-Country Center,
tel. 802/464-0999; White
House Cross-Country Center,
tel. 802/464-2135

Road conditions:
tel. 800/429-7623

Towing: tel. 802/464-2276
or 802/464-2166

FIVE-STAR FAVORITES
Best run for vertical: Free Fall

Best run overall: Uncle's

Best bar/nightclub:
Wilmington Village Pub

Best hotel: The Hermitage Inn

Best restaurant:
Inn at Saw Mill Farm

Condos at Mount Snow Resort are mostly down a ways from the mountain near Snow Lake Lodge— once the resort centerpiece, now a bit worse for wear. A spiffy new time-share hotel that's being built on the southern edge of the main base lodge complex is your best bet for ski-in/ski-out convenience. Otherwise, accommodations are in Dover, essentially a strip along Route 100, and in the town at Route 100's junction with Route 9: old-fashioned Wilmington. It's only a couple of miles from the mountain, but the traffic is fierce at day's end, and it can take a half hour or more to get back to your digs on weekends.

HOW TO GET THERE

By Plane
The airports nearest to the resort are **Bradley International** and **Albany County,** both roughly two hours away (*see* Getting to Vermont Resorts, *above*).

By Car
From either north or south, get off I–91 at Exit 2 and pick up Route 9 heading west into Brattleboro. Follow it for 19 miles into Wilmington, then make a right at the light onto Route 100, heading north 9 miles to Mount Snow. From the south you can save about 25 minutes of travel time by taking I–91 to Route 2, heading west at Greenfield, Massachusetts. Watch for the sign to Colrain, Massachusetts; switch to Route 112 heading toward Jacksonville, Vermont; then pick up Route 100 north into Wilmington, Vermont. Turn left onto Route 9 west for a short time and pick up Route 100 again at the traffic light. Make a right and continue to Mount Snow.

You can also take the New York Thruway (I–87) to Albany, New York, then I–787 north to Troy, New York, where you get Route 7 and Route 9 (begins at the Vermont state line) east to Bennington, Vermont. Follow Route 9 east for 21 miles to Wilmington, turn left onto Route 100, and continue to Mount Snow.

Most major car-rental companies are at the Albany County Airport and Bradley International Airport (*see* Getting to Vermont Resorts, *above*).

By Bus
Vermont Transit (tel. 802/864–6811) has scheduled service into Brattleboro.

By Train
Amtrak (tel. 800/872–7245) serves Brattleboro, 19 miles from Wilmington.

GETTING AROUND
With so many of the area's attractions, accommodations, and restaurants spread around the rolling countryside, it's best to have a car. However, the **Haystack Express** (tel. 802/464–8501) provides regular free shuttle service between Haystack and Mount Snow every half hour from 8 AM to 4:30 PM weekends; 9 AM to 4:30 PM weekdays. The shuttle takes between 10 and 15 minutes, but it doesn't stop at Carinthia and doesn't make many stops at the accommodations. A free local shuttle runs between Snow Lake Lodge and every base lodge at Mount Snow and Haystack, including Carinthia, running continuously from 8 AM to 4:30 PM.

THE SKIING
Mount Snow Resort's skiing ranges from dead-easy to drop-dead difficult, with enough in between to keep a skiing family of widely different abilities happy. Here, black diamond is correctly labeled MOST DIFFICULT, no doubt about it. What you see is what you ski. You can start the day on a long and winding beginner's run, follow the sun to a south face, then head north and work your heart and thighs on one of the steepest, gnarliest, narrowest, and occasionally iciest bump runs anywhere. And that's all before lunch.

Where to begin? If you're a beginner, intermediate, or crowd-hating advanced skier, consider starting at relatively uncrowded Haystack. It has 43 short trails that add up to 12½ miles of mainly intermediate, mainly sunny skiing with a few diminutive diamond runs thrown in to keep you on your toes.

Haystack is unusual in that it has two base lodges, one serving only a beginner's area below and entirely separate from the intermediate and expert trails. The rest of the area is composed of two peaks, the Witches and Haystack Mountain. The Witches is by far the steeper, with a number of short but reasonably steep trails that become less difficult as you progress from south to north on the peak.

On Haystack Mountain itself most of the terrain ranges from high beginner to low advanced. You can enjoy a stunning and almost guaranteed solitary view of the surrounding mountains if you remove your skis at the ski patrol hut at the summit of Haystack but take your poles for balance and then walk a few hundred feet down a pretty wooded trail to a cliff top overlooking the ice-covered Haystack Pond. Bargain hunters can pick up substantially cheaper tickets if they're willing to ski only Haystack—ideal if you like sun and don't need a lot of terrain. (The resort sells an even cheaper Haystack-only family ticket.)

Carinthia is a novice-intermediate mountain with a few short and rather unterrifying black-diamond runs. Most trails are straight shots from the top of the slow-moving Carinthia double to the base lodge. That base lodge, now known as Planet 9, has been positioned as a family activity center, with a pool table and video games. It's a good place to start your day on busy weekends.

The Main Mountain, catering mostly to intermediates and experts, is the most crowded section of the Mount Snow complex. Still, there are ways to beat the crowds. When the trail you're skiing suddenly fills with other skiers, move over to the next trail. Time after time you'll see masses of skiers fighting for space on, say, Sundance, while the equally salubrious Hop, Ridge, and Uncle's are all but empty.

The same goes for lifts. Mount Snow has duplicate lifts for almost every part of the area. When one is backed up, switch to the one next to it. (There is one exception to this rule. Both the line and the ride on the Clipper move much faster than on the much slower Summit triple. When the weather's cold or windy, stick with the Clipper.)

Snowboarders have access to the mountain as well as to the Gut, Mount Snow's 400-foot competition-size half pipe, which is lighted from 5 PM to 10 PM daily for night riding; there are also ice skating and sledding.

Novices

Haystack, Carinthia, and the Main Mountain have an abundance of beginner and intermediate terrain. You'll find plenty of options from any of the base lodges, and except for Haystack, all the mountains are connected by trails and lifts.

The beginner's Mixing Bowl chair, at the bottom of Mt. Snow, is a piece of ski history, a holdover from the mid-'50s that is still running. If you're a tall beginner, duck when you ride it or risk a hit in the head from one of the weirdest lifts ever built. The gentle slope of the Children's Learning Center, on the Main Mountain, is served by two novice lifts, a rope tow, and a handle tow. Both Long John and Deer Run—which you reach from the top of the Clipper, the only detachable quad at the resort—are long, gentle, narrowish beginner's runs winding down the mountain. Deer Run is easier, but it snakes across some more advanced trails, so watch your back because when it's busy, speedy skiers often barrel through much faster than they should. Sweet Sixteen is a bit wider and steeper and will take you to Carinthia by way of Seasons Pass, another wider, steeper trail.

The Ski Baba chairlift, serving the beginner's area by the Carinthia base lodge, has a vertical rise of exactly 50 feet and gives access to a wide, gentle slope perfect for very young new skiers.

The most interesting trail on Haystack is Outcast, a 125-foot-wide beginner's trail that wanders for almost a mile through deep woods, revealing lovely vistas of the area as you go. Between Haystack and the Witches is a beginner's trail—Flying Dutchman—that runs from the top of Haystack to the upper base lodge. The final and northernmost Witches run, Shadow, is fine for beginners.

Intermediates

Carinthia is your best bet, with slopes such as the forested, beautiful, and narrow Ryan's Run. The terrain on Carinthia won't give strong intermediate skiers anything to worry about, with one small exception—when the blue-square Upper Iron Run turns into Lower Iron Run, it becomes a narrow black-diamond bump trail. If you find yourself suddenly sweating as you stare down the last 100 yards to the base lodge, you'll know you've found it. But fear not. Instead, back up 10 yards and take Detour down to the bottom.

From Carinthia, less-than-advanced skiers can move in two directions: They can cross the ridge from the top of the Carinthia double on Sun Spot to the warm intermediate trails of Sunbrook or keep heading northwest to the Main Mountain on Long John.

Over on the Main Mountain, most of the trails are labeled MORE DIFFICULT, but in fact they are for the most part good, solid intermediate runs. The Sundance chair and the Clipper high-speed quad take you to the three runs down the front of the mountain: narrow Ego Alley, Sundance, and Sapbucket—long, straight, and not too steep.

Don't leave the Main Mountain without at least one run on Snowdance, reachable from the Clipper quad or the Standard double. This is the ultimate intermediate cruiser, wide enough for the QE2 to tack from one side to the other. With its breadth and moderate pitch, it would be hard to have a bad time here. Then, for variety, take a run on One More Time, a narrow woods trail and the last one before North Face, Mount Snow's most ferocious area.

Not tired yet? Take the Clipper quad and blast down Exhibition, a trail wide and varied enough to bring pleasure to skiers of all abilities. If Clipper is superbusy, move over to the next lift, the Sundance triple, and take Uncle's, a winding trail of multiple pitches varying between fairly steep chutes and nearly flat plateaus—it may be Mount Snow's best-kept secret.

After lunch head for sunny Sunbrook, which has its own quad and the most sunshine in the area—perhaps the most in Vermont. Sunspot, Moonwalk, and Big Dipper all are relatively wide, relatively gentle runs down heavily wooded south-facing slopes. Ski Thanks Walt, which is gentle at the top and steep in the middle, and Cloud Nine, which goes straight down the fall line, continuing to play on their easy backs for a few more runs. They tend to be less crowded and open up a different, south-oriented vista.

If you want to try the Witches, on Haystack, take the short Spellbinder, an honest intermediate that's more or less straight, more or less wide, and not too steep. Last Chance from the summit is a narrow, winding run that takes you to the base of the Oh No lift. Next time down, traverse south and wind your way down Dutchman to the top of Needle, which is not steep enough for black-diamond designation but will give you an adrenaline surge nonetheless.

Experts

For the expert the North Face is where your tour begins. To get to the North Face, either take the main lift, also known as Lift 11, also known as the Clipper detachable quad, to the summit. Or take the Canyon quad to River Run, which gives an easy cruise to the bottom of the North Face. It's best skied in the morning; the light is better, and the snow hasn't yet been skied off.

The North Face is laced with good, challenging expert trails. Olympic is winding and fairly steep, with moguls on top followed by lips to catch air, followed by flatter terrain near the bottom. It's a sweetheart of a trail but definitely not for sleepy cruising; it demands attentive skiing the whole way down. Olympic's next-door neighbor, Fallen Timbers, is very fast, with a lot of different pitches but flat-surfaced. Challenger winds through a forest, then flattens out near the bottom. When Free Fall, which runs right under the lift, has moguls, it's perfect for showoffs and masochists who get off on public humiliation. Chute has killer bumps, but only part of the way down.

The toughest runs at Mount Snow are Jaws of Death and Ripcord. If you want to study them without actually skiing them, take River Run from the Canyon chair. It runs along below the steep stuff, permitting a cool and considered judgment before you take the plunge. Ripcord, Mount Snow Resort's only double-black-diamond run, is a 1,300-foot mogul field tilted like the back of an unloading dump truck— one of the toughest expert runs in New England. Should you find yourself at the top and suddenly remember that you hate being dumped, there is an alternative route to the bottom. Just to the right of Ripcord is the aptly named Second Thoughts, which will give you a kinder, gentler, and considerably slower descent.

The best strategy for advanced skiers and 'boarders on Mt. Snow is to start at the far north and work your way south. This way you minimize crowds and maximize snow conditions. Start on Fallen Timbers or on Chute for the warm-up run, up the ante on Olympic, and then play your hand on the serious bumps of Plummet. If you're feeling really lucky, have a run at Ripcord.

Next, head over to the toughest trails on the all-intermediate Main Mountain for a descent of the fairly steep and narrow Upper Choke, followed by a turn on untrammeled and snowy Ledge, followed by the pleasure of wide-open giant-slalom cruising on Standard (though it's sometimes crowded).

If you're ready for another bump run, try your legs on Sunbrook's Beartrap, an expert slope that comes equipped with an eight-speaker, 600-watt sound system that plays music all day long. You ski wall-to-wall bumps and listen to wall-to-wall rock and roll.

At the bottom of Beartrap is a snack shack (open when weather permits) that saves you the long circle back to the front of the mountain. And since you're skiing one of the least crowded (and certainly the sunniest) spots on Mt. Snow, you may never want to leave. Beartrap is also the site of the annual Glade-iator of the Year contest. Despite its name, it's not a tree run but a bump-skiing freestyle competition for telemarkers, 'boarders, and skiers. If you're at the resort the last weekend in March, be sure to catch it.

If you want to ski only expert trails all day, start on the North Face, then jump on the shuttle and ski Haystack's Witches; here the steepest and southernmost trail is Gandolf; by the time you work your way across Cauldron, Merlin, and Wizard, you'll be up for the challenge.

WHERE TO STAY

Condos are the mainstay accommodations closest to the resort, but at the base is the new Grand Summit Hotel & Crown Club, and within a 10-mile radius there are distinguished inns, classic B&Bs, and homey lodges. All accommodations can be booked through Mount Snow central reservations (tel. 800/245–7669) or Snow Resorts (Mountain Park Plaza, Box 757, Rte. 100, West Dover 05356, tel. 802/464–2177, fax 802/464–3809).

Expensive

Grand Summit Hotel & Crown Club
Time-shares make a lot of sense for skiers who want the permanence of a second home without the maintenance headaches, and they're a feature of several of the American Skiing Company properties. This one is breaking ground at press time, in preparation for a winter 1997 opening with all the luxuries. Units range in size from studios to three-bedroom layouts, all complete with a kitchen, and will be available for rent when not occupied by the owners. For ski-in/ski-out convenience, this is the place. *Rte. 100, Mount Snow 05356, tel. 802/464–7788 or 800/451–4211, fax 802/464–4192. 203 units. Facilities: restaurant, pool, hot tub, sauna, exercise room, concierge, child care. AE, D, DC, MV, V. $139–$800.*

Greenspring at Mount Snow
These extralarge two- to four-bedroom condominiums are just across Route 100 from the resort and have an exceptional view of the mountain. Reminiscent of Vermont farmhouses, they are built in traditional New England style with vertical pine board and batten. Units are individually decorated, many in early American style and some surprisingly modern. All the units have three levels, a spacious living and dining area, and a fireplace with free firewood. *Box 540, West Dover 05356, tel. 802/464–7111 or 800/247–7833, fax 802/464–1114. 140 units. Facilities: pool, hot tub, sauna, exercise room, video games, shuttle. AE, MC, V. $260–$495.*

The Hermitage Inn
Imagine a 24-acre mountainside country retreat, complete with a stately dining room, intimate bar, exquisite wine cellar, decoy collection, and art gallery. All rooms have fireplaces; four are in the main building, four are in the carriage house, and seven more are in the wine house, which has a wine store on the first level. Also on the property are a hunting preserve, sugar house, and 50 kilometers of cross-country ski trails. *Coldbrook Rd., Box 457, Wilmington 05363, tel. 802/464–3511. 15 rooms. Facilities: restaurant, bar, cross-country skiing. AE, D, DC, MC, V. $225, including full breakfast and dinner.*

Inn at Saw Mill Farm
Architect Rodney Williams transformed this old farm complex into a tasteful and stylish inn. Rooms may have canopy beds and comfortable armchairs—some come with a fireplace and a balcony (no phones or televisions, however). *Mount Snow Valley, Crosstown Rd. and Rte. 100,*

Box 367, West Dover 05356, tel. 802/464-8131, fax 802/464-1130. 20 rooms. AE, MC, V. $340-$425, including full breakfast and dinner.

Seasons Condominiums

These ski-in/ski-out painted-clapboard condos managed by Mount Snow Resort offer a choice of one-, two-, or three-bedroom units, all with lots of space. Owners have decorated individual units in their own styles, everything from traditional country to ultramodern, with such nice touches as original art and brightly colored bed covers. All units come with a fireplace, a dining area, and a washer-dryer. *Mount Snow Lodging, 299 Mountain Rd., Mount Snow 05356, tel. 802/464-7788 or 800/451-4211, fax 802/464-3808. 70 units. Facilities: indoor pool, hot tub, sauna, recreation room, ski-in/ski-out. AE, D, DC, V. $103-$700.*

Moderate

Inn at Mount Snow

This small white-clapboard country inn is right next to the ski area. Half of the rooms have spectacular mountain views. Every room is decorated differently, many with floral patterns. The living room is comfortable with a large fireplace and big picture windows. The billiards room has an antique pool table with leather pockets. The owners have recently purchased a 30-room lodge next door to the inn that is ideal for families and groups. *Rte. 100, Box 1546, West Dover 05356, tel. 802/464-3300 or 800/577-7669, fax 802/464-3396. 45 rooms. Facilities: ski storage, shuttle. AE, D, MC, V. $80-$323, including full breakfast.*

Nutmeg Inn

This handsome 1770s farmhouse on the west side of Wilmington was turned into a country inn in 1957. The rooms, which have woodwork and selectively exposed brick, are furnished with brass or iron beds, Laura Ashley-style bed covers, handmade quilts, colorful throw rugs, and antique or reproduction furniture. *Rte. 9, Box 818, Wilmington 05363, tel. 802/464-3351 or 800/277-5402, fax 802/464-7331. 12 rooms, 2 suites. Facilities: library, lobby lounge. AE, D, MC, V. $88-$175, including full breakfast.*

West Dover Inn

This traditional Greek Revival building with a quiet setting was built in 1846 and is on the National Register of Historic Places. It's full of original charm. Every room is different: Some are decorated with antique lamps, armoires, and brass beds with hand-sewn quilts; the suites have fireplaces and whirlpool tubs. *Rte. 100, Box 1208, West Dover 05356, tel. 802/464-5207 or 800/732-0745, fax 802/464-2173. 8 rooms, 4 suites. Facilities: restaurant, bar, library, meeting rooms. AE, MC, V. $80-$200, including full breakfast.*

White House

On a grassy knoll just east of the village of Wilmington is this stately colonial-style mansion. Rooms, some with handsome brick fireplaces, are done in early American style, with polished hardwood floors, rich area rugs, and well-crafted wooden furnishings. Next door at the farmhouse are seven additional rooms, decorated in the same elegant style, though a bit smaller.

Rte. 9, Wilmington 05363, tel. 802/ 464–2135 or 800/541–2135, fax 802/ 464–5222. 16 rooms. Facilities: restaurant, bar, indoor pool, sauna, hot tub, cross-country skiing. AE, DC, MC, V. $108–$178, including full breakfast.

Inexpensive

Four Seasons Inn

This hotel outside Wilmington, 2 miles from Mount Snow, offers colorful rooms with bright wallpaper and cheerful print bedspreads. All rooms are carpeted; deluxe rooms come with a refrigerator. *Rte. 100, Box 6, West Dover 05356, tel. 802/464–8303. 24 rooms. Facilities: dining room, bar, sauna, ski storage. AE, D, MC, V. $45–$85.*

Gray Ghost Inn

This inn set within a mile of Mount Snow has a comfortable family feel. Some rooms are paneled with tongue-and-groove cypress; local pottery and art embellish others. Handmade quilts, maple nightstands, and lace curtains in the rooms and the fireplace in the main lounge lend a real country inn flavor. *Rte. 100, Box 938, West Dover 05356, tel. 802/464–2474 or 800/745–3615. 26 rooms. Facilities: dining room, sauna, library, piano. AE, D, MC, V. $32–$47, including full breakfast.*

Old Red Mill Inn

This 19th-century structure on the creek near the intersection of Route 9 and Route 100 in Wilmington used to be a sawmill, and it shows: As you put your feet up on the huge open hearth, you can study the original machinery (check out the huge old bellows), the massive beams, and the slightly lurchy wide-board floors. The

rooms upstairs are fairly basic, with sturdy wooden furniture and beds that (like many in the local hostelries in these parts) will have you longing for your own. But the price is right. And the restaurant downstairs is downright pleasant. *Rte. 100, Wilmington 05363, tel. 802/464–3700 or 800/843–8483, fax 802/464–8513. 26 rooms. Facilities: restaurant. AE, D, DC, MC, V. $40–$80.*

Snow Creek Inn

This gray-and-white barn-board motel, 1½ miles from the mountain, offers large, clean rooms with homemade pillows and quilts and a small refrigerator. Efficiencies with kitchenettes are also available. *Rte. 100, Box 1008, West Dover 05356, tel. 802/ 464–5632, fax 802/464–0829. 19 rooms, 2 units. Facilities: lobby lounge, laundry facilities. AE, D, MC, V. $60–$100.*

WHERE TO EAT

In and around the resort there's an excellent choice of restaurants. Wilmington and West Dover offer a wide variety of cuisines.

Expensive

The Hermitage Inn

Just above the Haystack ski area, this secluded country inn serves elaborate dinners in several distinctly different dining rooms—one of my favorites is the intimate porch. The inn's owner raises deer, pheasant, and wild turkey on the premises. The menu includes such delectable dishes as roast pheasant with hunter's sauce (mushrooms, tomatoes, tarragon, and Madeira) and venison sautéed with bourbon, shallots, and cracked pepper. The wine cellar houses some 40,000 bottles. *Coldbrook Rd., Wilmington, tel. 802/ 464–3511. Reservations essential. AE, DC, MC, V.*

Inn at Saw Mill Farm
The chef here is Brill Williams, son of the inn's owner-architect. The dining room, part of an old barn, has wide-plank floors and toile wallpaper hung with 19th-century portraits and landscapes in massive gilt frames. The linen, sterling, and crystal on the table set a perfect stage for such complex fare as pheasant breast *forestière* and steak *au poivre*. *Mount Snow Valley, Crosstown Rd. and Rte. 100, West Dover, tel. 802/464–8131. Reservations essential. AE, MC, V.*

Le Petit Chef
Charming and unpretentious, this French restaurant occupies an early 18th-century white farmhouse. Laura Ashley wallpaper decorates the walls above the wainscoting. The menu, which changes seasonally, may feature chicken breast with pignoli nuts and grapes and roast beef with green peppercorn sauce. *Rte. 100, Wilmington, tel. 802/464–8437. Reservations essential. MC, V.*

Two Tannery Road
Fireplaces warm each dining room of this 18th-century house, formerly a Roosevelt summer residence. The quiet, attentive staff serves traditional fare such as seafood stew, shrimp scampi, steak au poivre, and fresh Long Island duckling in black cherry sauce. *2 Tannery Rd., West Dover, tel. 0802/464–2707. MC, V.*

Moderate
Dover Forge
This family restaurant has a blacksmith theme, complete with a brick floor and a fireplace flanked by bellows and forges. You select your base entrée—pasta, fish, pork, chicken, or veal—and then choose from a spectrum of sauces and preparation styles. *Andiron Lodge, Rte. 100, West Dover, tel. 802/464–2114. D, MC, V.*

Fannie's
A cathedral ceiling towers above the dining room of this rustic restaurant built as a house in 1838. Among the steak, chicken, and fish dishes are such entrées as Yankee grilled chicken and barbecued St. Louis ribs, as well as many other steak, chicken, and fish dishes. *Rte. 9, W. Main St., Wilmington, tel. 802/464–1143. Reservations essential. AE, D, DC, MC, V.*

Poncho's Wreck
This architectural anomaly in the middle of quaint Wilmington is a strange cross between Victorian San Francisco, a beachcombers' Hall of Fame, and the medal room of the New York Yacht Club. The food, as imaginatively whimsical as the decor, includes not only familiar south-of-the-border specialties, but also steak, chicken, ribs, and seafood dishes that shift with the ocean breezes. Sunday brunch is a monster. *S. Main St., Wilmington, tel. 802/464–9320. AE, D, MC, V.*

Inexpensive
Dot's Restaurant
Dot is renowned locally for her great home cooking and baking, not to mention her daily specials, which include baked stuffed sole, chicken

stuffed with jack cheese and broccoli, pasta, homemade soups, sandwiches, and burgers. Nifty movie stills and other memorabilia adorn the knotty pine walls. *Main St., 8 mi south of Mount Snow, Wilmington, tel. 802/464–7284. MC, V.*

The Silo

This landmark silo, hay barn, and 19th-century windmill is a good bet for steaks, chops, and burgers from the grill, homemade meat loaf, fried chicken, New York cheesecake, and chocolate mousse. *Rte. 100, West Dover, tel. 802/464–2553. AE, D, DC, MC, V.*

Tony's Pizza

You can either eat it in, take it out, or have it delivered—the *it* being hot and cold subs, pasta, homemade soups, salad bar, and of course, pizza. *Rte. 100, West Dover, tel. 802/464–8669. No credit cards.*

Best Bets for Breakfast

The Bakery

For the absolute best selection of breakfast baked goods, the Bakery is the place to be. There's room to sit down and enjoy, or you can choose and go. There are excellent muffins, sweet breads, croissants, fruit-filled pastries, and some of the best coffee in the area. *Rte. 100, West Dover, tel. 802/464–5914.*

White House

This marvelously formal, sun-filled dining room is in the stately, colonial-style hotel of the same name. The atmosphere is quiet and contemplative. Blueberry pancakes, eggs champignon, and French toast made from homemade honey-wheat bread are signature items. *Rte. 9, Wilmington, tel. 802/464–2135. AE, D, MC, V.*

NIGHTLIFE AND ENTERTAINMENT

Après-Ski

Deacon's Den

When you've had your fill of the slopes and want to warm up, you can come here for free soup and a drink. There are airplane props, a carousel horse, and other paraphernalia on the walls and live rock or blues on weekends. Or you can shoot pool, shoot hoops, or just shoot the breeze. *Rte. 100, West Dover, tel. 802/464–9361. AE, D, MC, V.*

Loud and Lively/Dancing

The Silo

This sprawling entertainment emporium has two dance floors, loud music (occasionally live), and two large fireplaces surrounded by big comfortable chairs. In the early evening it's a family crowd, but later on the average age plummets. *Rte. 100, West Dover, tel. 802/464–2553. AE, D, DC, MC, V.*

Wilmington Village Pub

Busy and lively, this sports-bar-cum-dance-emporium is decked out in all the appropriate jock memorabilia. There's pool and pinball and multiple satellite-linked TVs. Upstairs is calmer, with a large fieldstone fireplace. *7 S. Main St., Wilmington, tel. 802/464–2280.*

STOWE MOUNTAIN RESORT

STOWE MOUNTAIN RESORT

5781 Mountain Rd., Rte. 108
Stowe, VT 05672
Tel. 802/253-3000

STATISTICALLY SPEAKING
Base elevation: 1,280 feet

Summit elevation: 4,393 feet

Vertical drop: 2,360 feet

Skiable terrain: 480 acres

Number of trails: 46

Longest run: 3.7 miles

Lifts and capacity: 1 gondola,
1 quad, 1 triple, 6 doubles, 2
surface; 11,465 skiers per
hour

Daily lift ticket: $48

Average annual snowfall:
250 inches

Number of skiing days
1995–96: 157

Snowmaking: 350 acres; 73%

Terrain mix: N 16%, I 59%,
E 25%

Snowboarding: yes

Cross-country skiing: 150 kilometers (accessible from
Stowe Mountain Resort Touring Center)

Stowe Resort covers two mountains, Mt. Mansfield and Spruce Peak. Geographically, Mansfield and Spruce look like siblings of different ages and, perhaps, different fathers. Mansfield is big—by Vermont standards, *very* big. At 4,393 feet, it is the highest peak in the state and by far the most renowned. When northern Vermonters talk about a day on Mt. Mansfield, they say, "Wanna go ski the Mountain?" Mansfield is a hill among hills, high as the sky, broad as a Vermont barn, and as laced with ski trails as a summer cottage in March is with cobwebs.

Spruce Peak is a comparatively diminutive 3,300 feet, and its one skiable face gazes southeast toward Mansfield as if looking up at a big brother. Spruce forms the southern gate of Smugglers Notch, a narrow, winding gap through the Green Mountains that used to be the lair of rum and cattle smugglers and is now, at least in winter, the exclusive domain of cross-country skiers, snowshoers, and peregrine falcons soaring the thermals above their heads.

The first recorded descent of Mt. Mansfield was in 1914. One of the earliest ski resorts in the East grew almost organically—because people kept on skiing down the mountain. The first Stowe winter carnival was held in 1921; it marked the beginning of skiing as a tourist attraction in the area, long before lifts were built. Events included ski jumping, snowshoeing, skating, and bobsledding. During the Depression, Perry Merrill (a skier and director of the Vermont Forest Service) convinced the federal government that ski trails were roads, and so the Civilian Conservation Corps built the first ski trail on Mt. Mansfield in 1932. In 1934 they cut Nosedive, which is still in use (*see* Experts *in* The Skiing, *below*). In 1940 the longest chairlift in the United States opened on Mansfield and broke down on its first run, stranding the governor and other dignitaries. Nowadays the lifts on both mountains are considerably more reliable.

Stowe the town, a much-photographed symbol of New England village life, looks like a Currier & Ives engraving, complete with white-steepled church and old-fashioned general store. Discreetly tucked away in this 19th-century setting are such 20th-century amenities as four golf courses, 50 tennis courts, 51 restaurants, 64 lodgings, and 75 shops. If it's not typ-

USEFUL NUMBERS

Area code: 802

Children's services: day care, instruction, tel. 802/253–3000

Snow phone: tel. 802/253–3600 or 800/247–8693

Police: tel. 911 or 802/253–7126

Hospital: Copley, tel. 802/888–4231

Stowe Area Association: tel. 800/247–8693

Road conditions: tel. 800/429–7623

Towing: Willy's Auto, tel. 802/253–8552

FIVE-STAR FAVORITES

Best run for vertical: Goat

Best run overall: National

Best bar/nightclub: Bert's Place

Best hotel: Green Mountain Inn

Best restaurant: Cactus Café

ical Vermont, Stowe conveys the *air* of Vermont—the Vermont of Laura Ashley wallpaper, of Swiss fondue restaurants, and of shops called Nothing But Cows, all domiciled in wooden clapboard houses built before the Civil War.

The village is the hub of Stowe, the visual and historic heart of the town. Two major roads meet here, each with a distinctly different character—Route 100, the highway that connects most of the state's ski areas, and the Mountain Road. Route 100 is the classic American strip, but with antiques stores instead of used-car dealers. The Mountain Road and its environs, the newest commercial development in the area, is yuppie heaven, with a colorful mix of inns and eateries, sport shops and boutiques, wine stores and gift emporiums strung out between the highway and the frozen West Branch of the Little River.

Accommodations at the resort include one on-mountain lodge and range from a youth hostel and simple bed-and-breakfasts to lush spas and upscale inns nearby. All are sprinkled on or just off the Mountain Road and up and down Route 100 from the center of town.

HOW TO GET THERE

By Plane

The **Burlington International Airport** is a 45-minute drive west of the resort (*see* Getting to Vermont Resorts, *above*).

Shuttle Services

Transfers from Burlington Airport to Stowe are available from **Lamoille County Taxi** (tel. 800/252–0204, ext. 3) and **Peg's Pick-up** (tel. 800/253–9490). Advance reservations are required for both services.

By Car

Stowe is 45 minutes east of Burlington Airport (*see* Getting to Vermont Resorts, *above*) and 15 minutes from I-89. Get off at Exit 10 (Stowe/Waterbury) onto Route 100. Follow Route 100 north to the intersection of Route 100 and Route 108, in Stowe village. Take Route 108 north (the Mountain Road) for 6 miles to the Stowe Mountain Resort. Stowe is six hours' drive from New York City and less than four hours from Hartford, Boston, and Albany. From Montreal, Stowe can be reached in approximately 2½ hours.

Car rentals are available in Stowe at **Stowe Auto Service** (tel. 802/253-7608).

By Bus
Vermont Transit Company (tel. 802/864-6811) and **Greyhound Lines** (tel. 802/864-6811) provide daily service to Burlington and Waterbury. If you arrange it in advance, some inns offer pickup service from Waterbury. Otherwise, taxis are available.

By Train
The **Amtrak** (tel. 800/872-7245) station in Waterbury, Vermont, is 15 minutes from Stowe, and round-trip transfers are available to most hotels. Many lodges in Stowe will arrange to meet your train. Stowe Preferred Round-Trip fares are available on Amtrak's *Vermonter* from Washington, D.C., Philadelphia, and New York.

GETTING AROUND
By Shuttle
The $1 shuttle bus (tel. 802/253-7321), operated by Stowe Mountain Resort, runs continuously all season long between the village of Stowe and the resort, with stops along the way. You can pick it up roughly every 15 minutes during peak hours and then every hour until 10 PM at key locations, including the Gondola Barn, the Midway Base Lodge, the Spruce Peak Base Lodge, the Vermont State Ski Dorm, and H.H. Binghams, the restaurant at the Toll House lift.

By Taxi
Stowe Taxi (tel. 802/253-9433) serves the town.

By Car
When traffic is heavy on the Mountain Road, as it almost always is on holiday weekends, you'll crawl the 6 miles between the village of Stowe and the parking lots for Mt. Mansfield and Spruce Peak. Your best bet at these times is to use the shuttle service.

THE SKIING
On the ski area map, Stowe is two mountains, Mt. Mansfield and Spruce Peak. On the skier's internal map, Stowe is numerous mountains, each serving different types of skiers. Although most of the areas are on Mt. Mansfield, there's little geographical and even less functional overlap among them. Spruce Peak is a mountain devoted entirely to beginning and intermediate skiers. The pace is slower here than on Mansfield, and so are the skiers and the lifts (the Big Spruce Double was built in 1954). Mt. Mansfield accommodates skiers of every type, from never-evers to the most fearless in North America.

The bottom of Spruce is a broad expanse of practice slopes ranging from the fairly precipitous Slalom Hill to the aptly named Easy Street. In addition to slow pace and gentle terrain, Spruce has the advantage of afternoon sun. In December and January, when the sun leaves Mansfield's north-northeast-facing slopes early, Spruce is the place to be. Unfortunately, all that sunshine added to a complete lack of snowmaking on Upper Spruce means that in snow-lean times the Big Spruce lift is roped off, with a CLOSED sign dangling from the rope.

Stowe is great for cruising; there are great runs for everyone from novices to experts. Another skiing mode at Stowe is night skiing, which began here in 1991. The resort has lighted the top of Perry Merrill, the length of Gondolier, and the breadth of the beginner slopes by the Midway Café. The gondola gives access to the lighted slopes and, for beginners, the surface lift at its base. Dress warmly and wear goggles with clear lenses.

To get the most out of your ski time at Stowe, consider these tips: The best the resort has to offer begins on the gondola or quad at 7:30 AM holidays and weekends and at 8 AM during the week. This is when you'll find the best light, the smallest crowds, and every peak and trail on both mountains bathed in sun. At 11 AM Nosedive begins to lose light, and those around it soon follow. Start working your way to the right toward Toll Road.

When the lines at the quad and the gondola go on into next Tuesday, the triple chair is virtually empty. Yet it gives access to a long beginner's trail (Lullaby Lane), wonderful intermediate trails (Gulch, Standard, North Slope), and the lower half of an expert trail (Hayride).

Another Stowe specialty is Stowe Hosts, volunteers who know and will show you where the day's best skiing lies. Stowe Host tours start daily at 10:30 AM and 1:30 PM at the top of the Forerunner quad.

One final bit of insider's information: At the top of the Spruce Peak lift is a closely guarded Stowe secret: a little-known trail (not on the ski area map) that gives you access to the Smugglers Notch Resort, on the north slope of Mt. Mansfield. You reach Snuffy's, the groomed and patrolled connecting trail, by skating over Ster-

ling Pond. Stowe and Smugglers let one another's customers have one ride free. The views from the top are spectacular, and the trail across Sterling Pond is still an adventure that 99% of Stowe visitors never even hear of.

Like most of the mountains of northern Vermont, Stowe is scrupulously honest about its trail categories. If signs say, MORE DIFFICULT, you need to make linked stem turns to enjoy the trail. If they say, MOST DIFFICULT, expect steepness and/or moguls. If a sign says, EXPERTS ONLY, believe it.

Snowboarders have access to the entire mountain and to all lifts. There's also a half pipe and three terrain parks off the Forerunner quad, the Mountain triple, and the Easy Street double.

Novices

If you're a first-time skier who's going to be spending some time in these parts, has Stowe got a deal for you! You take a beginner's lesson (for $48), and when you're good enough to ski down from Stowe's two easiest lifts, the Mighty Mite (9) and the Easy Street double chair (8), you're given a season pass good for the Toll House double on Mt. Mansfield.

On Mansfield, start with the gentlest run, Toll Road. It's beginner's bliss, novitiate's nirvana. To reach it, take the Forerunner quad from the main base area. Toll Road is Stowe's easiest trail, 3.7 miles of wide curves slowly meandering through the woods down to the Toll House double.

Toll House, the easternmost lift at Stowe, gives access to the bottom third of Toll Road and the straight and deliberate Easy Mile. It is the lift closest to the village and may be the best-equipped beginner's area in the world, with its own restaurant (H.H. Binghams), tavern (the Broken Ski), hotel (the Inn at the Mountain), and condos (the Lodge and Mt. Mansfield Townhouses). It also has its own parking lot, so if traffic is heavy, you can stop here and use the chair to reach the rest of Mt. Mansfield.

When there's natural snow, beginning cruisers can try Main Street on Spruce Peak. The least crowded areas for beginners are Spruce Peak and Toll House.

Intermediates

On Spruce Peak you have a choice of three winding trails through the woods—Sterling, Whirlaway, and Upper Smugglers—plus one wider ski highway, Main Street. All are true intermediate trails, with no unexpected ultrasteeps or nerve-racking narrows to ruin your day.

On Mt. Mansfield when you graduate from beginner to intermediate status, it's time to ride the Toll House double for the last time and ski down Lullaby Lane to the Mountain triple. Lullaby Lane is nearly as gentle as Easy Mile, but from the triple you can get to the low intermediate Tyro and the solidly intermediate Standard and Gulch. As you ski them, you (and your knees) will feel the difference in terrain. Stowe's trails are laid out so that intermediate skiers have a safe way down from any lift. But bear in mind that as you leave Toll House and work your way left across the mountain section served by the triple and the Forerunner quad (the area known as the Main Mountain), the trails grow progressively steeper.

You can continue left on Rimrock to "the world's fastest eight-person gondola." This technological marvel, separated by a deep, forested bowl from most of Mansfield's trails, rockets out of the Gondola Barn, past the Midway Lodge and Café, and up a steep pitch to the Cliff House Restaurant. From there the intermediate Cliff Trail leads back to the main mountain, or you can cruise straight back to the barn on Gondolier. Other good cruisers are Sunrise (gentler) and the lower half of Nosedive. The least crowded runs for intermediates are Upper Spruce, Lower Standard, Gulch, and Lord.

Experts

The Front Four are the trails that gave Stowe its fierce reputation. Usually groomed, Lift Line starts with a steep drop-off, briefly levels off midway, and plunges straight down at the end. National is even steeper and more challenging, and the remaining two members of the Front Four go well beyond challenging. If you ski Starr or, worse, Goat, make certain that: There's plenty of snow cover, you really are an expert, and your insurance is paid up.

The oldest and best-known expert trail is Nosedive, built in 1934 and widened and somewhat tamed in 1966. It's still a steep and exhilarating challenge at the top and a fine cruising trail lower down.

From the gondola three expert trails lead back to the barn: The hardest is Chinclip; the two others are winding, frolicking Perry Merrill (1½ miles) and Switchback. Depending on what's been groomed that day, any one of these trails could have gentle moguls, but none is allowed to turn ferocious.

From the quad Lord and North Slope are good warm-up runs. Hayride gives you some more challenge. For experts, the least crowded trails are any that are away from the quad and gondola lifts.

Stowe's worst-kept secret is the glades. Stowe has no shortage of trees and no shortage of glade skiing. Yet except for one short dogleg of a trail labeled Slalom Glades, cut in the mid-1930s, and two trails—Tres Amigos and Lookout Glades, cut recently—they don't appear on the trail map. This is because officially they don't exist. To find these "nonexistent" woods, follow the experts between Chinclip and Gondolier, through gaps in the trees off Cliff Trail, and anywhere else you see skiers darting into the forest. Note well that as these glade trails don't officially exist, you ski them at your own risk. Your ticket won't be pulled by the ski patrol, but you are not encouraged to go in. If you do, go with a buddy. Nonexistent woods are terrible spots to get lost in alone.

WHERE TO STAY

Few resort areas in New England offer the variety of accommodations that you'll find at Stowe, although precious little of it is actually slope-side. There are large resort hotels, modern condo complexes, smaller lodges, basic inns, and motels, plus a wide selection of typical bed-and-breakfast establishments. When choosing where to stay, consider that the town is 5 miles from the ski slopes on Route 108 and that traffic to and from the village and the mountain can be terminally slow and frustrating. All reservations can be made through Stowe Central Reservations (tel. 800/253-4754).

Be sure to inquire about package rates: Most establishments will offer multiday packages that in many cases include meals and lift tickets for considerably less than the posted daily rate. All accommodations in this section are in Stowe and have a zip code of 05672.

Expensive

Green Mountain Inn

This classic three-story inn, built in 1833 right in the middle of Stowe village, is one of five in Vermont named a Historic Hotel of America by the National Trust for Historic Preservation. The character is obvious when you enter the lobby—polished pine floors, comfortable sofas, soft lighting, and classical music. The rooms have modern facilities, but the historic theme continues with period wall coverings and stencils, four-poster or canopy beds, and watercolors by a local artist. Afternoon tea is served in the lobby. *Main St., Box 60, tel. 802/253-7301 or 800/253-7302, fax 802/253-5096. 50 rooms, 14 suites. Facilities: 2 restaurants, bar, sauna, steam room, health club, shuttle, laundry service. AE, D, DC, MC, V. $89–$189.*

Inn at the Mountain and Condos

If you must ski in and ski out, this 70-year-old three-story hotel and the condos nearby are your only choices. Original Grandma Moses artworks and dark-wood fixtures decorate the inn lobby. The inn rooms are spacious if uninspiring. For the space and privacy of condo living, the tree-shrouded minivillage surrounding the inn is a good bet. The units have one, two, or three bedrooms. Each has a fireplace, a full kitchen, a dining area, a washer-dryer, and a deck. *5781 Mountain Rd., tel. 802/253–3000 or 800/253–4754, fax 802/253–3604. 28 rooms, 7 suites, 13 town houses, 23 units. Facilities: 2 restaurants, health club, cross-country skiing. AE, D, DC, MC, V. $150–$350, including full breakfast and dinner.*

Topnotch at Stowe Resort and Spa
One of the top-rated resort hotel/spas in the Stowe area, the Topnotch exudes old-world substance and style. Its 120 acres of grounds are ringed by mountaintops. Dark woods and Tudor furnishings set the tone; rooms are individually decorated in hunter green and maroon with antiques, original art, and well-crafted mahogany furniture. In addition to the hotel, the sprawling complex has town houses and a full-service health spa. In the two- and three-bedroom town houses, which are as luxurious as the hotel, decor varies according to the owner's taste. *Mountain Rd., Box 1458, 2 mi from mountain, tel. 802/253–8585 or 800/451–8686, fax 802/253–9263. 90 rooms, 3 efficiencies, 17 town houses. Facilities: 2 restaurants, lounge, spa, indoor pool, cross-country skiing, ski shop, guided tours, baby-sitting, laundry service. AE, D, DC, MC, V. $188–$525.*

Trapp Family Lodge
On a hilltop, surrounded by 2,200 acres of pristine, rolling meadows and woodlands and built (and rebuilt after a fire in 1980) by the legendary Trapp family, who inspired *The Sound of Music,* the lodge is wonderful, elegant, and Austrian in style. The rooms have dark-wood furnishings, bright and stylish accents in rich colors, and nice touches such as fluffy goose-down bedcovers. If you want more space, you can try getting one of the private houses on the property, which are available for weekly rental on a limited basis. *42 Trapp Hill Rd., tel. 802/253–8511 or 800/826–7000, fax 802/253–5740. 86 rooms, 5 suites, 100 houses. Facilities: 2 dining rooms, indoor pool, sauna, massage, fitness center. $85–$340.*

Moderate

Edson Hill Manor
This brick and finished-log manor house was originally a private mountaintop estate fashioned after an 18th-century French country house in Québec. It sits on 225 acres of woodland, open to cross-country skiing, horseback riding, and sleigh rides. Rooms are in the manor house and in four newer satellite guest houses; all are decorated with antiques, elegant wooden furnishings, and area rugs and tapestries. Most rooms have a fireplace. *1500 Edson Hill Rd., tel. 802/253–7371 or 800/621–0284, fax 802/253–4036. 25 rooms. Facilities: restaurant, bar, cross-country skiing, horseback riding, snowshoeing. AE, D, MC, V. $55–$105 per person.*

Golden Eagle Resort
Since 1963 this family-oriented facility has evolved from a modest motel to today's 80-acre, 10-building hospitality and recreational miniempire, complete with mountain and pond views. There are standard hotel rooms with a double or queen-size bed and slightly larger efficiencies with limited cooking facilities. The condos sleep six and have a full kitchen, a living room, and two baths. There's nothing exceptional about the decor or the furnishings here, but everything is

spotless and well maintained. *Mountain Rd., Box 1090, tel. 802/253–4811 or 800/626–1010, fax 802/253–2561. 71 rooms, 12 efficiencies, 5 units, 3 houses. Facilities: 2 restaurants, indoor pool, sauna, whirlpool, exercise room, fitness center, cross-country skiing, ice skating, billiards, laundry, nature trails. AE, D, DC, MC, V. $79–$299.*

Mountain Road Resort

This wonderfully modern and stylish resort complex is nestled in the trees and meadows just off Mountain Road. Accommodations range from basic single rooms to suites to two-bedroom condos, and all rooms are no-smoking. Regardless of size, everything is well furnished—brass beds, attractive fixtures—and well equipped. All units come with a small fridge. *Mountain Rd., Box 8, 3 mi from resort, tel. 802/253–4566 or 800/367–6873, fax 802/253–7397. 25 rooms, 6 suites. Facilities: indoor pool, sauna, Jacuzzi, outdoor hot tub, gym, wine bar. AE, D, DC, MC, V. $89–$325, including full breakfast and après-ski snacks.*

Siebeness

Nestled in the foothills of Mt. Mansfield, this place is homey without feeling cloistered. The main, two-story Colonial building is distinguishable by the stenciled drawings lining each shutter. Though not especially big, rooms in the main building are decorated with tasteful pine and maple antique furnishings, small artifacts, pieces of art, and such personal touches as duvets or quilts. The main inn has a comfortable sitting room with a large fireplace. There is also a full-service cottage that sleeps four. *3681 Mountain Rd., about 2½ mi from*

resort, tel. 802/253–8942 or 800/426–9001, fax 802/253–9232. 11 rooms, 1 cottage. Facilities: lounge, outdoor hot tub, game room. AE, D, MC, V. $70–$180, including full breakfast.

Inexpensive

The Gables

This rustic, comfortable B&B is housed in a classic, rambling 1856 farmhouse complete with a front porch. Barnboard, exposed beams, and antiques set the tone in the large sitting area warmed by a giant fireplace and filled with overstuffed chairs and couches. The room furnishings are a bit patchwork and vary wildly from room to room, but they're comfortable without being overly fussy. *1457 Mountain Rd., tel. 802/253–7730 or 800/422–5371, fax 802/253–8989. 13 rooms, 2 suites, 4 carriage house rooms. Facilities: outdoor hot tub, game room, snowshoeing. AE, D, MC, V. $100–$175, including full breakfast and après-ski snacks.*

Innsbruck Inn

A Bavarian handcrafted bell tower and Austrian-style murals set this inn apart from other big motels. The rooms are exceptionally large; most have a queen-size bed and a living area complete with a sofa and comfy chairs. Each efficiency sleeps eight and has a kitchenette; the house has five bedrooms, two baths, a full kitchen, a sauna, and four more bunks in the basement. *4361 Mountain Rd., tel. 802/253–8582 or 800/225–8582, fax 802/253–2260. 20 rooms, 4 efficiencies, 1 house. Facilities: restaurant, bar, spa, hot tub, sauna. AE, D, MC, V. $29–$69 per person, including full breakfast.*

Ten Acres Lodge

This charming New England–style clapboard lodge in a pastoral setting is warm and inviting. Rooms are stylish and elegant, with colorful print wall coverings. Some rooms come with a fireplace. The cottages have more sleeping space, a kitchenette, and a fireplace. *14 Barrows Rd., tel. 802/253–7638 or 800/327–7357, fax 802/253–4036. 16 rooms, 2 cottages. Facilities: restaurant, bar, outdoor hot tub. AE, D, MC, V. $40–$70 per person, including full breakfast and après-ski snacks.*

Vermont State Ski Dorm

This former Civilian Conservation Corps site camp offers bunk-bed accommodations. Not only is it the lowest per-night price in the area, it's the closest to the mountain—less than a half mile. The common room is warmed by a fireplace. There is a surprisingly good breakfast and a dinner that varies depending on who is the current manager. *6992 Mountain Rd., tel. 802/253–4010. 24 bunk beds. Facilities: dining room, lounge, sauna, game room, guided tours. AE, D, DC, MC, V. $20 per person; $24 with full breakfast; $29 with breakfast and dinner.*

WHERE TO EAT

Although there's no shortage of restaurants in the Stowe area, there's definitely a lack of innovative dining spots. Good, hearty, wholesome dining seems to be the mainstay, with a few exceptions. Stowe Mountain Resort is unique because it purchased a Maine seafood company, complete with lobster pound, to ensure quality seafood at low prices through the lean winter months. It supplies the restaurants at the Inn at the Mountain with lobster, crab, mussels, steamers, little-neck clams, oysters, shrimp, and other fresh fish.

Most of Stowe's restaurants are strung out along the Mountain Road (Route 108) between the resort and the village, but there are many right in town as well.

On the Mountain

Broken Ski Tavern

It's a bright, cheery tavern with ski memorabilia decorating the walls, a blazing fireplace, and sit-down service with sturdy stews and chili, mountain-size burgers, and a variety of daily specials and sandwiches. *Inn at the Mountain, tel. 802/253–3000. AE, D, DC, MC, V.*

Cliff House Restaurant

This is the most refined dining on the mountain—linen, silverware, tableside service, and a spectacular view. The lunch menu includes a selection of daily entrées, soups, and salads. *Top of gondola, tel. 802/253–3000, ext. 3365. Reservations essential. AE, D, DC, MC, V.*

Expensive

Blue Moon Café

This stylish restaurant in the middle of Stowe Village headlines innovative Vermont cuisine. In a restored village home, the intimate café offers light jazz and original paintings by local artists as a setting for the masterpieces that arrive from the kitchen. A good choice is braised Vermont rabbit with wild mushrooms and roasted garlic or marinated leg of lamb with pine-nut crust and braised sweet onions. There's also an excellent pan-roasted bluefish with lime glaze, roasted peppers, and pine nuts. *35 School St., tel. 802/253–7006. Reservations essential. AE, D, MC, V.*

Cliff House Restaurant

This restaurant atop Mt. Mansfield also serves dinner, and you still have to take the gondola to get there. When you call for a reservation, leave your phone number so restaurant personnel can call back in case high winds or lightning storms prevent the gondola from running. The prix fixe menu is $39.95, including the gondola ride, appetizer, salad, entrée, and dessert. Entrées may include sautéed salmon in fresh herbs, rack of lamb with Dijon mustard, or marinated Vermont venison with cherry port-wine sauce. *Tel. 802/253–3000, ext. 3365. Reservations essential. AE, D, DC, MC, V.*

Edson Hill Manor

Dark knotty-pine wainscoting and walls and ceiling adorned with hand-painted ivy contribute to a tranquil and somewhat formal atmosphere in the dining room here. The menu is heavy on game—local, of course—and may include grilled rabbit or barbecued quail with black bean ragout. *1500 Edson Hill Rd., tel. 802/253–7371. Reservations essential. AE, D, MC, V.*

Foxfire Inn

The Foxfire is a restored country farmhouse complete with wainscoting in its dining room and a living room warmed by a cozy fireplace. Both northern and southern Italian dishes are served here, many with a country flavor. There are several veal dishes—including parmigiana and marsala—a good selection of pastas, and an excellent eggplant Parmesan. *1606 Pucker St., 1½ mi north of Stowe Village on Rte. 100, tel. 802/253–4887. Reservations essential. AE, D, MC, V.*

Île de France

The only French restaurant in town is a good place for a special night. There are two dining rooms, both done in the style of Louis XIV, with high-back chairs and crystal wall sconces, crystal and linen place settings, and ever-so-attentive service. Such haute cuisine specialties as chateaubriand (for two) with a rich béarnaise sauce, frogs' legs sautéed with garlic, butter, herbs, and white wine, and English fillet of sole with lemon butter and white wine head the menu. *1899 Mountain Rd., midway between village and mountain, tel. 802/253–7751. Reservations essential. AE, D, DC, MC, V.*

Moderate

Cactus Café

In an early 19th-century brick house, this Mexican restaurant does a good job of imitating a Southwestern pueblo, right down to the soiled patina on the walls and woodwork. It's a local favorite and can be a tad cacophonous at times, but if you like basic Mexican dishes, you'll find nachos, guacamole, enchiladas, and burritos. If you crave something a bit American, there are baby-back ribs, fresh stone crab, and chicken breast stuffed with roasted red pepper and goat-cheese boursin. *Mountain Rd., ½ mi outside village, tel. 802/253–7770. MC, V.*

Gracie's Restaurant

This place has a fun and funky feel to it, with its dog theme and casual and lively atmosphere. The decor features light butternut wood, with a large wooden bar off to the side of the dining area, and a blazing fireplace. The mainstay of the menu is the lineup of "Just Doggone Good Burgers." There are more than a dozen varieties offered, including the Chihuahua, with tomato and guacamole, and the Blazing Beagle, with spicy Cajun seasoning. There's also a strong lineup of fresh fish (swordfish, scrod, salmon, scallops, and shrimp), which can be broiled, char-grilled, Cajun spiced, or served with different sauces, and a wide array of steaks trimmed on the premises. The baked goods are also available for takeout. *Rte. 100 behind the Carlson Bldg. in Stowe Village Ctr., tel. 802/253-8741. Reservations essential for 6 or more. AE, MC, V.*

The Shed

If you haven't been to the Shed, you haven't been to Stowe—it's one of those Stowe institutions that seem to have been around forever. It opened in 1965, but the original building dates from the 1830s. Old barn timbers are still evident in the bar, and there's also an atrium filled with knotty pine, skylights, and plants. The menu offers something for everyone: seafood strudel, country chicken stew, surf and turf, scallops with spinach, lamb with bourbon sauce, a varied array of burgers, and innovative salads. The original bar next door serves the same food, and it's usually less crowded, with a microbrewery offering golden to dark mountain ales. *1859 Mountain Rd., tel. 802/253-4364. Reservations essential. AE, D, MC, V.*

Whip Bar and Grill

Authentic early 19th-century decor is the name of the game here. The restaurant has been decorated along a tack-room theme, with a remarkable collection of buggy whips aligned to form a partition between the bar and the dining room. The walls are covered with a rich dark green Scottish plaid and accented by wood trim, carriage lamps, and 19th-century horse prints in gilded frames. The menu offers upscale pub food, with sandwiches, soups and salads, shepherd's pie, steaks, ribs, burgers, and trout, and even tofu-vegetable stir-fry. *Green Mountain Inn, Main St., tel. 802/253-7301. AE, D, MC, V.*

Inexpensive

Angelo's Pizza

When you're too beat to go out, call Angelo's. They'll deliver to your condo, hotel, or RV. The pizza is highly regarded by those in the know, and salads, pasta dishes, subs, and calzones are also available. You can also eat in the restaurant. *Stoware Common, Rte. 100, Lower Stowe Village, tel. 802/253-8931. No credit cards.*

Depot Street Malt Shoppe

At this 1950s-type diner you'll find burgers (try the La Bamba with chili and cheese), hot turkey and roast beef sandwiches, cherry cokes, ice cream, and egg creams. *57 Depot St., next to post office, Stowe Village, tel. 802/253-4269. No credit cards.*

Mr. Pickwick's Restaurant

From bangers and mash to wild boar, Britannia rules through and through at this antiques-filled, dimly lighted pub amid authentic brass-, copper-, and stonework. Other Brit favorites, served with astonishing authenticity, include fish-and-chips, beef Wellington, and Cornish pastry. There is also entertainment, including a resident table-side magician. If you're not a beer lover, try one of the Australian wines. *Ye Olde England Inn, Mountain Rd., ½ mi from village, tel. 802/253-7064. AE, D, DC, MC, V.*

Olives Bistro

This intimate restaurant is just the place for Mediterranean cuisine. Candlelight, linen settings, and tasteful burgundy-and-green tones set the atmosphere. Consider Greek lasagna, with layers of spinach, onion, feta cheese, olives, pine nuts, tomatoes, ricotta, and mozzarella; or a pan-seared sea bass topped with sautéed red and green bell peppers; or shrimp sautéed with sun-dried tomatoes, artichoke hearts, and kalamata olives, served on tomato and basil linguine. *Mountain Rd., Stowe Ctr. Complex, tel. 802/253–2033. AE, D, DC, MC, V.*

Best Bets for Breakfast

Midway Café and Bakery

This is a good, convenient location to grab breakfast at the mountain. It has a large selection of freshly baked croissants, muffins, and pastries. *Next to gondola at main base area, tel. 802/ 253–3000. AE, MC, V.*

Mother's Village Deli

This homey breakfast nook lives up to its name with its lace curtains and Cape Cod blue walls, not to mention the baked goods—fresh-baked muffins, pastries (try the cinnamon twist), sweet breads, and fresh bagels. You'll also find the best cappuccino and coffee in town. *Depot Bldg., Main St., Stowe Village, tel. 802/253–9044. MC.*

NIGHTLIFE AND ENTERTAINMENT

Après-Ski

Broken Ski Tavern

Conveniently located at the bottom of the Toll Road Run, the Broken Ski is also the first après-ski stop on Mountain Road as you head for the village. It's a classic, woodsy Vermont tavern

offering a wide selection of beers, with a blazing fire, a pool table, a jukebox, and an antique popcorn maker. *Inn at the Mountain, tel. 802/ 253–3000. AE, D, DC, MC, V.*

Jose's Cantina

This is a must after the last run, especially if you are skiing from the main base lodge area. It's loud, bustling, and filled with après-ski energy. There's music and a full Mexican menu. *Main base lodge area, next to gondola, tel. 802/253–3000. AE, D, DC, MC, V.*

Loud and Lively/Dancing

Bert's Place

Here you'll find a true mix of Stowe visitors and natives. The perfect place to meet, eat, drink, and play, it has the usual Vermont old-building feel. Beneath the exposed beams and ample lighting, you can play pool while choosing your favorite hits on the jukebox. There is, of course, a wide variety of hard spirits and beer, including two Vermont brews on tap (that change regularly), and light fare. *Mountain Rd., tel. 802/253–6071.*

More Mellow

Mr. Pickwick's Polo Pub

It's all Brit pub stuff: lots of dark and mysterious ales, stouts, and lagers (more than 150 kinds), a vast selection of port and Australian wines, good-natured barmaid banter, and the requisite dart boards. Local blues and jazz bands perform as well. *Ye Olde England Inn, Mountain Rd., ½ mile from village, tel. 802/253–7064. AE, D, DC, MC, V.*

STRATTON MOUNTAIN RESORT

STRATTON MOUNTAIN RESORT

R.R. 1, Box 145
Stratton Mountain, VT 05155
Tel. 802/297-2200 or
800/787-2886

STATISTICALLY SPEAKING

Base elevation: 1,872 feet

Summit elevation: 3,875 feet

Vertical drop: 2,003 feet

Skiable terrain: 500 acres

Number of trails: 90 (8 glades, 10 terrain parks on existing trails)

Longest run: 3 miles

Lifts and capacity: 1 gondola, 1 high-speed 6, 4 quads, 1 triple, 3 doubles, 2 surface; 21,020 skiers per hour

Daily lift ticket: $44 weekdays; $49 weekend

Average annual snowfall: 180 inches

Number of skiing days 1995–96: 150

Snowmaking: 375 acres, 75%

Terrain mix: N 35%; I 37%; E 28%

Snowboarding: yes (snowboard park)

Stratton Mountain opened to skiers in December 1961. It had 7 miles of trails, two lower lifts, and one upper lift. It was designed as a destination resort not a drive-in/drive-out ski area. It wasn't until the mid-'80s that ground for the master plan was finally broken and the centerpiece of the resort—the Stratton Village Square—took shape at the base of Stratton Mountain. The winding, street-lamped shopping arcade, with its chic boutiques, four-level parking garage, Stratton Village Lodge, and more than a hundred villas, is now the hub of Stratton's après-ski, shopping, and dining.

Top-quality instruction has been a Stratton hallmark just about from the start. In the '60s Emo Henrich was hired as director of the resort's ski school, and since then his name has become almost synonymous with Stratton Mountain. A native of Innsbruck, Austria, and an expert skier, Henrich had three rules: The ski school should concentrate on novice skiers with the goal of getting them onto the lifts and trails as soon as possible; all instructors should ski and teach the same way; and there should be live music in the base lodge every day. Not long after Stratton's lifts began carrying skiers up the mountain, Tyrolean oompahs began to float through what is now the Bear's Den, in the base lodge. The musicians? Austrian ski instructors, of course. These singing ski instructors still step out of their skis and pull on their lederhosen for après-ski in the Bear's Den on some evenings every week. Today, the Stratton Mountain ski school carries out highly polished, disciplined instruction.

Two special instruction features at Stratton. First, only private lessons are offered at Sun Bowl, so if you are interested in group lessons (for kids or adults), or if you plan to use the resort's day care, you need to park at the base lodge at the bottom of the main mountain. And second, you can sign up for Night Rider—skiing and snowboarding instruction from 6 PM to 10 PM on Friday and Saturday and during holiday weeks.

Just as Emo Henrich brought music to Stratton, so Jake Burton Carpenter brought snowboarding. While working as a bartender by night, J.B.C. spent his daylight hours in Henrich's garage designing and build-

USEFUL NUMBERS
Area code: 802

Children's services: day care,
instruction, tel. 802/297–4000
or 800/787–2886

Snow phone:
tel. 802/297–4211

Police: tel. 802/254–2382

Hospital: Carlos Otis Medical
Clinic, tel. 802/297–2300

Manchester Chamber of
Commerce: tel. 802/362–2100

Taxi: Manchester,
tel. 802/362–4118

Road conditions:
tel. 800/429–7623

Towing: Coleman's Inc.,
tel. 802/297–1950

FIVE-STAR FAVORITES
Best run for vertical:
Bear Down

Best run overall: Liftline

Best bar/nightclub:
Red Fox Inn

Best hotel: Equinox

Best restaurant: Mistral's

ing his boards. Under cover of darkness he'd hike the mountain for test runs. In 1983 Burton convinced Stratton's director of mountain operations to open the lifts and trails to snowboarders. Today Stratton offers Professional Ski Instructors of America (PSIA)–affiliated snowboarding instruction, season-long racing, and a 380-foot half pipe. The snowboard park, built in 1992, has been the site of the U.S. Open Snowboarding Championships since 1985. Besides the half pipe, the park boasts spines and elbows sculpted out of snow for catching air. There are also half-hidden objects like tires and giant wooden boxes for bonkin' and jibbin'. It has the largest pipe dragon (a machine for cutting half pipe) in the east, able to cut a 15-foot-diameter run. The snowboard park is closed to alpine skiers.

New in the 1996–97 season is a series of terrain parks and glades that add to the diversity of skiing and snowboarding possibilities on the mountain. The child-care center and the ski school headquarters are also in new premises. These changes are among the improvements begun by Intrawest, Stratton's owner since 1994 (and parent company of the Blackcomb resort in British Columbia and Mont Tremblant in Quebec). Plans over the next 10 years include increasing snowmaking coverage to 100%, building a mountaintop restaurant, and creating more high-speed lifts, glades, and terrain parks.

HOW TO GET THERE
By Plane
Albany Airport, in Albany, New York, is 1½ hours away, and **Bradley International Airport,** in Hartford, Connecticut, is about 2½ hours away by car. (*See* Getting to Vermont Resorts, *above*.)

By Car
From New York City and points south, take I–87 (the New York Thruway) to Albany and I–787 to New York Route 7 east to the Vermont border, where it turns into Vermont Route 9. Follow it to Bennington and pick up U.S. 7 north to Manchester. Turn east onto Route 11 and then south onto Route 30 to Bondville, where you take Stratton Mountain Road (the access road) on the right. Alternatively, from

New York City you can take I–95 east to I–91 in New Haven, Connecticut, and follow I–91 north past the Massachusetts Turnpike (on which you can connect from Boston) to Brattleboro, Vermont. Take Route 30 north 38 miles to Bondville and then follow Stratton Mountain Road 4 miles to the resort. New York City is 235 miles away, Albany 81.

By Bus
Vermont Transit (tel. 802/442–4808) has scheduled service from major centers into Manchester (25 miles away) or Brattleboro, Vermont (35 miles away), but nothing closer to the mountain.

By Train
Amtrak (tel. 800/872–7245) has scheduled service from major centers to Albany or Brattleboro.

GETTING AROUND
By Shuttle
Big white shuttle buses (tel. 802/297–2200) run a free service continuously from the parking lots to the skier drop-off area on the upper level of the parking garage. The wait is no longer than five minutes. A shuttle bus also runs about every half hour in a loop from the Stratton villas to the parking garage skier drop-off area.

By Car
If you're skiing Stratton just for the day and approaching the mountain on Route 30 from Bondville, park in the four-level garage. If it's full, try Lot 3 just across the road. Another option, especially on busy days, is Sun Bowl. Its parking lot is almost never full, and the walk to the lift is no more than 250 yards. If you're staying at the mountain, leave your car at your condo and take the shuttle bus.

THE SKIING
Stratton, at 3,875 feet, is the highest peak in southern Vermont. With 54 of its 90 trails falling into the intermediate/upper intermediate range and with many of these wide-open, relatively straight, fully groomed "supertrails," Stratton is definitely a cruiser's mountain. Stratton is also a one-mountain resort with no hidden ridges or peaks, so it's an easy place to get around. Its four areas are the Upper and Lower mountains on the main, north face, Snow Bowl to the west, and Sun Bowl to the east.

Although Sun Bowl has its own parking lot and base lodge, you can easily hop on the Sun Bowl quad and hightail it back across the mountain to the main base lodge. Sun Bowl is the place to be when it's cold or windy because it's the most sheltered section of the mountain. Another advantage is the extra half hour during the early season—until late January—that the Sun Bowl lift stays open, until 4 PM, longer than the upper lifts. You can grab a last run on the gondola at 3:30 and still have time for one more run on Sun Bowl. If you're an intermediate skier from the summit, take Black Bear to the Sun Bowl Express, then hook up with the Sunriser Supertrail to the bottom of the lift. Experts can use any way down they like, but a nice penultimate run is Black Bear to the short, steep double-diamond upper Downeaster, which empties right into the Sun Bowl area.

Stratton's 12-passenger (if they squeeze) Summit gondola is the only bottom-to-top lift on the mountain, moving 2,400 skiers each hour. It's the most popular and most crowded, with the longest lift line, but even on the busiest days the wait is no more than 10 minutes. A good alternative if you want to ski the top of the mountain, especially on warm, sunny days, is to take the Tamarack lift to the bottom of Grizzly or to the North American quad. However, when it's cold and windy, there's no question that the eight-minute gondola ride is pure pleasure.

If you want to beat the crowds, buy your lift ticket and pick up rental equipment any time after 3 PM the day before at the information desk or at the Welcome Center, which is open 24 hours. Save money by buying multiday tickets.

Novices

The Ski Learning Park, at the base of the lower mountain, was created in 1993 so beginners could learn to ski or snowboard without feeling intimidated by fast-moving objects. It has 45 acres of gentle terrain served by two surface lifts: Cub, a slow-moving platter, and Teddy Bear, a slow, low-to-the-ground handle tow, both of which allow you to keep your skis on the snow at all times. The boundaries of the park are clearly signposted to keep advanced skiers out. Inside the park is a terrain garden with a gentle bobsled run (the Flume) that has banked sides to teach the steering and pressuring movements of the turn; whale-shaped humps (Bear Backs) to encourage flexing, extending, and absorption (skills necessary to ski the moguls); and a 7-foot spiral tower (Treetops) for edging and giving a

taste of the steeps. A special lower-priced ticket is good only for lifts inside the park.

The first step up from the park is to take one of three chairlifts: the Villager double, the shortest; the Tyrolienne double; or for a longer ride that drops you off at the top of Lower Tamarack, the Tamarack triple. They're all slow moving and easy to get on and off and lead to gentle beginner trails such as Lower Tamarack, Mark's Run, and Daniel Webster and the glades Daniel's Web and Rosie O'Gladey, as well as the short intermediate trails Duck Soup and Spillway.

Novices can also get a taste of the Sun Bowl. Two of the sweetest beginner trails on the mountain are Lower Middlebrook and Churchill Downs. Both have an easy combination of very gentle pitches and near flats meandering through a beautifully wooded setting—in short, a novice's delight. To get to Sun Bowl from the Ski Learning Park, take the Tamarack triple and ski down the long, gentle 91 to the base of the Sun Bowl quad.

If you're at the Sun Bowl and want to get back to the main mountain, the easiest route is to take the Sun Bowl Access Trail to Way Home, past the Grizzly lift to Run Away, which leads directly to the top of the Ski Learning Park. From there take any of several lower mountain trails to the main base lodge.

One of the best things about Stratton is the ability of even a novice to ride the gondola and ski down from the top. Begin on Mike's Way, a short trail (while you're here, check out some of the best views on the mountain) that leads to the East and West Meadows. The Meadows are two wide-open, side-by-side cruising trails separated by islands of trees. There are no steep pitches, sudden drops, or otherwise threatening obstacles along the way. If you're heading back to the gondola, take Lower Wanderer, a narrower but still peaceful run, right to the bottom. Following this route, you'll have skied the longest run on Stratton: 3 miles.

For a shorter run, cut from Meadows onto Drifter Link to Old Log Road back to the gondola.

A third alternative for novices is to ski Meadows to Drifter Link, then take the Snow Bowl quad back to the summit. Skiing just the top two-thirds of Meadows is an especially nice way to capture the afternoon sun.

Intermediates

Stratton is an intermediate skier's dream. Virtually the whole upper mountain is a mix of wide, groomed cruising trails interspersed with some easy-to-avoid double-black-diamond runs. Many single-diamond advanced trails are perfect for high-intermediate skiers.

If you like making long, curving turns, take one of Stratton's supertrails—the Meadows (East and West), on Snow Bowl, and Kidderbrook and the Sunriser Supertrail, on Sun Bowl. The Sunriser Supertrail is Stratton's widest trail and can be skied many ways. As you're skiing down, hang to the left for some gentle bumps and a nice pitch on the bottom. If you want to cruise in and out among the trees, ski smack-dab down the middle. The new Glade Runner intermediate glade off to the left of the trail connects with Lower Downeaster for a sylvan run to the bottom.

Another classic Vermont trail for intermediates is the Drifter trio—Get My Drift, Upper Drifter, and Lower Drifter, in Snow Bowl, which you reach on the Snow Bowl quad. Snow does drift and collect on them, and gentle bumps may form, but the trails are wide enough to give you room to maneuver around the bumps if you're so inclined.

One of the most popular high-intermediate/advanced trails is Upper Standard, under the gondola. It's wide, with ungroomed bumps on one side only—the perfect trail if you want to practice in the bumps but don't want to commit to a double-diamond run with no option for bailout. You can also try the single-diamond Shred Wood Forest glade run just to the left of Upper Standard.

Running parallel to Upper Standard is North American, a single-diamond trail under the North American quad that's made just for show-offs. It's also the trail most often used for races.

The single-diamond Kidderbrook is a delight. A broad, expansive trail with surprising drops to keep you on your toes, it is pure fun. Lying on the easternmost shoulder of the mountain, it does pick up the wind, so you may want to avoid the Kidderbrook quad in cold weather.

Experts

There are six expert double-diamond trails spread out across the upper mountain. Bear Down and Free Fall can be reached from the summit or from the Kidderbrook quad, which also aims you for the new double-diamond Trees Release Me Glade, off Polar Bear. Bear Down, at 3,000 feet, is the longest expert trail, so don't take it if you're not prepared to stay because once on it, there's no escape.

The steepest bump run? The prize goes to World Cup; Upper Downeaster is a close second. World Cup is never groomed; the bumps spread from side to side and get really big; it can be seen from the Snow Bowl quad, so you can check out the action before you commit.

Be on the gondola when it opens and head to Kidderbrook for the first run of the day. Ride the Kidderbrook quad to ski Bear Down. Work your way to the Grizzly double and ski Tamarack to the North American quad. By this time you'll be ready for the banquet of bumps on Upper Spruce, Lower Slalom Glade, and finally, World Cup. Then another run or two on single-diamond Liftline to rest the knees, and you can take a break.

WHERE TO STAY

There's some excellent lodging in and around the Stratton resort, mostly condominiums but also some very good hotels. All have the advantage of access to the lifts in the morning without getting into your car. If you prefer a luxury hotel, a small intimate lodge, a classic Vermont country inn, or a designer bed-and-breakfast, the surrounding area, particularly Manchester, is a better choice. All bookings can be made through Stratton Central Reservations (tel. 800/787–2886).

All guests at the Stratton-operated accommodations have free access to the Stratton Sports Center, which has two indoor tennis courts, a 75-foot indoor pool, racquetball, aerobics, a fitness center with Nautilus equipment, a Jacuzzi, massages, and a steam room. Extra charges for certain services may apply. Some properties are individually owned and decorated, so although quality is consistent, styles vary.

Expensive

The Equinox

The historic, luxurious Equinox opened in 1769. Its white Federal and Greek Revival architecture sets the tone for the picturesque community of Manchester Village. Rooms and suites are decorated with sophisticated bleached-pine country-style furniture and muted colors accented by bedspreads and draperies in deeper colors. The public areas boast antiques such as grandfather clocks and writing desks. *Historic Rte. 7A, 17 mi from mountain, Manchester Village 05254, tel. 802/362–4700 or 800/ 362–4747, fax 802/362–4861. 126 rooms, 48 suites. Facilities: 2 restaurants, fitness center, health spa, indoor lap pool. AE, D, DC, MC, V. $169– $899.*

Ober Tal

These slope-side ski-in/ski-out one-bedroom units all have a wood-burning fieldstone fireplace, a complete kitchen, a washer-dryer, and a private deck. The units are comfortably decorated in a practical fashion, with Berber broadloom, big comfortable chairs and couches, and a nice blend of exposed brick and wood accents. There's a choice of one-bedroom or two-bedroom units. *Stratton Corp, Stratton Mountain Village, Stratton 05155, tel. 802/297–2200 or 800/ 787–2886, fax 802/297–2939. 50 units. AE, D, DC, MC, V. $90–$320.*

Stratton Village Lodge

A California designer attempted to replicate an Austrian Alpine village here, but the result is more West Coast than Old World. This ski-in/ski-out lodge has units designed to accommodate four people comfortably. Each has a microwave, mini-refrigerator, sink, and coffeemaker. They are decorated in a modern New England style. All amenities at the Stratton Mountain Inn, just down the hill, are available to the guests here. *Stratton Corp, Stratton Mountain Village, Stratton 05155, tel. 802/297-2260 or 800/777-1700, fax 802/297-1778. 90 units, 1 suite. AE, D, DC, MC, V. $99-$239.*

Village Watch

This five-story contemporary wooden condo complex comes with both mountain and valley views and has an elevator. The two-, three-, and four-bedroom condos are also ski- in/ski-out—they are between the Tamarack triple chairlift and the Village lift. The units have a complete kitchen, a fieldstone fireplace, and a sundeck. *Stratton Corp, Stratton Mountain Village, Stratton 05155, tel. 802/297-2200 or 800/727-2886, fax 802/297-2939. 35 units. AE, D, DC, MC, V. $130-$480.*

Moderate

Birkenhaus

This is the oldest inn on the mountain. The atmosphere is Old World Austrian—cathedral ceilings, stucco walls, and diagonal cedar paneling. The rooms are spacious and bright, with traditional Austrian handcrafted wood furnishings, floral patterns on drapes and bed covers, and Tyrolean bric-a-brac. The hotel is within walking distance of Stratton Village and the slopes. *Middle Ridge Rd., Stratton 05155, tel. 802/297-2000, fax 802/297-2002. 17 rooms, 1 suite. Facilities: restaurant, fireplace lounge, bar. AE, D, MC, V. $69-$159.*

Liftline Lodge

The only independently owned hotel on the mountain, it's directly across the access road from Stratton Village and the lifts. The classic European-style chalet has steep, sloping white stucco walls embracing sturdy timbers, paneling, and wrought-iron fixtures. The rooms are bright and white, with artfully placed wood accents, well-fashioned furnishings, and dark, richly colored carpets. The units have a fireplace, stove, refrigerator, and sink. *R.D. 1, Box 144, Stratton 05155, tel. 802/297-2600 or 800/597-5438, fax 802/297-2949. 80 rooms, 6 units. Facilities: restaurant, bar, café, 1 outdoor and 2 indoor hot tubs, 1 sauna, fireplace, living room, library, fitness center, game room, massage. AE, MC, V. $85-$275.*

Stratton Mountain Inn

Just a short walk from shopping and slopes, this large full-service hotel has lots of amenities, from a 24-hour concierge to room service to a health spa. The decor is traditional New England, with exposed brick and beams. The rooms are modern and well maintained, with solid wood furnishings. *Middle Ridge Rd., Stratton 05155, tel. 802/297-2500 or 800/777-1700, fax 802/297-1778. 117 rooms, 3 suites. Facilities: 2 restaurants, bar, lounge, indoor and outdoor hot tubs, sauna, exercise area. AE, D, DC, MC, V. $79-$169.*

Three Mountain Inn

This 1790s country inn integrates the feel and charm of the 18th century with modern conveniences for an especially personal and genuine atmosphere. There are rooms in the main inn and next door at the Robinson House. Across the street, the Sage House is also available for rent in its three-bedroom entirety. The rooms are bright and comfortable, with chintz wallpaper, wooden sconces, ruffled curtains, and colonial-style furnishings. *Rte. 30, Box 180, 10 mi south of Stratton, Jamaica 05343, tel. 802/874–4140, fax 802/874–4745. 16 rooms, 1 suite. Facilities: restaurant, pub, AE, MC, V. $85–$135, including full breakfast.*

Inexpensive

Haig's

This Early American pioneer decor lodge, opened in 1973, is a good deal. The rooms are large and well furnished in a thrifty Yankee style. Some even have a fireplace. *Rte. 30 at foot of Stratton Mountain Rd., Bondville 05340, tel. 802/297–1300 or 800/897–5894, fax 802/297–1301. 23 rooms, 3 suites. Facilities: 2 restaurants, sports bar, disco, indoor golf course. AE, D, MC, V. $65–$150.*

Inn at Bear Creek

This is a practical, all-purpose hotel complex that has large, clean, comfortable rooms in the hotel and more upscale two- and three-bedroom condo units with kitchen facilities. There is a two-night minimum for the condos. *Rte. 30, 4 mi south of Stratton, Rawsonville 05155, tel. 802/297–1700, fax 802/297–1701. 18 rooms, 20 units. Facilities: restaurant, lounge, shuttle. AE, MC, V. $59–$325.*

Red Fox Inn

This inn and restaurant has quaint, homey rooms in an early 19th-century farmhouse. The decor is country colonial style, with farming antiques and collectibles and sensible furnishings. *Winhall Hollow Rd., 1½ mi from access road, Bondville 05340, tel. 802/297–2488 or 800/870–2434, fax 802/297–2156. 8 rooms, 1 suite. Facilities: dining room, tavern, game room. AE. $60–$125.*

WHERE TO EAT

There's a variety of interesting dining establishments in and around nearby Bondville and Manchester, and it's worth the drive to experience them. There are also a number of solid if not spectacular eateries at the resort.

Expensive

The Colonnade

The dining room of the Equinox Hotel is named for the hotel's architectural claim to fame—the more than 285 feet of fluted columns added to the front in 1839. The restaurant has a hand-painted and -stenciled vaulted ceiling, crystal chandeliers, detailed floral rugs, starched white linen tablecloths, and richly colored velvet and brocade drapes. Dinner includes such classic Vermont dishes as maple-mustard-glazed lamb chops on roasted shallot wild rice or apple-roasted pheasant with wild rice and fresh berries. *Equinox, Manchester Village, tel. 802/362–4700 or 800/362–4747. Reservations essential. AE, D, DC, MC, V. No lunch.*

Mistral's

In the woods and on the way to Manchester from the mountain, this low-key, chef-owned restaurant overlooks a stream. The fresh, understated country French feel of the two dining rooms is reflected in a menu that offers such dishes as sautéed native trout stuffed with scallop mousse, and medallions of venison with sauce *au poivre*, accompanied by wines from an award-winning list. *Toll Gate Rd. off Rtes. 11 and 30, Manchester, tel. 802/362–1779. Reservations essential. AE, D, DC, MC, V. Closed Wed.*

Ye Old Tavern
Stepping through the yellow-and-white Federal and Greek Revival facade into this roadside inn is like stepping into a museum; parts date to 1760. The tavern serves lunch daily by the blazing hearth. The two adjacent dining rooms, open for dinner, offer such traditional American standbys as duck with blackberry sauce, lamb with cranberry-orange sauce, and salmon hollandaise. It also has steak cuts from the grill. *214 N. Main St., Manchester Center, tel. 802/362–0611. Reservations essential. AE, MC, V.*

MODERATE

Haig's
The dining room is bright, airy, and bustling, with two levels, a wall of glass, and hanging plants. It offers a complete salad bar and such basic entrées as surf and turf, barbecued chicken, lasagna, and baby-back ribs. *Rte. 30, Bondville, tel. 802/297–1300. AE, D, MC, V.*

Laney's
An antique two-wheeler presides over the dining room, and the bar bristles with vintage sports equipment. Owner Laney Davis's collection of posters, famous caricatures, and other memorabilia decorate the walls, while an old player piano tinkles in the background. The emphasis in the enormous portions of food is on quality and freshness, from the homemade bread to the selection of pizzas and the barbecued ribs. The atmosphere is 1,000-watt fun. *Rtes. 11 and 30, Manchester Center, tel. 802/362–4456. Reservations essential. AE, D, DC, MC, V.*

River Café
The restaurant has a beautiful view of the Winhall River, as well as hand-blown lamps, fresh flowers, and antique furniture. Italian specialties include seafood *possillipo* (clams, mussels, and other seasonal sea fare in marinara sauce) and veal *piccata* (sautéed in white wine with lemon, capers, artichoke hearts, and cream), as well as St. Louis–style spareribs and linguine with fresh whole clams. *Rte. 30, foot of access road, Bondville, tel. 802/297–1010. MC, V.*

Three Mountain Inn
The food served in this 18th-century inn's two fireplace-adorned dining rooms is well worth the drive. It's traditional New England, with homemade breads, salad dressings, and soups; filet mignon, fresh fish, venison, and chicken; and a fine selection of wines. *Rte. 30, 6 mi south of mountain, Jamaica, tel. 802/874–4140. Reservations essential. AE, D, MC, V.*

Inexpensive

L.L. Beastro
The short but tasty menu at this bright, cheerful new café-bar in Liftline Lodge includes chowders, bisques, and stews. *Stratton Mountain Rd. at Middle Ridge Rd., Stratton, tel. 802/297–2600. AE, MC, V.*

Mulberry St.

For pasta, pizza, and other Italian specialties in Stratton Village, try this simple restaurant with a sports bar next door. They fill take-out orders as well. *S. Village Sq., Stratton, tel. 802/297-3065. AE, DC, MC, V.*

Partridge in a Pantry

Amid charming antiques and miscellaneous cow paraphernalia, there's no shortage of great sandwiches, salads, soups, wine, beer, and cheeses at this deli and gourmet shop. Call in your lunch order in the morning, and just pop in during the noon rush for a quick pickup. *Village Sq., Stratton, tel. 802/297-9850. AE, MC, V.*

Best Bets for Breakfast

Double Diamond Café

This place serves the best coffee (in all its variations) in the area, plus a wide choice of muffins. *Village Square, Stratton, tel. 802/297-3431.*

Sage Hill

You can start the day with a generous buffet breakfast in a large, airy room with a window wall overlooking the valley. *Stratton Mountain Inn, Middle Ridge Rd., Stratton, tel. 802/297-2500. AE, D, DC, MC, V.*

NIGHTLIFE AND ENTERTAINMENT

Après-Ski

Bear's Den

There's live entertainment, dancing, free munchies, and a lot of strutting in a highly charged atmosphere. *Stratton base lodge, tel. 802/297-0012. AE, D, DC, MC, V.*

Mulligans

This is the center of off-slope fun and frivolity in Stratton Village. You can't miss the moose sporting a derby, who hangs over the fireplace, the imperial elk trophy on the wall, and the black bears (all stuffed) in the rafters. There's good bar food, too. *Village Square, Stratton, tel. 802/297-9293. AE, MC, V.*

Loud and Lively/Dancing

Haig's

This is where you'll find the hottest rock and dance music in the area, usually with a younger crowd. Deejay driven and video enhanced, the place sends the crowd to the dance floor in droves. *Rte. 30, Bondville, tel. 802/297-1300. AE, D, MC, V.*

More Mellow

Birkenhaus

The small, fireplace-warmed bar just off the inn's main lobby is good for a quiet nightcap. *Birkenhaus, Middle Ridge Rd., Stratton, tel. 802/297-2000. AE, D, MC, V.*

Taverne

This colonial tavern has a great stand-up bar, a fireplace, and a billiards table, all fostering its warm and laid-back atmosphere. *Stratton Mountain Inn, Middle Ridge Rd., Stratton, tel. 802/297-2500. AE, D, DC, MC, V.*

SUGARBUSH RESORT

SUGARBUSH RESORT

R.R. 1, Box 350
Warren, VT 05674-9500
Tel. 802/583-2381 or
800/537-8427

STATISTICALLY SPEAKING
Base elevation: 1,535 feet

Summit elevation: 4,135 feet

Vertical drop: 2,650 feet

Skiable terrain: 432 acres

Number of trails: 112

Longest run: 2½ miles

Lifts and capacity: 7 quad chairs (4 high-speed), 3 triples, 4 doubles, 4 surface lifts; 24,363 skiers per hour

Daily lift ticket: $47

Average annual snowfall: 350 inches

Number of skiing days 1995–96: 210

Snowmaking: 285.5 acres; 66% (80% planned)

Terrain mix: N 22%, I 46%, E 32%

Snowboarding: yes

Sugarbush opened for business on Christmas Day 1958, when a lift ticket cost $5.50 and the three employees rotated between selling tickets, tending bar, and washing dishes. There was one mountain, a gondola, a poma lift, and 10 trails. Since then a number of owners have come and gone at the Mad River Valley resort. And so have the celebrities—such as the Kennedys, author Gay Talese, and designer Oleg Cassini. The glitz and glitter inspired the nickname Mascara Mountain. Having overwhelmed neighboring Glen Ellen, Sugarbush now is two mountains—North and South. Currently under the aegis of Les Otten's American Skiing Company, it is the state of the art among American ski resorts, with a focus squarely on the quality of the skiing. In place of the gondola are 18 chairlifts, including four high-speed detachable quads—one of which swings high above the valley between South and North. Snowmaking covers more than half the resort, with plans for 80% coverage.

The original Sugarbush, now known as Sugarbush South, is known for the formidable steeps toward the top and in front of the main base lodge; it has a vertical of 2,400 feet. Sugarbush North, off Mt. Ellen, offers what South has in short supply—beginner runs. North also has steep fall-line pitches and intermediate cruisers off its 2,600 vertical feet.

Accommodations mountainside and in the surrounding valley and such towns as Warren and Waitsfield range from ultradeluxe hostelries and inns to low-budget ski dorms. Sugarbush Village, near the base of South (the original Sugarbush), is where the ski school, the restaurants, and the shops are. Nearby is the Sugarbush Sports Center, which has posh indoor and outdoor pools, a Jacuzzi, indoor tennis courts, a fitness center, massage, a sauna, and a games room (all free to guests at Sugarbush Resort lodgings). A car is a must.

HOW TO GET THERE

By Plane
Burlington International Airport is 45 minutes from the resort (*see* Getting to Vermont Resorts, *above*).

Children's services: day care, instruction, tel. 802/583-2385, ext. 378

Snow phone: tel. 802/583-7669

Police: tel. 802/496-2262

Medical center: Mad River Valley Health Center, Waitsfield, tel. 802/496-3838

Hospital: Central Vermont Hospital, Barre, tel. 802/229-9121

Chamber of Commerce: tel. 802/496-3409

Resort association: tel. 802/583-2301

Taxi: Morf Transit, tel. 802/864-5588

Road conditions: tel. 800/429-7623

Towing: Hap's service station, tel. 802/496-3948

FIVE-STAR FAVORITES
Best run for vertical: FIS and Lower FIS

Best run overall: Organgrinder

Best bar/nightclub: Mad Mountain Tavern

Best hotel: Sugarbush Inn

Best restaurant: Sam Rupert's

By Car

From Burlington take I–89 south to Exit 10 (Waterbury), then Route 2 east to Route 100 south to the Sugarbush Access Road. From New Hampshire, Connecticut, Massachusetts, and New York, take I–89 north to Exit 9 (Middlesex), then Route 2 east for a half mile to Route 100B south to Route 100 south to the Sugarbush Access Road.

By Train

Daily **Amtrak** (tel. 800/872–7245) service is available to Waterbury, Vermont, which is just a 20-minute drive from the resort. Shuttle service or rental-car pickups are available in Waterbury.

THE SKIING

South is the feature area, the expert's expert mountain that also has great beginner trails. It is bowl-shaped and is served by nine lifts—three triples, four doubles, and two surface. It is home to Castle Rock, among New England's most challenging collection of expert trails. Counterpoint to these steep, narrow runs are some good, wide intermediate cruisers such as Glades and Snowball.

North is 4,135 feet at the summit of Mt. Ellen, the highest peak in the Green Mountain National Forest. It is the cruiser mountain; the intermediate runs at North are generally wider. North is served by seven lifts—one high-speed quad, two quads, two doubles, and two surface lifts.

Trails on the two mountains are now connected by a high-speed quad that's strung high above a valley. Drop a ski pole, and it's gone forever—and watch out for frostbite when it's chilly. To get from one to the other, you can also take a shuttle bus. North is more north facing, so the sun hits the trails early and leaves early. South stays sunnier longer during the day. If it's a powder day, however, South is the place to get the first chair for fresh tracks on Castlerock.

As at all American Skiing Company resorts, Sugarbush has made a major commitment to snowboarding (in the form of its own half-pipe-cutting Pipe Dragon and a staff snowboard coordinator to direct board terrain maintenance and oversee snowboard events). The Mountain Rage Snowpark, served by the

Spring Fling triple and the Valley House double, is loaded with terrain features of all types, including gap jumps, tabletops, spines, and a half pipe.

Novices

South offers a learning area not intruded on by other lift systems. Here, never-evers are able to go from walking to taking the poma lift for a try down a low-pitched hill appropriately named First Time. The Village chair takes you to the wide Easy Rider. The third lift in the beginner's trilogy is Gate House Express, which carries you to Pushover, where you can let those muscles talk, and perhaps on a first blue-square run down Slow Poke.

There's not as much for never-evers at North. First-time skiers concentrate on the Ski School chair and runs like East Street and Graduation. With a diploma you can head up the superquad Green Mountain, for a run down the winding Northstar Trail.

Intermediates

It gets busy on the central corridor of South, accessed via the Sugar Bravo Express high-speed detachable quad. Most people take it to get to the center of the mountain. Use it between 10 and noon and then after 1:30. Try heading to the Valley House Base Lodge and concentrating on the two lifts to your left, Valley House and Spring Fling. These provide access to blue square terrain like Snowball, Lower Snowball, Spring Fling (half groomed, half bumped), and Moonshine. Take Reverse Traverse, off Snowball, and ski Murphy's Glade, which brings you back to the bottom

of Sugar Bravo. Lower intermediates can start on the trails from the Gate House Express. You'll also find lower intermediate trails off the Valley House chair. The Heaven's Gate triple reaches the summit of one of the four peaks at South: Lincoln Peak. Jester snakes down from the top of Heaven's Gate and provides access to the center of the hill via Birdland or Lower Jester. For a winding run 2½ miles down, take Jester to Snowball.

At North the main corridor is along the Green Mountain quad. Ride it early to the Summit Quad, which brings you to the top of Mt. Ellen, and ski Panorama to either the wide Elbow or the slinky Lower Rim Run. The North Ridge Express also gets you to Elbow (which can become crowded) but provides access to Cruiser, another wide-open trail, and Which Way, the site of Fat Bob, Sugarbush's snowboard park. Sneak over to Inverness via Northway for some time on Brambles, Inverness, and Semi-Tough. Intermediates who want to try bumps go to the Cliffs, at the lower end of the black-diamond scale.

Expert

Extreme skiers traditionally head to the Castlerock double chair. Respect the people who are there, and if you're not an expert, don't even think about it. Trails in this area were cut to the natural contours not bulldozed, and this fast and undulating terrain demands concentration and skill. Chutes and narrow spots like Rumble, only 15–20 feet wide, challenge speed lovers. The Valley House chair goes above the Mall, where exhibitionists showboat, to the narrow double-diamond Stein's Run. Spillsville and Paradise (it goes through a tree-speckled bowl) are narrow tests from the Heaven's Gate triple. Organgrinder drops 2,400 feet from top to bottom along the old gondola line. Toward the bottom, advanced intermediate skiers can handle it.

At North, double-diamond Black Diamond is steep and narrow, and Exterminator is wider, with Volkswagen-size bumps. People line up at the top of FIS to tackle the moguls on this short, wide, steep pitch. At the bottom, where it meets Rim Run, another set of skiers congregates to watch and eavesdrop on the expletives of those who have just made it down. Tumbler and Hammerhead leave no room for bailing out. Advanced intermediate skiers might want to try Encore, under North Ridge, where the consistent pitch leaves some room to recover and the bumps are negotiable.

Between South and North is Slide Brook Basin, 2,000 acres between Lincoln and Mt. Ellen, where 1½-mile-long trails wiggle down 1,600 vertical feet of completely natural double-black-diamond terrain with completely natural snow cover. These are open only on tours, with two guides per eight skiers, but it's the kind of wilderness skiing that's not often available in the East.

WHERE TO STAY

There are more than 6,600 beds in the area, most in condos and inns.

Expensive

The Bridges

These are the best condos in the area, very well maintained and managed. The privately owned one-, two-, and three-bedroom-with-loft units with white wooden exteriors come in six different floor plans. Decor and design vary from unit to unit, but all are spacious and bright, with lots of windows and complete kitchens, fireplaces, and decks. It's about a half mile from the village center. *Sugarbush Access Rd., Warren 05674, tel. 802/583–2922 or 800/453–2922, fax 802/583–1018. 100 units. Facilities: indoor pool, outdoor hot tub, sauna, 2 indoor tennis courts, aerobics, exercise room, recreation room. AE, MC, V. $150–$425.*

Hamilton House

This exquisite private mountain retreat a mile from the ski area is the perfect place to live out a fantasy of being a weekend guest of old-world gentry. A full English breakfast and English afternoon tea, included in the price, are served in either the formal dining room or the plant-filled conservatory. *R.R. 1, Box 74, off German Flats Rd. near Sugarbush Access Rd., Warren 05674, tel. 802/583–1066 or 800/760–1066, fax 802/583–1776. 2 rooms, 2 suites. AE, D, MC, V. $140–$200.*

Inn at the Round Barn Farm

A unique B&B away from the hustle and bustle of the Sugarbush Access Road, this early 19th-century farm complex created around a round barn offers luxurious rooms with antiques, fireplaces, and views. On a frosty January night you'll appreciate the down comforter on your bed. *R.R. 1, Box 247, E. Warren Rd., Waitsfield 05673, tel. 802/496–2276 or 800/537–8427, fax 802/496–8832. 11 rooms. Facilities: indoor lap pool, game room, ski storage. AE, MC, V. $115–$220.*

Sugarbush Village

When snow conditions are right, you can ski into and walk/ski out from most of the several hundred condos that make up Sugarbush Village (managed by two companies). All privately owned and decorated, they range in size from one-bedroom suites to four-bedroom villas. They all have a complete kitchen, many have a fireplace, and most have other standard creature comforts such as a washer/dryer, a sauna, or a Jacuzzi. *Sugarbush Village Association, R.R. 1, Box 68–12, Warren 05674, tel. 802/583–3000 or 800/451–4326, fax 802/583–2373. 155 units. AE, D, DC, MC, V. $80–$535. Sugarbush Resort, R.R. 1, Box 350, Warren 05674, tel. 802/583–3333 or 800/537–8427, fax 802/583–2301. 200 units. AE, D, DC, MC, V. $135–$505.*

Moderate

1824 House Inn

This quaint early 19th-century farmhouse is today both a home and a fine bed-and-breakfast. The house and rooms are appointed with no shortage of entertaining and eclectic antiques and modern paintings. With some 50 acres of woodland and hillside pasture, there is plenty of opportunity for sledding and cross-country skiing. *Rte. 100, Box 159, Waitsfield 05673, tel. 802/496–7555, fax 802/496–7558. 6 rooms. AE, D, MC, V. $105–$140.*

Mad River Inn

This bed-and-breakfast in a renovated wooden farmhouse with a slate roof has a Victorian interior that's well organized although a bit overdone with dust ruffles, lace, and Laura Ashley. The rooms, however, are comfortable, individually decorated, and come with antique featherbeds. *Tremblay Rd., Box 75, off Rte. 100, Waitsfield 05673, tel. 802/496–7900, fax 802/496–5390. 10 rooms. Facilities: outdoor hot tub, library with fireplace, lounge, pool table. AE, MC, V. $69–$125.*

Millbrook Inn

This blue Cape-style farmhouse with white trim has wide, worn pine plank floors in its entrance. The rooms are individually decorated with period furniture and subtle finishing touches, such as hand stenciling, antique objets d'art, and handmade quilts. The hearty breakfast and dinner in the great dining room are well worth the cost of the MAP. *Rte. 170, Box 62, Waitsfield 05673, tel. 802/496–2405 or 800/477–2809, fax 802/496–9735. 7 rooms. Facilities: restaurant. AE, DC, MC, V. $50–$70 per person, including MAP.*

Sugarbush Inn

This charming yellow inn with pillars and white trim is the accommodations flagship for the area—the only true full-service hotel. It has a great sitting room that's formal but comfortable, with a fireplace and a cozy library. The rooms are decorated with floral-print wall coverings, matching quilts, and first-rate antique reproductions. *R.R. 1, Box 350, Warren 05674, tel. 802/583–2301 or 800/537–8427, fax 802/583–3209. 46 rooms. Facilities: 2 restaurants. AE, D, DC, MC, V. $115–$150.*

Inexpensive

Hyde Away

This renovated farmstead with red tin roofs offers rooms, family suites (kids are welcome here), and dorms that sleep eight. Outside, you can go cross-country skiing and ice skating. *Rte. 17, R.R. 1, Box 65, Waitsfield 05673, tel. 802/496–2322 or 800/777–4933. 14 rooms, 4 suites, 2 dorms. Facilities: restaurant, TV lounge. AE, D, MC, V. $49–$89.*

Lareau Farm Country Inn
Porches surround this 1832 Greek Revival farmhouse-turned-B&B, painted gray with red and green trim. Inside, rooms are countrified and antique, with period wallpaper, hand-me-down collectibles, and the odd shapes and corners that century-old buildings tend to have. There are horses here on the farm, and sleigh rides are available. *Rte. 100, Box 563, Waitsfield 05673, tel. 802/496–4949. 13 rooms. Facilities: restaurant, sleigh rides. MC, V. $60–$125.*

Tucker Hill Lodge
Rooms in this blue clapboard hillside inn are simple, clean, and cozy. The mountain cabin charm is evident throughout the inn—from the knotty pine living room with its fieldstone fireplace through its two dining rooms to the cute and cuddly couch by the basement fireplace. *R.R. 1, Box 147, Waitsfield 05673, tel. 802/496–3983 or 800/543–7841, fax 802/496–3203. 21 rooms. Facilities: restaurant, lounge. AE, MC, V. $70–$115, including full breakfast.*

Waitsfield Inn
This 1825 inn in bustling downtown Waitsfield is within walking distance from shops, restaurants, and night spots. It's done in Federal style, with ornate woodwork and lots of country antiques. *Box 969, Waitsfield 05673,*

tel. 802/496–3979. 14 rooms. AE, MC, V. $79–$119, including full breakfast.

WHERE TO EAT
There are a number of good restaurants in and around the Sugarbush village area, plus a larger selection on the road between the resort and Waitsfield.

Expensive
Chez Henri
The restaurant, bistro, and nightspot is slope side on the edge of the Sugarbush Village, which means you can ski in for a stylish lunch, brunch, or après-ski meal. This romantic little French restaurant with a fireplace and white marble bar offers such lunch specials as cheese fondue or Cajun calamari. For dinner there may be frogs' legs or rabbit in red wine sauce or a scrumptious bouillabaisse. *Village at Sugarbush, base of ski area, tel. 802/583–2600. Reservations essential. AE, D, DC, MC, V.*

Common Man
Just off the Sugarbush Access Road is a quaint dining emporium situated in a mid-19th-century barn that was moved and reconstructed here in 1987. The atmosphere at Common Man is casual, but the fare is not so common. The candlelighted table settings, the crystal chandeliers, and the large fieldstone fireplace are a fit setting for the presentation of such dishes as fillets of trout steamed in parchment paper or medallions of beef tenderloin. *German Flats Rd., Warren, tel. 802/583–2800. AE, D, MC, V.*

Sam Rupert's

Dark wood, plants, wood-burning stoves, and white tablecloths with forest green napkins set the stage here for the eclectic contemporary American cuisine: rack of lamb with sun-dried tomatoes and green peppercorn sauce, lobster ravioli with blackened bay scallops and tomato cream sauce, pan-roasted salmon encrusted with sesame, ginger, and garlic. Despite the elaborate menu, the place is casual enough for children. *Sugarbush Access Rd., Warren, tel. 802/583–2421. Reservations essential. AE, DC, MC, V.*

Tucker Hill Inn

There's an understated Vermont style to this place with a skylighted terrace section. One of the culinary centerpieces of the Sugarbush area, it has wonderful ways with Atlantic salmon, wood-grilled swordfish, and Long Island duckling. *Rte. 17, Waitsfield, tel. 802/496–3983. AE, MC, V.*

Moderate

American Flatbread Kitchen

In the barn complex at the Lareau Farm Country Inn, they serve what they call Pizza with Integrity, baked on native Vermont soapstone inside a low, wide, hardwood-fired earthen oven. The dining room is rustic, with wide-plank floors and walls and a wood-burning stove. You can expect such creative toppings as their Medicine Wheel tomato sauce with onions, mushrooms, cheese, and herbs. *Lareau Farm Country Inn, Rte. 100, Waitsfield, tel. 802/496–8856. MC, V.*

Bass Restaurant

Right on the Sugarbush Access Road, this eclectic 1959 building originally designed for theatrical presentations today offers three separate levels for dining. The restaurant's central focus is a massive circular fieldstone hearth vented through a large brass-and-iron cone chimney. The cuisine is American with a hint of the Mediterranean; try the New England fisherman's stew, which includes lobster, shrimp, scallops, and black mussels in an herb-infused tomato broth. *Sugarbush Access Rd., Warren, tel. 802/583–3100. AE, D, MC, V.*

China Moon

This fine Chinese restaurant serves Cantonese, Mandarin, Szechuan, and Hunan dishes as well as such non-traditional dishes as lobster with spicy Szechuan sauce that capture not only your eye but also your palate. The dining room is full of beautiful natural woods, including huge overhead beams and oak tabletops. *Sugarbush Village, Warren, tel. 802/583–1024. AE, MC, V.*

The Den

A giant old bank safe is on the right as you enter this ever-so-popular eatery near Waitsfield Center. The main dining room is full of knotty pine, with a scattering of booths and tables. Lunches of burgers, pork chops, and sandwiches such as grilled avocado and cheese are offered. The local dinner favorites are the Texas rib appetizer and the steaks. *Rtes. 100 and 17, Waitsfield, tel. 802/496–8880. AE, MC, V.*

Olde Tymes

On the walls of the four dining rooms in this large, light, and airy restaurant, there are any number of antique knickknacks but no clutter. On cold winter days go for a table next to one of the two fireplaces or near a heat register unless the dining room is full. The fare is strictly American, with a good selection of seafood. *Rte. 100, Waitsfield, tel. 802/496–3875. AE, D, MC, V.*

Inexpensive

Grill Down Under

The grill is the central and highly visible component of this warm and friendly brick-and-wood bistro. The lighting is subdued, and small table groupings give a sense of intimacy. On the menu you'll find everything from plain grilled burgers, chops, and fish to dishes with interesting flourishes like a mustard-maple-syrup topping or lime-cilantro butter. No lunch. *Sugarbush Inn, Warren, tel. 802/583–2301. AE, D, DC, MC, V.*

Hyde Away Restaurant

This Route 17 restaurant is comfortable and casual, with a woodstove, lots of plants, and a menu that ranges from nachos and pasta to tuna, steak, and prime rib. *Rte. 17, Waitsfield, tel. 802/496–2322. AE, MC, V.*

Jay's Restaurant and Pizzeria

In this comfortable local hangout, with oak tables, plants, and an eclectic array of original local art, you can get a great deal on wholesome fare. Chicken comes Southern fried, parmigiana style, or sautéed with artichokes, mushrooms, and white wine. Or you could go for sautéed pork medallions, stir-fried duck, swordfish *puttanesca*, fish-and-chips, pizza, buffalo wings, or T-bone steak. And the lasagna is excellent. *Mad River Green Shopping Center, Rte. 100, Waitsfield, tel. 802/496–8282. MC, V.*

Miguel's

At the area's only Mexican restaurant, you'll find your favorite authentic south-of-the-border fare among cantina-style stucco and beams, bright posters, and wall hangings. Fajitas, tacos, and enchiladas are on the lineup—with a wickedly hot salsa—along with an interesting chicken breast stuffed with cornbread and pecans and a delicious vegetarian chili. *Sugarbush Access Rd., Warren, tel. 802/583–3858. AE, MC, V.*

Best Bet for Breakfast

Little Grocery and Deli

This takeout emporium with a counter offers a selection of ham, egg, and cheese combos on a choice of English muffin, bagel, biscuit, or croissant. The excellent home-baked muffins come in a variety of flavors. *Sugarbush Access Rd., Warren, tel. 802/583–2757. MC, V.*

NIGHTLIFE AND ENTERTAINMENT
Après-Ski

Green Mountain Lounge

This rustic ski-in/ski-out bar overlooking the mountains has high vaulted ceilings, a fireplace, and a huge deck. On weekends and holidays there is live music. *Sugarbush North Base Lodge, Warren, tel. 802/583–2381, ext. 464. AE, D, DC, MC, V.*

Wunderbar

This modern three-room bar has wooden shutters and a large mural of the local towns. There is live music on weekends, anything from Rockabilly bands to solo guitarists. *Valley House Base Lodge South, Warren, tel. 802/583–2381, ext. 464. AE, D, DC, MC, V.*

Loud and Lively/Dancing

Blue Tooth

Built in 1963 to resemble a Vermont sugar house, the Blue Tooth boasts the longest bar in the valley. The interior is blond board, open beams, antiques, and hanging plants. Live bands perform on weekends. *Sugarbush Access Rd., Warren, tel. 802/583–2656. MC, V.*

Mad Mountain Tavern

At this post-and-beam barn locals and visitors can eat, drink, dance, play pool or darts, and watch big-screen TV any night of the week. Live bands play Thursday–Saturday. *Rte. 100 and Rte. 17, Waitsfield, tel. 802/496–2562. AE, MC, V.*

More Mellow

Grill Down Under

In this comfortable, relaxed place, there are plenty of brass trim, a granite-top bar, 35 wines, and five local microbrews on tap at any given time. *Corner Sugarbush Access Rd. and German Flats Rd., Warren, tel. 802/583–2301. AE, D, DC, MC, V.*

Olde Tymes

Vintage skis, snowshoes, and other sporting artifacts decorate this warm, cozy bar. Wooden floors, a stone fireplace, and good jazz music make it an intimate spot for conversation. *Rte. 100, Waitsfield, tel. 802/496–3875. AE, D, MC, V.*

Wyoming is a marvelously wild slice of Americana that is home to the most impressive range of mountains on the continent. The 40-mile-long Teton Range, thrusting toward the sky in a dazzling array of jagged peaks and spires, comprises the youngest mountains of the Rocky Mountain system.

Seven of these granite giants top the 12,000-foot mark, and the tallest of them all, Grand Teton, reaches 13,770 feet. Circling this tight concentration of wind- and water-sculpted peaks are glacier-fed lakes and rivers shimmering like jewels on the flat plain known as Jackson Hole. Forming the walls of this scenic valley are the Yellowstone Plateau to the north; the Absaroka, the Washakie, and the Gros Ventre on the east; and merging to the south, the Hoback and Snake River ranges.

Sculpted and glacially etched from some of the oldest granite on earth, these peaks and pinnacles known as the Cathedral Group has been described as "Chartres multiplied by six." Your first glimpse of the Tetons is made dramatic by the absence of foothills. The Tetons shoot skyward with no geological preamble, resulting in some of the most stunning mountain vistas on the continent.

Beneath this riveting wall of granite, the Jackson Plain, dissected by 40 miles of the glacially fed Snake River before it winds its way 1,000 miles farther to the mouth of the Columbia River, is home to ranchers and elk, the latter outnumbering the former, with as many as 10,000 elk wintering in the area annually. This high alpine plain is an extension of the Yellowstone Park ecosystem, which occupies the northwest corner of the state, and the entire Jackson area is inside the boundaries of Grand Teton National Park.

Created in 1950 predominantly from land acquired by John D. Rockefeller, Jr., the park attracts more than 3 million visitors annually, including those who come to ski. There are a half-dozen ski resorts in Wyoming, but by far the best known and most spectacular is Jackson Hole.

JACKSON HOLE SKI RESORT

JACKSON HOLE SKI RESORT

Box 290
Teton Village, WY 83025
Tel. 307/733–2292

STATISTICALLY SPEAKING
Base elevation: 6,311 feet

Summit elevation: 10,450 feet

Vertical drop: 4,139 feet

Skiable terrain: 2,500 acres

Number of trails: 65

Longest run: 4.5 miles

Lifts and capacity: 1 aerial tram, 1 high-speed quad, 2 quads, 1 triple, 3 doubles, 2 surface; 9,995 skiers per hour

Daily lift ticket: $46

Average annual snowfall: 384 inches

Number of skiing days 1995–96: 121

Snowmaking: 240 acres; 12%

Terrain mix: N 10%, I 40%, E 50%

Snowboarding: yes

Cross-country skiing: 17 kilometers, plus mapped tours, guided backcountry tours, and trail system of Yellowstone National Park.

Technically speaking, Jackson and Jackson Hole, though closely related, are distinct entities. Jackson Hole is the name of the valley—or hole—that sits surrounded by the peaks and pinnacles of the Grand Tetons, the youngest and arguably the most spectacular mountains in the Rocky Mountain system. Jackson Hole is also the name of the ski resort, though the resort center at its base is called Teton Village. Twelve miles to the east is the community of Jackson, a bona fide Western ranching town that reflects the spirit of the entire region.

The resort, the town, and the ski area are all usually lumped together under the name Jackson Hole, but that's okay. The important thing is the way they fit together so perfectly, meshing beautifully with the surrounding mountains to form a whole greater than the sum of its parts.

This harmony of setting, town, and skiing is the reason I have such a profound fondness for this unique, isolated resort in the northwest corner of Wyoming. It just feels right. The town is authentic enough to be real but funky enough to be fun. Behind its facade of wooden sidewalks and movie-set storefront buildings, Jackson is in fact more grit than glitz; and yet the town also has a lively and cosmopolitan dining, entertainment, and cultural scene. The skiing at Jackson Hole Ski Resort is big and bold enough to spawn legends of derring-do but diverse enough to give us all a shot at the Jackson mystique. As for the surroundings—well, the Grand Tetons have to be seen to be believed. They rise abruptly in jagged spires, glistening with glaciers and at once overshadowing and protecting the ranch land of the valley floor, which is a winter home to the largest elk population in the world.

The 12 miles separating town and resort are an easy drive, facilitated by regular shuttle bus service. Teton Village itself is a curious blend of Western and Tyrolean styles, with a half-dozen slope-side hotels, a central mall with restaurants, bars, and shops, several condominium buildings, and all the other trappings of modern ski-resort life without the crass overdevelopment that blights so many other resort villages. It's neat, compact, easy to get around, and offers enough variety in accommodations and dining

USEFUL NUMBERS
Area code: 307

Children's services: day care, instruction, tel. 301/739-2610

Snow phone: tel. 307/733-2291 or 888/333-7766

Police: tel. 307/733-2331 or 911

Hospital: St. John's, tel. 307/733-3636

Jackson Hole Chamber of Commerce: tel. 307/733-3316

Cross-country skiing: Jackson Hole Nordic Center, tel. 307/739-2629; Spring Creek Resort, tel. 307/733-1004; Teton Pines, tel. 307/733-1005

Road conditions: tel. 307/733-9966

Towing: Teton Towing, tel. 307/733-1943

FIVE-STAR FAVORITES
Best run for vertical: Hobacks

Best run overall:
Rendezvous Bowl

Best bar/nightclub:
Million Dollar Cowboy Bar

Best hotel:
Spring Creek Resort

Best restaurant: The Range

to keep you quietly happy for more than a few days. If you like to be on the mountain first thing in the morning, it's definitely the place to stay.

If you prefer a little more action in the after-ski scene, you're likely to opt for the town of Jackson. Though it's not in the same league as Aspen, Vail, or Sun Valley, Jackson has a bustling nightlife, with lots of bars and saloons, a decent array of restaurants, and a number of cultural activities. Most of the action takes place along a six-block section of Old Town, an area that incorporates Jackson Town Square and its four massive elk-antler archways (don't worry: the elk shed their antlers naturally, and the discards are gathered by local Boy Scouts, who auction off the best ones to raise funds to maintain the elk wintering grounds).

Also in town is the Snow King Resort, Jackson's other ski resort. It is a modest day facility with mostly intermediate runs, an option on days when the weather is cold and windy at the big mountain or when you feel like having an easy day without driving too far.

Jackson is family-friendly, with diversions for those who don't want to ski every day. Yellowstone National Park is just 60 miles away, and numerous tour operators will give you guided tours of the park on everything from snowshoes to snow coaches.

For 30 years the ski area has gotten by without a single real change in lifts or facilities. In fact, that's what appeals to some people about this place—it's a down-home, no-glitz kind of place. But under new ownership now, the mountain is beginning to undergo some significant improvements. In 1996 the resort's first high-speed quad was added, and by the 1997 season a gondola will be in place, taking skiers from the base to Headwall to access the same terrain as the tram, minus Rendezvous Bowl. This is a much-needed addition, as tram lines can be up to an hour long on busy days. A 20-year plan, approved in 1997, calls for the replacement of every lift on the mountain as well as the addition of new lifts.

HOW TO GET THERE

By Plane

Jackson Hole Airport, 10 miles north of Jackson, is the only airport inside a national park anywhere in America. That necessarily restricts its volume, but even so, there are daily flights from Chicago via **American,** from Seattle and Boise via **Horizon Air,** from Salt Lake City (*see* Getting to Utah Resorts) via **Delta** and **Skywest,** and from Denver via **United** and **United Express.**

By Car

From Jackson Hole Airport it's a 10-minute drive to Jackson and 25 minutes to the resort. You can also drive from Salt Lake City, 200 miles southwest of Jackson. It's a fairly easy five-hour drive on interstates that are generally free of snow. Follow I–80 west from Salt Lake City and 189 north into Jackson. The following car-rental companies are available at Jackson Hole Airport: **Alamo** (tel. 800/327–9633), **Avis** (tel. 800/331–1212), **Budget** (tel. 800/533–6100), and **Hertz** (tel. 800/654–3131).

GETTING AROUND

A public shuttle bus runs between Jackson and Teton Village, and many of the hotels and resorts provide their own private bus service, but even so, a car is an advantage here. **Buckboard Taxi** (tel. 307/733–1112) services the town.

By Shuttle

The **START Bus** (Southern Teton Area Rapid Transit; tel. 307/733–4521) makes frequent stops in town, at certain points along the highway, and at the Teton Village area. It operates daily from 7 AM to 11 PM. The fare is $2 one-way between Jackson and the resort, $1 one-way within Jackson.

THE SKIING

If you go solely by its reputation, anyone but an in-your-face expert would steer clear of Jackson Hole. Tall tales about its staggering vertical abound. While it's true Jackson Hole has the highest vertical drop in the United States and the third highest in North America behind Blackcomb and Whistler mountains, in British Columbia, Canada, it is also true this is a good all-round intermediate-and-up ski mountain. Up is the key. Rendezvous Mountain, the higher of the two peaks that make up the broad-shouldered mountain hulk, is the one that gives the resort its savage reputation, for the terrain here is a mass of vertiginous chutes, couloirs, bowls, and gullies. But between the 4,000-foot-plus vertical of Rendezvous and the slightly lower and less precipitous groomed cruisers of Après Vous Mountain, there are 2,500 acres of varied skiing, including the mostly intermediate Casper Bowl area, which lies between the two summits.

It's a large resort, but it's easy to move back and forth between the three sectors on a well-designed series of cat tracks that actually slope in the direction you're going with no noticeable flat spots. Everybody starts from the compact base area, from which Jackson's aerial tram whips you to the Rendezvous summit: 4,139 feet of vertical in eight minutes; you can't do that anywhere else in America. It's steep, rugged, ungroomed, and uncompromising up here, and sacred areas such as Rendezvous Bowl, Corbet's Couloir, and the Hobacks are always discussed when serious ski addicts gather.

Fortunately, there's lots more of Jackson for the rest of us. Just a short distance from the tram are the lifts up to the Casper Bowl and Après Vous areas, virtually all of which are long, groomed blue runs with some black pitches and faces. This section is some of the most varied and challenging intermediate/upper intermediate/ expert terrain you'll find anywhere. Although experts push their limits on the tough terrain of the Rendezvous Peak, strong intermediates can sample the bliss of Jackson's pure fall-line skiing. Another bliss—for everyone—is the solitude. Jackson has one of the lowest skier-to-acreage ratios in the country. A busy day at Jackson is maybe 3,000 skiers spread over 2,500 acres.

Although there are no special features for snowboarders on the mountain, you'll find the same advantages as skiers do—rugged, limitless terrain and uncrowded conditions.

Novices

Aside from Snowbird in Utah, Jackson Hole is the only resort in America that I find totally unsuitable for raw beginners or low-end novices. If you fit into one of those two categories, I strongly recommend you look elsewhere and save Jackson for a time when you are at a steady intermediate level. It's not that Jackson doesn't have a fine ski school; and yes, there is a small beginners' area served by its own double chair, so you can certainly get started on skis here. But do yourself a

favor and go to Jackson when you can enjoy more of it.

If you do by chance end up at Jackson while you're still at the novice level, your options are limited to either the three short starter runs served by the Eagle's Rest double chair or the trio of slightly longer runs served by the Teewinot quad chair. These meticulously groomed, carpet-smooth extrawide novice trails are the only marked green runs on the mountain.

The next rung up is a fairly sizable one: to move to some of the gentler blue runs that start on the upper part of Après Vous. The Après Vous double (from the top of the Teewinot double) takes you there, and at that point, you are immediately dealing with steeper terrain. It's wide, well groomed, and goes in rolls rather than one straight shot, so easy, controlled plow turns will get you down, but you may find it hard work.

If you can't deal with that and want to bail out, you can follow the signs for the Togwotee Pass Traverse, a long, narrow cat track that winds back down to South Pass Traverse and eventually back to the top of the green runs on the lower part of the mountain. Take note: Once you get off the chair at the top, you have to turn left and immediately head down a short, fairly steep section that funnels you to the top of Upper Werner. From there the whole face of the mountain opens up, and you can see precisely what you are in for. The easiest terrain (still blue) is to your right, while the steeper pitches are to the left. You can catch the Traverse bailout about 500 yards down this stretch.

Intermediates

Intermediates will find some heads-up skiing at Jackson, the kind that will stretch you a little, throw you a few more challenges than normal, and even give you a greater sense of confidence at the end of the day. Your warm-up runs should, however, take place on the softer flanks of Après Vous Mountain, where the early sun will appear. Take the Teewinot lift to the Après Vous chair to the top. To the right (looking down) is a superb pair of groomed cruisers—Upper Werner and Moran—that roll and pitch sufficiently to get your legs warm fast. You can repeat them a few times or take the Togwotee Pass Traverse (from the top of Après Vous) over to the Casper Bowl chair, where it's a little steeper, less groomed, and just a little more unpredictable.

There are over 300 acres of intermediate terrain off the Casper chair, and it's made all the more interesting thanks to the trees and straight-ahead trail cutting that leaves dips, rolls, drop-offs, pitches, and glades as the fall line dictates. Campground, Timbered Island, and Easy Does It, which all start from the right side (looking down) of the Casper chair, are the widest slopes in this area and will give you a good ride back down to the bottom of the Casper chair. Avoid going down to the base area, where you'll have to take the Crystal chair back to midmountain. To the left of the top of the Casper Chair (looking down), you'll find narrower, more heavily treed trails. If you go farther to the right and follow the Amphitheatre Traverse, you can ride the Thunder chair and ski either the wide-open Amphitheatre Bowl area or play in the gladed runs in the Laramie (to the right, looking down) Bowl area. Both areas have good, steep fall-line bowl skiing, a pick-your-own-way-down buffet of options on some of the best intermediate terrain on the mountain.

Immediately above this is the summit of Rendezvous Mountain and the storied couloirs and chutes and rocky gullies that give Jackson its reputation. Good intermediates can push the envelope a little by trying some of the tamer blacks. Only the tram goes to the summit, but from the Laramie Bowl area you can take the Upper Sublette Ridge chair to a point just below the summit. To the right of the chair (looking down) is the steep entrance to a trio of tough black runs. You can avoid the drop-off access by taking the blue Hanging Rock, which winds easily down to the bottom of the Sublette Ridge chair to give you a sense of the terrain without actually getting you into any trouble. You'll find the black runs steep, treed, and ungroomed, with moguls on the left-hand side, but if you're a good strong intermediate, with some effort you should be able to cut your teeth on them.

Experts

Without a doubt your domain is Rendezvous Mountain with its 4,139 feet of vertical and some of the most demanding and rugged in-bounds skiing in America. You might want to warm up in the Laramie Bowl area first, but eventually you'll head for the summit on the tram. This is where you'll find the stuff that Jackson is famed for: ultrasteep couloirs, chutes, gullies, glades, and wide-open sweeping bowls. The most renowned of

Jackson's descents is precipitous, tree-choked Corbet's Couloir, which can only be reached by jumping from a cornice to land 15 feet below. If you're not ready for that, the Upper Rendezvous Bowl is a steep, wide-open screamer that gives you a taste of Jackson's vertical without the impediments of rocks and trees. You can ski this upper part of the mountain from the Upper Sublette Ridge chair to avoid going back to the village to ride the tram. Although there are a dozen or so named runs in this area of the mountain, they really do not convey the scale of the terrain; each named run has dozens of free-form options. The lower flanks of Rendezvous Mountain are the home of the Hobacks, a wide swath of steep, powder-packed cruising bowls that again dare you to discover all the different ways down. And when you've tired of this terrain, 20,000 acres of out-of-bounds skiing await you beyond the ski area boundaries. Just be sure to sign in with ski patrol at the shack at the top of the tram before heading out.

That's the beauty of Jackson for expert skiers: It offers virtually unlimited challenge and a kind of rugged adventure not found at resorts elsewhere. If you like to explore, cut new tracks, push the envelope—then you'll love Jackson.

WHERE TO STAY

There's a good range of accommodations at Teton Village and in the town of Jackson. A variety of resort-style hotels and small bed-and-breakfasts have sprouted along the 12-mile highway that connects Jackson and the mountain, as well as in nearby Wilson, about 9 miles from the resort.

All accommodations can be booked through Jackson Hole Central Reservations (Box 2618, Jackson, WY 83001, tel. 307/733–4005 or 800/443–6931).

Expensive

Alpenhof
Just 50 yards from the tram, this is an Austrian-style lodge with a twin-peaked stucco alpine-chalet exterior, and the old-world atmosphere positively oozes from the polished-wood-and-stone decor. The rooms share similar wood trim and colonial-style pine furnishings; some have stucco and stone walls, fireplaces, balconies, or whirlpools (or all four). *3255 W. McCollister Dr., Box 288, Teton Village 83025, tel. 307/733–3242 or 800/732–3244, fax 307/739–1516. 43 rooms. Facilities: 2 restaurants, heated outdoor pool, Jacuzzi, sauna, masseuse, laundry. AE, D, DC, MC, V. $89–$220.*

Rusty Parrot Lodge
This magnificent log-and-stone lodge is one of Jackson's best-known landmarks. Sturdy in its hand-hewed log splendor, with peaks and posts, balconies and beams, yet stylish inside with its handcrafted peeled-log furniture, stone fireplace warming its lounge, Western art, down comforters, and Jacuzzi tubs, the Rusty Parrot is pure Rocky Mountain elegance. The rooms are all individually decorated with pine and twig chairs and tables, Western-style fabrics and curtains. Half have fireplaces. *175 N. Jackson St., Jackson 83001, tel. 307/733–2000 or 800/458–2004, fax 307/*

733–5566. 32 rooms, 1 suite. Facilities: dining room, lounge. AE, D, DC, MC, V. $145–$450, including full breakfast.

Spring Creek Resort

This chic 1,000-acre log cabin resort is high atop the East Gros Ventre Butte 4 miles north of Jackson. It's really a minivillage, with three dozen honey-bronze log cabins and condo structures scattered around two central buildings. The spacious condo suites have hand-troweled plaster walls, handmade lodge-pole furnishings, large stone fireplaces, and down bed covers and kitchen facilities. *1800 Spirit Dance Rd., Box 3154, Jackson 83001, tel. 307/733–8833 or 800/443–6139, fax 307/733–1524. 86 units. Facilities: restaurant, lounge, hot tub, barbecue pits. AE, D, DC, MC, V. $150–$190.*

Wort Hotel

Originally built in 1941 and then rebuilt after a fire, this is Jackson Hole's landmark hotel. A noteworthy Western art collection enlivens the lobby and restaurant. Rooms aren't fancy, but the log beds, Indian blankets, and teddy bear in each room add a welcoming touch. The Silver Dollar bar is a popular watering hole, and the hotel's downtown location is ideal. *50 N. Glenwood Ave., Box 69, Jackson 83001, tel. 307/733–2190 or 800/322–2727, fax 307/733–2067. 60 rooms. Facilities: restaurant, bar, 2 Jacuzzis, fitness room, meeting room. AE, MC, V. $115–$325.*

Moderate

Best Western Inn at Jackson Hole

In a perfect slope-side location just 100 yards from the tram at Teton Village, this inn has some of the most comfortable, spacious, and reasonably priced rooms and suites at the mountain. The units range from standard hotel rooms to loft suites; most of the nonstandard rooms have kitchen facilities, and a few even come with a fireplace. *3345 W. McCollister Dr., Box 328, Teton Village 83025, tel. 307/733–2311 or 800/842–7666, fax 307/733–0844. 71 rooms, 12 suites. Facilities: 2 restaurants, bar-lounge, outdoor pool, 3 outdoor hot tubs. AE, D, DC, MC, V. $100–$225.*

Best Western Lodge at Jackson Hole

The massive log building, an easy walk from Jackson Square, combines new- and old-West touches: exterior timbers hand-carved with wildlife sculptures, leather-fringed chairs and couches, a log staircase, and antler chandeliers. The rooms, generous in size and amenities and tastefully done in soft pastels, with matching accessories and coverings, are a good choice for families. *80 Scott La., Box 30436, Jackson Hole 83001, tel. 307/739–9703 or 800/458–3866, fax 307/739–9168. 154 rooms. Facilities: restaurant, heated indoor-outdoor pool, sauna, hot tub, games arcade, shuttle bus service. AE, D, DC, MC, V. $79–$129, including Continental breakfast.*

Snow King Resort

This hotel and condominium complex is on Snow King Mountain, just six blocks from the Jackson Town Square. The largest full-service property in town, the hotel has a soaring atrium-style lobby with massive rough timbers and a 40-foot rock fireplace. The units range in size from standard hotel rooms to three-bedroom condos, and most are modern, with Berber carpets, textured walls, and Southwest-style furnishings. *400 E. Snow King Ave., Jackson 83001, tel. 307/ 733–5200 or 800/522–5464, fax 307/ 733–4086. 192 rooms, 12 suites. Facilities: 2 restaurants, lounge/nightclub, indoor ice-skating rink, outdoor heated pool, sauna, Jacuzzi, exercise room, ski shop, conference center. AE, D, DC, MC, V. $90–$345.*

Sojourner Inn

In a great location near the resort's base area—not quite ski-in/ski-out, but almost—is a comfortable stucco-and-wood Tyrolean chalet, but with slightly more contemporary decor and furnishings. The rooms are generally quite large, especially those in the newer section, which are furnished in a sleek, clean-lined modern style. Try for a mountainside room with a balcony. *3245 W. McCollister Dr., Box 348, Teton Village 83025, tel. 307/ 733–3657 or 800/445–4655, fax 307/ 733–9543. 96 rooms, 4 suites. Facilities: 2 restaurants, 2 lounges, heated outdoor pool and Jacuzzi, indoor sauna and Jacuzzi, laundry. AE, D, DC, MC, V. $85–$260.*

Inexpensive

Angler's Inn

A few minutes from Jackson Square, the rooms here are simply furnished and clean. Each has a morning coffee setup plus a microwave and a refrigerator. *265 Millward St., Box 1247, Jackson 83001, tel. 307/733–3682 or 800/867–4667, fax 307/739–1551. 28 rooms. AE, D, MC, V. $65–$95.*

Bunkhouse

In the basement of the Anvil Motel, this is good, clean, and basic bunkhouse-style lodging, with a central dormitory accommodating both sexes, a common living room with TV, and a kitchen area. *215 N. Cache St., Box 486, Jackson 83001, tel. 307/ 733–3668 or 800/234–4507, fax 307/ 733–3957. 25 beds. Facilities: indoor hot tub. MC, V. $18 per person.*

Elk Country Inn

This is a no-frills but clean and well-maintained motel and log cabin complex just a block off Jackson's Main Street, about a 10-minute walk from Jackson Square. There's a variety of motel rooms plus some larger cabin units with kitchen facilities and some lofts. *480 W. Pearl St., Box 1255, Jackson 83001, 307/733–2364 or 800/ 483-8667, fax 307/733–4465. 23 rooms, 7 suites, 13 log cabins. Facilities: indoor hot tub, laundry. AE, D, DC, MC, V. $38–$110.*

The Hostel

This has to be one of the best hostels in ski country, with its spiffy private rooms, all with private baths and maid service, and its furnishings a definite cut above the rustic style typical of hostels. In fact, the only typical hostel feature here is the price. You can choose from king rooms or twin rooms, which sleep four comfortably in a bunk arrangement. It's just 100 yards from the lifts. *3325 McCollister Dr., Box 546, Teton Village 83025, tel. 307/733–3415, fax 307/739–1142. 55 rooms. Facilities: 2 game rooms, play area, library, ski tuning area, laundry. MC, V. $44–$56.*

WHERE TO EAT

Jackson is not the culinary epicenter of Western skiing, but it does have an interesting collection of restaurants, dominated by traditional Western fare—beef and lots of it and various game dishes. It mostly has medium-priced places to eat, by ski-country standards, and the atmosphere is definitely blue-jean casual, with a few exceptions. There are a good number of restaurants in and around the Jackson Square area, plus others on the road to the resort, and, of course, at the ski village itself. Even if you're staying at the ski area and enjoy the convenience of walking from your accommodation, you would be remiss in not going into Jackson at least a couple of times a week.

On the Mountain

Casper Restaurant

A large stone fireplace flanked by two plush couches is the focus of the split-level dining room. Baked potato extreme (smothered in cheese and chili), seafood, and prime rib are menu regulars, but try the daily chef's specials, such as the tangy Cajun barbecued chicken pizza. *Mid-Mountain Lodge, top of Crystal Springs chair, Teton Village, tel. 307/739–2624. AE, MC, V.*

Nick Wilson's

At the base of the tram, Nick's has an outdoor barbecue on the deck on sunny days and live music après-ski. The menu is basic burgers, sandwiches, Mexican specialties, and hearty chilis and soups in a bread bowl. *Tram Building, McCollister Dr., Teton Village, tel. 307/739–2626. AE, MC, V.*

Expensive

Blue Lion

Spread over two floors of a renovated older house, the interior is spacious and modern in decor, with white walls, low-beamed ceilings, plants, and dusty rose table settings. The extensive menu, changed daily, focuses on fresh game dishes such as a tender grilled elk tenderloin smothered in a green peppercorn brandy sauce and a roulade of wild boar rolled in a mixture of smoked chicken, pine nuts, and red peppers and wrapped in phyllo. It's innovative and creative cuisine and ranks among Jackson's best. *160 N. Millward St., Jackson, tel. 307/733–3912. AE, DC, MC, V.*

Cadillac Grille

This hopping Art Deco bistro located front and center on Jackson Square is as close as it gets to slick glitz in Jackson. The tile, chrome, and glass decor complements the walls bedecked with avant-garde art. The fare is eclectic American with Southwestern accents and delicious original sauces. There's always a good selection of fish and game, such as pheasant stuffed with spinach and topped with boysenberry sauce, fresh Atlantic salmon with an orange-based sauce, or fresh ahi with crunchy pasta slaw. *55 N. Cache St., Jackson, tel. 307/733–3279. Reservations essential. AE, MC, V.*

The Granary

It's a large, softly lighted modern room with a spectacular starlit view over the valley. Linen and crystal place settings set a quietly formal tone here. The cuisine is an interesting mix of Continental, Western, and modern Southwestern. Game choices abound on the menu—from panfried Rocky Mountain trout to sautéed medallions of elk. Other entrées include marinated ahi in a peach and kiwi coulis and rosemary-seared rack of lamb. *Spring Creek Resort, off Spring Gulch Rd., Jackson, tel. 307/733–8833 or 800/443–6139. AE, DC, MC, V.*

The Range

This is Jackson's finest dining. The upstairs restaurant features an open kitchen and a striking East-meets-West decor, with black lacquer chairs and rice paper lights. The menu emphasizes regional American cuisine in original combinations. You might start with grilled scallops in Parmesan cheese cups with tomato-vodka sauce or a salad of fresh cactus, red pepper, purple onion, mango, and cilantro in a blue-corn tortilla cup. Entrées include daily game and seafood specials. *225 N. Cache St., Jackson, tel. 307/733–5481. Reservations essential. AE, MC, V.*

Snake River Grille

This spot is on the second floor of a clapboard plaza complex on Jackson's main street, opposite the town square. The atmosphere is contemporary casual, and the decor is upmarket rustic, with deep forest green carpets, earth-tone log walls, and a large wood-burning stone fireplace in the middle of the room. The menu is American/Italian with an emphasis on grilled trout, salmon, and swordfish and on regional game dishes such as grilled elk and buffalo chili. There's also a whole lineup of wood-oven pizza specialties. *84 E. Broadway, Jackson, tel. 307/733–0557. AE, MC, V.*

Moderate

Jenny Leigh's

This delightful small restaurant in the Inn at Jackson Hole has a hunter green and soft pink decor. You'll find steak or medallions of elk sautéed with lingonberry and green peppercorn sauce, venison Wellington, and bison steak, as well as seafood and pasta. *Inn at Jackson Hole, 3345 McCollister Dr., Teton Village, tel. 307/733–7102. AE, D, MC, V.*

Nani's

Hidden away on a side street, this gem of an Italian restaurant is a tiny white-brick cottage with maybe a dozen small tables, all covered with red-and-white checker tablecloths. The menu offers fresh handmade ravioli, creamy linguine *con vongole*, veal Florentine, as well as changing specials that emphasize a different region of Italy each month. *240 N. Glenwood, behind El Rancho Hotel, Jackson, tel. 307/733–3888. MC, V.*

Sweetwater Restaurant

This is a marvelous turn-of-the-century log cabin whose character arises from exposed logs, hand-hewed beams, sloping wooden floors, and wrought-iron lamps. Although small, it provides a touch of elegance with linen and crystal. The menu combines Mediterranean and Continental with traditional Western fare. Try large, succulent shrimp simmered in tomatoes and feta cheese or a Greek phyllo pie. For Western traditionalists, mesquite-grilled Idaho trout or salmon and the New York strip are good choices. *King and Pearl Sts., Jackson, tel. 307/733–3553. AE, D, DC, MC, V.*

Vista Grande

This pink adobe between the ski area and town has been a favorite après-ski gathering spot for almost 20 years.

The margaritas are excellent, and the food is a step up from traditional Mexican fare, with specialties like crab enchiladas, blackened chicken tostadas, and blackened tuna with pineapple salsa. *Teton Village Rd., Jackson, tel. 307/733–6964. Reservations not accepted. AE, MC, V.*

Inexpensive

Billy's Burgers
On the town square, it's not fancy here—a diner-style counter and about a dozen seats—but it's so central that it's always busy. If you love big, fat, juicy hamburgers, this is the spot. *Cadillac Grille, 55 N. Cache St., Jackson, tel. 307/733–3279. Reservations not accepted. No credit cards.*

Bubba's Bar-B-Que
You go to Bubba's mainly for the major portions of spareribs and baby-back ribs, hickory smoked and smothered in Bubba's secret special sauces and served with garlic bread. The decor is simply lots of beams, Western artifacts, separate booths, and brick floors. *151 W. Broadway, Jackson, tel. 307/733–2288. Reservations not accepted. AE, D, MC, V.*

Lame Duck Chinese Restaurant
This is an all-purpose Asian restaurant that manages to serve all the major cuisines—Japanese, Thai, and Chinese—without ruining any of them. The Japanese offerings are sushi and sashimi, limited in selection but fresh and well presented; the Thai dishes feature the spicy peanut and lemongrass accents of that country; and the Chinese selections run the full gamut from chow mein to sweet and sour chicken to *moo goo gai pan. 680 E.*

Broadway, Jackson, tel. 307/733–4311. AE, MC, V.

Mama Inez
This comfortable and lively white-washed Mexican eatery serves burritos, enchiladas, and tacos as well as chile relleños and chimichangas. All are available in small, medium, or large portions, priced accordingly. *380 W. Pearl Ave., Jackson, tel. 307/733–9166. Reservations not accepted. D, MC, V.*

Best Bets for Breakfast

Jedidiah's House of Sourdough
Mountain-size portions of light, fluffy flapjacks, a variety of sauces and toppings, and crisp golden-brown waffles with fruit toppings are the mainstay lure, but there are also the breakfast standbys of ham, bacon, sausage, eggs any style, home fries, and omelets. *135 E. Broadway, 1 block east of Town Square, Jackson, tel. 307/733–5671. AE, D, DC, MC, V.*

Nora's Fish Creek Inn
It's the log cabin with the huge fish on the roof beside Route 22. The pancakes and French toast are a local legend, plus there are monster-size portions of egg and meat dishes, lots of homemade biscuits, and great home fries. *Foot of Teton Pass, Rte. 22, 6 mi west of Jackson, Wilson, tel. 307/733–8288. D, MC, V.*

NIGHTLIFE AND ENTERTAINMENT
Après-Ski

Dietrich's Bistro
Dietrich's is a bustling après-ski bar that is a touch European in tone, with dark-wood surroundings and Bavarian styling. There's occasionally a rousing singing session and always

plenty of conversation. *Alpenhof Lodge, 3255 W. McCollister Dr., Teton Village, tel. 307/733–3242. AE, D, DC, MC, V.*

Mangy Moose

This is a crazy place, with two levels of controlled mayhem surrounded by some of the most bizarre antiques, collectibles, and junk that ever adorned one building—from trophy heads to antique sporting equipment. There's even an entire stuffed moose suspended from the ceiling. You'll find live entertainment on the weekends, loud music every other day, and definitely a younger crowd. *Teton Village, tel. 307/733–4913. AE, MC, V.*

Loud and Lively/Dancing

Million Dollar Cowboy Bar

This is Jackson's place to see and be seen. If the doorman doesn't like your face or dress, you may well be turned back. Inside, it's part electric cowboy, part Vegas glitz, and part Western rococo. Two parallel 75-foot bars on either side have saddle bar stools, mirrors, and backlighted art. The enormous dance floor is flanked by a stage with live Country-and-Western entertainment. *25 N. Cache St., Jackson, tel. 307/733–2207. No credit cards.*

Stage Coach Bar

On Sunday night it has live Western entertainment and jam sessions. The rest of the week it's a fairly low-key hangout with an old brick-and-wood funkiness, a long handmade wooden bar with log bar stools, three pool tables, and darts. It's the red building on the right-hand side of Route 22 as you enter Wilson. *Rte. 22, Wilson, tel. 307/733–4407. MC, V.*

More Mellow

Jackson Hole Pub & Brewery

Jackson's first brew pub has won awards at the Great American Beer Festival. A no-smoking environment, live jazz Tuesday night, English-style ales, porters, and wood-fired pizzas all add up to a pleasant place to hang out. *265 S. Millward, Jackson, tel. 307/739–2337. AE, MC, V.*

Silver Dollar

In the oldest hotel in Jackson—the Wort—the Silver Dollar is a cheerful lounge, with a pianist or guitarist and bartenders resplendent in wide-striped shirts and bow ties. The bar is inlaid with more than 2,000 original 1921 silver dollars. *Wort Hotel, 50 N. Glenwood Ave., Jackson, tel. 307/733–2190. AE, D, DC, MC, V.*

NOTES

NOTES

WHEREVER YOU TRAVEL, *H*ELP IS NEVER FAR AWAY.

From planning your trip to

providing travel assistance along

the way, American Express®

Travel Service Offices are

always there to help.

For the office nearest you, call
1-800-AXP-3429.

AMERICAN EXPRESS
®

Travel

http://www.americanexpress.com/travel